RAYMOND ARON

MEMOIRS

RAYMOND ARON

MEMOIRS

Fifty Years of Political Reflection

Translated by George Holoch

Foreword by
HENRY A. KISSINGER

HM

HOLMES & MEIER
New York   London

Published in the United States of America 1990 by
Holmes & Meier Publishers, Inc.
30 Irving Place
New York, N.Y. 10003

Originally published in French as *Mémoires: 50 ans de réflexion
politique,* copyright © 1983 by Editions Julliard, Paris. The English
edition has been abridged.

Interior design by Dale Cotton

The paper used in this publication meets the requirements of the
American National Standard for Permanence of Paper for Printed
Library Materials, Z39.48-1984.

Library of Congress Cataloging-in-Publication Data

Aron, Raymond, 1905-1983
    [Mémoires. English]
    Memoirs : fifty years of political reflection / Raymond Aron;
translated by George Holoch ; foreword by Henry A. Kissinger.
      p.   cm.
    Translation of: Mémoires.
    Bibliography: p.
    Includes index.
    ISBN 0-8419-1113-4.
    1. Aron, Raymond, 1905-1983. 2. Intellectuals—France—
Biography.
    3. Journalists—France—Biography. 4. Philosophers—France—
Biography. 5. World politics—20th century. 6. France—Politics
and government—20th century. 7. France—Intellectual life—
20th century. I. Title.
    CT3990.A76A313   1990   *LL749*
944.08'092—dc20
    [B]   89-7621
                                        CIP

MANUFACTURED IN THE UNITED STATES OF AMERICA

CONTENTS

PUBLISHER'S NOTE
ON THE ENGLISH-LANGUAGE EDITION

Many individuals lent invaluable assistance during the shaping of the English-language edition of Raymond Aron's memoirs, and we would like to acknowledge several persons in particular.

Professor Stanley Hoffmann's intimate knowledge of Aron's thought and works, as well as his generous editorial guidance at various stages of the *Memoirs*, influenced the overall quality of the volume. A special debt of gratitude is also owed to Mme Dominique Schnapper, Raymond Aron's daughter and a scholar in her own right, whose cooperation and painstaking review of the translation were helpful throughout the course of the project. Finally, Arthur Goldhammer's meticulous editorial preparation of the text for the English-language translation significantly enhanced the final book.

M.J.H.

FOREWORD

Henry A. Kissinger

Raymond Aron was a philosopher and a journalist. He wrote seminal works on the philosophy of history, on Clausewitz, on war and peace. He composed several trenchant columns a week, mostly for *Le Figaro* but also for an extraordinary range of other publications, philosophical, historical or topical in scope. And he maintained that pace with astonishing brilliance for nearly fifty years.

Raymond Aron was my friend. He was also my teacher. Few intellectuals have had a deeper impact on my thinking; none a greater one. Lest I burden his memory with my critics, let me add that he was on occasion less than satisfied with his student.

I met Raymond Aron in Paris in the fifties. It was in his apartment along the Seine—I a graduate student and he already a famous intellectual. At the time I was editing a publication called *Confluence*, a journal of limited circulation which I had launched in naive ignorance of the mechanics of publishing a small magazine, not to mention the financial vagaries. It was to be a medium through which European and American intellectuals could debate a series of issues of mutual interest. Aron seemed surprised at my youth; I was intimidated by his fame and somewhat skeptical manner. It was my initiation to Aron's characteristic mixture of intellectual rigor and emotional support. Though he had much better outlets, Aron not only wrote for *Confluence* but was also a great help in inducing other well-known French authors to do so.

Until his death some thirty years later, that first meeting set the tone of our relationship. I genuinely admired Raymond Aron; in turn, he gave me every indication of his regard, even of his affection, though in these memoirs he feels compelled—quite properly—to make clear that he was never one to surrender his judgment to the friendship of a Secretary of State.

In the Epilogue of these memoirs, Aron speculates about whether he was considered cold. Those who knew him had no such doubts. They realized that he was a man of passion, deeply committed to liberty, to Western culture, and to democratic ideals.

Aron was French and he was Jewish. He witnessed the decline and rebirth of France and the persecution and survival of the Jews. He lived through the confusion of prewar Europe; through exile in London during the war and all the tumults of internecine struggles, decolonization and internal debate of postwar Europe.

Through all this turbulence Raymond Aron maintained his sense of proportion and above all his sense of direction. Like a rock against which the waves hurl themselves, on the surface the very cause of their turmoil, in historical perspective Aron becomes the figure to illustrate others' transitoriness. What a record of steadfastness the writings of Aron represent in opposition to the conventional wisdom of his day! By the time the Second World War broke out he had already witnessed the fatuousness of a policy that sought to protect the small countries of Eastern Europe by a defensive strategy in the West. He warned against the failure to resist—in the name of peace and negotiation—the German reoccupation of the Rhineland, which gave Nazi Germany a glacis behind which it effected the overthrow of the existing European order. Aron understood that the British guarantee of Poland amounted as well to a guarantee of the Soviet borders since the German armies could not reach the Soviet Union without first crossing Poland. And he saw clearly that, therefore, paradoxically and unjustly, negotiations with Moscow would be rendered more difficult by Britain's decision at last to abandon appeasement.

In London during the war Aron supported the Free French. Throughout the postwar period, he was a staunch supporter of European unity, American friendship and Franco-German reconciliation. In the travails of France, he usually took the unpopular position. He was an early advocate of Algerian independence, recognizing that the "liberal" solution of greater autonomy would never satisfy on a continent where all colonies were on the road to independence.

Aron's friendship for America was deep but far from uncritical. Indeed, side by side with his defense of Atlantic partnership, persisted a masterful—occasionally scathing—critique of the policies by which this partnership was being implemented, including those of the author of this foreword. On Vietnam he deplored the extent to which America had staked its prestige even as he understood the struggle to extricate itself with honor.

Through the decades, Aron never wavered in his commitment to the cause of freedom. He never joined the Marxism in vogue with such contemporaries as Sartre and Merleu-Ponty, or the fashionable anti-Americanism of Malraux. He walked alone for the greater part of his life, only to be vindicated at the end by the turn of French intellectuals away from Marxism—though perhaps too late to give him the formal recognition of intellectual leadership which was his due.

Documenting Aron's intellectual life might easily overwhelm even the most devoted biographer, for how could anyone distill the passion, the honesty and the dedication behind such a stupendous output? Fortunately for posterity, Aron undertook the task himself at the end of his life.

In this intellectual biography, at once modest and moving, Aron steers the reader through the spiritual odyssey of his life using extracts from his own reader through the spiritual odyssey of his life using extracts from his own most significant articles and books as guideposts. One meets not only the author but also the extraordinary group of men and women he encountered on the way. The memoirs are profound, yet easy to read; they reveal a warm, caring personality whose commitment to the principles of freedom provided the impetus for his extraordinary labors.

For a man like myself, involved for many years in the mundane tasks of diplomacy, Aron's book is not always comfortable reading. Clearly, his judgment of my efforts as a statesman is less admiring than mine of his contributions to Western thought.

This is as it should be. The philosopher deals with truth; the statesman addresses contingencies. The thinker has a duty to define what is right; the policymaker must deal with what is attainable. The professor focuses on ultimate goals; the diplomat knows that his is a meandering path on which there are few ultimate solutions and whatever "solutions" there are, more often than not turn into a threshold for a new set of problems.

De Gaulle characteristically summed up the dilemma in a letter cited by Aron: "It happens that I am sometimes not convinced by what you write and I know that from the outset you have rarely approved what I do. However, please believe that I admire the way in which your mind attempts to encompass the great flood that is carrying all of us toward an apparently measureless and, in any event, unprecedented fate."

I last saw Aron in the summer of 1982. An obscure bank official from a small town in the south of France wrote to him that it was his dream to bring Aron and me to Draguignan for a dialogue. Aron took up this unusual request with his usual dedication. However, he had by then become quite frail, and my wife, Nancy, urged me not to delay accepting because she feared that he soon would not have the strength to go through with it.

So we went to Draguignan in June 1982. The organizers and a group of French veterans first took Aron and me to an American military cemetery at the edge of town as a symbol of their ties to America. The mayor of the town had refused to make a public building available, whether in protest against Aron or me I no longer remember. But a large tent had been erected and Aron questioned me before an audience of several thousand. He did so with a fierce tenderness, being both demanding and confident that I would withstand his rigorous cross-examination.

In the final years he had taken to kissing me whenever we met or parted— a sign, I felt, that he thought every meeting might be our last. A few months after Draguignan, Aron died, on the steps of a courthouse where he had gone to testify for a friend unjustly accused of collaborating with the Nazis.

It was an honor to have been his contemporary.

RAYMOND ARON

MEMOIRS

Political Education

1905–1939

MY FATHER'S WILL

I was born on the rue Notre-Dame-des-Champs in an apartment about which I remember nothing. On the other hand, the apartment on the boulevard Montparnasse into which my parents moved shortly after I was born has left some traces in my memory. I see, or imagine, a vast entryway that my brothers and I used as a skating rink; one of its walls was covered by three large bookcases, with books on the upper shelves, while the lower shelves held papers and brochures behind doors. It was there, when I was about ten, that I discovered the materials on the Dreyfus Affair that my father had accumulated.

There were three of us—"the little chestnuts"*—almost the same age, born in April 1902, December 1903, and March 1905. Adrien was the eldest in every respect, the one who soonest escaped from the family or rather revolted against it, perhaps the one most loved by my mother (a year before he was born, a first son had died after a complicated labor; my mother sometimes said that he could have lived, and she blamed the doctor). He wasn't really spoiled any more than the others, but Adrien might have

*Trans. note: A pun on "marron," meaning "chestnut."

3

followed another path if my parents, my mother crying and my father excusing his own weakness, had not given him for so long the means to live as he wished, without working, and comfortably.

Before my birth, my mother had decreed that I would be the daughter she passionately desired. I was thus the little baby as Adrien had been the first-born. She sometimes suffered from the harshness of the grown-ups, the ones she called the Arons. She would take me by the hand, and I loved to share her solitude, in tender complicity. My father, on the other hand, gave me another mission which weighed on my entire life, even more than my barely conscious intimacy with my mother during my earliest years.

On the first page of my recollections, my pen spontaneously evokes Adrien. Why him, who had no place in my existence either between the end of my studies and the war, or after my return from England in 1944, and until his death in 1969? Around 1950, one of my cousins said: "Before 1940, when I was asked if I was related to Aron, people were talking about the bridge and tennis player; now they are wondering about my connection with you." In fact, Adrien enjoyed a certain celebrity, or at least notoriety, in the world of sport, particularly in Paris. Ranked ninth as a tennis player toward the end of the 1920s, at the time of the four musketeers, he was at the same time among the four or five best bridge players in France, perhaps the best along with Pierre Albarran. He participated in the then celebrated match of the Culbertson team against the French team. Although he was not a professional in either game, he earned a living from them, especially bridge. After 1945, he gave up tennis and cards; he bought and sold stamps, as an amateur again. To his last day, he lived on the margins of society, for whose hypocrisy he felt contempt, gradually shading into cynicism.

We hardly saw each other any more in the 1960s. After an operation for a strangulated hernia, he expressed the wish to live in our apartment; our hesitations irritated him, and our meetings became intermittent. I remember a brief conversation in May 1968; he reacted to the events with his usual mixture of contempt for men and retreat into himself. In November 1969, he phoned me and said, in a tone that was more mocking than anxious or sad: "This is it, I feel a hard ball in my stomach, it must be cancer." He was not mistaken. Within ten days, he was dead from the spread of cancer. He smoked two or three packs of cigarettes a day; he coughed with a smoker's cough whose origin was obvious even to a layman. I visited him every day at the American Hospital—except the last day of his conscious life. I was making my candidate's visits to the professors of the Collège de France— visits that seemed to me all the more absurd because Adrien's death contrasted with the social comedy that he had never performed, and whose glitter he did not regret. He did not fear the end, which he awaited in his usual manner, without a hint of obvious fear, rather with impatience; on the other hand, he was afraid of pain. He had begged me to spare him from it. He had asked his doctor for a bottle of aspirin, which he did not use. He did not hasten the end; the spread of the disease was rapid, but he faced the denouement, faithful to himself, without qualms of conscience, with a kind of detached, objective summing up of his sixty-eight years.

He remembered the first part of his life, before 1940, with satisfaction. Not the satisfaction of duty or work accomplished, the satisfaction concerned only himself; women, money, sporting success, he had had everything he had wanted. At that time, he drove a Lancia (that he loaned me several times); he was elegant, and he frequented the wealthy circles of tennis and gambling clubs. He was a perfect embodiment of the man of pleasure, a type of man for which my philosophical self felt contempt and which a barely conscious part of myself, humiliated by his sovereign frivolity, admired or envied.

The defeat of France had put an end to his youth. All of a sudden, he, too, found himself to be a Jew. Not that he encountered anti-Semitism among his associates, seizing the opportunity to give free rein to suppressed feelings. As far as the statements he made in his hospital bed allow me to reconstruct his experiences, he was surprised, offended by the indifference to the fate of the Jews (indifference being the best reaction) shown by his sporting and gambling associates (the few real friends of his that I knew were loyal to him).

He gave up tennis after a hernia; he gave up bridge the day he discovered that the game was beginning to bore him. During the Occupation, he had stayed at first in Cannes; later, he reached Switzerland, where he discovered stamps. His postwar years, he told me, did not repeat the perfection of those before the war. In fact, this lazy man worked hard several hours a day on his stamp collection, or should I say his profession, to which he applied the same talent he had applied to bridge. Without the war, he told me, he would have found a "position" with the help of one or another of his "friends." Those friends with whom he spent time and who disappeared because of events.

In these last moments, he regretted nothing, or almost nothing; he deplored the fact that circumstances, independent of his will, had deprived him of certain pleasures during the last years of his life (besides, he thought he had already lived too long). All things considered, he had chosen his "intelligible character." For him, as he had wanted himself to be, old age meant nothing. Not that he was as detached from his fellow creatures as he pretended to be. The family, in a certain sense, was in his bones. When my father died in 1934, all three of us cried before his corpse (the first I had seen, I think), and he asked Robert and me: "Am I guilty?" My father had lost his entire fortune in the stock market crash of 1929. Among the three of us, only Adrien had enough money to help our parents. I had suggested it to him, and he had replied that his apparent luxury reflected the constraints of his way of life. In any event, I do not know how my father would have received such an offer. Robert and I did our best to assuage his remorse.

I have left out a detail, or perhaps the essential thing: he was gifted with exceptional intelligence; he put it at the service of bridge and stamps. After normal studies in the lycée, he entered the preparatory course for Polytechnique. After a few weeks, he rebelled against the work. My father proposed another choice, a *licence* in law and a *licence* in mathematics. He did get a *licence* in law. In the three weeks before the exams, he learned the texts by heart, and did the same thing for each of the three years. He dropped the *licence* in mathematics after a failure in a preliminary examination. He preferred tennis lessons to lessons in math. He continued to live with my parents until the early 1930s, and then moved into a ground-floor apartment on the rue Marignan that had been set up by one of his friends. When he died, he was still living in this same small apartment whose style, that of the 1924 exposition, was buried in disorder, dirt, and worn-out carpets and hangings—negligence, not necessity.

Bridge and tennis. In the garden of the house my parents had built in Versailles between 1914 and 1915, there was a tennis court. We played there several times a week. Adrien was the most gifted, Robert, the middle son, the least. In the same way, I started playing bridge when I was about ten. For years, my father and his three sons played bridge every night, or almost every night. My parents had decided that we should not "work" after dinner. The evening games lasted until Adrien started looking for other diversions away from home. As for me, I lost the passion for bridge and tennis from the moment I discovered philosophy and the world of ideas.

The memories that have first come to mind risk giving a false impression of my family. It now seems to me banal, classic; it belonged to the solid French Jewish bourgeoisie. My paternal grandfather, whom I did not know, had established a wholesale textile business in Rambervillers, a Lorraine village, where his ancestors had settled by the end of the eighteenth century, or so I was told. The business he ran with his brother Paul (father of Max Aron, the Strasbourg biologist) prospered and moved to Nancy.

I know nothing about him, except for two statements that were reported to me, one by my parents, the other by a Lorrain living in Mexico who had served under him. My grandfather Ferdinand is said to have predicted that I, the baby with his name, would have a great career.[1] In 1961, in Mexico City, I met a man who was over eighty and who had worked for "Aron frères." He recounted the lesson he had learned from his boss. "One night, around midnight, Ferdinand let us know it was time to leave. 'Let's go to bed,' he said, 'it's not late, but we'll get up earlier tomorrow.'" My grandparents, Jews of Eastern France, were intransigent patriots. I do not believe that they ever asked themselves the now fashionable question: Are we first of all Jews or Frenchmen? Even my father, as far as I remember, even though he was disturbed by the Dreyfus Affair more than by any other historical event, never budged from his positions: a freemason in his youth, without religious concerns, hardly following Jewish ritual, he differed not at all, at least superficially, from his student friends, Catholic or atheist, vaguely on the left.

My grandparents on both sides "had money" as they say, but not a great fortune. My mother, whose father owned a small textile factory in the northern part of the country, had provided a dowry. Before 1914, my paternal grandmother owned a large automobile, driven by a chauffeur with a cap; these external signs are not deceptive. My parents, then, received several hundred thousand francs from each side. After they received an inheritance at the death of my paternal grandmother, my parents decided to leave Paris for Versailles, first into a rented house, then into a house designed by an architect friend, a stone house, at the time the last house on the street. On the other side of the garden wall was a soccer field.

In a way typical of Jewish families, my father decided young not to join the family business. He was a brilliant student, first in his class in Lyon, in competition with a classmate who later taught French literature at the Sorbonne. He saved some of his philosophy papers and his rhetoric and Latin poetry exercises, which I read much later. In his first year in law school, he won first prize in a competition among the best students in Paris, or indeed in France. For reasons that I have reconstructed as well as I can, he failed at his career. He prepared for the *agrégation*, choosing as subjects Roman law and the history of law. There was an examination every two years. He came in second in an examination for which there was only one position. At first he agreed to teach in the law faculty at Caen, then he gave up the *agrégation* and returned to Paris where he accepted a lower position in the law faculty, one that was eliminated a few years later. He remained a teacher of law, in the Ecole supérieure d'enseignement commercial and the Ecole normale supérieure d'enseignement technique. Given his ambitions and his talents, this was a failure. He could have entered the judiciary. He held to teaching which he converted in his own eyes into a vocation, the most wonderful profession in the world, he said.

Was he sincere? Until 1929 and the great depression, I remember him as a happy man, expansive, comfortable in his skin. Afterward, little by little, I wondered. He had published some legal works when he was preparing the *agrégation*. Once he was married and the father of three children, he stopped "working." He published a little book, *War and the Teaching of Law*, which was of little significance. He left Paris to get away from "worldly life," Parisian dinners (at least that is how the decision was explained). He hardly made better use of his free time in Versailles; from time to time, the sense of failure, suppressed by his taste for life and his willed resignation, returned to the surface. More often, he said to himself and to others that he was devoting himself entirely to his children. Gradually, as my own aging allowed me to understand him, no longer as an all-powerful father but as a humiliated father, I felt myself to be the bearer of the hopes of his youth, entrusted with the task of providing him with a kind of compensation; I would cancel his disappointments with my successes. He died a few weeks after the birth of my daughter Dominique; it was his last happiness.

Once more, the memories that come back to me are those of the dark years, between 1929 and his death, in other words after he had lost everything, his fortune and my mother's dowry. At that point, at the age of sixty, for the first time since his marriage, he had to earn his living, to rely exclusively on his earnings. As a bourgeois of the turn of the century, he spent more than he earned, which was not a sign of irresponsibility. Why should he not spend the income from his capital? But I am afraid he had developed the habit of spending more than his income and salary combined. I remember a conversation between my mother and father in Versailles, thus well before the disaster. "I thought we weren't spending more than our income," said my mother. And my father answered: "No, we're spending more."

My mother was not extravagant. Probably the way of life to which my parents had become accustomed—a cook, a chambermaid—became too onerous in the 1920s while the three sons still depended on the family finances. After the war, during the inflationary years, my father developed the habit of speculating in the stock market. Speculation is perhaps an exaggeration; he bought stock options, and kept the shares in his portfolio if the price fell. At least he did that at first; gradually, he became involved well beyond his means. In 1929, the crash on all stock exchanges hit him like so many others. But he was struck more than many others because he thought himself guilty and, for thirty years, he had had no ambition but family happiness and the future of his children.

He remained my father, and I couldn't ask him any questions. Once, to a half-question, he answered: "If I sell, I'm ruined." He was, but he didn't want to admit it; he continued to hold the shares he had bought, which added to his losses and expenses. Robert, the middle son, who was already working for the Banque de Paris et des Pays-Bas, should have advised him. He did nothing of the kind; neither he nor my father was capable of reversing roles.

I cannot recall the last years of his life without a feeling of guilt and enormous sadness. He did not deserve the fate brought upon him by his own mistakes. He let himself be taken in by all kinds of "tipsters" (I remember one of these operators who brought him into a deal in which he lost thousands of francs). He didn't show his unhappiness. Courageously, he gave private tutoring and helped students prepare for exams. One day, when I dared ask a question, he told me: "I'm earning a living."

Already as a child I had felt guilty. During the war, my mother started collecting tin soldiers and, if I remember correctly, she collected in particular the helmets of all the allied armies; I was worried about the expense. In 1922, my parents returned to Paris, partly because of me; then they went back to Versailles and finally sold the house (it was worth a half million francs at the time)—the last folly. Of course, my parents decided, not I. But I could not consider myself innocent since our desires—mine—weighed so heavily on their decisions. Robert and I also agreed to be supported while we were students. Once my father remarked to me: "This sport is expensive," when I asked him for a check for dues for an indoor tennis club.

The word *bourgeois* has come from my pen as often as the word *Jew*. Was my family more typically bourgeois than Jewish? I have no idea, and perhaps the question makes no sense. My mother was very close to her two sisters; my father did not get on well with the older one (for good reasons), and quarrels about money finally led to a break (over the small textile factory that belonged to my maternal grandfather). Relations with my father's sister were from time to time interrupted by "spats" that did not seem attributable to my father, who was of a generous character.

If I were to play the sociologist, I would say that my parents were products of large families (in my grandparents' generation, six-children families were frequent), and brothers and sisters suffered when they were separated from one another, since they were emotionally too attached to ignore each other. They "quarreled," another way of living together. It seems to me that my generation took one further step. Parents aside, we chose among our cousins, even among our brothers and sisters, those we wanted to keep.

A few words about money, so that I won't have to say any more about it. For most of my life, after completing my studies, I had no capital; I lived on my salary. By chance in a conversation with Alain, I alluded to the contrast between an old-style bourgeois childhood and my current position, that of a bourgeois without reserves, as André Siegfried would have said; I confessed to him that I derived some satisfaction from this, or rather, that I felt unburdened; I would not have to worry about money, I would spend what I earned like a wage-earner, while deriving some benefit from the intellectual capital accumulated in the course of my studies. Alain answered that I had been fortunate first of all to benefit from the security provided by a well-to-do family, and then by receiving only the inheritance that everyone receives from his mother and father. An inheritance of being, not possessions. Perhaps I would never have the fear of want which constantly troubles those who have experienced real poverty; at the same time, I would not be obsessed by what the Americans call keeping up with the Joneses.

Alain was right. When I returned from England in 1944, I hadn't put a penny aside, and without much thought, I refused the chair of sociology at the University of Bordeaux that the dean had offered me with the assurance that my colleagues would all welcome me. Since then, I have regretted my refusal, which delayed my return to the university for ten years, but I see it as an expression both of frivolity (I am my father's son) and of a certain confidence. After all, outside the university, what career was open to me? Journalism, of course. But I hadn't written a single article for a daily newspaper before the war, and my philosophical works, difficult, obscure, gave no indication of the very different talents of a newspaper columnist.

Perhaps I owe to my father my ambiguous relationship to money. But I have also contracted a debt to him that I will never repay. As a candidate for the Ecole Normale and the *agrégation*, I carried my father's hopes for a second chance. In a vague way, every time I felt or feared that I was ruining my life, that I was not accomplishing what I was capable of, I thought of my father, as though life were inflicting a new defeat on him; the son who was to rectify injustices, to whom he had confided his message, like his father, and with fewer excuses, was choosing the easy way or failure, because of the same defects of character. With fewer excuses, I might add, because he had long been happy despite failure, and I would not feel the same.

In Jerusalem a few years ago, I received a doctorate *honoris causa* from the university. I had forgotten that I was supposed to reply to the laudation of the Israeli professor. The day before, I delivered a lecture at the Weizmann Institute. That morning, before getting in the car for Jerusalem, I hastily wrote my response—and my last words were addressed to my father who would have been fulfilled by my election to the Collège de France and the doctorate granted by the University of Jerusalem. A friend, Dan Avni, wrote to me that I had given a lesson in Jewishness: paying homage to the father for the honor granted to the son. Jewishness? Psychoanalysis might hazard another interpretation. Perhaps I evoked the debt that had weighed on me for fifty years at this time, in this place, to convince myself that I had finally repaid it.

I was a typical good student; I entered the Versailles lycée in the *huitième*. A tutor, Mlle Lalande, taught me to read and write. The private lessons I had gotten had not brought me to the level of the *huitième*. I caught up rather quickly and, especially from the *sixième* on, I was always eager to be classed first, as though that were my right. In short, I was afflicted with a vanity that I cannot remember without shame.

I liked to learn, and I took pleasure in working. But before the year of philosophy, I don't think that studies themselves excited me. Latin, Greek, mathematics, history, geography—none of that touched my inner life, my own interests, my pleasures. My bicycle (I dreamed of being a champion cyclist) meant more to me than Latin or history. Perhaps because we lived in Versailles, we went less often to the theater, museums, or concerts than we ought to have. There were the inevitable piano lessons but, in general, at the age of fifteen, I was first in my class (in a lycée inferior to those of Paris), but less cultivated than other future students of the Ecole Normale Supérieure. I became aware of my deficiencies when I entered the preparatory class at the lycée Condorcet.

Did I read a lot, beyond what I was required to read? Probably when I was eleven or twelve. I remember *War and Peace*, Prince André lying on the ground with his eyes fixed on the sky. Several times I looked for the emotion I felt on first reading, and I was disappointed. I expected too much from this passage of the book, which thereafter lost its charm. Indeed, I have often experienced these anxious expectations, always unsatisfied. The dialogues of Horace and Curiace, which I recited to myself, raised me into a sublime universe.* For several days before the performance of the tragedy at the Comédie-Française, I experienced in advance the joy with which the actors' voices would fill me; I would see and hear the heroes whose lines I repeated to myself: "I know you no more . . . I know you still. . . ." The miracle did not take place. Because of the staging, the actors? I don't think so. Several years later, I read Proust, and understood the banality of my disappointment; one does not experience perfect moments on order. Proust gave me a few, but I hesitate to reread certain passages of *A la Recherche du temps perdu,* for fear of not reliving those perfect moments or even of spoiling their memory.

Aside from the novels—from *The Three Musketeers* to *War and Peace*—that I devoured while still a child, my father's library, or rather the closed cabinets below the bookshelves, offered me books, tracts, and newspapers on the Dreyfus affair—*J'accuse;* a brochure by Jaurès. I plunged into the affair without seeing it as a challenge to the Jews and their status in France. It was during the war, and my parents shared the patriotic passions of everyone. Passions? Yes, parents, uncles, and aunts had given their gold to the nation. My father, forty-three when war was declared, mobilized in the national guard, spent a few months in a barracks in Toul. Demobilized during the winter of 1914–15, he resumed his ordinary life. I remember with some shame my indifference to the unhappiness of others, to the horror of the trenches. Indifference? Yes, in the sense that my studies and my games—

---

*Trans. note: The reference is to Corneille's *Horace,* a standard text in the French *lycée* curriculum.

skating on the Versailles park canal—concerned me more than official communiqués or newspaper stories. I joined the Maritime and Colonial League because our teachers asked us to. A national and quite natural act. I raised no questions about the colonies and civilizing mission of France and, in an essay that every school child had to write on the profession of his choice, I praised the greatness of the "little captain."

The Dreyfus affair had no effect on my feelings as a little Frenchman. My father surprised me when he made connections between the war and the Dreyfus affair: the affair, even more than the war, had been a test, an opportunity to judge men and their character. Of course, I knew that I was a Jew, and I often heard bourgeois Jews say: "It's that kind of people who create anti-Semitism." What kind of people? People who were called vulgar, who talked loudly in public, laughed loudly, called attention to themselves. One aunt detected those who were "responsible" for anti-Semitism especially among my parents' friends or the friends of another closely related family. These statements embarrassed me, irritated me in a way I could not express. I could no longer stand them when I reached the age of reason. The reaction of many French Jews to the arrival of German Jews after 1933 made me indignant but not surprised. After all, it was true that they were "Boches"; most of them had lived with their people—the people they had thought to be theirs—and they too had said *Gott strafe England*. Most French Jews had no feeling of solidarity with German Jews. They did not know, they wished not to know, that their time would come; with assimilation, they had alienated the freedom to choose themselves.

I am perhaps inclined to present myself as too naïve, before my contact with pre-Hitler Germany, barely aware of belonging to Judaism, a completely serene French citizen. And yet. . . . A right-wing history teacher, close to the Action française, dealt with the Third Republic in one of my last years at the lycée. He taught us that it was unknown, even in hindsight, whether Dreyfus had been guilty or innocent, and that, in the end, the question hardly mattered, that the affair had created the opportunity or the pretext for unleashing partisan passions, the passions of the enemies of the army and religion. The "ignoble" regime of the Radicals and the *fiches* had come afterward. I argued as well as I could with my teacher, who, in addition to everything else, had been wounded in the war, and everything came up: the original telegram ("le petit bleu"), the "patriotic" forgery, the trial in Rennes, the final decision of the appeals court. The teacher replied with standard formulas: "It's more complex than you think." He also made use of falsehoods: "The appeals court was not legally required to decide on the merits; it did so to put an end to the polemics that were tearing the nation apart." In this dialogue with my teacher, neither one of us, as far as I remember, had mentioned or, in any case emphasized, the fact that Dreyfus was a Jew and that I was too. In 1920 or 1921, there still remained something of the *union sacrée*.

My fellow students were of course aware that I was Jewish. With what feelings? I did not know at the time and I probably didn't want to know. When I was eleven or twelve, outside school, I remember being called "dirty Jew" or "yid." Struck, or frightened, I reported the incident to my parents. The next day, a "big boy," my brother Adrien, scared off the little ones.

I was fourteen when the Treaty of Versailles was signed, and I probably had serious family discussions about world events: the Russian Revolution, the occupation of the Rhineland. My parents let us participate in all conversations, even with noted professors. They were fond of saying that they treated us as equals; they naïvely believed that they were thereby "liberating" us. In fact, they made our liberation more difficult. Some of my parents' friends called me "the lawyer," because I argued with such facility. I am completely incapable of saying what I argued in the years 1918–21, between the ages of thirteen and sixteen. I long ago reconstructed my intellectual biography: before the class of *philosophie*, darkness; thereafter, light. I entered that class in October 1921. Patriotic fervor was subsiding; the left was recovering its strength and its ideas. The Chambre *bleu horizon* was suffering the effects of the disillusionment of victory. My father was returning to his earlier moderately left views. He had voted, I think, for the National Front in 1919; he certainly voted for the Cartel des Gauches in 1924. In the meantime, a reader and subscriber of *Le Progrès civique*, the weekly that had led the campaign of the Cartel des Gauches for the 1924 election, he became again the Dreyfusard of his youth, and never supported Raymond Poincaré, who had taken so long to "free his conscience"; he gradually moved away from war propaganda and, prudently, became receptive to notions of reconciliation with the enemy.

The 1921–22 school year, which I consider decisive in my life, was, historically, marked by the last convulsions of the crisis of war and revolution. I learned nothing about politics, economics, Bolshevism, or Karl Marx, but I glimpsed, for the first time, the enchanted universe of speculation or, simply, of thought. I had chosen the classics section, less out of a taste for ancient languages than out of fear of mathematics. A few years earlier, I had been traumatized by an incident that I have not forgotten. I had not found the solution to a problem. The teacher had written on my paper in red ink: "How could you not find the solution to such an easy problem?" I retreated before the obstacle; in other circumstances I have perhaps evaded obstacles. Writing essays, signing contracts for derivative books, are these not forms of evasion?

The study of philosophy revealed my vocation and the austere pleasures of reflection. But the exaltation of thought as such is not without danger.

Philosophers often develop the bad habit of attributing to thought in itself, without information or proof, the capacity to grasp the truth; others exclude from thinking analysis or scientific demonstration. The fact remains that a few months spent with a genuine teacher of philosophy, who initiates young people into Plato's Ideas or Aristotle's syllogism, Descartes's *Meditations* and the transcendental deduction of Kant, have a profound effect on their minds and give them something that is irreplaceable. Perhaps I am getting ahead of myself. It may be that I am mixing up the last year of the lycée with the four years of the Ecole normale supérieure. The decision to prepare for the ENS came naturally out of the class of *philosophie*. The scientific *grandes écoles* were closed to me by my choice of the classics section. I was unaware of the combination of a law degree with study at the Ecole libre des sciences politiques. Although my interest in public affairs had been awakened, I had no thought of a political career. Later, while I was at the Ecole normale, I thought of it more than once, but rather as a temptation, a risk of falling. Journalism too, as much as, or more than, the profession of politics, seemed to me a confession of failure, a refuge for sterile minds.

My childish vanity had already been sublimated, purged, after having been taken down a peg by experience. In the *khâgne* class in the lycée Condorcet, I made no attempts to be among the first to be admitted to the ENS. It was enough that I was admitted to that illustrious school. Four years later, for the *agrégation* exam, the predictions were that Jean-Paul Sartre or I would come in first.

When it turned out that I was first on the list (ahead of Emmanuel Mounier and Daniel Lagache), I attributed this success, with melancholy foresight, to academic virtues. In none of my essays or oral presentations had I demonstrated any originality. The *agrégation* was at the time what it has remained; candidates demonstrate philosophical knowledge and rhetorical talent.

Should I say that the class of *philosophie* led me to the Ecole normale and the *agrégation* because that was the path of least resistance? I devoted myself to the intellectual exercise for which I was apparently most gifted. I think that this harshness is excessive. The class of *philosophie* had taught me that we can think our existence rather than submitting to it, we can enrich it by reflection, carry on a dialogue with the great minds. A year of familiarity with the work of Kant cured me once and for all of vanity (at least in the deep sense). On this point, I still feel very close to Léon Brunschvicg. On 22 September 1892, he wrote in his diary: "It may be that I have not been unfaithful to a dual imperative: to aim for the highest and to judge myself clearly." In a letter to his daughter Adrienne, he quotes this phrase and comments: "That seemed to me to define me completely, without illusions about myself, but attached to meditation on and commentary about the greatest geniuses of humanity." In my defense, I do not claim such fidelity, but I have devoted a good deal of time to the "defense and illustration" of those who are greater than I; I willingly attributed to them ideas I had not gotten from them but that seemed to me at least implicit in their work.

Why did the class of *philosophie* also bring about my conversion to the left? The year 1921–22 coincided with the renewal of the bourgeois, academic left, which had until then been suppressed by nationalist fervor. I nevertheless believe that philosophy in itself provides a lesson in universality. Men think, they are all capable of thinking. They must therefore be taught, persuaded. War denies the humanity of man because the victor has demonstrated nothing but his superior strength or cleverness. The climate of a class of *philosophie*, whatever the opinions of the teacher, usually fosters feelings of the left.

This class revealed to me the universe of thought; notwithstanding Descartes, it provided me no rules of method, which the "philosophers" of the Ecole normale need so much. It taught me to think but also, above all, to learn, to study. Bachelard says somewhere that only philosophers think before they have studied. For ten years, I asserted political opinions; in fact, I preferred certain men to others. My sympathies were toward the humble and the oppressed, and I detested the powerful who were too confident of their rights; but between philosophy and my feelings there was a gap— ignorance of society as it is, as it can be, and as it cannot be. Most of my contemporaries have not filled, have not even tried to fill, that gap.

I seem to remember having written a "Machiavellian" first article, signed Landhaus, the name of the street on which was located the Französisches Akademiker Haus.[2] Sartre's reaction was simple, as reported by a mutual friend: "Has my little classmate become a bastard?" This was the time when I discovered the autonomy of the political realm, to use philosophical language. Politics, as such, differs from morality. "What a wonderful discovery!" you might say. Yes, of course, everyone knows this, but my education in the lycée and the university, as I received and absorbed it, did not prepare me to understand politics, Europe, and the world. Academic idealism led me to condemn the Treaty of Versailles and the occupation of the Ruhr, to support German demands and the parties of the left, whose language and aspirations corresponded to the sensibility maintained, perhaps created, by the taste for philosophy. Has my sensibility changed since then? I am not sure, even though my reason—or what I think is my reason—has gradually taken command over my feelings.

How much of this reconstruction is based on memories, how much on the idea I have created or tacked on to my past? Conversion to philosophy and to the left at about seventeen; fixed opinions, political enthusiasms (joy at the victory of the Cartel des Gauches in 1924), emotional participation in all events, in the French parliament as well as in world history. In this respect, I do not think that my intellectual memory has distorted or disfigured my authentic experiences. But I am getting ahead of myself; I am still in the class of *philosophie*, at the lycée Hoche, when I chose my career because of facility, my tastes, my success in school, and the revelation of philosophy. Did I imagine that I would be a lycée teacher for the rest of my life? Was I already dreaming of a "work"? Or of a thesis, the normal step after the *agrégation?* I don't know, and perhaps I didn't know at seventeen. In Versailles, I bore a close resemblance to a provincial, to the good student who heads toward Paris without looking beyond examinations, the ENS, and the *agrégation.* Only competition with others, in *khâgne* and afterward, would tell me about my chances for the future. In any event, contrary to the impression that many classmates had of me, examinations frightened me, and successes did not give me genuine confidence, I mean the confidence to create. I envied Sartre's confidence and, in my heart, I accepted his certainties and my doubts, whose authenticity he had difficulty in admitting.

I have almost left out of these pages my memories of my mother and my brother Robert. How can I speak of my mother unless I recount the vague memories of my earliest years, which I am neither capable of doing nor willing to do.

My parents presented to the end the image of a united couple, even though the marriage had been "arranged" by their families. My mother had not continued her education (she frequently referred to a young woman who had taken her baccalauréat and who was known as the *bachelière des Vosges*). She had difficulty detaching herself from her mother and her sisters; she was devoted to her husband and her children. But she could not help my father in his career or his business affairs. I have been told that she disliked Caen, and that, eager to return to Paris, she urged my father to accept a marginal teaching post (more marginal than it is now).

A victim of the fate assigned to her by the customs of the time, a child until her marriage, in tears on the day of her wedding to a man she hardly knew, she was happy as long as her children remained in the family nest; she suffered from Adrien's rebellion and harshness; she suffered from our financial ruin. She never criticized my father, she gave him everything she owned, her few jewels, her rings. After my father's death in 1934, without resources, she depended on her sons, whom she would have liked to "spoil" to the end. She did not get as much from her only granddaughter as she had hoped. She would have liked to have played fully the role of grandmother, for which she was suited by her conception of life, which came from a vanished world. She could not offer a substitute family since, alone, she no longer had one. In June 1940, having taken refuge in Vannes, she died alone.

I often think about the fate of the three "chestnuts." As far as I can judge, my two brothers had received genetic gifts comparable to mine. Adrien could probably have entered Polytechnique. Robert wrote well and quickly. The former devoted his intelligence, which always struck me with its acuteness, to bridge and to stamps. I deplored what seemed to me the waste of a rare talent. I could not help but make a moral judgment on his way of life before the war; he violated no laws; those who played with him regularly recognized his superiority; hence, in the long run, they were bound to lose money. Nevertheless, Adrien, whose amorality shocked and saddened me, remained my brother, often affectionate and helpful. In his last days, it was with me that he awaited death, without anxiety.

Robert, caught between the two extremes, one brother who excelled in sports the other in his studies, never fully overcame his initial handicap. He took simultaneously a *licence* in law and a *licence* in philosophy. At that point he should have made a decision: either prepare for the *agrégation* in philosophy or leave the university and look for a job after his military service. He did not have the courage to choose, and he spent another year on a diploma in philosophical studies. His thesis was, as a matter of fact, excellent: a classic comparison between Descartes and Pascal which concluded with an original interpretation of the "wager," which was published in the *Revue de Métaphysique et de Morale* (with his name as author, it was sometimes attributed to the author of the *Histoire de Vichy*, sometimes to me; the real author was ignored).

After his military service, he joined the Banque de Paris et des Pays-Bas, with the help of the Bank's director, with whom I played tennis. He spent his whole life there, except for the Occupation, when he was excluded. He returned on the day of the Liberation, and he climbed the hierarchical ladder to the position of director of the analysis sections. He never married, and, to my knowledge, did not have a permanent companion; I do not know how he experienced his condition, chosen and then accepted. Respected and admired by his colleagues (some of them have told me of their warmth toward him), he was one of the first professional financial analysts in France.

But I doubt whether he had the qualities necessary for success in the context of the bureaucratic rivalries of a large enterprise. Emmanuel Monick, who appreciated his competence, several times gave him the task of preparing the annual report for the stockholders' meeting. But Robert had the feeling that he was used, exploited by the management, without receiving the rewards he hoped for, less money than status. He told Adrien more than me about his various conflicts. In a sense, as a bureaucrat, he was the right man in the right place, but kept in the background. The presidencies of subsidiaries, to which he felt entitled, went to others. He did not have the profile of a chairman of the board. Robert would have been an extraordinary teacher, and he conducted himself as a professor toward his colleagues.

After the departure of Emmanuel Monick and the first signs of the illness that gradually paralyzed his body and then his mind, his position at the bank deteriorated, and his character soured; we saw him less and less. Perhaps he had given up the *agrégation* of philosophy because he would have been a candidate at the same time that I was. If he had succeeded on his first attempt, he would have done so a year before I did, but the oral exam included the translation and commentary of a Greek text: he had never learned Greek. I probably made his life difficult, from the very beginning. He demonstrated no less talent in financial analysis than I did in my various professions. The difference between us had nothing to do with the obscurity of one or the notoriety of the other. He was fighting in a jungle for which he was not equipped; he lost more often than he won.

Robert's last years may darken the portrait. For a long time, even in the first ten or fifteen years after the war, he seemed to have kept his youthful friends; he loved Dominique, the only child of the three Aron brothers; he gradually drifted away, and like Adrien, and in the same way, he sank into solitude. He wrote detective novels that I was unable to find after his death; he had begun a history of the 1944 landing to correct the mistakes of official versions. His character and his spirit were gradually wounded by the disappointments he experienced in his professional life, identified with his existence as a whole. There followed the years of decline, the loss of movement, of memory, and then of consciousness.

My father died in January 1934 from a heart attack a few months after a first attack; he had been killed by a guilty conscience and excessive work. I repeated to myself in the funeral parlor, crying without tears: he died from misery, which was almost true. Robert entered into darkness long before he died; he had conducted his affairs in an apparently normal manner. His hidden life perhaps resembled the open life of our father.

Adrien found the death he wished for. With pleasures at an end, alone, resolute in the solitude of egotism, he awaited the end not with stoicism but with impatience—with no company but his little brother, for whom the cynic, tempted by the worst, nevertheless felt genuine affection mingled with respect; I loved him, too.

NOTES

1. I was named Raymond Claude Ferdinand.
2. I have not been able to locate it. Perhaps I am thinking of an article entitled "Propos de politique réaliste," published in *Libres Propos*.

2

STUDIES AND
FRIENDSHIPS

I entered the *khâgne* of the lycée Condorcet in October 1922 with the timidity and the ambitions of a provincial arriving in the capital. Why Condorcet and not Louis-le-Grand or Henry-IV, which every year produced the largest number of *normaliens?* My father had made a choice on the advice of some university friends. Perhaps its proximity to the gare Saint-Lazare was the decisive argument: my family was still living in Versailles and neither my parents nor I were attracted by the idea of my being a boarder.

With hindsight, I am trying to judge the education I received, which for the current generation, for my grandchildren, belongs to the past. The reduction of mathematics in section A (Latin and Greek) had been carried to absurd extremes. Yet this section attracted a number of "good students" not all of whom thought themselves incapable of understanding a demonstration or finding the solution to a problem. Today, the pendulum has swung too far in the other direction. What remains of section A has become a dead end. Section C reigns without challenge, the royal way taken by almost all the young people who will be the elite of the future. Mathematics has become the touchstone, the preeminent selective device. Traditional humanistic education survives on the fringes, and perhaps it is dying.

Aside from history (barely) and civic instruction (insignificant), we learned nothing or almost nothing about the world in which we lived. In essence, subject matter and programs came directly from the tradition of Jesuit colleges. The celebrated reform of Léon Bérard tended not to bring things up to date but rather to set the clocks back, to restore, for the best students, the lycées of the last century. Is the classical lycée of my youth, and of the youth of my daughter, to be condemned without reservation? In the course of the last twenty years a "cultural revolution" has taken place, and mathematics, old or new, has replaced Latin and rhetoric on the throne. The revolution was in part legitimate: mathematics is a language whose rudiments it is important to learn early. Language, languages remain the means of expression for all men, even for mathematicians. Between the two languages, of symbols and of words, there is no need to choose; both contribute to the shaping of thought. Sometimes I even wonder whether the isolation of lycées from the outside world didn't have more advantages than disadvantages. A teacher likes to provide an example of detachment, he represents an arbiter, a witness, he judges according to the truth. As soon as he discusses politics, he has difficulty in raising himself, even when he attempts to do so, to that serenity he demonstrates with ease when he translates or interprets Caesar's commentaries on the Gallic wars.

My first impression of the ENS, I confess at the risk of appearing foolish, was wonder. Even today, if I were asked why, I would answer with complete sincerity and naïveté: I have never met so many intelligent men assembled in such a small space. These good students, prize winners, did not all seem to me devoted to the exploits of thought. But even those whom some of us sometimes judged harshly gave life to their culture with a youthful intelligence. Perhaps this did not always survive the class routine and the correction of essays. I avoid reunions of old students in order to preserve the memory of what they were. They were not always inferior to the ones who made a career for themselves.

Leaving aside the classmates whose names I cannot recall when I look at the school photographs, let us turn to my two contemporaries of whom we all expected a great deal, who did not disappoint their admirers. One of them did not have the time to complete his work, the other, plunged into darkness as I wrote these lines, was following his path, more moral than political. I am not unaware of the traps into which I can fall. There is a risk that images of Sartre will be superimposed on one another in the student, the teacher after years of study and before success, the prophet of existentialism and the communist fellow traveler, the protector of the *gauchistes* and finally the old man at the Elysée, supported by Glucksmann, next to me.

Sartre and Nizan both came from Henri-IV, bound together with ties of friendship rare even among young men. Both were devoted at the same time to literature and philosophy; both were recognized by their classmates as out of the ordinary; they were themselves aware of their gifts and set on their path (Sartre was free of doubt, Nizan perhaps not). Even so, they participated happily in the life of the school, not at all separating themselves from the others. Sartre willingly took the lead in "hanging" new students, sometimes with a ferocity that shocked me. Neither one stood out from the crowd through his academic successes. We sensed that each of them carried within himself a work or a destiny.

I remember the satisfaction of my vanity when I learned from someone else that both of them had placed me on the right side of the barricade, among those they had not consigned to outer darkness.[1] From time to time, they subjected their classmates to new tests, and refined their judgments. Their friendship, it seems to me, maintained a special quality, compared to Sartre's relations with Pierre Guille or me or my own relations with Nizan. But after two years at the ENS, Nizan left for Aden (from which he brought back a book) as a tutor for the family of a rich Englishman. He married Henriette Halphen even before he had finished his studies. Thus, in the fourth year, the year of the *agrégation,* I found myself sharing rooms with Sartre and Guille. It was during this final year that Sartre and I became closest; my period of closest friendship with Nizan was the year before.

There are already several biographies of Paul Nizan. I don't think I have anything new to contribute about him, aside from a few indiscretions that are not worth reporting. Just a few memories.

Along with several others, I attended his "deliberations": Should I accept the offer from the English businessman, a long stay in Aden as his son's tutor? Nizan no doubt hesitated; to interrupt his studies and delay for a year the examination for the *agrégation* might appear, to his parents and perhaps to himself, as hardly reasonable. Nizan wrote to several more or less famous men of letters and visited them in search of advice. He did not take the statements of his elders seriously. He repeated for us, mockingly, the words of Georges Duhamel: "If you are asking the father of a family what you should do, I will say: finish your studies first. But if you are speaking to the man, he answers you: leave, young man, discover the larger world. You will learn more there than in all the books." Nizan, at bottom, had made his decision alone and immediately.

His rounds among the writers were characteristic of a *normalien* and they presaged his career as a man of letters. There was a hint of the practical joke ("*canular*") in these conversations in which a young man presented to a mature man less a moral dilemma than a personal choice. But the *normalien* took a literary pleasure from this joke. At the time, I had no doubt that Nizan would become a writer. I thought he was inferior to Sartre in intellectual force and philosophical power; on the other hand, I thought he had talent as a writer that did not seem obvious in Sartre.

What attracted us to Nizan was the mystery of his personality. He had been tempted by Action française, by the blue shirts of Georges Valois, before taking root in communism. But in 1926 and 1927, political opinion played little part in our relations. The mystery was located beyond his material elegance, beyond his humor, beyond his extraordinarily quick wit. One suspected that he was anguished, determined to overcome his anguish through action or serious thought, despite the intermittent gaiety beneath which he concealed himself.

Acute appendicitis, on the very day of his wedding, almost killed him. There were no antibiotics at the time. He developed peritonitis, and I shared with Henriette those days of dreadful anxiety. Later our paths diverged. He was committed, without reservations, to communism. I met him rarely during the 1930s; I liked and admired *Aden Arabie; Les Chiens de garde* (I'm not sure I read it to the end) displeased or rather shocked me. Our teachers did not deserve those insults for the single crime of not being revolutionaries. Why should they have been?

I often wonder now why we set Sartre and Nizan apart, even though neither one had yet written, or rather, published anything. The answer I can offer, for want of a better one, does not differ from the one I gave myself later when I was considering the chances of a student. Wrongly or rightly, we have a "gut" reaction to the abilities of a young man, we think he can obtain an *agrégation* easily or, on the contrary, only through hard work. Beyond that, we believe him capable or not, one day, of having something to say. In this sense, whatever our theory about the respective influence of nature, we attribute to genetic inheritance at least a negative causality; despite all his efforts, a person cannot go beyond the resources programmed in his genes. Mathematicians, I have been told, can discern their own limitations.

Did I have the conviction that Sartre would become what he did become, philosopher, novelist, playwright, prophet of existentialism, Nobel prize winner? In this form, I would answer no without hesitation. Even in another form: will he be a great philosopher, a great writer? The answer would not always have been the same nor would it ever have been categorical. On the one hand, I admired (and still admire) the extraordinary fertility of his mind and his pen. We teased him about the ease with which he wrote (at the time, I wrote with difficulty, and I was haunted by the blank page and the immobile pen). No more than three hundred fifty pages in the manuscript begun three weeks earlier: what's going on? we said to our classmate. Aside from his ease in writing, the richness of his imagination and capacity for construction in the world of ideas dazzled me (and dazzles me still). Not that doubts did not cross my mind. Sometimes he developed an idea at length in speech or in writing, simply because he had not fully grasped it and found proper expression for it. He built up theories whose flaws it was easy to grasp.

I envied his self-confidence. A memory comes back to me of a conversation on the boulevard Saint-Germain, not far from the Ministry of War. He revealed, without vanity, without hypocrisy, his idea of himself and his genius. To rise to the level of Hegel? Of course, the ascension would neither be too arduous nor would it take too long. Beyond that it might be necessary to struggle. Ambition, he said, took on two forms in his imagination: one was a young man in white flannel trousers, with his shirt collar open, slinking catlike from one group to another on a beach, amid charming young girls. The other image was a writer lifting his glass to answer a toast offered by men in evening dress standing around a table.

Sartre wanted to become a great writer, and he did. But in the meantime, he lost interest in evening dress, banquets, the outward signs of fame. Even at the time, although he rarely discussed politics, he already scorned the privileged and detested with all his heart those who proclaimed their rights, confident in their competence or their position of authority, the "bastards." He thought he had encountered them in the bourgeoisie of Le Havre, which I knew as well when I replaced him for a year (1933–34); at the tennis club, two courts were reserved for the "gentlemen from the Exchange."

The image of the ephebe touched on one of the subjects of our conversation: how to deal with one's own ugliness. Sartre spoke willingly of his ugliness (and I of mine), but in fact his ugliness disappeared as soon as he began to speak, as soon as his intelligence erased the pimples and swellings of his face. Besides, short, stocky, vigorous, he walked the tightrope, bowlegged, with a rapidity and ease that astounded everyone.

Sartre has stated, in a recent interview, that he was influenced by no one, perhaps a little by Nizan, certainly not by Aron. In essence, he is right. For two or three years, he took pleasure in subjecting his ideas to my criticism. Perhaps he derived some profit from our dialogues, but that has nothing to do with an influence. Let us take an example: psychoanalysis was for long a theme of our debates. He rejected it, once and for all, because psychoanalysis was involved with the unconscious and for him this concept was equivalent to the squaring of a circle; there was no separation between psychic life and consciousness. I finally gave up the hopeless debate on the conceptual problem, but I suggested that he should keep in mind the materials of psychoanalysis, even if he rejected the unconscious. The notion of "bad faith" provided him with the solution. He was the one who recognized it, and probably he would in any event have recognized the necessity to integrate some aspects of psychoanalysis into his universe, instead of excommunicating it altogether and once and for all.

Another of Sartre's concepts is in some way connected to our conversations. My thesis for the *diplôme d'études supérieures* was on the intemporal in Kant's philosophy, a subject that dealt simultaneously with the identifiable choice of one's character and the ever-present possibility of conversion, which allows everyone to redeem, or rather at a stroke to transfigure past experience. There is something of these theories in *Being and Nothingness* and in his plays. Indeed, he combined the two ideas in the identifiable choice of character and the freedom of conversion in his own way. Despite the existential choice of oneself, Sartre prides himself on beginning anew, at every moment, as though he refused to be a prisoner of his own past, as though he were denying responsibility for his acts or his writings, once they were completed.

I might support, with qualifications, his idea that he owed nothing to anyone by another memory. In a presentation in Léon Brunschvicg's seminar, he sketched his vision of the world. The question he had been asked concerned Nietzsche. Léon Brunschvicg was working on *The Progress of Consciousness in Western Thought* and was troubled by his chapter on Nietzsche. Should he be considered as a philosopher in the strict, almost technical, sense, or as a literary figure? Sartre chose the former and, by a device I no longer remember, he sketched the opposition between the *en-soi* (in-itself) and the *pour-soi* (for itself); things, these trees, these tables mean nothing, they are here or there, without reason, without finality, and by contrast, consciousness, at every moment, signifies and gives meaning to those blind, massive realities that negate it and that nevertheless exist only through it.

Sartre's vision of the world is not entirely his own. Quite obviously, it owes a good deal to Husserl and Heidegger. The former gave him much more than a vocabulary; thanks to phenomenology, he analyzed lived experience, the opening of consciousness to the object, the transcendence of the ego; thus the *pour-soi* becomes the subject in its immediacy, not the ego. Thus he borrowed from Heidegger's interpretation of time, of anguish, and of the world of objects. Perhaps through Merleau-Ponty he became aware of certain Hegelian ideas, as interpreted by Alexandre Kojève, the idea of love dreaming in vain of taking hold of a freedom, or that of the master who wants to gain recognition from the slave—a recognition that cannot be authentic since the slave has been deprived of freedom. There is no doubt that he seized ideas as they passed within his grasp. In 1945, Merleau-Ponty told me that he was careful not to tell Sartre of his ideas.

In *Les Mots*, he presents himself as without a father (one of my school friends smilingly noted: no father, born of a virgin, and himself the Logos), but in asserting that he had experienced no influence, he did not mean to deny his debt to Husserl and Heidegger; he borrowed, absorbed, integrated many concepts, themes, approaches of past and present philosophies. If he rejects the very notion of influence, this is because it suggests the passivity, even partial or temporary, of the one who experiences it.

His failure at the *agrégation* in 1928 affected him not at all, nor did my success lead me to revise my judgment about him or myself. I had come in first, substantially ahead of the second, Emmanuel Mounier (about 10 points out of 110 for the seven tests, oral and written). Of course, I was not indifferent to this success, I would be lying if I said so today; I preserved something of the character of the good student. I was not unaware that my success was due to strictly academic qualities (of an advanced level, to be more indulgent). The best of the three essays was the third, on the history of philosophy (Aristotle and Auguste Comte). Neither of the first two demonstrated the slightest originality. On the oral, I was given a passage from Aristotle's Physics which I had explicated in Léon Robin's seminar. I commented a Latin text by Spinoza, and I committed a misinterpretation of which I became aware as I was justifying it. I showed so much conviction in arguing for my mistake that the jury allowed itself to be convinced for the moment. The following day, it recovered its wits and common sense and took a point off (my teacher in *khâgne*, André Cresson, who was on the jury, told me the story).

I don't wish to be misunderstood: as a means of selection, the *agrégation de philosophie*, in the end, was as good as any other. Most candidates who deserved this piece of paper got it. Sartre's failure was remedied the following year when he came in first, with a higher score than mine. In 1928, he had not played the game; he had set out his philosophy of the moment. The following year he allowed himself to be persuaded to give the examiner what he wanted.[2] Afterward, everyone could go his own way.

Success in the *agrégation* did not at all make me vain. A few weeks later, even more after eighteen months, after my military service, the results of my years in the ENS seemed disappointing to me; at twenty-three in 1928, at twenty-five in the spring of 1930, what had I learned? What was I capable of doing? I hadn't worked very much during my first two years. Not having registered at the Sorbonne before entering the ENS, I had to spend two years on my *licence*, which left me some free time. I played tennis, read novels, great ones or fashionable ones, frequented the Louvre. I started to attend Edouard Le Roy's course in analysis at the Collège de France, but not for long. I took up large tomes on civil law, and gave them up after a few weeks. I began the study of mathematics texts with no more persistence. In retrospect, the last two years seem more fruitful, although I might have thought differently in 1928 or 1930. The subject of my thesis for the *diplôme d'études supérieures* required me to study Kant's works from before the *Critique of Pure Reason* down through *Religion within the Limits of Reason*. Every day I read the *Critiques*, for eight or ten hours a day. I don't know what I learned, nor what my understanding of Kantian thought was worth. The copy of the thesis I gave to Sartre and Nizan (Kant was on the *agrégation* syllabus the following year) was lost. I regret it only because of some curiosity. No doubt, the thesis deserved to be relegated to the ferocious criticism of the mice.[3]

I retain a memory of austere exaltation from my year lived in common with a philosopher. I continue to believe that I derived much more profit from it than from the book by Victor Delbos (standard at the time) or from any of my courses. Of course, if it's only a matter of passing examinations, mediators save a good deal of time and effort, providing students with an all purpose summary, the philosophical equivalent of ready-to-wear fashion. But nothing can replace, even for those who are not committed to philosophical labors, the deciphering of a difficult text. For years, after my year with Kant, all books seemed easy to me. I judged the level of books according to the mental tension each one demanded.

The year of the *agrégation*, I was obliged to study seriously Aristotle, Rousseau, and Auguste Comte. I read almost all of Comte's works a second time about thirty years later to help candidates for the *agrégation*, where Comte was once again on the syllabus. The history of philosophy occupied a substantial place in our studies, and it could hardly be otherwise, at least at the time.

Of the four certificates in philosophy, only one—logic and general philosophy—evoked current debates. The two others—psychology, and ethics and sociology—had more to do with the social and human sciences. Thus, the history of philosophy, even more than logic and general philosophy, put us in touch with the *philosophia perennis*. It is hardly necessary to add that there was no equivalent of the "new philosophers"; that the best professors, aside from Bergson, rarely appeared in the national press. To find a master to inspire us, whom we could attack, or whose work we could continue, we could only choose among Léon Brunschvicg, Alain, and Bergson (the last had already given up teaching). In the Sorbonne, Léon Brunschvicg was a mandarin among mandarins; he "philosophized" more than the others, and his work—the *Stages of Mathematical Thought, Human Experience and Physical Causality, The Growth of Consciousness in Western Thought*—could not fail to incite our respect. We could not judge his mathematical competence, but he gave us (I should say me) the feeling that he joined together scientific and philosophical culture. He shed light on moments in the history of Western philosophy with parallels from mathematics and physics. He did not break with tradition, he did not fall into the platitudes of idealism or academic spiritualism. He did not set himself at the level of the greats, but he peopled his life through his contact with them.

Given all that, what did he teach? Today, to reduce the jargon to a minimum, I would say that his interpretation of Kantian thought tended to reduce philosophy to a theory of knowledge. The *Critique of Pure Reason* demonstrated, definitively, that we know reality through the forms of the senses and the categories of understanding. We know only the world constructed by our minds, and there is no means of apprehension that would allow us to go beyond physics. In this sense, there is no metaphysics; science leaves to philosophy no specific subject other than science itself. In a different language, analytic philosophies present a closely related thesis: philosophy reflects on science or language; it reflects on all human activities. It does not bring a knowledge of reality outside of or beyond science.

Presented in this way, Brunschvicg's thought might seem to be derived from positivism. But I have omitted the other side of this neo-Kantianism: the idealism it proclaims and the moral attitude with which it ends up. It does not preserve the table of categories from Kant's *Critique*, nor does it accept the solution of the Third Antinomy (immanent determinism, transcendental freedom). Platonic and anti-Aristotelian, it aims toward the suppression of all obstacles to the progress of science, the fiction of immutable concepts. Einstein's renewal of the notions of space and time, far from contradicting the Kantian conception of the forms of sense experience, confirms their inspiration; the mind constructs reality through science, and science consists essentially not in elaborating concepts or deducing their consequences, but in judging.

This broad summary is designed only to suggest the kind of impasse toward which apprentice philosophers had the feeling they were being led. My philosophy teacher in Versailles took his inspiration from Brunschvicg when he devalued juridical concepts as opposed to judgment. In other fields, disciples of Brunschvicg, almost inevitably, had to reflect on the progress of science in relation to philosophical positions or else to rise to the most fundamental problems of the theory of knowledge.

Despite his rejection of traditional metaphysics, Léon Brunschvicg often resorted to a religious vocabulary, for example in one of his last books, *On True and False Conversion*. Hence, the frequently asked questions: Was he an atheist? Was he religious? The answer to the first question seems to me beyond doubt: he did not believe in the God of Abraham, Isaac, and Jacob, in the Christian God, or in the Trinity. He had no concern about the salvation of souls after death. Both the dogmas of Catholicism and the alliance of the Jewish people with its God were foreign to him.

Why did he use the expression "true conversion"? At the risk of simplifying or vulgarizing his thought, I would say that he did not want to concede to the churches the monopoly over religion and conversion. True conversion meant the liberation of the spirit in each individual, from egoism, from egocentrism. Religion also preaches this conversion, and this is why Brunschvicg was a tireless reader of Pascal and Spinoza. But true conversion does not hang on a decision by God; it is carried out by the individual's effort to rise above himself, to in some degree depersonalize himself. In the last analysis, isn't the consciousness of eternity, for Spinoza, the consciousness of grasping the truth? True conversion does not hope for salvation, it *is* salvation.

Humanity finally discovered that the earth was not at the center of the solar system; it has given up the notion of the absolute, unreal observer measuring time and space while discounting his own position. Similarly, moral progress is expressed by detachment from the self, by true dialogue, with everyone putting himself in the other's place. Spiritual conversion is inspired by the virtue of the scientist. The attitude of the pure scientist would lead to justice.

A harsh, almost stoic philosophy, Alexandre Koyré said to me once, which would even have some grandeur if it were expressed in a different language. When Léon Brunschvicg, at the meeting of the Société française de philosophie, replied to Gabriel Marcel, "I am less interested in the fate of my person than M. Marcel is in his," he anticipated, so to speak, the *Antimémoires* of Malraux. Religious in a sense, but removed from all established religions, a negator of metaphysics, he embodied a way of philosophy despite a rejection of systems that was carried to extremes. Thought is judgment, concepts are only stages toward the conquest of truth or the construction of reality. The same thought weaves relations among people who do justice to one another. We might add, for those who would call this immense work simplistic, that all the philosophy of the past remained latent, alive, in his books and his lectures.

While Léon Brunschvicg dominated the Sorbonne, between the two wars, Husserl's phenomenology and the thought of Heidegger had "gone beyond" or displaced German neo-Kantianism. As surprising as it may seem today, French and German philosophers were hardly aware of one another. The book by Georges Gurvitch, *Tendencies in Contemporary German Philosophy*, with a preface by Brunschvicg, came before the famous lectures Husserl gave in France, under the title of *Cartesian Meditations*. In addition, except for Jean Wahl, the French hardly knew more of contemporary Anglo-American philosophy; do they know it any better today? What is the explanation for this corporation of philosophy professors closed in on itself, ignorant of foreign developments?

The teaching of philosophy in lycées and universities, as it was presented to my generation, is subject to many reservations. The post-Kantians—

Fichte, Hegel—were not ignored, but they were never on the syllabus for the *agrégation*, on the pretext that their principal works had not been translated into French. The demigods of the postwar period—Marx, Nietzsche, Freud—did not belong to the pantheon in which were enshrined the authors of the *agrégation* syllabus. At least the ordinary philosophy teacher of the time maintained respect for the texts and a demand for rigor. The three demigods, geniuses every one, have said, or authorized the saying of, almost anything. It is easy to interest students by commenting on ideology, the eternal return, the death instinct. But these concepts, quintessentially ambiguous, defy precise definition; they suggest ideas that evade refutation, that are not susceptible of 'falsification', as contemporary English analytical philosophers would say. Commentary on the analysis of the *Critique of Pure Reason* maintains an educational value, it helps to shape the mind. Commentary on the aphorisms of *The Will to Power* stimulates the mind; it does not help young people to make good use of their reason.

In addition to Léon Brunschvicg, while I was at school, I spent time with another philosopher, Alain. I came to meet him several times outside the lycée Henri-IV and walked with him to his apartment on the rue de Rennes. I must have established personal relations with him through the intermediary of some of his students.

As far as I remember, I was more impressed by Alain's personality than by his philosophy. A volunteer soldier from the outset, he detested war and could stomach it only by living through it with the combatants. He had not betrayed his calling, had not participated in the avalanche of anti-German propaganda (even Bergson had not escaped the hysteria). At the time, most of us were in revolt against the war and our elders. There were few communists among the students of the ENS; those who thought of themselves as on the left, adhered to the Socialist Party, at least in spirit. The Catholics represented the right. Alain and his students were independent, neither communist nor socialist, but the eternal left, the left that never holds power, since it is defined by the resistance to power, which by its very essence leads to abuses and corrupts those who hold it.

I do not think I was ever entirely convinced by his thought, or rather by his political attitude, particularly by his refusal of an officer's stripes. Perhaps I would have passed the examination at the end of my military training if I had not been divided on this point. At the time, I admired *Mars ou la guerre jugée*, often splendid, but in the end a deeply unjust, or at least partial book. It may be true that certain leaders find in the exercise of command a compensation for the dangers and rigor of combat, but junior lieutenants, lieutenants, and captains in the infantry lived with their men, in the same trenches; they left their shelters together. To judge war on the basis of the intoxication of exercising command seems to me unreasonable, or even, to tell the truth, low. Simple soldiers sometimes love war. Certain officers, without loving it, conscientiously carry out their job. The physical and moral distance between the front and headquarters was never as great as it was from the time the fronts were frozen in September 1914 until 1918. This peculiarity of the operations should not serve as the basis for a philosophy of war which amounted, in reality, to a psychology of the military order.

Why were we so dominated by the authority of the soldier who, unlike all our teachers, had rejected both the *union sacrée* and rebellion? At the ENS in the 1920s we called into question the recent past. Heretics challenged the exclusive or predominant responsibility of Germany for the origin of the war.[4] Opinion on the left condemned the occupation of the Ruhr and called for reconciliation. Young people could no longer understand the statements that had been made a few years earlier by the most prestigious of our elders about Germany and the Germans. Alain, at least, had kept silent in the midst of the collective madness.

Alain's politics, as formulated in *Man against the Authorities*, which I later harshly criticized, was something I had never really adopted; it did not correspond to my intellectual temperament. I used it at a time when I knew nothing of societies or of economics, when, more or less badly, I found reasons to justify my feelings; pacifism, horror of war, adhesion to ideas of the left, universalism in reaction to the nationalism of our elders, hostility to the rich and powerful, a vague socialism (the Radical Party was becoming less and less acceptable); and an intellectual, especially a Jewish intellectual, is obliged to sympathize with the misfortune or the dignity of the humble. Alain's politics tempted me to the degree that they spared me the trouble of learning about reality, of imagining solutions to the problems posed to the teachers. A citizen against the authorities immediately assumes an irresponsible stance. Once I had overcome the uncertainties of my youth and the limits of my academic training, I took an extreme position on the other side. I considered myself responsible at almost every moment, and I was always inclined to ask myself what I could do in the place of those in power.

After the war, more out of indignation against my past than against Alain, I wrote two articles on his politics. I made the mistake of not recalling Alain's experiences at the front. What prevented him from living, what provoked his impotent fury, was the fate of the young men who wanted to live but who felt condemned to death. I have inscribed on the blade of my Academician's sword a Greek sentence from Herodotus: "No sensible man can prefer war to peace since, in war time, fathers bury their sons, while in peace time sons bury their fathers." Never has the tragedy of the generations been illustrated so forcefully as by the events of 1914–1918; few witnesses experienced the tragedy with his nobility and compassion. Even today, when I read Alain's last remarks before his enlistment, or his appeal to the enemy in 1917, I tremble with respect for his greatness.

Aside from politics, what did Alain contribute to us? Sartre, who was already thinking about perception, the image, the imaginary, took up Alain's argument about the essential difference between the perceived and the imagined. He freely cited Alain's question to those who claimed to *see* the Pantheon when not in front of it: "How many columns do you see on the facade of the Pantheon?" The radical heterogeneity of perception and imagination is found in Sartre's book on *The Image* and in *L'Imaginaire*.

What do I retain from Alain? He helped me to read the major authors, even though I subscribed neither to his method nor to its results. If one were to believe his disciples, if not Alain himself, the authentic philosophers, Plato or Descartes, were never mistaken; they had all said more or less the same thing. He drew a link between Kant, who lifted his hat to temporal authority without morally submitting to it, and Auguste Comte who accepted the rule of force and moderated it through spiritual power (public opinion, women), and he discovered a deep connection between them. What both of them had thought, preached, or taught was in the final analysis, the philosophy of Alain himself.

One day, Léon Brunschvicg, with more irritation than irony, told me of the presentations by Alain's students in an examination in which they had been asked to comment on a text by Descartes. "Let us remove, they said, the heavy layer of commentaries and exegeses that separates us from the text itself. Let us reconsider the text itself, as it was written, in its purity and truth. And then," Brunschvicg went on, "they recite what Alain has taught them." The contempt for history affected by Alain, communicated to disciples who lacked his genius, fostered a kind of obscurantism.

He himself was not taken in by his quips, his excesses, his excommunications. In 1931 or 1932, when I told him of my intention to think about politics, he replied: "Don't take my remarks on politics too seriously. There are men whom I do not like. I have spent my time in letting them know it." He was not unaware that he "missed" the historical dimension by always referring to human nature, a constant whose essential characteristics were immutable. He rejected Einstein and relativity, he rejected psychoanalysis. Out of ignorance? Out of lack of understanding? I don't think so. As far as relativity was concerned, the rejection had principally to do with lack of competence, but also with his intellectual hygiene: one must not shake the foundations of the temple of reason. He called psychoanalysis "monkey psychology," an expression that was infelicitous, at the least. He did not want to interpret men from below. He would have sympathized with the idea of the *Antimémoires* of André Malraux (but he certainly did not share Malraux's cult of the hero). He also would have had contempt for the "little pile" of secrets everyone carries within himself. As a moralist, he addressed the same man for whom French moralists have written through the centuries. But the moralist also taught philosophy in *khâgne*, as a professional philosopher and master thinker of the Third Republic.

In a private conversation, Marcel Mauss called him a "sophist." Without hostility, without passion, without contempt: a sophist in contrast with scientists or perhaps even with philosophers. He treated everything in terms of probability; he denied sociology in order to speak of public affairs in his own manner. He taught the young his vision of the world. With more severity, Dennis Brogan, around 1940, wrote a sentence that I used as an epigraph for an article on Alain in *La France libre:* "The prestige of a sophist like Alain foretells the ruin of a state." And yet colleagues like Elie Halévy and students like André Maurois saw the spark of genius in him. I think it was Elie Halévy who said: "He has a little genius, but I am not sure he makes the best use of it." Many others who knew him, either directly or through the intermediary of his disciples, hold obstinately to their belief in his genius. "A teacher of the *khâgne*, raised almost to the level of genius," I said on a television program devoted to him. His fervent disciples criticized me for the statement just as they reproached me for having pointed out that Alain has been infrequently translated and read in other countries. Even now, I hesitate to draw conclusions.

There is no doubt that he did not want to know some of the intellectual conquests of his century; he remained within the "eternal philosophy," as that was conceived by the body of teachers of philosophy in the lycées and universities of France. But the *Système des Beaux-Arts, Les Idées et les âges,* the *Propos* (on education, on happiness), the books on the novelists he loved, all this philosophical literature reveals a writer, even though his style in the end is irritating. Too much a syncretist to be recognized as an original philosopher, he remains a moralist and a serious writer on ideas.

Georges Canguilhem may have provided the connection between Alain and me. We were linked by a solid friendship, different from the one I had with the Nizan-Sartre group, but nonetheless solid. He had been taught by Alain at Henri-IV and shared his convictions at the time, particularly his pacifism. Through him, I came into closer contact with Alain's students, shaped by their master more than other students at the ENS were by theirs. We met again in Toulouse in 1939, where he demonstrated to my wife, who remained alone when I was in the army, the affection and kindness of his true character, which was often masked by the brusqueness he adopted for his official duties. We met yet again at the Sorbonne in 1955; sometimes he terrified the students, but he was always respected by them. A medical doctor, a historian of medical and biological thought, he worked, taught, and wrote (all his lectures were written out) much more than his publications would indicate. Thus careful readers are not deceived by his modesty: they grant him the rank he deserves. I say no more about him: he would be angry if I attempted a literary portrait, hardly compatible with a half-century of friendship.

Politically, the ENS contained two coherent groups: on one side the socialists and their sympathizers, on the other the Catholics. Lucien Herr, who ruled over the library during my first two years, inspired the first group, in which Georges Lefranc was very active. Lefranc played an important role in the noncommunist CGT, in the training institute for militants, and wrote a number of books on workers' movements and the Popular Front. Pierre-Henri Simon belonged to the other group, the Catholics—called the "talas"—who at the time leaned toward the right perhaps in the limited sense that they did not rebel against the virtues and patterns of thought that had ruled wartime France.

I was more politicized at the time than Sartre or Guille. From time to time, I became excited by the events of parliamentary life. I took part in family discussions on Herriot and the crisis of the franc; an uncle who worked for a stockbroker once silenced me: "I'll listen to you when you speak of philosophy; you know nothing of finance, so keep quiet." This memory of humiliation and a few others of the same kind are for me like Proust's madeleine; I feel the humiliation a second time, or perhaps I sympathize with my vanished self. I have never relived pleasant experiences with such intensity.

I can find some scattered evidence of my interest in politics. In 1925 or 1926, through the intermediary of an association for the League of Nations that I had joined, I spent two weeks in Geneva during the annual meeting of the General Assembly. I heard a speech by Paul-Boncour, who passed for a great speaker and whom I admired. He argued for the cause of universal peace. It was in Geneva that for the first time I met Betrand de Jouvenel, only a few years older than I but already a celebrated journalist.

What place did politics occupy in my thought of the future? The day when I witnessed the parliamentary assassination of Herriot, did I dream myself of mounting the speaker's platform? I don't think so. On the other hand, the emotion provoked in me by oratorical contests helps me to understand militants, crowds, and party loyalists. Susceptible to the eloquence of Paul-Boncour or Herriot, later to that of Déat, I trembled while listening to them, I felt with them the hostility they declared against their adversaries. Herriot seemed to me an innocent victim in the lion's den. A few years later, I understood enough of financial mechanisms to arrive at a totally different judgment of Herriot, the events, and my opinions at the time.

It was in 1925 or 1926 that I joined the SFIO, the local section of the fifth *arrondissement.*[5] Why did I join? I must give an answer at which my readers can only smile: we had to do something for the people or for the workers. I imposed membership on myself as a contribution to the cause, the cause of amelioration of the unfortunate classes. A clear memory comes back to me: a letter to a comrade named Blanchet whom I had met in Geneva and liked. I described to him my hesitations, my consciousness of a kind of obligation—today we would say the obligation is to commit oneself—with the conclusion that I was going to join the SFIO.

In the first issue of *Les Temps modernes*, I was still talking about the chances for socialism (in a mediocre article). A Jewish intellectual of good will who chooses the career of letters, estranged from his fellows who remain in textiles or banking, can hardly do anything but will himself, feel himself, to be on the left. I might almost say, paraphrasing my colleague Robert Escarpit, that I was born on the left, conditioned by psychosocial determinants. I remained there, at least as long as I had not created my own, autonomous thought. Have I remained there to the end?

I spend little time with the great men of our society, the men in power, the heads of great national or international companies, sometimes I visit one of them, or one of them comes to see me. They are no different from ordinary mortals, they seem to me neither more human nor more inhuman than their fellows. Big capitalists are reluctant to accept the fact that one can argue in favor of capitalism while criticizing some of their practices. To be sure, there has been no lack of businessmen and government officials who have been pleased by or who have congratulated me for the influence exercised by my writings. But there remains between us the inevitable, unbridgeable distance between the men of state or economic power and a free intellectual.

On one point—an important one—my sensibility is in harmony with that of the "real" left. Above all, I despise everyone who thinks he is of another essence. I remember two quarrels that almost degenerated into street brawls: one with a bank officer, the other with a diplomat who resembled Proust's Norpois. Both occurred during the Algerian War. One said: "I'll get my own hunting rifle to bring the Algerians back into line." "You don't consider the Algerians to be people like us," said the ambassador, in the presence of Paul-Henri Spaak, at a lunch among friends. I am not sure that, on either occasion, I maintained the tone of polite Parisian dialogue.

NOTES

1. I was perhaps more moved by this "recognition" on the part of Sartre and Nizan than by the praise given me by Léon Brunschvicg for a presentation on the ontological argument in St. Anselm and Kant.

2. He recognized the effectiveness of my technique on the exam and asked my advice.

3. Since then, Mme Lautmann has found a second, uncorrected copy among her old papers. I have not yet managed to read it.

4. Léon Brunschvicg never wavered on this point: to an exorbitant ultimatum, Serbia had given a moderate response. Austria had rejected that response and bombarded Belgrade. From that point on, in the absence of a miracle, the system of alliances provoked a general conflagration. At the time, I real Alfred Fabre-Luce's first book, *Victory,* so heretical that it provoked a scandal. He attempted to apportion responsibility for the war between the two camps.

5. Georges Lefranc assures me that I never joined the SFIO, only the Etudiants socialistes. But since I remember a meeting with mature men, I conclude that I attended these section meetings without ever getting a party card.

3

THE DISCOVERY
OF GERMANY

I will pass over the eighteen months of my military service (from October 1928 to March 1930), most of which I spent at the fort of Saint-Cyr, used by the weather service of the army air corps. After a few weeks in Metz in an engineering regiment, I was transferred to Saint-Cyr where I learned the rudiments of meteorology that instructors taught to draftees, most of whom were sons of good families. Thanks to my intervention, Sartre also did his military service there. Put off by the job of telephone operator in national headquarters in Paris, I returned to the fort, where I taught two groups of students the little I knew about cloud formations; I tried to communicate the art of distinguishing among cumulus, cirrus, and other kinds of clouds.

This parenthesis between school and life remains in my memory as an empty time, in the strongest sense of the word. I had failed the examination for which military training was a preparation; success would have led to admission to a school for officers and reduced my time in uniform by six months. Influenced, without really being persuaded, by Alain, I had not determined either to succeed or fail in the examination. My mistakes in reading military maps and my ineptitude in leading a patrol accomplished the rest.

Was it immediately after the *agrégation* or after this parenthesis that I had—for the first but not the last time—the feeling that I was wasting my life? Was I going to fail in the duty I had assigned myself in my dialogue with myself: to make myself while making something else (an expression borrowed, I think, from a philosopher)? Of course, during my student years, I let myself go during the summers, from one tennis tournament to the next, but at the end of every vacation, a feeling of guilt suppressed the memory of amusements. In any event, in the fall of 1928 and the spring of 1930, rich in certificates and poor in true knowledge, I questioned myself.

If I had limited my ambition to teaching philosophy in a lycée for the rest of my life, there would have been no further obstacle to overcome. During the first years, I would have been a good, probably very good, teacher. I was passionately interested in philosophy, and I expressed myself with facility, more in speaking than in writing. At the time, I managed to make the most abstruse controversies among philosophers understandable to listeners who were usually indifferent or bored. My teachers, my classmates, and my parents decreed that I was destined for another career, that of a university professor, indeed as a philosopher. But at the age of twenty-three or twenty-five, what had I gotten from my six years of study after the baccalaureate? Perhaps the ability to learn; in that respect, the time spent reading the great philosophers had not been fruitless. But how was I to direct my personal thinking? Since the choice might determine my entire existence, what should I choose as a thesis subject?

Why did I first choose biology, then the notion of the individual? I did not want to follow the example of many of my classmates, even the most brilliant among them, like Vladimir Jankélévitch, for example: minimizing risk by writing a thesis in the history of philosophy. I might have written a good book on Kant or Fichte. My only master at the Sorbonne, Léon Brunschvicg, left little room for metaphysics or the perennial philosophy. If philosophy aspires to its own truth, that truth will not coincide with the truth whose conditions, methods, and limits have been revealed by exact science. Through what miraculous faculty can philosophy attain a metaphysical truth, essentially different from scientific knowledge and superior to it?

Psychology occupied a substantial place in lycée courses, as a survival. If it is admitted that psychology has not yet reached, and perhaps never will reach, the level of rigor of physics, should philosophy devote its energies to filling in the provisional gaps in scientific knowledge?

Bergson did nothing more to open a path for apprentice philosophers. He too referred to scientific truth and developed a kind of metaphysics on the basis of a critique of certain results of science. At the time, we knew almost nothing of phenomenology or analytic philosophy. I would probably have been attracted to the method of the analytic philosophers. It did not, so to speak, come within our ken.

Since philosophical reflection was supposed to be applied to a scientific discipline, I chose biology, about which I knew little and which did not require mathematical training (I suffered all my life from this ignorance). Did I begin before or after my military service? Before, I think, but I'm not sure. All my papers from before the war were destroyed during the hostilities, and I now rely less on my memory of the facts than on my memory of ideas or even of individuals.

I sometimes went to the laboratory of the ENS; I read many books and came upon genetics. Etienne Rabaud still held the chair of general biology in the Sorbonne, and he had declared war, once and for all, on Mendelism, genetics, and experiments on the fruit fly that had permitted mapping the genes on the four chromosomes. What was the source of this, peculiarly French, stubborn refusal, while in the rest of the world, Mendelism had been integrated into accepted knowledge, and while French scientists, like Lucien Cuénot, had contributed to the rediscovery of the laws of heredity? The answer, discounting for nonscientific motives, finds some clarity in Thomas Kuhn's celebrated theory: the structure of chromosomes, of hereditary matter, the atoms of heredity that constitute the genes, did not fit with Etienne Rabaud's paradigm, a paradigm of a living totality, of the harmony between organism and milieu. One day, Marcel Mauss, who considered himself a scientist, told me on a bus platform: "I don't believe in Mendelism." As for Charles Blondel and Célestin Bouglé, they did not "believe" in psychoanalysis; they did not discuss it, they rejected it.

There was no need for extraordinary prescience to see, in 1930, that genetics was opening the royal way to the analysis of living matter, and also toward manipulation, for good or ill of the hereditary characteristics of vegetables, animals, men. But as my wonder at the perspectives of biology grew, I lost all confidence in my enterprise. What could I say about the procedures of a geneticist that he could not say better than I, once he was indeed to reflect on his work? What more is there to say about the biological individual than what biology teaches or will teach us? I could have followed the path taken, brilliantly, by Georges Canguilhem: the history of biological thought, the elaboration of concepts, the transformation of paradigms. I gave it up before having seriously tried, for two very different but convergent reasons.

In the spring of 1930, through the intermediary of the service of French culture in foreign countries headed by Jean Marx in the Foreign Ministry, I obtained a post as teaching assistant in French at the University of Cologne, under a well known professor, Léo Spitzer. The relatively heavy obligations of courses and seminars did not leave me enough time to absorb the knowledge demanded by my project. The other reason, decisive in itself, had to do with my existential choice, to use an expression that became fashionable after 1945. Ever since the class of *philosophie*, my studies had not been confined to academic exercises; transcendental deduction does not resemble a Latin translation and demands a totally different intellectual effort. Despite everything, my reading of the great works, the dialogues on idealism or realism, interested only my mind, not my heart. Rebellion against Léon Brunschvicg had something to do with my second choice, which was definitive. Brunschvicg's ethics, those of Socrates as he and Elie Halévy interpreted them—with demands for universality and reciprocity—I accepted without trouble, as I still do today. But taking as a model and a foundation for existence the attitude of the scientist in his laboratory left me unsatisfied. The scientist practices the ethics of the scientist only in his laboratory (even so, sociologists have demystified this excessively flattering image of the scientist). A *fortiori*, the man in each of us is not a scientist; "true conversion" belongs to the realm of cliché. I therefore searched for a subject of investigation that would simultaneously interest the heart and the mind, which would demand an attempt at scientific rigor and, at the same time, would engage me entirely in my research. One day, on the banks of the Rhine, I decided for myself.

I have recalled this meditation so often that in the end I am afraid I may have confused my actual experience with my later reconstruction. I nevertheless remember that, exalted by the joy of discovery, I wrote my brother Robert an enthusiastic and barely intelligible letter. Broadly speaking, I had the illusion or the naïveté to believe that I was discovering the historical condition of the citizen or of man himself. How, as a French Jew, situated at a particular moment in time, could I understand the whole of which I was one of many hundreds of millions of atoms? How could I grasp the whole except from a point of view, one among innumerable others? There followed from this a quasi-Kantian problem: to what extent was I capable of objectively understanding history—the nations, parties, and ideas whose conflicts filled the chronicles of the centuries—and *my* time? A critique of historical or political knowledge should answer this question. This set of problems involved another dimension: the subject, in search of objective truth, is immersed in the material he wants to explore (it penetrates him), in the reality from which, as historian or economist, he extracts the object of scientific analysis. I gradually grasped my two tasks: to understand or know my time as honestly as possible, without ever losing awareness of the limits of my knowledge; to detach myself from immediate events without, even so, accepting the role of spectator. Later, when I became a commentator in the daily press, my tendency to look at events from a distance, to present the world as it was, not the ways of changing it, constantly irritated many of my readers. I will return to my experience as a journalist. I was far from it in the spring of 1931, when I was lecturing to German students about *Le Désert de l'amour*, *Le Baiser au lépreux*, and the *Journal de Salavin*.

In 1930–31, the department of romance languages in the University of Cologne, headed by Léo Spitzer (surrounded by a coterie of charming young women), lacked neither warmth nor brilliance. Enrico de Negri, the reader in Italian, who remained, through the years and despite separations, a dear friend, and who also had philosophical training, woke early every morning to translate Hegel's *Phenomenology*. I had a few quarrels with Léo Spitzer, for which I was entirely responsible (I sometimes get carried away), but in general I liked the atmosphere of the University: students in lectures and especially in seminars seemed to me warmer, more open, less reserved than French students. I have no memory of any incident that might be referable to my Jewishness. Besides, Léo Spitzer was also Jewish, assimilated as they said. After Hitler's rise to power, he complimented me on a moderate article on National Socialism in *Europe;* he criticized me for not having sufficiently stressed the "new civilization" carried by National Socialism.

In the university year 1930–31 I gave a course on the French counter-revolutionaries Joseph de Maistre and Louis de Bonald; I read Claudel and Mauriac with the students—most of them shared the feelings these works provoked in me. From my contacts with these young people—despite the nationalistic passions of the time—I derived a lasting impression, a kind of friendship for the Germans, a feeling that was suppressed by Nazism and returned after 1945. In Tübingen in 1953, as a *Gastprofessor* for a few weeks, I rediscovered German students, entirely different and yet so like their predecessors. As un-Hitlerian and un-nationalistic as possible, they loudly agreed when I improvised this definition of world history: *die Weltgeschichte, diese Mischung von Heldentum und Blödsinn* (world history, a mixture of heroism and stupidity).

It was during this year at Cologne that I read *Das Kapital* for the first time. At the Sorbonne, I had given a presentation on historical materialism. Célestin Bouglé, probably correctly, criticized me for having softened Marx's thought; I used Engels and his notion of "in the last analysis." I had also studied the Italians: Mondolfo and the two Labriolas; I was reluctant to attribute to Marx a determinist explanation of *all* human history; at the time, I was not familiar enough with the early works or the *Grundrisse* to recon-stitute the Marxism of Marx, as I tried to do at the Collège de France in 1976–77, almost half a century later.

In 1931, I did not have enough knowledge of economics to understand competently or to judge *Das Kapital*. But two questions governed my reading. One was economic: Does Marxist thought help to explain the great crisis? The other was more philosophical: Does the Marxism of Marx, as a philosophy of history, free us from the heavy obligation that is nevertheless a constituent part of our humanity, of *choosing* among different parties? If the future is already written, inevitable and redemptive, only those who are blind or confined by their personal interests will reject its advent. In the contemporary interpretation of Marxism, it was the philosophy of history that simultaneously attracted and repelled me. Did the contradictions of capitalism necessarily lead to socialism through the intermediary of a revolution or progressive reforms? Did the great depression that was ravaging the world and tragically affecting Germany confirm Marx's predictions? And, similarly, did it justify the communist movement, and the Soviet Union as well? I don't want to give the wrong impression: I was not looking to *Das Kapital* for a confirmation of my rejection of the Soviet Union; on the contrary, I was hoping to find there a confirmation of socialism as the next necessary phase of history.

A reader of today will, justifiably, consider these questions primitive. But I had barely begun to study social science. Professional economists, insofar as we understood them, were agreed neither on the diagnosis nor on the treatment of the crisis. All historians now consider the restoration of a balanced budget in response to deflation and depression to be senseless; observers at the time did not all condemn the strategy. Franklin Delano Roosevelt was elected in 1932 with a program that included a balanced budget. The literature on the crisis that I read in Germany—the work of essayists rather than of specialists—accused the "structure" of the German economy, "overindustrialization," and the agriculture of eastern Germany. My ignorance of economics in 1931 and 1932 was demonstrated in articles I published in *Libres Propos* and *Europe*. To prepare this chapter, I reread them, without pleasure but without humiliation. To become a commentator on history in the making, I had a lot to learn.

An anecdote of 1932, after the return of Edouard Herriot to the Foreign Ministry, comes to mind frequently: it is as vivid now as it was fifty years ago. Emmanuel Arago, who frequented political circles, and whose brother was my brother Adrien's best friend, introduced me to an undersecretary in the Foreign Ministry, Joseph Pagnon. I had spoken to Arago about my anxiety in the face of political developments in Germany, because of the nationalistic furor that had seized the entire people and the threat of war that Adolf Hitler's rise to power would cause to hang over Europe. The undersecretary asked me to speak, and I delivered a lecture, brilliant I suppose, in the pure style of a student from ENS. He listened to me attentively, apparently with interest. When my speech had ended, he answered me, by turns ridiculous and to the point: "Meditation is essential. Whenever I find a few moments of free time, I meditate. So I am grateful to you for having given me so many subjects for meditation. The prime minister, minister of foreign affairs, possesses exceptional authority, he is a man out of the ordinary. The moment is ripe for all initiatives. But you, who have spoken so well about Germany and the dangers appearing on the horizon, what would you do if you were in his place?" I do not remember my answer; I am sure that it was embarrassed, unless I kept silent. What should I have said?

This lesson from a diplomat to a future commentator bore fruit. Fifteen years later, in the offices of *Combat*, I asked Albert Ollivier, who had criticized the government in an editorial: "What would you do in its place?" He answered, more or less: "That's not my problem; it has to find what to do, I have to criticize." As often as possible, I have tried to carry out my role as a commentator in an entirely different spirit, to suggest to governments what they should or could do. Sometimes I knew that my suggestions were inapplicable in the short term. At least, in influencing public opinion, I helped to facilitate action that seemed to me desirable (as I did, for example, during the Algerian war).

I originally thought of entitling this chapter "The Discovery of Germany and of Politics." The two discoveries went together. My pacifist and moralistic obsessions, derived from Alain, were also fostered by a conviction about history: "The interest our country takes in the German crisis comes . . . from a profound intuition: whether we like it or not, the fate of Germany is also the fate of Europe." I took up this subject again immediately after the defeat of the Third Reich in 1945. In delivering the *laudatio* when I received the Goethe Prize, Ralf Dahrendorf was not far wrong when he said that Germany was my fate.[1]

I am now attempting to reconstruct the feelings I had during my earliest encounters with German culture. When I arrived in Cologne in the spring of 1930, I could puzzle through the newspapers; I had trouble understanding the German of Spitzer, the teaching assistant, and the students; and I struggled through philosophical works. During the academic year 1930–31 that I spent in Cologne, I developed enough competence in the language so that it was no longer a barrier between me and people I talked to. I was aware of the distress of German youth, and of the warmth that characterized personal relations; even the students who were more or less close to National Socialism did not reject dialogue. Those whom I approached, in Cologne and Berlin, did not resemble the monsters that are depicted today. We would drink together on the banks of the Rhine or the Spree, and suddenly there was a gust of love or friendship that transfigured the evening. But it was

German culture rather than the young Germans I met that captured me forever.

It was a shock that may at first appear surprising. I had spent an entire year with Kant. Although an inadequate knowledge of Hume had limited my understanding of the three Critiques, I had absorbed a precious, perhaps the most precious, element of German philosophy. I never forgot the categorical imperative, the essence of ethics; nor did I forget religion within the limits of reason. But I had translated Kantianism into the neo-Kantianism of Léon Brunschvicg. Kant fit easily into the historical universalism of French thought, at least as it was expressed in the Sorbonne.

My unsystematic reading oscillated between two poles; Husserl and Heidegger on the one hand, and the sociologists, the neo-Kantian school of southwest Germany, Heinrich Rickert and Max Weber on the other. Both gave me a feeling of extraordinary richness, compared to which French writers suddenly seemed to me mediocre, almost empty. A half-century later, I am inclined, to say the least, toward a more reserved judgment. The conceptual richness of the language and of the German philosophical tradition easily create an illusion. The *Sinnhafte Zusammenhänge* lose something of their charm when they become "significant groups" or "networks of meaning." At the time, I felt an admiration for Karl Mannheim that now surprises me. A few years ago, I devoted a seminar session to *Ideology and Utopia* and reread the book for that purpose: I wondered why it had enjoyed such renown. But back to the past.

Simone de Beauvoir has recounted how I spoke to Sartre about Husserl and awakened in him a feverish curiosity. In studying phenomenology, I too experienced a kind of liberation from my neo-Kantian training. At the time I had already, so to speak, repressed my metaphysical impulses; I was less impressed by transcendental phenomenology or the *epoché* than by the method, the way of looking, of the phenomenologist. I meditated on History and the immanence of meanings within human reality—a reality that lent itself to deciphering. It seemed to me that Dilthey had lacked a philosophy like Husserl's in order to clarify his intuitions. Grasping meanings in history in the making led me, or led me back, to Max Weber, whose greatness I gradually came to admire as I discovered that I was linked to him by a *Wahlverwandschaft,* an elective affinity.

Why was it that, in my contact with the Germans and particularly with Max Weber, I was drawn to sociology, while Emile Durkheim had repelled me? To answer this question, I must, to repeat an expression I have already used, go in search of a past which, although it's mine, is hardly less foreign and objectified than if it belonged to someone else.

At the Sorbonne, between 1924 and 1928, Paul Fauconnet and Célestin

Bouglé taught sociology. The former was an orthodox disciple of Durkheim; the latter was also a disciple, but more free-spirited, less of a "sociologist." Neither one created disciples. Neither one had teaching assistants. Students at the ENS, convinced of their superiority, did not frequent classes at the Sorbonne. I must have gone to Bouglé's course from time to time, since, as I have already said, I gave a presentation there on historical materialism.

Of course, I read the major books by Durkheim and his disciples, but the spark did not appear. At the ENS, I was moved sometimes by Kant (even by Descartes), sometimes by Proust (or, but I'm not sure, by Dostoevsky). Then, I escaped from myself, from my doubts, from the judgment of others; I became identified with the understanding of the reason within me. At one point, in *A la recherche du temps perdu*, I rediscovered the difficulty of living, the slavery to which one is reduced by one's obsession with the judgment of others, the inevitability of disillusion. I have retained my admiration for Proust, although I have not reread *A la recherche* for many years. Kant or Proust, transcendental deduction or Mme Verdurin's salon, the categorical imperative or Charlus, intelligible character or Albertine. Compared to these two, neither *The Division of Labor*, nor *Suicide*, nor *The Elementary Forms of the Religious Life* touched my heart. They were simple objects of study that I could discuss in case of need. A good *agrégé* in philosophy in my time could discuss anything at all.

I am afraid, once again, that I am embellishing. In addition to Kant and Proust, there was also politics. I almost never talked about politics with Sartre, Nizan, Lagache, or even Canguilhem; I did a little more with less intimate friends, friends of Robert's rather than mine, whom I saw from time to time. Politics awakened my passions; even long after my education in Germany, I shared the feelings of crowds in public meetings. I remember a meeting early in the period of the Cartel des Gauches: Paul-Boncour was greeted with acclamations; Herriot began to speak: "He has finished speaking and you are still listening to him"; more applause. I confess, to my shame, that much later I was carried away by the eloquence of Marcel Déat, totally different from that of Paul-Boncour or Edouard Herriot, more reasoned, less emotional, and fueled by an extraordinary elocutionary talent.[2] But the taste for politics represented for me an equivalent of weakness, the inclination of "the Arons" for the easy path.

Durkheim's sociology did not affect me in my role as apprentice metaphysician, nor as a reader of Proust, eager to grasp the comedy and tragedy of man in society. Durkheim's formula: "God or society," shocked or angered me. The explanation of suicide by means of statistical correlations left me unsatisfied. Ethical teaching on the basis and in the name of society seemed to me a counterpart to Catholic teaching, and a fragile one for the simple reason that society did not constitute a coherent whole.

Right now, a kind of neo-Durkheimism has been joined with a variety of Marxism: the dominant ideology has replaced society as the ultimate force. This sociology suggests an interpretation of collective life that is in some ways close to that of Durkheim. Durkheim postulated a unified society, so that the same values were imposed on all classes. Those who use the notion of dominant ideology describe a class society; they emphasize the omnipotence of the dominant ideology and reduce its moral authority by attributing it to the privileged or ruling classes. Durkheim, on the contrary, hoped to restore morality to the dominant position that it had lost. The denunciation of the dominant ideology leaves me as bemused as I am by the divinization of society. The same theory does not work for both totalitarian and democratic societies.

For some reason, Max Weber provoked my sometimes passionate interest, unlike Emile Durkheim. I was more open in 1931 and 1932 than I had been between 1924 and 1928. At the ENS, still a student, I had not yet broken my ties with my family, the country, and the banalities of the university. Max Weber also objectified the lived reality of men in society, but he did so without "reifying" them; he did not, as a matter of method, leave out of account the rationalizations that men give for their practices or their institutions. (In fact, Durkheim pays more attention to the motives or impulses of social actors than his methodology would suggest.) What struck me in Weber was a vision of world history, his enlightening perspective on the originality of modern science, and his reflection on the historical and political condition of mankind.

His studies of the great religions fascinated me; sociology understood in those terms preserved the best elements of its philosophical origins. It proposed as its task the reconstruction of the meaning men had given to their existence and of the institutions that had preserved religious messages, had transmitted or ritualized them, and the ways in which the prophets had shaken, revitalized, and renewed them. Perhaps Max Weber's sociology of religion is not so opposed to that of Durkheim as I thought a half-century ago. But, reading Max Weber, I heard the rumors, the creaking of our civilization, the voice of the Jewish prophets and, as a sardonic echo, the ravings of the Führer. Bureaucracy on the one hand and the charismatic authority of the demagogue on the other—that conflict recurs throughout history. In 1932 and 1933, I glimpsed for the first time, in the constructions of the sociologist who was also a philosopher, my ethical dilemmas and my hopes.

Durkheim had not helped me to philosophize in the light of sociology. A secular ethics as a replacement for a failing Catholic ethics—this was the civic mission that Durkheim had given himself—left me cold, to say the least. A disciplined man, with a strict morality, Kantian in his life and his writings, he compels respect. He was perhaps right in thinking that revolutions do not transform societies in depth and create more noise than good. During the 1930s, Marxism and the Soviet Union troubled me and National Socialism threatened France and Judaism throughout the world. Sociology that did not see revolutions in a tragic perspective floated in a space above our real conditions. Max Weber had misunderstood neither social systems nor the irreversible and fatal decisions taken by men of destiny. Thanks to his philosophical consciousness, he had linked awareness of history with that of the present, the sociologist and the man of action. Thanks to him, my future course, glimpsed on the banks of the Rhine, took shape.

In addition to these two reasons for my attraction to him—the immanence of meaning in social reality and the closeness to politics—there was another: his concern with the epistemology that was specific to the social or human sciences. He, too, was a neo-Kantian. He was looking for a universal truth, in other words a form of knowledge that would be valid for everyone in search of such a truth. At the same time, he was acutely aware of the ambiguity of human reality, of the multiplicity of questions that the historian is entitled to ask of other men, of the present or the past. This plurality of questions explains the renewal of historical interpretations that Max Weber attempted to limit. Hence, the duality of *Sinnadäquation* and *Causaladäquation* (the understanding of meaning and the understanding of causality): it is not enough that a relationship is intellectually satisfying, we must also demonstrate its truth. Of all the motives that caused the Germans (which Germans?) to vote for National Socialism, which were determinative? What causes provoked those motives? From this oscillation between the plurality of plausible interpretations and the concern for a true explanation—an oscillation that I saw as the center of Weber's thought—came my own work in my two theses.

This is how I explain to myself my allergy to Durkheim's sociology and my wonder at the discovery of German sociology, with a background of the torment of the German people and the rise of Nazism. A sociology designed to establish civic instruction in teachers' colleges seemed colossally irrelevant in the face of the catastrophe that was brewing in the beer cellars and the stadiums. What a tragic irony—as Marcel Mauss himself recognized—that Durkheim's idea of the birth of religious faith in collective trance, in torchlight, was incarnated in Nuremberg, with thousands and thousands of young Germans adoring their own community and their Führer.

Max Weber created the concept of the charismatic leader, and in the name of axiological neutrality, he applied it to the Jewish prophets as well as to American demagogues like Huey Long. Would he have refused to put Hitler in the same category as the Buddha? Would I have protested at the time against the refusal to differentiate between values and people? I am not sure.

Often, in the course of the years 1931 and 1932, I wondered whether I was not getting lost in all directions; after the event, once I had returned to France, I had the feeling that I had learned a great deal.

I witnessed the final years, the agony of the Weimar Republic. In Cologne, I lived with a middle-class German family that rented me a room. I vaguely remember the head of the family, who frequently evoked the image of a Germany that had finally been defeated by a coalition of the entire world; his wife knew Jewish families that were *so anständig* (so acceptable). During my second stay, after an unfortunate choice (the wife had warned me in advance that her husband often came home at night a bit drunk), I found a comfortable two-room apartment, where I did not share meals with the landlord. I established connections not with my landlords but with students and other teaching assistants.

In Cologne, I met a young student whose charm enchanted me, Rudy Schröder. His father sold raincoats and umbrellas. We were very close friends during my stay. He detested National Socialism. Two years later, he came to Paris, where he lived with difficulty until war was declared. He joined the Foreign Legion; after the war, I learned from his wife, from whom he had long been separated, that he had joined the forces of Ho Chi Minh in Indochina. One day, I read an article in *Le Figaro* by Dominique Auclères with the title *Le Colonel SS Rudy Schröder*. Rudy had become a familiar, a favorite of Ho Chi Minh. I tried to reach him with a letter that he probably never received. In 1946, his parents had asked me for news of him; around 1960, I heard from some Germans that he was a professor at the University of Leipzig. If he is still living in East Germany, I would like to meet him. I doubt that life has changed him into a good communist. I am not surprised that he deserted the Foreign Legion and French order in Saigon or Hanoi; in the name of what could I blame him? I am naïve enough to believe that we could meet again.

In Cologne, with teaching and preparation for courses, the reading of *Capital*, conversations with students, time at the tennis club (where I was classed second or third), and the rich museum of painting from the Rhenish school, I had little opportunity to observe the unemployed or the poverty around me. In Berlin, I spent a good deal of time in the *Staatsbibliothek*. I nevertheless had direct experience of Weimar culture during the two final years before the catastrophe. As far as philosophy was concerned, I knew the essentials. Husserl and Heiddegger on the one hand, the survivors of the Second International, the Frankfurt School, and Karl Mannheim on the other, made up the two poles of philosophical-political reflection. After 1945, French philosophy continued phenomenology, *Existenzphilosophie*, and the Hegelianized Marxism that dominated German philosophy in the 1930s.

George Lukács's *History and Class Consciousness*, from 1923, a seminal work for Marxists in search of Hegel, was rediscovered in the 1950s by Maurice Merleau-Ponty, who, oddly, christened it a work of "Western Marxism."

We witnessed the final flowering of film and theater of the period. I gave French lessons to the famous director Max Reinhardt. We were charmed by the *Dreigroschenoper*, moved by *Mädchen in Uniform*. *Kulturbolschevismus* still flourished, and besides the châteaus and the museums of classical painting, we were offered the works of Klee and Kokoschka. A *fin de siècle* atmosphere? The threat of death hovered over this Republic without republicans, over a *marxisant* left-wing intelligentsia that hated capitalism too much and did not fear Nazism enough to come to the defense of the Weimar regime. A few years later, the sign of death was inscribed on France.

Of course, we were joined together by our anti-Nazism, and on election night we listened silently to the results. We went to the large public meetings: I heard Goebbels and Hitler several times. For my students, for many of my friends, my memories already belong to the historical past. Can I give them anything but old newsreel pictures? Who were these Germans who assembled in the *Sportpalast* and acclaimed the Führer? They apparently belonged to all classes. Many of them, to judge by their clothing and their faces, belonged to the comfortable bourgeoisie, sometimes even to intellectual circles. They nodded in approbation to Hitler's diatribes against the Jews, the French, or the capitalists. Once, I found myself in one of these meetings with an exceptionally gifted student named Schüle, who was very hostile to Hitler. He refused to stand when the flag-bearers came through the hall to stand at the foot of the platform. Insults and orders came from all sides; Schüle did not move, and no one struck him. In 1941, he was in Moscow as an attaché to the German embassy in the Soviet Union. He was killed on the eastern front. A diplomat told me that he had retained his outspokenness. In 1958 or 1959, a German student came to talk to me at the end of one of my classes at the Sorbonne: it was Schüle's son. His mother had kept some letters from me. I also located by chance some letters from him, after 1933. He had thus served the Third Reich, like millions of others, condemned to a fate that they did not deserve.

January 1933 did not change our existence as inhabitants of the *Französisches Akademiker Haus*. Demonstrations of anti-Semitism never touched me directly. With my blond hair and blue eyes, I did not present to the Nazis an image in conformity with their representation of the Jew. My friend Susini, Corsican, dark, Mediterranean, was sometimes insulted in the street; I never was. But once, a woman in a train confided to me that we were in the same camp: she did not like Hitler's slogan *Kirche, Küche, Kinder*, and I was a Jew. What struck me the most during the first weeks of the regime was the almost invisible quality of the great events of history. Millions of Berliners saw nothing new. A single sign or symbol: within three days, brown uniforms swarmed through the streets of the capital. At the student center, I observed without surprise formerly reserved companions rapidly donning uniforms. Many of these students had joined up during the first week. One of them, who had never joined the National Socialists and who, before the seizure of power, had shown some hostility toward them, had already decided to *mitmachen* (go along). You, he said to me, you will always be a spectator, a critical spectator, you will not have the courage to commit yourself to action that carries the movement of crowds and of history. He was right, but in the face of Hitler and, similarly, in the face of Stalin, it was necessary to say no. My temperament has protected me from the dishonorable writings or commitments of which a few men of my generation have been guilty, fascinated as they were by history or snared by it.

What also struck me was the spread of fear, without hundreds of thousands of adversaries or suspects being thrown into prison or concentration camps. During the first six months of the regime, the new masters, to be sure, committed some cruelties. The concentration camps inaugurated the arrival of the Thousand-Year Reich; they did not contain more than sixty or seventy thousand communists, liberals, Jews, or criminals: enough to create a climate of terror. And yet, in the political circles of the old Republic, among the Jews of course, and among the masses as well, there spread the feeling of omnipresent and mortal danger, the threat of arrest. We were no longer breathing the same air. In the spring of 1933, my friends, Jews or liberals, while the sun gleamed on the cafés of the Kurfürstendamm, said: "*Den Frühling werden Sie uns nicht nehmen*" (They will not take spring away from us).

My friend Manès Sperber, who at the time still belonged to the Communist Party, expected, despite everything, according to his memoirs, resistance on the part of the workers' parties, the German proletariat, once the pride of the Second International. In the small French community and the circles around the embassy, none of us thought popular rebellion possible. On May first, three months after Hitler's election as chancellor, workers and civil servants marched beneath the swastika, the same people who a few months earlier had marched beneath red flags, with or without the hammer and sickle, with or without the three arrows of the Front of Steel whose few successes are recounted in *The Rape of the Crowds* by Chakotin. What explains this collapse of the German proletariat? Why the disappearance of millions of voters who had, to the very end, voted for the Social Democrats or the Communists?

In retrospect, the answers are obvious: the Communists, under Stalin's order, fought the "social traitors" more than the Nazis; how could these two factions of the Marxist movement have come together in the underground, in armed action, when they had not been able to do so to prevent the victory of the man who would condemn both groups to the same concentration camps? Demobilization of the masses, aware of their powerlessness, a feeling of fate, of the irresistible wave: the time for resistance had passed. Beyond these classic arguments valid as far as they went, there was one obvious fact: neither the leaders nor the troops of the Socialist and Communist Parties dreamed of armed revolt against the police and the *Reichswehr*. They did not dream of it because they didn't have the means, namely the weapons, but also because Socialist, perhaps even Communist, voters, good citizens, respectful of authority, accepted the new order. Some of them were probably waiting for the failure of the Nazi experiment before acting. The fact remains, and it struck us at the time, that the Nazi victory was accepted by the German people even though the majority of voters had not come out in favor of Hitler before the Reichstag fire and the banning of the Communist Party.

Must it be said that the German people in 1933 ratified, so to speak, anti-Semitism? I doubt that it was won over by the invectives against the Jews, or that it took the insults and pronouncements of Nazi orators literally. I heard from intelligent people arguments that, at the time, did not seem absurd. "He will not challenge world Judaism. . . . He would bring down on the Third Reich the anger of the United States. . . . He will not expel the Jewish chemists and physicists without whom the Wilhelmine Reich would not have withstood the Allied blockade for four years." These arguments may appear puerile in retrospect but no one at the time could decisively refute them. All observers should have recognized that anti-Semitism was more than a propaganda weapon, more than an ideology for purposes of the election. But it seems to me that no one in the immediate circumstances suspected the radical character of the anti-Semitism that was expressed from 1942 on in the "final solution." How can one believe the unbelievable?

In the course of these years in Germany, I became acquainted with writers and I established connections with NRF and the Left Bank. Léo Spitzer invited speakers to Cologne: Georges Duhamel, André Chamson, André Malraux. Duhamel charmed the public and even the city's major newspaper; he asserted, with more seriousness than irony, that a language's loss of the mood of a verb was worse than a country's loss of a province. André Malraux's lecture, whose precise subject I have forgotten (it had something to do with cultures and their fate), impressed the public. When I suggested to him that his words may have been over the heads of his audience, he answered me— and he was right—that the audience had followed him to the end. Malraux had in fact seized, subjugated, fascinated the audience. In the last sentence of his lecture, the wind blew over the deserts in which, covered by sand, there survived the sacred stones of the dead gods.

Clara had come with André, and she was deliberately provocative. At the outset, she said to Léo Spitzer: "Er hat sich eine kleine Jüdin geheiratet." Without the reflexive *sich*, the sentence simply meant that he had married a little Jew. With *sich*, it became vulgar, it suggested that he had searched out and, as it were, bought himself a little Jewish wife. Léo Spitzer repeated the statement to me, more surprised than shocked. It suggested that, at the time, not without irony, Clara effaced herself for André; her charm and intelligence were all the more apparent.

It was at the Pontigny conferences, much more than at the Cologne lectures, that I had the opportunity to discover the distinguished intelligentsia of the time. Paul Desjardins had invited me to a conference in 1928, immediately after my *agrégation*. I delivered a presentation on Proust that had the good fortune to please Ann Heurgon. I liked these conferences; the formal proceedings themselves were full of interest, and besides, they only took a few hours each day. Around them there flourished a social life made up of endless conversations, not exempt from gossip: fifty intellectuals, more or less distinguished, were closeted together; how could they not have observed, praised, criticized one another, as though at a royal court—except that there was no sovereign. Paul Desjardins, even in his last years, occupied the center, the heart of the group. All the others never ceased to admire (in every sense of the word) the art, a mixture of sincerity and performance, that he displayed in his relations with others and with himself.

If it had not been for Pontigny, how could I have spent days with André Malraux and established a long and deep friendship with him? Roger Martin du Gard faithfully attended the conferences without even participating in the discussions ("since 'they' are all intelligent . . ."). Nevertheless, through his generosity and simplicity, he won over both the no longer young female *normaliennes* and the young, ambitious, and anxious *agrégés*. I also have a vivid memory of Arthur Fontaine, a distinguished civil servant and a friend of Albert Thomas and Paul Desjardins, statesmen and poets. The condition of the working class interested him as much as a balance sheet. A dialogue between André Philip and him, in 1928 I think, remains fixed in my mind, not in detail but in substance, in which he compared the factory of his youth with that of the present.

It was in the course of a brilliant conference in 1932 that I met Suzanne Gauchon who became the companion of my life. Nothing led her to frequent this retreat for intellectuals, aside from her studies at the lycée Victor-Duruy. Her father, the son of a peasant who also owned the village hotel, had had a rather haphazard education. He had joined the navy as a technical officer, and had left it at the end of the war to assume a rather significant position in industry. Suzanne had had as classmates in the lycée Christiane Martin du Gard and Edie Copeau, to whom she was very close. Roger Martin du Gard demonstrated unfailing affection for his daughter's classmate. He agreed to be a witness at our wedding in 1933.

Suzanne was also very close to Simone Weil, who was in her class for the last three years of the lycée. I hesitate to write anything about Simone Weil, since that exceptional woman has become so much a cult object; any remark not expressing admiration, which she certainly deserves, risks appearing indecent, inconoclastic. I met her for the first time at the ENS, when I was taking the *agrégation* and she was taking the entrance exam for the ENS. We had at most a student conversation. I remember no personal relations with her in the following years until Suzanne announced our marriage to her. She did not receive the news with pleasure; without knowing me, she had placed me in a category that she rejected, first in the *agrégation* of course, and inclined toward worldly or facile thought. She had fixed on me an image that she had created on the basis of fugitive impressions. She promised Suzanne that she would get rid of her prejudices since her friend had chosen me.

She joyfully welcomed the birth of our daughter Dominique as though it were her own. We saw each other several times; Simone and Suzanne remained loyal to their youthful friendship. I greatly admired the fine article she published on the condition of the working class, as well as the one on Roman imperialism, even though historians have legitimately criticized it. Nevertheless, intellectual interchange with Simone Weil seemed almost impossible to me. She was apparently unacquainted with doubt and, although her opinions might change, they were always thoroughly categorical. She approved the Munich agreement, not because of the balance of forces, but because resistance to German hegemony in Europe did not seem to her to be worth the sacrifice of a generation. After German troops entered Prague, she took another, equally firm position: since the Nazis were not satisfied with a traditional kind of hegemony in Europe, since they tended toward a colonization comparable to the European colonization of Africa, resistance was necessary, whatever the price. She was perhaps right in 1938 and in 1939, but this was open to discussion. Was it not possible to see in 1938 the way in which the Nazis appeared to her in 1939?

At the time, she kept her religious life, her faith, secret. Personally, I had an intuition of her vocation one day in the jardin du Luxembourg. We were walking, taking Dominique for a stroll, in glorious sunshine. The park was so beautiful that we seemed to be breathing happiness. Simone approached us, her face troubled, on the point of tears. She responded to our questioning by saying: "There is a strike in Shanghai,[3] and the army has fired on workers." I said to Suzanne that Simone must be aspiring to sainthood; to take on oneself all the suffering of the world has meaning only for a believer, or even, more precisely, for a Christian.

I saw her again when she arrived in London in 1943. For the first time, our conversation, a genuine one, lasted for two hours. She seemed the same; we talked about the war, the occupation, London, the privileged position of the French in exile. Some of the ideas of *L'Enracinement* came through in her conversations.

Let us return to 1933. Suzanne came to meet me in Berlin in 1932, and we returned to France in leisurely stages; we visited Bamberg and Würzburg on the way. The guides presented the attractions or the history of the monuments, often turning toward Suzanne who understood no German. One guide to whom I pointed this out, said: "Schöne Mädchen gibt es überall" (there are pretty girls everywhere).

Seen from Germany, until July 1932 France seemed capable of influencing events. From February 1934 on the situation was reversed. Germany had a government, hateful to be sure, but stable and strong. France, after some delay, was in its turn entering into the vicious circle: economic crisis, exacerbation of social conflicts, strengthening of revolutionary parties of right and left, erosion of moderate parties, paralysis of the government. The events of 6 February 1934 brought back from exile a former President of the Republic, the survivor of the parliamentary republic needed, from time to time, to overcome the obstacles created by its internal dissension.

As for me, I had passed a threshold in my political education—an education that will last as long as I do. I had understood and accepted politics as such, irreducible to morality; I would no longer attempt, through statements or signatures, to demonstrate my fine feelings. To think about politics is to think about political agents, hence to analyze their decisions, their goals, their means, their mental universe. National Socialism had taught me the power of irrational forces; Max Weber had taught me the responsibility of each individual, not so much with respect to intentions as to the consequences of his choices.

I had dreamed of playing a role in Franco-German reconciliation. The time for that had passed; it would return later. For the moment, France had to keep its powder dry and dissuade the potential aggressor. A French Jew who warned his compatriots against the danger of Hitler was not free of suspicion. Was he serving his coreligionists or his country? From 1933 to 1939, the Third Reich, just across the border, weighed on the atmosphere of our country. Refugees streamed in. At the same time, I finally went beyond my doubts, I shook off my fear of the blank page. The six years between August 1933 and August 1939, in the shadow of a feared and foreseen war were perhaps the most productive years of my life. Private happiness, public despair.

NOTES

1. I received the Goethe Prize, given every three years by the city of Frankfurt, in 1979. Ernst Jünger was the recipient in 1982.

2. Jean-Richard Bloch was also moved by Déat at the time.

3. I don't remember the city; it may have been another.

4

IN THE HEART
OF THE LATIN QUARTER

I had lived in a postwar world until my first trip to Germany. Between 14 September 1930, the first success of the National Socialist Party in legislative elections, and 30 January 1933, I moved slowly from revolt against the past to apprehension of the future. I left a postwar world to enter a prewar world. At bottom the same values inspired me, but, beyond the left and antifascism, it was now a question of France and its salvation.

In October 1933, when we settled in Le Havre, my conversion was nearly complete. The patriotism of my childhood, of my family, of all my ancestors won out over the pacifism and badly defined socialism to which I had been led by philosophy and by the postwar atmosphere. I still thought of myself as "on the left"; I was afraid of compromise with the right, in order not to be exploited by the opposition. This timidity had more to do with resistance, social rather than intellectual, than with the logic of politics. Later, much later, I often replied to those who criticized me for my questionable companions that one chooses one's adversaries, not one's allies. Moreover, I rather quickly got rid of the superstition that Sartre defended to his dying day: "the right are all bastards," or, in more academic language, that parties differ in the moral or human qualities of their militants or their leaders. Parties of the left probably find more recruits among idealists (in the banal sense of the word). When revolutionaries move to the other side of the barricades, do they long preserve their moral superiority? There are virtuous men in both camps; are there many in either one?

The Le Havre that Jean-Paul Sartre described in *La Nausée* and that I discovered in turn was suffering greatly from the crisis. A Protestant bourgeoisie, which dominated the cotton and coffee exchange, held sway; it was known as "the hill," because it had built its houses on the heights. The social hierarchy of the city infiltrated into the lycée, into the principal's office. Students' families were not unknown to the teachers or the administration. I was accepted at the tennis club as an equal of the "gentlemen of the exchange," not because I taught philosophy in the lycée, but because I was among the better players. A qualification for the second rank in France, in these circles, was better than degrees from the university.

I was also struck, at this time, by the inhumanity of the university hierarchy. Not all of the lycée teachers were *agrégés*, and some of them suffered from their permanently inferior status in relation to the status of the few who had overcome the last and highest obstacle, the *agrégation*. Before coming to Le Havre, I had no particularly strong feelings about the *agrégation*, I merely had pleasant memories of the year of preparation and the attentive, almost complete, reading of the works of Jean-Jacques Rousseau and Auguste Comte. In Le Havre, I sympathized with the "excluded," those who, for one reason or another, would never be *agrégés*, but who nevertheless deserved the title and its advantages as much as others did. More than thirty years later, these memories of Le Havre were the source of a series of articles in *Le Figaro* that made me, for a time, the number one enemy of the *Société des agrégés*.

During the year 1933–34, I worked harder than I have ever done, before or since; I wrote most of *German Sociology* (New York: Free Press of Glencoe, 1957) and the complementary thesis on German philosophers whom I grouped together under the theme of the *Critique de la raison historique*. Since I was simultaneously, and for the first time, teaching a philosophy course dealing with traditional problems about which I had not thought for years, I had to prepare my classes, which were certainly of uneven quality, to say the least.

I taught in a lycée for only one year, without being bored, indeed delighted by dialogues with the students. We had to deal with the entire syllabus; the contradiction between research on limited subjects and the encyclopedic knowledge demanded or presumed by the course bothered me and would have made the profession almost unbearable to me. Sartre managed to deal with it for about ten years, like our great predecessors, Henri Bergson and Léon Brunschvicg; Alain never left the *khâgne*, and he looked down on so-called higher education. What would I do today?

We returned to Paris in October 1934 and lived through some intense years, illuminated by the birth and early years of our daughter, Dominique, enriched by friendship with uncommon men, darkened by the decadence of the French economy and French politics, by obsession with the war we felt to be inevitable, but to which, despite everything, we did not wish to resign ourselves.

I went to work at the Center for Social Documentation at the ENS. There were evening lectures which were almost always very well attended. I remember in particular my lecture on National-Socialist Germany, published under the title: "An Anti-Proletarian Revolution: The Ideology and the Reality of National Socialism." I began my presentation with personal remarks on Hitler's anti-Semitism and my Judaism. Mme Poré—the indispensable, unforgettable secretary of the ENS—told me that the students greatly appreciated my declaration of faith. Célestin Bouglé, the director of the ENS, considered this preamble too long and practically useless, if not shocking. Anti-Semitism did not enter into his universe, and the questioning of his own condition by a French Jew troubled and irritated him; one might almost say that the subject seemed to him indecent. As for me, it was the first time in France, at the Ecole Normale, that I referred to my Jewish origins. From 1933 on, perhaps from my first encounter with National Socialism, I had understood that German anti-Semitism would call into question the existence of French Jews; I adopted once and for all the only attitude that seems to me appropriate: never to conceal my origins, without ostentation, without humility, without compensatory pride.

The text on the antiproletarian revolution, published in 1936, a year after the lecture, was finally stripped of survivals from Alain and of emotional flourishes, written in the style of political or sociological analysis, without adjectives, without indignation, with a few lines of explanation at the beginning: "How could I honestly assert my impartiality, when Hitlerism has always been anti-Semitic and while it is now multiplying the risks of war. If I say to you that I will try above all to understand rather than to judge, do not forget that the man who is talking to you has made a severe judgment against National Socialism."

At the end of the text, I returned to the essential: "French specialists in German affairs sometimes asserted, in 1933, that National Socialism was contributing to German recovery and that this was, in the context of European solidarity, a positive development. In my eyes, National Socialism is a catastrophe for Europe because it has revived an almost religious hostility between peoples, because it has propelled Germany toward its ancient dream and its perennial sin: in the guise of defining itself proudly in its singularity, Germany is lost in its myths, a myth about itself and a myth about the hostile world. Of course, we must understand and seek a neighborly agreement, but understanding demands a common language and mutual confidence: Can we honestly find the first and grant the second? Otherwise, there would remain only a fragile peace based on force and fear." By fear, I understood the fear of war as such.

Between my initial remarks and this conclusion, my analysis of the National Socialist clientele, the non- or antiproletarian masses, remains largely valid (and without any originality); also valid is the analysis of the reasons why, in 1935, the German people, far from being disappointed by the new regime, tended to support its new masters; particularly inadequate was my analysis of Schacht's economic policies and the reduction of unemployment (already cut in half by that time). I saw in the Autobahn only military preparation, I exaggerated the role of rearmament in the economic recovery, and I had not yet fully understood the mechanism of stimulation and the "multiplier" effect in an economy separated from the outside world by a system of variable exchange rates.

Bouglé had offered a place for the French branch of the Institut für Sozialforschung. The periodical appeared in France, published by Alcan, but the principal members of the Frankfurt School lived in the United States. I met Max Horkheimer, Theodor Adorno, and Friedrich Pollock on their visits to France. They wanted to expand their coverage of French books. They asked me to take over this aspect of the journal (after having asked for "essays" from several other possible contributors). I accepted all the more willingly because my salary as a new *agrégé* at the Center was far from munificent.

My participation on the *Zeitschrift für Sozialforschung* implied adherence neither to Marxism nor to the Frankfurt School. My initial reviews of books were often harsh and did not conform to university customs. On occasion, I mistreated mandarins, who showed me how a young man ought to behave. The historian Henri Hauser, whom I had criticized unrestrainedly, wrote a devastating review of my *Introduction to the Philosophy of History* (Boston: Beacon Press, 1961), without any analysis of the text. A few weeks later, at a meeting of the administrative council of the Center for Documentation, Bouglé criticized him for not having described the book before refuting it. A little embarrassed, Hauser was effusive in praise of me. Neither Kojève, nor Koyré, nor Weil, philosophically speaking, placed Horkheimer or Adorno very high. I accepted the judgment of my friends, whom I admired. I must admit as well, that thirty years later, I was not convinced of the genius of

Marcuse. I should add that Marcuse always appeared to me to be an *honnête homme*, courteous, without aggressiveness.

Max Horkheimer belonged to a rich family of the Frankfurt bourgeoisie. Pollock, who managed the funds of the Institute, and Adorno, the most impressive of all because of his culture, his knowledge of music, and the difficulty of his style, came from the same social milieu. All of them, including Marcuse, who at the time was not in the first rank of the school, considered themselves followers, in one way or another, of Marx. Politically, they supported neither the Social Democrats nor the Communist Party. They did nothing to save the Republic. When they were forced into exile, they did not hesitate about where they would go. They reconstructed the Institut für Sozialforschung in the United States, where they conducted sociological studies, the two most celebrated of which were devoted to the family and the "authoritarian personality." Horkheimer and Adorno, more philosophers than sociologists, blended economic and cultural criticism of capitalist society, as Marcuse did later; in the 1960s the students chose Marcuse as mentor and assured his fame.

None of the books written by Horkheimer or his friends had the impact of *History and Class Consciousness* of Lukács or *Ideology and Utopia* of Karl Mannheim. Mannheim and Horkheimer both taught at the University of Frankfurt but they were unaware of each other, or, in any case had no respect for one another: perhaps because of their relative proximity and their common antecedents. On the basis of a similar intention, to use Marxist concepts to interpret the society of their time, they arrived at very different theories. Mannheim's relationism—a theory of knowledge based on the inevitable rootedness of social knowledge in a class—is now forgotten, although the idea of *Wissenssoziologie*, the sociology of knowledge (of cultural works), remains as current as it was fifty years ago. The Frankfurt School arrived at a critical theory that can hardly be summed up in a few sentences. Criticism is thought to arise, so to speak, from reality itself, to the extent that reality is torn by contradictions. In the end, in his polemic against positivism, Adorno accepts the contradictions within the knowledge that emanates from a contradictory world. Positivism, sociology that claims to be empirical and objective, misconstrues the contradictions that condemn its scientific program to failure.

In general, critical theory, following the subtitle of *Capital*, takes as its object both capitalist society and the necessarily false consciousness that it has of itself. One might say that it is a Marxism rethought with the help of a renewed theory of knowledge. Marcuse was to remain faithful to the end to the Marxist idea of the socialization of the forces of production. But he recognized that in the East, the economic revolution did not bring about the cultural or human revolution that should have come with it.

After one's student years, dispersal does not break connections, but it loosens them; opportunities to meet become less frequent; the availability of the student gives way to the demands of one's profession; the family takes up a part of one's time. Friendships during the 1930s may not have held a lesser place in my life than during the 1920s, but they held a different place.

Paul-Yves Nizan had thoroughly committed himself as a novelist and a journalist to communism. Nothing remained of our intimacy at the ENS, although neither one of us, I believe, had forgotten or denied the time we spent together at Quiberon or the days following his wedding. We never discussed communism, though we may sometimes have discussed fascism, about which we were in agreement. I remember a presentation that Paul made at the *Union pour la vérité* of Paul Desjardins after a stay in the Soviet Union. It was more philosophical than historical and turned on a Marxist or para-Marxist concept that was fashionable at the time: total man or totality. Julien Benda, who was in the audience, greatly admired the presentation. Thirty years later, in his *Critique de la raison dialectique*, Sartre multiplied variations on this theme.

My relations with Sartre changed from the moment Simone de Beauvoir entered his life. She has recounted, better than I could, our philosophical dialogues; her memory is clearly superior to mine. Many episodes came back to me while reading her, for example the conversation in a café about phenomenology and Edmund Husserl. However, she did not meet either of us until after our time at the ENS; she had the impression and propagated the idea that, on every occasion, we threw ourselves into interminable discussion, usually concluded by my formula: "My dear friend, one of two things is true, either. . . ." She is probably right; the debates between us, in her presence, often took on this form. Sartre himself, in the film shot shortly before his illness and blindness, confessed that he had never discussed philosophy with anyone but Aron "who did me in." But our camaraderie at the ENS, that we shared with Pierre Guille, resembled more that of the other students, less a foretaste of the quarrels of our maturity. For a long time, Sartre was in search of himself, and he liked to present to me his ideas of the day or the week; if I took them apart or, more frequently, if I revealed their ambiguities or contradictions, he often accepted the criticism because he had just conceived them and had not yet fully adopted them. In the period that Simone de Beauvoir narrates, Sartre had perhaps already tested his ideas in dialogue with her; in any event, he defended them because he considered them his own, in the deepest sense of the term, and no longer as hypotheses formulated on the basis of chance reading or a sudden intuition.

During the year following his meeting with Simone de Beauvoir, Sartre prepared for the *agrégation* in the Cité Universitaire, and I did my military service. In our infrequent meetings, we did in fact take pleasure in the philosophical debates narrated by Simone de Beauvoir. We met again in the fort of Saint-Cyr, where I was serving as an instructor. Those months, for unknown reasons, have not left a pleasant memory. Nothing happened, but relations between us, compared to what they had been at the ENS, deteriorated.

During the 1930s, we met more than once as a foursome. The success or failure of the occasions depended on indefinable and apparently insignificant things. We had given up philosophical contests and spoke about this and that, without excluding Simone and Suzanne from our conversations. I remember successes, for example a lunch with Sartre and Simone after Munich. We were not in agreement, but there was an atmosphere of friendship and historical tragedy. I also remember a dinner, in early July 1939, in a restaurant on the *quais*, near Notre-Dame, whose beauty seemed more and more miraculous as night fell. We were waiting for the Nizans, who did not come. In my memory, that evening remains as one of those perfect moments that fortune sometimes grants us among the lost hours and missed meetings. After the ENS, our relations were dependent on these hazards of fortune.

My friendship with Malraux never resembled my school friendships, even the close ones. I have referred to our first meeting in Cologne in 1930 or 1931. I accompanied him to his hotel in a driving rain, carrying on a vigorous discussion as we jumped over puddles and slipped on the wet pavement. When I met him at Pontigny a year or two later, he humorously recalled our stumbling walk and our interrupted conversation.

In 1932, he had already published *La Tentation de l'Occident, Les Conquérants, La Voie royale*, while I was still struggling with the blank page. He was only four years older than I, but he seemed to belong to another generation and especially to a superior "class" (in the way the word is used in sports). I felt his superiority and admitted it to myself without bitterness. He spoke little of himself, of his little "bundles of secrets." He was already putting into practice in his life the ethics of the *Antimémoires*.

Unlike Sartre, who never really knew Suzanne, or at least was not interested in her, Malraux was immediately warm toward her, as early as our meeting at Pontigny. Until the years of the Spanish Civil War, the dinners or evenings with them showed no sign of deep tension between André and Clara. She had bet on me—as she later told me—she believed in my "success" (social as much as intellectual). She was very fond of Suzanne. The two women, all four of us, were also linked by our daughters, Florence and Dominique, who were the same age. From 1936 on, André could tolerate Clara less and less. She has written too much about it, he not enough, for a third party to get involved. Nevertheless, in deference to the honesty that is the unwritten rule of this narrative, I must say that our sympathy was with André. Not to say that one was right against the other (such notions have no meaning when two people separate), but, in our presence, Clara was the one who was most often unbearable. Willingly? Out of anticipation, desire, or refusal of the break? Out of torment? What good would a black and white answer do?

Jean-Louis Missika and Dominique Wolton, in interviews published in *The Committed Observer* (Chicago: Regnery Gateway, 1983), asked me how I could have established a genuine friendship with someone so different from me. They know only—and not very well—the Malraux of after 1945, propagandist of the RPF, and then a minister of General de Gaulle, lavishly installed in the little Hôtel de Boulogne. When he lived in his apartment on the rue du Bac, his kindness and humor held in check his taste for grandeur, assuming that the taste was as pronounced as it became after 1945. The two of us, or the four of us, spoke about politics, literature, each other. He did not reduce his companions to silence, even though I listened more than I talked, often dazzled, not always persuaded. His manner discouraged discussion, excluded the controversies characteristic of my exchanges with Sartre. I do not think he had philosophical training, in the academic sense of the term. Had he even opened the *Critique of Pure Reason* or the *Phenomenology of Mind,* had he ever read *Being and Time,* though he sometimes spoke of Heidegger (before or after the war)? In 1945 or 1946, he spoke without restraint about *Being and Nothingness* (had he really liked it?). He had read Nietzsche and Spengler much more than Kant or Hegel. I could not verify his knowledge of Sanskrit and other Asian languages. But on a frequently contested point, namely the authenticity of his cultivation, I can testify in his favor and against the prosecution. When I was able to verify, I was almost always struck by the precision and the pertinence of his knowledge of literature and history. At the time, he indulged much less than in *The Voices of Silence* and in his television series, "La Légende du siècle," in intellectual display.

He did not belong to the Communist Party, but he spoke and acted until the outbreak of war as a fellow traveler. I later met Frenchmen who had lived in Moscow (some of them at the embassy), who never forgave his almost Stalinist conformism when he visited the Soviet capital. However, Clara told me, in his presence, that after a great dinner (or debate) with Soviet officers, André passionately defended Trotsky and the role played by the exile in the 1917 Revolution.

Why did our friendship during the 1930s withstand our political differences? There is no lack of explanations. Hitler's rise to power had created a kind of sacred union of the left, based on antifascism. Despite Stalin, because of Hitler, we tended to place communism on the right side of the barricades. In private, Malraux spoke neither as a communist nor as a fellow traveler. He concealed neither from himself nor from others the harshness and the crimes of the regime, but he also praised its social accomplishments. He did not believe the lies of the Moscow trials nor did he discard Trotsky. In 1935 or 1936, when I met Manès Sperber at Malraux's apartment, that ex-communist, who had worked in the Party "apparatus," refused to denounce Stalinism in public: Hitler represented the immediate and therefore primary danger. I do not think we were right to choose or resign ourselves to a selective silence: the silence of 1936 paved the way for the silence of 1945.

What did André Malraux think of communism during the 1930s? I have only disjointed memories of the time, relating to different dates. He sometimes feared an alliance of all the capitalist countries, democratic and fascist together, against the Soviet Union. The Soviets show their childcare facilities and their schools to their visitors, he told me once, and this is a mistake. We have better equipped and more luxurious childcare facilities, but they have thousands of them. I do not think that Gide's *Retour d'URSS* shocked him, though he may have considered untimely this polemic against the USSR during the great days of antifascism.

If we wish to understand and not to judge, we should reconsider the passage in *The Conquerors* where he sets out a comparison between two kinds of men; one kind, men of faith, adhere to the content of the message, the dogma of the church; the others, men of action, do not subscribe to the doctrine but join the true believers in order to fight with them. He never took a party card, he never alienated his judgment, but he converted to the Party many young men in search of a cause to which they could devote themselves.

Until 1939, André Malraux made no distinction between his personal adventure and the revolutionary movement that was spreading around the world—a movement that was usually Marxist or quasi-Marxist. He left Marxism to the true believers, whom he called Romans. He had only to detach himself from the revolutionary movement to become freely available, without suffering pangs of conscience. He never went through the conversion of ex-communists or ex-Maoists; Marxism had never subjugated him. He did not even need a Kronstadt or a Budapest.

I am tempted to believe that his nationalism and Gaullism were much deeper than his quasi-Marxism. To be sure, he joined the General—the hero—much more than the RPF or even Gaullism. Communism continued to obsess him in the years immediately after the war. Late in 1945, in the National Assembly, when he pronounced the sentence that has so often been quoted against him, especially by anticommunists: "Freedom belongs first of all to those who have conquered it,"[1] he turned toward the Communist Party. During his entire speech, he addressed the Party as though the other parties did not exist. In 1947, 1948, and 1949 he more than once anticipated communist attempts to seize power through violence; he dreamed of fighting not with the CP or alongside it, but against it.

After 1945, communism was identified with the Soviet Union, and even more with the Soviet Army. This army imposed on the countries that it liberated a regime that was as despotic as the Nazi regime. The same concentration camps housed other "criminals," sometimes the same, since democrats and liberals suffered a similar fate under Stalin and under Hitler. Malraux, with his historical intuition, understood more quickly and clearly than Sartre that the revolutionary spirit was no longer embodied in the East; the subjection of the Poles, the Hungarians, the Rumanians, was an expression of *Realpolitik*. Stalin pushed his borders toward the West and strengthened his protected domain, indifferent to the desires of a hundred million Europeans. Adherence to the Stalinist Soviet Union in 1945 and 1946 required a strange moral blindness or an attraction to power. André Malraux, by contrast, was considering the role of the United States, heirs and protectors of Europe. A civilization would flourish around the Atlantic as Hellenic civilization had around the Mediterranean. These considerations, whatever one may think of them, were worth more than the analyses of Merleau-Ponty, who went in search of authentic intersubjectivity and historical reason in the depths of the Stalinist empire.

The return to France corresponded for Malraux to a genuine spontaneous impulse. Parliamentary democracy bored him: General de Gaulle formed a bridge between the prosaic character of democracy and the poetry of history. Before his first meeting with the General, he had, uncharacteristically, asked me what I thought of his joining de Gaulle: should he become a vassal of the General without the mediation of a party between the hero and himself? He was, I think, already dreaming of the meeting between Goethe and Napoleon when he was preparing for his first conversation with the Liberator. Twenty-five years later, when he visited General de Gaulle, who had returned to Colombey-les-deux-Eglises, he recalled the visit of Chateaubriand to Charles X, the exile of Prague, the last legitimate sovereign, the last of the kings who, in a thousand years, had made France.

In his eyes, the General transfigured France and politics. He tirelessly repeated that the Fifth Republic was not the Fourth plus the General. In a sense, he was not wrong. The Constitution had changed the style and even the nature of the Republic. The president, elected by the people, chooses the prime minister and exercises power, supported by a majority forced into coherence by the operation of political institutions; the Fifth Republic bears more resemblance to an elective, liberal, and democratic monarchy than to the Republic of the Deputies of the Third and Fourth Republics. But, after the end of the Algerian War, between 1962 and 1969, the Fifth Republic with the General was not substantially different from the Fifth Republic without him. Perhaps the General gave his ministers the feeling that they were living in History and not in everyday life, but the impression was deceptive. The Franco-African community was worn down; the African countries all became independent; some remained within the French sphere, others verbally rallied to Marxism-Leninism. France embraced the century. It ceased to appear as the sick man of Europe; under a finally respectable regime, it revealed to the outside world the successes that had until then been concealed by colonial wars and unstable governments. An honorable phase of the history of France, through the magic of the word and of press conferences, became a moment of universal history.

Let us return to the André Malraux of the 1930s, who constantly expressed extraordinary warmth toward Suzanne and me. An affectionate and charming companion, he told funny stories, apparently devoid of any "importance," in the sense that Alain used the word. Suzanne and I were friends of André and Clara. We had never agreed with Roger Martin du Gard, who said: "One must be desperate to marry Clara!" (André did not refrain from ironic remarks about Roger's marriage.) As long as her understanding with André lasted, Clara was more worthy than the image she later gave of herself in her memoirs or settling of accounts. And until 1940, and even long afterward, André remained the same man that Suzanne and I had met at Pontigny and who had adopted us as friends.

Aside from the ENS and Gallimard, I spent time at the Ecole pratique des hautes etudes and with Alexandre Koyré, Alexandre Kojève, and Eric Weil, three superior intellects whom I admired and against whom I did not dare measure myself. Of the three, perhaps only Kojève attained notoriety beyond a narrow circle of specialists or academics; he also seemed to me the most brilliant of the three, even though his personality and his deepest thought remained mysterious to me.

I did not regularly attend Kojève's now famous lectures on Hegel's *Phenomenology*; but during the final year, I became an almost faithful member of the groups of auditors that included Raymond Queneau, Jacques Lacan, Maurice Merleau-Ponty, Eric Weil, and Georges Fessard. Kojève began by translating a few lines of the *Phenomenology*, heavily emphasizing certain words, then he spoke, without notes, never stumbling over a word, in an impeccable French to which his Slavic accent added a certain originality and charm. He fascinated an audience of superintellectuals inclined toward doubt or criticism. Why? His talent, his dialectical virtuosity had something to do with it. I do not know whether the speaker's art remains intact in the book that records the last year of the course, but that art, which had nothing to do with eloquence, was intimately connected with his subject and his personality. The subject was both world history and the *Phenomenology*. The latter shed light on the former. Everything took on meaning. Even those who were suspicious of historical providence, who suspected the artifice behind the art, did not resist the magician; at the moment, the intelligibility he conferred on the time and on events was enough of a proof.

The distance was immense between what I tried to think and to write in the *Introduction to the Philosophy of History* and what was taught by Kojève (or Hegel). But Wilhelm Dilthey and even Max Weber belonged to Hegel's heirs, were tributaries of the problems he had posed and that he thought he had resolved. An epigone, I listened, speechless and skeptical, to the voice of the master, the founder.

There remains a question that I cannot evade. In 1938 or 1939, when he declared himself a "strict Stalinist," was he sincere, or more precisely, in what sense was he sincere? History leads to a universal and homogeneous empire; for want of Napoleon, Stalin; an empire that was neither Russian nor communist but encompassed a humanity reconciled by the reciprocal recognition of individuals. That red Russia was governed by brutes, its very language vulgarized, its culture degraded—he admitted all this, in private. Even more, he sometimes described it as a thing that was so obvious that only imbeciles could be unaware of it. Those who addressed imbeciles thought it had to be repeated. Did there remain in him a kind of Russian patriotism, hidden and rationalized? I don't doubt it, although there is no question that he served the French nation, freely chosen, with unshakable loyalty. He did not like Americans, because, as a Sage, he considered the United States the most radically unphilosophical country in the world. Philosophy for him was of course identified with the Greeks (the pre-Socratics, Plato, Aristotle) and the Germans (Kant, Hegel) and, between the two, the Cartesians. When he defended, against American pressure, the article of the GATT[2] that permitted the establishment of the European Economic Community, he preserved the autonomy of France and Europe. He had a reputation as a formidable negotiator in international conferences. The finance minister of Hong Kong, a British civil servant trained in Oxford or Cambridge, originally a classical scholar, with whom I had a conversation in 1971, had still not forgiven Kojève for the hostility that sophist or dialectician had shown to one of the last British possessions. He still had not understood the reasons.

At one of our lunches, in 1946 or 1947, he sketched an interpretation, compatible with his philosophy of history, of his personal development: the movement from his proclaimed Stalinism to the service of France and Europe. History was over, in the sense that nothing important had happened since Hegel; the circle of philosophical discourse was closed. But events were still occurring; a phase of regional empires (or common markets) would precede the universal empire. The organization of Western Europe belonged to this phase.

Why did he decide, after 1945, to join the administrative service, to become a civil servant in the Ministry of Economy and Finance, in the service devoted to international relations? He said to me one day: "I wanted to know how it [history] happened." To tell the truth, I find it hard to imagine him as a professor in any French university. He would first of all have to defend a thesis for the *doctorat d'Etat*. The reaction of a jury to one of his books, for example to his *Essai d'une histoire raisonnée de la philosophie païenne,* would have been stormy. At bottom, he probably thought he had said everything he had to say, and this everything coincided with the end, the totality of philosophy as he understood it. Like Plato, he wanted to advise a tyrant, in the shadows exercise influence over the visible actors, Olivier Wormser or Valéry Giscard d'Estaing. The former wrote in praise of his friend Kojève in an article in *Commentaire;*[3] an episode involving the latter comes to mind. Kojève told me that Giscard d'Estaing respected intellectuals and that, specifically, after having delivered a speech inspired by him, he said: "Well, Kojève, are you happy?" I might add that he took his profession very seriously, and was sometimes furious when one or another of his suggestions had not been adopted. He was all the more passionately concerned with these controversies over the international economy because this commercial diplomacy counted more for him, a good Hegelo-Marxist, than political or military affairs (at least in our time).

In the spring of 1982, in a conversation with Valéry Giscard d'Estaing, I mentioned Kojève, expressing my admiration for him and indicating that I placed him in the first rank. The president was surprised, but he had a precise memory of the negotiator whose sinuous procedures he described in a few words. He took indirect paths, said Giscard, but he finally arrived at his goal. Kojève had not abandoned the dialectic when he moved from the academy to diplomacy.

Have I justified my judgment of the genius of Kojève? Have I persuaded the reader? I doubt it. His book, *Introduction à la lecture de Hegel,* does not provide proof. Nor do the posthumous books, inspired by the same themes. Moreover, they have not been analyzed, or even read. It remains to me to recommend these books, a partial expression of the man, and to evoke some further impressions.

If I may risk a comparison that some will consider sacrilegious, he seemed to me, in a sense, more intelligent than Sartre. Sartre impressed me by his inventiveness, by the richness of his intellectual imagination, but his passions and his moralism, often inverted, limited his angle of vision.

The repression of the Hungarian revolt revealed the nature of Soviet domination, but given the nature of international politics, there was no reason to be surprised. The realm of the Gulag called for hatred; the restoration of order in Hungary fit in with the demand for the maintenance of the Soviet *imperium*. Kojève commented on the Soviet intervention in Hungary in a few words, Sartre in dozens of pages, as though the event had transformed his vision of the world, while it brought to the surface a reality that he could and should have known long before. A badly chosen example, the admirers of Kojève will say. You present him as a realist close to cynicism, indifferent to the suffering and indignation of simple mortals who have no access to the *Phenomenology of Mind*. It is true that Kojève easily adopted a White Russian attitude toward the many, unless this attitude was dictated to him by the ethics of the wise man, aware of his superiority and indulgent to the blind crowd. He never said anything foolish; I rarely had the impression that I was teaching him something, although, unlike most intellectuals, he was very careful to recognize the priority of those who had first expressed an idea with which he agreed. Because he thought he had assimilated the philosophical and historical totality encompassed by Hegel's system, he followed the ideas and events of our time with the detachment of the sage and also with the attentiveness of a high civil servant. When it was a question of politics or economics—our principal subjects of conversation—he was masterful. He asked for my opinion in various circumstances, for example, in May 1958 and May 1968. These were matters of French politics; perhaps he lacked the intuition, the immediate understanding available only to those who were born in the country (at least he thought so).

It is difficult for me to specify the influence that Kojève really had on French politics. From time to time, he drafted memoranda for the use of ministers or their subordinates. He sent me a great number of them, always suggestive, sometimes paradoxical. I remember a memorandum in which he explained that the Marxist theory of pauperization had been refuted not by economists but by Ford. On the other hand, he wrote, it is now economists who are going to convince businessmen that they should help develop the Third World out of self-interest.

For the twenty-three years between 1945 and 1968, the philosopher who had taught a generation of French intellectuals to read Hegel, remained, disguised as an *éminence grise* of government ministries, a Sunday philosopher; he wrote large books that have not yet all been published, all of which testify to his consistency. In an article in *Commentaire*, he expressed recognition of those to whom he owed something: Alexandre Koyré, Martin Heidegger, Jacob Klein, Eric Weil, but he disdainfully criticized those among them who had deviated from the royal road, the only road, the *Phenomenology of Mind*. Kojève had said the last word by rethinking Hegel, who had, before him theorized the end.

I still wonder how much of this was a game, intellectual or existential, for him. Rejecting once and for all the dialectics of nature, had Kojève really preserved the whole Hegelian system? After a trip and a love affair in Japan, he added two pages on the tea ceremony to a new edition of *Introduction à la lecture de Hegel*. Perhaps he thought that one of two things was true: either the philosophy of which I am the spokesman rather than the creator is true; or else humanity is living through a contemptible comedy interrupted by equally contemptible tragedies. Some time ago, Raymond Barre reminded me of something Kojève had said: "Human life is a comedy, we have to play it seriously." I also remember a statement he made once: "Men are not really going to continue indefinitely killing each other."

Eric Weil,[4] whom I had met in Berlin in 1932, left Germany shortly after Hitler's rise to power. He immediately understood the fate that awaited the Jews. Our friendship, man to man and family to family, was close in the prewar years, not free of stormy conflicts attributable sometimes to over-developed egos on both sides, sometimes also to political differences. At moments, for motives in which philosophy and immediate tactics were mixed, Eric Weil leaned toward communism. For example, after the Nazi-Soviet Pact, I was indignant that the philosophical spirit, instead of protecting him from aberration, threw him into it. At the end of the war years, which he spent in a prisoner of war camp, he once again declared himself, briefly, as a communist (Kojève, at the time, thought that this opinion was hardly suitable for a new French citizen).

His procommunism did not last. He lived in Lille because he did not like Paris and his wife worked for the European Community in Brussels. He rarely came to Paris, waiting for visits in Lille, and later in Nice. Separated by distance and by family dramas, we stopped seeing each other. During our last telephone conversation, he thanked me for having helped elect him as a corresponding member of the *Académie des sciences morales et politiques*.

I prefer to recall him as the man to whom I dedicated my principal thesis. He also attended Kojève's lectures, even though he had mastered the *Phenomenology* as well, or almost as well, as the speaker. He did not speak with the same charm as Kojève; conversations with him did not always flow easily. It was he who, to a large extent, brought me back to philosophical speculation or, at least, restored my taste for it. His knowledge of the great philosophers rightly impressed me; it did not seem to me inferior to that of Kojève or Koyré. The articles he published on the most diverse subjects in *Critique* demonstrate astonishing cultivation. On each occasion he knew as much as, or more than, the specialists. His principal books, *Logique de la philosophie, Philosophie politique, Problèmes kantiens*, enjoy a well deserved reputation in narrow circles; he still has, scattered about, passionate admirers. Kojève, rather than he, enjoyed a certain notoriety. An unjust fate? He too wrote an introduction to the reading of Hegel, but perhaps in order to return to Kant.

Alexandre Koyré, the patriarch of the group, had fought in the First World War (he never spoke about it). An admirable historian of philosophy and of science, he covered an immense territory, from German mysticism to Russian thought of the nineteenth century and studies of Galileo, rightly considered classic throughout the world. He spoke little, slowly, softly, but he expressed accurate and definitive judgments about events and people. He warned me against Alain's antimilitarism; he never allowed himself to be tempted by communism, even when the great depression seemed to confirm Marx's predictions. Among those exceptional minds, he shone not by his talent but by his modesty, by his scrupulous and patient search for the truth, by his ethical rigor. He took the university seriously; he hoped for a chair at the Collège de France; Martial Guéroult was chosen over him. Both deserved admission to this celebrated institution.

Reading the book by Zeev Sternhell,[5] I wondered whether I had misjudged the basis of the National Revolution that sprang forth in 1940 as a result of the defeat. Had I misjudged the strength of anti-Semitism and the threat of fascism? Was France, as Sternhell writes, "impregnated with fascism"?

I was aware of the extreme right press: *Je suis partout, Gringoire, Candide*. I didn't read these weeklies regularly, since they nauseated me; to preserve a cool head and to spare one's nerves, one must impose discipline on one's reading (so said Auguste Comte). These rags, with some talent, fostered by hatred, expressed a certain bourgeoisie, including those symbolized by the celebrated slogan: "rather Hitler than Blum!" I had nothing in common with that faction of the right, whatever may have come of their internecine struggles. Between me and them, communication remains impossible, even if we might agree on a specific subject.

Through the 1930s, Charles Maurras continued to give his morning lesson and his political directives to his disciples: minor provincial nobles, naval officers, a fraction of the Parisian intelligentsia. Several times I tried to develop an interest in this doctrinaire supporter of the monarchy, without success. He certainly held an important place in the intellectual history of France in the first half of the twentieth century. His success has more to do with the poverty of rival thought than to the richness of his own. His analyses of particular events were more than once penetrating. In my view, he served neither the idea of monarchy nor his country.

Supporting Salazar and Mussolini (with some reservations), he never showed the slightest sympathy for National Socialism, which he detested as

Germanic and Romantic, at the antipodes from the eminent order that remained for him the eternal model of wisdom and beauty.

The conversions or "deconversions" of men of letters, sometimes to fascism, sometimes to communism, provoked my curiosity or contempt rather than serious concern. Gide's adhesion to the communist cause, followed by the publication of *Retour d'URSS*, in my view had more to do with the biography of a writer concerned with his image than with world history.

I knew Emmanuel Mounier and read *Esprit* from time to time, without getting very much from it. As I remember, I published only one article there, entitled "Open letter from a young Frenchman to Germany." Dated January 1933, written before Hitler had come to power, it reveals my feelings at the end of my stay in Germany. "Pardon me, but I have no right to speak in the name of French youth. I am neither of the right nor the left, neither communist nor nationalist, no more radical than I am socialist. I do not know whether I will find companions. . . . Perhaps in reaction to German nationalism, I have become a French nationalist. . . ." I developed the thesis that Germany was going to be governed by right-wing parties, that dialogues on the contrasting cultures of the two peoples (order against dynamism, reason against enthusiasm) no longer made sense, that the invocation of ideals or moral principles had become hypocritical on both sides. No hope remained for agreements based on self-interest between great powers.

Esprit irritated me less because of its values than because of its manner. I saw there typically ideological writing, in the sense that it did not approach political problems in a style that would enable the reader to discern the recommended relations or choices. The governing ideas, variations on communitarian themes, reminded me of some German writing exploited by the National Socialists. When the test came, when events demanded decisions, the *Esprit* group was torn apart in 1938—which was understandable—and even in July 1940—which makes one wonder.

I did not take the books by Armand Dandieu and Robert Aron very seriously; pitiless critics of parliamentary and capitalist democracy, they protested against any relationship with fascism. As for the writings of those who explicitly claimed allegiance to the Italian and German experiments, Marcel Bucard, Georges Valois, Jacques Doriot, they were propaganda, and I looked at them as at party political publications.

Is Sternhell nevertheless right when he says that France was "impregnated with fascism" on the eve of the war? If I refer to the electoral or parliamentary situation, I cannot renounce my diagnosis at the time. The various leagues that were dissolved by the Popular Front government did not constitute a serious threat to the Republic. The February 1934 riots were provoked by various accidents, not by a plot. Thus the police, under the orders of a weak but legal government, did not hesitate to shoot at demonstrators of the right as well as the left. The leagues posed a challenge, they did not place the Republic in danger.

The argument may be made that the ruling classes were perhaps "impregnated" with fascist ideas, even though the Third Republic was not in a situation comparable to that of the Weimar Republic in the early 1930s. I would certainly take such an argument seriously. However, the parties of the right that inhabited the ranks of the National Assembly were not impregnated with fascism—at most, this was true of a few deputies of the extreme right; hence, it is not necessary to mobilize the Communist Party, the working masses, and the unity of a divided left to save the Republic. But parliamentary democracy, tied to capitalism, suffered from a kind of contempt that spread more and more widely, although those who shared the feeling were not at all fascist.

To be sure, one could find almost everywhere more or less successful attempts to combine themes borrowed from socialism with themes borrowed from nationalism. These combinations did not however lead to Hitler's National Socialism. Some right-wing socialists, who left the SFIO and provoked Léon Blum to the statement, "I am terrified," became more or less committed collaborators (Marcel Déat, Adrien Marquet). In the 1930s, the socialists recognized the emptiness of the Socialist International; unless they were blind, they had to decide on or resign themselves to action within the national framework. The groups that called themselves "planists," inspired by Henri de Man, neither thought of themselves as, nor wished to be, fascists or National Socialists; they were looking for a solution to the world crisis and to the impotence of parliaments.

There is no doubt that, in the late 1930s, ideas from the other side of the Rhine were widespread in France; anti-Semitism, as virulent in France as in Germany in the preceding century, derived from Hitler's example moral reinforcement and a kind of legitimacy. Finally and above all, the quarrel about the diplomatic approach that should be taken toward the Third Reich profoundly divided the nation; advocates of resistance were called warmongers by their adversaries, and those who were in favor of agreement with Hitler were suspected of fascist sympathies. There was an element of truth in the counteraccusations: those who favored a one-party state rejected a war that would have been based on the "defense of democracy." The most determined adversaries of the regimes of Mussolini and Hitler risked neglecting the principal thing in wartime, the balance of forces. Many men of the right clearly recognized the military inferiority of France; many men on the left had a clear vision of Hitler's ambitions.

The disdain that afflicted the Third Republic explains not only the National Revolution, but also the passive acceptance by the people—who were stunned—and by the ruling class, the established authorities, of the measures taken by Vichy on its own initiative to liquidate the Republic and to imitate certain aspects of Hitler's legislation. I was not surprised by the Vichy reforms. In June 1940 in Toulouse, as I was about to leave France, I said to my wife: "They—the ones who wanted the armistice after having rejected war—are going to do more quietly what the German occupation would have demanded." I was excessively optimistic: I did not believe that they would anticipate the desires of the Nazis.

The defeat, more than the ideological controversies of the 1930s, made Vichy and the National Revolution possible. But the old enemies of the Republic, Action française, provided a fraction of the personnel and the ideas for the first Vichy regime. Other men, other schools of thought, joined the founders. One cannot say that Pierre Laval was a fascist beforehand, or that he was influenced by the debates of the French intelligentsia. They had popularized an authoritarian philosophy, derived from both French traditions and foreign experiences.

I did not belong fully to any of the groups that I frequented, and they barely communicated with one another. Malraux was already celebrated, while Sartre, before the publication of *La Nausée*, was still looking for a publisher for his manuscripts. Academics and writers rarely came together outside the meetings of the *Union pour la vérité* and the Pontigny seminars. I derived benefits from both. I sometimes regret the lack nowadays of a circle like the one created by Paul Desjardins.

Alone among us, in charge of foreign affairs on *Ce Soir*, Paul-Yves Nizan participated in the ideological battle that raged on the Left Bank after 1933 and especially 1934. The men who were to dominate the postwar philosophical Paris were working on their books, the first of which appeared in the late 1930s. The fat volumes of *Recherches philosophiques* broke with the atmosphere of the 1920s, with the teaching that our generation had received. Perhaps postwar philosophy is now approaching its end; it ripened during the 1930s, outside the quarrels of the time, which were conducted by men of letters.

NOTES

1. When this was quoted, the expression "first of all" was frequently omitted. Did he make the statement? He confirmed it to me several times. Personally, I do not remember it, but I take his word for it.

2. This international institution, the General Agreement on Tariffs and Trade, created at the end of the war, establishes the rules for commercial exchanges, the conditions under which a common market or a free trade zone can be created.

3. No. 9 (Spring 1980).

4. In 1938 or 1939, Kojève, Weil, Polin, and I had read Kant together. Kojève and Weil were sometimes engaged in interminable controversies; one or the other, who was obviously wrong, argued indefatigably.

5. *Ni Droite ni Gauche: l'idéologie fasciste en France* (Paris: Le Seuil, 1983).

5

DESPERATE OR SATANIC

The two adjectives I have used as the title of this chapter come from Paul Fauconnet, who hurled them at me during the defense of my thesis on 20 March 1938. A few days earlier, in the course of the visit I paid him, in conformity with custom, he asked me, indiscreetly and benevolently, whether family matters influenced the tone of my writing. Tempted to laugh, I evoked the dangers threatening our country, the approaching war, the decadence of France. I had reassured him about my family, he reassured me about France. Yes, of course, France had passed its peak, the supreme height of its grandeur. This entirely relative decline, in keeping with the fate of nations, neither justified nor even explained my aggressive pessimisism. This sociologist, an unconditional disciple of Emile Durkheim, looked from a distance, almost indifferent out of scientific serenity, at the growth of a catastrophe whose dimensions I did not anticipate, although the mandarins of the time criticized me for a constantly gloomy outlook.

During my thesis defense, according to the summary published by the *Revue de métaphysique et de morale*, at the conclusion of my presentation, Paul Fauconnet, greeted with diverse reactions from the public, expressed himself in these terms: "I conclude with an act of charity, faith, and hope: charity by repeating to you my admiration and my sympathy; faith in the ideas that you condemn; hope that the students will not follow you."

A pure product of the Sorbonne and of positivist or neo-Kantian rationalism, I appeared to Fauconnet, and not to him alone, as a nay-sayer, less a revolutionary than a nihilist. A few years later, *L'Etre et le néant* did not encounter the same indignant surprise from the distracted professors.

In any event, Fauconnet's reaction, caricatural in its expression, did not differ fundamentally from that of the other members of the jury and, more generally, from that of the professors of the 1930s. My books, *Contemporary German Sociology*, *The Critical Philosophy of History*, and *Introduction to the Philosophy of History*, appeared between 1935 and 1938 while several German philosophers, expelled from or fleeing the Third Reich, were living in Paris. *Recherches philosophiques* published articles by these exiles. This peaceful invasion provoked reactions of rejection. I simultaneously profited and suffered from the circumstances. My books introduced one or more sets of problems that had come from the opposite bank of the Rhine. Fauconnet felt himself challenged by my critique of historical objectivity; all of them were surprised not to find in me one of their students, whom they greeted in advance as a member of the family. It is hardly necessary to add that Bouglé, out of friendship, and all the others, out of loyalty to their ethics, did not for an instant dream of closing the doors of alma mater to me.

Why did my books give off an aura of despair or "satanism"?

Between my thesis on Kant for the *diplôme d'études supérieures* (1926–27) and my year in Le Havre, I had read a good deal, in scattered directions. Aside from articles in *Libres Propos* and *Europe*, I had written nothing. Between October 1933 and April 1937, I succeeded in writing the three books I mentioned earlier.

I do not use the word "succeeded" to suggest my merits, the accomplishment of an exploit, but to recall my fear of the blank page, my difficulty in writing. It took me years to put reading and writing together, to prepare for writing by reading, to reread when I had already begun to write. Most of the time, I drafted the chapter concerning a writer without referring to the texts, by reconstructing his thought on the basis of the ideas I had drawn from his books. I added the references later.

What was, what is the value of *German Sociology?* I can say, without vanity, that this little book was useful even though it is hardly so today. Some sociologists included there are no longer of interest, and others, in particular Max Weber, who took up more than one-third of the book, no longer need an introduction. Several generations of students derived from the book a knowledge, that may have been superficial but was on the whole accurate, of some tendencies of German sociology at the moment when National Socialism interrupted its development. Robert Merton, in a seminar at the International Congress of Sociology, stated that this little book by an unknown writer had struck him. It has since been translated into Spanish, Japanese, English, and German—the last two after the war. It has recently been translated into Italian for reasons unknown to me,[1] and republished in the United States and Japan.

In 1935, most of the German sociologists whom I discussed were either unknown or little known. *L'Année sociologique* had reported on some work by Max Weber, particularly his essay on the Protestant ethic and the spirit of capitalism. Max Weber, for his part, had never quoted Durkheim but, according to Marcel Mauss, had a complete collection of *L'Année sociologique* in his personal library. In 1935, there was no general study on the personality of the political figure and the sociologist. Post-Marxist theoretical approaches, for example that of Karl Mannheim, barely touched the minds of a few French sociologists. My book followed the *Bilan de la sociologie française* by Célestin Bouglé and benefited from more favorable conditions than his book had. In a sense, it opened up an unexplored field. Thanks to it, I met Brodersen and Shils, with whom I still have connections today. What touched me the most, twenty-five years later, was the statement by a sociologist of Polish origin, Stanislav Andreski, that my little book had awakened his vocation.

I had written the book at the request of Bouglé, who had promised me, for the following year, a position in the Center for Social Documentation of the ENS. It was not a lucrative task (royalties were to be modest) but apparently aimed at students; it distracted me from my complementary thesis on which I was working at the same time. Was I later satisfied with having been forced to carry out the project? Even today, I am pleased that I completed my German pilgrimage with this book.

I was carrying on a short tradition: Durkheim and Bouglé had both visited German universities, and had then written articles, gathered together in books. I had not visited universities, I had barely observed von Wiese's circle in Cologne, glimpsed Sombart in Berlin. Unlike my predecessors, I concentrated on sociology in the narrow sense of the term. I presented not surveys of reading or of experiential impressions, but a systematic outline with the help of the antithesis between *systematic sociology* and *historical sociology*. Does the antithesis have any value beyond the pragmatic one as a useful device, so to speak? Oppenheimer, Alfred Weber, and Mannheim no doubt belonged to the same current; the first two suggested a global view of history, the third reflected on the implications of the social roots of the sociologist, all three in the shadow of Karl Marx. Each of them had chosen his own theme: Oppenheimer the origin of social hierarchy, of the exploitation of man by

man, attributable to the victory of the shepherds over the farmers; Alfred
Weber the duality of civilization and culture, of the technical and the
spiritual; Mannheim the conception of a new science, *Wissenssoziologie*, an
extension of the Marxist idea that each class sees social reality from a point of
view, a position that is peculiar to it.

Of the three, in 1932, Karl Mannheim had by far the greatest notoriety. In
Berlin, I wrote an article on him that I sent to him; I went to see him in
Frankfurt where I met Norbert Elias, whose books on the civilizing process
have recently been published to acclaim. Mannheim had misplaced my
article, which probably did not deserve a better fate. When I wrote *Contemporary German Sociology*, I had freed myself from the spell that *Ideology
and Utopia* had cast on me, and the chapter I devoted to him was far from
indulgent. I saw him again in Paris in 1935, and with much elegance and a
little irony, he congratulated me on my book which he "greatly appreciated"—"except for the chapter that concerns me directly," he added with a
smile. A young man writes his first book and tears apart the mandarin who is
almost famous in Europe and America, and the mandarin, far from being
indignant, compliments the rash young man. Mannheim was, as the English
say, a decent man. I saw him again a few times in London during the war.

The *Critical Philosophy of History* grouped together, for purposes of
analysis, four writers: Wilhelm Dilthey, Georg Simmel, Heinrich Rickert,
and Max Weber. Was this assemblage artificial, arbitrary, or justified by the
resemblance of their approaches, the relations among the questions they
posed? Wilhelm Dilthey, born two years after the death of Hegel, belonged
to a different generation from that of the three others, who were born around
1860 (1858, 1863, and 1864, respectively); none of the four had devoted his
life or his entire œuvre to the question I posed to that work. Wilhelm Dilthey
was a historian before "criticizing" his own profession. Simmel's
Geschichtsphilosophie occupies a modest place in his work. The great work
by Heinrich Rickert, *Die Grenzen der naturwissenschaftlichen Begriffs-
bildung*, although it is probably the best known of his books, was contained
within a neo-Kantian framework that was all-encompassing, and within
which the antithesis between the two kinds of science was only a small part.
Finally, Max Weber, although he was always concerned with the methods of
his knowledge as well as his knowledge itself, owes his fame to his work as a
sociologist.

It still seems to me that comparison of these writers is justified, as long as
the limited objective of the exercise is specified. It was not a matter of
presenting the whole of the thought of Dilthey or Weber, but of making
explicit and comparing the answers they had given to the same question.
Was the question exactly the same? Probably not, because it was expressed
by each of them in the language and within the framework of a particular
philosophy. But in rereading this difficult book after so many years, I can

understand both the value I attributed to it, rightly or wrongly, and the various reactions that it provoked.

Léon Brunschvicg's reservations about the *Critical Philosophy of History* and my foreboding of the approaching war prompted me to undertake immediately the book I had been thinking about for several years, ever since my meditation on the banks of the Rhine. Since I had devoted myself to the role of committed observer, I owed it to myself to bring into the open the relationship between the historian and the man of action, between the knowledge of history-in-the-making and the decisions that a historical being is condemned to make. I abandoned the idea of a second volume on the theory of history and, after having improved the manuscript of the first volume, I set to work in October and November of 1935 and began to write *Introduction to the Philosophy of History;* the book was finished after the Easter vacation of 1937.

I do not think I worked out the structure in advance. As I wrote, the *Introduction* took on a form that now irritates me: four sections, three of which contained three parts, each of which was in turn subdivided into four subparts. At the thesis defense, Emile Bréhier pointed out that this was a scholastic presentation, and he criticized me for breaking up the development, for dividing the theme into a succession of problems, and leaving to the reader the task of putting the pieces together. I answered, with some vanity, that the notion of development had nothing to do with philosophy; it was enough that I had analyzed the problems with a maximum of clarity. I would now be tempted to agree with Bréhier. The book also suffers from an obsession with symmetry; certain paragraphs and conclusions of sections and parts do not seem to be to be indispensable. Perhaps the method adopted by Alain in some of his books was still weighing on my mind.

I have no intention of either recanting or defending this book, written almost fifty years ago, whose history, in France at least, is perhaps not entirely over, an indication of the fact that I might have been a professional academic philosopher.

Before undertaking the thankless task of presenting the essential aspects of a book that defies summary, I would propose as a kind of epigraph the following remark on autobiography that I find in the *Introduction:* "I cannot possibly think again as I did at twenty, or at least, I have to go on a voyage of discovery almost as though I were talking with another person. Often, to rediscover my former self, I have to interpret expressions, works. We are hardly aware of this development of our minds, because we have accumulated the best of our experiences; the past of our intelligence interests us— apart from introspective curiosity—only to the extent that it is or would be worthy of being present."

I would replace "introspective curiosity" with autobiographical curiosity.

For the rest, my experience tends to confirm this analysis. I have several times reconsidered some of the problems treated in the *Introduction*, for example in *Dimensions de la conscience historique* (1961), without ever referring to my prewar writings. I thus assumed that I had kept within myself the essential aspects of the results reached in the course of earlier research. It was out of autobiographical curiosity that I reread the *Introduction*, in search of a text whose creation I would now have a great deal of difficulty in reconstructing and which would be even more difficult for me to write today.

First of all I looked for the few passages that could have incurred the wrath of Paul Fauconnet, and I found some judgments that would shock no one today:

A philosophy of progress . . . consists in agreeing that societies and human existence in general tend to improve, sometimes that this improvement, regular and continuous, must go on indefinitely. Essentially intellectualist, it moves from science to man and to collective organization; optimistic, since morality, in theory and practice, is supposed to go along with intelligence. Reaction against this doctrine has in the present taken on the most diverse forms. Doubt has been cast on the reality, or at least the regularity, of progress. Too many events have revealed the precariousness of what is called civilization; the apparently most certain acquisitions have been sacrificed to collective mythologies; politics, stripped of its masks, has revealed its essence to the most naïve. By the same token, there has been theoretical and practical criticism of the reasoning process that led from science to man and to society. An isolated activity, positive science develops according to a particular rhythm, while thought, not to speak of conduct, does not follow its increasingly rapid pace. Besides, what does this supposed progress mean? Between a communitarian society that takes itself as an absolute value, and a liberal society that aims to enlarge the sphere of individual autonomy, there is no common ground. The movement from one to the other cannot be evaluated except by reference to a norm that should be superior to historical diversity. But such a norm is always the hypostatized projection of what a particular collectivity is or would wish to be. And our era is too much aware of the obvious diversity it finds within itself to succumb to the naïveté of closed groups or to raise itself to the confidence of those who compare themselves to the past and to others with the certainty of their superiority . . . .

Such a challenge to the philosophy of progress on the eve of the Second World War should have scandalized no one, not even a Durkheimian stagnating in his belief in sociology. This text, moreover, was not the last word of the *Introduction;* it rejected the vulgar form of the belief in progress, based on a factual error—society as a whole does not change at the same rate and in the same manner as scientific knowledge—and based on a naïveté—progress can be evaluated only with reference to a transhistorical criterion. *Increase* in knowledge is observable, *improvement* in cultures is a matter of judgment, and which judge is impartial?

In 1938, the pluralism of cultures (or of civilizations) already belonged to the spirit of age. The salons repeated Valéry's declaration: "We civilizations now know that we are mortal." In spite of everything, the rejection of rationalist progressivism shocked the optimistic and idealist philosophy that still dominated the left of the Sorbonne. A passing remark on world history, banal as it may now appear, was probably attributed to "despair."

> Our period would thus appear to favor such an attempt [a universal history] since, for the first time, the entire planet is involved in a common fate. Objections will be made because of the accumulation of knowledge that cannot be assimilated by a single mind, the scientific rigor that condemns such extravagant visions; it will be pointed out that relations among diverse peoples still remain distant, their community thin, this unity partial and external. All these propositions are valid, but they do not reach the essential. If the West still had confidence in its mission, we would write, collectively or individually, a universal history which would show, on the basis of separate adventures, the gradual accession of all societies to the civilization of the present.
>
> What makes such a history impossible is the fact that Europe no longer knows whether it prefers what it contributes to what it destroys. It recognizes the particularities of expressive creations and of individual existences, at the moment when it threatens to destroy unique values.

The moderate left at the time still believed in "the civilizing mission" of France or the Western countries. I certainly set myself on the fringe, in France at least. In Weimar Germany, historicism—in the sense of the awareness of the pluralism of cultures and the historicity of values—fostered the pessimism and disarray of intellectuals. The ideas in which Paul Fauconnet renewed his faith on 26 March 1938 did not resist the years that followed.

A Durkheimian sociologist had to consider even more aggressive an analysis directed against the claim of Durkheim himself to establish the ethics of the teaching corps on the new science. I recalled, in the passage devoted to historical relativism *(der Historismus)* the link among diverse societies and their morality (in the Hegelian sense of *die Moralität),* and the diversity of moral obligations and ways of living that results. And I continued:

> On the contrary, the interdependence of ethics and society confirms the validity of our particular imperatives if society is by right as well as in fact the origin and basis of any obligation. Wasn't it Durkheim's intention to restore morality, shattered according to him by the disappearance of religious belief? The sociologists, democrats, free-thinkers, partisans of individual freedom, confirmed through their

science the values to which they adhered spontaneously. In their eyes, the structure of their present civilization (density or organic solidarity) somehow demanded egalitarian ideas and the autonomy of individuals. Value judgments gained rather than losing by becoming collective judgments. In complete confidence, they replaced God with society. In reality, the term "society" cannot be used without ambiguity, since it sometimes designates real collectivities and sometimes the idea or ideal of those collectivities. In truth, it can be applied only to particular groups, closed in on themselves, but, less than the words fatherland or nation, it calls to mind rivalry and war (it is hard to imagine a society encompassing all of humanity). It conceals the conflicts that divide all human communities. It permits the subordination of opposed classes to social unity and allows one to conceive a national morality that would be sociological without being political: but if this concept, stripped of all borrowed prestige, designates the partially incoherent whole of social facts, does it not seem that sociologism adds to unlimited relativity the reduction of values to a reality that is more natural than political, subject to determinism and not open to freedom?

The execution in a few lines of an idea dear to Durkheim, namely the renewal of the teaching of ethics in the Ecoles normales* through sociology, must no doubt have troubled the master's most faithful disciple. But I think the book or books as a whole shocked him. I gave the impression that I was breaking with rationalism—while my subsequent activity demonstrated the contrary; a break with the optimism of progress and faith in science—in which he was not wrong, although he was not entirely right. The meaning of the book itself remained ambiguous, if not obscure: each analysis was in itself perhaps clear, the intention and the conclusions of the whole led to controversy. To an extent, the form of the book bears responsibility for this, but I see other reasons.

In the introduction, I summed up the intention of the book in the following terms: "On a higher level, our book leads to a *historical philosophy* which is opposed both to scientistic rationalism and to positivism." Henri Marrou, in the review he wrote for *Esprit*, emphasized above all the antipositivism, the merciless critique of historians who harbored the illusion of attaining to truth in the naïve sense of reproducing the reality of the past, *wie es geschehen ist* (as it happened), according to the celebrated expression of Leopold von Ranke. A little further on, I explained the intention again: "A historical philosophy that is also in a sense a philosophy of history, on the condition that such a history is not defined as a panoramic vision of humanity as a whole but as an interpretation of the present or the past connected to a philosophical conception of existence." Again: "Philosophy develops in the endlessly renewed movement of life toward consciousness, from con-

---

*Trans. note: Schools created by the government of the Third Republic to train the "republican" teachers.

sciousness toward free thought, and from thought toward will." Although it had a rationalist inspiration, the book as a whole, in 1938, surprised our masters in the Sorbonne, who detected in it a manner of thinking, preoccupations, and subjects of reflection that were foreign to their universe.

I will pass rapidly over the two theories of understanding and causality that make up the largest part of the book, but that have to do with epistemology. I established at the outset a distinction between two modes of knowledge, a distinction I will illustrate with a simplified example. To establish the motive of an act in the vocabulary that I had adopted, was not to illuminate its cause. The understanding of an agent, whether it is accountd for by the logic of the situation or by an emotional impulse, is not opposed to explanation in the ordinary sense of the word, but to *causal explanation*. Understandings of an action, a work, an institution, share the characteristic of looking for meaning, and intelligible connections, immanent to the object. I would have accepted the enumeration I find in a working paper by a Norwegian philosopher: objects of understanding are people, their acts and their words, certain products of their acts and their speech, generally the manifestations of the human spirit (painting, sculpture, and the like), finally some objects that are called meaningful, like instruments, tools, and the like. The theory I set forth at the beginning was at the opposite pole from the presumably irrationalist conception of understanding, namely the affective participation of the consciousness in the consciousness of others. I designated understanding as the knowledge of a meaning that, immanent in reality, was or could have been thought by those who experienced it or brought it into being.

To illustrate my conception of causality, I will repeat the example I used: the origins of the 1914 war. For me, research on the causes of the 1914 war involves not only discovering the intentions of the actors, who, after the assassination of Archduke Francis Ferdinand, desired or accepted local or general war, but also discovering the acts that made inevitable, or at least probable, the explosion of August 1914. In a sense, the determination of the causes of the war can be compared to the analysis of the causes of an accident, the breakdown of an engine or the fall of an avalanche. The wearing down of an engine component or the collapse of a mass of snow each obeys the laws of nature, but an expert would find the cause among antecedent events to be the one that directly and immediately provoked the accident; either he focuses on an antecedent event that is so foreseeable that antecedent events as a whole rather than the last one, the detonator, bear responsibility for the accident; or else, on the contrary, he seizes on an unforeseeable antecedent so that the event does not appear to be implicit in the situation; the situation did not make the event inevitable or even probable, but it arose, as they say, from a combination of circumstances.

In the case of the origins of the 1914 war, the procedure seems to me both simple and difficult: we can observe, without the shadow of a doubt, that the crisis, the fear of approaching war, began with Austria's ultimatum to Serbia. But it would be obviously wrong to say that this was the *cause*, the detonation of the war. One may however evaluate the *probability* of war created by the *initiative* taken by the Vienna government. Retrospective calculations about probability never reach rigorous conclusions, but they allow for evaluations suggested by a comparison between what happened and what would have happened if a particular incident had not taken place. For each act (in this instance, the antecedents of war), one may ask the question: what were the consequences that the actor could and should have foreseen? Moreover, since, in human affairs, causality cannot be separated from responsibility or guilt, one must consider the extent to which the act constituted an *initiative*, whether it conformed to the customs and moral rules of the diplomatic world, and what were the intentions of the actor. In my view, the essential thing was to distinguish between understanding human behavior through motives or the logic of the situation on the one hand, and analysis of causality on the other. In the case of an event, unique, particular, it is a question either of historical causality or of sociological causality; in a vocabulary that I now prefer, either one attempts to establish the rule or the law that explains the event (the law establishes that event x occurs in circumstances a, b, c; if we observe that a, b, c were given, we consider event x explained); or one attempts to measure the respective causality of various antecedents by means of retrospective calculations of probability, without neglecting rules or general principles.

With respect to the origins of the 1914 war, analysis encounters all the more obstacles because the crisis extended over several days, with many actions and reactions. Some of these actions were subjected to particular investigation: the rejection by the Austrian government of the Serbian government's answers, the Russian general mobilization, and so on. In contrast to what some of my readers have seen in my book, research on the origins of the First World War does not seem to me to be characterized by a fundamental relativity, but it cannot lead to results that are both precise and demonstrable. Since Russia had established itself as protector of the southern Slavs, Austria clearly took the risk of a general war because of the system of alliances, but what was the degree of risk (or probability) of war? What were the intentions of the Vienna officials? To what extent were Vienna's demands legitimate? Contemporaries never achieve impartiality: historians do, but they cannot give categorical answers to the questions they ask as though they were prosecuting attorneys.

This simplified example gives an idea of the general propositions that I wished to confirm through the development of my research: "Understanding is connected to the intrinsic intelligibility of motives and ideas. Causality aims above all at establishing necessary links by observing regularities. To the extent that the sociologist attempts to discover causal relations, he legitimately ignores, he must ignore, the verisimilitude of rational connections; he treats historical phenomena as foreign material or, in the classic expression, as things." Shortly before this, I distinguished three kinds of intentionality; those of the judge, the scientist, the philosopher. The first is expressed by the question: Who (or what) is at fault? The second leads to the establishment of constant links of coexistence or succession. The third attempts to bring together, to unite, the two other kinds of research, placed in the context of historical determinism.

Only the conclusion of the section devoted to causality deserves to be recalled, namely that plurality is immanent in the historical world. Neither a society nor a historical process constitutes a totality. Just as we do not grasp the ultimate intention, the *Gesinnung* (or intelligible aspect) of a being, so we do not grasp in a single perception a large whole, a global culture, or even a macro-event like the French Revolution. This plurality is bound up with the plurality of human nature itself, simultaneously life, consciousness, and idea, and with the fragmentary nature of determinism (*momentary* in the explanation of an event, *partial* in the reconstruction of patterns). But all narratives, all interpretations, simultaneously use comprehensive understanding and causal analysis; fragmentary determinism hangs on a construction of facts and groups of facts; causal relations are accompanied and illuminated by intelligible connections. The understanding of causality and the understanding of meaning, according to the formulation of Max Weber and the practice of all sociologists and historians, strengthen and confirm one another, even though each of the two procedures has its own meaning.

More than a contribution to the epistemology of historical knowledge, the book fulfilled the intention that I presented to the reader. "In 1930,[2] I made the decision to study Marxism in order to subject my political ideas to philosophical review." The analysis of historical causality served as a basis for or an introduction to a theory (or rather a sketch of a theory) of action and politics. The book as a whole made explicit the mode of political thought that I adopted from then on, and that has persisted into the autumn of my life. In a slightly scholastic style, I distinguished three stages: choice, decision, the search for the truth.

"Logically, it is important above all to accept or reject the existing order: for or against what exists, that is the first alternative. Reformers are opposed to revolutionaries, to those who wish not to ameliorate capitalism but to suppress it. By destroying his milieu, the revolutionary attempts to reconcile himself with himself, since man is in harmony with himself only if he is in harmony with the social relations of which he is, willingly or not, the prisoner . . . the revolutionary has no program but a demogogic one. One may say that he has an *ideology*, that is, the representation of another system, transcending the present and probably unrealizable. But only the success of the revolution will allow us to distinguish between anticipation and utopia. If we were thus to confine ouselves to ideologies, we would spontaneously join the revolutionaries, who usually promise more than the others. The resources of the imagination necessarily triumph over reality, even when disfigured or transfigured by lies. This explains the intellectuals' prejudice in favor of the so-called advanced parties."

In this respect, I have not changed: I did not choose the cause of revolution (in 1937, as in 1981, this cause is identified with that of communism or Marxism-Leninism), because of what has been called my pessimism: "There is no doubt that the societies we have known until now have been unjust (measured against current representations of justice). It remains to find out what a just society would be and whether it is definable and realizable." In my inaugural lecture at the Collège de France, I confessed, or more precisely, I proclaimed the failure of all *sociodicies*. Today I would add that modern societies seem to us more unjust than those of the Ancien Régime appeared to their inhabitants. For a simple reason: modern democratic societies invoke ideals that are to a large extent unrealizable and through the voice of their leaders, they aspire to an inaccessible mastery over their fate.

What is the meaning of the priority given to the choice for or against revolution? In the first place, and above all, it calls for the most rigorous possible study of reality and the possible regime that might replace the existing one. Rational choice in political history as I understand it does not result uniquely from moral principle or ideology, but from an analytical investigation, as scientific as possible. An investigation that will never lead to a conclusion exempt from doubt, that will not impose a choice in the name of science, but that will protect against the traps of idealism or of good will. Not that, on the other hand, political choices are outside values or morality. In the last analysis, one does not choose liberal and capitalist democracy against the communist program only because one thinks that the mechanism of the market is more efficient than central planning (the relative efficiency of economic mechanisms is obviously one of the arguments in favor of one regime or another). One chooses on the basis of many criteria: effectiveness of institutions, individual liberty, equitable distribution, perhaps above all the kind of person created by the regime.

At the time, I distinguished between (and I have used this distinction several times since then) the politics of understanding and the politics of Reason: "*The politician of understanding*—Max Weber, Alain—seeks to preserve certain goods—peace and freedom—or to reach a unique goal, national greatness, in situations that are always new and that follow one another without organized patterns. He is like a pilot navigating without knowledge of the port. There is a dualism of means and ends, of reality and values; there is no current totality or predestined future; every moment is new to him. *The politician of Reason*, on the contrary, foresees at least the next stage of evolution. The Marxist knows that the disappearance of capitalism is inevitable and that the only problem is to adapt tactics to strategy, to harmonize accommodation with the current regimes with preparation for the future regime."

I presented the two terms—politics of understanding and politics of Reason—as ideal types which are not mutually exclusive in reality: "There is no immediate action that is not responsive to distant concern, no one who is confident in Providence who is not in search of unique opportunities . . . . Politics is both the art of irreversible choices and of long-range plans." The last sentence, barely modified, is equally applicable to the journalist or the political commentator: the interpretation of events is only valid to the extent that it grasps both the originality of the event and its place in a whole, whether system or process.

I called the second stage of action decision, that is, the commitment of the individual to a political choice. "Choice is not an activity external to an authentic being, it is the decisive act through which I commit myself and judge the social milieu that I recognize as my own. Choice in history is in reality identical to a choice of my self, since it has as its origin and its object my own existence."

By entitling this second section "Historical Man: The Choice," I was, in a sense, ennobling politics. Political or historical choice was also the choice everyone made of himself.

"In those rare quiet epochs, when private life flourished outside public affairs, when work had nothing (or almost nothing) to fear from the authorities, politics appeared to be a specialty, the domain of a few professionals, an occupation among others, more exciting than serious. It took war to teach men again that they are citizens before they are individuals: the collectivity, whether it be a class or a party, legitimately demands that each individual sacrifice himself for a cause. National defense or revolution, the individual who belongs to history is called upon to assume the supreme risk." I wrote these lines in 1937, while the Popular Front government was pitting the French against one another and while the shadow of war and the Third Reich was spreading over France. Fascism or communism, resistance to Hitler or submission, it was true that "if political choice risks bringing about the choice of a certain kind of death, this is because it means the choice of a certain kind of existence." The presence of Hitler and Stalin justified the insistence with which I asserted that political choice implied a choice about society as a whole, and that the decision affected the agent as much as his milieu: "In wishing for a certain social order, one wishes for a way of living . . . . I discover the situation in which I am living, but I recognize it as mine only by accepting or rejecting it, that is, by deciding on the one in which I wish to be. The choice of a milieu is a decision about myself . . . . The decision is as profoundly historical as the milieu. And it creates my spiritual universe at the same time as it establishes the place I claim as mine in the collective life." Despite the obsession with the tragic character of politics, I was already aware of the limits of its concerns: "Everything would not be overturned by a revolution. There would always be more continuity than the fanatics imagine. The mind is not entirely a prisoner of the common fate." At the same time, I emphasized the inevitable paradox, or perhaps one should say contradiction, between the absolute of commitment and the uncertainty of causes: "In our age of blind faith, it would be desirable that individuals remember that the concrete object to which they are attached is not revealed but constructed, according to probability, and that it should not, like transcendental religions, divide the world into two opposed kingdoms. One is tempted to emphasize the precariousness of opinions rather than the absolute character of commitment. As long as there is room for discussion, it is in fact better to remember that no humanity is possible without tolerance and that no one is granted possession of the entire truth." And yet, "for a historical task, man must assume the risk that, for him, takes precedence over everything."

The philosophy that comes through in the last four sections of the book implicitly contains a certain idea of man, above all of a man who is committed, who makes himself by judging the objective spirit he has internalized, who decides by himself by attempting to make his surroundings correspond to his choice: "Man who is aware of his finiteness, who knows that his existence is unique and limited, must, unless he gives up living, devote himself to ends, whose value he establishes by subordinating his being to them . . . . Thus, we neither give in to the fashion of pathetic philosophy, nor do we confuse the anguish of a troubled time with a permanent phenomenon, nor do we sink into nihilism, when we recall how man chooses himself and his mission by measuring himself against the void. This is, on the contrary, an affirmation of the power of the man who creates himself by judging his milieu and choosing himself. Only thus can the individual integrate into his essential being the history which he bears within himself and which becomes his own."

There remained, there still remains, the principal question: how are we to understand history—reality? Do human societies as a whole constitute a *unity*? Can one bring together the thousands of human groups, from the paleolithic bands and the neolithic tribes to the empires and the nations of our time, under the concept of History? I considered only the seven thousand years during which collective organizations or spiritual universes had developed and proliferated. And I asserted, not without hesitation and scruples of conscience, that man has a history, or rather "is an unfinished history." A formulation that was probably inspired by my memories of Kant.

It seems to me that these final pages reveal the tension between my immediate, emotional reactions to historical experience and my speculations: "Every human being is unique, irreplaceable in himself and for a few others, sometimes for humanity itself. And yet History horribly devours individuals in a manner that apparently cannot be avoided as long as violence is necessary for social change." Men are sacrificed for historical ends, and yet those ends are located in this world.

> The moral judgment that attributes the act to the agent appears ridiculous in the face of the monstrous sublimity of history, totally condemned if it is measured against the law of love or the imperative of good will: Should one subject the leader or the master to the usual rule? Since he is one among many, how can one not say yes? Since he is accountable for his work rather than responsible for his conduct in the face of the future, how can one not say no?
>
> Since the human condition is historical—a finite being who devotes himself to perishable works and wishes to attain goals beyond himself and his brief existence—how can one avoid the question of the end of history? Not the cosmological or biological end of humanity incapable of living or a continent rendered uninhabitable by the force of the elements on the folly of men, but the end that Kant and Hegel had envisioned: a state of humanity that would correspond to its destination and that would in a sense, bring to fruition the truth that men are in search of.
>
> This truth should be above the plurality of activities and values, or else it would sink back to the level of individual and contradictory wills. It should be concrete, or else, like ethical norms, it would remain at the fringes of action. Simultaneously theoretical and practical, in the image of the aim conceived by Marxism. Through the power acquired over nature, man would gradually arrive at an equal power over the social order. Thanks to participation in two collective enterprises—the state that makes each individual a citizen, culture that makes collective accomplishments accessible to all—he would realize his vocation: the conciliation of humanity and nature, of essence and existence.

And I added: "A no doubt indeterminate ideal since participation and reconciliation are thought of in diverse ways, but at last an ideal that is neither angelic nor abstract."

I rarely alluded to this idea of reason, to this end of history, in my later books, although I am still nostalgic for it. After the war, I criticized Sartre and Merleau-Ponty for having confused a particular aim with the end of history—a confusion that fosters fanaticism since it transfigures combat between classes and parties into the struggle, less eternal than final, between good and evil. Perhaps the style of the last lines of the thesis now seems to me excessively emotional: "Existence is dialectical, that is dramatic, since it operates in an incoherent world, commits itself despite time, seeks a fugitive truth, without any assurance beyond a fragmentary science and formal reflection." Neither Satanic nor desperate, I was experiencing in advance the world war that my judges did not see coming.

NOTES

1. *Main Currents of Sociological Thought* has been published in Italy. This large work reduces the interest of *German Sociology*.

2. 1931, I think, would have been more correct.

6

THE ROAD
TO CATASTROPHE

I took no part in political and intellectual debates between 1934 and 1939, but I followed events with so much passion during those dreadful years that I think it necessary to refer to them. I felt within myself the torments of the nation, and I foresaw the catastrophe threatening the French, pitted against one another so that even misfortune could not bring them together.

Most of my companions of the time are no longer alive. My current associates belong to another generation; they know the prewar period only through books. They have difficulty understanding what the decadence of France was like; the youngest among them even have some difficulty in imagining the atmosphere of Paris during the cold war. These pages are addressed to my friends, awakened to political consciousness twenty or thirty years after I was.

Between 1929 and 1931, France, which had been relatively little touched by the crisis, did not suffer from mass unemployment like Great Britain or Germany. In 1931, under compulsion, the national union government in London made the decision that freed, rescued the economy; it agreed to devalue the pound and to leave the value of the currency to the movements of the market. Since, at the time, most raw materials were priced in pounds, their prices were lower for countries, like France, that had not changed the exchange rate of their currency in relation to gold, or—which amounts to the same thing—in relation to the dominant currencies in the world market.

The level at which the franc should be stabilized was badly calculated in 1936 by Raymond Poincaré at too low a point; gold was accumulating in France. From 1931 on, the tide was reversed, gold fled from a currency that was now overvalued; the inevitable evils of this overvaluation followed in rapid succession. The protected sector, not in competition with international trade, maintained its prices; the sector open to world commerce lost its replacement markets in the empire and had to reduce its production costs and selling prices. From 1931 to 1936, against all challenges, all governments, from the moderate left (1932) to the center or the right, held to this policy. When Laval came to power, he pushed the old policy to extremes; he decreed the reduction of everything—government employee income, budgetary expenses, the costs of production—and he rejected the corresponding measure recommended by his advisers, by Jacques Rueff in particular, devaluation. The successive governments—Doumergue, Flandin, Laval—had all contributed to the desperate condition of the French economy. 1931: France, spared from the crisis, sitting on its pile of gold; 1936: France, shattered by widespread strikes, seemed to be drifting toward civil war. Alone among the industrialized countries, it had not moved out of the crisis in 1936; the 1929 level of production had not been restored, and our leaders—with the exception of Paul Reynaud—had not yet understood the absurdity of monetary patriotism.

This was the background for Robert Marjolin, a few friends, and me. The world crisis, the refusal of rulers—ministers and economic authorities as well—to make the decisions demanded by the devaluation of the pound and the dollar, condemned our economy to a prolonged case of lowering prices and to gradual weakening. Deflation sharply affected the condition of the workers. The permanent pressure exerted on the workers to produce at the best possible price had come about not because of the bosses' lack of humanity but through the constraints attributable to the overvaluation of the currency. Powerless and exasperated, we witnessed this suicidal aberration.

In the foreground, party rivalry continued, financial scandals unleashed press campaigns and overheated partisan passions. The 1934 riots did not reveal the activity or the plotting of an authentic fascist party. The Stavisky affair, the fanciful shifts of high officials from the *préfecture de police* to the Comédie-Française, the marches by Colonel de la Rocque's Croix-de-Feu, police forces that were in turn passive and violent, provoked one of those historic days, 6 February 1934, so characteristic of France (May 1968 evidenced the continuing vitality of this national tradition). In Le Havre, I looked on these events from a distance, already isolated by my obsession with the external threat. I was quite obviously an antifascist, but how could we resist against Hitler's threat if the government was supported by only half the nation?

Throughout the 1930s, I refused to join the committee of vigilance of antifascist intellectuals, for two principal reasons: first, there was no fascist peril in France, in the sense given to the term because of the examples of Italy and Germany. Colonel de la Rocque bore more resemblance to a leader of veterans than to a demagogue able to excite the fury of the crowd. Moreover, the group of antifascist intellectuals brought together disciples of Alain (pacifists for the most part), communists or fellow travelers, and conventional socialists. They all detested fascism and war but, on the essential problem, the attitude to take to the Third Reich, they differed. From 1935 on, after Pierre Laval's visit to Moscow and the joint declaration of the two governments (in which Stalin affirmed his understanding of the demands of French national defense), the Communist Party closed down the *gueules de vaches* column in *L'Humanité*, liquidated its primitive antimilitarism, raised the tricolor, and rejoined the antifascist coalition. We were already familiar with their "foreign nationalism," to use Léon Blum's expression; Alain's disciples were not alone in suspecting the intentions of their allies: was it a question of preventing war or of turning it toward the West? The Soviet Union had no border with Germany. Poland and Rumania were no less fearful of their pseudo-protector in the east than of their potential aggressor in the west.

I was in agreement with none of the parties, none of the motions. Each event—the restoration of military service in Germany, the war in Abyssinia, the entry of the German army into the Rhineland, then into Vienna in 1938, the Munich agreement—provoked one of those great debates that French intellectuals still relish and which confuse considerations of national interest with ideological passions.

Mussolini's expedition to Ethiopia in late 1935 imposed on French diplomacy one of those agonizing choices that symbolize the grandeur and the servitude of politics. To approve or excuse Italian aggression would have been to undermine the moral principles to which French foreign policy lay claim, to deny the speeches and the professions of faith of the statesmen who had argued in Geneva for the cause of our country and of peace. To apply effective sanctions against an Italy guilty of aggression would have been to break the front that had been established in 1934, on the occasion of the attempted assassination of Chancellor Dollfuss in Vienna, to push Italian fascism toward German National Socialism, to move away from the British government which, suddenly converted to the doctrine of collective security, wanted to mobilize the League of Nations against Italy and for international law.

In no way did the crisis create a serious risk of war. Fascist Italy—as the war later demonstrated—did not have the means to respond to an oil embargo or to the intervention of the Royal Navy. Would fascism have survived a victory of the League of Nations organized by Great Britain and France? The point was raised a half century ago, and the same response remains probable, though not demonstrated: fascism would not have resisted humiliation.

Thus the debate among intellectuals began even before that among diplomats. Shortly after the entry of Italian troops into Ethiopia, *Le Temps*, on 4 October 1935, published the manifesto of French intellectuals for *The Defense of the West and Peace in Europe*, from which I quote the following lines: "At a moment when Italy is threatened with sanctions that risk unleashing an unprecedented war, we, French intellectuals, declare to the whole world that we want neither those sanctions nor that war." In other words, the signatories of that appeal, with Henri Massis in the lead, assimilated sanctions to war—which was at the least improbable.

> When the acts of men who hold the fate of nations in their hands risk putting the future of civilization in danger, those whose work is devoted to the realm of intelligence owe it to themselves to make the demands of the spirit clearly and vigorously heard. Some want to launch the people of Europe against Rome There is no hesitation in treating Italy as guilty, on the pretext of protecting the dependence of a collection of uncivilized tribes in Africa, who are thereby encouraged to call on the great powers to enter a closed field. Through the offensive of a monstrous coalition, the just interests of the Western community would be injured, and the entire civilization would be placed in the position of a conquered force. To contemplate it is already the signal of a mental affliction which expresses a veritable surrender by the civilizing spirit.

A little further on, they evoked "the civilizing conquest," the coalition of "all anarchies and disorders against a nation in which, in the last fifteen years, some of the essential virtues of the highest level of humanity have been affirmed, heightened, organized, and strengthened." A eulogy of fascist virtues, of the civilizing mission of the West, this kind of writing has taken refuge, assuming that it still survives, in obscure corners of our country; at the time, it expressed the sensibility or the thought of a right-wing current that had been joined by Gabriel Marcel and Jean de Fabrèque.

The Catholics of the left or the Christian Democrats replied to this text with another appeal, which, with different arguments, led to the same conclusion: the rejection of measures that risked unleashing the war: "[W]e have to note as a fact that the world is powerless to intervene by force of arms in the Ethiopian conflict without risking even greater evils." It was tacitly admitted that Italy could only be stopped by force and the use of force against Italy would cause a conflagration in Europe. In addition, the Christian left recalled that the work of colonization was not "carried out without serious errors: . . . one must consider it a moral disaster that the benefits of Western colonization have been shown to those peoples with a brilliance unequaled by the superiority of its means of destruction placed in the service of violence, and that it is claimed at the same time that the violation of rights revealed by such a war becomes venial on the pretext that it's a matter of a colonial enterprise . . . . It is also important to denounce the sophism of the inequality among races. If one wishes to say that certain nations have a culture less advanced than that of others, one is simply observing an obvious fact.[1] But some move from that to the implicit affirmation of an *essential* inequality that would designate certain races or nations for the service of others and would change for them the laws of the just and the unjust." The moral condemnation of Massis's text left no room for doubt or ambiguity, but it did not suggest a political action clearly distinct from that advocated by the right. It discarded force and did not even mention the sanctions that would have been effective without recourse to the fleet or the army. The rejection of recourse to force, of war or even the risk of war, united all Christian intellectuals in the rhetoric of unreality.

As for the left, it responded with a manifesto calling for *Respect for International Law:* "The undersigned . . . are also astonished to find French writers asserting legal inequality among human races, an idea so contrary to our tradition and so ignominious in itself for such a large number of the members of our community. . . . They consider it a duty of the French government to join the efforts of all the governments struggling for peace and for the respect of international law . . ."

The members of the *Antifascist Committee of Vigilance* joined in this motion. It promised peace through respect for international law and refrained from responding to the argument of the other camp: should we impose respect for international law through the threat or the use of force? In a discussion, at the *Union pour la Vérité* I believe, when I analyzed the requirements of colective security, Jean Wahl was quick to distance himself: he refused force in every circumstance. On this point, all the intellectuals came together, incapable of following the logic of their respective positions, incapable of recognizing that the acceptance of an immediate risk might prevent a more serious risk a few months or years later.

The entry of German troops into the Rhineland took place while the Ethiopian crisis was still unresolved. Against his advisers' counsel, Hitler sent a few detachments of the *Wehrmacht* into the demilitarized zone, assuring the military leaders that the troops would withdraw if the French army responded to this violation of the Locarno treaty. The Sarraut government was a few weeks away from a general election; the Minister of the Army, General Maurin, asserted that mobilization would be necessary before the intervention of the French army in the Rhineland. Rarely have the leaders of a power that sill considered itself great had a comparable opportunity to influence the fate of their country and the world. The draft had been reestablished by Hitler in 1935; scarcely a year later, the transformation of a small elite army into a national army could not have progressed so far that the high command would accept a test of strength. To be sure, the Rhineland was German, and Hitler once again evoked the principle of nondiscrimination, which the ex-victors of the war no longer dared reject; but the occupation of the Rhineland constituted a violation of a treaty freely signed by Germany. The demilitarization of the Rhineland did not remove a province from the Reich, nor did it deprive its inhabitants of freedom; it provided the only precaution possible against the plans that the German chancellor had proclaimed in advance, when he was not yet exercising power.

What was the reaction of the intellectuals? One or two days after the movement of German troops, I met Léon Brunschvicg on the boulevard Saint-Michel. The conversation turned to the events. "This time, fortunately," he said, "the British are attempting to calm us." (The Minister of Foreign Affairs, Pierre Etienne Flandin, was then in London.) I tried my best to explain to him the implications of the remilitarization of the Rhineland, the collapse of our system of alliances, our incapacity thereafter to come to the aid of Czechoslovakia and Poland, the contradiction between our military apparatus, designed for defense, and our alliance obligations—a contradiction which, in our group, we frequently discussed. Léon Brunschvicg listened to me, half convinced, and concluded, with some self-irony and disillusionment: "Fortunately my political opinions have no consequences." Some thirty years later, at the defense of Julien Freund's thesis, Jean Hyppolite made the same comment about himself. It is easy to think about politics, but on one condition: recognition of and submission to its rules. I agree that thinkers should leave to others the thankless task of thinking about this activity, but they rarely resign themselves to that kind of abstention.

Were the reactions of the certified spokesmen of the intelligentsia of a better intellectual quality? The article by Emmanuel Berl in *Marianne* on 11 March was not lacking in good sense. Entitled "Dictators and Proceduralists," the article contrasted Hitler advancing his pawns with France, which was concerned only with procedure. "Hitler advances his troops toward our borders and he offers us peace. We should similarly offer peace, multiply troops, and demand assistance from the nations that have promised it. The worst thing would be to stimulate German bellicosity more and more, and to oppose to it ever more shallow trenches."

The most developed, representative, and dismaying text came from the Committee of Vigilance of Antifascist Intellectuals, directed by Rivet, Langevin, and Alain. I will not bore the reader with a reproduction of the complete text. It began with the following assertion: "Unilateral abrogation of the Locarno pact, whatever the arguments invoked to justify it, is politically, juridically, morally indefensible." A little further on one could read: "The present conflict is not between Germany and France, but between Germany on the one hand, and all the signatories of the Locarno treaty and the League of Nations on the other." Between point 1 and point 7, the declaration recalled the "particularly weighty responsibilities incurred by several of our governments in the sequence of events that have led up to the present situation"; it called on France to "break, in the most categorical fashion, with a long tradition of routine and mistakes, the most nefarious of which had been the occupation of the Ruhr basin." What was the conclusion? "The only solution that would be honorable for all and effective for peace would be for Germany to rejoin the League of Nations on the basis of absolute equality of rights and duties . . . ." Then, in point 9, to accommodate the demands of the Communist Party, there was the following explanation: ". . . if democratic France, overcoming its profound aversion to Hitler's regime, agrees, in the greater interests of peace, to negotiate and deal with the Third Reich within the framework of the League of Nations, it cannot grant to the Reich the right to present itself as a champion of Western civilization and reject all contact with the USSR, member of the League."

Well drafted and well argued, this manifesto, which Jean Guéhenno called "admirable," tragically illustrates the naïveté of antifascist intellectuals in the face of events. On 7 March 1936, the French government had to say yes or no, to act or to accept: all the rest was only words, words, words. The "return of the Third Reich to the League of Nations," all that verbiage, did not make any sense. Minds were operating in the void, with the sole purpose, unconsciously, of concealing renunciation. Most foreign ministries, outside France, understood the implications of the event. The Polish government let it be known, I believe, that it was ready to send its troops into Germany if ours entered the Rhineland. The intellectuals of the left did not or did not wish to understand this. Consider the article by Jean Guéhenno in *Marianne* on 13 March: "Once the first alarm had passed, the country immediately recovered its wisdom. . . . Such a declaration [that of the Committee of Vigilance] means that, from that very alarm, from those follies [those of Hitler], from that violence, peace can finally be born, real peace, 'Europe,' if France finally finds men capable of truly speaking for her, if France wishes it." France had lost without defending it the only guarantee of peace which it owed to the death of 1,300,000 of its children; the intellectuals praised a people that, a week after the "alarm," had recovered its "wisdom."

Perhaps we should quote Léon Blum, whose courage and moral rigor I certainly recognize, but whose blindness has been concealed by his biographers-hagiographers. He wrote this in *Le Populaire* on 7 April: "The literal texts of the Locarno pact can permit no doubt of any kind. Military occupation of the Rhineland is there identified in formal terms with unprovoked aggression and an invasion of national territory. The French government would thus have the strict right to consider the crossing of the Rhine by the *Reichswehr* as a flagrant violation, as an act of war, and even, I repeat, as an invasion. It has not done so. I do not think it thought for a moment of doing so;[2] I am not aware that a single political party, a single responsible organ of opinion, criticized it for not having done so. Instead of returning his passports to the German ambassador, mobilizing, calling on the guaranteeing powers immediately to fulfill their unquestionable military obligations, it has turned to the League of Nations. Between direct settlement by arms and the procedure of peaceful settlement through the intermediary of international action, neither the French government nor French public opinion hesitated. Make no mistake about it, this is a sign of the times. This is the proof of the immense change in which socialism can proudly claim its part." Did Léon Blum ever become aware of his aberrations, of the error committed by a statesman who sacrifices the interests and even the security of his country to his illusions, who confuses an abdication with a sign of a new world? In prison in 1941, after the defeat, he made a half-confession: "Because it was peaceful in essence, France wanted to believe in the possibility of 'peaceful coexistence' between the established democracies of Europe and the warlike autocracy that was taking root there. It made more and more costly sacrifices to that possibility, and they had no results but to weaken its prestige abroad and to compromise its internal cohesion, and hence to aggravate the danger."

A few months after the entry of the Reichswehr into the Rhineland, the Popular Front government came to power, and soon thereafter the Spanish Civil War broke out. Once again, diplomatic positions were determined by ideological preferences; the notion of the national interest was lost in the tumult of passions.

My sympathies were for the Spanish Republicans; among my acquaintances, the choice went without saying. André Malraux and Edouard Corniglion-Molinier had immediately left for Madrid, which remained the capital of Republican Spain. Among my friends in the university—Robert Marjolin, Eric Weil, Alexandre Koyré, Alexandre Kojève—there was no hesitation either. The generals were conducting a civil war after having undertaken a coup d'état that was half aborted. They were receiving aid and comfort from fascist Italy and Hitlerite Germany. Georges Bernanos, a disciple of Edouard Drumont, who had written a passionately anti-Semitic book, *La Grande Peur des bien-pensants,* wrote an indictment of the Spanish nationalists: *Les Grands Cimetières sous la lune.* Bernanos and Malraux compared their experiences of the crimes committed on each side. Salvador de Madariaga, whom I later knew well, held himself above the struggle, convinced—correctly—that he could not live in Spain regardless of which camp was victorious, neither in the Spain of Franco, nor in the Spain of the Republicans infected by the communists. Behind Franco could be seen Hitler and Mussolini; behind the Republicans, Stalin and his GPU, active behind the lines and already engaged in the task of the purge.

The diplomacy of nonintervention divided the two factions of the Popular Front, Socialists and Radicals on one side, Communists on the other. Even though, in André Malraux's circle, Léon Blum's policy was more frequently criticized than excused, I put myself in the prime minister's place, following the lesson given to me by Joseph Paganon, and I came to the same conclusion as he did. Can the leader of a democratic government commit his country to an action that involves a risk of war and that half the country does not consider to be in the national interest? Alexandre Kojève, in a conversation at one of Léon Brunschvicg's regular Sunday morning gatherings, explained that the Soviets were afraid that too visible a presence in the Mediterranean would trouble the British government and push it toward a rapprochement with Berlin. The dialectician met skepticism from the mandarin as well as from the young philosophers present. He was right on an essential point: the Chamberlain government hardly favored the victory of the Republicans, mortgaged by the control of the communists and thereby of the Soviets.

The victory of the Popular Front in 1936, a few months after the remilitarization of the Rhineland, resulted logically from the deflationary policy carried out to the bitter end by Pierre Laval, with as much courage as blindness, and with the support of the Chamber elected in 1932. Edouard Daladier, removed from power by the riots of 6 February, joined an alliance with the Communists of Maurice Thorez and thus contributed to the victory of the Popular Front. Our feelings, mine and those of my friends, like Robert Marjolin, did not fit with the programs of either of the two camps.

We knew, Marjolin and I, and a few others in small groups like "X crisis,"[3] that the immediate sudden application of the Popular Front program would doom the experiment from the outset. The increase in hourly wages, the limitation of the work week to forty hours, and the rejection of devaluation made up a cocktail that the economy could not absorb. Léon Blum believed that the forty-hour law would create jobs for hundreds of thousands of the unemployed. Even as it was launching an expansionist policy, the government reduced the physical productive capacity of an apparatus that had aged during the years of deflation and because of inadequate investment. Laval's policies had provoked a lowering of prices; a limited devaluation of the franc had been enough to restore them to international levels and to accelerate the recovery, begun before the Popular Front victory. Léon Blum was completely ignorant of world prices, of the relationship between world and domestic prices; he did not know—and perhaps his advisers did not know either—how many of the unemployed that had been identified (between 400,000 and 500,000) were in a position to resume work. Marjolin sent notes to Léon Blum's cabinet. He also wrote articles in *L'Europe nouvelle* in favor of Paul Reynaud, greatly scandalizing Célestin Bouglé, who saw it as the betrayal of a young man whom they considered as one of their hopes. Bouglé, whose absolute good faith was protected by his ignorance of economics, judged opinions on the subject not in relation to reality but in relation to political parties. When I irritated him too much—Mme Porée[4] told me—he predicted that I would end up as an economic columnist for the *Journal des débats*. Perhaps the death of that paper spared me the misfortune.

A few months ago, François Goguel reminded me of the article entitled "Reflections on French Economic Problems" that I had published in the *Revue de métaphysique et de morale* in 1937. He told me that at the time the article had made an impression because of the vigor and pertinence of its analysis. I reread it and was rather disappointed by this first exercise of a commentator on current events (although it is better than my "Letters" published in *Libres Propos*).

I still find the opening remarks on intellectuals pleasing:

> Intellectuals thus intervene, as they should, in political struggles, but one can discern two forms of this intervention: some act (or claim to act) as intellectuals with the sole purpose of defending sacred values; others join a party and accept the servitudes that that brings about. Each of these attitudes seems legitimate to me, provided it is consciously adopted. But practically, those who present themselves as antifascist intellectuals or interpreters of human rights behave as partisans. It is an inevitable shift: it is not every day that a Dreyfus Affair comes along justifying the invocation of truth against error. In order for them to be able to express their opinion daily as intellectuals, they should have some competence in economics, diplomacy, politics, and so on. If it is a question of inflation or deflation, of the Russian alliance or the entente cordiale, of collective bargaining or the level of wages, it is less a matter of justice than of effectiveness. On the other hand, in every party, writers and professors now appear as propagandists. They are asked less to enlighten minds than to influence hearts. They justify and fan passions, rarely purifying them. They are the heralds of a collective will. The masses, who have confidence in them, are unaware that an illustrious physicist, a celebrated writer, or a respected ethnographer[6] knows no more than the man in the street

about the conditions for economic recovery. Practicing a scientific discipline and calling oneself a positivist is not enough to escape from myths.

The rest of the discussion, marked by contemporary debates, preserves only historical interest: Alfred Sauvy's book, *Histoire économique de la France entre les deux guerres*, will teach the reader much more than my 1937 article. It nevertheless had one virtue; it pointed out the two essential causes for the failure of Léon Blum's experiment: the rejection of devaluation and the rigid application of the 40-hour law. "If, after the improvement of 1933, the economic situation of France deteriorated in 1934 and 1935, the essential cause, according to all serious studies, was the disparity between French prices and world prices. This disparity not only affected exports, but it exercised deflationary pressure on the entire economy. One fact is now indisputable: in every country on the gold standard, devaluation rapidly and deeply improved the situation; by setting loose a sharper and stronger increase in wholesale than in retail prices, it helped to suppress both the uncertainty of domestic prices and the disparity between them and world prices." The rejection of devaluation can be explained, at least in part, by the opposition of the Communist Party. As for the 40-hour law, I wrongly attributed it to the Popular Front program; it was not there at the outset, but it was in the Communist Party program. Most historians today would concur with the judgment I made at the time on this measure. "None of the necessary studies had been conducted at the time that the new principle [40 hours] was included in the Popular Front program, none of the necessary precautions was taken when the law was brutally applied to all branches of the economy. The strength of French industry had been overestimated, considered, without proof, capable of producing as much in forty hours as it had been in forty-eight. In fact, the scope of the recovery was reduced." The average work week in the industries surveyed was approximately forty-five hours. Léon Blum learned these figures at the Riom trial; simple citizens like me were capable of determining the length of the average work week.

Of course, this article, read today, calls for correction. I underestimated the immediate consequences of devaluation, the extent of the recovery it would have brought about if the 40-hour law had not reduced the productive capacity of the economy while simultaneously accelerating the rate of wage increases. Moreover, although the article was confined to the economic aspects of the Blum experiment, I should have emphasized the ethical, even more than the social, scope of the reforms: a half-century later, the left, loyal to itself, celebrates the Blum experiment, paid holidays, and its defeat.

Of course, I did not succeed in convincing the academics, who nevertheless ought to have understood. Maurice Halbwachs spoke amiably with me, but although he was one of the economic specialists of the Durkheimian group, he was not moved by our arguments. Only Léon Brunschvicg, whose wife was in the government, told me: "No intelligent person had believed in success."

Since then, the personality of Léon Blum has been transfigured, as that of Jean Jaurès had been between the two wars. His courage before his judges in Riom, the abjection of those who conducted his trial, the almost unanimous admiration that greeted him on his return from Germany, make it almost impossible for those who did not live through the 1930s to judge dispassionately the actions of the prime minister of the first Popular Front government. And at the time, the hatred provoked on the right by the grand bourgeois, the socialist, and the Jew—a hatred barely comprehensible to postwar generations—prevented us, so to speak, from providing with our critiques arguments for men or parties with which we had nothing in common. This is why I sent my analysis of the economic policy of the Popular Front to a journal with restricted circulation, the *Revue de métaphysique et de morale*.

Those on the left remember, wish to remember, only the reforms that were landmarks and survived: paid holidays, collective bargaining, now common negotiations between unions and management. In fact, legislation and social practice in France were behind those of the other democratic countries of Europe. The industrialists, the upper bourgeoisie, terrified by the factory occupations, detested the man who, while saving them from a revolution, had shattered the regal power of business leaders. Léon Blum's mistakes do not erase his virtues, each as unquestionable as the nobility of the man.

Moreover, he did not lack extenuating circumstances. France had no institute for the analysis of the economy. The statistics on unemployment were ambiguous. The Popular Front program had been composed by a commission in which the Committee of Vigilance probably played as important a role as the delegates of parties. Ignorance of the situation was not confined to politicians; the leaders of the economy demonstrated no greater lucidity. Despite all this, Paul Reynaud, advised by a French banker in the United States, André Istel, denounced the government's aberrations and, alone, spoke the simple truth. Léon Blum was not superior to the rest of the governing class in knowledge or judgment. After one year, the Senate put an end to the experiment, and the Socialist Party finally agreed to participate in a government that it no longer led.

After the failure of the first Popular Front government, events followed their course without surprising us. Radical leadership, with Camille Chautemps, replaced Socialist leadership. Inflation continued; the first devaluation, too long delayed, was followed by another. As a result of the fusion of the two union confederations, the Communists had assumed key positions in the CGT. Externally, Mussolini's Italy had tied its fate to that of the Third Reich. In the spring of 1938, when Hitler decided to annex Austria and to eliminate Chancellor Schuschnigg, the successor of Dollfuss who had been assassinated in 1934, France had no government and Mussolini resigned himself to the event that he had helped to forestall a few years earlier. From the day the *Wehrmacht* entered Vienna, the question of Czechoslovakia was on the table. Munich followed a few months later.

The name of the capital of Bavaria has survived in the political vocabulary of the entire world as a common rather than a proper noun: a symbol. Munich means to sacrifice an ally in the hope of sparing oneself a test of strength; it is the illusion that the aggressor will be satisfied with the victories won without a fight; it is appeasement as opposed to resistance. The so-called Munich policy thus means today both moral fault and intellectual error, cowardice, war delayed but thereby made all the more costly and inevitable. I make no claim to correct this interpretation; after all, despite the most carefully established facts, historians have not succeeded in overcoming the legend of the division of the world at Yalta.

Between 1936 and 1939, most of the French—or rather most politicians and intellectuals—had joined one camp or the other: for or against Italian fascism and the conquest of Abyssinia, for the insurrection of the Spanish generals, or for the defense of the Republic. The left as a whole did not understand that the reoccupationn of the Rhineland had radically changed the balance of forces in Europe: our army, in a defensive position behind the Maginot Line, lost the means to provide help to our allies east of the Reich. From 1933 to 1936, the left did not promote rearmament; in fact it declared the arms race lost in advance. It was converted to resistance, even military resistance, against Hitler by the war in Spain. Resistance to Hitler, in March 1936, contained a minimum of risks: we know today that there were none, and we should have known at the time that the danger was remote. Intervention in Spain was not without danger, at least for national unity. In September 1938, an alliance obliged us to declare war on Germany if it launched an armed assault against Bohemia. On this occasion, resistance involved the probability of war, but the alternative meant imposing capitulation on Prague, that is, detachment of the Sudetenland, and hence, the abandonment of its fortifications and supplies. After his peaceful triumph, Hitler informed the world of the magnitude of the booty.

Statesmen and simple citizens wondered whether Hitler was bluffing or whether he was determined to attack Czechoslovakia if it did not give in. If Hitler was bluffing, then resistance also meant peace. If he was not bluffing, resistance would provoke a war, at least local and probably general. Those who thought it was a bluff thereby gave themselves a good conscience: peace through courage and without war, who would not choose that with enthusiasm? But this language, which was certainly clever, seemed to me to be dishonest. The day after Munich, when I began my classes at Saint-Cloud, I devoted a half hour to reflections on the crisis. I commented on the "cowardly relief" of Léon Blum, and above all I denounced the "sleep merchants," following Alain's expression, those who pushed the French toward firmness while simultaneously reassuring them about the cost of their valor.

At the time I was acquainted with Hermann Rauschning, who had maintained connections with German military and conservative circles that were hostile to the Führer's adventure. He spoke to me several times about the generals' conspiracy; he assured me that the military leaders would have revolted if Hitler had ordered an attack on "Czechia," as the Führer called it.[6] I brought Rauschning to meet Gaston Palewski, Paul Reynaud's chief assistant, after the signing of the Munich agreements; Palewski listened to the former mayor of Danzig with visible skepticism. The plot existed, and Halder later spoke about it. But historians are still discussing it. Would the military leaders at the last moment have refused to obey the man to whom they had pledged their oath? Would they have deposed Hitler?

In any event, no one had the right to assert categorically that Hitler was bluffing, and we know today that he was not bluffing. He sometimes even regretted that Mussolini's intervention had prevented him from militarily destroying Czechoslovakia. Once the risk of war and the obligations of alliance were accepted, statesmen and citizens should have weighed the costs and benefits of the reprieve. Assuming that war was inevitable, that Hitler, despite his solemn declarations ("the last demand"), would in any event have pursued the application of the plans of *Mein Kampf* and of his speeches to the leaders of the armed forces in 1937, which date was preferable, 1938 or 1939? The passions that had been unleashed foreclosed this reasonable deliberation.

I do not except myself from the intellectuals to whom this critique is addressed. At the time, I did not think that Hitler was bluffing; I was anti-Munich, as they said, but out of feeling, without enough knowledge of the balance of forces, without reflecting on the serious, perhaps valid, argument in favor of the "reprieve." Those opposed to Munich applauded the conversion of English diplomacy after the entry of German troops into Prague more out of feeling than reason. I understood only later what any diplomat should have understood immediately: by signing a mutual assistance treaty with Poland, the United Kingdom automatically gave a guarantee to the Soviet Union without the slightest compensation in return.

It is an irony of history and a reflection of the folly of passion that the *Munichois* remain criminals, while those who applauded the "wisdom" of the French in March 1936 are never even accused. Conformism goes so far that Sartre, in *Le Sursis*, presents all the *Munichois* as "bastards," while he himself, because of his pacifism, approved the four-power agreement. The conversion of English policy in March 1939 is almost never a subject of debate, as though it did not belong to the sequence of acts and events that determined fate.

Everyone can construct in his own way the history that did take place and conclude that it would have been preferable to start the war in 1938, or reach the opposite conclusion. The Czech army was better than the Polish army, but Hitler was pleading the cause of the Sudeten Germans, who had a right to self-determination by virtue of the principles that the French invoked. Imperialist designs, beyond bringing together German population groups, were still a matter of doubt, and the Spitfires would not have been operational in a Battle of Britain undertaken a year early. There were, of course, among the *Munichois,* a number of those who later approved the armistice and supported the Marshal. But among them were also men who considered that resistance to Hitler in 1938 was showing itself too late (the Rhineland was occupied) or too soon: without a border on the Third Reich, the Soviet Union, armed and ready, would witness the battle of the West, preserving its ability to intervene later, to deliver the coup de grace, and to enlarge its domain of sovereignty or influence.

While I was composing this chapter, I read *Un Voyageur dans le siècle.* Before 1939, I hardly knew Bertrand de Jouvenel. He began his career as a journalist and writer much earlier than I did. While I was painfully freeing myself from the lessons of Alain, he was wandering through Europe and the world and encountering all the political figures of France and England. Through his father and his uncle Robert, he belonged from birth to the political class of the Third Republic; in his mother's salons, he met the founders of the "Europe of Versailles." In 1919, when the treaty was signed, I was living in Versailles and, lost in the crowd, I watched as the men who constructed the postwar world went by. He was probably in the Galerie des Glaces.

Two years difference in age—fourteen and sixteen—still meant a great deal when we both attended the lycée Hoche; they no longer meant anything five years later. We belong to the same generation, but he was already living the life of a journalist closely involved with the politics that was making history, while I was continuing conventional studies in the university or in Germany. I barely knew the friends of his generation whom he mentions with loyalty, indeed with admiration, in his Memoirs. I met only once Jean Luchaire, author of *Une Génération réaliste.* I have a vague memory of the conversation. I told him of some of my philosophical preoccupations; he answered that he had never heard a man of my age express such concerns. I was not dazzled by the talent that Bertrand attributes to him, perhaps out of generosity. I met Alfred Fabre-Luce several times in the 1930s. I regularly read the journal *Pamphlet* that he published for a year with Jean Prévost and Pierre Dominique, and then the *Europe nouvelle* of Louise Weiss, of which he became editor in chief. He asked me to contribute to the journal. Through him I once met Drieu La Rochelle, whose talent I admired. André Malraux had told me: "Of all of us, he is the one endowed with the most authentic and the most spontaneous talent as a writer." Drieu and Malraux remained friends despite the divergence of their political paths. Drieu and Jouvenel were friends, but not Jouvenel and Malraux (during the Occupation, they both ended up in the Corrèze with Emmanuel Berl).

I shared with the generation whose shipwreck Jouvenel sadly narrates their rebellion against war and *Poincarisme* and their desire for reconciliation with Weimar Germany. I was not tied, like Bertrand, to Czechoslovakia, the Europe of Versailles, and the League of Nations. Favorable in principle to the League, I had returned from spending a few days in Geneva during a session of the General Assembly with mixed feelings. Germany was not yet there; the United States held aloof. The parliamentary expression of relations among states seemed to me verbal, artificial, theatrical.

Until the spring of 1930, my feelings and opinions did not differ, in any essential respect, from those of Jouvenel's friends; none of us concealed from ourselves the fragility of the order established by the conquerors, immediately divided, and we judged harshly France's diplomacy toward the conquered. In 1930, I had the raw experience of Germany, drastically affected by the economic crisis and the withdrawal of American loans, humiliated, demanding, anti-French. The following year, in 1931, France, spared by the crisis, apparently dominated Europe; it was denounced by everyone—Americans, English, Germans—who attributed to France, immobile on its stock of gold, responsibility for everything. During this same year, National Socialism continued its rise, the bearer of a historic storm whose warning signs were proliferating. In seven years, between 1931 and 1938, the entire edifice collapsed; in October 1938, France was reduced to the dimensions of its population and its industry. Fabre-Luce created a scandal when he pointed out in an article that the population of our country represented only 7 percent of the population of Europe. It no longer had a choice between a war that the French rejected and a submission whose duration no one could predict.

During the years of decadence, we felt France's ills personally. I was inhabited by an obsession: how to serve France. It is in an atmosphere of national decline and partisan conflict that the rallying of Bertrand de Jouvenel and Drieu La Rochelle to the movement of Jacques Doriot becomes intelligible. I never saw or heard the mayor of Saint-Denis, the popular orator expelled by the Communist Party while he supported positions that the Party later adopted. In the Communist Party, to be right at the wrong time is the supreme crime. Supported by his troops, who preferred their chief to the Party, Jacques Doriot created a *Parti populaire français* (PPF) which, alone among the groups, leagues, and little sects of the period, created the impression of being a possible fascist-leaning party. Doriot ended his life in Germany, the victim of an Allied air attack.

The writers of the 1930s, even some who belonged to another generation, and who had earlier had no interest in public affairs, did not escape from the torrent of history. Almost all were ready to adopt as their own the statement attributed, I believe, to Napoleon: Politics is fate. It was no longer a matter of choosing between the two Edouards,[7] or even between Aristide Briand and Raymond Poincaré. From 1933, perhaps even from 1923, the population of France was torn away from its distractions. The wind was blowing from outside, from the East and from the West. Many prominent intellectuals knew little about Lenin, Hitler, the modern economy, American resources. André François-Poncet, along with many others, took Italy for a great power. What struck all of us—appropriately—was the contrast between the paralysis of democratic regimes and the spectacular recovery of Hitler's Germany, as well as the rates of growth published by the Soviet Union. What government could come out of the competition among parties that were lost in parliamentary intrigues and refused to open their eyes? Decline in fertility, decline in production, collapse of the national will: at times I even thought, and perhaps said aloud, that if we need an authoritarian regime to save France, fine, let us accept it, while simultaneously detesting it.

Unlike Drieu La Rochelle and Bertrand de Jouvenel, I did not run the risk of being drawn by despair into absurd commitments. I was protected not so much by my Jewishness as by the men among whom I lived, by my manner of thinking, by my constant rejection of the two one-party states.

Quite obviously, I was not touched by the fascist temptation. I might have been by the other temptation. Alexandre Koyré declared himself to be a "strict Stalinist," André Malraux behaved as a fellow traveler. But the former seemed to me in spite of everything a White Russian, a communist perhaps for world-historical reasons, but very distant from the Party. As for the latter, he in no way attempted to put pressure on me and considered me, I suppose, destined by nature for moderate opinions.

As for me, as soon as I returned from Germany I considered steps toward Franco-German reconciliation to be futile and even nefarious, with Hitler in power, while before January 1933 I had argued for this cause. I observed, without participating in it, the civil cold war unleashed after February 1934. I have already written that I did not believe in the threat of fascism in France, because one looked in vain for a demagogue, disintegrated masses, a conquering passion, in short any of the elements of the fascist crisis. The antifascists were pursuing an elusive enemy, and they did not agree about the essential point, the method to be followed against the real enemy, Hitler.

I retained from my memories of Germany, from the harangues in the *Sportspalast,* the conviction that the Führer of the Third Reich was capable of monstrosities. History proved me right, but I must confess that my judgment was based on a psychological or historical intuition, rather than on evidence. In September 1938, most Germans had rallied to the regime because of the successes it had achieved, that is, the elimination of unemployment, the creation of the Great Reich, the attachment of Austria and the Sudetenland *without war:* the accomplishment apparently went beyond Bismarck's.[8] If he had died suddenly after the Munich agreements, would he not have passed for one of the greatest Germans in history? In appearance, of course, for he would have left behind neither a regime nor a legal state. The Weimar Constitution no longer existed, that of the Third Reich did not yet exist. Moreover, Hitler had already promulgated the Nuremberg laws and raised up his people against a minority that was visible but powerless. It was after Munich that Goebbels organized the national pogrom of the Kristallnacht, as reprisal for the assassination of an official of the German embassy in Paris. Hitler's successor, whoever he might have been, would have overcome the constitutional chaos. The administration remained in place, the traditional leaders of the army still dominated the National Socialist officers. No one knows how the Third Reich would have developed after 1938 without Hitler. All that one can legitimately say is that Germany without Hitler in October 1938 would not necessarily have unleashed the European, and the worldwide, war.

NOTES

1. This factual observation expresses a "progressive" philosophy of history.

2. This was incorrect, the Council of Ministers had considered a military response.

3. An economic study group created by graduates of Polytechnique like Jean Coutrot, Jean Ulmo, and Alfred Sauvy.

4. Mme Porée was the secretary of the director of the school. One of the first typists before 1914, she typed innumerable theses for students. She knew everything about the school and enjoyed a popularity close to fame.

5. Paul Langevin, André Gide, Paul Rivet.

6. But did he use this term before Munich? I am not sure.

7. Edouard Herriot and Edouard Daladier.

8. Sebastien Haffner, in his remarkable book, *Bemerkungen zu Hitler,* develops this argument with talent.

The Temptation of Politics

1939–1955

7

THE WAR

$\mathbf{W}$e received the news of the Hitler-Stalin pact in Val-André, a village in the Côtes-du-Nord where the Bouglé family owned a large house very near the coast. Célestin Bouglé was dying, in unspeakable pain, from rapidly spreading cancer. We had rented a little villa from a fisherman who had retired from the navy. From a distance, we were following the negotiations between the French and English delegations and the Soviet authorities.[1] When a friend, overwhelmed, brought us the news that the German Minister of Foreign Affairs, Joachim von Ribbentrop, was going to Moscow to sign a nonaggression pact (secret agreements had been suspected but not known), my first reaction was a kind of consternation in the face of such cynicism, which, for us, meant war. This rather naïve indignation was followed a few moments later by reflection. The division of Poland between its two powerful neighbors reproduced a historical scenario. At the Société française de philosophie in June 1939, I evoked a possible alliance between the two totalitarian regimes, but I thought it improbable in the immediate future. I was wrong, and I soon understood the logic of the "meeting of the two revolutions."

The Soviet Union had no border with the Third Reich: Rumania and

Poland refused authorization to the Red Army to enter their territory to fight the Wehrmacht; they were no less suspicious of the armies coming from the east to their "aid" than of the invaders from the west. As for Stalin, he was above all afraid of Hitler and the Germans. The alliance between London and Warsaw gave Stalin the guarantee that he would perhaps have purchased at a high price. By committing themselves to fighting for Poland, France and Great Britain implicitly made the same commitment to the Soviet Union. Stalin's calculation, cynically correct if one hypothesized prolonged fighting in the west, was proved wrong by the rapidity of the French defeat.

In August 1939, I hardly speculated about the distant consequences of this diplomatic *coup de théâtre;* like most of the French, I gave in to resentment against Stalin who simultaneously made war inevitable and left all of its burden on the democracies. The argument that dissuaded me from expressing myself freely, without reservation, on the Soviet regime, collapsed of its own weight. At the beginning of September, I went to the mobilization center, in Reims I believe, and I left a few days later for the Belgian border, where the OM1 weather station was to be set up.

In September 1939, the weather station contained about twenty people, a disproportionate number for the missions with which we were charged. The captain who commanded the station, an air force engineer, was sent on a special mission after a few weeks; the lieutenant who succeeded him was also sent on a special mission; I became, as sergeant, the head of the station, although I was not the most expert in following the balloons with the theodolites.

Until 10 May, I had a good deal of leisure time; I worked on my study of Machiavelli and on preparing for publication the *Histoire du socialisme* by Elie Halévy. Near Charleville, where I would go for lunch on Sundays, I saw the *spahis,* on their little horses, leave for the east and return a few days later, apparently exhausted. Displacements began. By 13 or 14 May, the order to retreat arrived, and we were soon swallowed up by the swarm of soldiers from the Corap army. From that day on, the memory of the decade of 1870, as described by Zola, haunted me, and deprived of news, not reading the newspapers regularly, after a week or two I lost all hope. My memory of the facts is not sufficient to allow me to reconstruct the successive stages of our movements from Charleville to Bordeaux. I remember a few days spent in Brie-Comte-Robert, between the evacuation of Dunkerque and the battle of the Somme. It was at the beginning of June that my mother died in Vannes. I called Captain Léglise, who had commanded the OM1 and who was at air force headquarters. He refused me permission to go to Vannes. A few minutes later, he called me back and gave me an order that allowed me to arrive before the death of my mother, who was already in a coma. There I found my wife who, after an interminable journey, had finally managed to get from Toulouse to Vannes. I returned to the OM1, which had been perfectly useless from 12 or 13 May on; we transported our instruments, now without purpose, armed with old rifles, with no opportunity to use them except when German planes flew low.

We crossed the Loire at Gien, and we witnessed the bombers' attack on the bridges. The bridges were untouched, at least that time. I observed how accustomed the men had become to aerial attacks. The same ones who in Charleville, on the first day, had rushed for shelter when the Stukas appeared, remained quietly seated on the banks of the Loire, following almost with curiosity the dispersal of bombs around the target.

Around 20 June, we were close to Bordeaux, south of the city; I went to see Darbon, the dean of the faculty of letters at the University, whom I had met during the months when I had substituted for Professor Max Bonnafous. We were all stupefied by the suddenness of the catastrophe. André Darbon, one of those old-fashioned professors who were the honor and the conscience of the University, was accomplishing his task as usual, while simultaneously participating with all his being in the misfortune of his country.

I heard Marshal Pétain's speech. For a long time, I believed that I had heard: "We must *try* to stop the fighting. . . ." According to historians, the correct text did not contain the word *try*. Around me the speech was greeted with relief, as a decision that resulted naturally from the circumstances. In the chaos in Gien, we had lost a radio officer, wounded by shrapnel. We had crossed France from north to south, afraid of being taken prisoner by the Germans, who were always reported to be a few kilometers from any village where we stopped. I discussed the alternative with my comrades; capitulation of the army and transfer of the French government to North Africa, or else armistice. The second choice corresponded to the feelings of those around me. When I was in Toulouse for one night, I breathed an entirely different atmosphere.

Despite the influx of refugees, Toulouse maintained its customary appearance. I could still see the spectacle of the exodus, thousands and thousands of civilians and soldiers together, the automobiles of the rich, the wagons of the peasants, an entire people on the roads mixed with the soldiers of the routed army, like an endless caterpillar creeping along the roads of France. Decisively, my friends in Toulouse, those who, for one reason or another, were not in uniform, had already taken a position: against the Marshal, for the General, whose appeal they had heard. Some of them, like my friend Georges Canguilhem, were already preparing to modestly play a role—which was to be a glorious one—in the Resistance.

My feelings corresponded with theirs, but my political judgment was not yet fixed. I was not certain that the transfer of the French government to

North Africa and the surrender of the army to put an end to the fighting was the best solution. At the time, two questions obsessed me: with the army's surrender, several million soldiers would become prisoners of war. If the war were to continue for some years, what would become of the nation, deprived of so many of its mature men? The other question had to do with the resources of North Africa: it had no weapons industry. In the absence of Great Britain, could the United States resupply the French armed forces on the other side of the Mediterranean?

I discussed the decision that had to be made with my wife: to remain in France or to leave for England which, we thought, would continue the fight. Our judgment of the armistice, not yet concluded but probable, had little effect on our deliberations. A government that would negotiate with the Third Reich would be situated somewhere between the status of a satellite and that of an independent state. The arrival in power of men and parties who had denounced the "warmongers" left no room for doubt. Neither Marshal Pétain nor Pierre Laval would convert to National Socialism, but conquered France, reconciled with the Third Reich or subjected to it, would have no place for the Jews. We considered the two possible courses of action: either remain with my detachment, at my post, until the demobilization that would probably follow the armistice, then return to Toulouse to await the course of events; or else leave immediately for England and join the troops of General de Gaulle. My wife understood that I preferred to take my part, however small it might be, in the struggle that the United Kingdom would not abandon. Unlike some of those at the top of the military or political hierarchy, I did not think that Churchill would deal with Hitler, or that he would accept defeat even before he had repelled the foreseeable attempt at a landing. The success of the operation, the invasion of the island—inviolate since the eleventh century—demanded another kind of *Blitzkrieg* from that of the breakthrough of armored divisions supported by the Stukas.

I had traveled to Toulouse from south of Bordeaux on the back seat of a motorcycle driven by a soldier from the Nord, a mechanic by profession, with whom I had cordial relations.[2] I returned to my detachment, took leave of my comrades (some of them had put on their new uniforms in preparation for the Germans), and I left for Bayonne and Saint-Jean-de-Luz. I slept in a car attached to the train carrying the stocks of the Bourse. I had taken with me only a knapsack, which contained toilet articles, a razor, soap, a book (I think), and I had a curious sense of lightness. What did I care about things, furniture, even books, all of that was lost in the distance. In the national disaster, only the essential swam to the surface—my wife, my daughter, my friends. Through these attachments, I remained myself. The catastrophe itself revealed the futility of all the rest.

The next day, probably 23 June, I wandered through the port of Saint-

Jean-de-Luz with a few others in search of a ship sailing for England. I learned that a Polish division was going to be transported on a steamer, the *Ettrick*, at anchor a few hundred meters from the port. I took off the blue cape of the air force, put on the yellow cape of the infantry, and finally found myself in a boat taking me to the *Ettrick*. Among the refugees and volunteers was a distant relative of Marshal Foch who, if my memory does not deceive me, expressed some thoughts about the Jews, from which, of course, he excluded me (you ought to have a grudge against them, he said, or something along those lines).

I met René Cassin on the ship; I spoke with some Polish officers, one of whom recommended the condition and state of mind appropriate to the time: no family and joyous acceptance of solitary adventure. The war was going to last, who knew how long. Perhaps we would return to our country one day. In the meantime, let us gather rosebuds.

I have two memories of the crossing that seem worth recalling. I was in the process of clearing a table, cleaning the oil cloth, perhaps washing the dishes; I don't know why, but a middle-aged Englishman started a conversation and asked me what I did in civilian life; when I told him that I would be teaching philosophy in the University of Toulouse if the army had not taken me, he burst out in furious reproaches against the French and English governments, reproaches that he seemed to address to his wife: "I've told you for years that with this political stupidity we were going to lose everything. This is what we come to twenty years after the victory." The university professor transformed into a dishwasher became for him the symbol of society turned upside down, of the misery that the French and the English had called down on themselves.

The organization on the ship left a lasting impression on me. The thousands of soldiers came one after the other to receive their rations. There were no "tickets," no verifications, they had confidence in everyone and took no precautions against cheaters or line-jumpers. On the *Ettrick*, I breathed for the first time a British atmosphere, and I felt immediately at ease, even though I understood nothing of the English of the sailors and soldiers, and hardly more of that of the intellectuals.

What struck all of us coming from a country that had been turned upside down, with millions of refugees on the roads, haunted by images of the debacle and the bombing, was the peace and perfection of the English countryside. At a stroke, the war had disappeared: the lawns fully lived up to their legend. The first conversations with ordinary subjects of the king left us silent and grateful. "We'll get you your country back by Christmas," I was told by a little man living in a charming cottage. No one, at the top, was unaware of the danger; the people, too, expected air attacks and perhaps an attempt at a landing. The factories were running at full blast, and militias were organized to assist the army, whose men had been repatriated but without their heavy weapons. It was a strange impression; the nation was confident and, in places, almost unaware. We had learned of the signing of the armistice while we were on board ship. We discovered an intact country with great power; on it was weighing the threat of death, and the sun—the spring sun of 1940—shone on a countryside where everything was luxury, calm, and sensuality.

I found myself in London, with several thousand other French soldiers, in the Olympia Hall; we had nothing to do but to eat, to clean—in vain—our quarters, and to talk. The French of Olympia Hall belonged to all social categories and all political families. The armistice or the transfer of the government to North Africa? The same conversation took place among the French on both sides of the Channel. Most of the French had already adopted a dogmatic position; either the Marshal and his men were betraying France and her allies, or else the General and his men were separating themselves from the nation. Personally, I tested more than once, on chance acquaintances, an apparently paradoxical opinion: the Marshal's decision is not without advantages, I said, on the condition that England wins the war. A paradox, since the Marshal in Bordeaux was apparently counting on a German victory, while the General in London was counting on an English victory. And, in fact, the English victory led the General to power. But the armistice saved several million Frenchmen from prisoner of war camps; the unoccupied zone improved the condition of half the French; the aim of sparing French blood could legitimately influence the judgment of statesmen. In late June 1980, I met an old gentleman whose name I no longer remember who reminded me of a conversation in Olympia Hall. He told me that he was so struck by what I was saying that he asked me who I was. His surprise disappeared when he learned of my diplomas and my profession.

During my first stay in London, I again met Robert Marjolin, who was part of Jean Monnet's group;[3] he spent two days in the hell of Dunkerque and had accompanied the future "Mister Europe" to Bordeaux. He planned to return to France. Not that he hesitated about which side he was on, but he thought himself obliged in conscience to return to his family, his mother, at such a time.

Through him, I met the liberal economists of the Reform Club, Lionel Robbins (now Lord Robbins), Friedrich von Hayek, and others, with whom I had dinner almost every Thursday during the war. Our first conversation turned to the chances of England. Robbins, more optimistic than I, insisted on the chances of the West, on the condition that the attempted landing was repelled in the coming months. Once this moment of extreme danger had passed, Great Britain, helped by the United States, would again become unbeatable. Other forces would mobilize against the Third Reich. It was an impeccable analysis, which borrowed from the appeals of General de Gaulle, and was confirmed by events: if Great Britain refused Hitler's advances, if Hitler did not offer an acceptable peace to the occupied European countries, the war must spread. At the end of 1940, it was thought that either Hitler would attempt to defeat Great Britain, in reliance on Soviet neutrality, or else he would launch his forces against hated communism, in reliance on the semineutrality of the United States. In either case, the French defeat was reduced to the dimensions of an episode. In a system extended to the dimensions of the planet, France ceased to belong to the exclusive club of the great powers.

I visited an English family that I had met at Varangeville, that of A. P. Herbert, humorist, novelist, dramatist, sailor. I had become particularly well acquainted with his wife during the vacation of 1931. I read *Sein und Zeit* on the cliff; she painted; we struck up a friendship. I saw her again more than once in the course of the following years.

Once I arrived at Aldershot, the military camp, I went before a committee of two or three British officers, who offered everyone the following choice: either return to France and join the Free French forces or else remain in England. The immense majority of soldiers[4] chose to return to France. As for me, I chose the company of assault tanks of the Free French forces. There, I already appeared as a veteran: except for the officers, most of the soldiers were closer to twenty than to thirty.

Instead of getting into a tank, I was charged with administering the company accounts, and I became an expert in calculating pounds, shillings, and pence. From my stay in the camp, one episode remains in my memory. One late Sunday afternoon, a volunteer arrived. There was an empty bed in my room, and he settled in. We chatted in the afternoon and evening. The next morning he asked me the time in a still sleepy voice. "Twenty minutes to seven." I heard his answer: "Already twenty minutes to seven!" I left the room to wash; when I came back he was dead, his revolver at the foot of his bed. He had probably set seven o'clock as his final hour. He had reached England from Morocco to continue the fight. Why did he commit suicide? There was a coroner's inquest at which I testified, along with a medical aide, a medical student named François Jacob. The coroner concluded that it was a suicide, committed by one who had a "disturbed mind."

A few days before our embarkation for the Dakar expedition (the plan was an open secret, and I was not surprised that Vichy, informed, had the time to send some warships to Dakar), I went to London, to Carlton Gardens, the headquarters of the Free French forces, where I had an appointment with André Labarthe. This visit changed the entire course of my existence. For good or ill?

I met Labarthe at Carlton Gardens with his two colleagues, Mme

Lecoutre and Stanislas Szymanczyk (whom we called Staro); she was a Warsaw Jew, he a Pole from the Teschen region (annexed by Poland in 1938, at the time of Munich). André Labarthe presented himself as an instructor of mechanics at the Sorbonne. All three threw themselves on me and displayed all their charm, all their powers of persuasion. Labarthe was directing a still phantom service at headquarters; he had access to the General who, at the beginning, was very warm toward him and asked him to create a monthly journal. He told me that he had read the *Introduction to the Philosophy of History*, and he begged me to give up the tank company and the computation of wages. The reader can imagine his arguments. Many others could replace me as an accountant, but how many, in England at this moment, could compose articles? Cynically, Staro told me: "If you want a hero's death, you have time for that. The war will not soon be over." Labarthe belonged to the Gaullist movement; the military would not refuse his request to transfer Sergeant Raymond Aron to headquarters.

I deliberated for three days. A tempest in a skull, I said to myself sarcastically; I had not left France and my family to seek shelter (in that respect, the United States was safer), but to cooperate with those who were continuing the struggle. The humiliating experience of the French campaign was still present in my mind. I did not know whether I would hold up against the whistling bullets and exploding shells. A child during the First World War, I was still young enough to participate physically in the Second. Why did I finally accept Labarthe's offer? I can only recall the reasons I gave myself. I wanted to serve in a tank: I had been made a paper-pusher. I would accompany the real fighters, but I would not be one of them. Moreover, the choice that Labarthe urged me to make did not have a definitive character. Perhaps the journal would not last long, or else it would no longer need me. If I hesitated, it was because, in spite of everything, I was afraid that the choice was irreversible.

For a Jewish intellectual, being editor of a journal representing France in exile was not dishonorable, nor was it glorious. In 1943 and 1944, comparing myself to the pilots who risked their lives on every mission, like Jules Roy and Romain Gary, I felt myself to be in hiding; the gaze of those who defied death every day weighed on me. In the summer of 1940, and even more in the autumn and during the winter, I had no such pangs of conscience. Perhaps the great battle would take place in Great Britain: London was the target for the German air force.

Neither what is usually called the Blitz—the bombardment of London every night during the winter of 1940–41—nor the V-1 bombs of 1944 resembled, even remotely, the test of battle. I usually slept in my bed during the Blitz, except for one or two nights, "under the protection of the laws of probability," according to Dennis Brogan's expression. At that point, at least in appearance, the volunteers of London were suffering the assault, while the French of Toulouse followed from a distance, as spectators, the vicissitudes of the struggle. With the help of a good conscience, I slept better than usual. One night, to sustain the morale of the population, the English increased antiaircraft fire. The noise of the guns, more deafening than that of the bombs, kept me awake for a few hours, but it did not prevent me from later falling peacefully asleep. I was living at the Institut de France in Queens Gate, headed by M. Cru, famous for books in which he attempted to restore the truth about the First World War, on the battles as the infantrymen had really experienced them, and to dissipate legends (for example, about battles with blanks). He had organized a rotating guard for the inhabitants of the house during the alerts. He was killed and the house destroyed in 1943, during one of the rare serious bombardments conducted by the German air force against London after the beginning of the Russian campaign.

The V-1 attacks in 1944 shattered only fragile nerves. The V-1s acted by the displacement of air. Even in a house blown down by a flying bomb, a table was often enough to protect oneself against falling wood and stone, fragments of glass or steel. The noise of the motor increased more or less quickly. When the noise stopped, you knew approximately how far you were from the explosion. At the worst time, a hundred twenty V-1s fell on London in a single day: coolness, or better, indifference, in the face of this danger cannot serve as a test of physical courage.

In the course of the winter of 1940–41, London appeared to the eyes of the world as the symbol of resistance to Hitler. Justly so, provided the emphasis is on the symbol. The city was never struck physically in the way that German cities were.

La France libre was born and achieved success through the efforts of a staff of four, two of whom were not French. Staro was as indispensable as I, because he thought up or wrote the monthly analyses of the military situation, analyses of strategy which, more than all the other articles, made the reputation of the journal and gave it its intellectual authority. He could not do without me. And neither Staro nor I could do without Marthe, the moving spirit and the director of public relations, or André Labarthe, who was capable of outbursts of generosity and was finally naïve in his ambition. Without him, the journal would not have existed, even though he did not always write the articles he signed. Because of him, it lost direction.

It is difficult to emphasize the virtues of the journal without praising myself, but at a distance of forty years, I have enough detachment to talk about it without feeling a self-satisfaction that would be ridiculous. I will thus risk quoting Alexandre Koyré, who wrote to me toward the end of the war that the French in exile had produced little of value, except for *La France libre*.

Jean-Paul Sartre, to whom I had given a bound volume of half a year of the journal, wrote a laudatory article in *Combat* (we must consider the circumstances, our friendship).

> *La France libre* presents itself in the most thoughtful, calmest, and most balanced way. Written in the heat of the constantly shifting present whose very rhythm was unpredictable, it always seems to enjoy the benefit of historical distance. Banished, insulted in France, separated from their families, how were they able to maintain that objectivity without passion for four years, while they were at bottom assailed by hope and regret? Are there many military chronicles that one can read for years after the event with the same deep interest? The most varied articles on Vichy, the condition of France, Italian public opinion, or the German press, on problems of international law, along with battle stories by officers or soldiers, were grouped around three regular features of admirable intelligence: the chronicle by Raymond Aron (René Avord) which gives us a kind of ghostly analysis of National Socialism, that of the anonymous military analyst who, in order to explain the battles and the strategy of this universal war, was capable of adopting a world perspective and showing in each case how the military and economic struggles were closely connected; finally that of René Vacher (Robert Marjolin), the economist, who examined the problems of wartime and of the postwar world.[5]

Every month I wrote an article on the events and the condition of France, under the title "Chronique de France," and an article on political or ideological analysis; I translated or adapted into French Staro's military article, and I sometimes also wrote the editorial signed by Labarthe. In the literary section, which was often weak, we published work by Jules Roy and Albert Cohen. Sartre, reading one of Cohen's pieces, reacted vigorously; he detested its style and asked me: "Who is this Albert Cohen?" This was an article on the German army paralyzed by the Russian winter. Jules Roy also provided pieces of high quality. In London, I read the manuscript of *Une Education européenne* by Romain Gary, for whom I predicted a great literary career.

Thirty-five years later, Jean-Louis Missika, one of the two young men preparing the television series on me, was surprised by the tone of my "Chroniques de France," by our discretion on the Jewish question. At the time of these conversations, I went through some of these old articles.

For the contemporary historian, these articles are only a kind of testimony or document. I had access to the French press from both zones. One can find some information in a gagged press, but the German archives have revealed much more; the French archives probably contain many facts of which we are ignorant. What troubles me, at this distance, is the implicit criticism of a thirty-year-old Frenchman, of Jewish ancestry, a nonbeliever: Why such coldness? Why were there only three passages a paragraph or two long on the status of the Jews or the *Vel d'hiver* roundup?

I will defend myself on the tone of these chronicles. What made *La France libre* valuable and successful was precisely the fact that the journal was not war literature. The few articles that came close to that were criticized by our best friends. Not long ago, at a lunch in Oxford after I had delivered a lecture, Richard Cobb, the historian of the French Revolution, reminded me that he had already met me twice; he had brought about the first meeting by visiting me at *La France libre*, the only French publication, he said, that he could read at the time, a cultural journal, without propaganda, without excessive polemics, a French journal.

It is true that we avoided the use of adjectives of which today's "philosophers" are inordinately fond. To call anti-Semitism an "abject beast" would have seemed ridiculous to us. Anti-Semitism for us was not a horrible memory or a vague threat, it was reality. Should we have discussed it more, particularly in my "Chroniques de France"? Today, I would certainly answer yes. But between 1940 and 1943, perhaps even up to the Liberation, I was more concerned with the pro- or anti-German feelings of the men of Vichy than with their opinions in domestic politics. There were also anti-Semites among the Gaullists. I will not mention the name of a minister of the Fourth Republic who, in the fall of 1940, said to me: "I would not be hostile to the National Revolution, but not as long as the Germans are occupying the country."

In a French journal that tirelessly defended democracy, I did not need to multiply invectives against the Vichy men to demonstrate that I was not one of them. It is true that at least the first Vichy government generally did not act on German orders, they applied some of their theories; I knew that only defeat had allowed them to come to power, but I also knew that some of their ideas predated the defeat and would survive victory. To reconstruct France, it would be necessary to exclude as few "traitors" as possible. The collaborators were indeed traitors, those who supported the National Revolution were not. Those who today wholly regret that the purge did not affect all supporters of the National Revolution as such, are acting as promoters of civil war. Even in 1941, I did not give in to those low passions.

Let us consider the other criticism: I did not give enough space in my "Chroniques" to the persecution of the Jews. A simple argument led me to a relatively detached position toward the *laws* (but not the *practices*) of Vichy. If the Germans won the war, the Jews would disappear from France and Europe. If they lost it, the status of the Jews would not last; it would vanish with the war. There remains the raid conducted by the French police under the orders of the German occupation authorities. There remains the fate of all the Jews, from Drancy to Auschwitz. We knew that the occupation regime differed profoundly among countries, from west to east. Hitler's racial notions largely determined the patterns of occupation. Schools, lycées, and universities functioned more or less normally in the west in general and in France in particular. In Poland, the occupying forces prohibited higher education, as though the Slavs, an inferior people, ought to abandon their land to the *Herrenvolk* or work there under the orders and for the glory of their masters. We were not unaware of acts of resistance, nor of Gestapo repression, nor of the deportation of Jews. But to what extent did the organizations of Free France in London know that the transfer of Jews to the east had a different meaning from the deportation of resistance fighters captured by the Gestapo? There was a quiet and vague talk in London about the suicides of two leaders of the *Bund*,[6] who had ended their lives to call the world's attention to the genocide that was taking place in Eastern Europe, with no reaction from the two men—aside from the Pope—who could have spoken, Winston Churchill and Franklin D. Roosevelt.

If we had had the necessary information, would we have been able to use it in *La France libre?* We were not subject to censorship, although we practiced a kind of self-censorship. The journal did not indulge in *Greuelpropaganda*, the expression the Germans had created in 1914 to denounce Allied propaganda accusing them of atrocities. We considered the horror of the Hitler regime, of the Gestapo and their actions, to be self-evident. Beyond that, we did not enter into details. In 1944, after the liberation of France, I no longer participated in the production of the journal. About *The Last Secret*,[7] to name a now classic book, I knew or wanted to know nothing. I write "wanted to know nothing" to be scrupulous; I seem to remember references in the press to Soviets who refused to return to their country.

One doubt still haunts me. What did we know of genocide in London?[8] Did the English press refer to it? If so, was it a hypothesis or an affirmation? As far as direct awareness was concerned, my perception was something like this: the concentration camps were cruel, ruled by prisoner-guards chosen from among the common criminals rather than the political prisoners; mortality was high, but the gas chambers, the industrial assassination of human beings—I must confess that I did not imagine it, and because I could not imagine it, I remained unaware of it.

On a television program a few years ago, Jacques Attali accused the prewar generations who, deaf and blind, had foreseen nothing, had attempted nothing to forge their own destiny and escape from that imposed on them by the Nazis. The accusation, directed less against me than against a generation, wounded me. I could not do much for the German Jews because of my lack of personal wealth and connections, but I helped a few; Hannah Arendt did not forget the modest services I was able to give her; my friends and I had understood that after 1933, there was no more room for Jews in Hitler's Germany. Although I was "assimilated," I detested those Jews who saw Jewish refugees as "Boches" and the occasion for (or the cause of) renewed anti-Semitism. I sent a furious letter to one of my friends from the *Französisches Akademiker Haus* when he wrote that a law, affecting the latest immigrants from Poland, who were not yet assimilated, acceptable as such, would have permitted the preservation of the Jewish community that had been established for decades if not centuries. The attempt by French Jews to separate their fate from that of the "Polacks" disgusted me. But I did not attribute even to the Hitlerites the idea of the *Endlösung:* the cold-blooded murder of millions of men, women, and children; who dared to foresee such a monstrous operation carried out by a highly cultivated people? It will be said that the collectivization of agriculture in the Soviet Union caused even more deaths. The mad program of a tyrant who was determined to transform by force the agricultural world of an immense empire, agricultural collectivization, as the program of an ideological party, was not beyond the comprehension of ordinary minds, of Europeans of the 1930s. I cannot criticize myself for not having foreseen the execution of a plan of genocide, and for having written nothing about it in *La France libre.*

La France libre, created in 1940 at the instigation of the General himself, belonged to the movement of the Free French, but it was never a Gaullist journal. The first issue disappointed and may even have slightly irritated the General, since his name appeared only once, in a parenthesis.[9] He smilingly pointed it out to Labarthe. A few months later he sent a letter to the journal in which he praised its patron Paul Reynaud. In early 1941, Labarthe did not dream of breaking with the General: he wanted to be recognized by de Gaulle for the virtues he attributed to himself.

The personality cult of Charles de Gaulle was born at the same time as the movement itself. The armistice became the original sin which, once and for all, discredited the men of Vichy. The Gaullists immediately unleashed propaganda against the "accidental government" that was delivering to the enemy our weapons, our arsenals, our ports, and everything else (as though, had the army surrendered, the Germans would not have taken everything). The General, in one of his first speeches, accused or suspected the Vichy government of wishing to turn the fleet over to the enemy.

I did not have all the information necessary to express a categorical judgment on the armistice, but I inclined to the belief that it was inevitable. In any event, those who had signed or accepted it did not seem to me thereby dishonored. What weapons and ammunition would the French government have found in North Africa? The Marshal and Laval, who had declared that they would not leave France, would probably have formed a government. Which government would the air force and navy have obeyed? How many men in uniform would have been sent to German camps? The transfer of the French government to Algiers should have been decided by the end of May at the latest, and organized during the first weeks of June. Improvised at the last minute, would it have helped or hindered the Allied cause? Of course, those who finally won out in Bordeaux were responding to other concerns than the careful and tragic calculation of the advantages and disadvantages of military surrender and armistice: they despaired of democracy and of France and they longed for a "restoration" of an authoritarian regime. It was a political faction that had imposed the armistice; thereafter, the Gaullists denounced the "fascists" along with the armistice (which was called the "surrender," while the other solution would have involved surrender properly speaking, that is, the surrender of the army, which General Weygand stubbornly rejected).

The debate continues even now. The magistrates who prepared the case against Marshal Pétain did not include the armistice itself among the counts of the indictment. In his *Mémoires,* the General is unforgiving on this decision. Since he claimed legitimacy from 18 June 1940 on, since he carried that legitimacy with him to Colombey-les-deux-Eglises in January 1946, the armistice had to be criminal and the General's appeal the authentic expression of France, still unaware of itself. Events later ratified this juridical legend, but at the end of 1940, France as a whole, established institutions, the army, the fleet, the air force, took their orders from the Marshal. It was necessary not to excommunicate all the followers of Vichy but to return most of them to the cause of France and its allies.

After the elimination of the survivors of the Third Republic, the first Vichy, so to speak, the first group symbolized by Raphael Allibert, explicitly identified itself with counterrevolution, taking its inspiration from the ideas of Maurras. It was a reaction comparable to that of 1871 which brought a royalist majority to the National Assembly. From June 1940 on, the two voices of Vichy and London, leaving out of account the Paris radio directly controlled by the Germans, carried on a dialogue of irreconcilable enemies. The French did not all participate in this duel to the death (many believed in a secret agreement between the Marshal and the General). Until November 1942, France preserved the possibility of avoiding civil war.

In London, we often discussed the fate of North Africa. Most of the people I talked to used the simplistic argument: "The Germans tolerate the preservation of Vichy authority in Africa because it is in their interest." It was an argument based on the omniscience or total wisdom of the Hitlerites. I argued that both camps profited from this neutrality: the Germans economized the occupation troops that would have been necessary to control

North Africa directly; the Allies were awaiting the moment when they would have the means to make a landing. Since then, I have read in Clausewitz about the rational theory of implicit agreement among enemies: the superior party, which should attack, does not have a margin of superiority great enough to compensate for the intrinsic advantage of the defense. To an extent, the case of North Africa illustrates the argument: the stronger party, Germany, had no interest in assuming responsibility for those territories. The outcome of the war was being played out in Russia. Once the armistice with France was signed, the Germans and the Allies accepted the status quo. In the last analysis, this would favor the camp that was able to mobilize French North Africa for its benefit: that turned out to be the Allies. This explains what Churchill said to General Georges in Algiers in November 1942: "In the end, it's better like this; in 1940, we would have been able to do nothing for lack of troops and material." The statement was, of course, denied; I believe that it was made.

In 1941, as in 1942, we wondered what would happen when the Allied troops made their landing. I spoke about it more than once with the Canadian ambassador Pierre Duprey, who went back and forth between Vichy and London, his credentials accepted, *de facto* if not *de jure,* both by the Marshal's government and by the Free French. He analyzed the various Vichy factions and, although he did not predict that Vichy followers would join the Allied cause, he did not think it inconceivable. In November 1942, General Weygand,[10] cabinet ministers, and Jean Borotra urged the Marshal to leave for Algiers. Unsuccessfully, as we know. The Marshal had sworn never to leave his native soil; he thought he was capable, by his presence alone, of protecting the French people from the worst excesses of the occupation. In the absence of the Marshal, the officers and soldiers in North Africa ended up by recognizing the authority of the General. Vichy's anti-English propaganda delayed in particular the rallying of the Navy. Nor did the politics and propaganda of the Gaullist movement between 1940 and 1942 facilitate the coming together of the two factions of overseas France.

Without believing it, I hoped for the unity of the French when the Allied landing in Africa would deprive the Vichy government of its last weapons, the fleet and the Empire, and would strip away its legal facade. In Syria, troops loyal to the Marshal had fought courageously against the Free French and the English. Most soldiers, after the end of hostilities, had preferred repatriation to joining Free France. The Americans and the English did not share the secret of the North Africa operation with General de Gaulle, perhaps because they anticipated stronger resistance against the Free French than against the Allies, perhaps also out of hostility to the General himself. The Americans had bet on General Giraud, mistakenly believing that he was capable of rallying the North African forces to the Allied cause.

"The temporary expedient"—according to Roosevelt—the role of Admiral Darlan, did not scandalize me; it ended fighting among the French and their allies; it created a transition between the Marshal and the General. I detested civil war and did not fully share the passions of either camp.

Whether the armistice was inevitable or not, the clash between Vichy and London certainly was, because men on both sides claimed to embody the legitimate government of France. As René Pleven explained it to me one evening in 1941 at a private dinner, from the very beginning General de Gaulle had a choice between two paths: either he created a volunteer corps, and hence he would represent nothing, since their numbers would appear insignificant in the context of this worldwide war; or he established a political organization that had the vocation of becoming the government of France. He did not hesitate between these two paths, and the agreements reached between General de Gaulle and the British government, at the initiative of Winston Churchill, left no doubt: they granted Free France a unique status as representative of French interests outside France, they made General de Gaulle the leader of the French who were continuing the fight. The General was thus obliged to denounce the "imposture" of the Marshal. This explains the gloom of certain Gaullists in November 1942, when a semirallying by the men of Vichy made them fear the loss of their monopoly of Resistance.

I think that the General could not have chosen another path in July 1940, but he could have conducted the political struggle against Vichy a little less stridently. The war in Syria, which he recommended to the English, was not necessary; events worked for him. Even if the Marshal had gone to Algiers in 1942, General de Gaulle would probably have come to power, as heir of the Marshal. The General wished it to be otherwise, for France and thus for himself.

As early as June 1940, he considered himself the bearer of legitimacy. Hence his mission was transfigured in his own eyes. What he was apparently asking for himself, he was claiming for France. He considered the French who fought in the English forces as deserters because he embodied France, and in his eyes diplomatic battles against the Allies were no less important than the war against the enemy. The recognition that he achieved, "against all odds," was for the benefit of France which, thanks to him and through him, had never left the camp of freedom and victory. It was an epic and mythic vision of history that one might legitimately reject.

Not Gaullist, but close to the movement, *La France libre* developed an anti-Gaullist reputation after the quarrel between Admiral Muselier and General de Gaulle. André Labarthe, who had close ties to the admiral, certainly played an important role in this serious crisis. I am really unable to write anything new about this event, which Admiral Muselier presented in his way, and whose progress can be reconstructed from the General's writings. Labarthe didn't tell me everything that he did, and what he said was not always accurate.

Admiral Muselier, on orders of the General, took possession of the islands of Saint-Pierre and Miquelon in December 1941, or, using a more orthodox expression, raised the tricolor with the cross of Lorraine over these French territories, and expelled the representatives of Vichy. The operation was carried out in secret, without informing the British and the Americans. According to the General, the Americans and the Canadians planned to seize the island radio.

The Americans reacted with extreme ferocity, verbal of course, against the intervention of the Free French in a region covered by an agreement with the Marshal. Under certain circumstances, the authorities established in French possessions of the Western Hemisphere, taking their orders from Vichy, would not be disturbed. The coup of Saint-Pierre et Miquelon apparently violated that agreement. Outraged, the American secretary of state, Cordell Hull, spoke of the "so-called Free French." The statement provoked a storm in the press and in some sectors of Congress. It served the General, because Hull, who had ample grounds for legitimate complaint, had put himself in the wrong and had shocked pro-French opinion in the United States.

As for de Gaulle, as his telegrams of the time and his *Mémoires* demonstrate, he never had a moment's doubt that he had acted properly. In *Lettres, notes et carnets* (July 1941–May 1943), I find the following revealing sentence about his thought: "Although it happens, for opportunistic reasons, that our allies accept French neutrality, in general or locally, we do not accept it. At every opportunity, we do everything to bring this neutrality to an end, through persuasion or force, wherever we have the means to do so." He went on: "Moreover, we think that this is in the general interest." In other words, out of principle, he fought, even with force, against the Vichy authorities.[11]

The fury of the Americans did not trouble the General; he rather relished, as an artist, the spectacle of the storm he had provoked. At bottom, the British were not angered by the fact that the leader of the Free French had stirred up trouble and embarrassed the secretary of state, who was carrying on the policy later christened The Vichy Gamble by an American historian.[12]

The General congratulated the Admiral for the way in which he had carried out his orders and brought about the joining of the islands to Free France. The Admiral himself did not approve of the aggressive approach to the Americans that the General had imposed on him. When he returned to London, leaving Alain Savary in charge of civil administration and Louis de Villefosse in military command, it seems that he tried to change the operations of the National Committee, in order to assure that in the future such serious decisions would not be made by a single individual, without deliberation. (Was the decision about Saint-Pierre and Miquelon made in these conditions?) One can retrace the stages of the crisis through the writings of General de Gaulle. The Admiral resigns from his position as a member of the National Committee, but wishes to maintain command over Free French naval forces. The General relieves him of his command a few days later and replaces him with Rear Admiral Auboyneau. Demonstrations of solidarity with Admiral Muselier disturb the navy, particularly at headquarters. The British government puts pressure on the General, first to stop his dismissal of the Admiral, then, where the General had proven inflexible, to preserve for the Admiral a status worthy of his rank and the services he had rendered. The Admiral, after having been urged to take a rest away from London, did not answer the General's summons and broke with him. He rejected the title and the function of Inspector of Military Forces of Free France.

What was the exact role of André Labarthe in this whole affair, in this "plot," according to the frequently used expression? There is no doubt that he urged the Admiral to stand up to "the solitary exercise of power," but, in my opinion, he never foresaw a "dissidence" or a "secession" on the part of the navy, which was inconceivable despite the personal attachment navy officers felt toward the Admiral. In retrospect, the enterprise of Muselier and Labarthe appears puerile. The Admiral had no support in the National Committee. British support, on which both of them probably counted, was not lacking, but the General contemptuously rejected these interferences in the internal affairs of Free France, that is, of France itself. When calm had returned, the General made a concession to the English government: as I have noted, he offered the Admiral a position that was honorable and powerless; the Admiral chose to withdraw.

Louis de Villefosse nobly and disinterestedly remained loyal to the Admiral; so did the ship's captain Moret (whose real name was Moullec), but he had been closely tied to Labarthe, among those who had woven the web of the plot. As for the Admiral and André Labarthe, who, at bottom, wanted a larger place in the movement, by limiting the omnipotence of the General, they finally found themselves excluded. There were hardly any echoes of this crisis in *La France libre*, which nevertheless appeared anti-Gaullist because of the political activities of its director.

The distance between the Gaullist government and *La France libre* grew again in November 1942, when British and American troops landed in North Africa, and the Vichy authorities, after a token resistance for honor's sake, rallied to the allied cause. An equivocal editorial which suggested the union of all the French was bitterly criticized by the General's men. Jacques

Soustelle sent me a letter that I have not kept; it criticized us for breaking with the inspiration and the principles of France in arms.

This break might not have been definitive if Admiral Muselier and André Labarthe had not gone to North Africa to place themselves in the service of General Giraud. As far as I remember, the journal did not follow the turnings of the battle of the generals, but the director's choice of a position, placed *La France libre*, at least in appearance, on the side of General Giraud and, after he had been eliminated, among the non-Gaullist or anti-Gaullist exiles. In particular, one of my articles, "L'Ombre des Bonaparte" (1943), was considered shocking because it developed a comparison between Bonapartism and Boulangism on one side, and fascism on the other. I enumerated the traits characteristic of a situation governed by plebiscitary Caesarism: popularity of one man, or simply of a name; the bourgeois classes rallying to Caesar; disparagement of Parliament; divisions among the republicans and confusion in the popular masses; opportunities offered by the system of plebiscites. At the origin of the Boulangist adventure, the coming together of the same phenomena: "republic against parliament, and appeal to the people with the consent of the dominant class. General Republican and General Revenge: there crystallized around his name both the transports of a patriotism humiliated by defeat and the hope of democratic romanticism."

I responded to the two objections that had been made to the comparison between the Bonapartism of the nineteenth century and the fascism of the twentieth: the decisive role of the peasantry in the last century, and the economic crisis at the origin of National Socialism. "The role of the peasantry is one of the characteristics of French Bonapartism, but there is in addition a Bonapartism of the cities, that of the petty bourgeois, the artisans, even the workers, radical circles sensitive to a military appeal, nationalistic and rebellious, republicans who are at the same time in favor of strong authority. Moreover, the joining of extremes in the myth of a national hero, the rallying of the party of law and order to the adventurer adored by the mob, the explosion of ardor directed toward the charismatic leader, the mobilization of the drifting masses, all these characteristics common to the development of Bonapartism and of fascism justify the comparison." As for the second objection, the radical difference between the socioeconomic situation of the middle of the last century and that of the middle of this century, I replied with a question: "Why did France experience, before all the other countries of Europe, a particular form of popular Caesarism? The fear of the *partageux* created the same openness to Caesarism among the peasant masses, who had become conservative with their accession to property ownership, as the fear of proletarianization created among the masses of the German petty bourgeoisie after 1930."

The analytic conclusion was summed up in the following lines: "Bonapartism is thus both the *anticipation* and the *French version* of fascism. A French anticipation because political instability, patriotic humiliation, and the concern for the social conquests—blended with a certain indifference to political conquests—of the revolution, created at various times the conditions for a plebiscite in the country, even while capitalism was on the rise. A French version because, in favorable circumstances, there are always millions of Frenchmen willing to compensate for their ordinary hostility to their rulers with the formation of passionate groups crystallizing around a person who is chosen by events. A French version also because an authoritarian regime, in France, inevitably refers back to the great Revolution, pays a verbal tribute to the national will, adopts a left-wing vocabulary, and claims to address the whole people over the heads of the parties."

The article left the reader in no doubt about the meaning of this warning: "However deep and unanimous this aspiration to freedom, the nation will nevertheless, until its institutions have been reorganized, remain exposed to adventure. Surfeited with humiliations, it will be stirred by a combative patriotism." I transformed the analysis into a polemic because I used as an epigraph the words written by Louis Napoleon when he was living in London—in Carlton Gardens: "The nature of democracy is to be personified in one man." Maurice Schumann denounced the article as an "evil action"; Denis Brogan admired it very much. An English historian, a specialist in the Second Empire, confirmed the pertinence of the analysis. I now regret certain insinuations in the article rather than the article itself.

Where was the mistake? The General had obvious siimilarities with Louis Napoleon and all other candidates for supreme power. Alexis de Tocqueville describes Louis Napoleon as "more convinced of his legitimacy than the descendants of the kings of France." The General had attributed to himself an inalienable legitimacy, which he jealously preserved in his exile and his solitude. When he returned to power in 1958, he invoked the act of 18 June, even though the French had not all condemned the armistice or accepted the appeal of 18 June as creating a personal legitimacy that would persist after the restoration of the Republic. Like the Bonapartes, de Gaulle detested political parties and factions; he addressed the entire nation, and he used the plebiscite as Louis Napoleon had. Contrary to what his supporters maintained, he had never limited his mission to military victory; he had conceived the project—and why criticize him for it?—of giving France "good institutions."

But he had limited his power in advance, out of democratic conviction, and perhaps also in order to convince the English and the Americans of his republican orthodoxy. He had rejected the proposal of some resistance figures, like Henri Frenay and Pierre Brossolette, to prevent the reconstruction of the old parties and to bring the resistance movements together in an at least temporarily single party. The General arrived in France with a consultative Assembly and a legal Communist Party, cleared of its errors of 1939 and 1940. He certainly did not want to restore the Third Republic. The Radicals and the Socialists who published the daily *France* correctly sensed that the Gaullist Republic would not resemble the Republic of the deputies. Given the awareness of the flaws of the latter, why should this new perspective be rejected in advance?

"L'Ombre des Bonaparte," reread today, suffers less from what it contains than from what it leaves out. Neither General Monck nor the general of a coup d'état, General de Gaulle wanted to establish a constitution shaped in his image that would also be viable after him. He succeeded in 1958.

In the United States, as in England, the French who were hostile to the Vichy regime did not all rally to Gaullism. In New York, Antoine de Saint-Exupéry provoked the anger of the Gaullists, who called him a traitor, and he in turn was revolted by their sectarianism. After the Anglo-American landing in North Africa, Saint-Exupéry pleaded for reconciliation of all the French who wanted to fight the enemy. Jacques Maritain replied with a harsh letter that wounded its recipient.[13] One was a-Gaullist if not anti-Gaullist, the other Gaullist. The first saw all of the men of Vichy held by the throat by the occupation forces and driven to concessions to save "the children's milk"; the other, a merciless critic of the armistice, could conceive of no reconciliation with those who had played a role in Vichy. One rejected all politics and wanted to resume the fight; the other pointed out that the battle had to be led and the role of leader obviously devolved on the General himself. (On this point, Maritain was right.) This was the conflict between these two superior men, the two consciences of the French in America. Saint-Exupéry, who had gone to Africa, did not join the Gaullist movement, which he considered to be as sectarian in Algiers as it was in New York. With difficulty, he obtained authorization to pilot a Lightning, in violation of all the rules. He lost his life in an observation mission over France.

Another French personality, Saint-John Perse (Alexis Léger), held to the opinion he expressed from the very first day: there could be no government, not even a provisional government, outside the territory of occupied France. He refused the important position that the General offered him, and he continued to live modestly on the grant from his position as literary adviser to the Library of Congress, directed at the time by his friend the poet Archibald MacLeish.

For the most part, the French who refused to join the Gaullist movement had different motives from those of Alexis Léger, for example, the editors of *France*, the daily French paper published in London. They were in complete agreement with the Gaullist version of history. They considered the Marshal and Maurras as traitors. Out of partisan emotion, they sometimes denounced the men of Vichy with such violence that their propaganda took on an anti-French character. I remember a lunch to which one of the editors of the paper had invited the Czechs, Ripka among them. The conversation turned to President Hacha, who had signed the document in which his country asked for the "protection" of the Reich. Our guest answered discreetly, with a vague statement: "He is doing his best." A few moments later, the French journalist was vigorously attacking the Marshal, his ministers, and his supporters, as though none of them was doing his best, as though all of them were serving the occupying forces with docility if not zeal.

The group that edited *France*—Pierre Comert, Charles Gombault, Louis Lévy—came from the political class of the Third Republic; they were always suspicious of General de Gaulle, whose style, apparent affinities with *Action française*, and harsh statements about the regime that had been abolished all made him suspect.

The group that produced the radio program *Les Français parlent aux Français* was divided. Jean Marin had a reputation as an orthodox Gaullist; Pierre Bourdan kept his distance from orthodoxy, Jacques Duchesne, who led the group, nephew of Jacques Copeau, a professional actor who was not at all nostalgic for the Third Republic like the journalists of *France*, did not like the religious atmosphere that surrounded the General. Bourdan, the most gifted of them all, was stupidly drowned in 1947, after he had begun a brilliant political career.

After the Allied landing in North Africa, thanks to the proliferation of flights among occupied France, North Africa, and Great Britain, the French colony of London grew. Resistance fighters, political figures, and higher civil servants enriched Free France; in 1941, General de Gaulle, in my presence, had deplored the absence of men of quality in his ranks.

Robert Marjolin had returned in 1941, after Emanuel Monick, for whom he had been chief administrative assistant in Morocco, had been recalled to France at the demand of the Germans. He had known and admired General Weygand, but he soon learned that these feelings would harm anyone who expressed them. Most diplomats and political figures from Vichy rallied to General de Gaulle, and they were right. There were now two Frances, each one embodied by a group that, in its own eyes, represented *the* France. There was no third term, except for isolated figures. Moreover, the converted soon learned that former supporters of Vichy, once they had received Gaullist christening, were more easily accepted than those who had served the Allied cause outside the ranks of Gaullism.

At the time, the virtue attributed to adhesion to Gaullism shocked me, as I was shocked by the Gaullists' harshness toward the French who had joined the English army or resistance movements in direct contact with British intelligence. Now, a slightly more developed political education helps me to tolerate this logic of civil war (which I had always understood), or, if one prefers, of total nationalism. The French cause was not *separated* from the Allied cause, but it was not *identical* to it. Once the French army had been destroyed and France occupied, France's material contribution to victory could only be secondary. It was thus important to proclaim the importance of this contribution to the greatest possible degree; everything that was given to the allied cause without appearing as a particular contribution of France, that is, of Gaullism, was a failure of national duty.

For me, there was no question of joining the Gaullist movement, which was already victorious. Politics had been displaced from London to Algiers. André Labarthe was in the United States. In the face of the degradation of the Vichy regime, General de Gaulle had become, incontestably, the legitimate leader. Political life had nevertheless not been suspended; on the contrary, it was emerging from the shadows of exile and returning to reality.

During these years I lived in French circles, but I also entered into English society. The Reform Club and the liberal group—Lionel Robbins, Friedrich Hayek—welcomed me with a generosity that I remember with gratitude. Karl Mannheim, who was teaching at the London School of Economics, was my host on several occasions. Morris Ginsberg, the most prominent sociologist of the LSE, asked me toward the end of the war if I would accept a position that would soon become that of a full professor. I did not consider the offer seriously. During those years, although I had usually spoken French with the French, I had made enough progress so that lectures or courses in English no longer terrified me. The decisive reason for my choice almost went without saying: I would never change my country. I would be French or I would have no country.

Of course, I could have lived in another country, in Great Britain or the United States, and behaved as a good citizen. But I would not have found a country to replace my own. Language, symbols, feelings, memories, all the ties that bind an individual to a community are found in the first years of life; once those ties have been severed, we feel as though an essential part of our being has been amputated. Many French Jews have not forgiven France for the status that was imposed on them, more precisely, the status that separated them from *their* France, from their country as they knew it or as they wished it to be. As for me, perhaps to spare myself a painful reexamination, I at first believed that the status had been imposed on Vichy, directly or indirectly, by the Germans, then I asserted that Vichy was a parenthesis in the history of France, a war episode.

I met many of the French in London, particularly the personnel of the

Institut de France; I developed a deep and tender friendship with Louise Verrier. Among the fighters who had served in Africa and returned to London, I met General Edouard Corniglion-Molinier, André Malraux's pilot in the expedition to the capital of the Queen of Sheba. A native of Nice, a man of the *pays d'oc* near the Italian border, he frequently recounted startling anecdotes, but he never boasted. On the contrary, one of the only Frenchmen who had been a fighter pilot in both wars, he never spoke of his exploits, of the enemy planes that he had shot down. Nor did he mention his gifts as a musician, a violinist. Discreet about his qualities, expansive about successes of other kinds, he was for Suzanne and me an incomparable friend, loyal, helpful, disinterested.

By chance, thanks to André Labarthe's connections with some Americans, Suzanne and Dominique arrived in London on 14 July 1943. Our daughter Emmanuelle was born on 18 June 1944, and Edouard was her godfather. We rented two neighboring cottages, one for Corniglion and his current companion, the other for Suzanne and her baby. The Liberation did not separate us. He was several times a minister in the Fourth Republic, and he remained a close companion.

Several young Frenchmen who belonged to the commando units of the Free French Forces that were part of the first wave of the landing, were frequent visitors at the little house in Queensberry Gate where I lived alone when we were obliged to leave the Cromwell Gate apartment and Suzanne moved to the country. Two of them remain in my memory, Guy Hattu and Guy Vourch. The latter is now a well known anesthesiologist. We see each other rarely, but I maintain a faithful memory of those years of comradeship.

Jean Cavaillès spent a few weeks in the little Queensberry Gate house. I had met him at the ENS, where he was "head boss" (the first in rank of the most advanced class). We admired him from a distance; he spent a lot of time with science students since he was preparing a *licence* in mathematics. I have only one clear memory of him from those years: he approached Emile Bréhier to persuade him to withdraw his resignation. Bréhier had been offended by the fact that some students did not regularly attend the seminar he gave for the school's philosophy students (Sartre and Nizan were chiefly "guilty"). I was impressed by the ardor and the tone with which Cavaillès attempted to persuade the professor to go back on his decision. Several years later, when he was an *agrégé* preparing candidates for the exam, he asked me to speak about history in one of his seminars. He wrote me a generous letter about my thesis. On the eve of the war, we inaugurated a series of books at the scientific publishing house Hermann. The series included only one work, the *Théorie des émotions* by Jean-Paul Sartre.

We became friends in London. He talked to me about his family, his sister Gabriel le Ferrières. I admired the philosopher-mathematician without reservation, the strength of his mind and the firmness of his moral sense. We constructed projects for the future. Captured by the Gestapo, he was shot. If he had lived, the philosophical community, the intellectual community of France would have been different. I would have made fewer mistakes.

In London, I also knew that I was a Jew and that others knew that I was a Jew. But despite the rumors that circulated about the anti-Semitism of certain Gaullist circles, I never saw the slightest sign of anti-Semitism coming from above. Personally, I did not want to speak on the radio—except in special circumstances, for example, on the death of Bergson—in order not to provide ammunition for enemy propaganda; I was happy to return to France as anonymous and as poor as I had been when I left. In this I succeeded.

What was my state of mind in the summer of 1944, after the Liberation, on the eve of returning to France? How can I sum things up? I oscillated between feelings of guilt and innocence. Although I had not experienced the dangers of a fighting unit, I had contributed to a necessary task: a French cultural journal, distributed throughout the world, while the voice of France was stifled, or worse, distorted. According to some, it ought to have supported a more orthodox Gaullism; even today, I am not persuaded of that. Neither within nor outside France were the French divided between unconditional supporters of the Marshal or the General. The journal served ecumenical Gaullism better, at least until 1943, than would have a publication composed in the style and the tone adopted by the General's faithful supporters.

At the same time, I questioned myself, particularly about my inclination toward solitude. Would I always find more or less subtle reasons to remain marginal, outside any party, any movement? I remembered the German student in 1933 who criticized me for being incapable of *mitmachen*, of joining up.

Exile accentuates the most disagreeable aspects of politics: there is a proliferation of intrigues, gossip, hidden antagonism, superficial agreements. Controversies have to do with the future, with possibilities. The experience of London should have represented the last stage of my political education. It did in a certain sense, since for the first time I approached the men who make politics. I only gradually absorbed the lesson. My allergy to any mythical vision of history-in-the-making determined the destiny that has been mine for the thirty-seven years since the end of the war. I did not know this as clearly as I do today at the moment when, my heart pounding, I set foot on French soil. I still needed a few years to accept myself or, more precisely, to work out how much emphasis I should place upon analysis and how much upon commitment.

NOTES

1. Just before vacation, I had met Marc Bloch and Marcel Mauss. The former, with impressive rigor, demonstrated that war would break out within a few months. Mauss murmured: "The headquarters staff is waiting for the end of the harvest." We should have noted the many signs of diplomatic change in Moscow: the replacement of Litvinov by Molotov, the casual expressions ("we will not pull chestnuts out of the fire for others").

2. He came to see me once after the war; he was managing a small plumbing business; he showed me the countless kinds of faucets that he made; he had a hard time of it before the standardization of the 1960s and 1970s.

3. All the time, I was barely aware of the proposal of a Franco-English community offered to the French government that had taken refuge in Bordeaux. I thus did not have occasion to think about it then.

4. They had been evacuated from Dunkerque.

5. Sartre had read the volume covering the second half of 1941. Robert Marjolin wrote regularly for the journal during that period. He left, for the best of reasons, after a crisis involving the arrest of Admiral Muselier for leaking secrets about the Dakar expedition (he was on the admiral's headquarters staff).

6. Socialist party organized by Polish Jews.

7. Written by an American diplomat about the delivery to Soviet authorities of all Soviet soldiers and civilians in the West. The Americans and the British had committed themselves to this at Yalta.

8. The habit has arisen of using the word *holocaust*, which has a religious connotation; the word *genocide* seems more precise to me.

9. In the first issue, René Cassin condemned the armistice and called into question the legality and the legitimacy of Marshal Pétain's government.

10. At least at the beginning.

11. There was nothing left of the promise made to the volunteers of 1940 that they would not have to fight the French.

12. Walter Langer.

13. In the introduction that I wrote in 1982 to the *Ecruits de guerre* of Saint-Exupéry, I tried to explain the attitude of the pilot-writer who gave his life for his country.

8

THE NONLYRICAL
ILLUSION

$\mathbf{I}$ have chosen as a title for this chapter, devoted to the end of the war and the first postwar years, a reverse of the formula that André Malraux used to designate the first phase of a revolution. There was much talk of revolution in liberated France; on the front page of *Combat*, beneath the title, was the slogan "From Resistance to Revolution"; Georges Bidault launched the slogan of "Revolution through law." This phraseology meant nothing.

During the war, the decision had been made, by General de Gaulle himself, to encourage the reconstitution of political parties. Even today, I consider this decision to have been both wise and inevitable. In any event, the Communist Party had not ceased to exist underground; it had played an active role in the struggle against the occupation forces from June 1941 on. Since General de Gaulle had committed himself to allowing the nation to speak, in other words to organizing elections, it was indeed necessary that, in the face of the CP, the other parties and their representatives be able to function. Léon Blum and the survivors of the SFIO would not have agreed to dissolve themselves in a larger whole defined by the Resistance or the Republic. France was condemned to rivalry among parties if not against the regime. It was a struggle that was both hidden and distorted by the tactics adopted by the CP. As long as hostilities continued, it supported the General's government, and it urged workers to stay on the job, while at the same time it used the purges to settle scores with former communist or union militants in the union federations that were hostile to the CGT. Their ministers provided places for their men, and assumed the party's control over positions that last even now (Marcel Paul at EDF, for example).

The unity of the Resistance seemed to me deceptive. The behavior of the Soviet occupation authorities in Rumania, Poland, and Eastern Germany left little doubt about Stalin's intentions. Following the formulation he used in a conversation with Djilas, every army brings its ideology with it. By May 1945, the break between the CP and the other parties was only a question of time. By refusing to give a key ministry to the CP, the General had given expression to the radical difference he saw between it and all other parties. The tripartite alliance among the three great parties—the CP, the MRP, and the SFIO—could not last for long; it would not withstand the dissolution of the alliance among the three great powers.

Like the party struggle, the purge poisoned the first phase of rediscovered democracy. Inflation, partially suppressed during the war, was immediately unleashed. The expulsion of the invaders did not immediately cure the rifts in the nation; on the contrary, it gave free rein to resentment, to the contradictory aspirations of the various classes and parties; ordinary Frenchmen surrendered to gloom because reality had gone so far to contradict the hopes that had been fostered in the dark years. I remember the days of 8 and 9 May and the sadness of the capital. I exchanged a few words with Jules Roy, if memory serves, about the strange atmosphere, the absence of any enthusiasm. The massacres were coming to an end, in Europe at least; France was in the camp of the victors, but the people had not come together, and we were already wondering about the future. I was thirteen on 11 November 1918. My parents took my two brothers and me to Paris the day after the armistice was signed. I will never forget the joy of the Parisians, coming from houses, factories, and offices to fill the streets. Bourgeois and workers mingled, men and women kissed, everyone cried aloud, "We won the war," "we beat them." National unanimity did not last. But at least it expressed the pride the French derived from their heroism and their sacrifices, and the relief they felt at the end of the killing. I have participated in many demonstrations; none of them brought together Frenchmen of all conditions, none resembled the Parisian demonstration of 12 November 1918. On that day, they did not parade, they walked together, they lived together.

It is hardly necessary to add that France recovered more easily from the defeat of 1940 than from the sublime and superhuman ordeal of 1914–1918.

The meeting with André Labarthe at Carlton Gardens in July 1940 had determined my existence during the war years.

Another decision, made without qualms of conscience, almost without reflection, also influenced the rest of my life. The dean of the faculty of letters of the University of Bordeaux asked me to become a candidate for a vacant chair of sociology, and he promised unanimous support from his colleagues. I had been named *maître de conférences* at the faculty of letters at Toulouse, and my wife had received my salary from 1940 to 1943, when I was considered missing. The dean of the faculty was aware of the truth. I should therefore have gone to Toulouse as soon as possible to thank the dean and my colleagues for their attitude toward my family. I still cannot understand why I did not do this.

In 1938, as a substitute for Professor Bonnafous, I had gone back and forth to Bordeaux for most of the academic year. This practice, theoretically prohibited except in special circumstances (for example, if the wife—or husband—lived in another city), bothered neither the administration nor the dean. As I remember it, the dean who asked me to be a candidate made no demands as to residence. Perhaps my professional performance in 1938 had made a good impression in Bordeaux. It may also be that the Jews, persecuted in the past, briefly enjoyed a favorable position, at least in some circles. In the university, those who had been tempted by collaboration could almost be counted on the fingers of one hand. On the other hand, even in prison camps in Germany, many Catholic professors, for example Jean Guitton, remained devoted to the Marshal for a certain period.

My appointment at Toulouse in August 1939 had fulfilled my hope. In 1944, I had a choice between Toulouse and Bordeaux, since, if I had asked for it, I would have been restored to the position from which the Jewish laws had excluded me. The argument I made to myself came down to the question of residence. Having been cut off from my friends in Paris for five years, I was afraid of a kind of exile in Bordeaux, where my future colleagues, with a few exceptions, were strangers to me. In 1938, I had respected and admired Dean André Darbon, with whom I had a brief conversation in June 1940 right before boarding ship for England; I often spent time with William Seston, the historian of Rome, a Protestant to whom I felt close. Not wanting to settle in Bordeaux, I also rejected the prospect of going back and forth between the city where I would live and the city where I would teach. Was giving a day and a half each week to the university enough, was it proper?

Was this ethical objection the principal motive? To put it bluntly, I was infected by the virus of politics. Not that I dreamed of a political career when I returned to France. What convinced me to interrupt the academic career for which I was destined by my studies, my aspirations, and the memory of my father, was the change in my personality caused by the years I had spent in London, close to the protagonists of history, as a journalist. At bottom, although I did not admit it to myself, the university as I had known it and as I anticipated it would be, bored me. A few dozen students, to whom I would present *Le Suicide* and *Les Formes élémentaires de la vie religieuse:* I remembered my experience of 1938 with feelings that were completely different from those I had had at the time. In 1938, I had just ended a period of four years in which I had written three books, and I was resting without too many scruples. The results already attained, as modest as they were, would have delighted my father if he had lived four years longer. In 1944 and 1945 another ambition turned me away from what I would now call my natural place: the ambition to take part in national debates, to serve my country, not to sit on the sidelines if France once again went into decline. My country had been liberated, and everything remained to be done.

In London, I had argued for a liberal democratic regime, the regime I had criticized so bitterly at the Société française de philosophie. Would the new republic avoid the flaws that had led to the death of the preceding one? Would the same ignorance of economic affairs lead the authorities to aberrations comparable to those of the 1930s? How would France manage to adapt to the age of empires, to a system of state relations that was now worldwide rather than merely European? I do not think I am flattering myself, thirty-seven years later: I wanted to participate actively in the reconstruction of France otherwise than by an *Introduction aux sciences sociales* or a study of Machiavelli. My friends who are now thirty or forty years old have difficulty in imagining the mixture of humiliation and national will that inspired the men of my generation. The Gaullist epic had not erased the memory of the collapse of 1940, preceded by the years of decline. The defeat of the Third Reich had restored an opportunity to France, an opportunity that could not be lost.

Should I also incriminate the taste for journalism, the temptation of the facility with which London and *La France libre* had inoculated me? A serious book demands years of work; months go by before reactions to the published book reach its author. My authentic ambition, strictly intellectual, gave way for a time to the dream of public service and to political intoxication.

I rarely wonder what my life and work would have been like if I had occupied the chair in Bordeaux, which would probably have led me to the one in Paris, not in 1955 but in 1948. All, or almost all my books were affected by my attention to the present. *Le Grand Schisme* (1948) came out of the need I felt to formulate a general view of the world in order, so to speak, to frame my commentaries on international affairs. *The Century of Total War* (New York: Doubleday, 1954) was a sequel to *Le Grand Schisme*, responded to criticism, and deepened the analysis of certain problems posed by the world situation. Even books about which I feel more strongly, like *The*

Opium of the Intellectuals (New York: Doubleday, 1957), and *Peace and War* (New York: Doubleday, 1966), cannot be separated from history-in-the-making, even though I attempt in them to raise myself above personal experience and the vagaries of fate.

Having said that, I have no basis for asserting that, had I returned to the university in 1945, I would have pursued the research of the years immediately before the war, as though war, a simple parenthesis, had not fundamentally transformed me. As I was in 1944 and 1945, I do not imagine that I would have undertaken an introduction to the social sciences. The epistemological questions that interested me, sometimes even excited me, before 1939, left me almost indifferent in 1945. Reality, more than the various manners of approaching it, stirred my philosophical curiosity. In order to detach myself from events during the postwar years, I would have had to contain myself. It was entirely different ten years later, in 1955, when I aspired to return to the university, not for the prestige of a chair at the Sorbonne, but to liberate myself, at least partially, from journalism. After a few years at *Le Figaro,* I felt myself, once again, in the process of dispersing myself or losing myself—like my father.

My career as a journalist, in my view, did not begin until March 1946, on *Combat,* a daily that had come out of the Resistance, edited by Pascal Pia. I have nothing but incoherent memories that I can recall only with great difficulty about the eighteen months between my return to France in the autumn of 1944 and the time I started writing for *Combat*—so much so that, retrospectively, this period seems to me a great void. During the first months, I had an intense feeling both of joy in returning to my country and of the "disillusionment of freedom," the title of an article I wrote for the first issue of *Les Temps modernes.*

Simone de Beauvoir has told of the emotion with which Sartre and I resumed our dialogue, henceforth rarely philosophical, but always friendly. After the long separation, we were immediately close.

Sartre wrote a superb article for *La France libre:* "Paris sous l'Occupation"; he wrote it in one night, with the help of a stimulant, because I had given him a deadline. In the meantime, this date had been put off for a day or two, and I had not told him about it. When I did, as he was giving me his article, he answered with "Damn it." Of course, I was at fault (perhaps I had had no means of communicating with him). I am struck—and not only by this incident—by the degree to which he reacted as a moralist. Spontaneously Kantian, he was concerned with the intention of the other, much more than with the act itself, and he concluded with a definitive judgment, favorable or unfavorable, on the basis of the unstated motives he attributed to any particular individual.

Another of my joys was to renew a friendship that I have not mentioned in the preceding chapters. Not that it held a lesser place in my life or my feelings; I would rather say the opposite. Colette and Jean Duval had nothing to do with my studies; I met Colette for the first time in Praz de Chamonix, before she was married to Jean, to whom she introduced me. One of my friends from the lycée Condorcet was friendly with Colette's brother, Michel Lejeune the Greek scholar, and perhaps also with another brother, Jean Effel. Jean Duval, a colleague and friend of Jean Guéhenno, was above all an admirable being with a sensitivity and delicacy which would easily have made me feel like a peasant from the Danube, had he not carefully concealed with humor both his intimate feelings and those he had for others. Jean and Colette were a couple; a friend of one necessarily became a friend of the other. They spent two days with us during our year in Le Havre. We sometimes had four-way conversations, more often dialogues in which Colette or Jean would talk to one of us.

They had spent the war where they had always lived (their son André lives there still), on rue Monsieur-le-Prince. They had been part of the network of the Musée de l'Homme, miraculously saved. The Gestapo knew that there was a meeting on rue Monsieur-le-Prince; they had a suspect walk from one end of the street to the other in the hope that, in one way or another, by a sign, or facial expression, or a gesture, he would reveal the house. The prisoner withstood the ordeal and saved his comrades.

Malraux knew and admired the Duvals. One day, leaving their apartment with me, he spoke of these noble beings, devoted to a noble calling, cultivated, outside the battles and the vulgarities of the political and literary jungle, custodians of the tradition, and entrusted with the task of transmitting it. A victim of the "Cultural Revolution" and the loss of prestige of the humanities, André Duval no longer believes as much as his father did in this obscure and necessary task. His father believed in it, without devoting his entire existence to it. He spoke about poetry as no one else did; his students admired and loved him. He had an ambitious project, a book on Victor Hugo that he never wrote. After his death, his regularly kept (not daily) private diary was discovered. Malraux thought that a diary gradually devoured the writer. In the case of Jean, the explanation is not sufficient. Happy with Colette, as much as a man can be, satisfied with his profession, surrounded by friends, he suffered from internal contradictions that he did not want to admit to himself. He held firm to the end, happy and divided. Colette wrote charming children's books that have been translated into countless languages. She survived Jean for many years, always thinking of him, always young at heart and close to her grandchildren. I blame myself for not having seen her often enough in the course of later years, but when we did meet each other, time and distance disappeared and the same friendship united us through common memories.

In 1938, despite the success of *La Nausée*, Sartre's fame did not reach beyond literary circles. In 1944, he had not changed his way of being and living, but he attained glory. *L'Etre et le néant* had appeared, and *Huis Clos*, after *Les Mouches*, was greeted with enthusiasm by the theatergoing public. The fashion of existentialism and the cafes of Saint-Germain-des-Prés was beginning. Far from avoiding politics, he resolutely threw himself into it. He felt an unreserved sympathy for communism, which was rarely reciprocated. André Malraux had changed. Not in his relations with his friends, or at least with me; I saw the same simplicity, the same discreet affection; what startled me was his hostility, I would almost say his hatred, for communism. He never explained to me the reasons for his "conversion."

During the war, I had received only one letter from him, written while he was living in the Midi and writing *La Lutte avec l'Ange*. I remember a sentence, but not its exact terms: "It is said that I will work on *La Nouvelle Revue française* in Paris. There is no chance that I will." He did not join the Resistance until 1944, but he was certainly never tempted by collaboration or Vichy. He came to Paris from time to time during the winter of 1944–45, sometimes to warn the united Resistance movement against the maneuvers of the communists. He had not yet declared his allegiance to General de Gaulle, or I should say, he had not yet chosen de Gaulle as his leader. He looked on literary agitation and the creation of new journals with some contempt (Sartre's plan to create *Les Temps modernes* was well known to him).

A voluntary exile from the university, I continued to work on *La France libre* until the middle of 1945. As long as he had needed me, André Labarthe had used his charm, and had even shown me some affection, which he probably felt to the extent that an actor with sporadic sincerity was capable of such feelings. A mere employee of the operation, I had not asked for a different status at a time when he would not have been able to refuse. I had no choice but to leave when political and personal differences were exacerbated, beginning toward the end of 1943, when, after General Giraud's final failure, he left for the United States and tried to establish a journal in English there, a caricature of *La France libre*. I had become attached to the journal in which I had played a significant role, and I left it with a heavy heart. Today, my bitterness seems to me slightly ridiculous. A journal places a heavy weight on those who are responsible for it; I had given a good deal of time and thought to this ephemeral work—I could and should have found time for more substantial works.

Politically, during this period, I was *elsewhere*, at the fringes. There was no longer any question of anti-Gaullism. The General, who had come to power with the support of the reconstructed parties and the Resistance movements, hence with a coalition dominated by the ideas and the earnestness of the left, presented himself in two ways: as the man around whom the majority of the French came together, as the majority had done around the Marshal four years earlier, in 1940; and as the man who, thanks to his popularity, would restore the state and restrain the Communist Party, which, using the pretext of the purge, was liquidating adversaries in the name of doing justice.

It seemed obvious to me that in electoral terms the Resistance movements would not carry much weight and that the parties would quickly revert to their traditional role. I said this in two articles entitled "Révolution ou Rénovation";[1] I rejected the revolutionary vocabulary that was fashionable in the Paris of 1944–45 and that seemed to me devoid of meaning in relation to the historical and geographical situation of France. On the Resistance movements, I wrote in October 1944: "The Resistance is playing and will play a primary role in the initial period when it will support the government as the government will rely on it. But as soon as elections take place, it will come up against the parties; to transform *Combat* and *Libération* into parties is the path of least resistance that will probably lead to a fiasco. Establishing the Resistance as a single party is a pure illusion, because there is no political unity among those who, with a common passion, have fought for France. The Resistance has not brought to light new *parties*, it has prompted the appearance of new *political personalities*."

In August 1945, I explained why France was not on the eve of a revolution:

> The Communist Party? Convinced that in Western Europe, in the current historical situation, its time has not yet come, it relies on its restored legality and the circumstances to expand its positions, to maintain the fervor and calm the impatience of its rank and file. The Resistance? Some men of the Resistance organizations often indulge in extremist language. From one day to the next, they have been forced into a total reversal; just recently primarily concerned with obscurity and mystery, they are now calling for the full light of day. The law of clandestine activity is to remain unknown. The law of politics is to be known. One is not a political man until one's name has appeared often enough in the press.

In addition, I sketched the broad outlines of the necessary renovation, without revolution, within the framework of a parliamentary regime.

My first experience as a journalist was on an illustrated weekly, *Point de vue;* I never remember it without embarrassment, if not shame. Why did I agree to play at being an editorial writer for such a publication? We have to remember the Paris of the months following the Liberation and then the surrender of the Third Reich. Except for *Le Figaro*, all the prewar papers had disappeared; new titles appeared, sometimes retaining a fragment of a popular title *(Le Parisien libéré, France-Soir)*. Resistance networks *(Combat)* transformed a clandestine bulletin into a daily newspaper. Resistance personalities, at a moment when almost any paper would sell, also threw themselves into the press. Corniglion-Molinier and Marcel Bleustein persuaded me to write for *Point de vue,* directed by Lucien Rachline—a bedding manufacturer by profession who had held a command in the Resistance—and edited by Pierre Descaves. Whatever title I may have been given, my role was soon confined to writing a weekly article whose length and character was not significantly different from those I later wrote for *Le Figaro.*

I have reread some of these articles, which I had completely forgotten. They contain some ideas that are now banal or, better, obvious, which at the time went against the grain. Above all, I attempted several times to liberate the French from their obsession with Germany. Thus, on 4 April 1945, I wrote: "We French remain obsessed by the German question alone, as though the universe continued to gravitate around Europe. And when M. Vladimir d'Ormesson warns us against the mistakes of 1919, he proposes that we return to the division of Germany, that is, that we go back three centuries. Nineteen forty-five is the 1815 of Germany." A few weeks after the end of the war, I denounced the policy of the occupation authorities, their prohibition against soldiers fraternizing with the population: "In the West, there is an increase in severity, particularly verbal severity. There is an attempt to maintain the literally absurd rule of nonfraternization. Goering and Rosenberg have not yet been judged, but Tommies and G.I.s don't have the right to smile at little children."

Punish Germany? Hitler himself had assumed the task. Confronted with its destroyed cities, an economy in ruins, millions of refugees, the victors were charged by history, willingly or not, to reconstruct their beaten enemy and to offer him a future. "Hitler, by his mad obstinacy, has punished his own people more cruelly than a hardened supporter of Vansittart could have done. According to the *Neue Zürcher Zeitung,* the bombing of Dresden caused 200,000 casualties"[2] (4 May 1945). From that moment on, I did not believe in the restoration of German unity. "Everyone expects something different from unity. The Anglo-Saxons seem to hope that the iron curtain that has been lowered for more than two months on the demarcation line will finally be raised. But the Russians will see this as an opportunity to extend to the west of the Reich the spread of their ideas and the activities of their representatives. Who would gain more?" The expression "iron curtain" was not yet widespread. I think that Winston Churchill had not yet used it.

The division of Germany seemed to me to be established for a long time, and thereby the connection of France with the western fraction of unavoidable Germany. These common sense ideas had at the time a paradoxical or audacious character. Extreme anti-Germanism still dominated, at least in appearance, French public opinion. Thus General de Gaulle and his spokesmen called for amputations from West Germany comparable to those that the Soviet Union was inflicting in the east. A few years later, as president of the RPF, the General repeated the slogan: "Never again a Reich." André Malraux also supported this argument and repeated the formula in a published dialogue with James Burnham.

I wrote three articles for *Les Temps modernes:* "Les désillusions de la liberté"; "Après l'événement, avant l'histoire"; and "La chance du socialisme." The last article presented a perspective for the French Socialist Party more or less comparable to that of the Labour Party that had been victorious at the polls in Great Britain; I prefer to forget it, even though it expresses an idea that was true then and is true now. Socialism has no real chance in France unless it thinks for itself, decides to be a social-democratic party, and does not form an alliance with the Communist Party. In "Les désillusions de la liberté," I find a discussion—the first—of General de Gaulle's foreign policy: "Materially, we will depend principally on our American allies. An 'external' threat to our independence thus lies in the West rather than in the East. The French government has been led, by this kind of emotional logic, to proclaim its total sovereignty and its hostility to concessions, particularly toward those on whom it depends the most." These remarks, embarrassed and badly written, were aimed at the anti-Americanism revealed by the diplomacy inspired by the General.

It is quite obvious that the articles in *Point de vue* were unnoticed in literary and political Paris. André Malraux, the minister of information, rescued me from the impasse into which I had plunged by asking me to be his chief of staff. This was in December 1945, in the government established by General de Gaulle after the elections to the constituent assembly. For the first and last time, I occupied an official position, a modest one: the minister of information did not have extensive powers, even less his chief of staff. We should add that Jacques Chaban-Delmas was secretary-general of the government. How much brain power there was in this trio, for such small effects.

The government lasted for only two months, and André Malraux did not have the time to undertake any of the projects he launched twelve years later. At the end of 1945, the central question remained the authorization for publications to appear, the distribution of paper, the fate of previously banned newspapers and of printing houses seized shortly after the Liberation. I felt no sympathy for the "racket" of the newspapers, in particular provincial papers, whose former proprietors had been dispossessed, so that Resistance forces had seized control of the press. Perhaps the former owners deserved punishment (many of them were not subject to prosecution); did Resistance fighters deserve the reputation given to them by a paper whose title resembled that of the paper that dominated a region before the war? Some of the major provincial newspapers, the most prosperous in the French press, changed their names slightly and came under new ownership. Sometimes, groups of Resistance figures divided ownership in the business without gaining any profit; in other cases, a Resistance figure took the place of the owner of the paper.

When André Malraux assumed his post in the Ministry of Information, this transfer of ownership was a *fait accompli*. With a few exceptions, the prewar papers had changed hands and changed their titles. *Paris-Soir*, renamed *France-Soir*, became the property not of Jean Prouvost, but of its first contributor, Pierre Lazareff. Jean Prouvost took advantage of an authorization to publish held by the director of *France* in London, Comert, to launch *Paris-Match*, which, after difficult beginnings, achieved striking success, although it later declined. The old lion, on the eve of his death, was forced to sell *Paris-Match*, his beloved child, which, under more careful management, once again became a successful business. I had nothing to do with this situation, which I did not at all like. Among those who came to the ministry were some whose papers had been confiscated, including Jacques Chastenet. I told him directly that *Le Temps* no longer existed and that *Le Monde*, established in its predecessor's offices, would remain there. I refrained from making a judgment about the substitution itself; I observed that it was definitive.

Authorizations to publish and the distribution of paper were already the subject of polemics. Authorizations to publish, it was said, were bringing us back to the Second Empire, and perhaps even further back. One day, a directive from the prime minister's office asked us to prepare for the suppression of authorizations to publish. It was a praiseworthy initiative, but it did not remove the real obstacle to the return to a normal regime of freedom: the shortage of paper. As long as paper was distributed through administrative means, the suppression of authorizations to publish had no meaning, except if every new publication automatically had a right to a certain volume of paper. In my office in the ministry, I met Louis Gabriel-Robinet, overwhelmed when I told him, a day in advance, of the General's decision to resign. Malraux and I agreed to grant *Le Figaro littéraire* the authorization to publish.

The only decision of any importance that I made at the ministry, which, I believe, would have been in conformity with the public interest, came too late; Malraux had had nothing to do with it, and his successor Gaston Defferre reverted to what seemed to me an unreasonable solution that produced foreseeable consequences. Hundreds of printing presses had been seized by the public authorities or simply by Resistance groups, genuine or not. The ministry's legal officer, a specialist in and responsible for press law, and leaning toward the socialists, presented a simple proposal to me that seemed to me the least appropriate: the establishment of a single organization that would own and direct the entirety of this state-owned property. I objected that this quasi-governmental organization would badly fulfill its function: to assure the maintenance and the modernization of operations that were too diverse to be appropriately controlled by a single, distant, and badly informed authority. I suggested an entirely different law, which provided for the sale of equipment to new press corporations; the state would gradually be relieved of its burden. Moreover, since we wanted to return to a free press system, the nationalization of the printing presses was not in the spirit of our plans. The ministry's legal officer had more success with Defferre than with me.

What impressions remain from those few weeks? First of all, the number of people I had to meet every day. Perhaps the multitude of petitioners—an unjustly pejorative word since they often were seeking not a favor but an accommodation that in normal times they would not have had to request— was swollen by the exorbitant powers of the ministry. I might add that ten hours of work at the ministry seemed to me not as hard as four hours reading the *Critique of Pure Reason*. Another impression, probably more banal, that I have not forgotten: the personal rivalry among the various members of an administration or a staff, a rivalry that came out in quarrels about offices and cars. This improvised ministry, with bloated divisions, was probably a caricature of the ordinary practices of other government departments. I need hardly add that the minister's staff also expanded in the course of two months.

One more word on the minister. Those who have worked with him after 1958 know much more than I, but a brief account may be of some interest. When he arrived at his post, Malraux was even more ignorant than I about the functioning of governmental authorities; the distinctions among laws, decrees, and rulings was foreign and probably unknown to him. In a few days, he learned what he needed to know, and with the same speed, he absorbed the files on which the curiosity of journalists had been fixed. He imposed a rigorous schedule on himself and received journalists at the exact moment that had been previously arranged. He responded to precise questions with pertinent answers, which impressed ordinary journalists and saddened a figure like Georges Altmann, disturbed that Malraux was concerned with such trivialities. In spite of his nervousness, I never remember him raising his voice to any of his subordinates. He sometimes caused me difficulties because he promised a job or a favor to someone, and left it to me to fulfill his promise. I was not always in a position to do so.

This was the origin of my "quarrel" with Romain Gary, whose talent I had recognized in London and toward whom I felt friendly. André Malraux wanted to appoint him as cultural counselor at the French embassy in London; so did I. In his favorite style, Malraux assured him that "the decision had been made." But we still had to obtain the agreement of the General's staff. Gaston Palewski considered Gary too lightweight and too young for the position. It was my task to tell Gary. One morning, more than usually harassed, I told him over the telephone, more bluntly than I ought to have, not to count on London and to accept another position that was open to him. For years, he blamed me for a decision I had not made. In one of his letters, Roger Martin du Gard alluded to what Gary was saying about me. Long before his death, this misunderstanding had been cleared away.

One month after the General's first period in power, I joined *Combat*, which was at the time the newspaper most respected by the literary and political circles of the capital. The editorials by Albert Camus commanded extraordinary respect: a genuine writer was commenting on the events of the day. The editorial board included a constellation of intellectuals who had been involved in the Resistance and had not yet returned to their natural places; they included Albert Ollivier, Jacques Merleau-Ponty (a cousin of Maurice, who wrote a thesis on the *Cosmologies of the Twentieth Century* and now teaches philosophy at the University of Nanterre), Pierre Kaufman (who also teaches philosophy at the same university), Alexandre Astruc, Roger Grenier, and other writers and philosophers. There was an extraordinary disproportion between the intellectual abilities of these men and the editorial space available to them. I had seen a similar disproportion at the Ministry of Information. These writers and scholars were probably motivated by feelings similar to those that turned me away from an immediate return to the university.

The leader of the group, contrary to popular opinion, was never Albert Camus; it was Pascal Pia, an extraordinary personality, whose visible existence and public itinerary give no indication of what he did and what he could have done. A very close friend of André Malraux, who had dedicated one of his early books to him, possessing a literary culture that was both extended and profound, endowed with exceptional talent as a critic if not as a creator, he commanded respect from everyone because of what Wladimir Jankélévitch would call the *je ne sais quoi*. Resistance credentials? Others had the same. Modesty? Perhaps. As director in theory and practice, he worked from morning to night, but, as we said, he corrected commas and spelling mistakes. He refused to "arrive," in the social sense of the word, and had firmly resolved to settle into anonymity, while *Combat* offered everyone the opportunity to make a name for himself. What explained this urge to remain in the shadows? We talked about it among the staff. Some asserted that in the course of his study of history he had taken stock of the hazards of fame and had discovered the work of a writer who had sunk into oblivion—a work from which a still celebrated writer had derived the substance of his writings. The interpretation is too rational to be convincing. I do not know Pia's secret, and many others who knew him better than I probably know no more than I do.

It was at his request, perhaps in responding to a suggestion by André Malraux, that I began to write regularly for *Combat*.[3] My first articles dealt in succession with the various parties in 1946. For reasons I cannot explain, these articles were noticed. Albert Ollivier and many others praised me for them, not without a hint of surprise. In the small world of the press, they suddenly granted me a position that my prewar books, ignored by most journalists, had in no way promised. I became an editorialist, in the proper sense of the term, no longer merely a columnist. Alternating with Albert Ollivier, and more infrequently with a journalist using the name Marcel Gimond, I wrote the left-hand column on the front page.[4]

In the spring of 1946, the principal subjects of debate were the Constitution being drafted by the Constituent Assembly, the relations between the Communist Party and the other parties, economic difficulties, and the negotiations with Ho Chi Minh, more generally the relations of the metropolis with the French Empire, which had already been renamed the French Union.

On the Constitution, I prepared a study that appeared under the title of *Les Français face à la Constitution*. A young jurist, whom I hardly knew, briefly reviewed the various constitutions of France since 1789; a second, shorter, section, written by me, considered the new Constitution. I had such unpleasant memories of this text that it appears in none of the bibliographies prepared by my various assistants in the course of the last twenty years. A few days ago, I reread it and was rather pleasantly surprised.

Not that it was by any means original. It developed a certain number of ideas that were in the air, fashionable, and which were not taken up by the writers of the Constitution: strengthening of the President of the Republic through the method of his election and his powers (the right to dissolve parliament without the acquiescence of the Senate), granting to the government the right to end debate in parliament and to exercise greater control over the work of the Assembly; I expressed a qualified preference for single member constituencies with two rounds of voting, with no belief that this proposal had any chance of success.

I committed a cardinal sin: not declaring from the outset the political context of the constitutional debate, that is, the triangular battle that developed once the Gaullists had returned to France along with the consequences of the years of war and occupation. In appearance, from the Liberation to the election of the first Constituent Assembly, General de Gaulle governed the country with the support of the three major parties, the Communists, the Socialists, and the MRP (the latter won the majority of votes from moderates and Radical-Socialists). There had never been an organized center-right party under the Third Republic. Men of the right had sat on the National Council of Resistance, but when the people were consulted, the MRP was in the best position; it claimed allegiance to the General; its leaders had unchallengeable resistance credentials; it seemed able to resist pressures from the Socialists and the Communists.

The first constellation contained two concealed fundamental conflicts: the Communist Party against all the others, and all parties—or almost all—against the General. He never thought that his mission should come to an end with the Liberation and the election of the Constituent Assembly. He harbored the ambition to give France solid institutions and to govern it, at least for a few years. When he resigned early in 1946, he anticipated returning to power within a few months. I remember André Malraux, returning from a conversation with the General, saying to me: "We will return in six months."

Why did the General resign in January 1946? He believed that the parties would not succeed in governing the country, but he also thought, correctly, that the Constituent Assembly would not draft a constitution that would give him the position he intended to occupy in the Republic. All parties, including the MRP, understood more or less clearly that the General did not deny their right to exist, but he was determined not to receive his power from them. He did not want to govern the country as President of the Council of Ministers. Not that he was unable to do so: on the contrary, he had an innate talent as a parliamentary debater. I was in the Assembly when he spoke during a debate prompted by a proposal of André Philip,[5] when he hinted at his retirement. His intervention impressed the Assembly without converting it. Divided, by 1947, between communists and noncommunists, the parties were in the end united in voting for a constitution which the General considered incompatible with the interests of the nation and with his own ambitions.

Combat, as it was until the spring of 1947, was located on the left by its vocabulary and its positions on colonial questions, but some of its editors— Pascal Pia, Albert Ollivier—became more and more Gaullist in 1946 and 1947. In my editorials, I supported a "no" vote on the Constitution approved by the National Assembly, supported by the Communists and the Socialists. When the second version of the Constitution was submitted to the French, I suggested a resigned "yes"; the next day, Albert Ollivier responded with "Why not no?"

The Indochina War broke out in December 1946; the Vietminh made a surprise attack on French troops in Hanoi. I wrote an editorial that Sartre characterized as "embarrassed." I have reread it without too much shame or remorse. In London, I argued in favor of the *abandonment* of Indochina. The costs of an Empire scattered through the world exceeded the resources of a France that had been depleted by the years of war and Occupation. But in December 1946, in a daily article, when our soldiers had just barely escaped a massacre, I could hardly not support the socialist government of Léon Blum, who personally decided to send reinforcements. This explains the zigzag in my analysis, or rather in my adoption of a position.

At the beginning: "When our troops defend themselves against a deliberate attack, unleashed by surprise and according to orders, we feel solidarity with the French who are fighting and dying in a distant land." This was followed by an immediate qualification: "It would, however, be rather cowardly to stop there. It may very well be that, in the present situation, the assertion of force is an unavoidable necessity. If only to be able to negotiate tomorrow, we must today resort to arms. But it is impossible not to confess that this very necessity, given the hopes that inspired all of us after the Liberation, is a harsh disappointment, a bitter failure. The constitution that has just been adopted solemnly proclaims that France will take no action against the freedom of any people. We have recognized the independence of Vietnam within the framework of the French Union. Nothing allows us to think that our representatives want to question the principle. But the present battle only appears all the more disastrous, since we do not and cannot intend a military reconquest, and since Vietnam has until now not denied our rights." I did not distinguish between Vietnam and Vietminh: Ho Chi Minh represented Vietnam. Lacking precise knowledge about what preceded the Hanoi coup, I refused to share out responsibility among the various parties involved. I concluded by calling on the parliament to recall once again the French doctrine: "We have no doubt that those who are elected by the people will affirm the will to 'maintain,' but real French positions, not identified with sordid interests, those that the nation is determined to serve, cannot be maintained by force alone. To maintain by violence would not be to maintain France."

Despite the awkwardness of expression, the meaning seems unambiguous to me. There should be no military reconquest, for which we had neither the means nor the desire; we should honor our promise of independence; what France wanted to preserve was not the colonial regime of the past. The tone of Albert Ollivier the next day was different from mine, but his editorial referred to Léon Blum's speech to the Assembly. On the essential point, Ollivier quoted the socialist premier: "For the moment, we can only indicate our refusal to negotiate under pressure or, as Léon Blum very forcefully stated, 'before the restoration of peace, the necessary basis for execution of the contract.'"

As head of a transitional government, Léon Blum had to take charge of a situation whose responsibilities he had assumed, perhaps against his will, fully aware of their seriousness. He nevertheless used an expression that contained the seeds of years of warfare: "to reestablish peaceful order." The reestablishment of that order was equivalent to an attempt at military reconquest, an intention that was carefully denied. National feeling—not to use the ambiguous term *nationalism*—which was very strong in the country, and ignorance of real power relations explain, without excusing them, the decisions that gradually led France into the Vietnamese trap. The editorial of 29 January 1947, in which I commented on statements made by Marius Moutet on his return from Indochina, which is too modest for my present tastes, nonetheless emphasized this rejection of military conquest, and the need for conversations, not only with our protégés, but above all with those who had the people's confidence.

Aside from articles on current economic conditions, I wrote the majority, and perhaps the most important, of the editorials on Germany and on the Constitution. In the issue dated 26–27 January 1947, under the title "Is there still a German danger?" I once again analyzed the radical novelty of the immediate circumstances, the decline of Europe as a whole in the context of world politics, the definitive inferiority of the Central European countries in relation both to the Soviet Union and to Western democracies. A few days later, I emphasized the inevitable economic and industrial reconstruction of Germany, and I criticized the "ceilings" that had been placed on the production of some of its industries. Finally, on 7 February 1947, I evoked "another Germany." "The rebirth of Europe, that is, of the nation-states located between the Russian border and the Atlantic, is hardly conceivable without the reintegration of the Reich, or its successor, into a peaceful community." As for French policies, I said, by accepting the economic unity of Europe, France had virtually accepted a certain form of political unity. "Nothing stands in the way of the affirmation of a French doctrine, a positive and constructive doctrine, which has as its aim a reunited Germany in a peaceful Europe. I think that the reconstruction of Germany will go on against us if, because of us, it takes place without us."

I have reread most of the articles I wrote on the Constitution, or rather on the two drafts that were presented in succession, by referendum, to the people. We all agreed on the first draft: we rejected the proposed Constitution both because it seemed distasteful and because only the two "Marxist" parties, Socialists and Communists, supported it; and the Socialists did so with the greatest reluctance. The day after the "no" vote, I entitled my editorial "Saved by Defeat." I was speaking, of course, of the Socialists.

The debate on the second draft Constitution took place in totally different conditions because of the intervention of General de Gaulle. He delivered a speech in Bayeux on 16 June 1946 that has remained famous and in which it is easy to see the organizing principles of the 1958 Constitution. The key formulations are the same: the separation of powers, hence the executive does not "derive" from the legislature; the President of the Republic (to be elected by a broadened "electoral college") was to choose the Prime Minister. Governmental responsibility to the Assembly was not explicitly provided for. The General cleared away ambiguities on this essential point in later speeches.

Perhaps the portrait of the head of state as the General saw him can be seen more clearly in these statements of 1946 than in any of his writings.

It is thus from the head of state, placed above the parties, elected by a 'college' including the Parliament, but much broader than that and constructed so as to make him President of the French Union as well as President of the Republic, that must flow executive power. The head of state must harmonize the general interest with the directions emanating from Parliament. It is his mission to appoint ministers, principally, of course, the Prime Minister, who will direct the policy and the work of the government. It is the function of the head of state to promulgate laws and formulate regulations, for both involve the relation of citizens to the state as a whole. It is his task to preside over the councils of government and to exercise the influence of continuity that a nation cannot do without. It is his role to serve as arbiter above political contingencies, either routinely through the council of ministers or, in moments of serious confusion, by calling on the nation to make a sovereign decision through elections. If the nation were in danger, to him would fall the duty to be the guarantor of national independence and of the treaties signed by France.

A compromise between the Assembly's views and the General's plans seemed at the least improbable. The governmental system outlined in Bayeux condemned to death not parliamentary democracy but the Republic of the deputies (or the parties). The Communist and Socialist Parties would never accept a Constitution inspired by the General's doctrine. There thus developed, along with the "great schism" between the Communists and everyone else, a "lesser schism" between all the parties and General de Gaulle. I did not believe that the General would achieve victory over the parties in the near future; Léon Blum's immediate response to the Bayeux speech left no doubt about the attitude of the Socialist Party toward the General's constitutional ideas.

The editorial I wrote on 18 June, two days after the Bayeux speech, ended with the following words: "From now on, aside from the present regime, with which no one, even its leaders, is satisfied, there is at least one other possibility. A Constitution somewhere between British parliamentarianism and the presidential system outlined by General de Gaulle is probably not viable in a peaceful period; at least, it evidences an aim which the parties will not willingly accept, but to which some of them would, perhaps out of necessity, one day resign themselves." I should have written not that this regime would not have been viable in a quiet period, but that it would come to life only in a troubled time—a day when the parties would abdicate under compulsion. That day came only twelve years later, provoked by the Algerian War.

After the Epinal speech, a clear declaration of principle by the General against the second proposal, I predicted the victory of the parties in the coming referendum. "Thus, if there must be a 'test of strength,' the outcome does not seem doubtful. Party propaganda will evoke the threat of personal power rather than the merits of the Constitution. With a lower rate of participation, the 47% of yes votes in the first referendum will become a majority."

"What is to be done?" I asked myself on 10 September 1946. Nothing essential had been changed since May: "The executive remains a simple servant of the Assembly. The upper chamber does not even have a right to suspend temporarily the application of laws. There is no control over the constitutionality of laws. The President of the Republic does not really have the power to choose the Prime Minister or the right to dissolve the Assembly. No provision has been made to postpone a serious decision for several months or for such a decision to give rise to new elections. No institution with real powers is set up above the parties, that is, above the determinations of their leaders."

And I concluded: "For the citizen, abstention will probably be the only means to express his desire to go beyond provisional resolutions and his rejection of the Constitution that has been presented to him." At the same time, a "revisionist" party—the RPF—was to arise out of the approval of the Constitution by one third of the registered voters.

Against the constitution that the General wanted, the Communists allied themselves with the other parties, and they went even further: they wanted a single chamber, all-powerful, in control of the government that would be its servant, the agent that carried out its wishes. Even after the Communist Party had moved into opposition, the cleavage between the Liberator and the parties persisted with absolute clarity. It took the Algerian War to produce the circumstances that the General had been looking for ever since his return to France: the abdication of the republic of the deputies in the face of a legislator who, once and for all, would establish what, for want of a better term, could be called a consular republic. The loyal MRP, had it been loyal to the end, would probably not have supported, in a third Constituent Assembly, the constitution corresponding to the General's wishes. In fact, the

General claimed above all that the President of the Republic, not responsible to the parliament, held supreme authority. The 1958 Constitution would have been voted by none of the postwar Assemblies.

Many friends in the press and at the university have asked me about my experiences as a journalist in the course of the last thirty-seven years. I leave out of account my experience on *Point de vue,* which taught me nothing, since I was an outsider. I felt cordially welcomed by *Combat;* I can barely remember two or three quarrels. The assignment of editorials became a little more difficult when Albert Camus returned to the paper in the hope of saving it. On the other hand, one of the journalists, at the time of the "journalistic foot soldiers," now highly placed in the hierarchy of freelance writers, René Dabernat, in his own way, described to me the feelings that I provoked, the irritation that some felt because of the speed with which I composed editorials, and the sometimes rather critical commentaries, less on my work than on my personality. I only half believe him. The editorial board of *Combat* reminded me a little of the Ecole Normale. When we were not talking about literature and politics, we spoke about each other. I was probably like the rest of the group in this respect.

In 1947, when the financial situation deteriorated, I participated in many editorial meetings and meetings between management and the print workers. The administrator, Jean Bloch-Michel, also belonged to the category of intellectual-writer; he was not a professional journalist or a businessman. Because of his legal studies, he was more qualified than others to run the newspaper. The print workers had bitter discussions, as was their custom, with him and with Pia. They had no particular sympathy for apprentice managers inspired by socialist sentiments; confronting Resistance intellectuals, they made the same demands as they would against an aggressive boss. I remember a union member, after a long discussion, saying: "I wish we had a real boss!"

Why did the original *Combat,* the *Combat* of Pia, Camus, Ollivier, Grenier, and Nadeau, fail so quickly? We discussed it among ourselves. Everyone reads *Combat,* it was said in Paris. I replied: "Unfortunately, everyone represents only forty thousand people." The papers with titles from before the war gradually moved ahead of the pack. *Combat* was preeminently a journal of opinion, to use a prewar expression, and journals of opinion never have large press runs. If I remember correctly, at one point, *Combat* reached 200,000 copies. Circulation gradually declined in the course of 1946. Why? Some editors blamed Albert Ollivier whose Gaullism fit badly with the sensibility of a left-wing readership (this was our opinion without the benefit of readership surveys). Probably others accused my editorials. Thirty-seven years ago, as today, my analysis incriminated no one in particular. As a paper of the Resistance, *Combat* found no place in a regime of parties.

In 1944–45, the war was still going on, and the shortage of paper reduced newspapers to two pages, one sheet printed on both sides. The quality of the articles and the atmosphere of unity of the Resistance attracted a heterogeneous readership, brought together by temporary circumstances. After the end of hostilities, as the French returned to electoral politics, political divisions reappeared and hence an unclassifiable paper was exposed to a mortal danger for a daily: not fully satisfying any category of its readers. From one column to the next, the writers expressed contradictory opinions. The episode that became symbolic was the referendum on the second proposed constitution.

Of course, there is a readership that accepts free discussion among the writers on a single paper. It attempts to instruct, not to indoctrinate. In politics, at a moment of uncertainty, indeed of crisis, who can claim possession of the truth? To present one's own truth as *the* truth seems less than honest.[7] These are respectable arguments to which most readers would answer: "We don't need our usual paper in order not to know what to think. If the journalist doesn't know any more, he should keep quiet." There is more to be said: after thirty years of experience, from 1947 to 1977, on *Le Figaro*, I am convinced that a number of readers expect from their newspaper, as from broadcast news, a kind of security, the confirmation of their own judgments. Robert Lazurick, who headed *L'Aurore* until his accidental death, used to have a routine on the freedom of the press: "For almost my entire life," he said, "I've written for 'bought' newspapers—which means that financiers or industrialists owned the business and were very particular whenever their interests were directly concerned. Otherwise, they left us completely alone. Now, I'm running a paper that depends entirely on its readers. If I write one thing or another, they threaten to cancel their subscriptions or to stop buying the paper." In other words, every paper feels half imprisoned by its clientele; Pierre Brisson stopped François Mauriac's campaign in favor of the sultan of Morocco when the letters of protest reached the breaking point. Thanks to its exceptional position, *Le Monde* does not hesitate to challenge various schools of thought, one after another.[8]

Pia's *Combat*, at least the one I knew from March 1946 until the arrival of Smadja, combined anticommunism, anticolonialism, and a semi-Gaullism (or at least Gaullism on alternate days). Too Gaullist for the socialists, too anticolonialist for the moderates, too far to the left in its vocabulary and style for the MRP, it appealed to the marginal figures of all parties, but it looked in vain for a center, a hard core of faithful supporters. There were enough of them for a journal of opinion but not for a national newspaper. It might perhaps have won the gamble if it had been run by professionals.

In the weeks preceding the dissolution of the first editorial board, there was talk of getting financial support. I talked with two or three bankers. They criticized the paper's line on one point or another, in particular on the colonial question. Besides, I doubted if my colleagues would have accepted a management of which I would have been at least a part. Bloch-Michel did not allow me to forget it. He was probably speaking the truth, although his feelings about me were stronger than those of many others.

When Smadja and Claude Bourdet took control of *Combat,* I contacted Hubert Beuve-Méry and Pierre Brisson. I had known neither of them before the war. I had heard about the former's resignation from *Le Temps* at the time of Munich. As for Brisson, I had met him during the two months I spent at the Ministry of Information. A year of working for *Combat* had transformed me, in the eyes of the Paris political world, into a journalist or an editorialist. Once again, I had to choose, this time not between the university and the press, but between *Le Monde* and *Le Figaro*.

There was little difference in compensation. The choice was between a morning and an evening paper, between a historic paper that had been changed since the war and a postwar paper. I had cordial relations with Beuve-Méry and, in addition, in 1947, disagreements over neutralism and Atlanticism had not yet provoked a national debate. It was not obvious that the two papers asking for my collaboration would represent, two years later, the extreme opposites of noncommunist French thought.

I followed the advice of André Malraux; your relations with Pierre Brisson will be easier, he said, than with Beuve-Méry. I thought the same. I had trouble seeing the place that I would be given on *Le Monde*. A few strong convictions animated the editor of *Le Figaro:* anticommunism, the defense of parliamentary democracy, European unity. His convictions fitted with mine, and I therefore anticipated no serious divergences between the line of *Le Figaro* and my own opinions—a prediction generally confirmed by events, with a few exceptions: the RPF, decolonization, the virtues of Antoine Pinay's economic program.

Pierre Brisson, a Gaullist at the Liberation, who rejoined Gaullism in 1958, opposed the RPF with a kind of passion. He accepted the independence of Algeria only in the early 1960s, following the lead of the General.

In the spring of 1977, recovering from a heart attack in Cochin hospital, I received a letter from Beuve-Méry that touched me deeply. We had both arrived at an age that helps one look at the past with detachment; he evoked his dreams of 1944–45, he wrote, and always with nostalgia, "the hope I held for a moment to have you share the adventure of *Le Monde* after the failure of the first version of *Combat*. What happened to that hope? Putting aside all petty differences, the possible difficulties would have been of an entirely different order from those we face now." Perhaps. I am not sure that my participation in the adventure of *Le Monde* could have gone on for long. But after so many controversies and so many years, this sign of friendship moved me more than I would dare admit.

NOTES

1. *La France libre*, October 1944 and August 1945.
2. The figure is as high as 300,000. Since then, the English have condemned this inhuman act without military justification.
3. At Pia's request, I had written an article for *Combat*, as early as October 1944.
4. The usual location for principal editorials in the French press after World War II. (Trans.)
5. I believe the debate had to do with a reduction in the national defense budget.
6. The editorial of 20 March 1947, after the Assembly debate on Indochina, added nothing to its predecessors. It insisted on the ambiguity of the policy of the Ramadier government: With whom did he want to negotiate? How long would "pacification" last?
7. A friend has objected: "How can one do otherwise?"
8. An exceptional position for many reasons: its recognized authority, the space it offers to all political figures, the role it plays for teachers and students.

9

JOURNALIST
AND MILITANT

I was about to write at the top of this page: Ten Lost Years. When the war broke out, I was thirty-four; I had done a good deal of work since the end of my military service, and I could still count on a dozen years of intellectual enrichment and perhaps of originality. The six years from 1939 to 1945 had introduced me to other people, other events, another way of thinking and of living. Most professors leave their studies only to teach. It is an insulated universe, populated by children and young people, that carries the risk of fostering a kind of puerility. I saw politics in action at much closer range than most political scientists—and I am glad of it—but political analysis *in vivo,* far from fostering philosophical reflection, paralyzes it. The philosopher, confronting politicians and journalists, has the feeling that he will be ridiculed or that, like Plato's philosopher, he will tumble into the well.

In the last analysis, I myself chose the ten years during which I was a professional journalist, not a professor who wrote for the newspapers; I am even partly responsible for my failure at the Sorbonne in 1948, since I gave many of my future colleagues the impression that I was more attached to *Le Figaro* than to the Sorbonne and that, forced to give up one of them, I would

160

not give up journalism. Georges Davy interpreted in this way a statement I was supposed to have made when my candidacy was being considered; he repeated it to the professors' meeting, from malice or naïveté, and thus determined the outcome of a close vote.[1]

I remember my conversation with Le Senne, a typical representative of academic spiritualism, a courteous man of good will, not at all hostile to my political activity, or to *Le Figaro*. What you are doing, he told me, is honorable, necessary, and I don't hold it against you, but journalism is not, in my eyes, appropriate for a university professor. He must accept a modest existence, outside public tumult, that of an intellectual who finds in the exercise and transmission of thought, in the training of disciples, the meaning of his life and the fullness of his vocation: You no longer belong to our order.[2] He added, with complete frankness, that in spite of everything he would vote for me, because Georges Gurvitch, if only because of his imperfect French, was even less worthy of occupying the chair that Albert Bayet— who was also more of a journalist than a professor—had just left.

The *Figaro* that I joined in the spring of 1947, entirely different from the one I left in the spring of 1977, was Pierre Brisson's paper; under the Fourth Republic, it was perhaps not the most prestigious outside of France, but it certainly had the greatest influence on the political class. Pierre Brisson commanded an influence, I would even say a power, over politicians that Hubert Beuve-Méry never attained. The paradox is more apparent than real: *Le Monde* was, permanently, an opposition organ, hostile to the Atlantic Alliance and to German rearmament, typically in favor of European unification; it affected public opinion, particularly that of young people. More anti-American, at least in appearance, than anti-Soviet, it became the bible for an intelligentsia of the left that was comfortable with a critical attitude, without direct impact on events. Politicians in power resigned themselves to the judgments of *Sirius*,[3] to the decrees pronounced from on high by the incorruptible editor. Pierre Brisson, because he was in general agreement with the politics of the Fourth Republic, because he frequented ministers and deputies, inspired more fear. If necessary, he was the one who summoned ministers. It goes without saying that everything changed when General de Gaulle returned to power. *Le Figaro*, which had fought against the RPF, became the paper of the *Ancien Régime*. But Pierre Brisson deserves praise; he never regretted his reign; as a good Frenchman, he was as delighted as I that the country was finally decently governed, since he, too, was in the long run humiliated by the limitations of France which, at the time, appeared to be the sick man of Europe.

Struck by my articles in *Combat*, by analyses made in passing at lunch discussions (for example, I had told him, a few months in advance, that we had to get ready for a government without Communist participation), he put friendly pressure on me in the spring of 1947 and persuaded me to write a certain number of articles every month. While he was alive, I was paid by the article.

Pierre Brisson lived in and for his newspaper. He had not wanted to break with the owner, Mme Cotnaréanu, President Coty's first wife, who had received shares in *Le Figaro* as part of her divorce settlement. While recognizing the owner's rights, he intended to run the paper with complete freedom. His formula ("in agreement with capital, but independent of it") was rejected by Mme Cotnaréanu, or rather by her brother-in-law who directed the Coty firm in the United States; she demanded full exercise of her rights as owner, in other words, the right to oversee the administration and even the political orientation of the paper. Pierre Brisson rejected these demands, relying on the fact that the authorization to publish had been granted to him personally and to his group, not to the company *Le Figaro*. A law, known as the Brisson law, enacted by the National Assembly, was concerned exclusively with *Le Figaro*, and granted to those who had obtained the authorization to publish the right to use the title. In 1947, the conflict was still going on. It was not resolved until 1949, by means of a compromise that was valid for twenty years, whose terms had been worked out by Marcel Bleustein.

A holding company, the capital of which was held by the friends of Pierre Brisson, had the rights to the title *Le Figaro;* Jean Prouvost obtained half of the capital of the *Figaro* company; Pierre Brisson, with 2.5 percent of the capital, presided over the two boards. It was an unusual arrangement, more vulnerable than that of *Le Monde,* but it was not likely to create problems as long as two conditions were met: the prosperity of the paper and the presence of Pierre Brisson. Less than twenty years later, Brisson died. Twenty-five years later, the other condition no longer seemed to have been met.

Before the war, *Le Figaro,* a small-circulation paper (about 80,000) with an illustrious and scandalous past,[4] was edited by Lucien Romier and Pierre Brisson. A Vichy minister in 1943, the former died before the end of the war; the latter discontinued the paper after the German occupation of the free zone and went underground. Thanks to the disappearance of prewar papers, the worldly and academic *Le Figaro* became, in a few months, the national morning newspaper. Pierre Brisson was justifiably proud of this extraordinary success. He fully exercised his powers as editor; there were many rumors about his style of management: a dictator presiding over friendly anarchy, or despotism tempered by the anarchy of the staff. He possessed unquestionable and unquestioned authority; he took advice from André Siegfried, he held discussions with François Mauriac; the journalists recognized him as one of their own.

A Parisian through and through, he belonged to a France of the past. He spoke no language other than French, and he had no knowledge of foreign countries. His education and his publications, which were strictly literary, had not prepared him to shape the editorial policy of a national newspaper with an international vocation in a period of revolutionary transformations. From pure good luck, he adopted some positions that, in retrospect, appear correct and sensible, even though a large fraction of the intelligentsia and a number of men who were much more conversant than he with national politics criticized them harshly: anticommunism, reconciliation with Germany, the Atlantic Alliance, European unification. Of course, he sometimes pushed his anticommunism so far as to publish some rather absurd documents. After the Assembly defeated the European Defense Community, he wrote an editorial of incredible violence ("I am ashamed").

When Brisson died in 1965, *Le Figaro* was already in decline. The proportion of income derived from advertising had reached 85 percent, which created a certain vulnerability. The number of readers was declining; the press-run figures concealed this decline to some extent because of free subscriptions and distribution in hotels. Above all, the paper had not renewed itself. It still had about a hundred thousand subscribers; the paper's old readership, held by society announcements and traditional academic reportage, generally remained faithful, but dead subscribers were not all replaced. The bourgeoisie of the 1960s, with its postwar education, read *Le Figaro* on occasion, but did not find in it everything it was looking for. *Le Monde* had gradually taken the place of *Le Figaro* as a symbol of intellectual, if not social, status.

Like most of those who like their work to the point of being unable to imagine it without them, Brisson had not prepared for his succession. When he informed Jean Prouvost of his intention to appoint Louis Gabriel-Robinet as second in command, he added that the man he worked with every day should rise no higher. Wladimir d'Ormesson wrote to me later that Brisson thought I would be most qualified to take over *Le Figaro* if he were to die. But he had never told me, nor had he told his son Jean-François. In any event, I do not think I would have accepted the job; however, if he had told me what he had confided to Wladimir d'Ormesson, the situation would have been entirely different. One of the reasons that dissuaded me from any ambition in 1965 was the predictable resistance of the paper's management (except for Jean-François Brisson) and of a fraction of the staff. The resistance would at least have been reduced to silence if Brisson had explicitly designated me as his successor.

In 1947, three "great bylines" dominated the paper: François Mauriac, André Siegfried, André François-Poncet. With the first, there was no question of boundaries; nor was there with André Siegfried, who did not willingly discuss current economic problems—inflation, prices, wages—which would demand references to a theory or a scheme. He had probably not read Keynes; trained as a geographer, he described countries and their landscapes, analyzed their rises and declines, and explained the British crisis of the twentieth century or the great depression as a sociologist or an ethnographer, without using the tools of economic theory. François-Poncet wished, understandably, to maintain a monopoly over coverage of international relations. I did not agree to be excluded from this area. This rivalry disappeared: François-Poncet took the place of General Koenig in Germany (head of occupation authorities, and then ambassador to the Federal Republic).

In 1947 or 1948, I joined the RPF, to the great surprise, even the dismay, of those who remembered "L'ombre des Bonaparte" and the remarks, probably even more vigorous, that I had made in London. I had denounced a possible danger, and I forgot it when it became present? What explains this parenthesis of militancy in the midst of the thirty-seven years from 1945 to 1982, years spent not as a pure observer but in any event as an observer not engaged in any party? At the same time, Manès Sperber attacked me for joining a movement that seemed to him hardly democratic in its style and its aims, despite its declarations of faith.

The aberration has usually been explained by my friendship with André Malraux. He himself thought this was true. He was not entirely mistaken, but I do not think he reached the essential points, the memories and regrets of London on the one hand, and the impotence of the Fourth Republic on the other.

It should be clearly understood that I did not renounce my refusal to subscribe to the Gaullist legend of legitimacy acquired on 18 June 1940 and preserved in the exile of Colombey. I did not regret that, as late as November 1942, I had not rejected the possibility of the Vichy government going to Algiers—a step that would at least have attenuated the violence of the postwar purges. On the other hand, once the Allies had landed in North Africa and the inadequacies of General Giraud had been made clear, it was both inevitable and desirable that General de Gaulle assume the role of head of the provisional government. We thought that the General had no intention of withdrawing from politics, once France was liberated, and that he had conceived a Republic entirely different from the Third, and we were right. But, without joining the Gaullist movement, it was appropriate, by the end of 1943 at the latest, to see him as the unchallengeable and provisional custodian of the nation's destiny.

The Gaullism of 1946 or 1947 barely resembled that of 1941 or 1942. Aside from the General, who probably remained the same, the group surrounding the leader and the troops who followed him did remind me of the small band of the faithful, fixed in their devotion, who maintained the personality cult in 1940. At one of the few dinners to which he invited me in London, the General himself commented, without malice but also without complacency, on the poverty of Free France—not of the journal but of the French in London. He was not unaware of those whom I had christened the "upwardly mobile declassed." In Paris, the Gaullists were identified with the Resistance. André Malraux and Edouard Corniglion-Molinier had joined his "entourage," that mysterious entity, hateful by nature since the leader's sins fall on its shoulders, or rather emanate from it.

On several important points, I was not in agreement with the policies recommended by the General, in particular with his attitude toward Germany. I have a rather clear memory of the probably impassioned debate with Maurice Schumann in 1945 on the objectives of French diplomacy with respect to our former hereditary enemy. The Russians—for once I use this expression, because the General always used it—had amputated German territory in the east by annexing East Prussia themselves and giving Poland the territories east of the Oder-Neisse line. The French, to maintain the balance (what balance?) ought to do as much, detach the left bank of the Rhine (without annexing it), establish an administrative authority over the Ruhr that would control its production and maintain its opposition to Berlin,[5] and then, within the Western framework, to every institution that might suggest the reconstruction of a Reich. This accumulation of guarantees seemed to me slightly ridiculous, unacceptable to the Germans, and hence incompatible with the Franco-German reconciliation for which the General was arguing at the same time. Maurice Schumann defended the Gaullist positions with his usual fervor and eloquence. I did not have too much difficulty in convincing most of the audience, Etienne Gilson among them, that French ambitions would come up against a brutal veto of the English and the Americans. Troubled by the Soviet advance and the sovietization of the countries liberated by the Red Army, the Western victors would reconstruct a viable Germany, able to erect a barrier to the wave from the east. Maurice Schumann replied, in a categorical tone, that the Gaullists did not subordinate their plans or their activities to the approval of their allies. The debate was resolved not by eloquence but by the balance of forces. The General's attitude, exaggerated by the spokesman of France in arms, provoked acute crises with London over Syria and with Washington over Stuttgart and the Val d'Aoste.

In conformity with his philosophy, when the General returned to France, he placed foreign policy in the forefront. This primacy of diplomacy is not at all original; it had been erected into a dogma and a categorical imperative by the thinking of historians, particularly German historians, at the end of the last century. In a sense, I too would accept it, on the basis of the common-sense maxim *primum vivere*. The security of the nation, the independence of the state: Who would subordinate these fundamental requirements to any private or collective good? But when the primacy of diplomacy is expressed by really insignificant border adjustments, a great policy risks degenerating into petty squabbles over procedure. The immediate resumption of the Russian alliance, after the liberation of France, manifested for the first time a constant of Gaullist diplomacy or rather of the General's conception of the world. He did not see or did not want to see Europe as it had emerged from the storm, divided into two zones with opposed political cultures, and then into two military blocs; he almost always railed against the politics of blocs, just as the Soviets did. It is almost as though he did not know that the sovietization of Eastern Europe was equivalent to the formation of a Communist bloc, which implied, in reaction, the creation of a Western bloc. It should be added that at the time of the RPF, between 1948 and 1952, his antisovietism and anticommunism were more vigorous than those of the parties in power.

If the General had remained in power after 1946, would he have accepted the Anglo-American policies to which the leaders of the Fourth Republic, particularly Georges Bidault, consented (reluctantly)? The General would probably not have been able indefinitely to reject the establishment of the Bonn Republic. But I doubt that under his rule Jean Monnet would have had the opportunity to persuade the government and with its help to launch the coal and steel agreement and obtain the Assembly's vote in favor of the treaty of Rome. The French of today have forgotten that Jean Monnet and Robert Schuman prepared the way for Franco-German reconciliation through institutions that the General and the Gaullists fought against. Through these institutions, based on equality of rights, they broke not with the end— Franco-German reconciliation—but with the means of Gaullist policy. There was no longer any question of adopting the model of Russian policy and amputating the territory held by the West Germans. In 1958, the men of the Fourth Republic left a legacy of *faits accomplis* that the General could not reverse. He completed the Common Market, which he himself would probably not have begun. The ruse of reason was probably in our favor: the General would not have signed the treaties, the Fourth Republic would probably not have been able to apply them.

What drew me to the RPF was certainly not the General's German policy, but his rejection of the "regime of the parties" (or, more precisely, of the tendency of the restored democracy to fall into the practices that had drawn the Third Republic into the abyss). During the period immediately after the war, the establishment of proportional representation had fostered the success of the three major parties: Communists, Socialists, and MRP. In 1947, the tripartite agreement could not resist its internal tensions nor the repercussions on it of the conflicts between Soviets and Americans. The Communists soon became untouchables. Coalition governments resembled those of the Third Republic. Even a commentator deeply attached to democracy could not fail to measure the distance between the tasks of the state and the power held by government ministers, who were never certain of their future.

Of all the avatars of Gaullism, the RPF, by force of circumstances, was both the most parliamentary and the most resolutely anticommunist. It was General de Gaulle who coined the expression that Soviet troops were "two days' march from the Tour de France." He also presented himself as the man who was the most radically opposed to communism and to the Soviet Union, while in his eyes, the "third force," the parties in power, occupied the place that Vichy had between the collaborators and the resistance (an analysis that was certainly not valid).

What did my activity as a militant in the RPF consist of? In a hall in the fifth *arrondissement*, at a meeting presided over by Claude Mauriac, I gave a lecture on the international situation. A small group of *normaliens* had decided to prevent me from speaking. They succeeded without too much trouble; without a security service, a dozen boys, determined to interrupt the speaker in the midst of every sentence, can wear out anyone's patience. Claude Mauriac whispered to me: "Go on, go on." After forty-five minutes or an hour, the organization, with my agreement, gave in and closed the meeting.

André Malraux, director of party propaganda, reacted as he should have; he organized a larger meeting with a security service, which, it turned out, did not have the opportunity to intervene. Socialist and communist opponents let it be known in advance that they would not disrupt the meeting and I was recovering from a rather serious illness and, as I remember it, was not in my best form. The specific ideas of the RPF were not the inspiration of my talk; André Malraux was nevertheless satisfied with the victory: we had spoken again and demonstrated that we had the strength to enforce respect from our adversaries, to hold a meeting where and when we wished. But he sincerely regretted that the speech was hardly filled with strictly Gaullist ideas. I had emphasized my favorite themes—the union of the West or of Europe—rather than specifically Gaullist themes.

I was appointed by the General to the *Conseil national*, made up of various recurring personalities. At each session, the General presented a brilliant analysis of the national and international situation. It was at a meeting of the *Conseil national* in Vincennes in 1952 that the first split took place: a fraction of the RPF group in the Assembly had voted for Antoine Pinay, against the General's wishes. In any event, the split was obvious by the 1951 elections. Since those who were in opposition out of principle—Communists and Gaullists—did not together make up the majority, the parties of the Fourth Republic preserved their rule, forced to understand one another because of the threat of the two oppositions.

More curiously, at the national convention in Lille in 1949, I was asked to give the report on "association," a word the General used at the time for what was later called participation. The General sincerely believed in an intermediate formula between capitalism and socialism, between the jungle of unrestrained competition and tentacular bureaucracy, between private ownership of the means of production and nationalization of enterprises. Between these two regimes, he envisioned a third, which would put an end to class war without imposing on society the constraints of an all-powerful state. He knew the title, the source, and the aim of this regime, but he did not know the means of bringing it about. I did my best to concretize the idea of association, and I pointed to the possible directions: participation in management or profit. Thirty years ago, although less than now, there were already some more or less successful experiments of participation by workers in the organization of labor, by unions in the management of businesses, and by salaried employees in the profits.

I did my best, but I did not give my companions the feeling that I was a fellow communicant in their faith. I was criticized for my skepticism, with some injustice. What was meant by "believing in association"? Did it represent a doctrine comparable to socialism or to liberalism? Was it defined by gradual reforms or specific institutions? If association was to be a rival to socialism, I was indeed not among the believers. Once in power, in the course of eleven years, the Gaullists passed at most a few laws that fostered one or the other form of participation that we had envisaged at the time of RPF.

My second reservation had to do with the phase that the French economy was going through. This was in the late 1940s. Unlike many economists who were haunted by memories of the dark years and feared, at every point, the collapse of the French economy into stagnation, I leaned toward optimism. Despite inflation and governmental instability, reconstruction, supported by the Marshall Plan, was going well. But reconstruction—perhaps it should already be called growth—presupposed a high level of investment, hence a high level of reinvestment of business profits. Workers' participation in profits risked both reducing reinvestment and disappointing the beneficiaries.

Let us return to the RPF. In London, before Labarthe broke with the General, de Gaulle had invited me to dinner twice. I have two memories of our first meeting: the compliments he made for my articles in *La France libre*—compliments that could be called banal, but marked by a mixture of courtesy and seriousness probably characteristic of his approach to all his visitors—and during the course of the dinner, he improvised a brilliant analysis of the occupation regime in France: the *Wehrmacht* favored a traditional occupation respecting the rights of people; the Gestapo tortured; and there were more or less sincere partisans, like Abetz, of Franco-German cooperation. Together, these three groups determined the condition of the French, with the Gestapo increasing its influence as the Resistance developed.

At this dinner, or another, the conversation turned to the Vichy government. At the time, it was holding back from complete collaboration and attempting to obtain material improvements for the population without granting the enemy political advantages that would provoke strong reactions in Washington. Indirectly, I suggested that, given the situation in which they found themselves, the Marshal and his advisers could not act otherwise. The General grasped the meaning of my remarks and let me know that he did not accept that interpretation or that indulgence. That evening, or another, he said in passing, at the conclusion of his analysis, that the men of Vichy would follow collaboration to its conclusion. I made a common-sense objection: the fleet and North Africa were significant factors in world politics; at the same time they provided Vichy with its last weapons, its supreme arguments. Without them, the Marshal was at the mercy of the occupying forces. Why would he carry this out on his own? It was obvious, even in these informal conversations, that the General detested the role being played by Vichy as such, as though he wished that the situation were perfectly clear.

Another occasion was the night when the United States Department of State published the notorious communiqué which included the expression "the so-called free Frenchmen." The occasion was the liberation of Saint-Pierre and Miquelon by the ships under the command of Admiral Muselier. The General walked up and down in his living room angrily repeating, "They're wonderful, our allies." By his manner of addressing the United States, he, the embodiment of France, spontaneously raised himself to the level of the greatest power in the world. This dialogue of the General with himself remains fixed in my memory.

I saw the General several times during the RPF period; a narrative of these conversations, even if I were capable of reconstructing them, would add nothing to the writing that has been devoted to the "historic hero." When my wife and I were grieved late in 1950 by the death of our little daughter, who had been born in London in 1944, we received a letter of condolence from the General, the terms and especially the tone of which went beyond conventional formulas; I asked for an audience, and in the conversation I had with him a few days later, he spoke to me of his daughter Anne, "who had never been normal." He spoke with reserve, as though he were masking the feelings, the pain that attached him to the child, but at the same time he showed his sensitivity, or rather, his vulnerability. He was not offering me his compassion, but, by evoking his own ordeal, he brought himself closer to mine.

During the same year, 1950, the year of the Korean War, I spoke with him at length about international and domestic politics. "What are you going to do?" I asked him at one point. "What can I do?" he answered. "I have no troops, and if I did and I used them, you would not follow me." He commented on the retreat of the Eighth Army from northern Korea to the 38th parallel, and, on that occasion, evoked the retreat that General Eisenhower had ordered, which would have opened Strasbourg to Nazi reprisals had it been carried out. The Americans, he said, have a tendency to establish their distance much more than is necessary.

These details have only limited interest; they suggest the nature of my relations with the General during the RPF period. In 1953, I thought of being a candidate on an RPF slate in Paris; when Malraux raised the question among the leaders, the first places had long been promised to others. The General pointed out—and he was entirely right—that I had never breathed a word of my intentions to him—inclinations rather than intentions. I had trouble dealing with my life as a professional journalist and occasional teacher; at times, active politics seemed to me to be a way out, but in the jungle, mere inclination is harshly dealt with. One wants or does not want. If one dreams, one will dream for a long time. Fortunately, I soon gave up even dreaming.

I did not leave the RPF, it ceased to exist. At least I had the satisfaction of having given to it more than I had received. In 1953, while on vacation near Colombey-les-deux-Eglises, I rang at the gate of the general's property; since he was not there, I left my card and my address. A few days later, I received an invitation from him. My wife and I thus had the opportunity to enter the *Boisserie* and to learn its rituals: tea, then the General took me into his office, where he read me a passage from his *Memoirs*, the portrait of the Marshal. There followed a walk in the park. He alluded to a lecture I had given under his auspices; I remembered the remarks he had made after the lecture. In the course of the lecture, which dealt with the economic situation of France, I had formulated a rather banal idea: the French periodically make revolutions, never reforms. The General had appropriately corrected me: "The French only make reforms in the course of the revolution." And he recalled the reforms that had been carried out after the Liberation.

In 1959, when I wrote an article in *Preuves* entitled "Adieu au gaullisme," the General said to Malraux (I have been told): "He was never a Gaullist." He was right. I have never been a Gaullist like Malraux, attached to the General by a kind of feudal tie. Nor was I a Gaullist like Maurice Schumann, even though he had not followed the General during the RPF period. My relations with de Gaulle have always been ambiguous, even during the RPF years, for reasons that are both obscure and profound.

The intransigence that he boasts of in his *Memoirs* pushed him into war against Vichy and, at moments, to the brink of war with his allies. It was thanks to Churchill's support that he got from the English and Americans an occupation zone in Germany, which Stalin did not think France deserved; it was to Stalin that he showed the greatest courtesy after his return to France. Vichy set French public opinion against our allies; de Gaulle, too, in his way, set his companions against the English and the Americans. Except for the RPF period, General de Gaulle constantly engaged in diplomatic battles against the English and the Americans. In some of these battles, he was in fact defending French interests; but when he criticized the English and Americans for landing in North Africa, without contingents of the Free French, he was serving the interests of his legitimacy, not those of France; the experience of Syria had proved that Vichy troops and officers were more willing to join the allies than the General.

The visit to the *Boisserie* was my last conversation with the General. For reasons I myself have difficulty discerning, I had no further communication with him, even in writing, until 1958. Perhaps the loosening of my ties to Malraux unconsciously influenced my attitude toward the General. Perhaps, once the RPF was gone, I wished to step back after this incursion into partisan politics. I had returned to the University in 1955, and the last years of the Fourth Republic were troubled by the convulsions of decolonization. The Gaullist who was closest to me, aside from Malraux, Michel Debré, engaged in excessive polemics, not only against the Fourth Republic, but in favor of French Algeria. I did not confuse the General with those who proclaimed themselves his followers. I did not dare to ask him for an audience.

Some of my dearest friends prefer to forget my years in the RPF, a temporary deviation in an otherwise straight career. Others attempt to forget my attitude toward the events of May 1968. In both cases, I cannot bring myself to confess guilt without at least defending myself.

Was the General wrong to create the RPF? On his return to France, he came up against the parties whose reconstruction he had fostered during the Resistance. The first elections showed a shift to the left, as is customary after a war. The Communist and Socialist parties, despite hesitation on the part of the latter, opposed the General's constitutional ideas. For himself and for France, he wanted a strong president, cornerstone of the Republic. Perhaps he would have governed the country if he had accepted the role of prime minister, but, even though he was perfectly capable of winning out over his rivals in parliamentary contests, he did not for an instant consider joining in these games, poisons and enchantments of the regime of the parties. He embodied France, he ought not to squander his capital of public confidence by lowering himself to the level of head of a party.

The resignation of 1946 was never, in the General's mind, a farewell to politics or an admission of defeat. He believed that the parties, incapable of governing the country, paralyzed by their disputes, would turn to him, as they had called Raymond Poincaré to the rescue in 1926 and Gaston Doumergue in 1934. It was a calculation that was soon belied by events. But the General, as a good strategist, had two irons in the fire. By retiring on his own initiative, he set himself apart from party disputes, he remained a national figure of last resort, he preserved his legitimacy, exiled but not proscribed. What should he do? At the age of fifty-five, at the height of his powers, should he live in Colombey-les-deux-Eglises with no activity but the composition of his *Memoirs*? Or else should he speak and write as an elder statesman, offer his advice to the governors of the country, with no concern for himself or his own fortunes? In Colombey, he champed at the bit; since the parties stubbornly refused to turn to him, he would move toward them, not to correct their faults but to aggravate them and, by the same token, shorten the inevitable agony of the Fourth Republic.

If he were to descend into the political arena, as a party leader like Léon Blum, Maurice Thorez, or Georges Bidault, he risked losing his aura of charismatic leader. Aware of the danger, he called his party *Rassemblement* and gave it a national mission—revision of the Constitution. If he had remained in power rather than leaving it, he would have undertaken this battle in more favorable circumstances. The first draft Constitution had been rejected without the General having broken his silence. The second was approved despite the condemnation proclaimed by the Liberator, but with a very slim majority: no votes and deliberate abstentions together made up a majority. The General launched the *Rassemblement* while tension between the Soviets and the West, and, domestically, between the communists and the other parties was at its height.

Did General de Gaulle betray himself in 1948, when he attempted to create a situation in which the parties would give way before him and agree to reform the institutions of government? What he allowed his "unconditional" supporters to do ten years later seemed to me much more shocking. In 1947, there was no plot, there were no arms: the *Rassemblement* criticized a Constitution that no one was defending and a parliamentary practice that was making the country look ridiculous, with a clear purpose: to obtain enough seats in the Assembly to force the parties into a compromise. This procedure would have been less humiliating for the Republic than the capitulation of the National Assembly in 1958, in the face of the sedition of the armed forces and the threat of the praetorian guard.

As far as I am concerned, even in the 1930s, I have always defended a liberal regime against communism and against right-wing revolutionary movements, but I have suffered, like every patriot, from the decadence of the Republic and of France throughout the dark years. I was not contradicting my permanent convictions by associating myself with an attempt at calculated revision. When revision took place in the heat of the moment, I could hardly either approve or oppose: those who brought the General to power, the majority of whom were devoted to the preservation of French Algeria, had effectively excluded me because I was arguing for the Algerians' right to independence. To be sure, I had been told that the General, in private, supported me against Soustelle. But at that point, any inclination to take part in political activity had definitively evaporated. All things considered, I am not ashamed to have been a "militant" in the RPF, nor am I proud of it.

A militant in the RPF from 1948 to 1952, I was also, before and after, a militant for European unity and the European Community. Public meetings, conferences, study groups, were all too numerous during the cold war and in subsequent years for me to recall all of them.

It was also during my years as a journalist and a militant that I had the opportunity to leave France, not only to visit frequently the other countries of the European Community, but also to cross the Atlantic more than once, and also to spend a few weeks in Japan and India. Nevertheless, I should say that I was an armchair columnist.

To tell the truth, I took pleasure in these quasi-political activities, not without an occasional feeling of futility. Perhaps that feeling is stronger now than it was in the late 1940s and early 1950s. In the years after the war, up to the death of Stalin, we were engaged in a real battle in which the hearts and minds of men were at stake.

Today, these activities as a militant bring to mind the Congress for Cultural Freedom; I cannot avoid discussing its role, its influence, and finally the scandal associated with it. We thought that the Congress was funded by American foundations. In an investigation of the CIA, the *New York Times* named it as one of the organizations financed by the notorious Agency, for which the foundations were only a screen. From that point on, I distanced myself from the Congress, which, under a different name, and with subsidies from the Ford Foundation, survived for a few years.

Two questions arise for us—Denis de Rougemont, Manès Sperber, Pierre Emmanuel, and all the others who worked in some way within the framework of the Congress—should we have known or at least guessed? If we had known the origin of the money, would we have refused any collaboration? To the first question I am inclined to answer that we lacked curiosity, that many signs should have alerted us. But financing by the foundations was plausible and, in any event, when I participated in conferences or wrote articles for *Preuves*, I said or wrote what I thought. I was not paid by the Congress, it gave me the opportunity to defend and illustrate ideas which, at the time, needed defenders.

The second question remains: Would we have tolerated financing from the CIA if we had known? Probably not, even though, in the last analysis, this refusal would have been unreasonable: I wrote a number of articles for *Preuves*; I expressed myself there with the same freedom as in any other journal. *Encounter*, created by the Congress, remains the principal, the best monthly journal in English. Neither one of these journals would have prospered if they had appeared as instruments of the secret services of the United States. The Congress could accomplish its task—and it did accomplish it—only through camouflage or even, if you like, through lying by omission. This lie continues to weigh on my memories of the Congress, even though I have fond memories of conferences in Rhodes, Rheinfelden, and, much later, when the Congress had changed its name and was no longer receiving anything from the CIA, in Venice.[6]

Today, curiously, intellectuals who had nothing to do with the Congress refer to it without hostility, and sometimes explicitly approve it, while finding in that history a pretext for opposing an analogous organization recently created by Midge Decter, wife of the editor of *Commentary*, Norman Podhoretz. I accepted, with some hesitation, the honorary presidency of that organization[7]—the Committee for the Free World—which came into existence in an entirely different context. In 1950, when the Congress was born in Berlin, it was necessary to organize intellectual, much more than armed, resistance against the Soviet Union. In 1982, in France at least, the established intelligentsia and the best known figures of the younger generation are tempted neither by Sovietism nor even by the progressivism of the fellow travelers of thirty, twenty, or even ten years ago. To be sure, Marxism, or a vaguely Marxist vision of the world, in France, continues its dominance in the minds of the majority of primary and secondary school teachers. Most, or at least the most activist, of the junior faculty in the universities have not renounced more or less Marxist convictions. Whoever has lived through the twenty years after the war can measure the distance that has been traveled.

We can leave the task of evaluating the Congress to others. I do not regret having participated in it, because it had a far from negligible influence on European intellectuals. As for me, I particularly remember a few people. Michael Josselson, of Estonian origin, was the creator of the Congress, the intermediary between the CIA and the intellectuals. He deceived us, we might say, and he would have acknowledged it if we had had serious discussions with him. He probably would have added: How could I do otherwise? I still hold him in great respect. He believed in what he was doing. He lived from it as well, but his exceptional intelligence would have enabled him to find another position. He was something more and something other than an agent of the secret services. An intellectual gifted with a capacity for action, he bears responsibility both for the success of the Congress and for the original lie. When he retired, he began writing a book on one of the Russian generals who fought against Napoleon during the Russian campaign, Barclay de Tolly. He died a few years ago from a heart complaint from which he had long suffered.

Through the Congress I met George F. Kennan on a number of occasions. In another chapter, I present our dialogue after the Reith Lectures. I met him for the first time in Princeton in 1950, at a conference on France organized by E. Mead Earle. We always had personal relations that were both excellent and superficial. Unless I am completely mistaken, he valued my intellectual vitality, my taste for controversy, and also my skill in facilitating dialogue among people from various backgrounds. I spent several days with him at Rheinfelden, and I appreciated his courtesy, his knowledge, and his total lack of vanity or pretentiousness. Reserved almost to the point of being cold, a profound moralist, an "elitist" perhaps without knowing it, he was less and less fond of an America that was becoming more and more populist. His evolution, from the article he signed as X to his current positions, can probably be explained by his growing detachment from his own country. His article in *Foreign Affairs* had a lasting effect on the diplomacy of the United States and established the bases of the doctrine of "containment." Since then he has constantly repented his "finest hour," expiated his historical role. In 1978, I wrote a critique of Kennan's latest manner;[8] I have not yet had the opportunity to discuss it with him.

Robert Oppenheimer also participated in some meetings, for example at the Berlin Conference in 1960 for the tenth anniversary of the creation of the Congress. He created a strong impression by the contrast between the purity of his blue eyes and the nervous tension in all his gestures and his statements. Devoured by an internal flame or by the battles he was fighting with himself, he tended to take any episode of his existence not seriously but tragically. I can see him in his room, with his wife, discussing the latest conference presentations with me, as though he were disturbed by their possible banality. I did not get past the first phase of friendship with him either. Unlike Kennan, he established distance not by his rigor but by the personal divisions that he allowed one to glimpse. Father of the atomic bomb, against the creation of the H-Bomb, challenged because of his past and his imprudences, he carried a burden that even a less sensitive man would have had difficulty bearing.

Of all the major intellectuals I met through the Congress, Michael Polanyi remains in the front rank of my admiration and affection. He had a strange career: leaving the "hard" sciences of physics and chemistry at the highest level, destined for a Nobel prize, he decided one day to give up his research and to have his university change his appointment. He became a philosopher. The world had more need of wisdom than of knowledge. Man needed self-knowledge more than the accumulation of more information. He wrote books on freedom in economics and in scientific research. Above all he wrote a beautiful book, a great book: *Personal Knowledge*, admired by a few, unknown or misunderstood by most. His theory of knowledge, which implicitly contained a philosophy, perhaps even a religious conviction, was on the periphery of all the Anglo-American schools of the time, logical or analytical. His representation of the levels of reality, his antireductionism, the meaning he attributed to personal commitment in the acceptance of a truth, all led the reader, between the lines, toward belief—belief in the spirit, perhaps the Holy Spirit. Isaiah Berlin made an ironic comment on Polanyi's history. These Hungarians are strange, he said, here is a great scientist giving up the Nobel to write mediocre works of philosophy. Assuming that the philosophy is indeed mediocre—which remains to be shown— this judgment leaves out one dimension, which is perhaps the essential, the personal dimension. Michael Polanyi left scientific research in order to fulfil himself the better and to serve other people.

An English writer, in a book on the fellow travelers, outlines a comparison between the Congress for Cultural Freedom and the organizations of intellectuals created and manipulated by the Communist Party.[9] On both sides, prestigious personalities were appointed president, Jaspers on the one hand, Joliot-Curie, or, before the war, André Gide on the other, committed writers or scientists and party militants. Formal resemblances conceal radical differences. The Congress never systematically defended American diplomacy or American society. In Milan in 1955, a controversy arose among us between those who emphasized and almost exalted Soviet economic success and those who questioned the triumphal statistics. We wrote in *Preuves* as we did in other journals. We shared one thing, the rejection of communism. But pluralist anticommunism, which included social democrats at one extreme and conservatives at the other, was different in kind from the pro-Soviet stance of organizations of intellectuals that were condemned to dress up the truth (to use an understatement).

In my career as a journalist on *Le Figaro*, compared to American columnists,[10] I traveled relatively little even during the ten years that I was a professional journalist. Did my travels (apart from my frequent visits to the United States) give very much help to the "armchair analyst"? I am not sure. In essence, I have no information beyond that of my readers, what all of us find in news reports. Hence, everything depends on knowledge of the context in which an event takes place. It goes without saying that the analysis of domestic and international politics in a daily newspaper does not have as its goal the prediction of the course of events, even in the very short term. It ought to clarify events by including them in a larger context: explain an American decision by the views of Washington leaders, by the various pressures and constraints to which they are subject, or else explain the Soviet intervention in Czechoslovakia by the Soviet system, the world view and the code of conduct of the men in the Kremlin. Nietzsche's prophecy— great wars will be fought in the twentieth century for control of the world in the name of rival philosophies—has been confirmed before our eyes in the course of the last half century. Analysts of world politics, and French states-men in particular, were mistaken in the 1930s because they stubbornly persisted in seeing Europe at the center of the universe, considering the Third Reich as a not very unusual variant of the Wilhelmine Empire, and not believing that the Soviet Union was different in nature from Czarist Russia. Journalists of today learn, in journalism schools, skills, tricks, techniques, that anyone can learn in a few months in the field. On the other hand, these schools do not teach the essential: the history and culture of peoples, the theory and practice of Lenin and Stalin, the functioning of the American Constitution. If the reading of the paper is the morning prayer of modern man, in the words of Hegel, then the journalist is invested with a *weltgeschichtlich*[11] task, at a lower level. He must place the event within the planetary network and thereby express its meaning and its consequences.

While I was becoming deeply engaged in journalism, with a bad con-science, Golo Mann reminded me that Max Weber had challenged his academic colleagues to deflate their pretensions: he had reminded, or per-haps informed, them that they would not all be ready to replace, at a moment's notice, editorialists or mere commentators. The contempt of the professor as professor for the journalist as journalist seems to me, in fact, unjustified if not ridiculous. The learned are not all intelligent; even profes-sional economists do not always succeed in analyzing a situation or express-ing a thesis in a few pages. One who can do more can not always do less. Of course, an examination paper for the *agrégation* of philosophy requires more culture than an editorial in *Le Monde* or *Le Figaro*, but an *agrégé* does not always make a good editorialist. The fact remains that the average journalist usually feels that university professors look down on him, even though he may sometimes adopt an attitude of superiority toward them. When I said to Lazareff one day that, disgusted by the politics of the Fourth Republic, I wanted to return to the University, he looked at me as though I were about to commit suicide and murmured: "Oh, no, don't do that."

Before the war, Roger Martin du Gard, who was well disposed toward me, suggested that I had the necessary qualities for a political journalist. I replied that philosophy was worth more than journalism. He did not insist, but thinking of the mediocre or obscure condition of professor, he probably preferred, for me and Suzanne, another place in society.

Of course, once I was in that place, like everyone else—perhaps a bit more—I was ambitious for the highest distinction. I did not achieve it at *Combat* or *Le Figaro* because it belonged, in theory and practice, to Albert Camus or François Mauriac, each of whom was endowed with a literary talent that I did not have and which, moreover, did not fit easily with the rigors of economic or diplomatic analysis. Nevertheless, I was not starved for satisfactions of my vanity. I might even say that the temptations of the profession include, in part, the immediate praise that an article might receive well beyond what it deserves, while a book, more often than not, makes its struggling way among countless competitors.

The superficial pleasures of the profession, after a few years, made me anxious, bitter. It may be that I progressed from the time I joined *Le Figaro* in 1947 up to my departure in 1977. It may also be true that my passion gradually dimmed and that experience stifled my imagination. In my view, the profession of journalism is compromised by the possibility of excelling immediately and the difficulty of improving, by contrast with the profession of writer or scholar. Of course, the journalist, too, is forced to renew himself, whether he will or no, not to let himself be caught short by the course of events, not to hold fast to a representation of the world that, already, belongs to the past.

I have always lacked the taste for the new, characteristic of the journalist. I always admired in Lazareff, an incomparable editor, a talent, a way of being that are totally foreign to me. What is the good, except to create a sensation, to be eager to get the news a few hours before the others? If it is important, there will always be time to think about it; if it isn't, why get excited?

Was I suspected of looking down my nose at the professionals? Perhaps, but in this case, the suspicion was misplaced. How could I have generally despised those men and women—I am tempted to say those boys and girls, since they seemed to me to be, so to speak, young by profession? Among the newspaper staffs with which I am familiar, I have liked some, others not; some liked me, others not. When I was in charge of the very small economics staff of *Le Figaro*, the writers did not complain about our weekly meetings. With Roger Massip, who was responsible for foreign affairs, there was a daily risk of conflict: our collaboration was harmonious. Those on *Le Figaro* who liked me the least had, I believe, nothing to reproach me with but being what I was.

NOTES

1. I feel some hesitation in recounting episodes of university life. In fact, there were three candidates: Georges Gurvitch, Jean Stoetzel, and I; Stoetzel explained

that he was not a candidate against me, but he had the support of the head of the philosophy section, Jean Laporte. Votes for Stoetzel on the first round normally would have reverted to me. The remarks repeated by Davy probably shifted the few votes that assured the victory of Gurvitch.

2. I am certainly stylizing his remarks.

3. Pseudonym used by Beuve-Méry for major editorials. (Trans.)

4. The editor of the paper had been assassinated by Caillaux's wife in 1914. The paper had conducted a hateful campaign against her, with the publication of private letters. Mme Caillaux was acquitted.

5. The representatives of the four occupying powers met in Berlin. They attempted to create central administrations whose authority would extend through all four zones. The French representative vetoed all these attempts. Perhaps, in this case, he served the interests of the West as a whole.

6. The proceedings of the latter two were published. The last one, with the title, "History between Ethnology and Futurology," had not the slightest connection with political problems.

7. I now regret it.

8. *Commentaire,* no. 2 (Summer 1978).

9. David Caute, *The Fellow Travelers.*

10. Except for Walter Lippmann.

11. Placing him in contact with world history.

1 0

THE DIVISION
OF EUROPE

Immediately after the capitulation of the Third Reich I had come to a general view of the European, if not worldwide situation. I often surprised my interlocutors at *Point de vue* when I asserted that Germany would remain divided for a least a generation. Twenty years later I willingly made the same judgment. Moreover, the German danger, as the French had known it between 1870 and 1943, belonged to the past. As a state in the center, when the Reich held the principal place in Europe, it felt encircled and, at the same time, posed a threat to its neighbors to the east and the west. This was a genuine threat since there was no doubt that it could prevail easily over each of its neighbors taken separately. A protective alliance was imperative for France in order to counter German power. But, by the same token, the Franco-Russian alliance first, then the great alliance among the English, the Americans, and the Russians, encircled the Second and Third Reichs in turn with a ring of steel. Postwar Germany, with its eastern portion cut off, and a portion of its population subjected to a Soviet regime, no longer had resources superior to those of its Slavic neighbor—the Soviet Union, now in control of the countries that had in the past separated it from Germany; nor, as it had in 1940, did Germany outclass France or the Franco-British alliance; moreover, the Western alliance now included the United States. Germany as the backwater of the West no longer measured up to the giant of the New World.

For the short term, at least for twenty years, whether the French liked it or not, West Germany would necessarily belong to the same camp as France, the Western or democratic camp. The French and the Germans, inevitably, would experience or take on the same fate. The dictates of reason came up against strong emotions. During the war, had I written some articles that could be called anti-German, not merely anti-Hitler? There were not many of them, in any event. I also wrote articles, that may in retrospect seem ridiculous, which envisaged precautions against the "German danger" of the past. But, from the Liberation, or at least from the end of the war on, the division of Europe, the iron curtain, and the extension of Poland to the Oder-Neisse line once and for all rid me of the images of the past. The cunning of Reason offered me a second opportunity for the dream of my youth—Franco-German reconciliation—this time it could not fail. When I returned to Germany for the first time, in 1946, I hated the occupation regime, and I was ashamed of the "zone bombing," contrary to the laws of war, which had reduced entire cities to rubble without military effectiveness in proportion to the losses inflicted on the population.

In 1946, I delivered a lecture at the University of Frankfurt, surrounded by rubble, partly spared in the midst of an ill-nourished population. There I met Hans Mayer, who had not yet gone to the East (I met him again, a few years ago, after he had returned to the West). What struck me most were the looks of hatred directed toward me when, using the occupant's privilege, I went to the head of the line of Germans to get my railway ticket. A few years later, in Tunis, with the same spontaneity, I hated the colonial regime, although it was not one of the worst.

On the basis of this analysis, primitive but fundamental, I was systematically in favor of measures initiated by the English and Americans—creation of the dual zone, then the triple zone, the end of the policy of dismembering, the creation of the German Federal Republic, the rearmament of the Bonn republic, the equality of rights. Events developed as I had foreseen and wished for (with French resistance causing not too much difficulty). It is nevertheless legitimate to wonder whether I was right to encourage the developments, whether things could have happened differently.

Recall General de Gaulle's ideas in 1945–47: vetoes opposed by the French representative in Berlin to every measure leading to the creation of a single administration for the four zones, public declarations in 1947 condemning the decision made by the three great powers to create the triple zone and then the German Federal Republic. Even at that date, the General rejected the very idea of a Reich; he was in favor of a federation that would group the Länder together. He was wedded to a thesis of Bainville and Maurras, which, in the postwar situation, seemed to me anachronistic to say the least. The General reasoned, at least in appearance, as though Germany remained a possible source of trouble, while, quite obviously, that role had been taken on for an indefinite period by the Soviet Union.

The General's theories about Germany are clearly expressed in a press conference of 12 November 1947, held in response to a speech given by General Marshall, the secretary of state of the United States. The most important passages follow:

> European economic reconstruction is now the principal concern of those who wish to build the world in conditions that will allow it to survive and perhaps to live in peace. From this point of view, France cannot imagine that what used to be Germany will not enter into the economic cooperation in the process of being constructed. It is quite clear that France never wished to exclude, out of a spirit of vengeance, those who are German from the European economy. But that does not prevent France, after what has happened to it several times and which almost spelled its death, from feeling that it owes to itself and to others to make certain that Germany is never again a threat. The Germans must be reborn as men associated with mankind's common effort for its reconstruction, especially the common effort of the Europeans, but it must never again find the means to become once more a threat. In order to prevent this, France proposes a practical means, tested by history and corresponding to the nature of things: Germany must not again become the Reich, that is, a unified power, centralized around a strong force, and necessarily led into expansion by any means available. *We do not want a Reich.*

The General considered the two possibilities: agreement of the Allies on the reconstruction of *one* Germany, and the lack of agreement. But, in either case, rejection of the Reich remained the same overriding imperative: "If Germany must remain divided, West Germany must also be organized in that form." What did that form consist of? "The future of Germany, as we view it, is not the Reich, but a Germany reconstructed on the basis of the various German states. Moreover, we see no difficulty in a federation of those states in which each one would possess the rights that were in the past crushed by the Reich. This federation, with 'allied control to prevent egregious error,' particularly control over the Ruhr, and with particular provisions for the supply of coal, may very well be the future of Germany. France would have no difficulty in making economic treaties with the states of that federation; this is the very nature of things." Would the economic treaties be signed with the individual states or their federation? In any event, the General called on France not to "abandon the chips it held," in other words not to agree to the fusion of the three occupation zones, as long as the risk of a resurrection of the Reich persisted.

The General's conception obviously recalls that of Jacques Bainville and Action française, but the very notion of "no more Reich" remains ambiguous: if the German states established a federation among themselves, in what way would that federation differ from a Reich, which, despite the historical resonance of the word, implied nothing more, in 1946 or 1947, than the formation of a German state?

The General took the rejection of the Reich very seriously; as did André Malraux, who said to me from time to time: "They [the men of the Fourth Republic] want to let everything go." The General did not give up, as evidenced by the declaration he published on 9 June 1948 in response to the recommendations of the London Conference on the future of the Western occupation zones, in other words the formation of the tripartite zone, which, in the following year, became the Federal Republic of Germany.

The General correctly predicted that the Russians, in their own way, would also build a German state. But the rivalry between the two German states seemed to him full of mortal risks for peace and for France:

> A single question will dominate Germany and Europe: "which of the two Reichs will establish unity?" since it has been decided and proclaimed that "unity is the future of Germany." One can foresee the nationalistic competition that will thereby be set loose between Berlin and Frankfurt and the resulting international climate. If the disturbances that threaten to take place among Germans and among the great powers, as a result of rivalry between the two Reichs, do not soon lead to war, one can nevertheless anticipate which of the two German camps will be harsh and rigid enough domestically and supported enough from the outside to win the contest in the end. One may even imagine that, one day, German unity, once again organized by Prussia—but this time by a totalitarian Prussia, linked body and soul with Soviet Russia and the "popular" states of central Europe and the Balkans— would appeal to the lassitude, the insularity, or the illusions of the Anglo-Saxons as an "appeasement" solution.[1]

The Ruhr integrated with Germany, no guarantees of reparations, vague formulations about the duration of military occupation: "France would find itself in a permanently dangerous situation." And, a little further on: "We are on the edge of an abyss." After the indictment, came the objectives: "No more Reich! Because the Reich automatically constitutes a motive and a tool for Germany's instinctive drive toward power, *a fortiori*, when those instincts could be tempted to join with others." Once again, the General insisted, with even more forcefulness, on *several* German states, "each of which would have its institutions, its character, its sovereignty, able to federate among themselves and joining a European grouping in which they would find the framework and the resources for their development." The sovereignty of the German states and the notion of federation seem to be contradictory, in the ordinary sense of those words. In conclusion, the General recommended rejection of the London agreements and the resumption of negotiations.

I accepted neither the indictment nor the recommendations. Convinced that the separation between Western and Soviet Germany would last, I thought the demands about security with respect to an amputated and divided Germany anachronistic; considering West Germany alone, they seemed slightly ridiculous. As for the predictions of East Germany's inevitable victory over West Germany, I rejected them at the time, and events have until now belied them. When General de Gaulle returned to power in 1958, he had the intelligence to forget his notions that had been overtaken by events.

In 1949, the German Federal Republic was proclaimed, the Fundamental Law *(das Grundgesetz)* having finally been approved by the occupying authorities. In his declarations and speeches of 1949, General de Gaulle maintained his criticisms and his theses. However, discussion of the Atlantic Alliance eclipsed the question of the reconstitution of the Reich. In the United States, the most prestigious political commentator denounced American policy in Europe. Walter Lippmann rejected a policy based on the hypothesis of two Germanies, one Soviet, the other Western, and he asserted, with incredible self-assurance, that the Germans would never accept the division of their territory.

Reading Walter Lippmann's articles of the spring of 1949 thirty years later provides a lesson in prudence to those who accept the thankless task of reacting to events and immediately discerning their meaning, before their consequences become apparent.

Lippmann's persistent misinterpretation of the German situation remains almost unbelievable today. A visit to Germany would have been enough to dissipate some aberrations. In 1950, I delivered a speech to German students on the occasion of the chancellor's visit. I developed the argument that the division of Germany could not be separated from that of Europe itself and that the former would last as long as the latter. The next day, commenting generously on my speech, the *Frankfurter Allgemeine* criticized me for attributing to the West Germans an obsessive concern with their compatriots in the East. The defeat had been so total, the conditions of life remained so difficult, that the West Germans were more concerned with the reconstruction of their country than with reunification, which they considered for the moment out of the question. It may be that a number of Germans witnessed the establishment of a Republic in the shadow of the occupying armies with some skepticism. But none of them, or almost none of them, thought of secret conversations between the general secretary of the United Workers party of East Germany and Chancellor Adenauer, president of the Christian

Democratic party. It may be that the presence of a Rhinelander, not attuned to the Prussian tradition, at the head of the party facilitated the formation of the Federal Republic, where Catholics and Protestants were fairly equally represented. In any event, once the disagreement among the Four Powers over Germany was established, what could the English and Americans do, except what they did—construct a Western Germany? Now, thirty years later, that Germany remains loyal to the Atlantic Alliance and has not sacrificed its freedom to the hope of reunification, even though the Social Democrats, originally hostile to the establishment of the Federal Republic, are again touched by the temptation of the East.

I know French civil servants who had discussions with the Russians in 1945 and 1946 and who continue to believe that the break was not inevitable. Other historians insist on the responsibility of the French, who vetoed any measure that would have applied the principle, affirmed at Yalta and Potsdam, of a central administration in Berlin that would have overseen the four occupation zones. The French certainly made the Soviets' work easier; for the facts leave little doubt. The Soviets brought with them the German communists who were intended to govern the country; they immediately took steps to create *faits accomplis*. Two of these actions took on symbolic and political significance: the unification of the Socialist and Communist parties on the one hand, and the collectivization of agriculture on the other. The first step anticipated the disappearance of party pluralism, even if, by law and on paper, the noncommunist parties survived; the second inaugurated a Soviet-style social order. Nothing of the kind took place in the Soviet zone of Austria; this is why I always believed in Austrian reunification, never in German reunification.

In 1947, the French government resigned itself or adhered to English and American policy toward the Bonn Republic. In hindsight, it seems curious that the French decision was provoked by Stalin's refusal to accede to French demands on the Saar, namely, the attachment of the Saar mining basin to France (who is still interested in the Saar?). Perhaps Georges Bidault seized this opportunity to take France out of the impasse in which General de Gaulle had left it: in the end, France gained nothing by paralyzing the reconstruction of Germany, demanding precautionary or punitive measures that it had no chance of imposing.

The first great postwar debate took place over the North Atlantic Pact and neutrality. The two questions were connected but not identical. Rejection of the North Atlantic pact did not imply neutrality. The debate on neutrality (or neutralism) took place, with some confusion, between Etienne Gilson and *Le Figaro* (myself included), between Hubert Beuve-Méry and Pierre Brisson.

The survivors of the postwar years remember the "Gilson affair," only certain aspects of which I was aware of, and in which I was involved against my will. Let us begin with the texts. Gilson published several articles in *Le Monde*, three of which I would like to consider: on 25 December 1948, "A Just People"; on 2 March 1949, "The Alternative"; and on 6 March 1949, "The Ambiguity." In the first, he vigorously attacked the American press for the way in which it dealt with France. Americans tend to cover their opportunistic decisions with moralistic arguments. Thus, on China, "It is all the more curious to see newspapers and magazines now carrying out a moral execution of China and proving that it is proper to leave these barbarians to fight with other barbarians. It is not enough that it be a lost cause, they insist that it is a bad cause. They are not content with saying, as it would be so simple to do, that the situation can no longer be saved, they struggle to prove that it does not deserve to be saved, especially if, as it happens, they feel some responsibility for the situation." Analogous commentaries would have been pertinent during the last phase of the Vietnam War.

Gilson detected in the American press the first signs of an "abandonment" of this kind, of France or of Europe. "They might abandon us because we are unusable, but, since they are beginning to prove to us that we are guilty, this is a certain sign that they are preparing to abandon us." In conclusion, the philosopher himself expressed French resentment: "In 1914 and 1939, we were in the front lines. We are even corrupt enough not to wish for a repetition of the blow of 1939; if there must be an American world war tomorrow, the front lines can be neither French, nor English, even less German. It is the Americans' turn."

The resentments and the conclusion are perfectly understandable, but the United States benefit from a geography that they owe to nature, not to cunning or egoism. Nor do they bear responsibility for the 1914 war; the Europeans themselves launched the war whose outcome was determined by American intervention, even though they were neither morally nor politically obliged to participate in it. Should we criticize them for arriving too late or remember that, without them, we would have lost the war? In 1939, Hitler did not threaten the United States as he threatened France and Great Britain. There was no "coup of 1939." In 1949, the question arose in the same way: did the Soviet threat affect primarily the Europeans or the United States?

The second article had to do with the Atlantic Pact itself, and it clearly expressed the objection used by all the adversaries of the treaty: the United States honors its commitments but does not go beyond them. The formulations used in the treaty, vague enough to be accepted by the United States Senate, would have no value, either in themselves, or for the Soviets: "When the dangerously naïve Mr. Vandenberg asserted that the simple formal recognition of a 'community of interests in the event of an armed attack against the Atlantic community' would be an invaluable deterrent to war, he was deluding himself if he believed that the Russians would understand as well as we do the meaning of that article."

This led to his conclusion: "Our only choice is between a commitment, not moral but military, of the United States, with all the explanations required; or else, if the United States refuses to fight in Europe, which is its right, our refusal to sacrifice ourselves for the United States, which is our commitment." A year after the signing of the pact, the moral commitment had been transformed into a military commitment through the creation of NATO. In any event, Gilson's expression—"the United States is buying our blood with dollars"—seemed exorbitant to me. Rightly or wrongly, Europe felt threatened by the Soviet Union; it was Europe that asked for American protection. Would it have been enough to sever ties with the United States to assure our security?

The third article returned to the precise content of the treaty. The Senate did not wish the United States to be forced by the treaty to reply militarily to a military aggression in the North Atlantic region. Gilson took up the central idea that appeared almost everywhere in the writings and statements of statesmen and commentators: we do not want a third invasion of the West, "in comparison to which the two earlier ones would seem like picnics."

In 1949, this article by Gilson stimulated one of those great debates of which the French are still so fond. I tried to provide a rational basis for my own opinions in an article in *Liberté de l'esprit*, which the Gaullist editors hesitated to publish and which the General approved at least in part.

Did I, with this article, help to persuade General de Gaulle to not take a position against the Atlantic Pact? It may be, if we believe Claude Mauriac's narrative in *Un autre de Gaulle, Journal 1944–1954*.

On 17 March 1949, Claude Mauriac spoke to the General about "the article that Raymond Aron has sent me for the issue on the Atlantic Pact: I explained its essential points in a few words, fearing that it was opposed to his policy and that of the RPF. It consisted of a rather violent critique of the two articles by Etienne Gilson that accused the Americans of wanting to buy French blood with dollars. He criticized the Atlantic Pact for giving the French no guarantees about the timing and location of American intervention in the event of a Russian invasion of Western Europe."

"But Gilson is obviously right," exclaimed the General. "You have to understand that America is an essentially isolationist country, simply because it is an island. It has never felt in solidarity with Europe, from which, I must admit, it is separated by a great expanse of water. In the war of 1914, as in that of 1940, the Americans did not intervene because Paris was threatened. And if London had been occupied in 1940, America would certainly have deplored that fact, as it would if Paris had been occupied by the Soviet army, but it would not have made war to liberate London or Paris. It would choose its time, after due deliberation. Similarly, in the Atlantic Pact, the Americans have been careful not to say where and when their armies would intervene. The reality is that, with the weapons that now exist, the Americans think they don't have to trouble themselves, that they can make war with relative ease, without leaving home, with their Flying Fortresses, their rockets, and so on. If Paris and France were occupied by the Soviets, they would find it very regrettable, but that in itself would not justify American intervention."

A few days later, Claude Mauriac was convinced that the General was going to raise strenuous objections to the "timing of the publication of this text in *Liberté de l'esprit* in its current form."

> I was thus surprised by the words with which the General greeted me:
> "Well, it's not bad at all, that article."
> The truth is that the General seemed to have radically changed his conception of the Atlantic Pact in the course of a few days.
> When he told me that he was going to explain what it was all about, I thought that he had probably forgotten that he had expressed his point of view at length, and that I was about to hear essentially the same speech. But this is not at all what happened.
> "It is certain, and Raymond Aron was right to emphasize this point, that this pact, even in the absence of a precise commitment, is likely to make Stalin think. I am not saying that it is now certain that he will not intervene, but at least he now knows that if he occupies Western Europe, he will have war. We can be convinced that if such a pact had existed in 1939, Hitler would probably not have undertaken the Polish adventure. Obviously, it would have been better if Aron had insisted on the fact that a strong France would further lessen the chances of war. It's in the interest of Queuille and his government to have us believe that the pact in its current form takes care of everything. Nevertheless, this pact is better than none at all, and Raymond Aron was quite right to attack the weakness of Gilson's argument."

At the end of the conversation, the General concluded: "You now know what I think of the question. You are free, of course, to publish or not to publish the article, but I didn't want Raymond Aron to think that I disapproved of his position."

The General did not want to appear to me to be a censor. He did not want my article to be rejected because it did not agree with his position. But it should be added that his first tirade against the Atlantic Pact and American isolationism was so far removed from reality that the General would probably not have maintained such foolish positions if his interlocutor had offered common sense objections. In any event, he accepted the Atlantic Pact while criticizing the terms of the treaty. Ten years later, he had an entirely different opinion.

The debate seemed legitimate to me, and as Beuve-Méry said in a lecture in 1951, men who are in essence close to one another can differ about the best means to attain their common ends. "As for the anticommunists, they tend to approve the pact for the simple reason that the communists condemn it. It is thus fortunate that a Catholic philosopher, with a powerful article, has opened the real debate. I do not agree with M. Gilson on any point, and I consider some of his expressions to be senseless. Nevertheless, I am glad that, in the midst of this conspiracy of silence, a writer had the courage to express publicly his anxieties and his doubts."

One of Gilson's principal objections, as I have noted, had to do with the terms of the treaty. He did not consider them precise enough, imposing obligations on the United States that were clearly enough defined. (General de Gaulle had formulated similar criticisms.) My response was to call into question the importance of an exact definition of the obligations of the signatories. As long as American troops were stationed in Germany, the guarantee would depend more on that fact than on the texts. The Atlantic Pact would not change the behavior of the Americans or the Soviets:

> As for me, I think that the North Atlantic Treaty will not materially change the factual situation. Western Europe will be protected by American force tomorrow as it is today. The Atlantic Pact will teach Stalin nothing that he does not already know, namely that military aggression in Europe would, most probably, be a *casus belli*. The more precise the terms in which the commitment to mutual assistance is expressed, the more automatic the intervention implied, the more it will impress the realists in the Kremlin; we are quite willing to make this concession to Gilson's argument, but this is not the essential point, and it cannot be set out in the text of the agreement. The American presence, symbolized by a few regiments in Germany, and the industrial and atomic power in the distance are for now the guarantee of French security. This security will be maintained in the future to the extent to which the American presence continues in place and, on the other side of the Atlantic, as long as its potential strength remains superior to that of the potential aggressor.

Nevertheless I recognized the fact that the Atlantic Pact did not guarantee protection against invasion in case of war. What other policy would give us such a guarantee? Gilson invoked armed neutrality; but Western Europe was not armed, and would be even less capable of arming itself if it rejected the aid of the United States. It did not provoke the anger or the hostility of the Soviet Union because it allied itself with the United States through the Atlantic Pact. It displeased the Kremlin because the eastern countries, sovietized by the Red Army, looked to the West.

The debate over the Atlantic Pact took an entirely different tack, and a different tone, after June 1950, with the outbreak of the Korean War. It may be that the Pact would in any event have brought about the rearmament of Western Germany; the hot war in Asia, at the least, shortened the time between the reconstruction and the rearmament of the former enemy. The diplomatic debate was broadened, taking in the worldwide policies of the United States and the relations between Asia and Europe.

Even before President Truman's decision was known, I took a position in favor of United States military intervention in Korea, even in favor of immediate intervention. Aside from the Communists, no one in France severely criticized the American intervention, at least at the beginning.[2] What relaunched the debate on neutrality, or gave it a new bitterness, was the American demand for European rearmament and, as a consequence, the fear of American "warmongering" once that rearmament had guaranteed them unchallengeable superiority. The opponents of the Atlantic Pact who one day criticized the text for not imposing clear obligations on the United States, the next day expressed the fear of being drawn by American impetuosity into a war that did not concern them.

Until 25 June 1950, the phrase I had used as the title for the first chapter of *Le Grand Schisme,* "Impossible Peace, Improbable War," remained the governing idea of my commentaries. After 25 June, for a few months—as I noted in my next book, *The Century of Total War*—I was afraid that war had become less improbable (I evaluated the improbability differently from day to day, according to my mood). Unlike some American commentators, I never interpreted the Korean episode as the first stage in a global plan of conquest conceived in common by Stalin and Mao. The American response refuted one of the arguments of the opponents of the Atlantic Pact: in Korea, the Americans were honoring their commitments beyond the promises set out in white and black. The military reversals of the Americans during the first weeks, and again in November after the intervention of the Chinese "volunteers," contributed to defeatism and occasional panic in Europe.

The argument in favor of American rearmament compelled support from all the French, except for the Communists. In 1950, the United States had only a very few atomic bombs, and experience suggested that a nuclear threat was not enough to deter aggression on the part of a small Communist state closely connected to Moscow. After the science fiction that described peace through terror and the disappearance of large armies, history once again surprised its actors. Five years after the end of the great war, American GIs were fighting, thousands of miles from home, against the army of a half-country armed by their former ally. The leaders in Washington derived a valuable lesson from the event: they had been living in an illusion. A few atomic bombs and American industrial power were not enough to safeguard peace throughout the world. The United States was discovering its imperial role and the obligations of that role. They had to give up their tradition: a minimum of military forces in times of peace, an effort of total mobilization once war had broken out. Warlike peace, international obligations, in part inherited from the British Empire, condemned the American Republic to maintain a permanent, substantial military apparatus.

The question of European rearmament provoked different controversies. Shouldn't economic recovery of the European countries take priority? Massive rearmament would paralyze reconstruction; symbolic rearmament would not affect the outcome of a possible war. Some critics adopted the thesis of Senator Taft; instead of a treaty of mutual assistance, the United States would declare a unilateral guarantee of European security. Thus, under American protection, the Europeans would carry out their recovery before giving themselves the means of defense. Taft's argument, supported by some opponents of the Atlantic Pact, lost all support after June 1950: in the light of the Korean campaign, the principal objection to the pact—the United States might eventually liberate us but would not spare us from occupation—told even more heavily against Taft's solution.

Just as the European governments had taken the initiative for the Atlantic Pact or, at least, had asked Washington for a treaty of that kind, they wished for, as much as the Americans, the creation of NATO, that is, the organization of the North Atlantic Treaty, including the unified command. The question of European rearmament was on the agenda, and, as a necessary consequence, so was that of the rearmament of the Federal Republic of Germany.

In the autumn of 1950, Dean Acheson launched the project of German rearmament at a time when American troops were fighting hard against the North Korean army, supplied by the Soviet Union. Confronted with this imperative, the French leaders, René Pleven and Robert Schuman, made ingenious attempts to avoid a yes or no response. They correctly determined that French public opinion would not accept the reestablishment of a *Wehrmacht* that had been defeated five years earlier by overwhelming coalitions. On the other hand, they hesitated to reject a measure that corresponded to the logic of the situation, and not to a whim of the American leaders. The proposal of a European army, greeted at first with suspicion in Washington, was adopted by most Western diplomats, so that John Foster Dulles, in 1954, threatened France with a "drastic revision" if the National Assembly refused to ratify the European Defense Community treaty that had already been ratified by our allies' parliaments.

On 22 November 1952, I warned my friends in the "European party." I considered German rearmament inevitable, but the method that had been chosen was open to obvious criticisms. In the absence of a European government, that army would obey non-European, in fact American, commanders.

How could France simultaneously maintain divisions subject to European command and divisions for overseas under the exclusive responsibility of the French state? Through its excessive precautions against the reconstitution of a German army, could the European Defense Community ever succeed in uniting itself into a coherent body capable of fighting?

In private conversations, I was blunter. Quite obviously, German rearmament, imposed by the diplomatic context, could take place in a European or an Atlantic framework. To my American friends, I repeated that, instead of committing themselves without reservation to the European Defense Community, they should state openly that it was up to the Europeans themselves to choose between the European Defense Community and the integration of the German army into NATO. The first solution was most likely to be rejected by the coalition of opponents to a supranational Europe and opponents of German rearmament. The second would perhaps also be rejected if it were presented to the National Assembly before the first; it would be accepted out of resignation if the European Defense Community had first been rejected by the deputies.

Strict believers in Europe were surprised by my coldness; one of them told me that my positions were finally unpredictable. General de Gaulle's indictment of the European Defense Community on 25 February 1953 could not fail to impress both citizens and deputies: "In order for there to be a European army, first of all Europe has to exist as a political, economic, financial, administrative, and above all moral entity, and that entity has to be vital, established, and recognized enough to secure the instinctive loyalty of its subjects, to have its own politics, and, should the occasion arise, to have millions of men willing to die for it. No serious man would dare answer yes." And General de Gaulle recalled everything he had accomplished during the last war thanks to the authority the government had maintained over the armed forces: "Koenig would not have been at Bir-Hakeim, Juin would not have played his role in Italy, Leclerc would not have captured Le Fezzan and would not have been launched toward Paris at the right moment, de Lattre would not have defended Alsace or crossed the Rhine and the Danube, Larminat would not have eliminated the pockets of resistance on the Atlantic, Doyen would not have taken control of Tende and Le Brigue, the expeditionary force would never have left for Indochina. . . ."

The debate on the European Defense Community continued for more than two years between the time the text of the treaty was made public and the National Assembly vote that dismissed any consideration of the project. In response to the pathetic appeal of Edouard Herriot, who was partially paralyzed, a majority voted to cut off discussion. The European Defense Community was buried before its proponents had the opportunity to argue their case.

What remains of this debate of the 1950s that can be of interest to the French of the 1980s? The discussion, apart from the problem of the European army, focused on the "German danger," in the long run if not in the immediate. The same argument recurred in various forms: unlike the other states of Western Europe, the German Federal Republic is still a "demanding" state, not satisfied or fulfilled: it wishes both for unity and to recover the territories east of the Oder-Neisse annexed by Poland. In the course of the campaign against the European Defense Community, Jacques Soustelle discovered and emphasized the Polish origins of Breslau, a city that had been Germanized for centuries and had again become Wroclaw after 1945.

A rapprochement between the Federal Republic and Moscow in the national interest of the Germans was not an immediate danger in 1953, but it had some plausibility in the long term. From where but Moscow could the Bonn leaders hope for an improvement in relations between the two German states? The opponents of the European Defense Community presented the argument in its most unlikely form: a new Rapallo agreement, or a new German-Soviet pact, a new division of Poland. To this I responded that the sovietization of one-third of the Germans, in the GDR, assured Moscow both protection against an invader from the west, and an invaluable base for aggression against the West. Unless the Kremlin was forced to, it was no more likely to surrender Pankow than Bonn was to give up its freedom. Some historians think that immediately after Stalin's death, Beria and other members of the Politburo entertained the idea of a unified and neutralized Germany. In 1982, without deserting the Atlantic alliance, West Germany is cautious about displeasing the Soviets who hold millions of hostages in their hands. We should add that the 1955 rearmament had no influence on either side on the diplomacy of Bonn and Moscow.

The argument over the Atlantic Pact and the rearmament of Europe, including the Federal Republic, came to an end in 1954–55 while the Indochina war and the North African troubles were in the spotlight. Pierre Mendès France must be given the credit for succeeding in negotiating the Geneva agreements in the shadow of Dien Bien Phu and, after the rejection of the European Defense Community, in setting in motion the alternative solution.

I have reviewed the articles I published in *Le Figaro* during the months of the PMF government, to confirm or refute the legend that I had bitterly criticized him. In fact, on the essential points, I supported him. Pierre Brisson took up his pen to praise Mendès France's spectacular journey to Tunis, which led to internal autonomy. I myself consistently supported the "liberal" policy adopted toward the North African protectorates. When the Geneva agreements were signed, my article was entitled "A Successful Wager," and I congratulated PMF for the results he had obtained. The provisions of the agreement, because of the military and political situation, could not have been better.[3] Moreover, on 28 October 1954, I asserted that PMF's responsibility for the rejection of the European Defense Community was limited, and I approved the steps taken by the government to secure the Assembly's approval of the alternative solution, that is, the formation of a German army within the framework of NATO.

My reservations or criticisms had to do with the thirty-day wager (either the Geneva agreement would be concluded within thirty days, or he would return to the Assembly either to resign or to send conscripts to Indochina). This wager, without which PMF might not have been voted into power by the Assembly, involved obvious dangers: the existence of the French government thenceforth depended on the North Vietnamese, or rather the Soviets and the Chinese. If PMF won his bet, he would become suspect in the eyes of the Atlantic or European party: the Soviets would have assured his success so that he could defeat the European Defense Community. The fact is that, especially after the rejection of the European Defense Community, he lost the confidence of Adenauer, the "Monnetists," and the MRP. I also criticized him at the time for holding aloof from the scheduled debate in the Assembly on the European Defense Community. This was a rather unjust criticism that I soon rectified by writing on 3 September 1954: "The European Defense Community was moribund when PMF became Prime Minister; he could probably have saved it if he had been determined to do so." Today I am not sure that he could have saved it even if he had wanted to. But the attacks of the "Europeans" against him, when he tried to extract further amendments from the other five European powers, ruined the final chances. The most resolute supporters of Mendès France were among the opponents of the European Defense Community and even of German rearmament. He could not be asked to fight without reservation for a treaty that, at bottom, he probably did not approve. Another criticism I addressed to him was his promotion of relations with Great Britain at the expense of relations with the Federal Republic.

The article entitled "L'Echec des rassemblements," published after PMF's fall, certainly demonstrates no hostility either to the man or the statesman: "PMF has served the country: he brought about the armistice in Indochina that the entire nation wished for, he took the initiative in negotiations with the Neo-Destour—a courageous initiative that cannot be reversed and that indicates the only way forward. But on subjects that have as much influence on our future as Africa—relations with the East, European policy—it is not clear that he had definite positions beforehand, and after his government, it is impossible to determine his basic intentions." I never paid such homage to any other premier of the Fourth Republic. I proceeded to explain that he had been the victim of emotionally charged political propaganda: "The entire opposition had rallied around him—some wanting peace in Indochina, others reforms in North Africa, others negotiations with Moscow, others the dissolution of European integration, still others more government and more authority. There is no reasonable connection among all these desires. An Atlanticist has not more reason than a neutralist to be in favor of deposing the former Sultan of Morocco." After having presented PMF as a victim of his disparate majority, I concluded that "it would be unfortunate if he had no further opportunity to demonstrate the exceptional gifts that no one can deny." PMF had no further opportunity, but this was his fault, not that of his opponents. He never accepted General de Gaulle's return to power through a quasi–coup d'état, and he never accepted the Constitution of the Fifth Republic. *Le Figaro* had nothing to do with it; nor did I.

In 1955, the development begun in 1948 with the Marshall Plan or in 1949 with the North Atlantic Treaty, had reached fruition: one Germany, again sovereign and armed, belonged to NATO, while on the other side, in accordance with the Warsaw Pact, official unity had been organized among the armies of the Eastern European countries under the political and military direction of the Soviet Union. Twenty-seven years later, the two blocs still confront one another. Have we let opportunities slip by? Was the policy that I supported as best I could the only, the best one possible?

Even today, I find it hard to believe that the failure of the European Defense Community was a historical turning point, a European abdication, consent to American protection for an indefinite period. I am less certain about the crystallization of the two military blocs in Europe. I would like, first, to refer to a discussion organized by the Congress for Cultural Freedom in January 1958, with the participation, according to George Kennan's memoirs, of Denis Healey, Joseph Alsop, Sidney Hook, Richard Löwenthal, Carlo Schmid, Denis de Rougemont, and me. I remember this roundtable discussion, but I rely on Kennan's version, since he certainly had access to the transcript of the session.

Kennan had delivered the prestigious Reith Lectures at the BBC. He had argued a heretical position, the withdrawal of American troops from Germany on the condition of a similar withdrawal from Eastern Europe by Soviet troops. The simultaneous disengagement of Americans and Soviets was the heart of these discussions. The central argument was accompanied with other, equally questionable, propositions: the Europeans would not attempt to give themselves a military apparatus comparable to that of the Soviet Union; they would prepare for resistance and guerrilla warfare, which would deter the Soviets from any inclination toward aggression.

According to Kennan's summary in his *Memoirs,* I raised two principal objections. The situation, I said, is indeed abnormal or absurd, but clearly delimited: everyone knows where the demarcation line is. When something shifts on the other side of the iron curtain, nothing happens on our side. A clear division in Europe is considered, rightly or wrongly, as less dangerous than any other arrangement. In other words, an equivocal situation would create more dangers than this abnormal situation.

Kennan, who was at the time still in the diplomatic service, deplored the hypocrisy of the statesmen in Bonn and Washington, who claimed to have the goal of German unification while they in fact accepted the status quo. Even today, Kennan's indignation astonishes me. Western statesmen had no means to force the Soviets to allow free elections in the GDR. Simultaneously, they considered it neither useful nor necessary to accept, legally or politically, the status quo, that is, the presence of Soviet troops 250 kilometers from the Rhine. They rejected in principle the division of Germany and Europe, realizing that this rejection helped to maintain it. A few years later, when General de Gaulle attempted to break with this static policy, I wrote that the status quo would be destabilized once it was recognized. The consequences of the *Ostpolitik* and the Helsinki agreements confirm this analysis. The Germans, and Chancellor Schmidt, have turned their eyes to the east ever since the territorial status of Europe that came out of the war has been solemnly accepted.

In the discussion with Kennan, I merely said that it was a question of choosing among risks—the risks of division and the risks of a policy that would tend to overcome the current division. I added that my evaluation of the risks left me "for once, by chance and with great regret, on the side of the statesmen" and against Kennan.

The second objection had to do with the extent of the withdrawal of Soviet troops, and counterpart to the withdrawal of American troops. It seemed obvious to me, after the experience of the Hungarian Revolution in 1956, that Soviet troops would not hesitate to return to the socialist countries they would have left, if the regime that followed their ideology was in danger. "I was not impressed by this argument against my lectures," writes Kennan, "because, personally, I would not have considered a disengagement agreement acceptable if it did not give assurances against such events, together with the sanctions they would have implied; but I must now, in retrospect, give Aron credit for a very remarkable prophetic insight, for, in presenting his argument, he presented, ten years before the fact, a classic formulation of the Brezhnev Doctrine, publicly confirmed by Brezhnev himself under the pressure of the tensions of the Czech crisis of 1968. The Russians, said Aron, have formulated a new doctrine, which I would call a Holy Alliance. It consists of the right to provide 'disinterested help' to any communist government threatened by 'counter-revolution.'" My 1958 statements do not deserve all the praise that Kennan bestowed on them. After the experience of

Hungary, there was no need of prophetic insight to foresee that the Kremlin would occupy a "socialist" county, even if it had earlier been evacuated, if a revolt, by definition counterrevolutionary, risked bringing down or desovietizing the regime. What strikes me is Kennan's confidence in a Russo-American disengagement agreement. The agreement would never be officially violated, since there would always be a "worker-peasant government" which would call upon its Warsaw Pact allies for help.

Nevertheless, the Reith Lectures, reread today, still pose a question concerning American policy as a whole from 1949 to 1955—a policy that was moreover inspired at the outset by the Europeans themselves. From the Atlantic Alliance, one moved logically to the organization of European defense, then to the rearmament of the German Federal Republic, and finally to the crystallization of the two military blocs and the preservation of the division of Germany, and Europe. Was another policy possible, and when had an irreversible choice been made?

If we return to 1949, when the North Atlantic Treaty was signed, it then appeared that Western Europe, made up of conquered or exhausted states, was a void. The Soviet Union as well had suffered enormous losses during the war; it could not in reason take the risk of a major war against the United States, the only belligerent that had come out of the conflict not only intact but strengthened. At the time, these ways of thinking, convincing in themselves, did not dissolve all doubts. The Soviets had imposed their authority and their regime on all the countries of Eastern Europe; if they met no resistance, why would they stop? Might not a unilateral guarantee granted to Western Europe by a solemn declaration ratified by Congress have been enough to reassure the Europeans and deter any Soviet aggression? This is a *post hoc* objection that carries little conviction. If we return to the articles by Etienne Gilson and General de Gaulle's speeches, it is evident that the obligations of the signatories of the North Atlantic Treaty, particularly of the United States, were not clearly enough set out in the text. What would the critics of the pact have said if a solemn declaration had taken the place of the treaty?

We might add to these speculations about the past a common-sense remark that has too often been forgotten: the policy of the Marshall Plan and the Atlantic Pact was a striking success for the Western Europeans. Even France, despite its colonial wars, participated in the spectacular recovery of the old continent. It might be said that this policy sacrificed the Eastern Europeans and abandoned them to their fate. The passivity of the West in the face of the Hungarian revolution of 1956 is not attributable to the Atlantic Pact, but to the refusal of the American leadership to intervene. The Franco-British Suez expedition, launched at the very moment when the Hungarians were offering the first example of an antitotalitarian revolution, did not make the task of American diplomacy any easier. But in all probability the Americans would not have behaved differently if the French and English had not launched their mad enterprise. By 1956, despite the verbiage about "rollback" instead of "containment," the leaders of the United States had no intention of using military means to support dissidents or rebels in revolt against a Soviet regime in Eastern Europe. As at the end of the wars of religion, the political map coincided with the ideological map: east of a demarcation line, Marxism-Leninism reigned; to the west, the democratic-liberal idea held sway.

I have chosen 1955 as a turning point because it saw the establishment of the two military coalitions; I could have chosen 1956: the Hungarian revolt and the Franco-British expedition, with each of the superpowers bringing its allies back into line. The Hungarians lost all hope of liberating themselves by force, Great Britain any illusion of still figuring among the great powers.

More than a quarter-century later, does the West regret the decisions made between 1949 and 1955 that shaped the world in which we are still living? If they remember the "thirty glorious" years, the years of unprecedented economic expansion, why would they accuse themselves of having been blind? Thirty years of success justify political decisions. The state of the Atlantic Alliance and of the West, a quarter century after the crystallization of the two military blocs in Europe, does not condemn the work of the founders, Truman, Acheson, Eisenhower, and on the other side of the Atlantic, Jean Monnet, Robert Schuman, Adenauer, de Gasperi.

One may criticize the Americans for having done nothing to "liberate" Eastern Europe when they had obvious military superiority, but at the time the Europeans feared the aggressivity, not the passivity, of their protector. In the end, the events that are now fostering pessimism have nothing to do with the choices made during the cold war. Neither the Vietnam War, nor Watergate, nor the rise of the Soviet Union, nor the decline in the American defense effort, were implied in the Marshall Plan, the North Atlantic Treaty, or the rearmament of the German Federal Republic.

NOTES

1. Declaration of 9 June 1948.

2. However, Dean Acheson was criticized for having encouraged the aggression by not mentioning South Korea among the American positions in Asia that would be defended.

3. In his *Memoirs*, Khrushchev asserts that he was pleasantly surprised by PMF's proposals. He had not hoped for so much. I do not find this version of events convincing.

1 1

THE WARS OF THE
TWENTIETH CENTURY

Despite my choice of journalism in 1944–45, I had not given up teaching: some courses at the ENA and the Institute of Political Studies, lectures in foreign universities, namely Manchester and Tübingen, were evidence of nostalgic regrets. During this decade of exile or diversion, I tried not to lose contact with philosophical and sociological publications. But events, as well as my profession, engaged my passions. The reconstruction of France and Europe, in the midst of propaganda struggles, occupied most of my attention. Thus, I did not succeed in establishing a sharp distinction between my articles for *Le Figaro* on the one hand and my "scientific" works on the other; I took the path of least resistance. I wrote two books, *Le Grand Schisme* and *The Century of Total War,* an attempt at a kind of immediate philosophy of history in the making intended to serve as a framework and a basis for my daily or weekly commentaries and for the positions I took.

I cannot reread (or rather skim) these books without disagreeable feelings. I wonder why I let myself be drawn into this kind of writing, which was less common than it is today. If *Le Grand Schisme,* published in 1948, had some success in intellectual and political circles, this was because it provided a general outline both of the world political map and of the map of French politics. One critic, Roger Caillois, wrote that *Le Grand Schisme* contained three books, or the elements of three books: one on the world rivalry between the two superpowers, a second on the degradation of Marxism into Sovietism, and a third on the crisis of French democracy. In a sense, the structure of the work itself carried a lesson: the situation of French politics was explained in the light of the diplomatic situation and the ideological schism. I wanted to explain to the French, who had been separated from the outside world for four years, that their country belonged to a larger whole, Western Europe, which in turn belonged to what André Malraux called Atlantic civilization: a participation in world history different in nature from the role of great power that France had played in the European concert but one that did not reduce our diplomacy to negligible proportions. Europe could no more do without France than without Germany or, more precisely, it could not do without both countries, restored and reconciled.

The expression "impossible peace, improbable war," became fashionable; it remains true even though many Western statesmen often fail to grasp its meaning; or rather, influenced by "détente," they misunderstand its lasting truth. I risk quoting myself: "The European concert no longer exists, there is only a world concert" (p. 14); "The extension of the political scene has changed the scale of power. A nation that is significant in the European context is small in the perspective of the world" (p. 15); "Germany, even if one assumes that, within a few years, it will rise from its ruins and reestablish its unity, is already located in an inferior class." I thus established a reasoned basis for the policy of reconciliation with Germany for which I argued in my articles.

In a diplomatic field extended throughout the world, diplomacy becomes total: "The traditional notion of peace implied a limitation of diplomacy in two senses: limitation of what was at stake in conflicts between countries, and limitation of the means used when the cannons fell silent. Now everything is called into question, economic organization, political system, spiritual convictions, the survival or disappearance of a ruling class. Without a shot being fired, a country risks, through the triumph of its communist party, experiencing the ordeal of defeat. . . . The real frontiers are now those, in the heart of a formerly united people, that separate the American party from the Russian party. The electoral map has become identical with the strategic map" (p. 19). A simplistic description of a situation that was already more complex thirty years ago, but it retains a partial truth: it is within nations, not always by formal votes, that the struggle between communism and its enemies takes place. And this struggle has spread throughout the world, even though some regions of the world seem to have become stabilized (Europe, for example), even though conflicts between states and within countries are not all connected to the rivalry between the superpowers. In Europe in 1947–48, the duel between the two superpowers seemed to absorb all the others.

The "impossible peace" is not connected only to total diplomacy: "With or without International, with or without Cominform, the communist parties represent a permanent conspiracy, designed to open the way to Russo-Soviet imperialism. Unlimited aims and permanent war: with these two characteristics, Moscow's imperialism defines itself as essentially Soviet, not Russian. As long as the Russian people is confined in the prison of lies and the NKVD, as long as it suffers the constraints and privations of a besieged outpost, the cold war will perhaps go through ups and downs, but it will offer no hope for peace."

In contrast, or in addition, I noted: "The absence of peace is not war. A source of energy, previously unknown or unused, normally inaugurates an epoch in military art, and thereby in civilization as a whole. But between testing and perfection of a new weapon, time passes. . . . No one knows whether the atomic bomb is, or when it will become, the absolute weapon, the weapon which, by itself, will force an enemy to surrender. This explains the present balance, whose precariousness does not mean that it will not last" (p. 29).

Was Stalin another Hitler? "The National Socialist idea had to die with its founder, the communist idea preceded the man who was for the moment the most powerful if not the most well-founded of its interpreters, and it will survive him. Stalin's imperialism is no less grandiose than that of Hitler, it is less impatient" (p. 33).

In the preface to *Le Grand Schisme* I wrote: "This book presents neither a theory of the wars of the twentieth century, nor of totalitarian regimes, nor of parliamentary democracies, nor of capitalist evolution." I added that I hoped to develop these theories elsewhere with more rigor. I did in fact attempt this a few years later; *The Century of Total War,* published in 1951, contained a sketch of the theories I mentioned in 1948.

The first two parts, entitled "From Sarajevo to Hiroshima" and "Crossroads of History," point toward a philosophical interpretation, in the style of Auguste Comte and Cournot, of the first fifty years of the twentieth century. How did the 1914 war, which began like so many other European wars, become "hyperbolic," to use the term of Gugliemo Ferrero? The "technical surprise" caught civil and military leaders unaware. Modern society, at the time bourgeois and liberal, mobilized totally under state direction in order to provide, for many years, millions of soldiers with weapons and ammunition. From 1914 to 1918, Europe gradually discovered total war; and the war of materiel. After their failure on the Marne, the

Germans held fast to their positions. The trenches and the balance of forces prolonged a merciless struggle; under a deluge of steel, men died by the thousands for a few kilometers or a few hundred meters.

The Second World War grew through an entirely different process. Hitler's initial victories provoked worldwide expansion of the conflict. In 1918, assault tanks had contributed to Allied victories. In 1945, the atomic bomb provoked Japanese surrender. Different in their development and in their strategic and tactical style, the two wars of the twentieth century both led to extremities, the crushing of the conquered and, through their combined effect, a new world map.

The First World War, compared by Toynbee and Thibaudet to the Peloponnesian War, shattered the structure of the Republic of European States. The Second put a definitive end to the predominance of Europe. Nations on the periphery acceded to the first rank. One of them relies on a nineteenth-century ideology developed by a German intellectual from a family of converts from Judaism. The other remains faithful to the philosophy of the Enlightenment, in its Anglo-American variant. The Soviet Union and the United States both lay claim to the European legacy. Conflict is inevitable between the two states who together won victory over the corpse of the nations of Europe, while simultaneously the development of a weapon of mass destruction has profoundly changed the essence of war and relations among states.

The other parts of the book dealt with the present and prospects for the future. I attempted to analyze what was going to happen, following a method modeled on the one that I used to explain the first half of the century. The attempt was ambitious and almost unrealizable. In looking at the past, I had distinguished, insofar as possible, between necessity and accident. Turned toward the future, the same distinction led to a number of uncertainties. The principal question was whether the cold war was preparation, or a substitute, for total war. I inclined toward the latter idea, which has until now been confirmed. Unfortunately, I was not satisfied with analyzing the conventions of the cold war, the West's defensive strategy; I devoted more than a hundred pages to Europe, its chances of recovery, of creating a common defense, and of achieving unity. And my analysis made excessive use of ambiguity and disappointed readers because of my insistence on the uncertainty of the future.

Finally I added a few chapters at the end of the book, one of which ("Totalitarianism") was appreciated by Hannah Arendt and perhaps inspired by her; they made the book substantially longer. These chapters, under the general title of "The Stakes," gave the impression that the book was an ill-assorted collection of essays that presented no clear order or coherence.

In the United States, *Les Guerres en chaîne** achieved a certain popular, not only critical, success. To my great surprise, I learned in the fall of 1980 that a publisher wanted to reprint the book with the title *The Century of Total War,* perhaps more topical than the French title.

The theory that was sketched out on our thirty years war was opposed to the Leninist theory formulated in *Imperialism, the Final Stage of Capitalism*. But this opposition was neither the center nor the aim of the first part: "From Sarajevo to Hiroshima." I attempted to illustrate, with reference to a particular case, ideas that I had developed in *Introduction to the Philosophy of History* on the question of historical determinism. The very movement of the analysis gradually brought out the refutation of Leninism. The two wars of the twentieth century were marked by the nature of the societies that conducted them, and the wars in turn changed those societies, but neither the deep cause, nor the pretext, nor what was at stake in these wars lies in economic rivalry among the principal capitalist countries.

In both parts of the book, I pointed out the accidental character of events as they came to pass, at particular dates, in particular forms, and with particular details. At the same time, I distinguished the "profound causes" or the "global phenomena" that made probable, not inevitable, at a date not determined in advance, events comparable to those that did in fact take place. "Diplomatic failure": the unleashing of the First World War, which none of the principal actors consciously or directly wished for; "technical surprise": the continuation of hostilities that military leaders on both sides thought would last for a few months. The temporary superiority of defense over offense, fixed fronts, and the mobilization of industry and the entire population made possible the hyperbolic war from which came revolution and the exhaustion of all the European peoples.

If one chooses to think of the two wars as elements of a single whole, as episodes in a single struggle, one should not refer only to "eternal Germany" but to the tragic linkage of causes and effects and to the dynamism of violence. All "monist" theories, those that accuse the German nation and those that incriminate capitalism, are puerile. In the domain of history, they are comparable to the mythologies that stood in the place of the physical sciences at the time when mankind was incapable of understanding the mechanisms of natural forces. This is history in the full sense of the term, whose guiding forces are set forth in retrospect, without having the right to assert that the actual outcome was foreseeable in advance, implied by the *forces majeures* of our time. A local conflict, through the operation of balance of power diplomacy, was transformed into a European war, which in

---

*Published in the United States and Great Britain as *The Century of Total War* (Garden City, N.Y.: Doubleday, 1954).

turn, because of industry, democracy, and the relative equality of the forces engaged, developed into a hyperbolic war; and this in turn ended by wearing out the weakest link in the European chain. The Revolution erupted in Russia, the thrones of Europe and the last multinational empires collapsed. Bordered by a Bolshevik Russia, the Europe of bourgeois democracies and independent nations attempted to return to the pre-1914 world, which it persisted in seeing as normal. The 1929 crisis destroyed the currency and economic orders that had been laboriously reestablished. Unemployment opened the floodgates, and a revolutionary movement stirred the German masses to frenzy. From that point on, afflicted by conflicts among three ideologies as well as traditional power rivalries, Europe slid rapidly toward catastrophe. Begun in 1939 with the German-Soviet alliance and the division of Poland, this time the war spread throughout the world, reviving and broadening the war that had raged in China since 1931 or 1937. When the conflagration was extinguished after six years, the land had been devastated in Europe and Asia. Here and there, the two real winners, when the noise of the first atomic bomb had barely ceased, girded their loins in preparation for the final confrontation. This history is so clear that, in hindsight, it is surprising that we did not recognize it earlier. Rather, we must today resist a retrospective illusion of fatality. In the course of those thirty years, there were moments when destiny was, so to speak, at stake, when entirely different lines of development were possible. A few regiments would have changed the outcome of the battle of the Marne. A decisive German victory in the west would probably have shortened the duration of the war, regardless of Russian or British policy after the fall of France. Europe would once again have avoided the possibilities of hyperbolic war, as it had in 1870–71.

Even more clearly, a compromise peace achieved before the Russian Revolution would have evidenced foresight of two kinds: the Germans would have recognized that, supported only by Austria-Hungary, they could not militarily conquer the rest of Europe; and the Allies would have recognized that they could not force Germany to surrender. Nor was the drift from the First to the Second World War inevitable. To reach that point, what was required was an almost unbelievable combination of stupidity and bad luck. Lost in the preceding century, the British evoked the shade of Napoleon because Poincaré belligerently defended the interests of France and demonstrated indifference to the economic consequences of sanctions. French diplomacy was both formalistic and brutal toward the Weimar Republic, while generosity and reconstruction in common of divided Europe would perhaps have been fruitful. It was weak and resigned in the face of a Germany that would have understood only force and the determination to use it. After Hitler's rise to power, there were still opportunities to overcome fate. In March 1936, a military response to the entry of German troops into the Rhineland would at least have slowed the development of events, perhaps even provoking Hitler's fall. It is possible, though doubtful, that Franco-British resistance in 1938 would have persuaded the anti-Hitler conspirators (who included some military chiefs) to take action. During the war, the English and Americans could have maintained or resumed contact with the opposition to Hitler, tried to conquer Germany without destroying it, not pushed the war to the point at which the annihilation of the loser made a contest between the Allies inevitable. To spare an enemy when one is not sure of an ally has always been the lesson of an honorable Machiavellian tradition.

In the same style, I outlined the conjunction of historical series (an expression I borrowed from Cournot), which led to *Le Carrefour de l'histoire:* "The present constellation is located at the point of convergence of three series. The first is leading to world unity and a bipolar structure of the diplomatic realm; the second, to the diffusion in Asia and Europe of a secular religion of which one of the two giants proclaims itself the center; the third, to the perfection of weapons of mass destruction, to total war inspired by both modern science and primitive fury; the sniper and atomic bomb appear to be the extreme forms of unlimited violence." I added that each of these series contained both an element of logic and an element of chance—an interpretation that condemned me to the style of Claude Monet, to use Maurice Duverger's expression. Categorical on fundamental forces, I still feel divided and uncertain when it comes to speculating on the course of events, near or far.

André Kahan submitted written questions to me of a purely philosophical nature on the interpretation of historical determinism. These questions help to demonstrate the disparity between retrospective and prospective thinking. And his letter provides the occasion for evoking one of the purest figures of my generation. Small, apparently delicate, sickly, awkward in movement and speech, a member of the Resistance, André was captured by the Gestapo and deported to a concentration camp. His older brother, who was also an active member of the Resistance, suffered the same fate. André survived, while his brother died of typhus, shortly after the Allied victory. Both of them, innocent of the calculations of politics, inspired by moral instincts, with no shadow of egotism or self-interest, embodied the ideal type of the philosopher at war. André, whom I knew better than his brother, gave me the impression of being a kind of saint.

The philosophy of history that inspires the two books oscillates between Marx (perhaps rather Saint-Simon) and Spengler. Although wars have been unleashed by national passions—those that tore apart the Austro-Hungarian Empire, those that inflamed the Germanic masses and Hitler himself—it was the forces of production, set in motion by the mobilization of industry, which supported the monster of war from 1914 to 1918, and again assured world hegemony to the United States after the collapse of the Japanese and German empires. It was science itself, the foundation of technology, that introduced a new phase in the relations among states.

The theme of the worldwide dominance of technology belongs to Saint-

Simon and Marx as well as to Spengler and Heidegger. What was in question after the war, and remains in question today, is the future implied by the technological revolution, the fate that it holds in store for the West. In Marx's thought, science is in itself a force of production; once capitalism has been destroyed by its own contradictions, science will create a human society from which the exploitation of man by man will have disappeared. In Spengler's thought, the triumph of technology will bring about the proliferation of cities and democracy, masses or slaves, and simultaneously, the disintegration of cultural forms. I agreed with neither of these philosophies, which I confronted thirty years later in *In Defense of Decadent Europe* (South Bend: Regnery Gateway, 1977). Neither the nationalistic optimism of the one, nor the stoic pessimism of the other: an open philosophy that humbly admits the limits of our knowledge, escapes from Promethean pride and biological determinism, concludes neither with the certainty of victory nor with a cry of despair.

In the last lines of the chapter devoted to Europe, I foresaw the end of the European empires: "The lack of space creates for communities a danger comparable to the lack of oxygen for individuals. As long as the Russian army is camped two hundred kilometers from the Rhine, Western Europe will feel threatened with strangling. Whether it's a question of economic progress or intellectual exchange, there is no lack of tasks for the West, a privileged minority that has means of production and technological knowledge vastly superior to those of the rest of humanity. The Europeans have no need of colonial domination or of spheres of influence to maintain their presence and pursue their historical function. Europe should fear less the collapse of empires than the newly independent countries should fear the hostility of their former masters."

In a more brutal fashion, I condemned French policy in Indochina: "We have provoked (or were incapable of avoiding) what we should have feared above all: an interminable war against an Indochinese resistance, led by the communists, but with the support of the majority of nationalists. From the outset, we had a choice between two methods: either to grant freely to Ho Chi Minh the essence of his demands, that is, the independence of Indochina, union of the three nations, with a more or less vague connection to the French Union, or else, if we considered it impossible to deal with Ho Chi Minh, to bring into being a national government to which we would have granted essentially what we refused to grant to a Stalinist agent. Instead of resolutely choosing one policy and holding to it, we hesitated. We recognized Ho Chi Minh as head of the national resistance in 1946, we negotiated with him, we received him with formal solemnity. But while thereby increasing his prestige, we were apparently playing a double game. We should have wished for an independent and friendly Indochina. It may be that this objective was inaccessible from the very beginning, that an independent Indochina would have become communist. From the point of view of France, this outcome would have cost us less than the war." I went on: "France, without the means of defending its own territory, is squandering its resources in an enterprise that may be justified by an anticommunist world diplomacy but not by the specific interests of the country."

In London, I spoke openly about the future of Indochina: I hoped that France would grant independence to the three countries of the peninsula. In *Combat*, at the outbreak of the war (16 December 1946), the article I have cited earlier left no doubt about my feelings.

From 1949 on, and especially after the Korean War, France found itself in a trap. Formerly criticized by the Americans, it was suddenly receiving their support. We had committed ourselves to the Associated States and Bao Dai. Unless there was a serious military defeat, we could not abandon the Vietnamese troops that we had ourselves created, organized, and armed. From 1950 on, after defeats on the borders, the leaders of the Fourth Republic had no further illusions. They were looking for an opportunity for retreat. When they sent de Lattre de Tassigny to Indochina, they were hoping he would produce a report that would permit a reversal or at least a modification of their policy.

General de Gaulle did not make the government's task any easier. He had named as governor of Indochina Thierry d'Argenlieu, the priest-admiral, the man who attacked the generals who "did not want to fight," and who established the government of Indochina on orders of the Paris government while Bidault was negotiating with Ho Chi Minh in Fontainebleau. In his press conference on 14 November 1949, the General said: "France must remain in Indochina. It must remain there for Indochina, for without the presence and cooperation of France, the independence, the security, and the development of Indochina would be compromised. Moreover, as time passes, it becomes clearer that the events in Indochina are only part of a larger whole. In reality, the question is whether Asia is going to remain free. Once it is clear that it is useful for the free world to cooperate with a free Asia, I do not see why France should not cooperate with Indochina."

On 16 March 1950, he claimed the responsibility and the honor of having sent an expeditionary force to Indochina in 1945. Without the French army, Ho Chi Minh would have won, and "the Indochina of Ho Chi Minh would have been subordinated to the communist system. It is therefore necessary that France and the French army remain in Indochina. In order to do this they must have the resources to act." He even added that it was thanks to the presence of French soldiers in Indochina that "the French Union has begun to become a reality in the minds of observers throughout the world."

The following year, on 22 June 1951, he set out four military solutions:

"We can leave. We can limit ourselves to holding a few strongholds. These are defeatist solutions. As for me, I do not accept them." The third solution was the one adopted by the Fourth Republic. The last would be to "send new forces and new equipment. With this, we could definitively deal with the military question in Indochina." Did General de Gaulle believe in a military solution? If so, his belief was illusory.

To be sure, I have never hesitated to express opinions in contradiction with the General's theories on any subject, in particular on Germany. I hesitated even less in supporting the "Ho Chi Minh solution" because André Malraux, when I was working for him in the Ministry of Information in 1946, constantly said: "It would take ten years and half a million men to restore French authority." General Leclerc de Hautecloque shared this opinion. Malraux was too optimistic: it would have taken much more than ten years; the proof was established. Moreover, I never heard him promote war in Indochina. He dealt with the situation by using superficial and unchallengeable statements: "If the government chooses war, it should at least give the expeditionary force the necessary material means."

During the same years, I was already thinking of the book that became *Peace and War*, and I wrote several articles dealing with the theory or the method of international relations: "Tensions and Wars from the Point of View of Historical Sociology," "On the Analysis of Diplomatic Constellations," "On Historical Comparisons," "On Peace without Victory," "In Search of a Doctrine of Foreign Relations," "Can War be Limited in the Atomic Age?"[1]

A few ideas served as a kind of transition between the historical analyses developed in *Le Grand Schisme* and *The Century of Total War*, and the abstract or general considerations that led to *Peace and War*.

One idea, which is found in several of thse articles, was originally a response to an argument propounded by experts, or self-proclaimed experts, of Unesco: "war begins in men's minds";[2] or to a text signed by a group of experts on the possibility of eliminating war. Against the psychologists and psychoanalysts, Marxist or anti-Marxist, I argued that research should begin with war as an "armed conflict between two independent political entities by means of military forces organized for the purpose of furthering a tribal or national policy," a specific phenomenon that can be found in every civilization, in various forms, but always recognizable. In other words, I was arguing in favor of a historical sociology.

I enumerated the six questions that the analysis of a diplomatic constellation should address. The first three, which make up a first category, should be in the minds of statesmen: What is the diplomatic arena? What is the shape of power relations within that arena? What is the mechanism of war to which the leaders refer more or less clearly in order to assess the importance of a given position or relationship?

The first question was obviously suggested to me by the experience of the first half of the century. The statesmen and military leaders who led the people into the great war of 1914–18 did not consider the United States as one of the actors, indeed the decisive actor in the drama. A great power in a sphere limited to Europe and its dependencies, France was not a great power in a world perspective.

The second question came from the bipolar diplomatic arena that followed the destruction of the Third Reich and the Japanese "coprosperity sphere." The European concert of the nineteenth century or of the twentieth century before 1914 was based on a plurality of great powers, of comparable strength; changing alliances among them forestalled the rise of a "universal empire." The memory of the European concert functioned for me as an ideal type of a certain configuration of power relations. The gap between the United States and the Soviet Union on the one hand and all other political entities on the other characterized another kind of configuration, based on bipolarity.

The extension of the diplomatic sphere depends both on the size of states and on military techniques. New means of transportation made the decisive intervention of the United States in Europe possible in 1917–18. MacKinder had already been struck by the first two wars of the twentieth century, in South Africa and in Manchuria. At a distance of ten thousand kilometers, and the end of a single railroad, Czarist Russia had resupplied an army in combat; similarly, thanks to its mastery of the seas, England had supported an expeditionary force far from the metropolis. The atomic bomb, a revolutionary change in weaponry, implied unknown changes in international relations.

To these three essentially strategic-political questions, I added three ideological-political questions: to what extent did states in conflict recognize one another, so that only borders and not the existence of the states themselves were at stake in the struggle? What is the relation between the functioning of domestic politics and the decisions of statesmen? And what meaning did the latter give to peace, to war, and to relations among the states?

The first of these questions was concerned with the choice between imperial and national wars. Clausewitz wrote that before Napoleon, sovereigns did not believe in the possibility of great conquests in Europe. With Napoleon, and Hitler, the very existence of certain states was at stake in war. The nonrecognition of states takes place in various circumstances: when the conqueror aims to subject the conquered to his sovereignty, when he considers a population unworthy of independence, and finally when the belligerents jointly consider their regimes and their ideologies to be incompatible and thus adopt the objective of eliminating the regime and the ideology of the enemy.

The second question requires an analysis of domestic politics. The president of the United States does not conduct his country's foreign activities in the same way that the Politburo conducts the foreign activities of the Soviet Union. There are numerous American sociological studies on the operation of lobbies, pressure groups, the press, and Congress, a phenomenon that limits the freedom of maneuver of the president and his advisers (not to mention the rivalry among the various state organizations that have a role in determining diplomatic choices).

The last question was also inspired by the immediate situation. The Marxist-Leninists of the Kremlin do not describe events with the same words as those used by the leaders in Washington. According to Moscow, the establishment of the Fidelista regime in Cuba represents a stage in the liberation of the victims of American imperialism. Soviet diplomacy is inspired by a revolutionary theory and practice and is located in a global vision of history. American diplomacy combines a juridico-moral idealism with a realism that was often unaware of itself.

A few years later, I reconsidered these six questions in a study entitled "Analysis of Diplomatic Constellations," and I used them to clarify the postwar situation. In particular, I distinguished among the various forms of nonrecognition. In the early 1950s, the West did not recognize the GDR, and the United States did not even recognize the annexation of the Baltic states. For the Soviet Union, the Republic of Korea did not exist; for the West, the same was true of the People's Republic of Korea. The examination of diplomatic techniques which I added to the third question led to new forms of relations among states: the United Nations, GATT, and the like, just as the examination of military technology led to the historical consequences of nuclear weapons. Delbrück's analysis remains more pertinent than ever: the history of warfare can be understood only in the framework of the history of political relations.

In every situation, one can discern the *power relations*—limits of the field, structure of forces, military technology—and the *ideological meaning* of the intercourse, peaceful or warlike, among states, a meaning that results simultaneously from the links between domestic and foreign policy, the mutual recognition or nonrecognition of states, and the diplomatic philosophy professed by the various states. Power relations on the one hand, ideological meaning on the other, these are the two aspects of a constellation of state relations. When all states give the same meaning to diplomacy, it tends toward a historical type: ideologically neutral diplomacy which establishes relations and contests among states not seeking to destabilize one another from within. Religious or revolutionary diplomacy comes to the fore in periods when conflicts between parties or beliefs coincide with or complicate conflicts between states. After the wars of religion, Europe sought and found a refuge in the diplomacy of professionals and the subordination of churches and beliefs to *rasion d'état*. After the Revolutionary wars, it returned once again to a kind of state legitimacy, the basis for a traditional diplomacy. Since 1917, Europe has entered a new ideological phase in which it is still engaged, and it has brought the rest of the world along with it. In a doctoral thesis defended in Geneva, I discovered the concepts I was looking for to designate the two types of international relations: the *homogeneous system* in which states call upon the same principle of legitimacy, and the *heterogeneous system* in which states base themselves on antagonistic principles of legitimacy and, as a consequence, follow ideological or religious considerations outside the realm of power calculations. The author of this thesis, M. Papaligouras, served as a minister in the cabinet of Constantin Karamanlis a few years ago.

The two wars of the twentieth century had also led me to reflect on hyperbolic war, to use the expression of Guglielmo Ferrero, and on the will to fight to the end in order to impose peace conditions, though not necessarily oppressive ones. Thus, the Korean War seemed to me to be a turning point: for the first time in its history, the United States gave up an annihilating victory. After a half century of total wars, there began the half century of limited war (the title of an article I published in the *Bulletin of the Atomic Scientists*).

Once neither of the two belligerents aimed for a decisive victory, a negotiated peace—or a cease-fire—became inevitable. And the possible compromise amounted to the continuation of the two Koreas: "In the current state of things and of attitudes, it thus seems that a return to the *status quo ante* must be the futile, absurd result of a war that has lasted for more than a year." In fact, it lasted two years longer; the Americans ceased operations as soon as negotiations began, while the Russians and the Chinese, for reasons that remain obscure, refused to give in on the question of prisoners, who would not have the choice between North and South Korea, between Peking and Taiwan. They gave in a few weeks after Stalin's death, which at least suggests an explanation.

The conclusion of the Korean campaign became, in my view, the symbol of the East-West conflict in a global context: "The cold war is equivalent to a limited war in which each of the two camps uses only part of the resources at its disposal, but where one of the antagonists foresees a total victory, the other a partial victory. In Korea, the Western camp has achieved the kind of victory to which it aspires in the third world war. The West wants to destroy neither the Soviet Union nor the Stalinist regime, it wants the Soviet Union to give up its program of worldwide expansion." Was I right? Of course, I was right not to argue in favor of a warlike strategy, but should the United States, at a time when they held obvious superiority, have been satisfied with a draw? Should they have accepted the division of Europe? Can it not be said that Stalin, by simulating the will to conquer Western Europe, gave the

United States the illusion that they had achieved a victory through the stabilization of the democratic regimes to the west of the demarcation line, while he was achieving his goal: stabilizing the peoples' democracies imposed on the occupied countries by the Red Army?

I would like to say a word about the two other articles that followed the Korean War and "Peace without Victory." In an article in *Preuves* in 1953, I asked, "In the atomic age, can war be limited?" I argued in favor of a geographical limitation of conflicts and for moderation on the part of statesmen. To avoid escalation to the extremes, it is above all essential that military leaders and statesmen not give themselves goals that can only be attained by crushing the enemy. In considering the possibility of a world war, I concluded that, even there, limitations should not be excluded in advance. To be sure, "a war, in Europe, *a general war between the two camps, cannot not be atomic*. But that does not mean that the belligerents will hurl all their means of destruction against each other." Rationally, each would attempt to destroy the other's retaliatory forces. Atomic proliferation, the diversity of military uses of the atomic bomb, and the development of rockets compel us to envisage the continuation of the initial battle, without changing the idea that seems to us to be essential. "Once both camps have an equal ability to launch atomic attacks against cities, reason commands all of them to abstain. Atomic equality should once again make enemy armies the primary target." The argument has lost none of its value. It may even have become stronger. Oddly enough, in 1970, the Americans adopted the doctrine of mutual assured destruction. In other words, they reduced deterrence to the ability of each of the superpowers to destroy the other's cities. This deterrence is extraordinarily weak against any attack other than an atomic attack against one's territory. The Americans were led to this doctrine by the postulate that I had criticized in the article: every crossing of the nuclear threshold would necessarily lead to the extreme of total nuclear war.

Perhaps the title of an article that appeared in the *Bulletin of the Atomic Scientists* sums up my interpretation at the time: "A Half Century of Limited Wars." It does not catalogue the means of limiting wars, even those in which some nuclear weapons are used. It concentrates on the change in relations between the two superpowers. After having explained to an American public the reasons why the Soviets could not accept the Baruch-Lilienthal plan to internationalize both the atomic weapon and the atomic industry, I wondered about the consequences of the current or approaching equality of the two superpowers in nuclear arms and means of delivery. Deterrence summed up in the statement: "Stop or I'll vaporize you," makes more of an impression on the presumed aggressor than the statement: "Stop or we will die together." In 1956, the United States still enjoyed substantial superiority in what is now called "the central balance"; but I anticipated the future, and I discussed the implications of the doctrine that is now called mutual assured destruction. Each of the two belligerents would preserve, after a first strike by the other, enough retaliatory weapons to inflict on the aggressor destruction that would be, if not equivalent, of the same order of magnitude as that it had suffered. On this basis, I raised the question: What positions can only be defended by the threat of nuclear retaliation? Which should be defended locally because the adversary will not take the nuclear threat seriously? I then turned to two controversies that were becoming more and more prominent. Is it appropriate to maintain deterrence in its extreme original form or, on the contrary, should deterrence (that is the threat) be graduated and made proportionate to the significance of what is at stake? I argued in favor of proportioning the threat to the significance of what was at stake, and also in favor of the strengthening of conventional resources in circumstances in which the threat of massive reprisals remained barely plausible.

The conclusion is a fairly accurate reflection of the immediate situation. Nuclear weapons have the function not only of neutralizing each other, they also serve to prevent aggression in particularly important regions. They are not a diplomatic tool that can be used in every phase at every time. For the immediate future, at least, the political observer does not entirely agree with the physicists who deplore the fact that scientists have placed these monstrous weapons at the disposal of politicians. Of course, one cannot exclude the possibility that mistake or madness would unleash a war the horrors of which would go far beyond those of all previous wars. But, for the foreseeable future, it is probable, I said, that general and total war will not take place.

The gunshots of Sarajevo set in motion a chain reaction that ended with the atomic bombing of Hiroshima and Nagasaki. Are we not witnessing a contrary movement? A tendency to limit the space of conflicts and to give up absolute victory through the use of all available weapons? All these limited wars taken together involve an unlimited stake and always risk provoking a suicidal explosion.

I oscillated between meditation on the first half of the century and anticipatory reflections about the second half. Once I returned to the university, I tried to combine in a single work the lessons of the recent past, the analysis of the present, and advice to political figures. I was an observer, but I was committed, and I was obliged to conclude with a theory of action.

NOTES

1. All these articles have been collected in *Etudes politiques* (Paris, 1972).

2. A proposition that is obvious in one sense, but which falsely suggested that psychological intervention and education could eliminate wars.

1 2

"THE OPIUM
OF THE INTELLECTUALS"

The permanent installation of the Russian army in the center of Europe would have shocked the British and the French in the nineteenth century. Karl Marx would have denounced even more forcefully imperialism and the cowardly passivity of the West. The slow and moderate reaction of the Americans and the Europeans, the formation of the North Atlantic Pact, required by developing power relations, would have been no less necessary if the West were confronting a conventional government. Since Russia had become the Union of Soviet Socialist Republics, the diplomatic debate took on a totally different scope. Were we threatened by the Red Army, by the "specter haunting Europe"—communism—or by the irresistible rise of the socialist economy?

Rereading articles and books from the cold war period, produced by the most responsible writers, creates ambiguous feelings: Why did thoughtful minds think illogically about the Soviet Union even though they adhered neither to Marxism nor to Marxism-Leninism? Reason, common sense, the simple truth that two and two are four—are all these control mechanisms so fragile, so vulnerable in the absence of ideological passions?

I remember an economic correspondent on *Le Figaro*, enlightened, aware of practicalities, who seriously spoke about the approaching possibility of free bread in the Soviet Union. Why did he not think—without even referring to the poverty of Soviet agriculture—that bread (and wheat), if it were free, would be wasted as food for animals and would soon become rare? I would not say that fear governed the work of these journalists. I would rather say that these *ad hoc* analysts unconsciously wanted to proclaim their freedom of mind, their "progressive" stance. They were anxious to recognize the virtues and effectiveness of a social organization that they otherwise rejected, for other reasons.

Polemics between progressives and Atlanticists revolved around the respective virtues and faults of the Soviet system and American democracy. There is no shortage of writings from which to take one's pick.

The first surprise, in 1945 I think, which revealed the distance between me and Sartre and Merleau-Ponty, came to me from an article in *Le Figaro* or *Le Figaro littéraire;* Merleau-Ponty was discussing Sartre and existentialism, and he noted in passing that dissensions with communism had had to do with "family quarrels." They soon learned, with the Stalinists, what "family quarrels" meant. My first controversy with Merleau-Ponty had to do with *Humanisme et terreur.*

Merleau-Ponty's essay of 1947 shocked me, or more precisely, provoked my immediate indignation. The Moscow trials, as Koestler had presented them in *Darkness at Noon,* made up the center, the object, or the occasion for the book. Rubashov was generally identified with Bukharin, who became an existentialist. I have never read the following lines without irritation: "There is as much 'existentialism'—in the sense of paradox, division, anguish, and resolution—in the *stenographic record of the Moscow debates* as in all the works of Koestler." Curiously, the trials were called debates, as though Vyshinski and Bukharin were discussing, as philosophy professors, the relative role of necessity and accident, rationality and chance, in the course of history. Writer and reader end up forgetting that the trials were fabricated in advance, parts assigned, and that everyone, judges and defendants, recited speeches that had been written in advance. I felt close to the Danube peasant whose natural reaction was expressed by Khrushchev in his famous speech to the Twentieth Congress: "Why did the accused confess to crimes that they had not committed, unless because they were tortured?" Merleau-Ponty may have known this, but perhaps as a philosopher he also thought that these material elements took nothing away from the *debate* on the responsibility of the opposition.

The book also shocked me because of its timeless and futile refutation of an argument that its opponents did not support. Merleau-Ponty rejected the *Manichaeanism* of anticommunist propaganda. Violence exists on all sides, and the free or liberal world is not opposed to the communist world as truth against lie, law against violence, the respect of minds against propaganda. This may be so, but once one has accepted the thesis that all struggles are, to one degree or another, ambiguous, there remains the question of degrees. If every foreign policy contains elements of deception and violence, it does not follow that there is no moral difference between the policies of Hitler and Stalin on the one hand and those of Roosevelt and Churchill on the other. When Merleau-Ponty writes, as though it were an obvious truth, that "the moral and material civilization of England presupposes the exploitation of the colonies," he flippantly resolves a still open question. England has lost its empire without losing its moral civilization. Respect for the law may serve as a justification for police repression of strikes in America, but certainly not for "the development of the American empire in the Middle East."

Similarly, I had no trouble in accepting the fact that the combination of rationality and chance left a margin for individual decision and hence exposed men to the contradictions and even the condemnations of history. Agents sometimes no longer recognize themselves in the consequences or even the meaning of their acts. Their opposition to established power appears retrospectively as treason if it has favored the enemy cause. What shocked me was not this dialectic, which was in fact banal. Any opposition figure can, *post eventum*, appear to be a traitor. But every historical decision must be judged in consideration of the moment, the context in which it was made; if a historian had the right and duty to consider the involuntary and unforeseen consequences of a decision, these consequences should not form the basis for a moralist's judgment, even less for the verdict of a jury.

Finally, Merleau-Ponty's philosophy of history seemed to me, on the one hand, classical (rationality and chance), and on the other almost puerile: "Carefully considered, Marxism is not just a theory, to be replaced later by another, it is the simple statement of the conditions without which there will be no humanity, in the sense of a reciprocal relation among men, nor any rationality in history. In this sense, it is not a philosophy of history, it is *the* philosophy of history, and to reject it is to reject historical reason. Thereafter, there are only dreams or adventures."

Merleau-Ponty based his position of a-communism, or suspension of judgment, on doubt: "The construction of socialist foundations for the economy is accompanied by a regression of proletarian ideology and, for reasons that have to do with circumstances—revolution in a single country, revolutionary stagnation and the corruption of history in the rest of the world—the USSR does not represent the historical triumph of the proletariat as Marx had foreseen." He went even further: "There may still be a dialectic, but only from the standpoint of a God who knows world history. A man situated in his time does not see the proletarian in power as a 'man of universal history.'"

Tranposed into ordinary language, Merleau-Ponty's thought was not extremely subtle. The economic base of socialism was being built amidst sound and fury; universal man, the proletariat in power, had yet to appear. If history were definitively to contradict Marxism, historical reason would disappear along with it. There would remain nothing but the power of some and the resignation of the rest: "In the context of this unique philosophy, 'historical wisdom' appears to be a failure." But how long will we have to wait and, like theologians, have confidence in the last judgment, in an uncertain future?

A few years later, Merleau-Ponty grew tired of waiting for harmony between real history and the Marxist vision. North Korea's aggression led him to revise his diagnosis of the present situation. Between *Humanisme et Terreur* and *Les Aventures de la dialectique*, Merleau-Ponty had traveled a substantial distance, and although he was not in agreement with me, he had come closer to my positions.

Merleau-Ponty's *Les Aventures de la dialectique* appeared almost simultaneously with *L'Opium des intellectuels*. Sometimes it was put in the same bag and "executed" in the same style by communist writers of the time (Claude Roy, for example). Merleau-Ponty and I never quarreled and, on the other hand, Sartre replied to his friend through the pen of Simone de Beauvoir. To some extent, in fact, their break was provoked by dissension on the attitude to be adopted toward the Communist Party and, by the same token, toward the Soviet Union. In addition, and perhaps to a greater extent, it had to do with an essentially philosophical controversy over relations between class and party—relations that implied a dialectic between experiences and theory, between union activity and political action. I will return to this philosophical controversy after analyzing political positions.

As I noted in a 1956 article,[1] one has the feeling of a kind of ballet or musical chairs. The "new left" of Merleau-Ponty in 1955 resembles the *Rassemblement démocratique révolutionnaire* of Jean-Paul Sartre in 1948. The Marxist temporizing of the former is closer to the procommunism of the latter than to the a-communism set out in *Les Aventures de la dialectique*. In short, Merleau-Ponty was predisposed in favor of the Communist Party when he wrote *Humanisme et terreur*, and not when he wrote *Les Aventures*. To the contrary, Sartre severely attacked the CP in his conversations with David Rousset, and returned to the fold in "Les communistes et la paix."

It was the conversations between Sartre and Rousset that put an official end to our earlier friendship. Merleau-Ponty, after having read the statements directed against me, pointed out to Sartre that these attacks, in any event, would bring about a break between us. Sartre is supposed to have answered: "Yes, but we have nothing left to save." Perhaps he was right.

An early incident had placed us in opposition to one another. Under the Ramadier government, Sartre had gotten a radio program; he spoke freely with some of his friends. In one of his first broadcasts, he spoke about General de Gaulle. One of his interlocutors made a long comparison between de Gaulle and Hitler ("heavy lids"). Of course, the comparison created a scandal. That evening I was scheduled to meet Sartre and his opponents. I found myself in the midst of excited Gaullists like Henri Torrès and General de Bénouville, who attacked Sartre violently and insultingly. I remained silent, not being able to agree with Sartre's position and even less able to join the chorus of the "attackers." A few weeks later, I learned that Sartre had not forgiven me for my "silence," when he was alone in the midst of enemies.

In his 1974 dialogue with Simone de Beauvoir, he recounts the same story as he experienced it: "Aron, he's the whole history of Gaullism and a dialogue on the radio; we had an hour on the radio every week to discuss the political situation, and we had been very violent against de Gaulle. Gaullists wanted to reply to me face to face, particularly Bénouville, and someone else whose name I've forgotten. So I went to the studio; we were not supposed to meet before the dialogue began. Aron came; I think I had chosen him as a kind of arbiter, convinced that he would take my side. Aron pretended not to see me; he joined the others; I could understand his recognizing the others, not that he would drop me. From that moment, I understood that Aron was against me; in political terms, I considered his solidarity with the Gaullists against me as a break. There has always been a strong reason to provoke my quarrels, but in the end I have always been the one who decided to quarrel."[2]

Let us reexamine a few points: "We had been very violent against General de Gaulle." This is an understatement: they at length compared General de Gaulle to Hitler, complete with physical comparisons. Could I approve this out of friendship for him? A few months earlier, in his absence, I had defended him against Gabriel Marcel who criticized him for comparing the French occupation of Indochina to the Nazi occupation of France. The invitation, as I remember it, came from the radio station and not from him personally, but that hardly matters: when I arrived, Bénouville and Torrès were engaged in voluble invectives against Sartre, declaring that one could not carry on a discussion with someone who lowered himself to such attacks. Sartre did not respond to the invectives; he never liked direct confrontations.

To be sure, I could have found the means to behave otherwise, to show him my friendship without supporting his program broadcast the day before. I remember this brief scene as an unbearable moment: on one side Gaullists for whom I felt no sympathy, and on the other Sartre, impassive in the face of insults, and I was silent. Everyone left separately

That said, Sartre is right, friendship was dying by itself, inexorably. Our friendship, during the last two years of the Ecole Normale was nourished by intellectual complicity and student camaraderie. The first element dissipated with time, as did the second, for reasons that his 1974 dialogue with Simone de Beauvoir makes clear. After the ENS, he preferred female friend-ships; conversations among men seemed to him impoverished and quickly boring. We discussed philosophy as long as we did not write books. Sartre read the *Introduction to the Philosophy of History*, he told me he reread it before writing *L'Etre et le néant*, but he did not enter into a dialogue with me about it, nor did he ask me to criticize his own work. At least once I approached the theme of nothingness and the two different meanings of the concept that he does not distinguish: nothingness according to ordinary understanding, nonbeing, on the one hand, and the "for-itself," or the consciousness that can be called nothingness in opposition to the density and immobility of things on the other. He replied that the two meanings came together in the last analysis. We had neither political conversations, because we lived in different worlds, nor philosophical conversations, since he no longer took pleasure in controversy: there might have remained, as between Desanti and Clavel, that insignificant or essential thing, the pleasure of being together, even though one has nothing to say to the other; that happiness was never granted us.

When I learned that we had "quarreled," I went to see him one day with Manès Sperber, and I tried to justify my attitude, and especially to minimize the importance of the episode. With rather ill grace, he accepted my explanation. "Agreed, we'll have lunch one of these days," was the ritual conclusion of the conversation. The lunch did not take place. I joined the RPF and he created, with David Rousset, the *Rassemblement démocratique révolutionnaire* (RDR). In *Entretiens sur la politique*,[3] the two comrades attributed to me opinions that I had never professed. For example, "Aron's utopia is to believe that technical development necessarily brings about social emancipation." The example of the Soviet Union could have cured me of that illusion, had I ever taken it seriously. Sartre attributed to me car-icatured opinions that he took not from my writings but from conversations. I answered him in *Liberté de l'esprit*, and I don't think it necessary to repeat the debate.

Still more serious in his eyes than my "cynicism, which is not even intelligent," was my "fatalist" acceptance of war: "It would be romantic to believe that peace is still possible. Hence, by declaring war inevitable, one helps to bring it closer." In *Le Grand Schisme*, I had asserted exactly the contrary. This was the first occasion, not the last, on which Sartre felt the need to define his own political attitude by denouncing mine. It is true that I had not taken the *Rassemblement démocratique révolutionnaire* seriously, while Merleau-Ponty's "new left" in 1955 was not without some relevance. In the usual sense of these words, democracy and revolution contradict one another.[4] The very idea of preaching a proletarian revolution in France, different from the one symbolized by the Communist Party, had less to do with "revolutionary romanticism" (of which I had accused Rousset and Sartre) than with naïveté or ignorance. In any event, the RDR experienced the fate that history had assigned it from the beginning.

A final remark: Rousset and Sartre took their distance from the Soviets and the people's democracies: "We are not with the people's republics. We are not with them for precise reasons, particularly because we do not believe that those regimes satisfy the basic needs of the workers. I am sure that a substantial part of CGT strategy in strikes is dictated much more by distant military considerations than by obvious social objectives."[5]

The RDR was subjected to attack from all sides, from communists and Gaullists, without receiving any support from the moderate parties in power. Merleau-Ponty, and I have a distinct memory of this, seriously wondered one day whether this little group would later appear as the origin of a great movement, comparable to the Bolsheviks, who had also, at the beginning, been called a sect.

Between 1948 and 1955, I wrote some more or less successful articles, some polemical, others analytic, most of which were collected in *Polémiques* (1955). One of them, "History and Politics," originally published in *La Revue de métaphysique et de morale,* most fully escapes from obsolescence and the exhaustion of debates among intellectuals.

Unlike this collection, *The Opium of the Intellectuals* still has meaning for me. I wrote it between 1952 and 1954, slowly, with some difficulty. Perhaps a victim of journalistic facility, but especially wounded by personal unhappiness, between 1951 and 1955 I sought refuge in incessant and various activity, a flight into studious diversion, if this combination of words is not inherently contradictory. I had the impression, perhaps the illusion, of having cured myself, saved myself thanks to *The Opium of the Intellectuals.* I was almost indifferent to the attacks to which the book was subjected. I had come out of the darkness, and perhaps I would become reconciled with life.

The first of the three parts of the book, dealing with "three myths," the "left," "revolution," and the "proletariat," aimed at the heart of themes favored by many intellectuals, beyond the progressives and the para-Marxists who were my immediate target. I did not deny the fact that there was a distinction between the right and the left in the National Assembly. What I denied was that there was an eternal left, the same in various historical circumstances, inspired by the same values, united in the same aspirations. In France, the myth of "the unity of the left" compensates for and covers over interminable quarrels that, since the Revolution, have opposed Jacobins to Girondins, bourgeois liberals to socialists, socialists to communists. Ideologically, the left has never been homogeneous, sometimes anti-state, sometimes bureaucratic, sometimes egalitarian. Some may wish that it be simultaneously liberal, bureaucratic, and egalitarian, in the naïve belief that these objectives are compatible.

A historian will readily agree that certain ideas, like nationalism, for example, have moved from one camp to the other. There is no doubt that there is a pessimistic left, that of Alain, for example, which argues for the resistance of citizens against all authorities and never has confidence in the wisdom of the masters. If this liberalism based on suspicion belongs to the left, what does it have in common with the statism of the planners, eager to submit the rich and powerful to government control and unaware of the duty to guard the guardians?

Similarly, with reference to revolution and the proletariat, I attempted to bring the poetry of ideology down to the level of the prose of reality. Does the working class constitute "authentic intersubjectivity"? Can it become the ruling class? Is it liberated when a party exercises absolute power in its name while depriving it of the tools of the relative and partial liberation achieved in capitalist democracy? Why is revolution a good in itself? "The myth of revolution serves as a refuge for utopian thought, it has become the mysterious and unpredictable intercession between reality and the ideal. Violence itself attracts and fascinates rather than repelling. Workerism and 'classless Scandinavian society' never had the prestige in the European left, particularly the French left, that has been maintained by the Russian Revolution, despite the civil wars and the horrors of collectivization and of the great purge. Should we say *despite* or *because of*?"

Without setting myself up as an arbiter in the debate between Camus on one side and Sartre and *Les Temps modernes* on the other, on one decisive point I repeated Camus's argument or rather his challenge: "Yes or no, do you recognize the Soviet regime as the fulfillment of the revolutionary project?" To which Jeanson (speaking for Sartre, I presume) answered: "The Stalinist movement throughout the world does not seem to us to be authentically revolutionary, yet it brings together, particularly in France, the great majority of the proletariat; we are thus simultaneously *against it* since we criticize its methods and *for it* because we do not know whether or not authentic revolution is a pure chimera, whether it is not necessary in fact for the revolutionary enterprise to follow those paths before being capable of establishing a more humane social order." A strange answer: historical man, aware of his condition, cannot be unaware of the fact that he commits himself without knowing the ultimate consequences of his action or of the historical movement that he had joined; evasion of a decision about the Soviet Union, or a combination of yes and no, is quite obviously a violation of the imperative of commitment.

With a rather arrogant tone, I declared Camus to be right on the essential point of his polemic with Sartre and Sartrianism: "At the points where it provokes the anger of *Les Temps modernes*, Camus's thought seems banal and reasonable. If rebellion reveals to us our solidarity with the oppressed and the imperatives of pity, revolutionaries of the Stalinist variety have, in fact, betrayed the spirit of rebellion. Convinced that they are obeying the laws of history and that they are working for a goal that is both ineluctable and beneficial, they become, like their predecessors, with a clear conscience, executioners and tyrants."

Sartre responded with no more clarity to Camus's challenge; he used a style close to that of Francis Jeanson. He too rejected both breaking with and adhesion to communism. He wished to be both close to and critical of the Stalinist movement. Even after the repression of the Hungarian revolution, Sartre could see no embodiment of the revolutionary and socialist project outside the communist movement. Jeanson, in passing, considered the possibility that authentic revolution was a pure chimera, but he did nothing with this possibility and drew no conclusions from it. He maintained the hypothesis that, at least until 1970, served as the principle for Sartre's thought: the revolutionary project may have to follow this path to arrive at the end of prehistory, or at least at a society preferable to the one it is fighting against. Merleau-Ponty condemned this reasoning, characterizing it as theological: the last judgment of History will determine the virtues and faults of today's social actors.

The second part of the book dealt with "The Idolatry of History." In the first chapter, I analyzed the relationships between the "churchmen" and the "men of faith," in other words between the communists who accepted party orthodoxy, and the paracommunists, like Merleau-Ponty in *Humanisme et terreur*, or the progressive Christians (the worker-priests), who maintain the principal articles of the faith (the mission of the proletariat, salvation through the proletariat) without accepting the letter of party orthodoxy. The two succeeding chapters, inspired by the *Introduction to the Philosophy of History*, discussed the two versions of Marxism, more generally the two ways of interpreting the past: on the one hand, the sense of the past, whether seen in a single known action or in the development of humanity; on the other, the determinism that was said to govern the course of events and would permit foreseeing the inevitable end of struggle between classes and nations.

The last part, a more adventurous essay than the two others, attempted a comparison among intellectuals of various countries, their attitudes toward their country, the debates characteristic of each of these intelligentsias. I did not decree a definition of the category of intellectual; depending on the country and the moment, the category includes all, or almost all, nonmanual workers, or else, in a restrictive sense, those devoted to the creation and diffusion of thought and culture. In developing countries, all graduates belong to the intelligentsia (this accounts for the spread of the term in nineteenth-century czarist Russia). In industrialized countries, nonmanual jobs are proliferating, but lower level employees, who would in earlier times have been called scribes, no longer pass as intellectuals. *Experts* and *men of letters* make up the intelligentsia in the Soviet Union, for example. In the West, we may have a tendency to restrict even further the expansion of the category; does any elementary or secondary teacher deserve the label "intellectual"? Don't we demand that he examine his existence and his activity?

As for French intellectuals, I attributed to them a tendency to transform problems that were peculiar to our country into a universal debate. For historical and social reasons, a substantial fraction of the workers (between a third and a half) votes for the CP. Hence, the CP is no longer distinct from the proletariat, and Sartre, Merleau-Ponty, and Lefort discuss at length the link between class and party, the right of the latter to call itself the representative of the former. This is a debate that risks slipping into scholasticism or theology, once it has lost touch with reality. In Great Britain, quite clearly, the few thousand militants of the CP do not represent the English working class; in France, the CP represents a fraction of the French working class, while the party's enemy is not necessarily the enemy of the workers. The experience of Eastern Europe should have dissipated the clouds and brought the philosophers back down to everyday reality: the cadres of the party, after the seizure of power, become the political elite of the so-called proletarian regime. Merleau-Ponty violated a taboo when he was so bold as to ask whether the Czech workers did not feel nostalgia for their "servitude" under capitalism and for their unions.

L'Opium des intellectuels, one of many books devoted by an intellectual to the condition of the category to which he belonged, created a stir. The comparison with *La Trahison des clercs* occurred to several critics, either to crush my book under Julien Benda's monument or, on the contrary, to honor it by placing it in a glorious lineage.

In a sense, the criticism reveals the permanence of the split between right and left. Of all my books, this is the only one whose reception in the press followed rigid political, or rather partisan, concerns. The most widespread accusation against the book, even among the favorable critics, had to do with my "skepticism," and the totally negative character of the book. To begin with, this is a misunderstanding attributable to the conclusion, which I risk quoting:

> Does the critique of fanaticism teach reasonable faith or skepticism? One does not cease loving God when one gives up converting pagans and Jews by force of arms

and when one no longer repeats: "Outside the Church, no salvation." Will we stop wishing for a less unjust society and a less cruel common fate, if we refuse to transfigure a class, a technique of action, an ideological system? The comparison, to be sure, is subject to some reservation. Religious experience gains authenticity to the extent that one distinguishes more clearly between moral virtue and obedience to the Church. Secular religions dissolve into opinions as soon as dogma is renounced. Nonetheless, a man who does not expect miraculous change either from a revolution or a five-year plan does not have to resign himself to the unjustifiable. He does not give his soul to an abstract humanity, to a tyrannical party, to an absurd scholasticism, because he loves individuals, participates in living communities, respects the truth.

Perhaps it will turn out otherwise. Perhaps the intellectual will lose interest in politics on the day he discovers its limits. Let us accept this uncertain promise joyfully. We are not threatened by indifference. Men are not at the point of missing opportunities or motives for killing one another. If tolerance is born of doubt, let us teach doubt of models and utopias, let us learn to challenge the prophets of salvation and the prophets of doom. Let us pray for the arrival of the skeptics so that they may extinguish fanaticism.

The last sentence was taken out of context. In my eyes, skepticism did not mean the loss of all faith or indifference to public life: I wished that thinking men, once they had been freed from secular religion, would no longer be inclined to justify the unjustifiable. I admitted that they might lose interest in politics if they were to discern its limits. In our world, where the opportunities and motives for mutual slaughter proliferate, doubt about models or utopias at least holds out the promise of reducing the number of men eager to kill their fellows in the name of their faith.

Even with the misunderstanding cleared up, was the book not subject to the banal criticism: You have destroyed, what are you building?

I recall a dialogue with Père Dubarle. According to him I called for: "An end to the ideological age, a reasonable use of technological progress with the aim of establishing a currently viable human world, in which freedom would be as universal a reality as possible, even though it might turn out to be rather prosaic. In his eyes, it is probably the man in whom the passions of the mind have been dulled who is in the best position to use history well and to become successfully engaged in political action. Hence, the critique has ended by suppressing something of value on the pretext of correcting its unreasonable consequences."

I do in fact think that the organization of social life on this earth turns out, in the end, to be rather prosaic. Nightmarish in its Soviet version, imperfect and vulgar in its American version, industrial society remains the dominant type of our civilization. Those who expect or hope for the kingdom of God on earth transfigure men and institutions, they no longer see them as history has made them known to us. The petty bourgeoisie satisfied, the efforts of workers lightened by machines, a fiscal system that taxes the rich and provides the necessary minimum for the poor, all of that, indeed, appears prosaic. Is Soviet reality less prosaic because it is monstrous?

NOTES

1. After *The Opium of the Intellectuals*, I wrote two articles for *Preuves* responding to the criticisms that I took seriously: "Aventures et mésaventures de la dialectique," and "Le Fanatisme, la prudence, et la foi."

2. *La Cérémonie des adieux*, p. 354.

3. Gallimard, 1948.

4. One of my courses at the Ecole Normale d'Administration had the title "Democracy and Revolution."

5. *Entretiens sur la politique*, by Jean-Paul Sartre, David Rousset, Gérard Rosenthal. The quoted passage is by Rousset.

A *Professor* in the Storm

1955 – 1969

1 3

RETURN TO
THE OLD SORBONNE

In June 1955, I wanted to be appointed to the Sorbonne, and I could hardly conceal from myself the strength of my desire. Why? Had my ambition to make a mark in the university, diverted after the war by the drug of politics, reawakened? I concluded, perhaps wrongly, that journalism had already given me everything that it could. Youthful anxieties had returned: Was I not in danger of succumbing to facility, had I not been drawn into a path that was not, or at least should not be my only one? My prewar books did not suggest that I would become a regular contributor to *Le Figaro*. I remembered Célestin Bouglé's sarcastic forecast when my judgments about the Blum government offended his left-wing sensibilities.

I expected from the Sorbonne the discipline that I had lost. The birth of a mongoloid daughter in July 1950, and the death of Emmanuelle a few months later from sudden leukemia, had wounded me more than I could say. There is no apprenticeship for sorrow. I was a bad student, slow and rebellious. I sought refuge in work. The more I plunged into this illusory refuge, the more I lost myself. Aware that I was losing myself, I suffered more, beyond sorrow itself, from the wounds that time did not heal. I hoped for help from the Sorbonne, and my hopes were not disappointed. It did not restore what the year 1950 had forever taken from me, but it helped to reconcile me with life, with others, and with myself.

Appointment involved two stages: a department elected its candidate, then the assembly of all tenured professors of the faculty elected one of the candidates. The faculty did not always follow the recommendation of a department. In the Sorbonne of my youth, which had only about fifty voting professors, the system could conceivably be justified. The distance between disciplines, less pronounced than it is today, did not prevent most professors from knowing one another, and they all belonged to a restricted circle. Most of them had come from the Ecole Normale Supérieure, and most of the time, they followed the opinion of the scholarly elite. (Perhaps I am attributing to the Sorbonne that I did not know virtues that it did not have, or at least not to that extent.) In any event, as the assembly of professors grew to the proportions of a crowd, the election of a specialist by voting professors, the majority of whom knew nothing or almost nothing of the qualifications and the work of various candidates, became more and more haphazard. Personality conflicts, professors eager to leave for lunch, the quality of arguments, all sometimes had more effect on the vote than purely scholarly considerations.

The debates on the great days—that is, the days of major elections—attracted the public. The number of professors present at faculty meetings increased with the number of elections scheduled and with the significance attributed to the candidates and to the position. At faculty meetings, as in parliament, some speakers commanded silence. The remarks of others were lost in the murmur of private conversations. The style of presentation and of praise would have astonished an uninitiated listener. To praise the teaching abilities of a candidate for the Sorbonne was to condemn him to oblivion. By convention, praise of a professor suggested his weakness as a scholar. These tournaments of eloquence, in which I participated several times, vaguely irritated me: the speeches resembled funeral orations, and I never ceased to wonder at the fact that the French university system contained so many geniuses.

Denis Brogan, in an article that I have not been able to locate, commented on the electoral campaign that led to my appointment, a campaign that was inconceivable in Great Britain, according to him. Quite obviously, professors who were members of, or close to, the Communist Party were opposed to me. Some noncommunists of the left held against me the recent publication of *The Opium of the Intellectuals*. Georges Gurvitch, who, among other qualities, possessed those of a "university activist" (campaigning through phone calls and personal visits), proposed the candidacy of Georges Balandier, and asserted to anyone who would listen that my books and articles pointed me more toward a minister's portfolio than a chair of sociology.

I owe my final success to circumstances beyond my control and unrelated to my merits. I did not conduct a campaign, in the sense that the expression had taken on in the university. I visited colleagues in the division of philosophy and the heads of other divisions. My comrades from the lycée and the ENS filled the Sorbonne; they knew me better than Balandier, who was about fifteen years younger than I, and many of them paid no attention to my political opinions but voted for a comrade. Mlle Bonnefoy, the admirable secretary of the faculty, later said to me: "Perhaps you won because of your age." The journalist edged out the "kid." To prevent too sordid an impression, I should recall that, in addition to support from members of the philosophy faculty, I received that of H. I. Marrou, who, I was told, reminded the assembly of the recent appointment of a communist, in the course of an argument for the author not of *The Opium of the Intellectuals* but of *Introduction to the Philosophy of History.*

In the old Sorbonne, everyone claimed not to know—and in certain circumstances they forgot—opinions held by teachers outside their positions. In fact, the hostility of some professors toward me did not have that much to do with my political ideas. One, a moralist by profession, passionately declared that he would vote for the devil rather than for me. My crime? I had not played the game, I had refused to be "exiled" for a few years to a provincial university, I had detached myself from academic work and launched a career as a journalist. The reactions were understandable; after all, Georges Balandier had against him only his youth—a defect that would disappear more quickly than mine. Georges Balandier has remained loyal to Gurvitch—which has not interfered with our cordial relations. The election, preceded by visits to professors, is the equivalent of an initiation rite. Once the ordeal has been gone through and overcome, the candidate is accepted by all, opponents as well as supporters. Other disputes and other concealed alliances take the place of those that had been joined before and in view of the election.

In another chapter, I wondered whether and how my press colleagues welcomed me; I must pose the same question of university colleagues. As the prodigal son returning to his family? As an interloper intending to be both journalist and professor? As a journalist looking to the Sorbonne for some extra prestige who would compromise the illustrious institution in polemics that were hardly compatible with the dignity of the alma mater? From time to time, I felt reactions from one or another of my colleagues comparable to those that had come from some of my journalistic colleagues; I was outside the norm and all established bodies are suspicious of outsiders. The strength of these suspicions or resentments was perhaps exaggerated by my susceptibility, and time smoothed them over.

I had no trouble adapting to the profession, apparently new, since I had held a chair of sociology for only six months, in Bordeaux in 1938, when I replaced Max Bonnafous. My courses at ENA and the Institut d'Etudes politiques, the numerous lectures I had delivered in French, English, and German had, so to speak, kept me in shape. My facility in speaking, which had impressed my teachers in examinations, had not yet deserted me. My knowledge of Marxism made it easy for me to stand up to communist students. The librarian of the philosophy division, M. Romeu, known to generations of students, assured me that even the communist students respected my teaching.

The Sorbonne to which I returned after twenty-seven years of absence did not surprise me; it had not yet changed from top to bottom, as it did between 1955 and 1968 while I was teaching there. The philosophy division contained a dozen professors (who had split into two equal camps on the first two ballots of my election; on the third, one of the twelve had changed sides and given me a small majority). The number of students had increased, but not yet to the point of straining the institution to the breaking point. Each professor had an assistant who corrected papers, directed student work, and also presented courses.

What struck me most was the dinginess of the building and the institution. The chairs, in the tiny offices next to the lecture halls, could have come from the flea market. The rooms were gray, dirty, sad. I could not help recalling American and English universities, of which I had had some experience. In my eyes, the poverty of the building illustrated the decrepitude of the system.

Nothing, or almost nothing, had changed since the 1930s. The best students continued to take exams for their degrees without ever setting foot in the Sorbonne. The others were left to themselves, except for the help provided by the assistant. The professor, for the most part, did nothing but deliver lectures. My weekly schedule consisted of three hours, a light or a heavy burden depending on one's approach to teaching. At the Collège de France, the courses are supposed to be original every year. In the Sorbonne, the professor followed only his own conscience, renewing his teaching or, on the contrary, devoting his time to his own research. Compared to the great universities of the United States and Great Britain, the Sorbonne seemed to me a survival of the nineteenth century; the holder of a chair answered to no one; he knew personally the students writing, under his direction, the memoir for the diploma of higher studies or the thesis of the *doctorat d'Etat;* he had little to do, from lack of time, with students working for a *licence.*

In 1955, it was already true that most students had to fend for themselves in a world that was different from that of the lycée. Each year, as the number of students undertaking higher education increased, without a precise goal, without any particular vocation, the old pattern became more and more anachronistic. Many professors' courses were worthy of publication. Removed from any obligation or penalty, the professor sank beneath the burden of work or, on the contrary, respected the three-hour rule, and did not devote his time and energy to the preparation of classes or thesis defenses.

The Faculty of Letters of the University of Paris or, as it was still called, the Sorbonne, maintained a dominant position. Most doctoral theses were defended in Paris; the professor who, rightly or wrongly, had the reputation of being the dean of his discipline, exercised over the choice of subjects and the very direction of research an influence that was always excessive and sometimes stifling. The mandarins, denounced in May 1968, were not all figures of legend. Ernest Labrousse in economic history, Mme Durry in French literature, held a power over the young and their careers that they exercised vigorously. Sometimes, a great master of the Sorbonne was directing, on paper, several dozen doctoral theses, not to mention those at lower levels. The concentration of power rather than of talents scandalized me long before the students took to the streets.

I have on several occasions criticized the French system of higher education, in *Le Figaro* and in sociological journals (notably in *Minerva* and the *Archives européennes de sociologie*). The criticism focused above all on the *agrégation* and on the distortion of higher education that it caused. Faculties of letters had as their principal task the training of secondary school teachers, not researchers. Secondarily, distinctions among diplomas—*agrégation*, CAPES, *licence*—created within schools a heterogeneous teaching body, with duties and rewards determined not by present merit, but by examinations taken before entering the career.

What is the situation today? The *agrégations* have survived, hardly changed, as far as I can tell. Perhaps they no longer exercise the same tyrannical influence because of the multiplicity of university departments, relatively small groups, open to innovation, less trapped than in the past by programs and examinations, but they still evoke the same reservations: they are examinations that have nothing to do with intellectual or pedagogical ability. Because of the disproportion between the number of candidates and the number who succeed, the *agrégation* amounts to a method of selection, neither better nor worse than another. On the other hand, the rejection of selection for admission to the university has developed its logical and foreseeable consequences.

Along with many others, I denounced the equivocal character of the *baccalauréat*, both a diploma for completion of secondary education and a preliminary university degree. Gradually, during my years at the Sorbonne, the *baccalauréat*, which was revised several times, came closer to being a simple diploma for completion of secondary studies, without nevertheless losing its character as a first step in the university; in other words, everyone who passes the *baccalauréat* retains the right to pursue higher education. But a curious consequence of the system was that all the institutions of higher education, with the exception of the university faculties, set up a system of entrance requirements. Thus an ordinary *bachelier* cannot enter a business school or the Institut d'Etudes politiques without some other qualification or an examination. Even the Instituts Universitaires de Technologie, with two-year programs, make selections among candidates and offer an opening to careers. The only exceptions are faculties of letters or of law: for lack of anything better, they shelter thousands of the unemployed young.

Everyone could have predicted this consequence of the refusal of selection, and personally I argued in favor of "selection," the taboo word that simply designated a rejection of free access of all *bacheliers* essentially to the faculties of letters, and to a lesser degree to the faculties of law and economics (divided since 1969 into a multiplicity of departments). Among the hundreds of thousands of students who are enrolled, according to the statistics, how many seize their opportunities or take advantage of the benefits granted to students, without a definite plan, or even without the desire of completing their studies?

At the outset, when this process began, I was outraged by the irrationality of the system, the waste of scarce resources devoted to pseudo-students, who achieve no degrees and derive little profit from their hesitant efforts. I have not changed my mind, but I feel a little more indulgent. Of course, to maintain a system proportioned to this number of half-students means an indirect reduction in state funds available for genuine higher education and research. Already at the beginning of my time at the Sorbonne, all professors noted a decline in the number of students attending lectures, from 20 to 25 percent in the best cases, from the beginning to the end of the year. The students disappeared not only from the view of the professors, they no longer appeared in section meetings, they did not sign up for end of year examinations. Sociological investigations have not always found traces of these "deserters."

Between 1955 and 1968, from a sheltered position, I witnessed the transformation of the old Sorbonne. University theses were abolished, theses for the *troisième cycle* were introduced. I had a single assistant in 1955; ten years later, there were ten looking after the students. The increase in both teachers and students could be seen from year to year. The Descartes amphitheater was full when I gave my lectures; I was addressing hundreds of listeners whom I did not know. I decided to leave the Sorbonne at the end of 1967 and to become director of studies at the Ecole pratique des Hautes Etudes, because I had the feeling that the building was cracking, that we were paralyzed, sterilized, by a system at the end of its tether.

For sociology, the years 1955–68 were in many respects extraordinarily fruitful. The teaching of sociology in Paris, Toulouse, Bordeaux, and Strasbourg had hardly changed from what I had known and received (so to speak: I had not attended classes) a quarter century earlier. The courses dealt with the major authors, with the theories of the professors themselves, or with certain principal themes: classes or the class struggle, suicide, the division of labor, and so on. Sociologists were moreover beginning to undertake empirical research and did not feel concerned with the speculations or rivalries of Sorbonne professors.

During the period that I taught at the Sorbonne, there was the beginning of a rapprochement between researchers and the university. This was a simple coincidence, and there is no causal connection between the two. The number of students in sociology, the popularity of the social sciences, the decline of the humanities, all the circumstances favored the rise of sociology in the faculties, a rise that appeared after the fact as one of the causes of the events of May 1968. Personally, I lay claim to the responsibility—a virtue or a defect, according to one's perspective—for having created a *licence* in sociology in two years (extraordinary speed for an institutional reform).

In 1955, when I chose industrial society as the subject for my first public course, I broke with custom: five-year plans, agricultural collectivization, and the Moscow trials found a place in my studies. How could it be otherwise, since the Soviet Union embodied the ideal type of a regime of our time—a regime that had given itself the goal of catching up with the United States, of developing the forces of production in a social system? The evocation, in a Sorbonne amphitheater, of the concentration camps or the confessions of Lenin's companions brought so-called academic sociology closer to everyday political concerns. Gurvitch's courses, reflections of his books, rich in classifications and definitions, presented the contrary virtues; they drew students away from their everyday concerns and introduced them into a foreign realm, slightly mysterious, peopled by "small groups," animated by multifarious forms of sociability, and divided into many "levels of depth."

Which of us was right? The question probably makes no sense. It is good that sociology detach the student from his prejudices, from his spontaneous consciousness derived from his immediate experience. Nor is it useless for the professor to deal as objectively as possible with problems normally confined to journalism or propagandistic speeches. My first courses, *Eighteen Lectures on Industrial Society* (London: Weidenfeld & Nicolson, 1967), *Industrial Society and Social Stratification* (New York: Free Press, 1964), *Democracy and Totalitarianism* (New York: Praeger, 1969) in 1955–56, 1956–57, and 1957–58, did not attract crowds, only a few dozen students the first year; their number grew from year to year, less a sign of success than of the increase in the number of students. In any event, if they had few listeners, these courses immediately had thousands of readers through their publication by the Sorbonne.

This choice of subjects was not without danger. Wishing to remove myself from journalism, I risked falling back into it. But on the other hand, I wanted to use my courses as preparation for my magnum opus on Marx and Pareto, which I had been thinking about and even writing for several years. I wanted to demonstrate in practical terms the possibility of a synthesis of the theory of growth (Colin Clark, Jean Fourastié), the theory of regimes (capitalism, socialism), the theory of social classes, and finally the theory of elites in the three domains of the economic, the social, and the political. I am not sure that I thought out these three small volumes very clearly in advance. In the first year, I let myself be carried from one lecture to the next, without an overall plan. The miracle is that the result was not worse.

In another chapter, I will return to the content of these books. My state of mind at the time and my concern with my audience call for a few remarks. A number of students, Marxists or *marxisants*, were waiting to trip me up. I arrived with the reputation of a man of the right and a journalist; I had to tame the Marxists, to convince them of my knowledge, make myself recognized by all as a fully competent teacher. In *Dix-huit Leçons*, I more than once was less than candid about my judgment of the Soviet Union. To demonstrate my objectivity, I had to grant to the regime to which I was opposed the benefit of the doubt, to show it some indulgence. I sincerely believe that I achieved my aim. We should not forget that Khrushchev's speech to the Twentieth Congress dates from 1956, the year of my first course. The facts that I pointed to in my courses were confirmed by the general secretary of the Communist Party of the Soviet Union.

It is difficult for me to talk about my relations with the students, at least the students in their first two years. They rarely came to see me: they sought advice from the assistants. At the beginning, their small number allowed me to assign oral presentations, thus imposing on them the test of speaking in public in front of their comrades and the professor. I quickly gave this up. The students hardly listened to their comrade and relied on the professor's critique. I tried not to humiliate the student, even if he had performed badly. I considered it unworthy to make students laugh at the expense of one of their number. I am not sure that I never committed this mistake, which I abhor; at least I can say that I never did it deliberately.

In circumstances that I no longer remember, Pierre Hassner, who sometimes attended my courses, delivered a brilliant, astonishing presentation on Thucydides. I showered him with praise which was no less than what he deserved. I told him that never, as a student or a teacher, had I heard a presentation of comparable quality (Pierre was already an *agrégé* at the time).[1] At the end of the session, a student said to me: "I would have hated you if you had not recognized that what we have heard today was exceptional." The following week, I, too, spoke about Thucydides, with the hope of not falling too far below Pierre.

My relations with students working on their dissertations were without problems. I preferred to let them choose their subjects, particularly when it came to the doctorat d'Etat: "If you don't have a subject in mind, or at least a certain idea of your intellectual interests, why do you want to write a thesis? It should not, it must not, be an academic exercise; you will give it years of your life, do not give them to mere considerations of your career." This attitude still seems appropriate to me today; confronted by some masters and in some circumstances, students may surrender to commands or to the requirements of a career. In that event, the responsibilities are shared.

My relations with assistants in seminars or with older students defending their theses were more difficult. My daughter Dominique several times criticized me for putting assistants in a false position in front of the students. Thus Pierre Bourdieu, who was my assistant in the early 1960s hardly spoke when he attended my seminars. Several times I wounded Pierre Hassner (or at least hurt him) when we were supposed to conduct a seminar on international relations together. In fact, joint conduct of a seminar, which went smoothly with Jean-Baptiste Duroselle, did not suit the Aron-Hassner pair. By the 1960s, I had sufficiently overcome my intemperate manner of speaking and my desire always to be right to cooperate with a codirector, but Pierre Hassner is at his best when he expresses himself in complete freedom, when his monologue, by itself, encompasses both his arguments and the possible objections of his listeners. His subtlety and his feeling for nuance are so superior to those of others—myself included, of course—that dialogue with him becomes difficult. He has to be left alone to conduct the conversation in his own way; each of his listeners will grasp along the way the nourishment suitable to him (or the pearls thrown out at random by an inexhaustible wealth of invention and analysis).

That said, I remember my seminars, particularly those of the Ecole Pratique des Hautes Etudes where I was appointed director of studies in 1960, as free discussions, research carried out in common, without verbal jousting. Of course, sessions were of unequal value, as a function of the interest of introductory presentations and the dialogue that followed. People who are now classified by their peers as among the elite of the scholarly community enjoyed them and derived some profit from them (I think, for example, of Jon Elster, who defended a *doctorat d'Etat* at the Sorbonne, the first Norwegian to achieve that distinction for fifty years). A student who regularly attended the seminar, whose opinions were close to those of the ultra-left, sent me a touching letter of gratitude for the style of the conversations.

I have a more mixed memory of thesis defenses. I will say first of all that, unlike some of my colleagues, I read the theses attentively and completely. Precisely because my colleagues at first suspected me of not submitting to all the obligations of the profession, I made it a point of honor to match the most conscientious. But this professional conscientiousness was also expressed in a certain directness that was rightly seen as severity—not to mention that other judges accused me of seizing the opportunity to show off at the expense of the candidate who, for half a day, still remained on the other side of the barricade. The member of a jury uses and abuses the advantages of his position.

At the Sorbonne, everyone chooses his own style. One may choose to correct mistakes in spelling or expression or anglicisms, another, when the thesis permits it, may launch into a brilliant speech that allows neither the audience to evaluate the thesis nor the candidate defending years of work to plead his cause. I adopted once and for all a direct style: I attempted to discuss the central ideas of the work and thereby gained a reputation for rigor, and even for cruelty. To some degree, I deserved this reputation. The contest of eloquence is as much among the members of the jury as between the jury and the candidate. He risks being a victim of rivalries among colleagues.

Alain Touraine, in one of his books, has described the ordeal inflicted on him by Georges Friedmann, Jean Stoetzel, and me. I felt, and still feel, genuine affection for him. In the community of Parisian sociologists, he stands out through his elegance, his natural nobility, and his authenticity. I felt no hostility or resentment toward him. He asked me to be the director of his thesis when it was already completed. He wished to be judged by me, either because he placed me above the others, or because my presence would add to the splendor of the ceremony. After the discussion of his secondary thesis (an empirical study of class consciousness) by Labrousse and Gurvitch—a discussion that was prolonged by the former's habitual taste for eloquence—Touraine presented his thesis with the spirit of a conquistador, concluding with a poem in Spanish. The president of the jury turned to me, and I began by saying: "Let's come back to earth."

During the intermission between the two defenses, he had made statements (reported to me later) worthy of a duelist about to engage in combat: "I fear only Aron." I let the large audience feel my friendly feelings for him; my judgments on the thesis were all the more wounding to him. I was not settling old scores, but I criticized Touraine for indulging in analyses that were more philosophical than sociological, without having mastered the concepts, without philosophical training. Was I right or wrong? In such matters, there can be no proof. All I can say in my defense is that I had read and reread the work and had asked for the opinion of an eminent specialist. Perhaps my intervention would not have been so devastating if it had not encouraged Friedmann and Stoetzel to be even more severe. Taken aback, Touraine practically gave up defending himself. The atmosphere became oppressive; Labrousse whispered to me: "This is too much, it's not possible." Jacques Le Goff shifted around in his seat, tempted to challenge the judges: Friedmann, the master and protector who had suddenly become so harsh, and Stoetzel, who had come from another part of the academic world. Touraine relived this afternoon as a dream, or rather a nightmare, for weeks. That evening, he received the fashionable and intellectual Parisians he had invited beforehand. One lady told me that this initiation ceremony had been horrible. Paul Lazarsfeld appreciated the public discussion of the thesis. "Your improvisation could be published as is," he said (this was not true).

Even though I have expressed myself with the same frankness in other circumstances, no other thesis defense ever reached such levels of dramatic intensity. I had a discussion with Michel Crozier; my objections were not always pertinent, and his responses were frequently greeted with applause. My dialogues with François Bourricaud and Henri Mendras were calm and cordial.

Determined to fulfill completely my obligations as a sociologist, I created at the Ecole Pratique a research center with the title European Center of Historical Sociology. Pierre Bourdieu was the general secretary and, in effect, the director until the break provoked by the events of May 1968. I belong to a generation between that of the direct disciples of Durkheim and the one for whom the conversion from philosophy to sociology implied the conduct of empirical research. As a professor in Bordeaux in 1945, would I have undertaken investigations, carried out my apprenticeship in the field with my students? Perhaps, but I'm not sure. Friedmann did not complete his conversion. For me, the return to the Sorbonne came too late; I was fifty, and I did not want to give up journalism and political action; international relations (which have given rise to few empirical investigations) occupied half my attention and half my time. When Pierre Bourdieu returned from his military service, he had already worked in the field. At the time, he promised all that he has since realized, one of the "greats" of his generation; he did not suggest what he has become, the leader of a sect, sure of himself and overbearing, an expert in faculty politics, merciless toward those who might challenge him. Humanly, I hoped for something else from him.

My position at the Sorbonne led me to committees of the CNRS. There I experienced both bureaucracy and the struggle among pressure groups. The committee was supposed to examine candidacies and the work of researchers whose reappointment or promotion was in question. The sociologists, who for the most part had made a career of the CNRS, paid little attention to degrees (the *agrégation*, for example) that they themselves did not possess. Regardless of degrees, the proposals prepared by candidates determined, in principle at least, the selection that would be made. The members of the committee would not have agreed even if all of them had, in good faith, looked for the best. Political opinions, group connections, interest in one field rather than another, came together and clashed. The arbitrary nature of democratic management was glaringly obvious.

As president of the sociology committee for four years, I had some success in influencing our work for the better. When the members of the committee, even the communists, became convinced of my sincerity, they often followed my suggestions. What struck me the most was that almost all the members of the committee appeared to be pleased when they had made a fair decision together. It was a minor confirmation of my ineradicable optimism about human nature: these sociologists preferred justice over their passions and their affiliations, when they had the opportunity to do so.

The years 1955 to 1968, when I was most closely associated with the university, were also marked by three notable public stances: on Algeria, on the General's press conference in 1967, and on the events of May 1968. During these thirteen years, I published five of my courses on the basis of my notes;[2] I had presented part of *Peace and War* as a course, but I completely rewrote it; at the Institut d'Etudes politiques, I presented the first course ever given in France on nuclear strategy, and afterward, I wrote *The Great Debate* (New York: Doubleday, 1963) in three weeks. In 1957, under the title of *Espoir et peur du siècle*, translated as *On War: Atomic Weapons and Global Diplomacy* (London: Secker & Warburg, 1958), I collected three essays on *La Droite, La Decadence*, and *La Guerre;* in 1965, I wrote a book-length article for the *Encyclopaedia Britannica, Progress and Disillusion* (New York: Praeger, 1968), which did not appear in France until 1968. In contrast, I did not use a one-year course on the political thought of Montesquieu, another on Spinoza, one on Marx, and still another on equality. My teaching departed to some extent from the present, from the problems imposed by the time.

For me, I repeat, the experience of teaching was a blessing. It helped me to recover an inner balance, not through forgetfulness, but through acceptance. Was it also an opportunity for the students, for the Sorbonne, for the development of sociological thought in France? It is not easy for me to answer these questions. Nevertheless, here are some remarks that most of my colleagues will accept.

Through my courses and my writings, I helped to give the community of sociologists a certain prominence. In his secondary thesis, Durkheim presented Montesquieu and Rousseau as precursors of sociology. I interpreted *L'Esprit des lois* as a work that was already inspired by the principal concerns of sociology. This argument is in fact almost trivial, if one thinks about it, but it had been forgotten. Similarly, and more important, I reminded my students and my colleagues that Tocqueville belonged to them, that the author of *Democracy in America* was not a precursor but a pioneer of sociological thought. Tocqueville, forgotten by philosophers and by literary historians, who had not noticed that he was a great writer, now belongs to the sociologists, the Americanists, and the historians. François Furet has paid homage to *L'Ancien Régime et la Révolution* and has restored this magisterial book to its place in the historiography of the French Revolution. Of course, I do not claim responsibility for this enrichment of the historical consciousness of French sociologists, which would be both ridiculous and hardly compatible with sociological thought. I contributed to this enrichment, as I had contributed before the war to the understanding of the greatness of Max Weber.

Of course, in placing Montesquieu and Tocqueville among the seven major figures whose portraits I sketched,[3] I broke with Durkheimian orthodoxy, and Georges Davy, a loyal epigone, pointed that out in a critical review. An English sociologist, who was more indulgent, nevertheless reminded me, amid his compliments, that Durkheim was the sociologist par excellence. Granted, but his work also potentially contains all the errors of "sociologism": supreme authority given to the sociological interpretation over all others; the use of the concept of "society" as though it designated an all-encompassing, concrete, clearly delimited reality; the confusion, in this concept, between fact and value, to the point that he can see no difference between society and God as objects of religious faith. There can be no doubt about Durkheim's genius, nor about a kind of narrowness and fanaticism.

Davy criticized me for slipping from sociology into political science. Does the distinction between these two disciplines have any meaning beyond the barriers between academic departments? What is valid in Davy's criticism is the fact that Montesquieu and Tocqueville do not break with the tradition of classical philosophy, even if both emphasize the link between social conditions and the political system and hence shed light on the social conditions and consequences of that system. Unlike Comte and Durkheim, they do not postulate the supremacy of the social over the political, or, of course, the insignificance of politics in relation to social reality. It is not an accident that neither Comte nor Durkheim wrote anything of importance about politics, particularly on the regime that they would have considered in harmony with the spirit or the demands of modern society.[4] Because he was in the end concerned with politics, Tocqueville still has something to say to us.

Is there a necessary opposition between Montesquieu and Tocqueville, who investigate the social conditions and consequences of politics, and Comte and Durkheim, who begin with social totality and grant only a small space to politics? This may be true, but why should sociology be based on propositions elevated to the status of postulates without which it would not exist as a science? My virtue, in my eyes, was to maintain that sociology does not imply a "sociologistic" philosophy. My mistake was to fail to develop the analysis further and to fail to take a position in the debate over types of explanation and models of society. What I wrote on historical explanation and understanding, on international relations, on French society, or on means of development excluded the extreme forms of determinism and functionalism. In both the Sorbonne and the Collège de France, I should have addressed these questions of principle.

With a bit more hesitation, I see merit in my having given voice, in the august precincts of the Sorbonne, to immediate concerns; referring to Khrushchev's speech, I spoke of the collectivization of agriculture and the Moscow trials. The three courses on industrial society, which evoke in me a feeling of nostalgia for the book that could have been written, furnished a tool for the "dominant ideology." They did not disconcert those who came from a Marxist-Leninist background. They outlined the framework within which ideological competition took place. They raised more questions than they gave answers. Despite all their defects, they gave students and cultivated men a less coarse, less caricatural vision than Marxism-Leninism of developed societies, of so-called socialist regimes and liberal democracies.

Beyond these two virtues, the essential escapes me. Did I awaken minds? Did I help students to live their youth and overcome their anxieties? How many of them have remembered my courses and still have the feeling of having gotten more than the means of obtaining a diploma, the value of which has declined? Of course, my close friends among my students would certainly not deny that they have retained something from attending my seminars and from our conversations. Outside of this small group, it is impossible to say. A professor in France speaks to a silent skeptical audience. He sometimes wonders whether his listeners are following his oratorical exercises as though he were a circus tightrope walker. The French public, particularly the student public, has always seemed to me the most difficult, the harshest I have encountered in the world.

I have presented dozens of courses and lectures in English and German. With the exception of a few special cases, I never had any difficulty in capturing my audience, feeling it physically, so to speak. When one speaks to one's listeners—which I always did—rather than reading or reciting a prepared text, one senses their reactions, the moment when a subject bores them, when their curiosity is awakened, when they lose the thread. I have almost always found English, American, and German students sympathetic and, above all, grateful. They demonstrate gratitude with a delicacy and spontaneity that have always moved me, an old denizen of the Sorbonne.

At Harvard, I delivered a more or less improvised speech to a group of elite students. A few minutes later, one of them approached me and said: "I just called my girlfriend to tell her how much I enjoyed this evening with you." On the other side, the only parallel I can offer is a letter from a student who, after a lecture in which I had revealed my solitude in the face of hundreds of students ensconced in their convictions, wrote very movingly, as though to console or reassure me.

Why do French students almost never express the gaiety or friendship of English, American, or German students? The system of examinations probably has something to do with it. Perhaps the Sorbonne students were already a lonely crowd. They knew the assistants, hardly ever the professors. They did not show their feelings; perhaps they had the same ones as students in other countries. A few years later, a student, who is now a rector, spoke to me about my course on Montesquieu as an event in his intellectual life. In any event, the resistance of the usual French audience poses a challenge to the professor who is aware of his mission and eager to accomplish it. To the very end at the Sorbonne, I attacked my courses with a solid determination to conquer those hundreds of faces, those hundreds of young minds, some of whom were already won over; but others were rebellious, and I dreamed of uniting them, through speech, into a welcoming community.

During the years 1955–68, my situation in the Parisian intelligentsia and in the academic world, in France and abroad, changed gradually. The period 1945–55 concluded with *The Opium of the Intellectuals*, which provoked my condemnation for intellectual betrayal, but did not prevent my appointment to the Sorbonne. The period 1955–68 concluded with the scandal of *The Elusive Revolution: Anatomy of a Student Revolt* (New York: Praeger, 1968); it also brought me much recognition, perhaps more abroad than in France. The non-Marxist or ex-Marxist left read *Eighteen Lectures on Industrial Society; Annales* put together a symposium on *Peace and War.* Honorary doctorates, at Harvard, Basel, Brussels, Oxford, etc., consecrated my acceptance by foreign universities. In Great Britain I was invited to deliver "prestigious" lectures: the Gifford Lectures at Aberdeen, the Basil Zaharoff Lecture at Oxford, the Alfred Marshall Lectures at Cambridge, the Chichele Lectures at Oxford, and similar lectures in the United States, at Harvard, Chicago, and Berkeley. The Thomas Jefferson Lectures of 1963 became the *Essai sur les libertés* in 1965 (*An Essay on Freedom* [Berkeley and Los Angeles: University of California Press, 1966]) and so on.

As journalist and teacher, I had no ground for taxing the public or institutions with injustice. The day I was named to the Collège de France, and even more on the evening of my inaugural lecture, I recalled my father and mother, who ended their lives in sorrow. They would have been consoled by the success—that is what they would have called it—of their son. Personally, I was not sure that I had fulfilled my potential. In 1970, I still felt young or, more precisely, I did not yet feel the burden of age; I did not calculate the best use of the time that I probably had left. Perhaps, as my critics have said so often, I am a reasonable writer; I doubt that I have conducted my career and my work in a reasonable manner.

NOTES

1. Jean-Claude Casanova reminds me that I said: "I have not heard such a brilliant presentation since the one Sartre did for Brunschvicg." I think Casanova's memory is accurate. Indeed, Sartre's presentation pointed to the future, but it was not dazzling; I wanted to emphasize my praise and demonstrate my enthusiasm.

2. *Dix-huit Leçons sur la société industrielle, La Lutte des classes, Démocratie et totalitarisme, Les Etapes de la pensée sociologique* (the course had been titled *Les Grandes Doctrines de sociologie historique*).

3. In *Main Currents of Sociological Thought*, 2 vols. (New York and London: Basic Books, 1965–67).

4. This judgment on Durkheim is probably too harsh. In the *Leçons de sociologie*, he expounds very Tocquevillian ideas on intermediate bodies.

1 4

THE ALGERIAN TRAGEDY

In 1956, three events shook Europe and troubled the French intellectual world: Khrushchev's speech to the Twentieth Congress of the Soviet Communist Party, Nasser's nationalization of the Suez Canal, and, almost simultaneously, the Hungarian Revolution and the Franco-British expedition.

Khrushchev's speech stunned public opinion in the West, intellectuals, communists, and progressives. The shock was all the more brutal in our country because the French refused, for the longest time and with the greatest obstinacy, to recognize the reality of the Gulag and the nature of the Soviet regime.

In a sense, one might have said that this celebrated speech revealed no secrets. Neither the great purge, nor the Gulag, nor the deportation of whole populations, nor the Moscow trials were unknown to those who wished to inform themselves. After all, even Sartre and Merleau-Ponty, in *Les Temps modernes* of May 1949, recognized the fact that "there is no socialism when one citizen out of twenty is in a camp." But they wrote this only once, and they alternated this concession to reality with so-called philosophical commentaries, a few examples of which follow. "If our communists accept the camps and oppression, this is because they expect the classless society to come out of this through the miracle of infrastructures. They are wrong. But this is what they think." The Gulag was not enough to convince the existentialists that the USSR was on the wrong side of the barricades. "Whatever the nature of present-day Soviet society, the USSR is, broadly speaking, in the current balance of power, located on the side of those who are struggling against the forms of exploitation familiar to us." And the conclusion (so to speak): "The colonies are the labor camp of the democracies."

There was no lack of books in which the French could have discovered most of the "revelations" provided by the speech, books by ex-communists (Boris Souvarine, Anton Ciliga, Victor Serge, Victor Kravchenko) or by sociologists (David Rousset, Michel Collinet). At a stroke, the general secretary of the Communist Party authenticated the "propaganda" of primitive or systematic "anticommunists."

I can derive little satisfaction from rereading the articles that I wrote for *Le Figaro* about the nationalization of the Suez Canal and the Franco-British expedition. I was to some extent intoxicated by the warlike atmosphere, by the obsession with the resort to force that spread through the editorial offices of Paris newspapers. I was never in favor of a military expedition; at the moment of the Hungarian Revolution, the combined operation of Israel, France, and Great Britain seemed to me both senseless and outrageous. But I allowed myself to take ambigious positions, thinking that the threat of a reoccupation of the Suez Canal would prompt Colonel Nasser to negotiate an agreement with its users.

After the fact, I criticize myself for not having followed my thought to its conclusion. Yes, Colonel Nasser carried out the nationalization in a provocative manner; but nationalization posed no serious risk of blocking the free passage of English and French oil tankers through the Canal. I should have immediately denounced the commentaries on the "indispensable" role of pilots, even though I was completely ignorant of navigation in the Canal.[1] André Siegfried was largely responsible for the myth.

Fortunately, my intoxication did not make me lose all perspective; I never accepted the comparison between March 1936 and July 1956 or the argument that the events in the Near East would have a decisive effect on the Algerian War: "The comparison with March 1936 is fortunately erroneous in many respects; once German troops were established in the Rhineland, nothing but war could remove them, and the balance of power in Europe was definitively changed. Colonel Nasser does not yet definitively own the Canal, and even if he were to succeed in the course of the coming negotiations, which is improbable, he would still not have become the leader of a great military power" (4–5 August 1956).

On 2 November 1956, when the Franco-British expedition had been unleashed, I warned against illusions: "Force is only a means. In Algeria, it has been unclear for months what purpose is being served by the use of force. In the future, objectives must not be subject to doubt, they must be clear in the minds of our leaders, clear in the eyes of world opinion. It would be mad to combat nationalism that is called Arab or Muslim, mad to call into question the independence of Tunisia and Morocco, which has been declared and definitively won. In North Africa, France can have no aim but to strengthen the moderates who, aspiring to national independence, nevertheless wish to maintain ties of cooperation and friendship with France. We will not find in Suez the solution to the problems of Tunisia, Morocco, or Algeria. Our only hope, our only chance, is that the blow struck against the man who incarnated pan-Islamic fanaticism may give our interlocutors the supreme courage of moderation."

It is now difficult to understand why, in the midst of the historical process of decolonization, the British and the French threw themselves into such an adventure. The United Kingdom had graciously abandoned its Asian possessions. What significance would the road to India have once India was independent? Why would Egypt, in control of the Canal, not take steps to please its users in order to increase its income? In fact, as I wrote more than once at the time, the Suez affair involved two questions: free passage on the one hand, and the consequences throughout the Islamic world of Colonel Nasser's prestigious success in defying the West. The emotional reaction to Nasser's challenge had more influence than political calculation on the deliberations of the British and French governments. The British and the French would not and could not accept such a slap in the face. In both capitals, the immediate reaction was intemperate language and military preparation. Personally, especially in the autumn, several months after the nationalization, I had ceased to believe that the British and the French would take action; the threat was a negotiating ploy. In this spirit, I refrained from condemning in advance occupation of the Suez Canal. There is no doubt that I was wrong; the passion dominating the editorial offices of Le Figaro, particularly that of Brisson, does not excuse me, but it explains the ambiguity of my articles.

It was different on the day that Israeli troops attacked in the Sinai, while the governments of London and Paris sent an ultimatum to Cairo on the pretext of separating the belligerents. The collusion between France and Israel was not open to doubt; the response to the nationalization of the Suez Canal, which had been carried out several months earlier, now seemed to be nothing but a pretext for overthrowing Colonel Nasser. This scenario, which was morally unjustifiable, also lacked military merit. Everyone knew that for the operation to enjoy success it had to work quickly; several days went by between the ultimatum and the Franco-British landing. European diplomacy had not made certain of the tolerance of the American government. General Eisenhower, in the midst of his reelection campaign, exploded in anger. In London, public opinion rebelled against this gunboat diplomacy.

The pound suffered from attacks that may have been spontaneous or may have been orchestrated from Washington. The British prime minister gave in to American pressure rather than to the threatening letter from Bulgaria that referred to Soviet missiles.

In the course of those weeks, my articles, too, were less than generous to American diplomacy. The Americans had provoked Colonel Nasser not so much by the refusal to finance the Aswan Dam as by the style of that refusal. John Foster Dulles had maneuvered, from conference to conference, in order to dissuade the British and French from intervening. Finally, at the United Nations, he found himself in the same camp as the Soviet Union in condemning his allies, while simultaneously stirring a majority of the Assembly to condemn the Soviet intervention in Hungary.

The simultaneous crises in the Near East and in Eastern Europe impressed and informed me. The complicity of the great powers seemed to me to be obvious. Each of them had called its satellites or allies to order; of course, Hungary's aspiration to freedom differed fundamentally from Great Britain's vain desire to preserve its imperial positions, or France's wish to strike at the Algerian rebels by humiliating Nasser. A formal resemblance remained: the "people's democracies" of Eastern Europe could count on no external assistance; the European democracies, former great powers, no longer had the means to resort to force without the acquiescence of the United States.

The Guy Mollet government had thrown itself into the Suez adventure because the Egyptians were supporting the Algerian rebels and conducting a passionate propaganda campaign against France. French policy in Algeria turned out to be all the more dangerous; we were becoming the principal target of Arab nationalism. I asked for an audience with the President of the Republic—something I have done only two or three times in the course of my existence—in the hope of enlightening him on the inevitable failure of "pacification." René Coty received me cordially and began to speak, leaving me no more than five or ten minutes out of the sixty-five or seventy that our conversation lasted. When I left him, and he stopped talking, he seemed very satisfied with me.

La Tragédie algérienne appeared early in June 1957, two years after my return to the university; at a stroke, I was carried into a political uproar. At that moment, even opponents of the policies of Guy Mollet or Bourgès-Maunoury (the most forgotten of Fourth Republic premiers), the "liberals," did not use the word *independence;* they condemned repression and torture and recommended negotiations. Neither *Le Monde* nor *L'Express*, the bêtes noires of the government, specified the solution that they considered both desirable and possible. I had thus violated the rules of diplomatic obscurity and ambiguity. Or, to change the image, I had put my foot in it. Negotiations, of course, but let us have the courage of our thought and action: there will be no negotiations without recognition of the Algerians' right to independence; and this implied that at least a fraction of the French in Algeria would have to leave.

For a few weeks, this brief and harsh text created a scandal, all the more because I was its author: the commentator of *Le Figaro* was changing sides. Why? There were many colleagues who attempted to undermine me, either by seeing no value in my work (we knew all this already) or by attributing to me motives entirely different from those of the "left," and thus hardly honorable.

My position understandably surprised those who did not know me, and even those who thought they knew me. It did not represent a break in my thought, but it created that impression, for which I was perhaps responsible. In fact, in conversations with friends in London in 1943 and 1944, when victory was in sight, I made the argument that after the war France would not have the means to preserve its empire;[2] the war, carried out in the name of freedom, must inspire colonized peoples with the spirit of rebellion, free slaves from respect for their masters, and deprive masters of the instrument of force. The immediate abandonment of Indochina, or more precisely, the immediate offer to the three states of Indochina of independence within the framework of the French Community seemed to me to be the first indispensable step. Thereafter, we could devote the bulk of our resources to North Africa and black Africa to carry out, within a generation, the gradual emancipation of our colonies and protectorates. These ideas gave me a dubious reputation among orthodox Gaullists, not to mention the accusation of treason launched by those who claimed a monopoly on patriotism.

It is true that I had not taken part in the debate on Vietnam between 1947 and 1954. From 1954 on, I vowed not to continue my discretion of the previous years. In 1954, in a spectacular move, Pierre Mendès France granted Tunisia internal autonomy, which would obviously lead to independence. Pierre Brisson himself approved a historic decision which led to the evolution of North Africa as a whole. I wrote almost nothing about Morocco, but I gave as much help as I could to Edgar Faure, who was attempting to bring the sultan back from Madagascar to Rabat, a return that would almost certainly lead to the independence of the Moroccan empire. I was present at lunch at which Edgar Faure, then prime minister, "tried out," so to speak, on Pierre Brisson the idea of Sultan Mohammed's return. Edgar Faure presided over a heterogeneous cabinet in which the Gaullists, led by General Koenig, opposed a policy patterned after the one Mendès France had inaugurated—Tunisia. Pierre Brisson was subject to influence from opposite directions. To him, I argued for the inevitability of decolonization, which was moreover in conformity with democratic ideas. On the other hand, the old

"Africa hands" repeated to him—and they were right—that the return of
Mohammed implied the independence of Morocco, and would put an end to
the French enterprise in Africa, including perhaps Algeria. Brisson wrote an
editorial against the return of Mohammed, with the title "Never." I pointed
out the dangers of these declarations of faith, which posterity would cite as
examples of the blindness of participants and commentators. I have never
forgotten the "never" of Albert Sarrault in March 1936: France will never
allow the Strasbourg cathedral to be threatened by German weapons. How
many French leaders have rejected in words events which, at bottom, they
foresaw.

The Algerian rebellion began in November 1954, a few months after the
French defeat in Indochina, and a few months after Mendès France's trip to
Tunisia. These two events did not create the forces that swept away the
French Empire, but they set them loose, opened the floodgates through
which flowed national rebellions, supported by the Arabs, the Muslims, the
Soviets, and, within Western countries themselves, the countless enemies of
colonialism.

After the very limited victory of the Republican Front, the government,
led by Guy Mollet and not Mendès France, did not call into question the
independence of Tunisia and Morocco, but it succumbed to the pressure of
the French in Algeria and the supporters of "French Algeria" in France. Far
from choosing another line, it followed that of its predecessors and, since it
theoretically represented the left, it dared to send draftees to serve in
Algeria and thereby reactivated the old patriotism with a view toward preserving the last fragment of the empire. Or, more precisely, to preserve as
French the three departments that were, legally, an integral part of the
national territory.

I had no direct knowledge of Algeria, where I had never been. The few
weeks I had spent with a friend in Tunisia had not reconciled me to "colonization," even though the atmosphere, in 1949, was still relatively relaxed. I
had detested overpopulated Saigon, where soldiers of the expeditionary
force had filled the streets, bars, and hotels; "national" leaders, who were
weak, did not conceal the permanence of French authority. The military
occupation of Germany in 1946 repelled me.

What I had read and what I knew of French Algeria did not inspire any
sympathy in me, but my judgment and convictions were dictated above all
by reflection. Why would the Algerians accept a status that was inferior in
their eyes to that of Tunisia or Morocco? Why would the "educated," the
"Frenchified," not desire the independence that the elites of all colonized
countries had already achieved or were in the process of achieving?

Of course, the "Algerian problem," as it was called, differed from that of
the two protectorates to the east and west of it, because of the departmental

status of Algeria on the one hand, and on the other, because of the presence of a million French citizens. In Algeria, there was neither the embryo nor the residue of a state, which had survived in the two neighboring protectorates. As for French society, established in the midst, and especially on the periphery, of Algerian society, it could hardly maintain itself as it was on the day an Algerian government replaced the governor general and his administration. The departure, partial or total, of the French minority seemed the inevitable consequence of an Algerian Algeria.

My only virtue (or fault) was to have carried the analysis to its conclusion and to have set down in black and white what many liberals hesitated to admit to themselves and, all the more, to write. In 1955, *Le Figaro* had tolerated some of my articles describing the situation and emphasizing the dangers. In early 1956, I prepared a note for the Republican Front government. In the spring of 1957, I hurriedly wrote a pamphlet, haunted by the fear that France was for a second time about to throw itself into another doomed adventure, comparable to Indochina and even more serious. The government would not resist a continuation of the war for many years, and an absurd civil war seemed to be in prospect. I thought for a long time; I was afraid of predictable attacks, but I wondered about my duty.

Of all the commentaries on my pamphlet, *La Tragédie algérienne*, perhaps the most striking came from an anonymous writer, a few lines on an unsigned card in a hand characteristic of a simple man rather than an intellectual: "Objective, lucid, and penetrating analyses, fine and respectable in every way but perfectly ineffective in any matter that has to do with feeling, instincts, and reflexes."

I never thought that publication of *La Tragédie algérienne* required any particular courage. The physical risk was very remote, despite one or two anonymous letters that informed me of my condemnation by clandestine tribunals "of public safety." There was no moral or political risk, because, in intellectual and political circles, most people subscribed to the arguments and conclusions that I set out in black and white.

I experienced the danger to which I had exposed myself on the rue Madame, in the room reserved for Catholic intellectuals. Maurice Schumann and Edmond Michelet were supposed to speak after me. For a few minutes, I was able to speak in relative silence. Then, gradually, interruptions came from all sides. Tell me about Melouza (an Algerian village whose inhabitants were massacred by the FLN), one of the audience repeated in gentle tones. Exasperated, I made the mistake of replying: "There are also acts on our side which we cannot be proud of." This provoked an uproar. Schumann, on his feet, shouted: "I will not let French officers be insulted." He scored a victory, supported by the applause of most of the audience. Michelet survived the ordeal scarcely better than I. At the end of the meeting, the police advised me to wait ten minutes before leaving; a crowd of furious people had come together, probably not to manhandle me, but to humiliate me further, to give free rein to their anger.

The pamphlet created some stir; the argument for "abandonment" was no longer banished from the salons or the Assembly. In her friendly enthusiasm, our dear friend Jeanne Alexandre was wrong: "I said to myself at once that it was comparable to Zola's *J'accuse*. Everyone to whom I suggested this comparison agreed that it went without saying." No, the comparison does not stand. Zola was standing up against blind passions. The passion for French Algeria was shot through with doubts. Officers in the field discussed *La Tragédie algérienne*. Not all the colonels were followers of the theoreticians of subversive war, not all of them believed that a psychological technique could convert the Algerians to French patriotism. Jeanne Alexandre herself observed that a few months later the uproar had subsided. On its appearance, my pamphlet was not unrecognized abroad. John F. Kennedy quoted me in the Senate; an editorial in the *Economist* saw my position as a symptom of change in public opinion. In hindsight, I wonder. The pamphlet freed me from the absurd but common accusation of conformism. On the other hand, it did not cleanse me of another fault; I remained the heartless calculator, the cold thinker. I have never thought it appropriate to respond to this kind of remark. After the evening at the rue Madame, Henri Birault wrote me an admirable letter, some of whose statements, I hope, are not entirely false: "A sober fraternity that seeks above all to protect those one loves from great misfortune . . . writing *La Tragédie algérienne* so that not too many Frenchmen and Muslims would die for nothing in this war with no possible victory." Thus I justified my action to myself; in hindsight, I wonder if I succeeded. This is the frustration of someone who seeks to act through his pen.

In the summer of 1958, shortly after General de Gaulle's return to power, I received an honorary doctorate from Harvard, and I was invited to deliver one of the two commencement addresses (the other was given by the American secretary of defense, Neil H. MacElroy). The fall of the Fourth Republic, at least apparently, had been provoked by the fear of a diplomatic Dien Bien Phu. The crowds that had seized the headquarters of the French government in Algiers shouted *"Algérie française":* demonstrations of Franco-Muslim friendship, some of which were authentic, created for a few days or a few weeks the illusion that the believers were winning out over the calculators. Personally, I never vacillated. But at Harvard, I did not think it appropriate to recapitulate the argument of my pamphlet and, before a foreign public that was not very well disposed toward France, to denounce the blindness of my compatriots, their tendency to blame the Fourth Republic exclusively for the Algerian insurrection, inseparable from a historical movement that did not spare any of the colonies of any European nation. The excerpts of my speech transmitted by AFP made it appear that I had changed my views and that I had joined—or resigned myself to—the national and popular uprising of 1958. To clarify matters, and to avoid the propagation of the legend of a conversion, inspired by opportunism, I had long passages of my speech reprinted in Le Monde and, especially, I published another, more detailed pamphlet, L'Algérie et la République.

In 1957, as a guest of the French Canadian Institute of Public Affairs, I met the whole generation of politicians who are still generally in the front rank: Jean Lesage (the man of the quiet revolution), René Levesque, Pierre Elliott Trudeau, then in the full flower of his career as a playboy at the wheel of his Jaguar, if my memory is correct. After Canada, I accepted an invitation from Harvard and delivered three lectures, which were developed into Immuable et changeante, a book published in 1959, after the end of the Fourth Republic (France Steadfast and Changing [London: Oxford University Press, 1960]). In that year, 1957–58, my public course at the Collège de France dealt with the political systems of industrial societies. Published nearly ten years later, the course showed the influence, which I did not want to erase, of the events of 1958. The title of one chapter, "Fil de soie et fil de l'épée," referred respectively to expressions of Guglielmo Ferrero and General de Gaulle.

Legality had been formally respected, but the Fourth Republic had given way to a rebellion of the army and the French in Algeria, a rebellion to which General de Gaulle was not entirely unconnected (to say the least). Before 15 May, he himself had said nothing, but he had also not disavowed the wild propaganda of his most faithful companion.

In Le Courrier de la colère, Michel Debré went so far as to proclaim the right, even the duty, of revolt against a government that would allow French sovereignty in Algeria to be called into question. Gaullists were suspected of taking part in one or the other of the thirteen conspiracies that led to 13 May, one of which involved General Salan. All of this separated me from the Gaullists of 1958. Nevertheless, I did not identify the General with his followers; he himself had dirtied his hands as little as possible, even though he was not unaware of the intentions or the actions of some of the plotters. According to the perspectives of various commentators, he was the one who saved the deputies from defenestration, or he was the one who set the bombs of 13 May. In fact, he played both roles.

Besides, rumors reported statements by General de Gaulle that made him seem closer to the liberals than to the ultras. Someone assured me that the General himself, in a conversation, had agreed with me against Jacques Soustelle, particularly on the demographic problem. In any event, it was possible to argue that the General, thanks to his authority and prestige, had a better chance than anyone to find a solution to the conflict or to persuade the French to endure its continuation. In 1957 and 1958, I was attempting to persuade; from June 1958 on, I was relegated to the role of spectator or commentator. How could I have joined the Gaullist party, the UDR, improvised for the elections, defender of French Algeria, and led by Michel Debře and Jacques Soustelle? But, on the other hand, why should I assume an opposition stance while the meaning of the event remained ambiguous? André Malraux did not hesitate to join the service of the General, whatever the official doctrine may have been at any particular moment. It seemed to me inappropriate for an intellectual, who prided himself on being a political writer, to take part in the equivocations, the detours, and the perhaps necessary deceptions of a head of government. Since I had asserted my own doctrine, with complete clarity, I owed it to myself not to leave my solitude, and to interpret the General's progress without transfiguring it with rhetoric.

The second pamphlet, *L'Algérie et la Republique*, made very little stir, although it was much more rigorously argued than *La Tragédie algérienne*. In the first chapter, I demonstrated, with statistical support, why integration—Algeria becoming a province of France like the Ile-de-France or Lorraine—was impossible. The two populations did not share the same culture, and they lived in different demographic and economic circumstances. How could the same social laws be applied to both communities? Oil wealth would not be enough to close the gap between the conditions of existence to the south and the north of the Mediterranean. (Twenty years later, despite the twentyfold increase in the price of oil, the argument retains its truth.) Hence, I took a position in the strange debate opened by Germaine Tillion's book, *L'Algérie en 1957*, published a few weeks before *La Tragédie algérienne*. Thierry Maulnier, an unconditional supporter of French Algeria, cited Germaine Tillion in support of his conclusion: "France or famine." He drew from the ethnologist's work much more than she asserted. Nevertheless, she had posed the question: "Is anticolonialism in the process of becoming an alibi for immiseration?"

I recognized that "apparent liberalism can be a disguise for egotism. In the case of Algeria, two interpretations are possible: one who proposes a dialogue with the Algerian nationalists may be an idealist calling on the right of peoples to self-determination or dreaming of friendship with the Muslims. He may also be a capitalist, concerned with reducing expenses and indifferent to the poverty of an independent Algeria. (It goes without saying that anyone on the left belongs to the first, noble, category.) It is from love for Ali and Mohammed, from love for the most destitute of the Kabyles and Arabs, that the former governor of Algeria, whose heart is inexhaustible, finds himself miraculously in agreement with the superior minds and elite charac ters of Roger Duchet, Alain de Sérigny, and other contributors to the *Echo d'Alger*. If Le Brun Keris and Etienne Borne condemn my cynicism, this is because Christian feelings compel them to rescue the Algerians from poverty and the tyranny of the FLN."

In the second chapter, "The Crisis of French Consciousness," I tried to persuade my compatriots that the loss of the empire did not condemn our country to decadence. "Defeat is to despair of reconciliation with the nationalists. Abandonment is to reject cooperation with countries destined for independence. Who is blocking the future but those who claim that the aspiration of peoples for self-government is incompatible with France's attachment to Africa? Decadent nations are those that refuse to adapt to a changing world. The gravediggers of the nation are those who, on the pretext of preventing decadence, direct patriotism into a dead end."

The third chapter, "The May Revolution," presented a sketchy analysis of the events of May 1958, the return of General de Gaulle to power and the fall of the Fourth Republic. In passing, I discussed the ideas Albert Camus had presented in an article:[3] "Despite his desire for justice and his generosity, M. Albert Camus has not succeeded in raising himself above the attitude of a colonialist of good will." He rejected the legitimacy of Arab demands: "It must, however, be recognized that, as far as Algeria is concerned, national independence is a purely emotional formulation. There has never been an Algerian nation. The Jews, the Turks, the Greeks, the Italians, the Berbers, would have as much right to claim leadership of this possible nation." To which I replied: "These Muslims have not been a nation in the past, but the youngest among them want to create a nation. Is this an emotional demand? Of course, like all revolutionary demands." Camus recommended the same measures advocated by the defenders of French Algeria: improvement in the standard of living, "personal federalism" (in other words, civil and political equality of the Muslims and the French). He wanted the government "not to concede any of the rights of the French in Algeria," he presented "the Algerian nationalist demand in part as one of the manifestations of the new Arab imperialism, over which Egypt, overestimating its strength, claims leadership, and which, for the moment, Russia is using in its anti-Western strategy."

These texts have been forgotten; his Stockholm speech, or rather a statement made to a journalist, has, on the other hand been remembered: "I believe in justice, but I will defend my mother before justice."[4] The statement is finally meaningless. The Algerian rebellion posed to all the French, particularly the French of Algeria, a question of conscience. Why did Albert Camus find an answer to this question in his love for his mother? We understand that he was torn between his attachment to Algeria, his filial love, and his concern for justice, that he refused to choose sides between the two warring camps. But the confrontation between "mother" and "justice" seemed to me a clever phrase, not a judgment on a tragic conflict. I have no intention of tarnishing the justified fame of Camus: I call into question neither the nobility of his soul nor his good will. What remains instructive, for those who did not live through those years, is the rejection, even by a Camus, of Algerian "nationalism," of the will for independence that drove an active minority and that was probably supported by a majority of the population.

I was close to the mark on General de Gaulle's constitutional plans: "General de Gaulle no doubt sincerely wishes to restore the Republic and even a parliamentary Republic. The Constitution of the Fifth Republic risks being less a compromise between presidential and parliamentary government than a return to a semiparliamentary monarchy. The government will be responsible to the Assembly, but the prime minister will be chosen by the President of the Republic, and the latter, like a monarch, will retain certain prerogatives that kings themselves have lost in this century's parliamentary regimes. This step backward may serve some purpose. The Constitution, inspired by the Bayeux speech, does not provide a lasting answer to French problems, but it offers an institutional framework within which General de Gaulle will be able to exercise an absolute and limited power." (The expression "absolute and limited" comes from Maurras.)

Even though I had been shocked by the circumstances in which General de Gaulle had returned to power (on 15 May, he had lent his moral authority to the Algiers "insurgents"), in July 1958, a few weeks after the May revolution, I recognized that he had opportunities no one else would have had: "More than anyone else, General de Gaulle has the means to restore peace because he is capable of waging war and because he has a reputation for generosity." I described the General not as the representative or the leader of the colonels or the May conspirators but, on the contrary, as the statesman who might initiate dialogue with the Algerian nationalists: "What the ultras and the conspirators want goes against historical necessity and the long-range hopes of the majority of the French. The May revolution may be the beginning of the political renovation of France on the condition that it hastens to devour its children."

After this pamphlet, I frequently wrote articles for *Preuves* on the Fifth Republic and particularly on the General's Algerian policy. In the first article I published, in November 1958, I referred to my 1943 article in *La France libre*, in which I had analyzed the background for Bonapartism: "An atmosphere of national crisis, with parliament and parliamentarians discredited, and the popularity of one man." I did not fail to recognize the differences between the causes of the national crisis (social conflict in 1848, military defeat in 1940, loss of the empire in 1958) nor the differences among the men around whom popular feeling crystallized: "The beneficiary of the Bonapartist movement, whether he is named Louis-Napoléon, Boulanger, Pétain, or de Gaulle, whether he is an adventurer, a time-server, an old man, or an authentic great man, has to possess a particular virtue: to transcend French disputes, to be simultaneously of the right and the left, to unite pre-Revolutionary with post-Revolutionary France."

I am not unduly embarrassed when I reread my analysis of the 1958 Constitution—perhaps not very different from the one Marshal Pétain had prepared. Georges Vedel congratulated me, in a friendly letter, for my analysis of the moment and the Constitution, and he presented details that have a certain bite: "The Constitution of Pétain that you imagine," he wrote, "existed at least potentially. You will find that text and indications of sources in the seventh edition of the collection of constitutions by Duguit and Mounier. On page 10, you will find the following: 'The head of state derives his powers from a Congress comprised of those elected by the nation and delegates of the territorial units of the nation. He personifies the nation and determines its fate. As arbiter of the supreme interests of the country, he assures the functioning of institutions by maintaining, through exercising the right of dissolution if necessary, the bond of confidence between the government and the nation.'" Vedel added that this unwitting correspondence between the abortive plans of the Marshal and the General's conception proves nothing either for or against the 1958 Constitution.

My diagnosis of the Fourth Republic and the situation of 1958 remains the same today, often repeated by present-day historians: "Hostility to the Fourth Republic resembled the hostility against the Third Republic that was observed in 1940. This severity, which is not without injustice, at least expresses a healthy feeling: the French had had enough of being the world's laughingstock because of governmental instability. Whatever the consequences of that instability, even if they were less than is ordinarily thought, the frequency of governmental crises discredited the regime in the eyes of the French and others. In the long run, a country cannot obey those for whom it has contempt."

On the other hand, I made a positive judgment of diplomatic accomplishment (the Atlantic Alliance, reconciliation with Germany, the organization of Europe) and economic accomplishments, which exceeded the hopes fostered by the optimists at the Liberation. Did the French reproach the Fourth Republic for having lost the empire or for having attempted to save it? For having identified the loss of empire as a national disaster or else for having failed to recognize its importance? "The Fourth Republic stumbled on the obstacle of the Algerian war, incapable of pursuing it, of winning it, or of ending it through negotiations; it has surrendered the reins."

At the time, I presented the Constitution as that of a parliamentary empire—a diagnosis confirmed by later events—and I cannot find in this article the systematic anti-Gaullism that, with more reason, was later attributed to me: "Because it has not integrated the plebiscite into the democratic system, as the English and Americans have, France oscillates between the anonymity of second-rate parliamentarians and the vivid presence of the charismatic leader. General de Gaulle is a perfect example of the charismatic leader, but he has historic ambitions comparable to those of Washington." In the autumn of 1958, Boris Souvarine, a friend of Jacques Chevalier, informed me of the negotiations that de Gaulle had attempted to arrange with the FLN, through intermediaries. These negotiations failed.

In May 1959, I wrote an article on the government's economic policies. Jean-Marcel Jeanneny, a minister at the time, sent me a note: "I have just read your article in *Preuves* on our economic policies. It is the best—the only good—presentation that has been made of them. Thank you, and thank you for having noted that I am not a 'liberal.'"

On the occasion of the first anniversary of the new regime, I published another article in *Preuves:* "One year later: Charles de Gaulle between the Ultras and the Liberals." Once again, consistent with my earlier positions, I analyzed the General's Algerian policy with indulgence: "[T]hose who thought it just to recognize Algeria's right to self-determination, those who considered the desire to maintain colonial domination contrary to the vocation of France in the twentieth century, have no reason to repent. The fact that, at the present moment, the President of the Republic can do nothing but what he is doing does not imply that one should now approve what one had earlier condemned. Or else, we should apologize and regret the attacks directed against Guy Mollet." As for my attitude toward the General himself, it took the form of inevitably qualified, and indeed equivocal, expressions. I deplored the temptation of internal exile (that of Mendès France, for example): "The Fifth Republic exists, and in present-day France, General de Gaulle is the best possible monarch in the least bad of possible governments. He possesses personal power, but he restored the Republic in 1945. He manipulated the 1958 revolution in order to produce an authoritarian republic, not fascism nor a military despotism. He wants to save the remnants of the French empire, but he has granted the territories of black Africa the right to independence. He is making war in Algeria, but he does not exclude further developments." The conclusion was that we would like to help him but we continue to see the movement toward Algerian independence as irresistible. In the meantime, let us allow him to act.

Subsequent articles in *Preuves,* the last of which was completed on 20 April 1962, reflect my hesitations in judgment, or perhaps even more, the fluctuations in my mood. In the autumn of 1959, after de Gaulle's 16 September speech on self-determination, I foresaw, without risk of error, that the FLN and the GPRA would reject the proposal to end the fighting and take their chances in the electoral arena. The General proposed a middle path between "French Algeria" and "abandonment," at the end of which Algeria would be closely associated with France, autonomous within a French framework. But did this middle path exist?

In March 1960, after the crisis of the barricades, I admired the General's action in an article entitled "A single man, a man alone," at the same time recalling that proclamation of the principle of self-determination would not be enough to bring hostilities to an end. The FLN fighters would not surrender their weapons as long as the government had not specified the conditions in which the principle would be put into operation. In the absence of negotiations with the FLN or the GPRA, there was no way of escaping from the framework established by Guy Mollet's notorious three-part proposition (cease-fire, elections, negotiations). At the same time, the title of the article written in praise of "a single man, a man alone" illustrated my doubt, my anxiety: Is it appropriate to replace democratic legitimacy with the legitimacy of a man chosen by History? "The more the General insists on the personal character of the legitimacy that he possesses, the more he weakens the constitutional edifice that he has himself established. General de Gaulle has been led almost always to do the opposite of what he would like to do. He has a horror of rebellion, and he began his political career as a rebel. He has a horror of military coups d'état, and he returned to power in May 1958 thanks to a military coup d'état that threatened the legally constituted government. He has a passionate desire to unify the French in which he never succeeds because this unity is contrary to the nature of the tasks that have had to be carried out in the course of the past twenty years." This explains his program of national legitimacy, embodied in a single man, through the most extraordinary changes in direction.

In the autumn of 1960, I inclined toward more severity, and I entitled an article "Presumption," comparing the General's claims when he returned to power with the situation two years later: "General de Gaulle is a liberal, if that means a man who considers the evolution of Algeria toward existence as a nation inevitable, in conformity with the ideas of the time, and compatible with the preservation of French interests. But he is an ultra, if that means a man who refuses negotiations with the combatants. The only ones who have a right to independence are those who ask for it politely." It was an unjust article, composed during my time at Harvard University. Georges Friedmann, with justice, criticized its tone: "In the current situation, I see no one other than de Gaulle who can preserve the basic freedoms that you have spent your life defending. He still has a chance of succeeding. I am surprised that you seem (this is how many have interpreted it with pleasure) to have lent the authority of your name to those who exist only to break his power.

Knowing you, I am convinced that, if you were in France, you would have corrected your judgment after writing 'Presumption.'" In the next article, after quoting Friedmann's letter, I explained myself: "I never doubted the fact that, of all the French, the General was the most capable of operating on the Algerian abscess. A single man and a man alone is preserving our freedoms and has set himself between confusion in men's minds and chaos." The General's November 1960 speech took one further step: "The 'Algerian Republic' has come after 'Algerian Algeria,' and that Republic will have an independent diplomacy." The General was thus offering to Algeria a status similar to that of the states of the French community, but he left the crucial point obscure: Who would take charge of the Algerian Republic?

My concern was always focused on the same point: "Everything finally comes down to the question that observers have been incessantly asking for two years: Given that General de Gaulle, philosopher of history, considers French Algeria dead and independent Algeria inevitable, how long will General de Gaulle, head of state, reject the dialogue without which the tragic contradiction between his strategy and his tactics, between the conclusion he foresees and the rejection he maintains, will continue?" And at the end of the article, written in Cambridge in reply to Friedmann, I concluded: "We can probably do very little. We risk compromising him by approving him and weakening him by criticizing him. It is not entirely useless to declare openly that General de Gaulle bears our hopes, our last hopes for an honorable peace—that is, a peace that would reconcile France with the Algerian nationalists without provoking armed conflict among the French themselves."

After the plot of the "quartet" of generals and the press conference of 11 April 1961, I no longer doubted that the head of state belonged to the party of "abandonment," determined to negotiate with the FLN on the basis of recognition of Algerian independence: "After three years of hesitation or illusion, at the conclusion of slow and tortuous preparatory work, General de Gaulle resigned himself or determined to negotiate with the FLN about the future of Algeria, against his frequent promises without considering the feelings of the army. Isn't it 'governing *à la florentine*,' as used to be said, to choose as prime minister, with the duty of receiving Bourguiba, the editor of *Le Courrier de la Colère?* Isn't it 'governing *à la florentine*' to blame the Fourth Republic, on 15 May 1958, for 'the distress of the fighting forces,' while one has oneself the intention of doing what the distress of the army (usually called sedition) is designed to prevent?" A little further on, I put myself in the place of the "dupes": "The victors of 13 May, when self-determination was proclaimed in January 1960 and independence granted in April 1961, had the feeling that they had been had. They had been deprived of the revolution that the Gaullists had stolen from them. If the right of insurrection was legitimized against the Fourth Republic's party of abandonment, if, as the Prime Minister used to say, the duty of obedience ceases on the day the government considers giving up a part of the national territory, why are the four generals criminals and not unfortunate heroes? Personally, I have no doubt that they were criminals."

I changed direction, in a way I cannot explain, with an article mistitled "Farewell to Gaullism." What is the explanation for this verbal violence? The Bizerte episode had outraged me; perhaps I was wrong to place complete responsibility on the French government, but this bloody lesson administered to a Muslim head of state, who was a sincere friend of France, seemed to me unjust, cruel, and against our national interest. At the same time, the General's strategy, which consisted in granting bit by bit, through unilateral concessions, the very elements that were at stake in the conflict, seemed to me in the end to be unreasonable. This explains the barbs that may have been sharp, but were in any event discourteous: "One does not decolonize in the style of Louis XIV. Bidault would have waged war to the bitter end to serve the French empire. General de Gaulle is making war in order to preserve the style of his abandonment." At that point, I was criticizing Gaullist strategy as a whole: "The General agreed to sit at the negotiating table only after having carefully given up all his cards—nothing in his hands, nothing up his sleeves. Then what will he do if the GPRA asks for the Sahara?"

The FLN was negotiating as though it were the victor: "The Algerian nationalists may have lost all the battles in the field, but they have won the war, since the French government has recognized the justice of their demands, has declared itself ready to satisfy them, and wishes for 'disengagement.'" This was a foreseeable result that I had predicted as early as 1957. "If the ALN succeeded in holding 400,000 French soldiers in Algeria, it would give the GPRA the 'military victory' it needs. For it was predictable that, in the long run, the French people would grow tired of a war whose very duration demonstrated its injustice and futility."

As for the last lines of the article, the polemical violence of which still troubles me, they nevertheless contain a valid message: "The General has spoken of disengagement and not only of decolonization, suggesting that total abandonment—regrouping and repatriation of the French of Algeria and the Muslims who wish to remain French—would be, in the absence of an agreement with the GPRA, the inevitable solution. Whether this agreement comes about or not, it is clear that nothing, or almost nothing, of what could have been saved two or three years ago will be saved." Today's reader will be tempted to respond: Could he have saved anything?

I would still sign the following article, the last of the series, since it was in a sense a critique of the preceding ones. "Those who have followed the chronicles of the Fifth Republic in this publication are not unaware of the hesitancy in my judgments. It was only the necessity of putting an end to the Algerian war that seemed to me to justify the paternalist monarch introduced under the cover of the 1958 Constitution. In my eyes, only negotiations with the GPRA offered a chance of reaching that end, since the slogan of self-determination had no function but to camouflage the predetermination of the fate of Algeria, established in fact by the agreement between the French government and the GPRA. When Gaullist presumption seemed to close off the path of negotiations, exasperation won out over hope. Hope was reborn with the January 1961 referendum. It gave way again to exasperation last summer, after the absurd drama of Bizerte." I did not hold back from the praise due to the man who, "convinced that disengagement corresponded to the interest and the vocation of France, risked both his life and his fame in order to carry decolonization to its conclusion (a decolonization that his followers had called abandonment)." But "'governing *à la florentine*' in the twentieth century also involves a negative component. Accusing a man of action of having paid too dearly for his success is easy. Concealing the cost of deception and duplicity would be still easier."

This was an intermediate position that aimed for evenhandness. I quoted the attacks of the ultras and the liberals, without accepting or rejecting any of them. On the one hand, "was it necessary to prolong 'pacification' for three and a half years to end up engaging in the inevitable and indispensable political negotiations? Was it necessary to break off the first Evian negotiations on the Sahara question, only to declare suddenly, in a press conference, that no Algerian government would give up its sovereignty over the sand and the oil?" On the other hand, "what was the purpose of visiting the troops? Why allow officers to make solemn commitments to the population if it had been decided that they would not be able to keep their oath? From 'I have understood you' to the April 1962 referendum, a Louis Terrenoire sees only a straight line, without deviation or detour—*sancta simplicitas*. The French of Algeria and the officers see a sequence of hateful betrayals or cynical tricks."

To this indictment, which I did not simply dismiss, I countered with a simple but decisive argument—success, reality: "As long as the Prince is trapped in his own machinations, the critics have a free hand. Once he has disengaged himself, he is in possession of an irrefutable argument: the road may have been long, but at least it has led me to the goal. If I had taken a shorter road, would I have succeeded? The Machiavellian who has succeeded *invokes reality* against adversaries who *evoke possibilities*. Does anyone have the right to criticize the government for the civil war and the OAS rebellion if they were the price that had to be paid for the end of the war between the French and the Algerian nationalists?"

Once again I defined myself against the ultras of both camps:

The General's unconditional supporters acclaim the events, even when the events mock their earlier promises. The adversaries denounce General de Gaulle, even when events are accomplishing their earlier hopes. Is one a Gaullist or an anti-Gaullist if one resembles neither? In the pamphlet entitled *La Tragédie algérienne*, which provoked the anger of Louis Terrenoire, Jacques Soustelle, and Maurice Schumann, I had used the expression "the herosim of abandonment." And yet General de Gaulle pushed the will to abandonment to heroic extremes. The easy course was to continue "pacification," the superior interest of France was not to hang on desperately to the last fragments of empire. General de Gaulle maintains, and he will rightly maintain, the historic virtue of having convinced the country that decolonization meant change, not defeat. He did not take the initiative in this task, which his supporters had for long paralyzed. But he brought it to a successful conclusion in Algeria, where the risk of a tragic outcome was great.

Nearly twenty years have passed since the Evian agreements and the precipitate withdrawal of the French from Algeria. The population of Algeria has reached twenty million, which confirms, if confirmation is necessary, the argument advanced by the adversaries of integration. The massive increase in the price of hydrocarbons has substantially changed the bases of the calculation that I used in *L'Algérie et la Republique*. If France had maintained sovereignty over the Sahara, it would be paying for some of its oil in francs, or would compensate for purchase of oil in foreign currencies by its sales of surpluses of other kinds of hydrocarbons. Whatever certain historians and polemicists may have written, my anticolonialism and my support of Algerian independence were governed not by economic considerations but by convictions that may be called moral, political, historical, or even, if one likes, of national interest.

I do not know whether, after two thousand years, we ought to condemn the Roman conquest of Celtic Gaul. At the least, conquerors should consider every day Montesquieu's maxim: "It is up to the conqueror to remedy some of the evil he has done. I define the right of conquest in these terms: a necessary, legitimate, and unfortunate right that always leaves an enormous debt to be paid in order to make amends to human nature." The conquest of Algeria in the nineteenth century required at least twenty years, and some of the enlightened figures of the time considered it anachronistic, doomed to failure. The potential benefits brought about by conquest necessarily disappear when, nearly a century after their apparent victory, the conquerors must again take up arms to perpetuate their precarious domination. The Algerians, despite their heterogeneity (Arabs and Berbers), despite the absence of a tradition of the state comparable to that of Morocco, legitimately demanded the right to build a state and to affirm their identity. Their demand coincided with the historical movement of ideas and the enlightened self-interest of France: demography and economics made the policy of integration, the only alternative to independence, impossible.

I do not think that the large quantity of material published on the Algerian war in the last twenty years can lead me to revise the judgments I made a generation ago. We know more about the secret visit of the leaders of a *wileya* to the Elysée palace, about the internal exhaustion of the guerrilla struggle. The OAS and the attacks against the *pieds-noirs*, as soon as the French Army stopped protecting the lives of citizens, precipitated the sudden exodus of the French from Algeria—an outcome prepared by the decisions of 1955 and 1956. In 1957, I stated that, one day, after years of warfare, the country would give up the fight without saving anything. This was the way things turned out. Tragedies unfold, inexorably, to the end. Most of the *harkis* were abandoned to the vengeance of the victors, perhaps on the orders of the General himself, who, through words, transfigured the defeat and concealed its horrors.

Most of the insults directed at me from all sides seemed to me, because of their public character, almost anonymous; they rarely affected me. In the late 1960s, I met a woman refugee from Algeria several times. Finally, feeling comfortable, she said to me frankly: "How we detested you when you published *La Tragédie algérienne;* now we wonder how we could have been so blind. In the end, you were the only one who was concerned with us. You told us: 'When France abandons Algeria, it will not find for you the money it is now squandering to wage war.'"

NOTES

1. I remember a letter from a captain of a long-distance vessel who denounced this myth: navigation in the Canal involved no difficulties.

2. If I had used ideological arguments, I would have convinced no one.

3. Reprinted in *Actuelles III* (Paris: Gallimard, 1958).

4. In *Les Illusions retrovées,* published in 1982, Claudie and Jacques Broyelle place this statement in context and explain Camus's positions.

1 5

INDUSTRIAL SOCIETY

I chose as the theme of my first course in the Sorbonne in 1955–56, *La Société industrielle*. I had already treated the same subject in German at Tübingen, but more briefly.

The germ of this course went back several years, in fact to the end of the war. I had been struck by the contrast (and the similarity) between the theories of the ruling class and the theories of the social classes. Italian Fascism made great use of the Mosca-Pareto concept of the ruling class, while the Marxists were aware only of social classes; they made no distinction between the socially dominant class and the ruling class. But the Bolshevik party, the holder of power, represented not the working class, but a ruling class that had risen to the first rank after the elimination of the old ruling class.

To be sure, the Soviet revolution, unlike Fascism and even National Socialism, had transformed production relations in industry and agriculture, had eliminated factory owners, and then, through agricultural collectivization, had eliminated the owners of the land. However, this Marxist-inspired revolution did not lead, as the Marxists had prophesied, to the dictatorship of the proletariat, but rather, in conformity with Pareto's pessimism, to the

265

accession to power of a new ruling class. Disciples of Pareto could thus easily interpret the Bolshevik adventure according to their scheme. On their side, the Marxists interpreted Fascism according to their scheme: a pseudo-revolution since it did not disturb production relations and because the "moneyed powers" were content with delegating agents to the State, and they exercised their domination through the intermediary of another form of government.

In the 1940s, I had begun work on a book dealing with the confrontation between Marx and Pareto, a confrontation which led to a comparative analysis of the revolutions of the twentieth century, of the right and the left, of fascism and communism. A few hundred pages of this manuscript survive in a closet. I let it sit when, at the Sorbonne, after Tübingen, I undertook the task of reintroducing the concept of industrial society.

Several ideas came together in my plan. Like many others, I had been impressed by Colin Clark's book, *The Conditions of Economic Progress*. Calculation of gross national product made it possible to place national economies, Soviet as well as capitalist, on a single rising curve. Modern economies, despite the diversity of regimes and ideologies, contain certain common characteristics, particularly the potential for growth. The Soviet Union, through its five-year plans and the triumphant production of the rates of growth of gross national product, had in a sense posed a challenge to the West. It intended to demonstrate by action the superiority of its regime; it would win out against capitalism through the irresistible growth in its gross national product and its productivity.

Three years later, the three courses became *Dix-huit Leçons sur la société industrielle*, *La Lutte des classes*, and *Démocratie et totalitarisme*,[1] encompassing the themes that had excited my interest for a decade; comparison of the economies and societies of both parts of Europe, the diversity of regimes and patterns of growth, social structure as a function of the regime and the stage of growth, the relative autonomy of the political system, and its influence on style of life and class relations.

I will refrain from boring the reader with a summary of the ideas of these books which, for the most part, are of value because of the specific studies that they used or inspired, and not in themselves. It is preferable simply to outline the organizing ideas of the three courses.

Let us begin with the notion of industrial society itself. The expression comes, of course, from Saint-Simon and Auguste Comte. In the early nineteenth century, those who were interested in the philosophy of history—the subject was fashionable—inquired into the meaning and the originality of the society that had come out of the French Revolution. Saint-Simon and his disciples presented an interpretation of the new age, an interpretation that spread through Europe and exercised a lasting influence. According to them, what characterized modern society was, from here on in, industrialism, a system of labor or production. The managers of industrialism, the bankers, the engineers, made up the ruling class, while legislators, diplomats, and the military seemed, if not parasites, at least to be unendowed with some irreplaceable competence. Coming from the Saint-Simonian school, Auguste Comte developed a global system. The industrial type of society was contrasted to the military type of the past; exploitation of natural resources replaced enrichment through conquest and booty. After a transitional phase, peaceful work could put an end to war, a legacy of the theological and military era.

It is not illegitimate to present Marx as a successor to the Saint-Simonians, despite the Hegelian language that he used. He, too, posited civil society, the equivalent of industrial society, as the substantial reality of which the state was only an expression. Conflicts within civil society became, under the name of class struggle, the engine of historical movement, but just as for the Saint-Simonians, it was the industrial system which constituted the anatomy or the structure of the community as a whole. Only radical transformation of the industrial system would bring about a genuine revolution, unlike a crisis, violent or not, affecting only the holders or the exercise of state power.

Circumstances encouraged me to reconsider the concept of industrial society. Of course, the Soviets call their social formation socialist and that of the West capitalist. But this antithesis is based on the postulate that the economic and political system is defined or characterized by the type of ownership of the means of production, by the method by which surplus value is extracted, and by the technique of regulation—plan or market. Without questioning the legitimacy of the antithesis between state and private ownership, a comparison among the industrial systems respectively characterized as capitalist and socialist seemed to me equally legitimate. The notion of industrial society served as an organizing idea or a conclusion to this comparative study.

Although use of the term "industrial society" has become common, the notion itself, as I used it in my courses and as it has entered into everyday speech, is open to controversy. The expression designates an abstraction, a concept, or an ideal type. It is important to specify the characteristics that define an industrial society, which can be found in both capitalist and socialist societies. It is the definition of industrial society as such that may or may not justify use of the notion.

I outlined a definition on the basis of the unit of production: a society would be industrial when large businesses were the characteristic form of the organization of labor. From the nature of these businesses could be deduced the separation between the family and the place (the unit) of work. Large-scale enterprise introduces not a radically new but an intensified version of the division of labor. The technical division of labor is added to the traditional division of people among distinct tasks. Large-scale enterprise presupposes a certain accumulation of capital, imposed by the exigencies of competition. The necessity of economic calculation is derived from organization and competition. Finally, the growth of business enterprises brings about a concentration of workers which, in turn, almost inevitably brings about tension between workers and employers, and the existence of unions, able, thanks to their large membership, to carry on discussions with the management.

In every economic system certain functions must be performed: the division of collective resources among various jobs, the regulation of relations among producers. The five characteristics I have noted as definitions of industrial society leave out of account two characteristics that differentiate socialism and capitalism, that is, the ownership of the means of production, and regulation, by plan or market, of relations among business entities.

Historians have outlined the principal stages of what they call the industrial revolution; sociologists of the early nineteenth century placed themselves above events. Personally, I followed the lead of Auguste Comte, and more often than not, I was tempted to identify the application of science to production (and the resulting growth) as a distinctive characteristic of our time (even though, in the fifth lesson, I did not emphasize the link between science and production, it was nonetheless implicit in the nature of business, in concentration, and in rational calculation). In many circumstances, I also insisted on the predominance of the industrial spirit, which appears not only in what is now called the secondary sector (steel, automobiles, generally the production of manufactured goods). Auguste Comte had foreseen that agriculture would become as industrialized as industry in the narrow sense of the term.

The Soviets fiercely attacked the notion itself, which seemed to them incompatible with their Marxism. Would Marx himself have rejected the principle of comparative analysis? No one can say with certainty. In fact, Marx, in a famous passage,[2] suggested the exemplary value of English development and, in other places, suggested on the contrary that capitalist development, inevitable for humanity as a whole, could take on different forms according to the past of various precapitalist societies. Moreover, since the so-called socialist revolution had taken place in a country that was barely capitalist, it does not seem to me contrary to the spirit of Marxism to compare homologous phases of Soviet and American development, the phases being determined by per capita production or by the division of the labor force among the various sectors.

The Soviets did not understand matters in that way. Placing socialism and capitalism in the same category or connecting them to a single type was to commit the crime of *lèse*-Marxism. There obviously had to be an abyss between capitalism and socialism. The two systems could not be situated on the same level, each one with its virtues and vices. Socialism, according to Marxism-Leninism, has overcome the contradictions of capitalism and is leading humanity to the end of prehistory, even though present-day Soviet socialism lags behind the United States, which is at the head of the group of industrialized nations.

Delivered in the year 1955–56, the *Dix-huit Leçons sur la société indus-trielle,* was published in 1962 in the *Idées* series edited by François Erval. The typescript of the *Cours de la Sorbonne,* which reproduced my oral delivery almost without correction, had sold several thousand copies;[3] I refused to publish the courses as they were in book form. I saw them as a sketch for the real book that would deal simultaneously with the two themes, historical and theoretical, Sovietism-capitalism, Marx-Pareto. The appearance of the *Idées* series offered me a solution which I still considered provisional: published in an inexpensive format, the lectures could be revised, developed, clarified by the serious work of which I continue to dream.

As always in such cases, unexpected success came about through a combination of circumstances. Following the Hungarian revolution and Khrushchev's speech, a wave of defections left a number of disappointed communists stranded, looking for a replacement ideology. The *Eighteen Lessons* to some extent satisfied that need. Not that the book was of a kind to present an object of faith or a global vision; it shed light on our world, simultaneously homogeneous and divided. To my great surprise, it still happens that I meet intellectuals, and sometimes scholars, who assure me that this pamphlet, essentially a work of vulgarization, greatly helped and educated them.

The second course, the one that seems to me to have the greatest scholarly value of the three (most competent readers agree), analyzes production relations, to use the Marxist vocabulary, social classes, to use a more neutral vocabulary. It is in answer to a major question: In what sense is there a class struggle in Western-style industrial societies? In Soviet-style societies? To answer this question, I had to run through the stages of the theory—the inexhaustible theory—of classes. All modern industrialized societies are complex; hence, the obvious observation: the millions of men and women at work occupy different positions, some in the factories, others on the land, others still in shops or government departments. The majority of them, a majority all the greater because of continued growth in the national product, was made up of wage earners; in other words, they were integrated into businesses, organized hierarchically. In present-day France, slightly more than 83 percent of manpower is made up of wage earners. This results in a plurality of criteria of social differentiation: manual and nonmanual workers, salaried employees and independent contractors, heads of enterprise (or managing personnel) and wage earners, farmers and workers, and so on. Of all possible differentiations, one still dominates the thinking of most observers: the owners or managers of the means of production on the one hand, the proletarians on the other, the latter being the wage earners working with means of production that they do not own.[4]

Between employees and employers there develops a more or less vigorous conflict that in reality, has to do with the division of the income (or of the surplus value) of the enterprise. More generally, an open or concealed struggle over the distribution of the national wealth troubles all Western-style industrial societies. The struggle between wage earners and employers (or the state) takes on particularly visible forms and seems, at first, to resemble the class struggle conceived by Marx. In fact, this is far from being true.

In order for the rivalry between social groups for the division of the national wealth to become an authentic class struggle, two necessary conditions have to be met: first of all, class consciousness on the part of the wage earners or proletarians, and then demands from them going beyond material or psychological improvements of their condition. To illustrate these two conditions in straightforward language: Are the workers aware that they constitute a single collectivity, distinct from others within the society? Does this awareness of separation (or of a particular identity) go along with hostility to other groups or to the society as a whole? Is it true that workers have no fatherland? Finally, is this class, given reality by the consciousness of those who make it up, inspired by a desire for rebellion? Has it risen up not against one aspect or another of the present order, but against the system itself?

In all Western societies, class struggle for the division of the national wealth is the normal condition. Generalized unionization brings about a chaos of protests and demands; to the vertical conflicts between employees and employers are added the horizontal struggles among different categories of producers. This kind of class struggle, the surface of modern democracy, does not appear in Eastern European societies. Not that Soviet society has reached such a homogeneous state that all conflicts of interest have disappeared. The apparent homogeneity derives from the political and social system itself. Pressure groups do not exist or, at least, have no legal existence. Workers' unions confine the masses rather than expressing their demands. Socialism *à la sauce tartare* in fact eliminates this kind of class struggle not through reconciliation, but by reducing dissident groups to silence. As for the vertical form of class struggle, employees against employers, it too is stifled by the authorities and by ideology. Strikes, which are equivalent to rebellions in Eastern Europe, since they are forbidden (Poland is a case apart), are evidence of a banal reality: it is not enough for the state to take charge of the ownership and management of enterprises for the tension between workers and managers to disappear. The vertical class struggle apparently disappears in Soviet-style societies, not thanks to the restoration of harmony or the disappearance of classes, but through the omnipotence of the state and the suppression of freedom, in particular the freedom of association. The rise of Solidarity in Poland revealed the secret reality of societies that had claimed to be classless.

The principal, and perhaps least banal, idea of the second course was to establish a connection between social structure and political system—an idea derived from my reflection on Marx and Pareto. To the extent that class struggle implies class consciousness and class organization, it depends on the state, on legislation, whether that struggle will manifest itself and even, to some extent, whether it will exist. It is probable that Soviet workers also make the distinction between "us" and "them," the latter being the leaders, the privileged who live differently from the workers and control their labor; but it may be, in the absence of freedom of the press and of organization, that the proletarians have not moved from consciousness of their identity to consciousness of opposition, challenge, and revolt.

To be sure, a good deal depends on the manner in which "we" see "them." In Western societies, "they" are the "bosses," the heads of enterprises who are seen as possessors of the means of production, even if they are legally only salaried employees. If the Soviet system were to accomplish its ideal, "they" would be different in nature from Western heads of enterprises or bosses. All indications are to the contrary: the managers appear to the workers as managers, bosses, privileged. But unlike Western bosses, these Soviet heads of businesses are indistinguishable from the government as a whole, the state, and the party. As members of the *nomenklatura*, they are hardly less distant from the workers than the bosses of Renault or General Motors.

There is no reason not to interpret the Soviet system with the help of Marxist concepts. Private or juridical persons, flesh and blood bosses or corporations, have lost ownership of the means of production, but the workers have not acquired that ownership except through the intermediary of the party, which is theoretically identical with them. The state itself, controlled by the party, has become the nearly exclusive owner of the means of production; the bureaucracy of the party and the state "exploits" the workers as private owners had in the past. But this interpretation suggests that the state is not always the expression of those who possess the means of production; here, on the contrary, it is the state, or rather the minority that holds political power, that controls the means of production.

The Marxist-Leninist revolutions illustrate Pareto's conception of the ruling class and of revolutions. A minority seizes power by force of arms or, more rarely, through quasi-legal means, and reorganizes society according to its ideology. Fascist revolutions are different in no essential respect as far as the seizure of power is concerned. Once the new elite has been installed, it does not apply the same ideas. It goes without saying that Marxist-Leninists detest the Mosca-Pareto theory of ruling classes, just as they reject the very notion of industrial society. The Marxist-Leninist system, according to its adherents, is not an example of a general form, a particular expression of a type, but a historical conclusion, a unique expression of humanity, which it is indeed, but in the realm of darkness.

To compare regimes on the basis of the minority that rules the state is also to commit a crime of *lèse*–Marxism-Leninism: it is to place regimes based on the omnipotence of the party in perspective, to deprive them of their absolute originality, to associate them with all other regimes while recognizing their particular characteristics. The synthesis of Marx and Pareto can be carried out without major difficulty. In every modern industrialized society, there exist leading categories, by which I mean minorities who occupy strategic positions and exercise an influence on the minds of others and on the direction of the society. I enumerated, as leading categories, owners or managers of the means of production, the political class in the narrow sense of the term, upper-level bureaucrats, leaders of the masses (heads of unions and of mass parties), intellectuals, the dignitaries of the church, and the heads of the armed forces. In communist regimes, party personnel see themselves simultaneously as the political class, managers of the national economy, and priests of the secular religion. In other words, they tend to accumulate in their hands temporal and spiritual power, the exercise of purely political power and of administrative power. In the Eastern European countries, a kind of pluralism, especially in Poland and Hungary, has gradually asserted itself. On the other hand, in the Soviet Union, the regime of the party persists without significant changes.

In Western regimes, different ruling categories are not united in a single party; depending on the country, relations between the managers of the means of production and the leaders of the masses are more or less antagonistic. Similarly, depending on the country, relations between the managers of the means of production and the political class are more or less intimate. At the time of the "radical" republic, politicians did not come from the same social circles as industrialists or bankers. Under the Fifth Republic, before 1981, the political class was hardly distinguishable from the upper levels of the bureaucracy, which was in turn hardly distinguishable from the leaders of the economy. In a sense, these ruling categories tended to coalesce into a ruling class in the banal sense of the term. The various ruling categories, because of their common origin and their constant cooperation, took on a certain consciousness of their identity, of their common interests. The autonomy of the leaders of the masses and constitutional rules preserved individual liberties.

The opposition between a single party and a plurality of parties as a criterion of classification is open to question, but it still seems acceptable to me. Legally organized competition for the exercise of power in fact constitutes the reality of modern democracy. Democracy not only requires the existence of more than one party, it also demands that the winning party accept in advance the possibility of its defeat at the next election. It is also necessary that the party provisionally exercising power does so in conformity with constitutional law and with ordinary law. This is why I named Western regimes with the perhaps barbarous term "constitutional-pluralist," in contrast to one-party regimes, whose perfect form is represented by the Soviet regime, where the party seizes supreme authority, secular and spiritual or ideological.

There is no lack of regimes that fit neither into the category of constitutional pluralism nor into that of one-party totalitarianism. But the fundamental contrast that I established in the theory of political systems of industrial societies expresses not only an empirical fact: it was on the basis of the monopolization of power by a single party, which declared itself the sole master of the state, that the adventures of Hitler and Stalin developed. Moreover, the pluralism of parties symbolizes one of the preeminent democratic values—dialogue. The single Marxist-Leninist style party reserves to itself the right to legitimate expression. On the other hand, the diversity of legal parties legitimates the diversity of languages and permanent dialogue among citizens and between them and the holders of power.

The three little books, spoken rather than written, would not have replaced the book I had been thinking about for years, even if I had published them in a single volume. Because of the audience I was addressing, I neglected to some extent the most intellectually difficult problems, for example the distinction between the analysis of *historically particular regimes*, in their concrete characteristics, and the analysis of *ideal types;* similarly, I used the concept of industrial society without taking much trouble to define its status and its nature. The division among courses was problematic: relations among elites, parties, and governments are dealt with briefly, not in a single course but in several. In the *Eighteen Lessons*, growth is observed and described without any clear explanation of its mechanics or the factors that bring it about. In *Democracy and Totalitarianism*, the regimes I dealt with in the fourth (unpublished) course are missing. The conceptualization of the third course (in particular the recourse to Montes-quieu's two notions of the *nature* and *principle* of regimes) contrasts with the conceptualization of the first two volumes.

I delivered the third course during the 1957–58 academic year. I gave in to the temptation to allude, from time to time, to French political events, the crisis of the Fourth Republic. The principle of the constitutional-pluralist regime was defined, I said, by two feelings, or principles in Montesquieu's sense: respect for the law and a sense of compromise, if only under the pressure to find a majority. Compromise in domestic affairs involves losses but rarely ruins the collectivity; in foreign affairs, the refusal to choose most often brings about the combined disadvantages of all possible decisions. The Third Republic confronting Hitler, the Fourth Republic confronting the Algerian crisis, slid from half-measure to half-measure. At the beginning of 1958, I devoted a lecture to the corruption of the Fourth Republic, and I concluded with the following words: "In what sense is constitutional reform really, as everyone says, the vital question for France? France is going through a political crisis whose cause is well known, the Algerian war. The obsession with constitutional reform is a means either of forgetting the problem that has to be resolved or of looking for an essentially different government capable of resolving it."

In the following lecture, entitled "Fil de soie et fil de l'épée," I dealt with possible solutions. I took as my point of departure politics as it was con-ducted by the Fourth Republic: "I doubt that, in the immediate future, a policy different from the one that is being carried out is possible, a policy that is a reflection of the country, the Parliament, and the regime." A policy that reflected the division of the country but that was doomed to failure. What were the solutions? I enumerated three: the first was tyranny, the second dictatorship in the Roman sense, the third to wait for events, in one way or another, to decide the debate.

"The tyrannical solution," I said, "is the one we all dream of in our sleepless nights, on the condition that it would give power to those who think like us." I then mentioned the solution of dictatorship, in fact the appeal to General de Gaulle: "The second solution, which is often evoked, is an appeal to the *legal savior* or, if one prefers, the Roman dictator. Everyone knows his name today. Press organs of every opinion advocate this final recourse, but so many people of contradictory opinions are thinking of him that it is necessary to consider two possibilities. The judgment of this legal savior, inevitably, will disappoint one or another camp, since the representatives of all camps have appealed to him." I evoked a miraculous, improbable solution, which would reconcile opposing groups each of which was convinced that it was right. And I concluded with a remark that was confirmed by events: "Had the opposing parties agreed on the name of the savior, our adversaries would still not rally to his support." In this lecture, broadcast on the radio, I carefully refrained from expressing my own opinions; I argued for the *silken thread*, an expression used by Guglielmo Ferrero to designate legality, the fragile barrier protecting the state from civil war.

That year, the last lecture was delivered on 19 May 1958, a few days before General de Gaulle's official accession to power; I did not pronounce his name, but I was clearly referring to him at the end of the lecture: "Will constitutional legality survive? Will the transition from this regime to another be legal? In the twentieth century, France has developed the art of legal *coups d'état*. The current situation is characterized by an inextricable mixture of legality and illegality. It is complicated by the existence of a unique personality, to whom contrary meanings are attributed, according to the moment and to individual preference. The Roman Republic had an institution that corresponds to French needs, the *dictatorship*. This candidate for the dictatorship, that is, for legally sanctioned omnipotence, does not wish to prolong the current regime but to transform it; thus, he must be not only a dictator, but, to resurrect old concepts, a legislator."

I noted, once again, that "the *dictator*, desired by the people, would not maintain the support of all those who were acclaiming him on this date, 19 May 1958. But the adventure inaugurated by the reign of the dictator-legislator answers to a need. How could the government in place pursue a policy in Algeria in which they do not believe? To conclude, I have a single wish. There is only one protection against civil violence: a few months ago I called this single protection the silken thread, or legality. This silken thread has not been broken: let us pray that it never is."

There is no longer a possibility of writing the book that I might have written instead of these lectures. There is little point in mentioning the mistakes or filling in the gaps. It makes more sense to reconsider the ideas dealing with the French, the Soviet, or the world situation, and to submit them to the most severe critique of all, that of time. What confirmations or contradictions have the events of the last twenty-five years produced?

The comparison between Soviet and Western regimes in no way implied their convergence, to use the term that sums up a briefly popular theory. Despite the legends, I never subscribed to this thesis. A few passages of the *Eighteen Lessons* might create confusion: Soviet planners in the future would make more use of market mechanisms; the proportion of income distributed by the state in Western economies is already a considerable proportion of the total; the state sector of the industrial apparatus might grow in Western countries. In this sense, certain economic contrasts could become less pronounced. I did not deduce from these structural developments the probability or the inevitability of convergence; in the *Eighteen Lessons*, and even

more in the two subsequent volumes, I asserted that these possible economic convergences (which, in passing, have still not taken place) would
scarcely reduce the distance between two essentially different types of
society.

I cannot deny that the revival of the Saint-Simonian concept of industrial
society coincided with the East-West competition over rates of growth, with
postwar economic expansion, and with the success of the theories of the
stages of economic growth developed by Colin Clark and Jean Fourastié. But
I did not confine myself to economic analysis, to the statistics on growth in
East and West; I tried to establish a relationship between class structure and
the political system on the one hand, and economic development on the
other. Just as Tocqueville, while accepting the inevitability of democracy, left
men the possibility of choosing between freedom and servitude, I asserted
that industrial society imposed neither a one-party state along the lines of
the Soviet model nor the pluralism of parties and ideologies on which the
West prides itself. The only significant question, then, comes down to this:
Are there enough common characteristics in Soviet and Western societies to
justify the comparison and thereby the concept of industrial society itself? I
think an affirmative response remains valid.

The division of the labor force among various occupations is basically the
same in East and West, although at equivalent phases of their development
the United States and the Soviet Union did not need the same quantity of
merchants, bank employees, or jurists. The Soviet Union buys Western
factories, keys in hand, though it has long had the aim of catching up to and
overcoming the United States (on this point, Brezhnev declined
Khrushchev's legacy: the aim was displaced toward the military balance of
forces—not without success). The two parts of Europe belong to a single
type, and at the same time, they present two versions of the type, which are
very different from one another.

The Saint-Simonians correctly foresaw the rise of the industrial order that
would spread to agriculture and services. In this sense, they had a broader,
deeper vision of modern society than Marx, who, obsessed by the conflict
between employers and workers, shaped by the English economists, finally
came up with an impoverished utopia (on the pretext of replacing the
government of men with the administration of things, socialism administers
men, including their minds). The greatest of the Saint-Simonians, Auguste
Comte, confirmed the irresistible expansion of industrialism (in the broad
sense), but he did not succumb to the illusion that industrialism would
suffice to establish harmony in the life of men in society.

To return to a more prosaic level, is it not obvious, blindingly obvious, that
all governments, East and West, accept responsibility for management of the
economy? On election day in the West, candidates hurl production and

budget statistics at one another; in Moscow, the party's general secretary never tires of citing figures in his report, blaming one bureaucrat or another for delays or inadequacies. On both sides, the economy occupies a dominant position in political speech, although the oligarchs of Moscow have demonstrated by their actions that they prefer guns to butter and military force to the prosperity of their people.

With respect to the past, to all the complex societies that we know, I continue to believe that the Saint-Simonians saw clearly and that Marx distorted their philosophy by substituting capital (or capitalism) for industrialism; I also believe that what is now called postindustrial society should be interpreted as an original phase in the application of science to production, and more broadly to the very life of man.

This discussion of concepts is, in the end, of little importance; what is important is the vision of history, the theory suggested by the concepts; a quarter-century ago, I thought that the development of the Soviet Union belonged to the great wave of world industrialism and that it offered the example of another form of industrialism, a form whose distinctive characteristics would survive even when the standard of living in the East came close to that of the West. In other words, I agree—it seemed self-evident— that the Bolsheviks had in their way carried out primitive capital accumulation, but that they would not consider their task accomplished when per capita production reached several thousand dollars. I was not wrong, but I may have understated the truth on an essential point: of course, the theory of immiseration, absolute or relative, has no more application to the Soviet regime than elsewhere (for what it's worth, the standard of living in the Soviet Union has improved in the course of the last twenty-five years), but I underestimated the implications of overarmament and the inefficiency of the Soviet economy.

The final chapters of *Democracy and Totalitarianism*, influenced by the thaw (the course dates from 1957–58), evidence an optimism that, twenty-five years later, appears unfortunately excessive. I reviewed the changes that had taken place since the death of Stalin: the extreme form of terrorism, the great purge, had disappeared; intellectual life had taken advantage of the thaw; the police no longer exercised their power at the expense of party members. In counterpoint to these changes, I indicated the permanent elements. The style of de-Stalinization remained Stalinist; Stalin bore no resemblance to the grotesque and feeble character who was depicted as incapable of following military operations on a map. "It is creating a new mythology when one reduces the man whom one worshiped a few years earlier to a subhuman category." The great purge was over, but permanent small purges continued. The system of party control over ideological orthodoxy and the monopoly of politics is still in place. The oddnesses and excesses attributable to the former general secretary have been eliminated. I summed up my thought in the formulation: "Until now, there have been changes in the regime, but there has not been a fundamental change of the regime itself."

To sum up my thought at the time, or rather the attenuated expression of it that I presented to the students, I will quote a few lines of chapter 17 of *Democracy and Totalitarianism:* "The foreseeable changes, connected to industrial development and to improvement in standards of living and culture, do not imply elimination of the one-party state and ideological orthodoxy, any more than they imply the disappearance of the bureaucratic hierarchy common to the society and the state. Possibilities of bourgeois stabilization? Why not? Economic rationalization? Why not? Attenuation of terror? Probably. Abandonment of pathological forms of violence? Plausible. Introduction of multiple parties and liberal institutions as in the West? Possible, but there is neither a demonstrable necessity nor even a probability that the development of industrial society will bring about these desirable consequences."

In this passage, I would today change above all the idea that Western-style liberalization of Soviet society was possible. Not that I am now tempted to replace "possible" with "impossible" (there are more things in heaven and earth than are dreamed of in our philosophy), but I would say that such a liberalization would bring about the downfall, peaceful or otherwise, of the regime itself. The regime, as it has stabilized itself, does not tolerate challenges to its ideological principle, Marxism-Leninism, even though most Soviets no longer believe in it. The regime does not tolerate what I call economic rationalization: attempts like those of Professor Libermann were brought up short. On the other hand, the people's democracies, Hungary in particular, have adopted many Western economic concepts.

In the spring of 1958, while I was speculating on the future of the Soviet Union, we found ourselves at the beginning of the Khrushchev period; the oligarchs of Moscow still presented themselves as rivals of the United States, boasted about their rates of growth, and indicated the date of inevitable victory of Soviet GNP over that of the United States. I never let myself be taken in by these boasts, and I never feared the economic superiority of the Soviet Union. It is in this framework that the analyses of 1958 (some of which I have just quoted) should be located.

If the analysis of Soviet society was excessively optimistic, could the same reproach be addressed to the analysis of Western societies? Haven't I wrongly identified the years of postwar expansion with the ordinary developments of capitalist economies? Doesn't the much-discussed notion of "the end of ideology" find its origin in an overestimation of economic growth, a rosy perspective on the future of the industrialized countries, an optimism undermined by the world crisis that began in 1974? The criticism contains an element of truth, but only to a limited extent.

In the 1950s and 1960s, like many others, I was struck by the rates of growth in European countries (between 5 and 6 percent, expressed in terms of the gross national product), a rate roughly double the one that had, over the long term, led the United States to the first rank. Hence, I concluded that these rates would not continue indefinitely.

The "1985" commission assumed that the postwar rates of growth would continue until that date. The most eminent of French economists, Edmond Malinvaud, tended toward the argument that a mutation had taken place between the prewar and postwar periods because of various factors (among others, improvements in the managers of the economy), and that the new rates (5 to 6 percent) might represent the new norm. When I was invited to testify before the "1985" commission, I immediately expressed my doubt about the continuation of this annual rate of growth, which had been hypothesized to continue through 1985. At the time, I had no decisive argument on which to base my skepticism, which was greeted with politeness and indifference.

If I did not convince the commission, the fault is entirely mine. Like the commission, I did not mention the fact that the low cost of energy was one of the circumstances that fostered rapid growth in industrialized countries. I emphasized other factors that explained the "miracles": the introduction of techniques of production and organization derived from the United States and the advantage of following the example of a pioneering country, the creation of a large market in Western Europe, the chance of overcoming the delay attributable to war and to the disruptions of the interwar years. It nevertheless seemed plausible to me that European growth would diminish as productivity in Europe approached that of America.

Why did neither the commission nor I (as far as I remember) mention oil and its price? We all know that the consumption of petroleum products was growing at a rate of 12 percent per year. It was easy to foresee that, well before 1985, annual world comsumption would exceed three billion tons. The continuation of this curve confronted insuperable obstacles before 1985; at least the inevitable price increases for petroleum products would, well before 1985, change in one way or another the conditions of the European miracle. In 1956, following the Suez Canal crisis, in the introduction to *Espoir et peur de siècle* (published 1957; English translation *On War: Atomic Weapons and Global Diplomacy* [New York: Doubleday, 1959]), I observed that for the first time Europe no longer controlled the networks of supply for its industry: "compared to the Soviet Union and the United States, Western Europe, with the third highest level of industrial concentration, displays a

radical inferiority: it derives from elsewhere a substantial part of its food
(Great Britain buys half of its food abroad), its new materials (nonferrous
metals, cotton, wool); finally, since the last war, it has depended on the
outside world for energy supplies. Given the indispensable imports of energy and raw materials, doesn't the Suez crisis mark another stage in the
vassalization, the satellization of Europe?" I stated the obvious, that in the
course of the succeeding decades, Europe's dependency with respect to
energy and raw materials would increase. The United States would buy more
and more raw materials, either because their own mines were exhausted
(iron and copper), or because they wished to spare their reserves (oil). Not
foreseeing an absolute penury, I predicted "a bitter competition for political
control over the sources of energy and raw materials."[5] I maintained, despite
the dramatic events of 1956, the central argument: "Fallen powers, France,
Great Britain, Germany, like Holland, can live through their imperial decline in prosperity."[6]

I corrected this assertion with another: "In losing their empires, their
capacity for action abroad, the Europeans have been turned over to the
discretion of the powerful state whose citizens are rich, of the powerful state
whose subjects are poor, and of the weak states whose masses are impoverished."

My optimism about economic growth never went so far as to suggest the
disappearance of class struggle, in the non-Marxist sense, that is, the conflict
between classes or social categories over the distribution of the national
wealth or the improvement of working conditions; what I denied was the
thesis of a working class, conscious of itself and of its revolutionary will,
aspiring to another society in which the reign of the proletariat would
succeed that of the bourgeoisie. In a sense, I do not think I was wrong about
the essential: the growing economy, even in the absence of a radically
different distribution of income, tends rather toward a querulous satisfaction
than toward rebellion and violence.[7] I wrote the book entitled *Progress and
Disillusion* (New York: Praeger, 1968) in 1964–65, before the student explosion, well before the oil crisis of 1974. This circumstantial book was written
for the *Encyclopaedia Britannica*, which had become American. On the
occasion of the second centenary of the famous encyclopedia, the editors, in
particular Professor Robert M. Hutchins, ex-president of the University of
Chicago, decided to prepare, in addition to the usual volumes organized
alphabetically, long articles, called roof articles, which were in fact books of a
few hundred pages each.

I seized the occasion to present the dark side of so-called developed
society that I had neglected in the three courses. Using three concepts—
equality, socialization, universalization—I presented the three *projects* of
modern civilization, each one of which involved a dialectic, or in simpler

terms, contradictions. The aspiration for equality comes up against inde-structible realities: social stratification, whether or not it is identified with a class society; the aspiration of each individual for a unique, irreplaceable personality fits badly with the socialization of individuals through social institutions, family, school, peer groups; it fits no better with the inevitable hierarchy of the industrial order, or more generally the system of production. The dream of a united humanity, the ideology of a reconciliation among peoples and states, has not yet transformed the traditional anarchic system of states, a system based on power, not on law.

In short, *Progress and Disillusion* did not contradict the apparent op-timism of the theory of growth but rather limited its scope. The period of economic expansion after the war has taught us that economic progress and the increase in worker productivity can improve everyone's condition; that common resources, increased from year to year, permit giving to Peter without taking from Paul. But it did not teach us that growth eliminates or even necessarily reduces inequalities, that it reconciles men with one an-other, not to mention ideologies. The de-Stalinized Soviet Union remained an enemy of the West. The unionized worker, protected by social insurance, is still subject to the vagaries of the economy and reduced to repetitive labor.

Men manipulate material forces by means of technology, but they cannot do the same with social forces. History continues; it accentuates the contrast between the partial mastery that science has granted over nature and the impotence of planners in both East and West.

In what sense did these analyses of industrial society suggest the ex-pression "the end of ideology," or more precisely, "the end of the ideological age" (with a question mark)? This was the title of the concluding chapter of *The Opium of the Intellectuals*. My friend Edward Shils used the title "The End of Ideologies" for the report he published in the *International Herald Tribune* of the 1955 Milan conference of the Congress for Cultural Freedom. Daniel Bell used the same expression as the title for a collection of articles. In the United States, a debate on the question went on for several years. One writer produced a collection of articles on the debate.[8] The explosion in the 1960s of the students and their ideologies undermined, in appearance, this peaceful interpretation of political and intellectual life.

The discussion would have required an agreement on the meaning to be given to the word ideology. If ideology is understood as what Pareto calls derivation, in other words the various forms of justification used by orators, militants, and rulers, it goes without saying that ideologies may change in style and content, but they do not disappear. One ideology displaces an-other, ideologies do not die. I took the concept of ideology in a more precise, more limited sense: an ideology would be a global representation of society and its past, a representation announcing salvation and prescribing a liberating course of action. The decline of Marxism-Leninism, which I sensed in the mid-1950s, intensified in the 1960s and 1970s, in France at least, despite an apparent revival around 1968. I saw no replacement that was as all-encompassing as Marxism-Leninism. The critique of industrial society, as it was developed in the 1960s demonstrated that human passion can easily do without a systematization of the indictment. In the United States, Japan, Germany, and France, the students rebelled not so much in the name of Marxism-Leninism as in the name of the fundamental needs of human existence; one might even say that they were expressing an impassioned reaction against the worker's alienation and the anomie of the individual and a disgust with consumer society. The students of the 1960s, sometimes close to a kind of para-Marxism (Marx, Mao, Marcuse), embodied a romantic rebellion against industrial rationality—a rebellion that Marx had predicted would go along with the development of capitalist society. I would correct this to say along with the development of modern or industrial society.

If one accepts the meaning I gave to the term "ideology," my analysis still seems to me to be generally true today. But the limiting definition of ideology gives rise to justifiable criticism. Nationalism, or even liberalism, are not organized into a total world system, not even into a total system of world history, but they are not radically different from socialism or Marxism-Leninism, even though the latter lay claim to scientific status and, so to speak, to totality. If we must fear the excesses of true believers, ready for everything in order to save humanity, it is their faith rather than their ideas that we should blame. The communist party transforms young rebels into party militants or bureaucrats; some of those who escape from party discipline are tempted by terrorism.

Why did I evoke the end of the age of ideology as early as 1955? Two considerations guided my judgement: Marxism-Leninism, identified with the Soviet regime, would decline along with that regime; and the West would in the end lose its illusions both about the doctrine and about the party that proclaimed it. There could be no other ideology of such total proportions. Max Scheler correctly stated the case: in the intellectual Empyrean, there are only a small number of ideologies. Marxism has seized most of the mobilizing themes of our time, the salvific role of the proletariat, the technological production of abundance, the insoluble contradictions leading capitalism to collapse and death. Without this systematization, other versions of socialism lose their aura and sink into a series of reforms. Why should there be enthusiasm for collective ownership, for planning, when these prosaic measures, in themselves, no longer come together into a whole transfigured by historical reason? Once Marxism-Leninism has been compromised by Soviet failure, there still remain, of course, valid criticisms of the industrialized West: the pollution of lakes and of minds, the loss of being in favor of acquiring, the spreading of the mercantile spirit, the persistence and renewal of inequalities, and so on; these themes would be enough to foster the indignation of the young, but they do not make up an ideology capable of rivalry with Marxism-Leninism.

In the course of the ten years that followed the appearance of *The Opium of the Intellectuals,* I defended myself against my critics in three articles, collected in a small volume, *The Industrial Society: Three Essays on Ideology and Development* (New York: Praeger, 1968).[9] All three related the interpretation of contemporary socioeconomic development to the theme of ideological erosion, that is, my Sorbonne courses (which were published in 1962, 1963, and 1964) to *Opium.*

I restated the banal idea that the problems confronting societies change with the phases of growth, and that the same methods do not necessarily answer the needs of every phase. The dialogue between East and West, I wrote in 1964, is taking place on four levels. First of all, the traditional controversies are continuing over the respective virtues and vices of market economies and centrally planned economies. Soviet propaganda continues its ritual denunciation of monopoly capitalism, but if the only question is production and consumption, one wonders why the West would sacrifice its freedoms in order perhaps to accelerate growth (far from blackening the adversary, I treated him with excessive indulgence).

On a more elevated plane, Westerners and Soviets discuss the social, political, or human consequences of each regime. I chose social mobility as an example. Does the Soviet system foster the advancement of children of disfavored classes more than Western democracies do? Supposing that this is the case, what importance should be attributed to mobility? Should the continuity of families through the generations be considered a positive or negative characteristic of a social order?

On another level, there is a conflict between two theories, both of which could be called quasi-Marxist, of historical development: the Marxist theory, more or less modified, of the movement from capitalism to socialism, and the Colin Clark–Walt W. Rostow theory of the stages of economic growth, not to mention the more primitive theory of convergence toward "democratic socialism" proposed by Maurice Duverger.

The Soviets have no difficulty in refuting a certain version of Western evolutionism, according to which the development of productive forces (measured by per capita gross national product) determines the economic and social system. The theory of convergence is based on technological or productivist determinism. But the Western theoretician can and must confine himself to a *probabilistic evolutionism.* Each stage of growth *fosters* a certain regime; the Soviet system has more chances of becoming established during the takeoff stage than in a society that has already been industrialized; the elevation of the technological level and the standard of living of the population reduces the risks of the extreme forms of Stalinism. But these chance relations have only a limited interest; they do not permit a total understanding of societies. The comparision between the industrialization of Great Britain in the late eighteenth and early nineteenth centuries on the one hand, and the industrialization of Japan in the last third of the nineteenth and the early twentieth centuries on the other, presents fewer re-semblances—and less meaningful ones—than differences.

The Soviet theory of historical development has even greater difficulty in reconciling itself with reality. The Soviet Union must "catch up" with the United States, even though its socialism "comes after" capitalism; there is thus no parallelism between the phases of economic growth and the sequence of governmental systems. Why should underdeveloped countries follow the Soviet path? Because conversion to Marxism-Leninism does not correspond to historical necessity, the Soviets must henceforth demonstrate that a socialist regime, reduced to its essence, purified of any trace of the personality cult, is superior to Western regimes, in terms of both economic success and human values.

We thereby arrive at the fourth level: Do industrial societies tend to move in the same direction? In an Auguste Comte lecture, *War and Industrial Society,* I discussed the naïve optimism of the founder of the positivist school. The scientific exploitation of nature will make the exploitation of man by man useless and anachronistic; wars will disappear with the disappearance of the theological-military regime. Today we wonder; what is the aim of production? And hence, ideological dogmatism has given way to ideas.

The reference to dialogues between Soviets and Westerners seemed to me necessary to point up the difference between American and European discussions of the end of ideology: "The anti-ideology of American writers, from the very beginning, was different in character from the anti-ideology of a Camus, who was a communist as a young man, or my own, and I had never stopped carrying on a dialogue with Hegelian-Marxist thought. In the United States, 'liberalism' (that is, left-wing thought) has hardly been influenced by Marxism and has rarely been systematized, developed into a philosophy of history. After 1945, the 'liberals,' with a few exceptions, have been strongly anticommunist. The Americans have experienced neither the conservatism of a Burke, nor the Marxism of a Kautsky or a Lenin, nor even a *progressivism* like Sartre's. Their doctrine of free enterprise has rarely been expressed in a theory in the style of Mises or Hayek. In coming back from ideology, the American anti-ideologists did not have far to travel; some of them merely returned from Europe."[10]

NOTES

1. There is a fourth, devoted to the countries of the Third World, which I did not consider worthy of publication. I still have the typescript.

2. The preface of *Capital*.

3. My daughter, Dominique Schnapper, corrected and improved the text of the course.

4. Sociologists in France today generally use a tripartite distinction: the upper or ruling class, the middle classes, the lower classes.

5. P. 384.

6. P. 362.

7. At bottom, this analysis repeats that of Lenin a half-century earlier.

8. Chaim I. Waxman, *The "End of Ideology" Debate* (New York, 1968).

9. The first, entitled "Théorie du développement et idéologies de notre temps," was written in 1962, on my return from a trip to Brazil. The second, "Théorie du développement et philosophie évolutionniste," was written in 1962 for a conference sponsored by Unesco and the Ecole Pratique des Hautes Etudes. The third, "Fin des idéologies et renaissance des idées," dates from 1964. It continued the controversy over industrial society and the end of ideology.

10. *Trois Essais sur l'âge industriel,* 200–201.

16

THE GENERAL'S
GRAND DESIGN

André Siegfried frequently said to
Pierre Brisson: "The General's return to power means the end of the Atlantic
Alliance." To which I would answer: "No, the General is too intelligent, too
concerned with the balance of powers to break with the Alliance or with the
United States and to push the Americans out of Europe. He knows very well
that Moscow's objective is to separate the Europeans from the Americans;
can he give himself the same goal?" This was my conviction for most of the
period from 1958 to 1968, particularly from 1962 to 1968, when, through his
speech more than his action, he was shaking the pillars of the diplomatic
edifice that had been constructed after 1947, after the dissolution of the
grand alliance against the Third Reich.

Even before the end of the Algerian war, French diplomacy confronted a
major problem: what attitude should be taken toward Great Britain's candidacy for membership in the Common Market? From 1960 to 1963, I wrote
many articles on the Anglo-French dispute that expressed less intellectual
uncertainty than mixed and even contradictory feelings. I remembered
England, alone and heroic in 1940, and the service it had performed for the
common cause of the West; I noted the decline of proud Albion, forced to

knock on the door of the Community whose leadership it might have assumed fifteen years earlier. As a title for my article in *Le Figaro* of 22–23 December 1962, I chose "The Injustice of History." Readers reacted strongly: some considered History unjust, others thought it was just. The former referred to England in 1940, fighting alone against Hitler, the latter denounced the diplomacy of perfidious Albion between the two wars.

In the style taught for hundreds of years to students of rhetoric, I began with a parallel between the two countries. On the one hand, the United Kingdom "understood the aspirations of the colonized peoples and agreed to imperial withdrawal. The withdrawal was as gracious as the empire had been glorious. Unanimous during the hostilities, the British nation never experienced major division during the years of reconstruction. The British evidenced all the virtues that the wise have praised for centuries or millennia. And here they were humiliated by the young president of the United States,[1] knocking on the door of the European Community, uncertain of themselves and their future."

In contrast, France: "The disaster of 1940, the conflict between Vichy and Gaullism, governmental instability, entrapment in colonial wars, quasi-rebellion of the army, still unresolved conflicts between the Guide and the parties, none of the misfortunes recounted in the chronicle of the dark ages has been spared us. And yet, the franc is solid and the pound under challenge, it is France that is setting conditions in Brussels, it is France that, with decolonization completed and European unity in process, seems to have mastered its fate."

The origin of this apparent paradox was British refusal to understand fully the inevitable consequences of the war: "Great Britain has been the victim of its victory of 1945, as France between the wars was the victim of its victory of 1918, for the two victories had one trait in common: they were military and not political, illusory and not authentic." Continental Europeans, all defeated, torn from their habits and traditions, set out for a new future. Great Britain did not see the necessity for renewal: first came the alliance with the United States, then the preservation of the commonwealth, and only thirdly cooperation with the Europeans. Churchill and the Conservatives argued in favor of Franco-German reconciliation, but all the leaders, Labour or Tory, were offended by the actual functioning of the Treaty of Rome. They had not taken the plans for European unification seriously. When they understood their mistake, they launched the idea of a free-trade zone, an initiative obviously designed to paralyze the formation of the Common Market. After the rejection of the free-trade zone came the candidacy that we could interpret less as a conversion to the community then as a subtle method to destroy it, or at least to reshape it according to their conceptions and their interests.

Toward the end of 1961, I spent two weeks in London to take the pulse of the ruling elite and of British opinion. I met Prime Minister Harold Macmillan and admired his art of saying nothing and making his interlocutor speak; Edward Heath, responsible for negotiations with Brussels, no doubt belonged to the converted, the "Europeans" (I found "Europeans" here and there, but not many). Harold Wilson did not conceal his hostility to British membership. He used arguments close to those that Mendès France had used against French membership; the British economy is unable to stand up to continental competition; it must first reform in order later to be able to profit from that competition. A third school was represented by my friend Hugh Gaitskell, with whom I had lunch in Paris a few weeks before his unfortunate and premature death. This Labour Party leader, whom I liked for his simplicity, obvious honesty, and frankness—characteristics that are relatively rare in professional politicians—granted only secondary importance to the Common Market. In favor of membership if we obtain good conditions; let's remain outside if the Six impose on us sacrifices that are disproportionate to the foreseeable advantages. In any event, he said to me, the real drama of the future is taking place elsewhere, far from the Old Continent, in India or, better, in Asia and Africa where the formerly colonized peoples are making their voices heard and defying their former masters.

I returned from this investigation in a state of uncertainty. The British were not enthusiastic about participating in the European Community, but they hated the idea of being excluded. The Common Market seemed to me to be still too fragile to accept immediately a new member whose objectives and interests certainly did not coincide with those of France. On 4 September 1962, I expressed myself bluntly: "[T]hose for whom Europe is to be a fatherland cannot avoid recognizing that in British eyes (except for a small minority), it will never be anything but a means for something else. With a slight shift of perspective, like that adopted by one of our English colleagues, one can attribute to continental Europeans the opinion that Great Britain in the Common Market would be a Trojan horse for the United States. It is fairly clear what the Europe of the Six would be like (it would necessarily expand after the entry of Great Britain). All the changes brought about by the entry of Great Britain will go against French conceptions, I would even say against the conceptions of all French parties. It is thus hardly surprising that our representatives often appear intransigent to our British friends." At the same time, I tried to defuse the conflict. "If Great Britain does not join the Common Market, the Atlantic Alliance will not thereby be condemned. In the end, there is no lack of politicians in Great Britain, Australia, and other Commonwealth countries who would rejoice if the Brussels negotiations failed. How can one call General de Gaulle anti-English solely on the pretext that he perhaps shares the hopes of Lord Attlee?"

The last sentence, perhaps too politically clever, nevertheless pointed to an unchallengeable fact: British candidacy did not express the common feeling of the political class, a clear and solid wish of the nation. Many of the British who were hostile to joining found objective allies among French functionaries who, according to a current witticism, reversed the American formula, "when there is a problem, there is a solution," and said jokingly: "when there is a solution, there is a problem."[2]

At bottom, General de Gaulle was right, even though the style he adopted in the famous press conference of 8 January 1963 increased the resentment of our Common Market partners, the anger of the British, and the irritation of the Kennedy administration. In the course of the years 1961 and 1962, the Atlantic Alliance had been troubled by two disputes: Should the Common Market admit Great Britain? and what will be the consequence of the establishment of a French strategic nuclear force? The January 1963 press conference contained two spectacular *Noes* addressed simultaneously to London and Washington.

The Kennedy administration had a grand design. Economically, the Common Market, enlarged by British membership, would establish closer connections to the Atlantic zone and would reduce the customs barriers of the Six, who would now have become Seven, in conjunction with similar reductions in barriers protecting the United States. Politically, a united Europe and the American republic would make up the two pillars of the Atlantic edifice. Kennedy had made the mistake of intervening in a debate that concerned only the Europeans. He had committed a second mistake by offering Great Britain, as a replacement for the Skybolt air-to-surface missiles, Polaris missiles that would arm the nuclear submarines constructed by the British. He offered the French government an agreement identical to the one he had reached with the Macmillan government. General de Gaulle seized the opportunity to increase the effect of his double veto by his staging and the eloquence of his speech. Aside from the political arguments, General de Gaulle's rejection of the offer made at the Nassau conference[3] was also dictated by technological considerations. The French had established a nuclear weapons program; in 1963, Polaris could have no place in that program. Moreover, if billions of francs were going to be spent to perfect nuclear weapons and their targeting, it was better that the French arsenal be totally French, conceived by French engineers and manufactured by French workers. The Kennedy administration, out of passion and for theoretical reasons, was committed to an American monopoly not so much of weapons as of nuclear strategy in the Alliance. General de Gaulle had no intention of granting it this monopoly, Franco-American agreement was thus impossible. André Malraux, who came to Washington between the Nassau conference and the General's veto, suggested to President Kennedy that a Franco-American dialogue was about to begin. At least, this is how Kennedy understood Malraux's statements. (Kennedy mentioned this to me in passing and concluded from it that those who were closest to the General did not always understand his intentions.)

In the course of the weeks and months following the General's *no*, I had the opportunity to explain and comment on his policies; in *Le Figaro*, my commentaries were measured and sometimes "unsupportive," as the General would have said.

In 1966, the decision to remove French troops from the unified command of NATO symbolized Gaullist diplomacy and strongly affected public opinion. In 1967, the position adopted with respect to the Six-Day War scandalized a fraction of the public; the trip to Quebec also provoked some reactions.

The 1966 decision followed so logically from Gaullist thought that I barely commented on it. Military agreements between the French command and NATO headquarters replaced integration without too many difficulties. The relatively vague terminology of the North Atlantic Treaty—which General de Gaulle had severely criticized—helped the President of the Fifth Republic to carry out his plans. France alone would decide what help it would provide to one of its allies that was the victim of aggression. If hostilities originating in Africa or Asia risked reaching Europe, France would preserve a better chance of not being drawn into a war that was not its war.

I refrained from commenting on General de Gaulle's trip to Quebec, particularly on his exclamation: "Vive le Québec libre!" I was not surprised by the event. As I have already noted, as a guest at the annual meeting of the Institut des Affaires publiques in 1957, I had met all those who played significant roles in Quebec and Canada over the course of the succeeding years. Jean Lesage, the man of the quiet revolution, René Levesque, and Pierre Elliott Trudeau were there, along with many others who have disappeared from the political scene. The political shift of the Québecois—the rejection of the Duplessis regime, a North American style electoral machine—had appeared on the horizon. Nationalism was moving from defensive to offensive positions; the French-speaking population were no longer satisfied with preserving their language and their laws, they had the ambition of taking their fate into their own hands. The English speakers of "la belle province" were in control of the economy, major enterprises, and the higher positions in the administration. The renewal of the educational system, a major element of the "quiet revolution" increased the number of graduates, or, if you like, of "intellectuals." And they became both spokesmen and militants for the independence party.

After my visit to Sainte-Adèle in 1967, I continued to observe political movements in Canada. I accepted an invitation from the English Institute of Public Affairs, on which the French Institute had been modeled. I was struck by the absence of community between French- and English-speaking communities and by the innate precariousness of Canadian unity. In response to the attacks of the independence forces, I wrote an article for *Le Figaro* on 24 April 1964 with the title: "Will Quebec be Independent?" "The French will refrain from deciding whether it is desirable for the state of Quebec to attain independence. In a certain sense, the French Canadians have always been nationalists, if one understands by this ambiguous term the desire to preserve the originality of their culture and to conduct their own affairs. But as long as the French Canadians remained a peasant population, tightly controlled by the Church, cut off from urban and industrial civilization, nationalism was defensive, and the federal arrangement, whose centenary approaches, allowed for peaceful coexistence, if not psychological unity, between the two ethnic groups." Today, French-speaking Canadians are rapidly becoming urbanized. They have discovered that in the province in which they make up the majority of the electorate, English speakers dominate the economy and even the administration: "The English generally have a 'good conscience': haven't they left to the French their religion, their laws, their customs, their language, and even extensive autonomy for the last century? They look on supporters of independence as fanatics or demagogues, more ridiculous than dangerous. But I fear that they have forgotten the essential. They have not given to their French-speaking follow citizens what they can least do without: the feeling of being recognized. The English Canadians, who have been the most orthodox of the British in their anti-colonialism, are incapable even of imagining that the French Canadians consider themselves victims of 'colonialism.' And yet, if every ethnic group, even an autonomous one, is or feels itself to be a victim of colonialism when it occupies an inferior position in a binational state, how could the French Canadians fail to see themselves to some extent as having been colonized?" The feeling of inferiority is all the more painful the more they participate in modern life. My friends, particularly Eric de Dampierre, made fun of me and of the independence of Quebec. On the other side of the ocean, the article created a great stir and provoked debate. The major English-language daily, the *Montreal Star,* devoted a two-column editorial to me, from top to bottom of the front page. It considered the violent attacks of the "independents" to which I had referred of little importance (as did the French-language press). It presented me as so celebrated a personality that President Kennedy had summoned me for a consultation (which was not true), and it criticized me for granting probability, or at least plausibility, to an unreasonable enterprise. Since Raymond Aron takes the independence forces seriously, they have attained one of their principal objectives; they have come out of the ghetto and have become respectable. I also received a substantial number of letters from English-speaking Canadians, all outraged, all more or less violent, against my article (which had been reprinted in full in a French-language paper, *Le Devoir*, if memory serves).

If a single article had troubled the English of Canada, one can understand the effect of the General's trip and the scandal provoked by the final cry launched from the balcony of the Montreal city hall: "Vive le Québec libre!" The slogan of the extremist independence party. In his press conference of 21 November 1967, he retraced the epic of the French Canadians, 60,000 at the time of the Treaty of Paris, "who, of peasant origin, simple people cultivating the soil, grew magnificently to hold their own against the mounting wave of the invaders." The General also recalled the first period, of passive defense to preserve their language, their traditions, their religion, and their French solidarity. Now they were claiming, like any other people, the right to master their fate: "Industrialization has been accomplished, so to speak, over them." The Anglo-Saxons controlled the resources of the country and "placed the French in a more and more inferior position." Hence, the movement for liberation was completely understandable.

The General then recounted, in his finest style, his trip, his conversations with his hosts, and the supreme moment: "In Montreal, the second largest French city in the world, the expression of liberating passion was such that France, in my person, had the sacred duty to respond directly and solemnly." The General did not hesitate to explain the conditions necessary for a solution to the Canadian problem. "The change of the present structure of Canada will result in the accession of Quebec to the rank of a sovereign state, master of its national existence." The second condition was "that the solidarity of the French Community takes shape on both sides of the Atlantic."

I, too, had been moved by the endurance and the awakening of French Canada, but I was not sure that the independence and sovereignty of Quebec was the solution. My friend Pierre Dupuy, who had gone back and forth between Vichy and London between 1940 and 1942, told me: "I would refuse to live in an independent Quebec, I would go back to France." The conversation dates from 1967; I had come to Montreal to deliver a lecture on the occasion of the World's Fair. On my return, I wrote a series of articles, as objective as possible, presenting the arguments of the various parties.

At first and above all, I noted the effect of the president's try: "He created neither Québecois nationalism nor the independence parties. The two principal parties, the National Union and the Liberal Party, are now seriously considering the 'independence option' (an expression that I had heard and read on many occasions). The relations between French and Québecois were strange. The descendants of the French who had been 'abandoned' by the Treaty of Paris of 1763, now six million strong, are enthusiastically saluting their country of origin as embodied in the man who symbolizes both the old and the new France. The synthesis of tradition and modernity that Lesage's 'quiet revolution' wanted to accomplish is embodied in their eyes by General de Gaulle, simultaneously Catholic and Republican. Thus, the French reaction to the journey of their head of state seemed incomprehensible to most Québecois." The fact that the General's trip, "triumphant in the eyes of the Québecois," was harshly criticized in the French press, should warn us about possible misunderstandings.

A nationality comparable to that of the Americans in the United States did not take shape in Canada. The two founding peoples, as they are called, lived together without mixing with one another. "The French Catholics, concentrated in Quebec, wanted to remain themselves. They paid no attention to France, which reciprocated. The Church supported resistance to the Anglo-Saxon world; at the same time, it inhibited adaptation to modern life, while French Canadians in the course of this generation have experienced rapid and profound changes; as they have become urbanized, they have discovered their inferiority in their own province and the inferiority of their province among the provinces of Canada."

I then posed the major question: "What are the aims of the French Canadians after Lesage's 'quiet revolution,' after the surprising victory of Johnson's National Union over Lesage's Liberals? The economic aims were to accelerate and control the economic progress of the province. The cultural aims were to preserve the French language in Quebec, to encourage bilingualism in Ottawa and in the other provinces. As for the political aim, it is the essential subject of the debate. For a long time the speech of the Québecois has been considered as a dialect used by an inferior population: set in competition with a universal language, it can resist only with the help of the public authorities." I mentioned another aspect of the situation: "The French Canadians now define themselves in relation to the Americans and the neo-Canadians as much as in relation to their former British masters. This explains their hesitation between 'special status' and 'separatism,' the feeling that neither solution may be capable of preserving the future. Will Quebec preserve its national identity in the Canadian federation if the federation does not preserve its own identity, if the neo-Canadians are absorbed neither by the British nor the French, but the Americans?"

In the third article, I presented the advantages and the risks of each of the two solutions: "Either separatism, which implies the abandonment of a million French Canadians who have settled outside Quebec, with the danger of economic decline or of an 'interdependence' more determinative of the outcome than theoretical independence, or else a supreme effort to give content to Canadian nationality, to accelerate the movement toward bilingualism, or 'biculturalism,' to protect the French character of Quebec." René Levesque or Pierre Elliott Trudeau. Neither one had yet succeeded in 1982.

France should support the Québecois as much as possible in their desire to remain North American and French. It should not work actively for a dissolution of the Canadian federation: the dissidence of Quebec would probably provoke similar movements. In any event, the decision belonged to the Québecois, not to the European French.

In 1967, the General's statements provoked conflict with the Jewish community and the Israelis. He declared in advance that he would condemn whichever of the two parties first had recourse to arms; he thus condemned the Israelis without recognizing extenuating circumstances. Moreover, for reasons that still escape me, he placed part of the responsibility for the Six-Day War on the United States. After sketching the outlines of his own solution, he concluded on a pessimistic note: "It is hard to see how any agreement can be reached, not on the basis of some imaginary formula, but involving real concerted action, as long as one of the four great powers has not extracted itself from the hateful war it is conducting elsewhere. For, everything hangs together in today's world. Without the Vietnam drama, the conflict between Israel and the Arabs would not have become what it is; and if peace were to return to Southeast Asia tomorrow, the Middle East would soon achieve the same peace thanks to the general détente that would follow."

Everything in this analysis seemed to me artificial, arbitrary, simply false. What relation was there between the concentration of Egyptian troops in the Sinai or the closing of the Tiran straits and the Vietnam War? We now know that the withdrawal of American troops from Indochina is not enough to bring peace to the Near East. The Arab-Israeli conflict began before the American intervention in South Vietnam, and it continued afterward. After the Six-Day War and the Israeli victory that the General himself, according to what he said at his press conference, had foreseen, France voted with the Soviet Union and the Arab countries in the United Nations. On this occasion, I wrote an article entitled "Why?" which unrestrainedly criticized the General's diplomacy.

The first criticism: was French activity contributing to peace in the region? "If the aim of French diplomacy is to foster a lasting solution, the least that one can say is that French acceptance of Soviet-Arab arguments does not seem likely to lead to that result."

The second criticism: "Let us speak the language of pure realism. The countries of black Africa with moderate leaders are anxious or indignant. The shipment of Soviet arms to Algeria and the so-called revolutionary politics of Boumediene provoke anxiety in Tunis and Rabat, where the leaders, who understood French neutrality, do not understand pro-Soviet militancy, the conscious and deliberate support given to all of those in the third world who profess the most hostile feelings toward the Americans and the West."

What do the preceding pages suggest about Gaullist diplomacy?

First of all, we should leave the war years aside. As long as he was not recognized as head of the provisional government of the Republic, his activities had to do with both domestic and foreign politics. He attained his goal because he wanted above all for Free France to become official France. In his military operations against positions held by authorities loyal to Vichy—Dakar, Syria, Madagascar—he had no success. Soldiers and bureaucrats resisted the Free French more stubbornly than they resisted the English and the Americans. Would a different kind of propaganda, less aggressively against those who followed the Marshal have attenuated, if not eliminated, the civil war among the French? No one can say. Events at least justify the hypothesis that the Manichaean interpretation of the armistice, asserted at the outset and maintained through thick and thin, is a legend or an epic fiction. At the Liberation, neither the magistrates nor the French as a whole subscribed to this epic vision. The appeal of 18 June retains its moral and political significance, but the speeches that came immediately after the appeal were already those of a party leader rather than a spokesman for the defeated country.

Let us pass over the quarrels with the English and the Americans, especially with the latter—quarrels which, in early 1943, came close to provoking a break between the Western Allies and the leader of the Free French. Let us consider the beginnings of the General's diplomacy when he had returned to France as leader of his nation. His first gesture, simultaneously symbolic and effective, was the treaty with the Soviet Union, a treaty directed against Germany, at a moment when no one could be unaware of the consequences of the war: the permanent presence of the Soviet Union in the center of Europe, and the definitive weakness of Germany. In these circumstances, what was the sense of this Franco-Russian treaty against the Third Reich or the country or countries that would be its successors? The defenders of the General will reply that, through this treaty, the president of the provisional government of the Republic was demonstrating his independence from his powerful Western allies. We can accept the reply, but we should remember the other episodes.

In Syria and Lebanon, countries to which he had promised independence at the moment when his troops began their campaign against those of Vichy, the General found himself involved in a bitter quarrel with Great Britain, to the point that, according to his memoirs, he declared to Ambassador Duff Cooper: "You have failed France; if I had the means, I would make war upon you." A war with Great Britain over territories which, in any event, were to achieve independence? I prefer not to take this martial, not to say warlike, pronouncement seriously.

What seems to me most striking is his attitude to Germany, an ambiguous attitude whose ambiguity he himself may not have recognized. On the one hand he invited the new Germany to join the new Europe, and he sketched the broad outlines of a Western Europe united under French leadership. But which Germany? For General de Gaulle, while calling for Franco-German reconciliation, resurrected, in a totally different context, the theses of Bainville on "the Germanies."

In Berlin, where the Tripartite Commission met, the French representative vetoed every measure that might favor the reconstitution of German unity. The three Great Powers had envisaged an administration of the four zones by civil servants or organizations chosen in common by the four occupying powers. The French veto, motivated by inveterate hostility to the Reich, played into the hands of the Soviets,[4] who, as early as September 1945, indicated by measures inspired by their ideology (agricultural collectivization) that they intended to stay. There is more to be said. While the French doctrine of many Germanies was out of date, and the dilemma posed was whether there would be one or two Germanies (one Soviet and the other Western), the General and André Malraux continued to repeat the old refrain "no more Reich," as though the Reich, in 1945, meant anything other than the state. Confronting a Germany cut off from the Soviet occupation zone, the General continued to fulminate against the Reich and thereby against the union of the three Western zones in the Federal Republic of Germany. International control over the Ruhr, in which the Soviet Union demanded a role, the detachment of the Rhineland, all these precautions against the Germany of the past were major themes of the General's thought, as though he had not fully understood the obvious revolution. The disturber, the country that threatens the Old Continent with universal monarchy, is now and for the foreseeable future not Germany but the Soviet Union.

When the General returned to power, after having fought hard against the Anglo-American policy of "German reconstruction," he recognized that nothing remained of his plan of 1945. He recognized the circumstances, accepted what had occurred, but reverted to another of his guiding ideas, even more vigorous than historic hostility to the Reich, that is, the refusal to place France in one of the two blocs, the one led by the United States. Once the Algerian war was ended, a tragic but finally provincial affair (decolonization, or at least the decomposition of European empires, was reaching its conclusion), the General launched himself into what the Germans used to call *die grosse Politik*. France should measure itself against the great powers, not with the GPRA or the Tunisia of Bourguiba. The close alliance with Adenauer's Germany, the manufacture of nuclear weapons (in which the Federal Republic might participate financially) would create the foundation for an autonomous Europe, no longer reduced to the inferior condition of a fragment of the Western bloc. In the service of his grand design, the General carried off some victories: he opposed British entry into the Common Market without provoking its breakup; he put in place a strategic nuclear force that would in the future permit a policy of deterrence "in every direction," and hence total independence of the two blocs. The Germans did not follow the Gaullist program, insofar as they understood it. The Bundestag added to the perpetual Franco-German treaty a preamble that emphasized the priority of the Atlantic Alliance. Thereafter, the General was no longer interested in the "perpetual treaty," even though it existed and Franco-German cooperation continued.

Between 1963 and 1967, the grand design changed its means of operation. To escape from the Atlantic vise, the "domination" of the United States, the General turned toward the Soviet Union. Of course, during the Berlin and Cuba crises, he demonstrated his solidarity with the West, but he changed his language from 1963 on. Perhaps one should say that he reverted to a language he had been holding in reserve: "Europe from the Atlantic to the Urals," "détente that will follow understanding and cooperation." The normalization of relations with the Soviet Union and the satellite countries of Eastern Europe was justified, in the eyes of most of the French, without any reference to the Gaullist "grand design." In fact, the common characteristics of the "perpetual alliance" with Germany and "privileged relations" with Moscow had more to do with the psychology of the General than with any political analysis. Along with Germany and the other continental countries of the Community, France had potentially reached the status of a Great Power. Thanks to the permanent dialogue with Moscow, without leaving the Atlantic Alliance, it had risen to world ranks.

In leaving the integrated command of NATO, France established its distance from the Federal Republic on the always decisive question of defense. The General signed no compromising agreements in Moscow. Nor did he obtain any material or moral advantages. Trade increased, but France had no monopoly on it. Although he visited Warsaw the year after he visited Moscow and encouraged his hosts to turn their eyes beyond the Soviet world, he came up against Gomulka's blunt rejection. General de Gaulle, acclaimed everywhere, a historic, almost legendary hero, did not shake the Soviet bloc, but he did trouble the Western bloc which was by nature more unstable.

Chancellor Adenauer had said to a minister of the Fourth Republic: "If you make the pilgrimage to Moscow, you should have no illusions: The Germans will do the same thing, the day after, if not the day before, you do." Détente in the General's style implied definitive resignation by the West to the consequences of the Second World War, according to the terms of the Soviets—a resignation expressed in the Helsinki accords several years after the General's death. And the General's successors are not wrong to recall at every opportunity that Gaullist France played a decisive role in East-West détente and hence encouraged West Germany to follow its *Ostpolitik,* its reconciliation with the East. Does France have any reasons to congratulate itself for this?

The strategic nuclear force, the Franco-German alliance, nonparticipation in the integrated command of NATO, these three decisions, only the last of which was excluded under the Fourth Republic, belong to the General's legacy and are still exempt from challenge, for obvious reasons: no government can simply junk such costly and prestigious weapons; every government wants to modernize the nuclear force in order to preserve credibility; the Franco-German alliance has become an integral part of normal French diplomacy, although the relations between Georges Pompidou and Willy Brandt lacked warmth. Finally, rejoining the integrated command is out of the question in the foreseeable future; it would provoke a great debate in the political classes and hence in the nation itself.

The legacy of the General is not limited to these three measures that a majority of public opinion approved and still approves. It was General de Gaulle who legitimated anti-Americanism. In moments of crisis, he demonstrated his solidarity with the West, but more often than not he represented France to be threatened equally by the two Great Powers. He attributed responsibility for the Six-Day War to American involvement in Vietnam. He gave the French the habit of seeing the wrong enemy, of taking the Soviet Union as an ally and the American Republic as a Great Power threatening French independence. Today, twelve years after the General's death, French diplomacy remains partially paralyzed by this inversion of roles, by a vision of the world that I consider contrary to reality.

In hindsight, can we explain the General's grand design or decode his secret? Was there a grand design or a secret? I have never agreed with the argument of Jean Paulhan, who imagined that General de Gaulle dreamed of playing the role of Lenin after having realized some of the ideas of Maurras. What can be verified is that, after the failure of the Franco-German treaty, the General had as his principal objective the greatest possible distance from the Atlantic Alliance without destroying or abandoning it: in his arguments against the blocs, he used language imitated from that of the Soviets. Certain legitimate questions were therefore raised: Did he want the Americans to withdraw; did he believe that the evolution from detente to understanding and cooperation would be fostered by the withdrawal of American troops? Did he harbor the illusion that the French strategic nuclear force would be enough to replace the American force? I cannot answer these questions categorically.

I can willingly agree that, in the long run, the General counted on change within the Soviet Union. Trained before the 1914 war, he frequently repeated the formula used by Stalin: Nazism will pass, the German people will go on. Most often, he spoke of Russia rather than the Soviet Union. He probably did not grasp the specificity of the Soviet regime, in his eyes a despotic regime like others that would experience the fate of the others. But this putative "agreement" among the Latins, the Gauls, the Germans, and the Slavs, from the Atlantic to the Urals, this newly discovered European balance—was it a distant vision or a political object that had to be pursued? Did the General believe in the dream of a unified Europe, no longer dependent on a non-European power (the United States), or did he simply want to transfigure a more prosaic policy? How could he be unaware that Western Europe could not contest Soviet imperial power without the support of the United States? Did dissolution of the blocs in order to return to the diplomatic exercises of sovereign nations represent movement toward a new future or a return to the past?

We can leave out of account the press conferences and consider only the most significant diplomatic initiatives taken by de Gaulle after the end of the Algerian war in 1962. After the abortive attempt to establish a close alliance with a Western Germany that, it was anticipated, would weaken its ties with the United States, the General wanted to appear not as a partner of the Western bloc but as a great power dealing with the others on an equal footing. At the same time, he maintained the advantages of the Atlantic Alliance, since German and American forces were placed between Soviet forces and the French border. It may be that the General considered leaving the alliance altogether. It is possible that he considered a "defense in all directions," a thesis of General Ailleret, which led to neutrality and was soon abandoned. What remains from Gaullist diplomatic activity is, on the one hand, an autonomous defense of France thanks to its strategic nuclear force, and on the other, dialogue with the Soviet Union: the General, and Georges Pompidou as well, felt assured of a role as intermediary between the Soviet Union and the West, a role that no one else could assume in their place. Immediately after the General's resignation, the German coalition government initiated *Ostpolitik*, which, a dozen years later, has compromised the German-American alliance and contributed to a profound transformation of the diplomacy and the public opinion of the German people. The preservation of détente seemed to the public to be the primary objective. Can the General's aggressiveness toward the United States, more verbal than actual, be explained by the overwhelming power that he attributed to the American republic? Was he pretending to side with the Soviets in order to restore the balance? I do not think I am capable of answering these questions.

I did not reject the General's policies as a whole: I approved the establishment of a strategic nuclear force; I called into question the "European" convictions of the government and people of Great Britain; the Franco-Israeli alliance lost its basis with the end of the Algerian war. What led me to these perhaps excessive criticisms was the General's very style; and it is style that assured his success. Positive results could have been achieved without scandal, without exasperating our partners and allies.

Style and content, in the end, fused together. General de Gaulle seemed in the world's eyes, particularly in the Third World, to be the representative of a country that had stood up to "American imperialism." I thought at the time and I continue to think that the Atlantic Alliance remains a necessary condition for European security as long as the Europeans refuse to take charge of their own defense.

I have always been less troubled by the excessive power of the United States than by the instability of a continent-nation, cast by the fortunes of war into world politics, whose leaders, most of them unaware of the historic fate of the Republic, are driven by the changing currents of public opinion. Would the General today fear the superiority of the American Power?

When the General withdrew from the world of politics, he may very well have still thought of the American Republic, bogged down in Vietnam, as the only superpower.

NOTES

1. Kennedy had canceled the Skybolt (an air-to-surface missile) on which the British had been counting to maintain their deterrent forces, made up at the time of bomber planes.

2. In May 1971, on the eve of the decisive meeting between Heath and Pompidou, I wrote an article which ended with the following lines: "The probable entry of Great Britain into the Common Market presents the opportunity for a new departure, but on the condition that our statesmen have no illusions about the interests of our future British partners, even further removed than those of our German partners from the arguments that French negotiators have, until now, been using."

3. The Anglo-American conference that produced the Polaris agreement.

4. This judgment is open to challenge. Another policy would also have encouraged Soviet influence in West Germany.

1 7

PEACE AND WAR

I began to develop a sociological interest in war in the course of my years in London. As in many other circumstances, remorse, or at least regret, was at the origin of my decision. By what right had we, before the war, expressed categorical judgments about diplomacy, while we knew almost nothing about military reality, the balance of forces, the chances of victory, or the risks of defeat? I had studied economics in order to have a rational basis for my judgments of capitalism and socialism. Why had I neglected what the Germans call *Wehr-wissenschaft?*

At the close of hostilities, the appearance of the atomic bomb filled everyone with fear and stupefaction; the question was posed to civilians as well as the military: How could this instrument of destruction, of a power incomparable to the weapons that were now called classic or conventional, be integrated into traditional international relations. As a commentator on international events for *Le Figaro*, I felt the need to study both the military and historical context of the decisions that, as a journalist, I was supposed to understand and interpret. The American word *deterrent* entered into every-day speech. The notion gave rise to a complex of problems in the United

States, which led to the production of dozens of books: Who can deter whom, from what, by what threats, in what circumstances?

In the period from 1945 to 1955, I had thought through the consequences of the two wars of the century, and in *The Century of Total War* I raised the question of whether the cold war was a replacement or a preparation for total war. The particular characteristics of the international scene were obvious to everyone: a world concert rather than a European concert; dispossession of the former great powers, notably the Europeans; a distinction between the superpowers and all the others; a rivalry between the two superpowers and the two halves of Europe that was both ideological and political; the improbability of global war because of the existence of nuclear weapons.

In an earlier chapter, I referred to my first conceptual essays on international relations. I was already thinking of the book that became *Peace and War*, not yet of the little book *The Great Debate: Theories of Nuclear Strategy* (New York: Doubleday, Anchor Press, 1965), but in my articles I participated to some extent in what was called on the other side of the Atlantic the debate on nuclear strategy—an inaccurate term, since the discussion had less to do with strategy than with the possible or actual use of a weapon. Now, if a weapon as revolutionary as the nuclear weapon changes the whole of international relations, by itself it does not exhaust strategic thought: reflection on nuclear weapons makes up only a part of strategic thought.

At the Sorbonne, after my three series of courses on industrial society, I devoted the two following ones to international relations. These two courses, which were recorded and transcribed, correspond to the first two parts of *Peace and War*, that is, theory and sociology. I then took a year's leave from the Sorbonne and spent a semester as a research professor at Harvard. On my return, I drafted the last two parts, entitled "Histoire" and "Praxéologie." (This last term exists in both French and English, is equally rare in both languages, and has been criticized by a number of commentators.)

I had thought about this book for approximately a decade. I had spent a semester at Harvard precisely in order to write it. When it was published, I thought it was significant, and I probably exaggerated its value.

Peace and War confirmed the reconciliation—even more than my election to the Sorbonne—between the University and the journalist. *Annales* organized a kind of written symposium: Pierre Renouvin, Alain Touraine, and others wrote articles on the book or the subject. Pierre Nora was kind enough to say that I had substantiated my second thesis. In a sense, he was right; so many circumstantial works seemed to university figures, Alexandre Koyré for example, to be deplorably close to journalism. Even *Peace and War* would never have been written, if I had not commented on international affairs, week after week, from 1947 on; this time, however, the work went beyond journalism, though journalism had nourished it.

The review in the *New York Times* was written by Henry Kissinger, who called the book "profound, civilized, brilliant and difficult." The adjective "difficult" did not surprise me, but I do not think it is justified, unless an eight-hundred-page book is by definition difficult. In a personal letter, Leo Strauss, whom I admired deeply, and whom I had met in Berlin in 1933, but whom I had not seen since then, wrote that after reading *Peace and War*, he thought that it was the best book on the subject.

Even though I emphasized the changes brought about by nuclear weapons, and attempted to locate these weapons within customary diplomatic conduct, did I succeed in establishing the necessary balance between the monstrosity of the weapons and the banality of international relations? The formula "to survive is to conquer" now seems to be more equivocal than it was then, although I am still inclined to justify it, at least in part.

I can be criticized and I was—for describing today's world in terms of the past and for concentrating on state relations at the expense of transnational, international, or supranational phenomena. To be sure, in some sense I helped create these distinctions, but I did very little with them. As for the transnational—economic, ideological, or religious society that ignores and often downplays borders—I identified it conceptually and mentioned it here and there, but I did not analyze it in any depth. One might say (wrongly) that the strategic and diplomatic conduct that makes up the central theme of my book has become a sector of lesser importance in the world of international relations. I placed nuclear weapons in the context of diplomacy with respect to the "transnational," the world economy. I wanted to write a treatise on war and peace in the ordinary sense of those words—bloody war, waged with weapons. I denied neither the war of the airwaves, nor that of trade and currency, or ideology; I even considered certain aspects of these wars, or rather these rivalries; but in 1961 and 1962, the confrontation between East and West was in my eyes the center of relations among states. I would maintain this proposition today, but I should have justified my choice and summed up other development with a view toward joining the analysis of the system of relations among states with the analysis of the world market (of the two economic systems, capitalist and socialist).

I also neglected an aspect of diplomatic reality that has become more and more important, namely, the dependence of the diplomat (I used this term to mean the one who made decisions about external actions) on various influences from the political class or from the society itself. In his book, G. A. Allison asserts that finally, despite reservations and qualifications, I maintain the notion of the "rational actor," or, in other words, that I accept the identification of a collectivity with an "individual actor." Extensive research in the United States on decision making demonstrates that the president of the United States does not resemble the strategist who, removed from all constraints or pressures, magisterially calculates his resources in the light of the goal he has set for himself. American presidents—and this was true to some extent for Stalin and Hitler—derive their knowledge from more or less autonomous bodies, they deliberate with advisers, particularly military leaders, before making decisions. And these advisers, or these informers, in turn are not rational actors fulfilling their mission with no motivation but the truth or the national interest. They belong to an organization, loyal to the CIA or the Air Force and not directly to the United States. They provide conflicting advice because, at least in part, they are acting with reference to the interests of their own organizations. Perhaps nowhere outside the United States does the struggle between organizations provoke such passion and take on such an institutional form. But the more or less attenuated equivalent can be found in other countries, in the present or the past. Anyone who has made even a superficial study of the days preceding the 1914 war can have no illusions about the chaos of opinions, interests, and passions out of which finally arise a few decisions, bearing the weight of millions of deaths.

Of course, I was not aware at the time of the gap between the "rational actor"—France, Russia, Germany, Austria-Hungary—and the responsible individuals in each of these countries who concretely made history. Particularly in the second part, I should have presented a more thorough analysis of this aspect of diplomacy, which was not new but had become more prominent in our time. I thereby would at least have provided an illustration of a subject designed for sociological analysis—not the macrosociology of Sorokin—but empirical analysis applied to all sectors of society, to all patterns of behavior of social man.

I also reproach myself for the inadequacy of some chapters of the second part, particularly the one entitled "The Roots of the Institution of War." My knowledge of the literature on wars in so-called archaic societies was certainly inadequate.

I will stop here with this sketch of a self-criticism. In France, and in other countries, the book provided if not a "definitive work" or a "monument," at least a systematic analysis not of all but of many of the problems and aspects of international relations (particularly in our time). American professors, for the most part, did not find that they could derive much use from this attempt at a synthesis; many of them remarked only on its defects or lacunae. Elsewhere, professors and students appreciated and still appreciate the attempt, and judge it less severely. For this retrospective view, the practical conclusions are more important than any judgment on the scientific virtues or defects of the work.

Next I must consider simultaneously the essay *De la guerre (On War)*, which was a part of *Espoir et peur du siècle*, and *The Great Debate*. The chapters on "deterrence" and on the "deadlock" in Europe in *Peace and War* seem less satisfactory than *The Great Debate*.

With many others, I had participated in the conceptual elaboration of what the Americans call "nuclear strategy." First phase: "unilateral deterrence": the United States alone possesses both delivery systems (the heavy bombers of the Strategic Air Command) and atomic bombs. Second phase: the Soviets also have atomic bombs and bombers that have sufficient range to reach American territory. Third phase: on both sides, thermonuclear weapons supplement or replace atomic weapons and missiles are added to the bombers. We have arrived at the late 1950s and early 1960s, the time at which I wrote *Peace and War* and *The Great Debate*. Since then, the number of nuclear warheads has massively increased thanks to the technology of MIRV, and the precision of the missiles (ICBM). The celebrated article by Albert Wohlstetter, "The Delicate Balance of Terror,"[1] had again become relevant.

The great debate in the Atlantic Alliance began toward the end of the 1950s: Once the Soviets had a capacity to destroy the enemy more or less equivalent to that of the United States, was the threat of responding to aggression in Europe by bombing Soviet territory still credible? Deterrence, a key concept in American thinking about nuclear strategy, in the end has to do with psychology. To give apparent rigor to speculations about the credibility (or lack thereof) of deterrence, all writers used the terms rational or rationality. In launching the Strategic Air Command in response to the crossing of a demarcation line by Soviet troops, would the president of the United States be acting rationally? Would he be ready to sacrifice New York and Washington to save Hamburg and Paris? An incessant discussion: to discredit American deterrence, some strategists began assuming the failure of deterrence, that is, a Soviet aggression in Europe; others placed themselves in imagination before the aggressive conduct and considered the possible decision by the Soviets to invade Europe, without recourse to nuclear weapons, to be irrational, thereby leaving to the Americans the advantage of a first strike.

While at Harvard in 1960, I had attended and participated in the joint seminar of Harvard and MIT that developed the ideas that were adopted by the Kennedy administration. In the light of the experience of the 1950s, these professors had concluded that the United States could not and should not try to deter all possible aggressions from the Soviet Union or its allies and satellites by the threat of recourse to nuclear weapons. They thereby abandoned the doctrine of "massive retaliation" and were looking for another doctrine, which was named "flexible response." This doctrine was applied specifically to the European situation; in a broad sense, it was extended to American strategy as a whole; in the American arsenal, nuclear weapons became the weapons of last resort. Hence, the Americans implicitly rejected the possible notion that nuclear weapons might be decisive and not only deterrent, designed to conclude and not only to prevent wars. On this point, I agreed with the Americans; today, I wonder.

At the time, the discussion focused on three principal points:

1. Assuming that nuclear war represented the supreme danger, the Americans developed a strategy that, should hostilities occur, would reduce the risk of escalation to the minimum. They asserted, and demonstrated, by argument and experience, that the principal distinction that enemies would spontaneously respect, without explicit agreement, would be the distinction between conventional and nuclear weapons. On the basis of this general thesis, the so-called McNamara doctrine foresaw for Europe a strengthening of conventional defenses in order to delay as long as possible the use of nuclear weapons. Under the direction of President Eisenhower, the American army had organized a first division trained to combat with or without nuclear weapons. This enterprise was abandoned when John F. Kennedy adopted the ideas of the professors: tactical nuclear weapons were stockpiled, and the decisions as to their use would henceforth be that of the President alone.[2] According to the Americans, once the nuclear threshold had been crossed, there would be no stopping. The escalation to extremes would become not inevitable, but very probable.

2. Would the doctrine of flexible response weaken the effectiveness of American deterrence? Would the Soviets read it as a symptom of a lesser determination to protect Europe, even at the cost of a nuclear war? Or else, on the contrary, by providing themselves with a conventional defense, would the West not be adding one deterrent to another? Proclaiming in advance that one will immediately unleash the apocalypse is a bluff; preparing oneself both for combat and for the use of nuclear weapons as a last resort is to adopt a rational attitude that will be taken more seriously by the other side than would a bluff ("stop or I'll do something terrible").

3. The French exploded their first atomic bomb in 1960, and General de Gaulle gave priority to the so-called *force de frappe* or, according to the official formulation, a strategic nuclear force. Strategists and the military were forced to develop a doctrine that would justify a small nuclear force in opposition to a large one. This is the origin of the notion of deterrence by the weak against the strong that remains the official doctrine of France.

The reader who is curious about the great debate will find in the book of that title the arguments that were made at the time. As for my positions, this is what seems to me to come out in my books and articles of the time. On the first point, I adopted the McNamara doctrine or, more generally, I gave up the doctrine of massive retaliation. The Korean campaign had demonstrated that a superpower with a formidable arsenal frightened neither North Korea nor the People's Republic of China. Statements by John Foster Dulles after the Korean armistice that seemed to revive the original doctrine of massive retaliation convinced no one. What remains in controversy is the relative effectiveness of the two doctrines as messages of deterrence with particular reference to Europe.

I have never accepted the dogmatism about tactical nuclear weapons in the McNamara doctrine, at least as it was applied to Europe. To be sure, the implicit agreement between enemies on the limitation of hostilities requires intelligible messages from both sides: the atomic threshold represents a stopping point that is immediately understandable to everyone. There are no others so clearly visible. On the basis of these propositions, it did not seem to me legitimate to conclude that the use of tactical nuclear weapons would lead *necessarily* to the extreme, the worst, in other words to the reciprocal destruction of cities by the belligerents.

On the question of the relative effectiveness of the two doctrines, I never adopted a dogmatic attitude, for reasons that seemed to me stronger and stronger. Any theory or rhetoric of deterrence rests only on speculations, which do not become scientific simply because they are illustrated by models. The disproportion between the gains and losses of a diplomatic conflict on the one hand and the cost of a nuclear exchange on the other is so great that numerical models lose all value. Moreover, I almost always feel a kind of repugnance toward abstract theories of deterrence.

Let us consider the defense of Western Europe as a whole. A direct attack against the NATO armies seemed to me at the time to be totally improbable. Such an attack was conceivable—and is still today—only in the context of a war involving the United States, hence a general war. The passion of the transatlantic debate between 1961 and 1963 thus had an artificial character. And, after 1963, after the Cuban missile crisis and the dissolution of Khrushchev's pseudo-ultimatum, the debate died out, only to resume fifteen years later.

In fact, the American doctrine of flexible response was accepted by NATO; the bizarre plan for a multilateral force was abandoned; a special committee including representatives of the principal allies was given the task of establishing the outlines of nuclear strategy, or at least of informing the Europeans on the subject. On all sides, mental reservations remained: Was the scenario of a graduated response the best deterrent? Did the West have enough conventional forces for a prolonged defense without the use of tactical nuclear weapons? Wouldn't these weapons, stockpiled in a few locations, be destroyed before they could be used? Would a Soviet attack take place in accordance with NATO predictions?

The Great Debate was well received in the United States and used in several universities. Robert McNamara had my book on his desk when I saw him in the Pentagon. He told me that among the countless books on the subject he preferred mine (flattery to a journalist? Kissinger told me that McNamara had said the same thing to him). It hardly matters. This little book, written in the country in three weeks, immediately after the course I had given at the Institut d'Etudes politiques, hardly contributed any original ideas (was this possible?), but it undogmatically shed light on a controversy that led finally to psychological speculations. Some details sharpened the analyses: Were the Soviets, by rejecting the hypothesis of limited war, not playing poker, although they were masters at chess? Weren't the Americans, by multiplying on paper the intermediate stages between all or nothing, between apocalypse and capitulation, dreaming of a strategic chess game? Did the Americans wish to confront an adversary who was conversant with the subtleties of strategic thought, or on the contrary, an adversary who was ignorant of American thought? In short, would they invite a Politburo member to take courses at the Rand Corporation?

Robert McNamara discussed one of my sentences that had struck him; among allies, I had written, it is desirable to avoid misunderstandings and to foster reciprocal understanding; on the other hand, uncertainty, if not misunderstanding, ought to continue between enemies. The secretary of defense, inclined toward rational thinking, had difficulty in accepting the ambiguity of relations between enemies. However, an element of bluff seems to me inevitable in diplomatic crises. To be sure, looking at history, one can attribute to lack of communication some responsibility for the outbreak of wars, particularly the 1914 war. If the Austrians had known that the Russians would take the risk, or the initiative, of a major war in order to support Serbia, they might have acted otherwise. But in fact, from the very beginning, the Austrians were playing for high stakes: to punish Serbia according to their lights and, strengthened by the total support of Berlin, to intimidate Russia and force it into passivity. They were not unaware of the possibility of general war, but could they attain their objective without accepting this danger? The fact remains that, in present crises, in the shadow of the nuclear apocalypse, the actors will draw from uncertainty, from the unpredictability of the enemy's response, conclusions that are more favorable to peace. As long as the powers are in opposition, have incompatible objectives, and exchange threats of the use of force to accomplish their aims, dialogue is not reduced to the level of a debate, still less to that of a game: there remains a conflict which will not necessarily degenerate into war to the death, but which escapes from a total rationalization and excludes transparence applied to the intentions of the participants.

What explains the burst of passion between 1961 and 1963 and, after two or three years, near indifference? European statesmen and journalists were generally unaware of the development of American ideas in universities and think tanks. Kennedy introduced these ideas with his academic advisers. Since most ministers and commentators still held to the original doctrine of massive retaliation and of the simple *casus belli* (the crossing of the demarcation line), the apparent subtleties of the new doctrine were badly understood, or at least interpreted in a manner that was least indulgent to the Americans. The Germans understood that the new doctrine presupposed, and thus accepted, the occupation of part of their territory; the French questioned the value of American deterrence. The thesis of General Gallois—no state can protect another—became popular: the United States would not sacrifice their cities to save those of their allies.

This thesis made up the final subject of *The Great Debate:* the French deterrent force and its effectiveness. I have already discussed the subject in the preceding chapter, with reference to my articles in *Le Figaro*. In *The Great Debate*, the discussion was more abstract.

Does the nature of nuclear weapons justify the notion of deterrence by the weak against the strong? There can be no question that when the subject is weapons any one of which could provoke a catastrophe, the concept of equality or balance changes its meaning. A small power can, in certain circumstances, deter a great power, despite the disproportion between the harms he could create and those he might suffer. And yet, we should not push this plausible idea to extremes. A weaker power must also convince its enemy that it is really ready to accept death in return for the wound that it would inflict. A rational formulation of this possible deterrence is not particularly difficult: the prize represented by the small power is not worth the risk that would be taken by the aggressor. But what is the "value" of the small power? What is the "risk" that the great power would understand? Alternatively, what French president would send Mirage IVs to Moscow if France had not been attacked with nuclear force?

Once the abstract plausibility of deterrence by the weak against the strong had been accepted, it was appropriate, in 1961–63, to examine the historical circumstances, not through a scheme or a fictitious calculation of the cost of what was at stake, but in a concrete presentation of the facts. Geographically, France has no border with the Soviet Union; politically it belongs to the

Atlantic Alliance. In the early 1960s, would the strategic nuclear force of France have deterred the Soviet Union from an attack against France alone? Aggression of this kind was, and remains, inconceivable.

It is now 1982, not 1962; we should pause a moment to recall the changes that have taken place in the course of the last twenty years.

During his election campaign, John F. Kennedy had denounced the "missile gap," the advantage the Soviets had achieved in the production of missiles. Once elected, he discovered that the "gap" did not have to be rectified, because it did not exist. The Soviets, far from producing the greatest possible number of intercontinental weapons, had deployed—in 1962—several hundred intermediate range missiles and a small number (a hundred more or less) of intercontinental missiles: "The Soviet Union has not mass-produced strategic bombers capable of reaching objectives located in the United States, nor has it produced the hundreds of intercontinental missiles that were feared by the American experts in 1957–1958. Either from lack of resources, or in order to shift the task to the succeeding generation of missiles, the Soviets are content with balancing the immense American apparatus with a certain capacity to retaliate (a capacity in which they felt complete confidence, no matter what the circumstances) and with their superiority, in conventional forces and intermediate range missiles, over the retaliatory or defense capacities of Western Europe."[3]

The American doctrine of graduated response was based on American superiority in the domain of intercontinental missiles, and more generally on their "mastery over escalation." If American superiority grew along with escalation, the strategists of crisis on the American side thought they had the power to determine the level at which hostilities would begin.

The situation in Europe, and in the world, has profoundly changed for two sets of reasons, some political, the others technical. In their scenarios, American doctrines assumed that aggression would come from the Soviet Union and that the latter should rationally use its superiority, that is, conventional weapons. The Americans, hypothetically, were in control of escalation. In their military works, the Soviets did not explicitly consider the Americans' preferred scenario. They treated American discrimination and their strategic analyses as ruses of imperialism. They supported the proposition that war, on the day it might occur, would be total, and that nuclear weapons, once used, would exercise a decisive influence on the outcome of hostilities.

In 1981, the Soviet Union had not only preserved but also increased its superiority in conventional weapons; its divisions were assisted by battalions specialized in chemical and nuclear weapons. At the level of intercontinental missiles, it had at least reached equality, perhaps even a "theoretical" superiority in that, on paper, the nuclear warheads on large Soviet missiles, the SS18s and SS19s, could destroy the functioning of American ICBMs. In 1960 or 1961, the missile gap did not exist; there was, or may have been, one in 1962, in favor of the USSR.

In addition to the change in the balance of forces between Americans and Soviets, there was also progress, if not a revolution, in technology: the precision of targeting even intercontinental missiles. The missiles of the first generation, were directed toward extended areas, because the average distance from the target was measured in kilometers. This distance is now measured in hundreds of meters. Hence, missiles, even long-range missiles, once again became weapons of combat and not exclusively deterrents. In 1961, I had already commented on the asymmetry of Soviet and American doctrines: the Soviets, taken literally, held to the notion that there would be total war or none at all; the Americans multiplied distinctions among various scenarios of crises and hostilities.

Twenty years later, the asymmetry of doctrines remains, but it has changed. Soviet military texts, translated under the auspices of the American Air Force, maintain Clausewitz's formula, consecrated by Lenin's approval, according to which war is the continuation of politics by other means. Nuclear war, a catastrophe for humanity, would nevertheless be in conformity with this principle: it would signify the supreme and decisive phase of the life and death struggle between the two social regimes; and it would end with the victory of the socialist camp. The Soviets, who do not place the concept of deterrence at the center of their thought, assert that nuclear war can and should be won, and not only prevented. The Americans on the other hand have thought and written much about the means of avoiding nuclear war, and relatively little about what they would do if war involving nuclear weapons were to come about.

Of course, Soviet military texts are always a mixture of theory and propaganda (at least from our perspective). Nothing proves that the members of the Politburo or the military writers seriously think that a nuclear war can be won. But everything depends on the meaning given to "nuclear war." Each of the great powers has the means to devastate the other's cities, even if evacuation and civil defense were to reduce human loss. The capacity for mutual destruction greatly weakens the rationality, and hence the credibility, of the nuclear threat. But precision targeting of missiles allows for the incapacitation of the adversary's missiles or, in the European theater, a strike against the vital centers of NATO defense without reducing Western Europe to radioactive ruins. Everyone can imagine scenarios which conclude not with mutual destruction but with the capitulation of one of the camps or with a negotiation before the apocalyptic orgy of violence.

The Great Debate would have to be rewritten, or have several chapters added to it. France now possesses nuclear submarines armed with missiles, which seemed to me, twenty years ago, the substance of an authentic strategic nuclear force. But the missiles, according to official declarations, are still targeted on major cities, in the absence of the precision necessary to select strictly military targets. Moreover, the political fate of France cannot be separated from that of the rest of Western Europe. The threat of recourse to nuclear weapons perhaps protects our country from invasion, but how can one imagine a free France in a Sovietized Europe? Our deterrent force would give us at least a reprieve so that we could adapt to the circumstances.

NOTES

1. *Foreign Affairs*, 1959.
2. Or else, in the "two key" system, of the president of the United States and the head of state of the European country in which the tactical nuclear weapons were located.
3. *The Great Debate* (New York: Doubleday, 1965), pp. 150–51.

1 8

"HE HAS NOT UNDERSTOOD US," OR MAY 1968

Like all the revolutionary *journées* of French history, the events of May 1968 are not lost in the mists of the past but remain present, heroic or burlesque according to the observer's mood, and they continue to provoke passions, even, or perhaps especially, among sociologists. Sociologists provided so many ideas and words for the speeches of the rebellious students that they felt directly concerned and therefore more troubled than others may have been. What was the meaning of this earthquake that, for a few days, threatened to tear down the imposing edifice constructed by ten years of Gaullism? Even foreigners are still discussing the question today. A review of several books on the French May in an English journal was still wondering about the merits of my little work;[1] the best or the worst of what had been written on the subject? In 1979 again, when I was awarded the Goethe Prize, Ralf Dahrendorf spoke of my attitude toward the "events" with so much circumspection that one could only guess at his feelings: affected by my feelings, I had been unworthy of and perhaps unfaithful to myself. I veiled words, he called for indulgence and granted me extenuating circumstances.

I was not suited, at least in appearance, to defend the old Sorbonne and the mandarins. In my journalism, I had always criticized the French organization of higher education; I had criticized the *baccalauréat* as too difficult for an examination for the completion of secondary studies, insufficient as a means of selection for admission to the university; I had criticized the *agrégation* because it did not guarantee the quality of education nor did it provide training in research; I had criticized the total autonomy of the professor, the uncontested master in his chair, often ignorant of what his colleagues were doing.

On the other hand, I tended toward the "right" on the question of "selection," a word that, since 1968, has taken on an incredible charge of blind passion and resentment. The educational system is everywhere selective, from primary school to the *agrégation* and the *grandes écoles;* the boys and girls enter the system at the same age (give or take a year); some of them leave at sixteen (perhaps even at fourteen), others at nineteen, still others at twenty-five. The word *selection* was reserved for the passage from secondary school to the university. I argued for selection in admissions to the university and, as a counterpart, a *baccalauréat* reduced to an examination for the completion of secondary studies. My arguments remain valid today: neither the *Instituts Universitaires de Technologie* nor the business schools accept all holders of the *baccalauréat;* only faculties of letters accept all *bacheliers* who wish, even without a clear direction, to continue their studies and accept being warehoused in these caretaking establishments; university diplomas have been devalued and those of the *grandes écoles* have gained prestige; selection operates after one year at the university. Thus, considerable resources are devoted to tens or hundreds of thousands of students who will not go beyond the first year and will not even appear at examinations at the end of that year.

During the first term of the 1967–68 academic year, my colleagues had given me the role of director of the sociology section. I had been led to talk to students and to understand more clearly the consequences of the immediate application of the new systems of study. Some risked losing a year, or more precisely, requiring another year to obtain the *licence* and the *maîtrise* (or its equivalent in the old system).

Nothing obliged me to intervene in the crisis shaking the Sorbonne (which I had left on 1 January), which did not spare the sixth section of the Ecole Pratique des Hautes Etudes; however, directors of studies* could look on from a distance, calmly, from their offices. During the first week of May, after the police had entered the Sorbonne courtyard, on Saturday the fourth, I

*Trans. note: Directors of studies (directeurs d'études) are professors at the Ecole pratique des hautes études. They do not have the same obligations as professors in the universities, and are entitled to select their own students.

observed, without surprise but anxiously, the escalation of violence, the demonstrations, and the clashes between students and police. I spoke once on Radio–Luxembourg, more to explain the troubles than to condemn or approve them. The Saturday morning after the night of the barricades, passion had reached those who ordinarily focused on their work and were uninvolved in usual university politics. I participated in a meeting with Claude Lévi–Strauss, Charles Morazé, Jean–Pierre Vernant, and many others. Without enthusiasm, I signed a motion that, as I remember it, essentially condemned violence.

The same Saturday, I was approached by officials of the radio and television authority; I think Yves Mourousi was their spokesman, unless he was acting on his own initiative. They asked me, I think, to make some reasonable remarks that would help calm the situation. The general secretary of the Elysée, Bernard Tricot, was supposed to have said, so I was told; "You can't impose rules or limits on Raymond Aron." After a few hours' reflection, I refused the platform that was offered to me. Given the state of people's minds on that Saturday, 11 May, I didn't really know what to say. Was my refusal also determined by a few unpleasant episodes? Because of the bad feelings the General had toward me, at least according to widespread rumors, Gaullists and television had kept me at a distance as though I were a dangerous outlaw. To refuse to speak for such a motive was hardly honorable. Guiltless or not, I was obligated to do my best to help extinguish the conflagration. But what impact would my intervention on television have had?

I had a seat reserved on a flight to New York on the following Tuesday. I had three appointments: a lecture on human rights at a university in the state of New York; an annual banking conference in Puerto Rico where I, an amateur, was to address the best specialists in the world on monetary problems; finally, the conference of the American Jewish Committee, where I had agreed to talk about Vietnam. I did leave on that Tuesday, the day after the general strike and the massive demonstration, the day after the reopening of the Sorbonne. From a distance, I anxiously followed the multiplication of strikes, demonstrations, and riots. On 20 May, I could wait no longer, and decided to return to France, canceling my commitment to the American Jewish Committee. The plane landed in Brussels, since French airports were closed. Fortunately, an executive of a major company was traveling in the same plane as I. The car waiting for him in Brussels brought me to Paris.

I walked around the Latin Quarter; once or twice I went as far as the Richelieu amphitheater in the Sorbonne where speeches followed one another without interruption in an atmosphere of revolutionary festivity; on the rue Saint-Guillaume, I had discussions with students from good families who were touched by grace. As for everyone else, the General's televised speech on 24 May seemed to me beside the point. Seeming old, the General launched into pseudo-philosophical considerations of the same variety as the speeches that were mobilizing hundreds of thousands of French citizens. The printers began to censor *Le Figaro*. I wrote an ironic article, using quotations from Tocqueville.

After the Grenelle negotiations, the agreement promised to lead to the gradual end of the strikes and thus of the social crisis, if not the student crisis. The Communist delegates of the CGT were shouted down by the workers at Billancourt; on Monday the twenty-seventh, everything was called into question, and the regime itself seemed to stagger. On the twenty-ninth and thirtieth, I too, was afraid that the rebellion was sliding toward revolution. We listened at home with some friends to the General's speech. I think I cried out: "Vive de Gaulle!" We all had the feeling that this time he had hit the target and that he had won. Kostas Papaioannou and I went toward the Champs-Elysées where a crowd was beginning to gather. At the paper, I learned of the declaration of the head of the Communist parliamentary delegation, Robert Ballanger, to the National Assembly: "We will have elections." Speaking on Saturday, 1 June, on Radio-Luxembourg, I used the expression "psychodrama," which provoked the indignation of union members who were present.

The following week, I began a series of articles on the crisis in the university. A few readers accused me of jumping on the bandwagon of the winning side. It was an unjust criticism: before the dissolution of the Assembly and the end of the political crisis, these articles might have been refused by the printing workers; in any event, they would not have interested the public. France had to be put back to work and to have a government again before reconstruction, particularly of the university, could be placed on the agenda. Moreover, the announcement of elections, which the young rebels had identified with "treason," had neither calmed the *enragés* nor emptied the Sorbonne. The professors were not teaching, the students were not studying. Even the rectors, the administrative authorities, were not exercising all their functions, not doing what they no longer had the means to do.

The appeal that I addressed, "in the name of those who are silent," to teachers at all levels helped to change the climate. The general secretary of the Ministry of Education, Pierre Laurent, told me (how much was politeness?) that without my campaign in *Le Figaro*, he would have been unable to organize the *baccalauréat* examinations. The address that I had given in *Le Figaro*, the Centre Européen de Sociologie, provoked my break with Pierre Bourdieu. His disciples had spread through the Sorbonne, distributing tracts based on the gospel according to Bourdieu and Passeron, calling for the institution of "Estates General of teaching"; the students, for their part, used and abused the ideas of the book *Les Héritiers*. Some sociologists immediately interpreted the events or took an active part in them. Claude Lefort was an *enragé* in Caen, if we are to believe the rumors. Many teachers seemed to change character, as though suddenly, in an organized carnival, each one rejected his social character, his conventional appearance, liberated himself from his obligations, from the rules of his profession, and gave free rein to the dreams each of us has buried deep within ourselves. In a general assembly of the VIth section, I observed these sudden and temporary conversions with a mixture of sympathy and irony.

My articles, even before *La Révolution introuvable*, made me, even more than after the pamphlet on Algeria, an actor, not merely an observer. *Le Nouvel Observateur* placed under my photograph the caption *Le Versaillais*, "distracted by reason." Jean-Paul Sartre published a text of incredible violence against both General de Gaulle and me.

I had only one contact with the official actors of this month; a conversation with Pierre Mendès France on the morning of the Charléty meeting. I tried to convince him that the student movement represented a detonator and not a force. There are, I told him, only two camps: on one side, the Republic, the government, the assemblies, possible elections; on the other, the Communist Party, which did not seem eager to cross the Rubicon. The intellectuals, the armchair revolutionaries, criticized the Communist Party for not following the lead of Cohn-Bendit, Geismar, and Barjonet. If we supposed that republican legality were to collapse under the pressure of stone throwing and crowds, only the CP would fill the void—much against its will. I remember that Mendès France accepted my analysis. That afternoon, two hours later, he was acclaimed by the students. The only argument he offered me to justify his attitude amounted more or less to the formula: we should not discourage the Latin Quarter. The future elite of the nation, the students of today should not come out of this crisis with their hopes frustrated, bitter, resigned in spite of themselves to a world they look on with disgust.

Before discussing the polemics provoked by my articles in *Le Figaro* and by *The Elusive Revolution, Anatomy of a Student Revolt* (New York: Praeger, 1969), I would like to pause a moment on the events themselves and distinguish the history and the sociology of the crisis, explain the diversity of interpretations to which it has been and continues to be subject, by reason of the very heterogeneity of the totality christened the "events of May."

Let us begin with a narrative history. The "events" can be divided into four phases. The first began with the entry of the police into the Sorbonne and lasted until 13 May, the day of the general strike and the reopening of the Sorbonne; the second was marked by the spread of the strikes, spontaneous at first, later provoked or supported by the Communist Party, leading to the Grenelle negotiations and the agreements between industry and the unions under the aegis of the government; the third phase lasted for only a few days, with the apparent rejection of the Grenelle agreements by the Billancourt strikers, the challenge posed to the President and the Prime Minister, the announcement by François Mitterrand of his candidacy for the presidency if the General were to resign, all of which was dramatized by the disappearance of the President of the Republic for several hours and crowned by the speech he delivered on Thursday the thirtieth, followed by the massive demonstration on the Champs-Elysées; the final phase lasted for a few weeks, and included the restoration of order, the elimination of pockets of rebellion in the Sorbonne and the Odéon, and the legislative elections that gave the majority a decisive victory—more decisive, it may be noted, in the number of seats won than in the number of votes cast.

For each of these phases, the historian is led to pose two kinds of questions: "historical" and "sociological." For example, during the first week while the Prime Minister was traveling in Asia, decisions were made that inflamed the situation: calling the police on Saturday the fourth, loading dozens of students into police vans, the prosecution of a few students, and finally, and especially, the return of Georges Pompidou on Saturday the eleventh, after the night of the barricades, and the reversal of policy. Instead of applying the agreement negotiated by Louis Joxe and Alain Peyrefitte with representatives of the student unions, the Prime Minister, who was in a sense above the factions, since he had been away from Paris during the preceding week, gave in to all the demands of the "students" (the quotation marks are justified because only a fraction of the students participated in these movements led by small revolutionary groups).

Of those decisions which had significant consequences, the one made by Georges Pompidou on 11 May seems to me the most serious, the one that, even today, remains full of ambiguity. The student carnival began on Monday the 13th; it provided a model for the workers. The Gaullist formula: "The state does not retreat" was made ridiculous by the hesitations, the back and forth movements of the government. The letter that Georges Pompidou sent me a few weeks later—a historic document, it seems to me—reveals the thinking of the Prime Minister and the unfolding of the crisis.

My dear friend,

I have read with interest and greatly appreciated your articles on the May crisis and the problems of the university. However, an assertion that appears in your article on Edgar Faure's speech leads me to write to you to rectify things, not for your readers, but *strictly for yourself*. You write: Pompidou has gambled and lost with appeasement. Permit me to tell you that you are mistaken. I did not gamble. There was, in my view not one chance in a hundred that my decisions of 11 May would stop the process. And then? you say. Then I did what a general does when he can no longer hold a position. I retreated to a defensible position. And I presented this retreat as "voluntary" both in order to save appearances and because of public opinion. Let me explain myself. When I returned from Afghanistan, I found a situation that seemed to me desperate—the Parisian public was entirely behind the students. The 13 May demonstration had been announced. I thought then (and today I am certain of it) that if we did not give up the Sorbonne, this demonstration might bring about the fall of the government (and the regime), but at the very least the demonstrators would take over the Sorbonne. Can you imagine that a cortege of 500,000 people marching from La République to Denfert (and the route of the march was accepted by the leaders of the demonstration on Sunday, only *after* my decisions) would not make a detour to the Sorbonne guarded by the CRS? And who has ever prevented a crowd of that size from entering a place like the Sorbonne? Even the army could not have done it, and besides, who would have ordered soldiers to fire on such a crowd?

From that point on, with the Sorbonne reoccupied by the students despite government decisions, the situation was without a solution and condemned us to surrender or to a war that public opinion would not have accepted.

For, and you know this very well, everything in an affair of this kind depends on public opinion; by giving them the Sorbonne, I took away the demonstration's strategic objective; it would no longer become a riot, but had to remain a "demonstration." But above all, having done what public opinion expected, I had shifted responsibility. From then on, it was the "students" who were in the wrong, who became provocateurs rather than innocents defending themselves against government and police provocations. I had only to gain time, to contain the evil, then to take the offensive painlessly when public opinion was fed up. This was my line of conduct from beginning to end.

In an affair of this kind, there are two solutions—either, from the beginning, to rely on the most brutal and determined repression. I had neither the taste nor the means for this. Even if I had had them, the revulsion of public opinion would have forced us to retreat, that is, to disappear. A democracy can use force only if public opinion is behind it, and that was not the case for us.

Or else one has to give ground, cut one's losses, and gain time. The students might grow weary and accept a compromise. They might also dig in, which they did. In that event, they would be fewer and fewer and more and more unpopular. This is what happened. And, at the appropriate moment, I painlessly took the offensive.

Make no mistake about it, I won the political battle on the evening of 11 May. There might have been another battle to win or lose if the Communist Party had decided to move to violent revolution. But then, in contrast to what happened with the students, the government had the option of using force, because public opinion would have supported it and the army would have been unhesitatingly loyal. In any event, the CP held back from adventurism.

I ask you to keep these quick reflections to yourself, but I was anxious to enlighten you about my tactics.

I would be happy to meet with you in the fall to discuss the university. I am concerned by many of the things that Edgar Faure said and, of course, I cannot take a public position.

Please accept my best wishes.

This letter, written at the end of July 1968, not only justifies the decisions of 11 May, it explains the "management" of the crisis, the responsibility for which fell much more on Georges Pompidou than on the General. The secret departure of the General on 29 May, and the dissension between the two men, came indirectly from the clash between the president and the prime minister on the evening of 11 May, the evening when the latter took change of maneuvers and prepared the victory—his victory.

A historian reading Georges Pompidou's letter cannot refrain from asking one question: what would have happened on 11 May if, instead of capitulating, the government had held firm? No one will ever know the answer for certain, but no one can question the conclusion that Georges Pompidou's decision was at the origin of the prolongation of the troubles and of the final success.

Questions of the same kind could be raised about other "events." What would the public reaction have been if a few young people had been killed by CRS bullets? Had the disappearance of the General for a few hours and his brief radio speech on 30 May created a climate in which the resolution of the crisis became easy, without violence? In fact, in the course of those weeks in May, there were a few "key events," about which one wonders: What would have happened if . . . ?

A sociologist is more interested in the antecedents of the events, in the general situation that amplified the repercussions of disturbances that were at the outset rather minor. What causes made the situation explosive? Answers differ according to whether one considers material facts or takes the rebels' statements literally.

Let us consider a theme that gave rise, in student palaver, to countless variations: democratization (or not) of the university. The book by Bourdieu and Passeron, *Les Héritiers*, became, so to speak, the students' bible. But what can we deduce from this fact? That the students, who were themselves heirs, were longing for a night of 4 August, anxious to renounce their privileges? Or else, not being heirs, did some of them consider themselves unjustly relegated to second-class disciplines, without career possibilities commensurate with their ambitions? Or else, heirs incapable of pursuing the prestigious subjects, were they rebelling against the system into which their personal mediocrity had cast them? Individual cases can be found to support each of these hypotheses: children of the petty bourgeoisie or the lower classes attaining higher education for the first time, felt lost; privileged students, for lack of anything better, sought refuge in psychology or sociology and transmuted their resentment into ideology. Which of the three categories was the most numerous? What meaning should be given to ideologies?

Some of the most serious sociological investigators emphasize a generational phenomenon: students from families without experience of higher education, disoriented in these new surroundings, uncertain of their choices, were afraid of not finding a job after having struggled for a diploma. They were living through, in anguish and solitude, a precarious condition. In the end, they joined more well-off comrades in the cry: "Down with the consumer society!"

Invectives against competitive examinations were an integral part of the revolutionary experience. They were not necessarily the causes of the explosion, but they illustrated the form taken by this "vacation." Groups of students of various political tendencies developed plans for the renewal of the university: professors and students who in ordinary circumstances rarely spoke to one another were on familiar terms, and they eventually reversed roles, since the students wished to be part of examination panels and even to participate in the appointment of professors. This carnival was not exclusively French; there were signs of it in student revolts in other countries, but here it took on a typically French form.

The distance between professors and students is greater in France than in English or American universities; the authority that a Sorbonne professor sometimes exercised over an entire discipline has no real equivalent in other countries because there is no equivalent to Parisian centralization. The mandarins of medicine were not invented for demagogic reasons, or to feed rebellion. Circumstances encouraged the explosion, sometimes legitimate, against abuses and aberrant expressions of the hierarchy.

If one moves from the students to the workers, analysis reveals, there too, distinctions among causes, motives, and ideologies. Among the causes of the initial strikes, there has been mention of the relatively rigorous policies pursued by Michel Debré during the year before the events. The lowest-paid workers had fallen behind the average wage level. The minimum wage had not been reevaluated in relation to the increase in all salaries. The Grenelle agreements eventually led to a devaluation of the franc in 1969, but even now, some, including Raymond Barre, would argue that the French economy could have, without devaluation, absorbed a 20 or 25 percent increase in wages—which suggests at least that they had been excessively restrained during the preceding period. But, whatever role the level of wages may have played at the outset in the spontaneous strikes, once millions of workers were idle, the speeches went well beyond ordinary demands: the structure of business, the style of management, self-management, consumer society, the struggle against pollution, and conviviality, all became themes in the debates in which hundreds of thousands of French citizens, who had been liberated from work (Marx's "kingdom of necessity"), participated.

This sudden diversion from everyday tedium, a quasi-revolution played out rather than carried out, created sympathy, and indeed enthusiasm. Street battles that degenerated into riots, clashes between demonstrators and police, always accused of violence, were immensely pleasing to the perennial Punch and Judy spectators delighted with the misfortunes of the police; the joyful cohort of young people who went off every evening to the "demo" warmed the hearts of adults—as long as their cars were not put out of commission. The colorful crowd filling the lecture halls and corridors of the university buildings, the nonstop public meetings, the spontaneous orators who, unconsciously for the most part, reproduced the gestures and the statements of the great ancestors, amused and attracted the curious. In the universities, and even in the lycées, professors entered into more or less passionate conflict with one another, some following or even leading the angry students, others raising a dam against the wave of demagoguery, utopianism, or dreaming, inflated by the illusion of living in historic times.

Between 15 May and 30 May, national life was effectively paralyzed, most factories were not operating, workers were occupying their factories and carefully maintaining their machines; the strike even reached public services; here and there, kinds of communes led by workers or union leaders sprang up. Until the last days of liberty, good feeling triumphed over the violence characteristic of this kind of social explosion. None of this was entirely serious. There was an element of play, it was not quite "for real." Toward the end of the month revulsion against disorder gradually replaced sympathy for the "admirable youth": the fear of a real revolution spoiled the pleasure of the spectacle.

At this point, a new question arises. What in fact happened? During the final days, between Monday the twenty-seventh and Friday the thirty-first, the regime trembled, or seemed to tremble. It may have been a student carnival. But who can forget the National Assembly sessions? Edgar Pisani had to take the floor for the government as representative of the majority; he delivered an opposition speech, to the outraged astonishment of Georges Pompidou. In a press conference, Valéry Giscard d'Estaing suggested that the prime minister resign. On 27 May, at another press conference, François Mitterrand declared that the departure of General de Gaulle after 16 June (the proposed date for the referendum), if it did not take place beforehand, would necessarily produce the disappearance of the prime minister and his government. "In that event, I propose that a caretaker provisional government be immediately established." A little further on, he wondered about the President of the Republic. "Who will be President of the Republic? The voters will decide. But I can tell you right now, because the decision may be made eighteen days from now, and it is part of the present battle, I am a candidate." These remarks implied a violation of the Constitution, which provided that if a president resigns, the prime minister remains in office and that the president of the Senate carries on the role of the President until the election of his successor. By asserting that the resignation of General de

Gaulle would bring about that of his prime minister, Mitterrand foresaw and advocated an unconstitutional, or if one likes, a revolutionary solution.

To preside over the provisional government, he suggested Pierre Mendès France, who allowed himself to be drawn into the adventure. On Wednesday the twenty-ninth, at 9:00 P.M., when the General had arrived at Colombey and was getting ready to return to Paris, Mendès France "did not reject the responsibilities that might be offered to [him] by the left, the united left." "As far as the transitional government is concerned, it will not be neutral but progressive, oriented toward a juster and more socialist society. It will have to make immediate decisions, which we have discussed this afternoon, and which we will continue to discuss in the next several days in order to establish a complete agreement." The scrupulous republican was already working on the composition of a cabinet coming out of the riots, with the president and prime minister having resigned or been driven out. Having fallen behind developments, he still believed in a revolutionary solution, while the General was preparing his counteroffensive, and his followers were organizing the 30 May march, Alfred Fabre-Luce published an article in 'Le Monde entitled "Mendès à l'Élysée."

There was thus, beyond the strikes and student speechifying, a genuinely political crisis, whose many symptoms I observed. Civil servants deserted the ministries, some deputies of the majority attacked the president, others attacked the prime minister; they called for the resignation of one or the other. The political class was afraid of a reversal: a brief speech calmed the anxiety of the men in power and ruined the hopes of those who, as in 1830 and 1848, wanted to take the place of a government that had been over-thrown by street demonstrations.

Why is there still so much passion for or against the "May events"? The answer to this question now seems to me relatively simple. The historian or the sociologist constructs an object, "the May events," which was so hetero-geneous that, as a function of the elements considered, the problem and the explanation changed.

Any interpretation tends to focus on a single aspect of the events: either the student revolt, or the proliferation of strikes, or the originality of the French May in relation to comparable phenomena in other countries, or else on the ideological speech of the students or the workers.

The student revolts that occurred throughout the world in the 1960s, from Japan to Paris, including Berkeley and Harvard along the way, can in each case be explained, aside from the effects of imitation, by particular national problems. There was no "Vietnam War" in France, just as the United States had no equivalent to Parisian centralization or the crowding together of thousands of students in antiquated structures. It is a simple matter to locate the causes, common to all industrial countries, for this explosion of youth, to establish the social origin of the most active militants in the movements, for example, the leaders of the SDS in the United States. Since the children of liberal (in the American sense) parents, from good middle-class families, made up a relatively large percentage of SDS, one can draw the conclusion that the rebellion was animated by relatively privileged students. Similarly, sociological research has identified the field of study from which SDS members, and similar students in France and Germany, were recruited. In France, in particular, sociologists have acquired a reputation as protesters, either because sociology, critical by definition, stimulates student revolt, or because naturally rebellious students choose to study such subjects.

To be sure, the student revolts that spread throughout the noncommunist world, from Dakar to Berkeley, Harvard, and the Sorbonne, revealed or meant something, even though their causes may have been different. They revealed at least the weakening of adult authority, of the authority of teachers and of the institution itself. The challenge to authority in the Catholic Church and in the military hierarchy reflected the same state of mind. The cultural revolution that reached its apogee in the 1960s makes up the context, the background, to the disturbances. After all, the demand for free access between girls' and boys' dormitories at Nanterre was one of the warning signs of the coming revolt.

The libertarian ideology of 1968, met a sympathetic response among many students; René Rémond names *Les Héritiers* as one of the books that caused or symbolized the events, while Didier Anzieu refers to the *Critique de la raison dialectique*, with its notion of the "group in fusion," for example, the crowd that seized the Bastille. 1968: an intellectual revolt of *us* against structure, of Sartre against Lévi-Strauss (French politics remain stubbornly literary), of "praxis" against institutions, of leftism against the Communist Party. The student movement in the United States also had libertarian sources (any rebellion that seeks to undermine power and not to replace it has libertarian sources). But in most universities, the movement had precise, and for the most part accessible, goals.

The ideological language of May, from students or workers, cut across party programs. It revived and popularized themes that could be found in books of cultural criticism, *Kulturkritik* as the Germans would say. *One-Dimensional Man* by Herbert Marcuse contained most of the themes that stirred the students: commercial society, forced consumption that was indispensable for the industrial apparatus, pollution, social repression, waste confronted with poverty, and so on. In this domain as well, the revolutionaries made friends by popularizing an ideology that did not coincide with the ideology of any of the parties: quality against quantity, a comfortable life against the pursuit of a high standard of living. The cult of the rate of growth sank beneath public contempt.

French workers launched a massive strike following the Parisian disturbances, provoked by the students, while the workers in every other country
did not even provide moral support to the students. In the United States in
particular, blue-collar workers and the unions did not lead the fight against
the Vietnam War. Even in France, student efforts to mobilize workers for a
common action generally failed. The Communists succeeded in preserving
the labor movement from libertarian infection, even though the Grenelle
agreements disappointed the rank and file, precisely because these agreements sought to put an end to "unusual" strikes and demands by "ordinary"
means.

If one considers the strikes, what is noteworthy is that they were less the
expression of the oppressed masses, the exasperation of Polish workers in
cities suffering from shortages of meat, fruit, and vegetables, than of the
dissatisfaction of workers whose working condition and living standards had
significantly improved over the last generation and who were free to elect
their own union leaders. All of this gave rise to the classic interpretation:
either one invoked "Tocqueville's Law"—when suffering diminishes, griev-
ances proliferate and an explosion takes place—or else the development of
qualitative demands after elementary needs are satisfied; or else, the persistence in French society of a rigid hierarchy, of a style of command that was
less and less accepted. All these interpretations are based on facts and
speeches; none of them can claim to be exclusive and total; they may have
operated in combination.

The French May displays particular national characteristics: elsewhere,
years of diffuse disturbances; here, disturbances concentrated within a few
weeks; all universities together, not one after another; more vague speeches
than precise demands. A final explanation: there was only one university.
Paris set the tone. Intellectuals took part in the celebration, and the students
took inspiration from the writings of their teachers.

Students and workers, simultaneously but separately, in a state of revolt;
confrontations between police and demonstrators day after day, with no shots
fired on either side; one police officer, the victim of an accident rather than
an intentional assault, one boy who drowned while trying to escape from the
police, these were the only two deaths of these weeks of nearly daily riots;
finally, aside from the battles, there was often an atmosphere of gaiety, as
though it were a holiday. The graffiti reflect a state of mind very different
from that, *tot ernst*, of the leftist Berlin students that I had met a few years
before May. "It is forbidden to forbid," a contradictory slogan, illustrates the
pleasing abnormality of the ideology of 1968.

This ideology was not substantially different from that of the SDS groups in
the United States and Germany: at one extreme, the three M's (Marx, Mao,
and Marcuse) threatened to load bourgeois kids into the Baader-Meinhof

gang and urban guerrilla warfare; at the other extreme, they led to ecology, the return to the land, the hippies. Some of the disciples of the three M's were tempted by violence. In his pamphlet on revolutionary strategy, André Glucksmann dreamed of a European conflagration extending from Lisbon to Moscow. After May, Trotskyist parties or sects continued their action, but most intellectuals who professed and lived through leftism in 1968 spontaneously stopped themselves on that slide. They became aware of the danger; direct action, intimidation in large meetings, urban guerrilla tactics—was all of this the realization of democracy or the beginning of fascism? The testimony of Soviet dissidents, of Solzhenitsyn especially, soon impressed the left that had adopted the notion of the "group in fusion." During the weeks of May, the leftists attacked the Communists, who accepted the "treasonable" elections and who paralyzed the revolutionary spirit of the masses. A few years later, the Communists seemed to them to be not only functionaries fixed in dead organizations, but also jailers in a potential Gulag, the prison guards of free men; from leftism to the defense of human rights.

What conclusion can be drawn from all this? There is not *one* sociological interpretation of May 1968, just as Karl Marx and Alexis de Tocqueville did not develop *one* interpretation of the revolution of 1848 and its consequences. Both wrote narrative histories illuminated and deepened by class analysis. A sociological narrative of May 1968 seems to me both easier and more difficult than a similar narrative of the events of the last century. Easier because student and worker movements were distinct and there was no revolution; more difficult because the students, the leaders, were not attached to any class, even though they proclaimed their attachment to the working class, which did not accept them. As for the workers, their conduct depended in part on the tactics of the Communist Party and in part on their own feelings. Were the workers of Billancourt who shouted down the representatives of the CGT and the CP following their own inclinations or the direction of some Communists who were inclined to cross the Rubicon?

Before writing the following pages, I have reread the articles I published in *Le Figaro* between 15 May 1968 and the days following the victory of the right in the elections, in early July. From this distance, considered coldly, these ephemeral pieces certainly do not appear earth-shaking; they warn against the techniques of subversion, they outline the limits of student participation in the governance of universities, they attempt, despite everything, to argue the cause of the old liberal university, the one that I had criticized so much. I have few memories of the attacks that were provoked by the positions I took.[2] I remember a statement by a student, quoted in *Le Monde*, which forbade me ever again to speak at the Sorbonne, or rather told me that I would never again do so.

A personal attack whose tone was extreme remains in my mind—an article that Sartre published in *Le Nouvel Observateur*. I think it necessary to quote the essential passages and to discuss them. The article was entitled "The Bastilles of Raymond Aron"; it was published on 19 June 1968, and it denounced the government: "At the summit, we see the politics of cowardice. But at the same time, among the rank and file, there is a call for murder. For de Gaulle's call for the creation of civic action committees is precisely that. It is a way of saying to people: join together in your neighborhood to beat up those who, in your opinion, are expressing subversive opinions, or who are behaving in a way that threatens the government." The "call for murder" launched by the President of the Republic: not even a vulgar demagogue would have used such an expression in reference to General de Gaulle, to a government that had tolerated the "demos," the semi-riots that had gone on day after day.

Turning to the case of the students and me: "The students have become so numerous that they can no longer have the direct relations with the professors, difficult as they may have been, that we used to have. There are many students who never even see their professors. They merely hear through a loudspeaker a totally inhuman and inaccessible figure delivering a lecture whose interest for them is completely beyond their comprehension. A university professor is almost always—as he was in my time—a gentleman who has written a thesis and recited it for the rest of his life. . . . When the aging Aron endlessly repeats to his students ideas from his thesis, written before the 1939 war, while those listening to him have no opportunity to exercise any critical control over him, he is exercising a real power, but one that is certainly not based on scholarship worthy of that name."

I can only agree that there are difficulties of communication between the professor and too many students. The notion that most professors recite their thesis throughout their lives is, in general, not true. It is absolutely inapplicable to Léon Brunschvicg: we were hardly aware of his thesis. The statement that I personally endlessly repeated my thesis at the Sorbonne is purely and simply a deliberate lie. Nothing in my thesis contained the books *Eighteen Lectures on Industrial Society, Main Currents of Sociological Thought*, or *Peace and War*. Similarly, the phrase "that implies that one no longer considers, like Aron, that thinking alone at one's desk and thinking the same thing for thirty years represent the exercise of intelligence" aims to be insulting; it indicates above all Sartre's indifference to the truth, at least when he is the prey of anger.

In the same article, Sartre discusses the question I had raised in my article about the selection of teachers by students or the participation of students in examination juries. In theory, in a world different from ours, it is in fact conceivable that students could have a voice in the appointment of professors. In the real world, the world of 1968, rebellious students would have chosen not on the basis of scholarly or pedagogical qualifications, but on the basis of the political opinions of the candidates. What the most activist militants wished to achieve was the expulsion of professors with the reputation of being reactionary or fascist. Similarly, in other circumstances, one can imagine students participating in examination juries. In the climate of May, juries filled with representatives of the students, hence of the unions, would have completed the "politicization" of academic life and would have discredited diplomas. On this point as well, Sartre spoke as a demagogue, either to play up to the young or out of total ignorance of reality.

Finally, there are the notorious sentences: "I would bet my right arm that Raymond Aron has never challenged himself, and that is why, in my eyes, he is unworthy of being a professor. . . ." And in conclusion: "This assumes above all that every teacher agrees to be judged and challenged by those whom he teaches, and that he says to himself: 'They see me entirely naked.' It's embarrassing for him, but he has to go through it if he wishes to again become worthy of teaching. Now that all France has seen de Gaulle in his nakedness, students must be able to see Raymond Aron in the same way. He will be given back his clothes only if he accepts the challenge." These remarks seemed to me both vulgar and arrogant. In the name of what does Sartre give himself the right to decide whether a man is worthy or unworthy to teach?

In his conversation with Michel Contat, on the occasion of his seventieth birthday, he justified these 1968 articles in these terms: "When I saw what he thought of the students he had had and who were challenging the entire university system, I thought that he had never understood anything about his students. It was the professor that I was attacking, the professor who was hostile to his own students. . . ." The justification is worth no more than his insults. What did he know of the professor? If he was intent on attacking him, why insult him with lies?

But let us come to the essential question, the necessity of challenging oneself. Whoever has taught, in a lycée classroom or a university lecture hall, knows that he is "judged and challenged" by his pupils or students—as a lecturer or actor is by his audience. No ordeal is more difficult for a teacher than the hostility of his listeners. If so many professors capitulated to the rebels in 1968, the principal reason was the fear of later suffering ostracism from the students, or at least from the activists among them. In this sense, no professor refuses to be challenged, because it is not up to him whether he will be or not. As for challenging himself, that is an entirely different matter. We are all threatened by stagnation, and we all risk closing ourselves off from others and from their criticism in order to give ourselves a kind of intellectual comfort. I do not think that I have adopted fixed positions or failed to recognize the progress of knowledge and the inevitable and rapid obsolescence of our few feeble ideas.

What struck me in 1968, and still strikes me today, is the case of Sartre himself, a man of monologue, even though he laid claim to the dialectic. He responded himself to Albert Camus, but with the cleverness and perfidy of a polemicist. I deserved no more than a philippic by Jean Pouillon. Lévi-Strauss's objections were brushed aside with a word, absurd or stupid: the ethnologist had mistaken himself for a philosopher. As for Sartre, on political questions, he did not always express the same opinions or judgments, but he never criticized himself. His doctrine of freedom—renewed at every moment—relieved him, so to speak, from all responsibility for his past. In 1968, he referred to summer courses for workers and factory apprenticeships for students, and he added: "This already exists in countries, like China and Cuba, where they have begun to understand that this is real socialism." 1968: the ruins of the Chinese Cultural Revolution were still smoking. He never challenged any moment of his own past (before the dialogue with Benny Lévy).

A reader might criticize me for not having responded to the *Nouvel Observateur* article in 1968. "Were you waiting for him to be gone before settling accounts with him?" I am not settling any accounts, I am reflecting on the man Jean-Paul Sartre, leaving his genius to one side. At the time, I felt no anger and, for once, my sensitivity was not even disturbed. Defend myself, as I have just done, reply that I had never repeated, much less "recited" the *Introduction*, that Sartre was systematically lying, that the courses of the professor who was "unworthy to teach" had been translated into a half-dozen languages and used by thousands and thousands of students? That I conducted a dialogue with my listeners to the extent permitted by the material circumstances, that my seminar at the Ecole des Hautes Etudes was open to all challenges? I had no intention of playing the role of the accused, as though I had granted Sartre the right to judge me; nor did I intend to lower myself to the low and vulgar level to which he had fallen. It was up to my friends to defend me, if they thought it necessary; and it was up to Sartre's friends, if they were concerned with his dignity, to warn him against his passions.

Today Sartre, the writer as well as the man, remains present among us, in Paris and throughout the world. We have the right, I would imagine, to speak and write freely about him. In search of an ethics throughout his life, why did he accuse General de Gaulle of launching a call for murder? Why did he insult me as the hated symbol of a university that he was no longer familiar with? It may be that he should be granted the privilege of genius. But he himself did not lay claim to such a privilege: the last words of *Les Mots* were: "A whole man, made up of all men, as good as all of them, and no better than any of them"; why did he not grant to General de Gaulle or Raymond Aron (forgive the comparison; it comes from him) the consideration he offers to everyone?

To try to understand, we might recall what Arthur Koestler reported about

Sartre and Simone de Beauvoir. Both of them said that the Communists would be better than the General. In this case, we have to have recourse to the least satisfying explanation: ignorance leading to out-and-out foolishness. The philosopher of liberty never managed, or resigned himself, to see communism as it is. He never diagnosed Soviet totalitarianism, the cancer of the century, and he never condemned it as such. He saved his worst invectives for those who did not share in his aberration. In *Nekrassov*, he ridicules Soviet dissidents, not the cultural functionaries in thrall to Stalin or Khrushchev.

What explained his anger against me? Of course, Sartre remained throughout his life a "nasty kid." At the ENS, he shocked me more than once by his harshness (in words) toward comrades or "caimaus." He sometimes spoke of his grandfather with apparent indifference: "The 'old guy' has gotten his second wind," he said sardonically one day, as though he were waiting for the death of the "old guy" or were surprised by his survival. Immediately after the publication of *La Nausée*, he wrote a series of literary studies for the *NRF* on some of the novelists of the preceding generation—Giraudoux, Mauriac. These studies were bursting with talent, but they were also merciless executions. He was clearing a space. His article on François Mauriac has remained famous: "God is not an artist, nor is François Mauriac." Armed with his theory of the novel, he decreed that the author of *Le Désert de l'amour* violated the rules of the game. To Dos Passos, lost in distant America, went all the praise he denied to his peers or his rivals.

In considering discrediting interpretations (of which I am not fond), how could I have offended him?[3] Toward the end of the 1940s Jean-Jacques Servan-Schreiber had wanted to entitle one of his articles "J.-P. Sartre and Raymond Aron." Lazareff objected that the two were not on the same level— in which he was not wrong. In 1968, the comparison of two old companions had become less eccentric; but I did not dream of comparing my works to his. We met once by chance in 1960, after I had taken a public position on Algeria. He approached me: "Hello, little friend." Suddenly, memories flooded my mind, or rather dictated my words: "We really screwed up" (or something of the kind). "We should have lunch." That was his conclusion. The lunch never took place. During the 1960s, we were not "reconciled," but we were not engaged in a polemic. Once again, in 1968, what explains this explosion of calculated rage or real anger?

Sartre was violent only in the face of his blank page. He did not like direct dialogue, and he never agreed to a public dialogue with me (or anyone else). The dialectician of the monologue never lowered himself to respond directly to Merleau-Ponty's *Adventures de la dialectique:* Simone de Beauvoir was given the task. But the tone of the article "Raymond Aron's Bastilles," reverted to the prewar period, to the extreme right weeklies *Gringoire* and

Je suis partout. He was authentically generous to those close to him, but Camus and Merleau-Ponty only benefited from this after their death.

Did France make good use of its revolution or pseudo-revolution? I would risk losing the thread of my narrative if I were to attempt an analysis of the consequences of the events. There is no doubt that the economy recovered rapidly from the shock. Some themes of *Kulturkritik* were popularized; the whole society became aware of low wages, of the scandal of the minimum wage; technocrats became receptive to human aspirations and suddenly called into question the received wisdom about growth (sometimes going to the other extreme and denouncing the consumer society). Business executives may have drawn some lessons from the days and weeks of demonstrations. Order was reestablished in the workplace as elsewhere; it is probable that this order is superior to the old order.

In the university, the crisis continued; the debate resumed when Edgar Faure's bill came under discussion. The day the Assembly reached the question, *Le Figaro* published a front page article of mine with the headline "The Illusionist." Faure took me to task for it in a private letter: "By calling me an illusionist, in large type spread over several columns on the front page of the most important French daily, on the eve of a decisive debate, you failed, if not friendship (since you are not obliged to feel any toward me) at least equity (for, whatever you may think of the underlying merits, my efforts did not deserve this insult), and the moderation that is dear to the gods."

Unfriendly remarks, sometimes attributed to Faure, sometimes to me, by the *Nouvel Observateur* added to the bitterness of these "debates among princes." When, in the fall of 1968, students broke the windows in a room where I was participating in a thesis defense and shouted "fascist, fascist" at me in the courtyard, Edgar Faure called to assure me of his disapproval of these intolerable excesses. Time passed, quickly if I may say so, and our cordial relations survived the storm created by his bill.

I had little liking for this bill, adopted by a nearly unanimous vote. The autonomy granted to the universities corresponded to my preferences, but it was inevitably limited, since the Ministry of Education retained financial control, and it was accompanied by an electoral system that seemed unreasonable to me. Student participation in elections was weak; the best organized and most active of student unions (those with a communist tendency) took on an influence that was disproportionate to the number of their members. To the academic quarrels about people, succeeding generations, and scientific schools, were added strictly political conflicts. Departments and universities were put together on the basis of political affinities. The politicization, simultaneously increased and openly expressed, of the academic world seemed to me to be one of the legacies of the May events; one of the least doubtful and most unpleasant. One division of the University of Paris pushed "reaction" so far as to attempt to go back to before April; the "reactionaries," who were adepts of economic liberalism, sometimes showed the same partiality for which they justly criticized the militants of *SNE-Sup.* At least in the faculties of letters, the virtues of the old university have not been restored.

Moreover, the division of universities was an improvement over the pre-1968 situation. Teachers had some freedom of action thanks to the new, smaller departments. Seen from the outside, teaching in universities both benefited and suffered from the earthquake that demolished the worm-eaten edifice. Hundreds of thousands of young students joined the new departments that had replaced the old faculties of letters, which were without a defined program; a still very high percentage (more than half) leaves without any diploma.

For the rest, the consequences of May affect universities much less than does the crisis of recruitment. There was almost no room for the best students of the younger generation. Up until about 1972, the simultaneous increase in the number of students and teachers and the weakness of the public authorities facilitated the careers of all, good or bad. Today, the best students of the ENS obtain the *agrégation* and vainly look for jobs as teaching assistants. The culture of the humanities is dying: almost all good lycée pupils specialize in math. The literary section of the ENS is sinking into mediocrity: condemned by the absence of suitable jobs for its students, it is questioning the school itself about its functions, its *raison d'être*. Even several years after 1968, students at the ENS caused a public stir. I canceled a lecture to which I had been invited by a group of them. An extreme left group had let it be known that it would prevent me from speaking (which caused me difficulty). Library books had been thrown out of the window at the end of one demonstration or another. Gradually, calm returned—what did not return was life. Compared to the ENS of my youth, the buildings, the laboratories, and the living conditions today are a sign of economic progress. But the letters section of the ENS is no more.

NOTES

1. *La Révolution introuvable* (Paris: Fayard, 1968). English title, *The Elusive Revolution.*

2. I barely remember my enemies. And yet . . .

3. Friends have told me that it was because he knew I was right. Quite frankly, I do not believe this explanation, also suggested by some Polish figures.

1 9

"SURE OF ITSELF
AND OVERBEARING"

In the spring of 1967, I was among the
"French of Jewish origin" who were profoundly moved by events in the Near
East: the threat to the state of Israel, then the Six-Day War, the enthusiasm
at the Israeli victory that stirred most Jews and a number of the French as
well, and finally General de Gaulle's press conference: "an elite people, sure
of itself and overbearing."

In the little book[1] that I published in early 1968, I reprinted the articles I
had written for *Le Figaro* before, during, and after the war. The diplomatic
analyses, it seems to me, still stand up. On 21 May, I thought, logically, that
none of the protagonists should wish for war. Nasser's Egypt, with part of its
army bogged down in South Yemen, was in a weak position. Syria by itself
did not have the means to challenge Israel. But I rectified this optimism in
the conclusion: "Thus, once it is agreed that no one has an interest in
provoking a major crisis in the current situation, uncertainty nevertheless
persists, for two principal reasons: the Arab governments do not have total
control over terrorist activities; the dialectic of mutual intimidation would
seem less unpredictable if the rivalry between the great powers did not
create the risk of upsetting the logic of the local balance of power."

Four days later, after the closing of the Gulf of Aqaba, the tone of the article in the next day's *Figaro* was darker: "On the morning of 25 May, the poker game is still being played at the diplomatic level. Israel will not accept the closing of the Gulf of Aqaba, and on this point the United States and Great Britain unreservedly support the Israeli government. . . . But it would take a robust optimism to believe that negotiations among ambassadors or ministers will lead to a solution. President Nasser will not back down from the mining of the Gulf of Aqaba without receiving some compensation. Unless Moscow is offered something, it has no reason to put pressure on Egypt. In short, either a military confrontation between Israel and the Arab countries, or else a strategic and diplomatic confrontation between the Soviet Union and the United States seems a necessary condition for a resolution. The first is already present on the ground where the mobilized forces are confronting one another, the second has not yet gone beyond merely verbal expression."

On 28 May, the doubt disappeared: "By provoking the withdrawal of UN forces and closing the Straits of Aqaba, Nasser launched a challenge both to the United States, which was solemnly committed to not tolerating a blockade of Elath, and to Israel, which had declared that this blockade would amount to a *casus belli*. It threw onto the enemy—Israel and its protectors— the potential responsibility for hostilities. . . . If the aggressor is the one who fires the first shot, the Egyptian operation, favored by the striking irresponsibility of the Secretary General of the UN, condemned Israel to the role of aggressor. . . . Since 1948, the leaders have never had to make a decision so weighty with consequences, so charged with 'blood, sweat, and tears.' They cannot maintain their army—10 percent of the total population—mobilized for weeks, or even for many days. Now, what the Soviet Union, Egypt, and France want Israel to do is to give in diplomatically." I entitled the article "The Hour of Truth." The last lines of the article gave an intimation of war: "These are thus the few men responsible for two and a half million Jews who have built the state of Israel, confronted with their fate and with their conscience. They are alone. Through the voice of President Nasser, the threat of extermination has been heard again. What is at stake is no longer the Gulf of Aqaba, it is the existence of the state of Israel, the state that all the Arab countries consider a foreign body that must sooner or later be eliminated." I then weighed the arguments for and against war: "Even victorious battles would resolve nothing, they would only offer a respite like that of the last eleven years. On the other hand, surrender would prepare, in the near future, another confrontation in perhaps even more unfavorable circumstances." And I left my readers in no doubt: "Everyone who knows the Israeli leaders senses the probable conclusion of such a deliberation."

These diplomatic analyses differed very little from analyses of other crises.

My feelings came through clearly at moments, but I do not think that they distorted the interpretation. On 4 June, on the eve of hostilities, in my old farm in Branney, I wrote an article for *Le Figaro littéraire* which was sharply different from my usual tone. One passage, in particular, has been frequently repeated: "The fact that President Nasser openly wishes to destroy a state that is a member of the United Nations does not trouble the delicate conscience of Madame Nehru. Staticide is, of course, not genocide. And the French Jews who have given their souls to all the black, brown, or yellow revolutionaries are now crying out in sorrow, while their friends are calling for blood. I suffer like them, with them, whatever they may have said or done, not because we have become Zionists or Israelis, but because there has arisen among us an irresistible movement of solidarity. It hardly matters where that movement comes from. If the great powers, following a cold calculation of their interests, permit the destruction of a little state that is not mine, this crime, modest in scale, would remove my will to live, and I think that millions and millions of men would be ashamed of humanity."

I criticize this article principally not for the passage just quoted (preceded, incidentally by the confession of a "de-Judaized" Jew who was passionately French), but for its omission or misunderstanding of the balance of forces. Israel remained the strongest; if it attacked first, there was no doubt that it would win. I should have known this, and, in a certain sense, I did know it, unconsciously, since in the earlier article, I had suggested the irrationality of another war from the point of view of Nasser's Egypt itself. Between 1956 and 1968, the enemies of Israel had not progressed enough to rely on the force of arms. Pierre Hassner did not like the pathos of the *Figaro littéraire* article, and he was probably right. Even at that point, I should have kept a cool head. Emotive and passionate by nature, there are times when I do not grant my intellect a monopoly over my speech.

Let us leave this burst of Jewishness (I will come back to it), which exploded into my consciousness as a Frenchman. And let us return to the past.

I have already noted that I received no religious education. The lessons that the rabbi of Versailles gave us—my brothers and I were the three pupils; Adrien had shown interest in it—were not a substitute. The occasional anti-Semitism I encountered in the lycée had no effect on me. I was excited by reading about the Dreyfus Affair, but the Affair, retrospectively, seemed to me to be an edifying story: truth had won out, and the French had been torn apart over a man and a principle. There was hardly any anti-Semitism at the Ecole Normale; it was in any event buried, almost clandestine. The shock of Hitler revived my Jewish consciousness, the awareness that I belonged to a group (or to a people or an international) that is called the Jews.

From the early 1930s, the influence of German historicism, in particular of

Karl Mannheim, dissipated my illusions of abstract universalism; I already felt very distant from the preceding generation, the generation of my father and Léon Brunschvicg, who refused to know anything about their Jewishness. I did not go so far as to reflect on Judaism or my Jewishness. Moreover, the birth of the State of Israel in 1948 provoked no emotion in me. I understood the aspiration of some Jews to create a state in which they would not be an always threatened minority; but, without any particularized knowledge of the Middle East, I sensed the inevitable consequences: a prolonged war between the Jews, who had become Israelis, and the Muslim world. In the course of my first visit to Israel when I saw, in a military office, a series of maps of the kingdom of Israel, from David down to 1956, I was not won over; on the contrary. I remembered the bas-relief maps of the Italian empire that Mussolini had built in the Roman Forum during the 1930s; the historic sequence from David to Ben–Gurion and from Trajan to Mussolini made me think of a banal theme, the power of myth in history. Israel belongs to the descendants of Abraham in the imagination of believers—strange believers, who do not always believe in God, but in the Bible, the Jewish people, or the vocation of Israel.

I had read Sartre's *La Question juive*, and I had spoken with him about it. I raised objections on two fundamental points. The first had to do with the very basis of his analysis: the Jew was claimed to be designated as such only in the eyes of the other. It was a rather facile remark that could be applied to any interpersonal relation. For example, I am arrogant only in the eyes of others; it remains to be seen whether or not I behave in a way to deserve such a characterization. If one takes as a model a Jew like me, de-Judaized, an unbeliever, nonpracticing, of French culture, with no Jewish culture, it is true to state that the Jew is a Jew for and through others and not for himself. But the Jew with earlocks, rocking back and forth as he says his prayers before the Wall of Lamentations, belongs to a historic group that is appropriately called Jewish, Jewish in itself and for itself.

My second objection had to do with the portrait of the anti-Semite. Sartre dissolved the being of the Jew, reducing him to a phantasm of non-Jews. On the other hand, he hardened the being of the anti-Semite to the point of attributing an essence to him. Of course, in his philosophy, existence precedes essence. Strictly speaking, the anti-Semite does not have an essence, but he is penetrated through and through by his anti-Semitism; this hostility is intimately connected to his existential choice, to his status as a property owner. In my view, there are many ways of being an anti-Semite, and Georges Bernanos who was one in his way, like his master Edouard Drumont, bears no resemblance to the portrait sketched by Sartre; Bernanos never possessed anything.

The little book that I published in 1968, a collection of articles written in various circumstances, does not demonstrate a clear pattern of thought; it is open to divergent if not contradictory interpretations. I leave aside my emotional states, the shifts in my Jewish consciousness, in my feelings toward the State of Israel. But I think it is neither impossible nor inappropriate to bring together a few ideas that can be found in all my writings devoted to the Jews and to which I remain committed.

A Jew of French culture, from a family that has been French citizens for several generations, is required by no human or divine law to consider himself as a Jew. Roger Stéphane, from whom I was estranged for a few years following the notorious press conference of 1967, rejects any solidarity with the Israelis or with the Jews. On what ground can he be condemned? A Catholic who loses his faith leaves the Church, and no one is surprised. A *fortiori*, why should a Jew who has never frequented the temple, who shares neither the beliefs nor the practices of the Jews, be treated as a traitor or a deserter? One cannot betray or desert a community unless one has belonged or wanted to belong to it.

Similarly, I refuse to join those (who are too numerous) who insult or express contempt for a Jewish intellectual like Maxime Rodinson, who has taken a position against Israel in the Arab-Israeli conflict. Only Orthodox Jews assert the right of the Israelis to Palestine with intransigence. This right, based on a sacred book, can affect only those who adhere to the faith. Old Jerusalem belongs to the three religions of the Book. Temporal priority does not establish the rights of the Jews in the view of the disciples of Christ or Mohammed. By granting a national home to the Jews of Palestine, the British, with a stroke of Lord Balfour's pen, and later the Americans, disposed of part of a land that the Arabs considered their own. Many Israeli patriots recognize the "originalism" of the Israeli State in the eyes of the Arabs. In the special issue of *Les Temps modernes* devoted to the Arab-Israeli conflict, my friend General Harkabi wrote that, unfortunately, the Israelis could accomplish their national aspirations only at the expense of the existing population of Palestine, or more accurately, in doing wrong to that population. The controversies about respective culpability—the Palestinians were driven out, according to some; they fled at the urging of their leaders, with the hope of returning as conquerors—are of little importance. All arguments contain an element of truth. The fact is that the Israelis reconquered a land in which Jews had always lived, but in which, immediately after the First World War, there were more Arabs than Jews. An observer who wishes to be impartial, whether or not he is Jewish, can argue in favor of the Arab position.

The Jew is born a Jew because his parents were Jews, but he freely chooses to remain a Jew or not. Is this freedom different in nature from that of a French Catholic or Protestant? The question is a difficult one. At least in our secularized states, the state declares itself to be separate from all churches. A defrocked priest becomes a citizen like other citizens, although he may be quarantined by the members of the community he has left. As for nationality, a French citizen can exchange it for another by emigrating to a country that, with more or less ease, will grant him citizenship. A secularized Jew, who rejects all ties with other Jews, is not repudiating any part of himself; he is rejecting neither his language, nor his morality, nor his way of life, since all of that comes to him from what is called his milieu, the country in which he is living and the state whose laws he obeys. But he remains a Jew in the eyes of others.

This leads to the abstract and yet essential question: What does the "Jewish people" mean? Does it exist? Can we speak of the Jewish people as one speaks of the French people, or of the Basque people? The only valid reply seems to me to be that if one speaks of the"Jewish people," one is using the notion of people in a sense that applies only to this particular case.

Those who are called Jews are not, for the most part, biological descendants of the Semitic tribes whose beliefs and transfigured history are chronicled in the Bible. In the Mediterranean basin, just before or during the first century of the Christian era, there existed dispersed Jewish communities that had been converted to Judaism, not necessarily composed of emigrants from Palestine. Nor did all the Jews of Romanized Gaul come from Palestine. Jews and Christians were close to one another before the victory of the Christians and the conversion of Constantine. Pogroms began in the Rhineland in the eleventh century, on the occasion of the First Crusade. Has history made Jewish communities—as it has become customary to name them—into a single community?

The concepts that we use, in history and often in sociology, escape from ordinary forms of definition. The Jews have not lived through the same fate in Muslim and Christian countries, in Eastern and Western Europe, in the nineteenth and twentieth centuries. Most frequently, over time, the various Jewish communities maintained connections, out of fear of the constant threat of persecution and in order not to forget their particular faith. But these communities had none of the chracteristics that ordinarily make up a people: neither a land, nor a language, nor a political organization. Their unity was based on their Book, their faith, and certain practices. The phrase "next year in Jerusalem" expressed a millenarian hope, not political will. Modern Zionism, the source of the State of Israel, is contemporaneous with assimilation and secular anti-Semitism, closer to the nationalism of modern Europe than to the perennial faith of the Jews exiled from their Jerusalem. At the present time, the World Jewish Congress brings together various national committees, all the Jewish communities of the diaspora maintain more or less close connections with one another, stimulated by the American

Jewish Committee, the most powerful and the richest of all. The representatives of the World Congress speak of the Jewish people and identify as one of the threats under which it labors mixed marriages, assimilation. This is the first contradiction: while the Jews assert that they are a people and that they wish to preserve their unity, they demand simultaneously all the rights of other citizens in their state of residence and the rights or duties implied by the fact of belonging to a people distinct from that of their state. Given that state of affairs, there is no lack of Jews who have come to fear the total disappearance of anti-Semitism, a disappearance that would foster the assimilation of the Jews and hence the disappearance of the people itself. To the fear that anti-Semitism would disappear, the Germans would respond with irony: *Ich möchte ihre Sorgen haben* (I should have your worries). It is true, however, that mixed marriages should normally increase as young Jews spend time with their compatriots, Jewish or not, and as they move away from their practices, which are inseparable from their faith.

In fact, the renewal of Jewish consciousness that has recently been observed by sociologists, the curiosity of "assimilated" Jews, in France at least, about their origins and the culture of their ancestors, should calm these paradoxical fears. In no country are the Jews close to forgetting yesterday's tragedy and tomorrow's uncertainty. What is more interesting to me is the hostility to mixed marriages and the concern with preserving identity—is it religious, cultural, or ethnic? I can understand that those who think of themselves as Jews by heritage might wish to assume that identity actively. But even though I do not deny my own Jewish heritage (I do not know what it consists of, but I agree that others can see it from the outside), for lack of a desire to be a Jew, and not knowing the Jewish particularity that ought to be served, I have no reason to condemn mixed marriages.

At this moment, the cult of (or the taste for) differences has caused Jacobinism to recede. Militant supporters of Corsican or Breton micronationalism play with plastic explosives; Alain de Benoist and his friends have rehabilitated a certain right; hostile to the uniformity imposed by the central government or modern industry, they praise the old mythologies of the Celts and the Germans. As a consequence, they accept, at least verbally, other differences, that of the Jews, for example, even though Jewish monotheism, adopted by Christianity, seems, in this historical vision, to be the principal cause of fanaticism. If the diversity of cultures is a good in itself, an asset for humanity in itself, why should one not draw the logical consequence in favor of Judaism, that is, all the communities that consider themselves an integral part of the Jewish people?

It may be that in France now the Jews are profiting from the fashion for, the cult of difference. Why should Jewish difference not be tolerated or even proclaimed like that of other ethnic groups—Basque, Celtic, or Occitan—

that have revolted against the straitjacket of Jacobinism? But the Jews, genuine Jews, do not place themselves on the same level as the micronationalists or the ethnic groups for which French culture has not erased particular characteristics. They believe in one God, who has imposed exceptional obligations on the Jews, but who rules over all mankind. The many Jews who do not believe in God while preserving the community's way of life, are inclined, consciously or not, to associate their Judaism with any group—Breton or Corsican—that has demanded a separate "cultural" identity. Is this identity enough to form the basis for a people?

It is indeed a weak foundation. Let us agree that the communities of the diaspora, despite everything, maintain certain common peculiarities, more or less pronounced according to the place that each of them occupies in the surrounding society. Most of the time, the Jews of the diaspora agree to, or rather wish to, live as citizens of the country in which they have chosen to settle; even Jews who are believers for the most part do not wish to emigrate to Israel, nor do they consider themselves citizens of a Jewish *nation*. Russian, English, German, and French Jews, even though they may speak the same prayers, do not speak the same language, and understand each other badly, more shaped by their respective national cultures than by reference to a genealogical history that is more mythical than authentically historical.

I repeat, the notion of a people does not have a single definition and is open to various meanings. But I do not hesitate to maintain, at the risk of provoking passionate protest, that, if there is a Jewish people, there is no other people of the same kind. The Jewish religion survived as a minority in the areas of civilization dominated by the two other religious of the Book. Hence, those who were faithful to Jehovah and the Law, even if they did not all descend from the biblical tribes, laid claim to a common origin and were loyal to the principal articles of their faith and to ritual practices. Because they suffered a similar fate in various countries, they were perhaps marked by certain moral or social characteristics. A single visit to Israel is enough to dissipate the physical image of the Jew popularized by literature that still obsesses certain minds. As for the prototype of Shylock, the man of commerce and money, allergic to military virtues, the Israeli soldiers have swept it away. They are now known as the Prussians of the Near East.[2]

Objectively, according to the criteria customarily used to identify a people, the Jews of the diaspora are not a people; they are made up of minorities who profess the same religion, an irritant for the Christians of all churches; they continue to have a certain feeling of solidarity toward one another, for the most part related to the state of Israel, as a symbol of their capacity to create a nation, to be something other than second-class citizens of the societies in which they live. French Jews in the 1930s called their co-religionists from Germany "Boches." The Jews of the United States seem to me to be Americans. Of course, the memory of genocide for a time changed the psychology of the socially solidly established bourgeois Jews of France or England. They acquired or rediscovered an awareness of their Judaism if not of their Jewishness. Assuming that they accepted their belonging to a Jewish people, this belonging imposes almost nothing on them, and the "Jewish people" remains for them entirely abstract, since they do not contemplate sharing the land, the language, and the fate of Israel—not even always the religion; in the younger generation, there is no lack of militants for Judaism or Israel who are unbelievers.

My own course now appears, when I look to the past, to have been divided into several phases. The first lasted up to my first trip to Germany: awareness that I was a Jew, but weak and possibly suppressed; reading the writings of Jaurès and Zola during the Dreyfus Affair excited me but did not awaken Herzl's temptation.

Then came the war years: sacred union ruled all feelings and left no more room for the reservations of minorities. In class of *seconde*, a professor whom I have not forgotten, Ziegler, commonly a target of unruly students, who was delighted that year to have both quiet and conscientious students, turned one day to the question of tolerance. I had the impression that he was turning toward me, speaking to me. He developed the idea that the word *tolerance* did not express an appropriate feeling toward those who were "different": respect would be better than tolerance, which suggests a hierarchical relationship.

From 1933 on, in order not to conceal my Jewishness out of cowardice, I asserted it, as much as possible without ostentation. During the 1930s the university was not attacked by the gangrene. Bouglé, Halévy, even Rivaud (who was for a few weeks minister of education at Vichy, probably because he had written a book on National Socialism before the war) did not seem to fear the dissemination of anti-Semitism from across the Rhine. But I sensed the climate, I heard the cries of "Jew" when Léon Blum appeared on the screen. Gerard Mandel, Jean Zay, both assassinated under the Occupation, were members of the cabinet; they suffered attacks from weeklies of the right and extreme right, denounced as warmongers out of Jewish solidarity rather than from concern with French interests.

During and after the war, one could hardly attribute my positions to my Judaism. I took no part in the purges; my writings (with the possible exception of articles on writers)[3] did not present a Manichaean image of France. From the surrender of the Third Reich on, I argued for reconciliation with Germany. Anti-Semitism, because of Hitler's crimes, disappeared from the political scene, perhaps to survive in obscure and clandestine ways. Bardèche's book on the Nuremberg trials may have created a scandal, but it had little effect.

I took note of the birth of Israel in 1948, without experiencing a feeling of victory; I had no awareness of a world-historical event. I did not identify with the pioneers who were clearing the earth and building a state. War accompanied the birth of Israel, or rather made it possible. It was only beginning. The circumstances in which the Israelis triumphed over the coalition of their Arab neighbors—Syrians, Jordanians, and Egyptians—resulted from an improbable sequence of accidents. Israel would be a military state.

I visited Israel for the first time in 1956. What struck me the most was the appearance, in the twentieth century, of a nearly forgotten political entity. The republic of citizen-soldiers. From a distance, the observer sees two or three million Israelis lost in an ocean of tens of millions of Arabs. He risks forgetting (as I did) that, except perhaps for 1948, the Israeli army as it was mobilized held both a quantitative and a qualitative advantage over the armies of its coalition enemies. It was only after 1956, rather than 1948,[4] that I was brought to comment on Near Eastern politics in accordance with the ethical demands of my profession: objective to the extent possible, with reference to French interests and to the rules, however ambiguous, of political morality.

In theory, the Franco-Israeli alliance assured my intellectual comfort. But this had certain limits: in 1956, I was troubled by the Franco-British Suez expedition, the collusion of the French with Israeli ministers, and the fact that this Machiavellian operation coincided with the Hungarian revolution. Pierre Brisson reproached me for my criticisms: "For once we're doing or trying to do something, you are criticizing, and moreover, as a Jew, you are criticizing the Franco-Jewish alliance." The day the ultimatum was sent to Nasser, Michel Debré, André Frossard, and their wives had dinner at our house. Michel Debré doubted success "under such a regime." We were all skeptical, perplexed, hostile. Had the French and the English decided to overthrow Nasser and to replace him with another military figure? English radio spoke of Naguib on the first day of the expedition. He had been chosen as leader or spokesman by the officers who had organized the plot against King Farouk, and he was pushed aside a few months after the fall of the monarchy.

The French—Guy Mollet, Christian Pineau—probably thought little about opening the Suez Canal: with the case of Israel put to one side, why should the Egyptians deprive themselves of the resources they derived from the passage of freighters and oil tankers? The French were hoping to strike at the heart of the Algerian rebellion, which was indeed supported by Nasser;

even Nasser's resignation and the rise to power of a less anti-Western leadership would not have blocked Arab support for the FLN.

Throughout the years from 1954 to 1960, I was aware of the precariousness and the incongruity of this alliance. By accident, France and Israel were both at war with the Arab world: France because of Algeria, Israel because of the Palestinians and Arab rejection. But the Algerian war ended before the other war; neither country had adopted the other's struggle "for better or worse." In 1956, in the course of my travels through the country, I had the opportunity to meet Ben-Gurion, at the time out of power and living in his *moshav*. An undecorated white room, almost a monk's cell; on the bookshelves along the walls, I noticed Marx, the *philosophes*, Spinoza, Kant, and Jewish literature that I could not identify. We talked: the conversation turned to Algeria and he told me in grave tones: "I read the press; yesterday twenty-three died, the day before thirty-four, today eighteen. But you will have to go." I did not contradict him.

This conversation took place in May 1956, before the nationalization of the Suez Canal, before the Sinai campaign. The remarks of the old statesman, with his weather-worn face and white shock of hair, who spoke as a philosopher, while occasionally revealing his fighter's temperament, revealed with complete naïveté the misunderstanding between France and Israel that would sooner or later come to the surface. Israel bought arms from France and sent its atomic engineers there, and in return helped us as much as possible at the United Nations and refrained from criticizing the Algerian policy of the Fourth and Fifth Republics. Many Israelis, private citizens or public figures, believed neither in French Algeria nor in pacification. Once France had found a solution, probably independence, it would return to the pro-Arab policies it had shown in 1948 by the several days it had hesitated before recognizing the state of Israel. Even before oil supplies became a question of life and death, because of its national interest, in the banal sense of the term, it should at least follow an intermediate line, a kind of neutrality between the Israelis and the Arabs.

Of course, when Ben-Gurion paid an official visit to France in 1960, he was greeted by General de Gaulle as a "friend and ally." In the course of their conversations, the General insistently asked the Israeli president about his plans for expansion. He did not believe Ben-Gurion's denials, and at the time, he did not declare himself to be hostile (perhaps he was not) to conquests that would strengthen the security of the small Jewish state. It was in the course of this third phase, the alliance between France and Israel, in my view temporary and precarious, that I published an article on Jews and Israelis in *Le Figaro littéraire*.

I had not written this article for *Le Figaro littéraire* or for any other weekly; I had responded to the request of an American group that was putting together a book of essays in honor of the first president of Israel, Chaim Weizmann, the man who had extracted from Lord Balfour the declaration on the national homeland for the Jews, who had negotiated with King Feisal, the head of the Hussein dynasty, the only Arab sovereign who did not adopt an immediate and inflexible position of hostility to the settlement of Jews in Palestine. Ben-Gurion, in a recent speech on *aliyah*, the return of the Jews of the diaspora to Israel, had declared that only in Palestine could the Jews live a fully Jewish existence. That assertion had irritated me, and perhaps in response, I wrote the article that appeared in *Le Figaro littéraire* on 24 February 1962. It expressed one of the extremes of my thought on the Jewish question and, as a contribution to a tribute to Weizmann, it had a provocative character.

The article doubled the sales of *Le Figaro littéraire* in Paris and provoked a fascinating correspondence (unfortunately lost), covering the entire range from approval to condemnation. With respect to my predictions about the future of Franco-Israeli relations, some accused me of pessimism and others accused me of mistiming my description of what the future held in store. "This is not the time," said René Mayer, in an unfriendly tone. I never understood why the moment was badly chosen. If the Israelis had read me carefully, they would have spared themselves the unpleasant surprises of 1967.

Otherwise, that is, on the essential questions, I defended two theses: everyone in the world belongs to a single nation; a Jew does not betray his Jewishness if he obeys the Law, even if he does not follow ritual practices, if he retains in his thought and his life the better part of the spiritual heritage of Israel. Now, I would not reject either thesis but I would formulate them in a less abrupt style. Besides, when I reprinted the article in the collection *De Gaulle, Israel and the Jews,* I indicated in footnotes my own distance from this article that had been written five years earlier.

A few years later, I was invited by the New School for Social Research to take part in a debate on the subject "Is Multicitizenship Possible?" Was it possible? On the purely legal level, the fact cannot be denied that there are many people with dual citizenships. When they reach draft age, for example, the French who were born in England are obliged to choose. They lose their French citizenship if they do not answer the call. Many French people have acquired Israeli citizenship without losing their original citizenship. But these relatively few cases do not resolve the political and moral question.

I remember a discussion, somewhere in Paris, among a dozen Jewish personalities, on the occasion of one or another Near Eastern crisis. At one point, one of the participants asked himself and the others: What should we do if the quarrel between France and Israel becomes acute? A retired general was among the participants. He was asked: "Would you obey if the government ordered you to conduct operations against Israel?" The general answered sensibly, shocking some of those were present: "I am a French general, and I carry out the missions assigned to me by my superior and, in the last analysis, by my government." If Jews lay claim to equality of rights, they cannot serve two Caesars at once; the extreme case still seems unlikely, but after 1967, and the break in the de facto alliance between France and Israel, some officers felt a painful contradiction between their duties as French officials and their preferences as Jews. The question of dual allegiance would in fact arise if a French Jew determined that he was an Israeli *first of all*, and only secondarily an officer of the French state.

On the other hand, in a democratic regime, national allegiance does not have a totalitarian quality, and it should not. Many Frenchmen, loyal to France, have no hesitation in feeling particular affection for one country or another. In the nineteenth century, Catholics supported the diplomacy of the pope, who, at the time, was also the temporal sovereign of Rome. The vast majority of communists, at least the active militants and the "regulars," have often demonstrated in practice the priority they grant to their attachment to their ideological fatherland. But the Jews certainly do not wish to be assimilated to the communists, unconditional servants of a foreign power.

In the United States, lobbying is an ordinary part of political life. President Carter's brother was registered as an official agent of the Libyan government. The American Jewish Committee exercises a permanent influence on public opinion and the leaders of the United States in favor of Israel and Israeli diplomacy. Up to now, even though American Jews on the Committee do not approve all the positions and activities of Menachem Begin, Jewish organizations have maintained a common front, a facade of unanimity. It has often been said that France has no equivalent of lobbies, of the Jewish, Irish, or Greek vote. The people of the United States, made up of immigrants, remains oddly heterogeneous, even though all ethnic groups have been partially shaped by the American milieu. Citizenship transforms them into members of the nation, it naturalizes them legally, but it does not erase the diversity of their ethnic origins. In France, immigrants are integrated more through language and culture than through citizenship. The divisions among the French, constantly renewed since the Revolution and perhaps since the Reformation, are considered normal and inevitable; dual allegiance and dual citizenship remain suspect. When a Jewish movement, the *Renouveau*, in opposition to official organizations, launched the idea of a "Jewish vote," opposition appeared on all sides.

In my own case, I have tried my best to respect the political and ethical rules of a *French* political commentator. My commentaries always contain more analyses then value judgements, but they never reach the state of total objectivity. Most often, they suggest the decision that seems to me the best either for France or for peace, or the most ethical decision. My commentaries on the Middle East presuppose Israel's right to exist, without denying the fact that the construction of the state had wounded the Palestinian population and the sensitivity of the entire Arab world.

Given these basic assumptions, I judged each crisis in itself, distributing responsibility, mistake, or blame among the various protagonists as equitably as possible. I condemned the French and English in 1956 more harshly than the Israelis, because the former took the initiative, while the Israelis simply seized the opportunity to even old scores with Nasser's Egypt and to assure secure borders for a few years.

In 1967, I blamed Egypt, because Nasser had consciously taken steps that would provoke the Israeli attack that he expected. Closing the Straits of Tiran, creating a joint Jordanian-Egyptian Command, the concentration of Egyptian divisions in the Sinai: three *casus belli* that the leaders of the Jewish state had identified in advance. To speak bluntly: "They wanted it, they got it."

Neither in 1956 nor in 1967 did I participate unreservedly in the enthusiasm of the Jews of France or the rest of the world. On the second day of the Sinai invasion in 1956, I spoke to a study group in Paris organized by Rabbi Feuerwerker. In the course of the debate, I expressed my doubts and my objections; a young man—I can still see him, about twenty-five, as unlike the conventional image of the Jew as possible, with carefully pressed trousers, a light-colored jacket, an open face—exclaimed at the end of a muddled discussion: "Having said all that, the logic of the stronger is always the best." Uncharacteristically, for once, I propounded a moral lesson, with passion and anger. A Jew should be ashamed to adopt this slogan, which was too often true, and worthy of a French Machiavelli. How often had the Jews been the strongest? How long would they remain so?

The policies carried out by the Israelis from 1967 to 1973 led predictably to a new fight. I said this to my Israeli friends at each visit. Neither Egypt nor the other Arab countries would tolerate a great Israel. I criticized the stationing of Israeli troops on the Canal, for both military and political reasons. The Suez Canal did not form a solid barrier, and it forced the Israelis to fight relatively far from their bases. Politically, the occupation of the Sinai, the Gaza Strip, and the West Bank makes Israel into a regional imperial power. The escalation in weapons used developed inexorably from one battle to the next.

I considered the Syrian-Egyptian attack of 1973 normal, like the Israeli attack of 1967 (normal in the sense of in conformity with the practice, custom, or ethics of *Machtpolitik*). After the cease-fire, despite the Israeli successes in the last phase of the battle, I was pleased with the success won by the Egyptians during the early days—success that may have allowed President Sadat, once the wounds of pride had been healed, with his pride finally restored, to choose the path of peace.

Without too many illusions, I supported the Camp David process, and I criticized the thesis of a greater Israel, colonies on the West Bank, and Begin's policies in general. I also criticized French diplomacy, which replaced the Camp David process not with another process, but with theoretically irreproachable declarations that were effectively inapplicable. Of course, had I been a diplomat rather than a detached commentator, I would have had to conform to a policy that I would not have agreed with. Many non-Jewish diplomats have found themselves in the unpleasant situation of having to carry out a diplomacy they deplored and to argue for its appropriateness.

In short, I respected the code of ethics that I had imposed on myself, which provoked frequent irritated or even insulting letters, some from Jews, and some from non-Jews; from the former because I expressed reservations about Israeli policies; from the latter for opposite reasons. Letters from anti-Semites left me as indifferent as I could be when confronted by blind, visceral hatred; letters from Jews affected me more, without in the slightest shaking my convictions. I am a French writer; a Jew who reacts or thinks first and above all as an Israeli is living an internal contradiction. Why should he not live in his country?

The passage from the General's press conference devoted to the June events contained an expression that had been noticed and commented on: "an elite people, sure of itself and overbearing." Men whom I respect and admire, like Father Riquet, refused to suspect in the General's remarks anything but admiration for an elite people, even if, on this occasion, this people had abused its inclination toward domination. As for me, I had no doubt—and I remain convinced that I was right—that the General had wanted to deliver a message to the Jews of the diaspora, he was not attacking the Jews of Israel alone. Probably what had irritated him was the attitude of French Jews toward the victory in the Six-Day War; large demonstrations, pro-Israeli positions of certain press organs going as far as the publication of false news, pro-Israeli feeling of the mass of the French inspired by propaganda and by unarticulated emotions, sympathy for Israel—David threatened by Goliath—but also a hardly conscious desire for revenge against the Arabs, after the abandonment of North Africa, identified as a national defeat.

At the time, I hesitated for a long time as to whether I should intervene in the debate, just as I had long hesitated before publishing my opinions on Algeria. General de Gaulle had never been an anti-Semite, at least since his entry into politics in 1940. Why should we take tragically a few words, which, after all, did not exclude a favorable interpretation? In the General's thought, "overbearing" and "sure of itself" were so many compliments. This interpretation was all the more improbable because the adjective "overbear-ing" *(dominateur)* had been constantly used by French anti-Semites for example, by Xavier Vallat, High Commissioner for Jewish Affairs during the last war. The *Protocol of the Elders of Zion*, the notorious forgery perpetrated by the Czarist police, had the same source and propounded the same accusation: the Jews' will to dominate.

I spent a week in Israel in the month of August, and on my return I wrote three articles whose principal arguments have not been undermined by later events. In the first, I reported my dialogue with Prime Minister Levi Eshkol: "An embarrassment of riches," he said, "Jerusalem, the Gaza strip, the Sinai, the West Bank of the Jordan. This time we have the best cards: the others have to wonder how to react." I interrupted the prime minister: "Are you emphasizing the *embarrassment* or the *riches?* If you are talking about negotiating cards, you certainly are not lacking in them. If you hold on to your conquests, will they really be signs of riches?" I observed that the Israelis, divided about means as well as ends, had agreed on a strategy, not a political policy. For the moment, they were holding onto everything they had conquered and were leaving the Arabs a choice between the status quo and negotiation, which amounted to waiting and watching: "What does every Israeli fear the most? Spiritual pollution of the nation because of its con-quests? Military insecurity following evacuation of the occupied territories? The loss of Jewish identity through the growth of the Arab minority? If I did not feel compelled by my duty of discretion, I could identify the hierarchy that each of my interlocutors established among the various dangers, without his necessarily being aware of it. But politicians and soldiers always came back to a diplomatically impeccable formula: "if the Arabs were to accept a peace agreement, everything would be possible." It took one more war, in 1973, the initial Egyptian military successes, and a statesman in Cairo in order for direct negotiations to take place between an "Arab" country and Israel.

The two articles of the third part differ less in their substance than in their tone, style, atmosphere. At the end of the first article was a quotation from Sartre, who in turn quoted Richard Wright: "Thus, there is no black problem in the United States, there is only a white problem." Sartre added: "In the same way, we can say that anti-Semitism is not a Jewish problem; it is our problem." I certainly do not agree with this aphorism, which is at least oversimplified. Contemporary Jews cannot evade this problem: to define themselves as Israelis or French; Jews *and* French, yes; Israelis *and* French, no, which does not prevent them from having particular sympathy for Israel. On the other hand, I would not now easily excuse Simone Weil from the accusation of anti-Semitism, as I did in this article. Her proposal even though it was expressed in conditional terms, to forbid unmixed marriages in order to eliminate Judaism, is equivalent to a desire for ethnocide. In spite of everything, this article contains the two pillars of my faith: "A Frenchman of Jewish origin seems to me to have a legitimate right to preserve his faith and the elements of the traditional culture to which he is attached. Why could a Jew be a good Frenchman or Englishman only by losing, through assimilation, the beliefs and practices of his forebears? The only ones who demand this alienation as the price of citizenship, are the doctrinaire supporters, open or hidden, of totalitarianism." The other pillar I borrow from Spinoza: "Rereading the *Tractatus Theologico-Politicus*, I believe that 'nations are distinguished from one another, I mean with respect to their social systems and the laws under which they live and govern themselves,' but that 'all of them, Gentiles as well as Jews, have lived under the law, I mean the one that has to do with true virtue, not the one established for the purposes of each state.' I believe more than ever that 'with respect to understanding and genuine virtue, no nation is different from any other, and hence there is none that God has elected over the others.' Hence, Jews today have nothing to claim that would set them above all other nations." Nothing, I will add, but misfortune; nor is there anything that ought to place them below other nations.

The other article, as I have said, was in some sense a response to a remark of Ben-Gurion's: "The Jews can only reach fulfillment in Israel." Rereading the article, I felt the need to correct a few assertions that were too categorized, too simple. I put these corrections in a footnote. I had written that Zionism in Europe had not a religious but a political inspiration; my footnote stated: "This brusque formulation requires at least some nuances." An important correction, but of a historical nature. The sentences that I criticized in 1967 all belong to the same category. "For believers, and even for the orthodox, isn't the best, the only way to be good Jews to obey the Commandments in letter and in spirit?" My note: "Simplification of a complex problem." "The Israeli state is secular." Note: "Not an entirely correct formulation. Relations between the State of Israel and the religious authorities would require extensive study." "For authentically religious Jews, the State of Israel is not essential." Note: "Too simple." "The Israeli enterprise is, in the context of the twentieth century, provincial." Note: "Today, I would no longer write that sentence."

If the reader considers the series of statements and corrections, it is clear that almost all of the latter are concerned with the nature of Israel, the role of religion and politics in the Jewish state, in its inspiration and its structure. I had sinned through an excess of simplification; the first Zionists, in particular the founder of the movement, an assimiliated Austrian journalist, were reacting to anti-Semitism, provoked by the entry of Jews into society, and did not share the faith of their fathers. But gradually, Zionism, a counternationalism confronting European nationalisms, was enriched by the religious feelings awakened by the millennial nostalgia for the Temple and Jerusalem.

The reader can thus see that these revisions do not affect the essential core of my consciousness as a Jew, of French nationality and culture, concerned not to uproot himself, respectful of the beliefs of his coreligionists—beliefs that he does not share. It is thus the first part, "The Time of Suspicion," a polemic against General de Gaulle's press conference that makes up the heart, the *raison d'être* of this little book.

What had I been trying to say in this book, unique in the body of my work? Above all to demonstrate, with support from the text, that the notorious phrase, far from honoring the Jewish people, transmitted the echoes of an old tradition of anti-Semitism. General de Gaulle had said: "Some even feared that the Jews, who had until then been dispersed, who had remained what they had always been, an elite people, sure of itself and overbearing, would, once they had come together, change the moving desire they had expressed for nineteen centuries—*Next year in Jerusalem*—into an ardent desire for conquest." That the Jews of the diaspora had remained a people sure of itself and overbearing seemed to me such an aberrant and extravagant assertion that I could hardly believe my ears. Sure of themselves, the Jews who had been confined to ghettos for centuries, excluded from most professions, and constantly threatened with persecution (that they had themselves "provoked" or rather "stirred up," to quote the General again)? Xavier Vallat, Commissioner of Jewish Affairs during the war, in a commentary on my book, saluted the return of ideas that he had always supported and applied. I did not accuse the General of anti-Semitism, I accused him of making it, if not honorable, at least legitimate. I did not criticize him for detaching France from the alliance with Israel: "Any French government, after the independence of Algeria and the end of decolonization, would have attempted to reestablish so-called traditional ties with the Arab countries of the Near East"; I criticized him for condemning Israel alone, while aggressive diplomatic initiatives were taken by Nasser (closing the straits of Tiran occupation of Sharm-el-Sheik after the withdrawal of UN troops, troop concentrations in the Sinai). Of course, General de Gaulle had declared in advance that he would condemn whoever drew the sword first and that he would come to the support of Israel in danger. "And," according to Georges Gorce, "a promise by the General is worth something." What would he have offered to Israel other than a press conference?

The General held against Israel the fact that it had not followed his advice. He was probably all the more angered by the Jews of France because they had demonstrated their joy and their "solidarity" with Israel.[5]

> "The pro-Israeli enthusiasm of last June," a dear friend said to me, "seemed to have an ambiguous character, and was even in some respects unpleasant." "Inde-

cent demonstrations," according to the signatory of an article in *Le Monde*, whom no one imagined to be an arbiter of decency. I agree: I liked neither the groups of young people marching down the Champs-Elysées to cries of "Israel will win," nor the Jews in front of the Israeli embassy. I did not like the former supporters of French Algeria, or those who were nostalgic for the Suez expedition—they were continuing their war against the Arabs by means of Israel. . . . We should accept censure from the men who, last June, maintained throughout their cool-headedness, who never felt the slightest anxiety about the life of the Israeli population. . . . In a civilization nourished by Christianity, how could the fate of the people from which Christ sprang not stir in everyone, believer or unbeliever, childhood memories and confused feelings? That may well be so, says an opponent of good will. I understand that Christian Europe, which has for twenty years wanted to forget rather than understand, has so to speak been liberated from its problems of conscience by denouncing in advance the genocide with which it, wrongly, thought the Israelis were threatened. But shouldn't French Jews (who, like you, assert that they are and wish to be French citizens "like the others," and those who were repatriated from North Africa and preferred France over Israel), have held back and avoided words and gestures that might lead to the accusation of "dual allegiance"? What occurred during those frantic days, made the reversal of which General de Gaulle was more the interpreter than the initiator, inevitable. Of course, my brother, you are so wise, like all men, when you speak for others. It would have been better . . . the Jews should not have . . . All of that goes without saying. I confess that after the sun of June, I expected the frost of November. . . . It is easy to forget a major fact that by itself explains the near unanimity of French Jews: because the sympathies of the majority of the French were with Israel, the Jews experienced joy and wonderment at the reconciliation of their French citizenship and their attachment to Israel; they were not separate from the French but a part of the nation. It was too good to last; they, too, believed in Santa Claus.

I pointed out that the Jews of France do not all belong to the same social class and do not profess the same opinions; some are on the right, others on the left, and many of them are pro-Palestinian, "anti-imperialist," and hence hostile to Israel, a "colonial phenomenon." "Nevertheless, the fact remains that the Jews of France have for the first time given the impression that they form some kind of a community." For myself, not a Zionist, principally because I do not identify myself as a Jew, "I know, more clearly than yesterday, that the possibility of the destruction of the state of Israel (which would involve the massacre of part of the population) would deeply wound me." Many intellectuals of the left went through the same experience. For a time, they forgot "imperialism" and the "colonial phenomenon," and they remembered their origins, finding themselves, to their surprise, to be Jews. "Intellectuals of the left of Jewish origin have not abandoned the realm of universalism for Israeli nationalism, although Jean-Marie Domenach has, uncharitably, accused them of doing so. They have had the same experience as Camus. In some circumstances, an intellectual would try in vain to arrive at a position on the basis of reflection, weighing the pro and contra, confronting the arguments of each side, referring to the abstract rules of justice. He remains silent, as he chooses his demon. Jews or non-Jews, this is what intellectuals of the left did last June, although they finally returned to their usual stance." Perhaps one sentence best sums up my position: "As a French citizen, I claim the right, granted to all citizens, to combine allegiance to the state and freedom of belief or sympathy. For Jewish believers, Israel has a totally different meaning from the one it has for me; but I would despise myself if I left them alone to defend a freedom that I could do without more easily than they."

As for General de Gaulle himself, I raised questions without answering them: "Why did he do it? For the pleasure of provoking a scandal? To punish the Israelis for their disobedience and the Jews for their occasional anti-Gaullism? To prohibit, solemnly, any inclination toward dual allegiance? To sell a few more Mirages to the Arab countries? Was he aiming at the United States when he struck at the Jews? Did he want to submit his unconditional followers, who had suffered under Charles de Gaulle, to a new test? Was he acting as an heir of Louis XIV, who did not tolerate the Protestants? As an heir of the Jacobins, who loved liberty so much that they forbade the citizens to have other feelings? I don't know. I only know that any kind of nationalism, pushed beyond a certain limit, ends up by pushing certain Jews (of whom I am not one but whom I do not want to desert) into a choice between rejection and betrayal of themselves."

The May events in the following year, the General's retirement in 1969, and his death in 1970, muffled the echoes of the press conference. In retrospect, I acknowledge that the polemic was useless; in any event, the problem of "Israel and the Jews" was bound to be raised sooner or later. A writer with whom I have had intermittent but always cordial relations wrote to me: "My wife, who objects strenuously to the slightest distinction between Christian and Jewish French citizens, was horrified by the behavior of the *great majority of French Jews*. It is as though an abyss has opened beneath her feet. Thus, these people placed Israel before France. Problems that seemed to have been resolved, like the problem of anti-Semitism, were once again immediately raised. You are mistaken when you write that you are indifferent to the fact that you, Raymond Aron, by asserting so strongly your *Jewish particularity*, supply arguments to the anti-Semites." Aside from these lines, which touch the essential point, the same correspondent asserted that Israel had decided before the summer to break the back of the Arab countries. "*The popular reactions* that provoked your enthusiasm[6] in the month of June shocked and saddened me. I saw in them the perennial stupid inclination of the French toward revenge."

I would like to end this chapter with a few remarks on the posthumous book by Father Fessard, entitled *La Philosophie historique de Raymond Aron*—a moving book for me, unique among my friend's works; an interpretive essay of my intimate, almost secret, thought, as it is revealed, here and there, by a turn of phrase or in a moment of feeling.

Father Fessard—as far as I can judge myself—is not mistaken about essentials: my career as a teacher and a journalist after the war does not imply a break with my prewar philosophical essays. My books—on international relations, or ideological and sociological analysis—did not necessarily flow from the *Introduction to the Philosophy of History*, but they were nevertheless one of its logical consequences.

The *Introduction*, which arose from an analysis of my political consciousness, contained, aside from epistemological investigations, a theory of action in history and a search for meaning in history. It goes without saying that I attempted to put into practice this theory of action, which Father Fessard compared to the *Exercises* of Ignatius of Loyola. I chose my original position, after 1945, as I had suggested it in 1938, not according to a chance whim, but on the basis of as scientific a study as possible of the types of society among which we may choose.

Father Fessard repeated the criticism that Léon Brunschvicg had made when I defended my thesis: I made history into "a drama without unity." He wanted both to defend me against the criticism and to understand me better than I understand myself, in the light of my practice if not my theory, to bring me closer to him without making me unfaithful to myself. In the *Introduction*, I distinguished natural history from human history; I did not categorically eliminate supernatural or sacred history; I considered its possibility or, if you prefer, its absence. Father Fessard fills the void with his faith in Christ.

Nothing in the formation of the state of Israel or in the persistence of the Jewish diaspora challenges the ordinary modes of historical explanation. Close to the Christians during the first centuries of our era, gradually confined to the ghettos, victims of pogroms that began on the eve of the First Crusade, "liberated" by the Revolution in France and gradually throughout Europe, deicides for centuries and a pariah people, the Jews lost, in the slaughterhouses of Buchenwald and the gas chambers of Auschwitz, the illusion that they could become, at least in the foreseeable future, citizens like any others in the nations in which they live and to which they belong. It was in response to modern anti-Semitism—not an anti-Semitism of religious origin, one nourished by dark passions, clothed in pseudo-scientific ideology—that Jews, the majority of them from Eastern Europe, despaired of "assimilation" and dreamed of a state that would be their own.

The fact that most Jews experience a feeling of "kinship" with Israel, even if they reject Zionism, even if they have determined that they are, unconditionally and without reservation, citizens of another country, does not in any way imply the "mystic" unity of Jews throughout the world. What I wrote in May and June 1967, on the eve of the Six-Day War, remains written. Anyone may interpret in his own way the eruption of emotions that are repressed in calmer times. I cannot prohibit Father Fessard from seeing them as a proof, or at least a symptom, of my "Semitism."

On one point, and not a minor one, I surrender to the good father. When I wrote about the Jews and my Jewishness, I had a tendency to rely on a simplistic alternative: either the universalism of the Law and the message of Israel, or else the nationalism implicit in the alliance, whatever the moral sense, subtle and authentic, of the destiny of Israel. Between the universal goals of humanity, and the "superstitions" of human groups are located peoples, each one convinced that it bears and contributes an irreplaceable treasure to the common wealth of humanity. The Jews, too, also possess their treasure, but aside from the Bible and their faith, they do not participate in a single culture. Once again, if they wish to be a people, this people does not resemble any other.

In conclusion, I return to the antinomy, which I have never resolved, between the historical diversity of values and ways of being on the one hand, and on the other, the vocation which I sometimes attribute to humanity. I have not given up the idea of a single destiny for the human race, nor have I given up the plurality of cultures, each one of which believes itself to be—correctly for those who are within it—irreplaceable. My attachment to the French language and French literature cannot be justified; it is, I live it, because it is identified with my being. Is my "solidarity" with Israel intellectual or organic? Perhaps both. In any event, this "solidarity" does not rise to the level of sacred or supernatural history, whose place is reserved for believers and to which I have no access.

NOTES

1. *De Gaulle, Israël et les Juifs* (Paris: Plon, 1968). English-language edition: *De Gaulle, Israel and the Jews* (New York: Praeger, 1969.)

2. An absurd comparison in any event: Prussian discipline, the strict hierarchy of the Prussian army and state bear no resemblance to Tsahal and Israeli democracy. The Israeli army is a citizen army.

3. Henry de Montherlant, Alfred Fabre-Luce, Jacques Chardonne.

4. Why not in 1948? I had not yet been assigned to writing diplomatic commentary in *Le Figaro*. The Arab-Israeli conflict was not yet linked to East-West rivalry. In 1958, it was still an episode in the British withdrawal.

5. What follows reproduces the text of "The Time of Suspicion."

6. This is not correct; I, too, saw the excesses in these demonstrations and the ambiguity of pro-Israeli feeling.

The Years of the Mandarin

1969–1977

FROM PIERRE BRISSON
TO ROBERT HERSANT

The year 1969 marked a break in French politics and in the troubled history of *Le Figaro*. General de Gaulle withdrew from public life after his defeat in the referendum that he had wanted to hold in 1968, and which he had given up on the advice of Georges Pompidou. *Le Figaro* ceased publication for two weeks because of a strike of the editorial staff—a strike that was provoked by a disagreement between one of the shareholders, Jean Prouvost, and Pierre Brisson's designated successors.

An earlier crisis had shaken *Le Figaro* at the death of Pierre Brisson. The agreement reached in 1949 between the owners and the Brisson group came to an end in 1969. Would the paper return to the ordinary laws of ownership, or would the editorial staff retain some or all of the freedoms guaranteed by the 1949 agreement?

Someone—perhaps Jean d'Ormesson—told me that Brisson considered me the most qualified to assume leadership of the paper as his successor. To know where I stood, I wrote to Jean's uncle Wladimir d'Ormesson, and this is the substance of his reply: "It is indeed true that I had a conversation with Brisson in his office—it must have been in 1963, or perhaps in the spring of

1964—I could find the date in the diary I have kept for the last fifty years, but I don't have it here. If you insist, I could do the necessary investigation. In the course of this conversation, Brisson spoke to me of his future and the future of *Le Figaro*. He said more or less the following: 'When the agreement expires, I will be of such and such an age. Logically, I should retire at that point, since there are times when I am extremely tired. It is, however, possible that I could continue running *Le Figaro* for a few years. In any event, when I give it up, Raymond Aron seems to me the best choice to succeed me.' He mentioned *no* other name" (1 April 1971).

The details of the long quarrel about Brisson's succession would hardly interest the reader; besides, I have forgotten them. The compromise that was finally negotiated did not grant to Gabriel-Robinet all the powers and advantages that Brisson had held. The presidency of the editorial group was given to Jacques de Lacretelle.

Since then, I have wondered about my conduct immediately after Brisson's death. Was I right to resist Jean Prouvost's active participation on the paper? I argued for the continuation, for a few years, of the peculiar juridical status of *Le Figaro*—a status that left the owners with financial responsibilities, but forbade their slightest intervention in the content of the paper. In theory, I remain in favor of such an arrangement, but it requires that two conditions be fulfilled, one necessary in any country, the other peculiar to France.

What should be done when a newspaper runs a deficit? The *Times* has experienced this unfortunate condition for years. But the illustrious London daily, an institution of the world, not simply of England or London, finally found, in the vast Anglo-American world, an Australian who agreed to cover the deficit. *Le Figaro*, a Parisian, barely national, institution, had to bring money to its owners, not ask them for it. Another, nonmaterial difficulty, more deeply serious, seems to me peculiar to France. The editor in England, the one who is responsible for the production of the newspaper, normally enjoys a freedom in relation to the owners not usually enjoyed by editors in France. In France, the owner, even if he does not intervene daily in management or editing, expects or demands conformity between his preferences and the opinions of his newspaper. The dialogue between the owner and the editor, delicate by definition, cannot be separated from the dual nature of the paper, a commercial enterprise and a means of providing information or opinions.

Gabriel-Robinet died in February 1974, and Jean d'Ormesson appeared on the scene. Prouvost suggested that d'Ormesson become president of the editorial board. At first surprised by the advice—Jean lacked journalistic experience and political knowledge—I welcomed him warmly when he paid me a visit. He, too, asked me whether I had ambitions for the position. I answered him, once again, that I had no such ambition, all the less because I was teaching at the Collège de France, and because, for the last few years, I had witnessed the decline of a once prestigious newspaper. I thereupon promised him my support, and I defended his cause in meetings of journalists. He might have wished for arguments different from those I offered. I reassured the editorial staff about their future director by pointing out that no one knew of any fixed or original opinions he might have in the realms of politics or economics. A conservative, as well as a classical liberal in economic matters, his perspective fit with that of *Le Figaro*.

I have no memory, during our years of almost daily collaboration, of any serious dispute, despite the efforts of certain journalists to provoke a crisis, which they had claimed was inevitable. "You will not be able to work with Aron because of his character." Jean has thousands of friends in Paris, and I don't know of any genuine enemy. Comfortable in his skin, a cheerful extrovert, aware of his origins but capable of forgetting them when he confronted those whom his illustrious family might have irritated, happy in his status and his activity, fulfilled by a series of prominently reported successes (*La Gloire de l'Empire*, the Académie française, *Le Figaro*), he managed *Le Figaro* more in the style of Robinet than in that of Brisson. He did not read the newspaper, which, like others, had become monstrous in size and in the disproportion between the quality of paper and the quantity (sometimes the quality) of reporting. From time to time, he wrote political editorials that, in my view, suffered from verbal facility but also gave indication of his talent as a writer. He displayed an apparently authentic modesty, and he demonstrated admiration for me well beyond the respect due to the old intellectual. We were separated by one generation; although, on occasion, he might have considered me arrogant, this caused him no displeasure. Perhaps he smiled at the situation. Compared to me, he had so many advantages deriving from history and nature that he was not offended by the superiority I felt and expressed over him, as a philosopher or a writer on politics. Why should I not add that he feels genuine friendship toward me, perhaps not unusual among the numerous friendships he has cultivated, and perhaps it is authentic.

In 1975, under pressure from the banks, Jean Prouvost resigned himself to selling *Le Figaro*—he had become its sole owner by buying out Ferdinand Beghin. It was said that *Le Figaro* had lost money in 1973 and 1974, especially because of the massive increase in the price of paper. The newspaper in fact was still a good business, I am now convinced; I didn't know that in 1975. Every year, it lost a few thousand readers in Paris. The press run has continued to decline since 1977. When I left the paper, sales in the Paris region fluctuated between 90,000 and 100,000. Those figures have declined by about 10,000.

Three possible purchasers appeared one after the other, and each of them visited me in turn: André Bettencourt, Jean-Jacques Servan-Schreiber, and finally Robert Hersant. The first, encouraged by members of the government, gave me the impression that he both feared and hated the task they wanted to impose on him. He knew little about the press and did not think himself capable of directing an editorial staff, still less of firing journalists or reducing the salaries they had given themselves. A friendly conversation left me with the certainty that he would engage neither his fortune nor his time in an enterprise that seemed hazardous to him.

I spoke next with Jean-Jacques Servan-Schreiber, with whom over the years I had had sometimes cordial and sometimes tense relations. When he was quite young, at the time he was writing brilliant articles for *Le Monde*, he came to see me, and I felt sympathy for this agitator of ideas, a man who was sure of himself and determined to become someone by doing something. When he founded *L'Express*, he informed me of his plans and suggested a possible collaboration. According to events and the editor's whims, *L'Express* treated me with kindness or severity. In 1975, he displayed all his charm for me. Twenty years ago, he told me, there were only two analysts in the press who counted, Maurice Duverger and you; today there is only you (at the time, Duverger wrote only rarely for *Le Monde*). I gave him a warm welcome and the assurance that I would in no way oppose his taking on the positions of owner and editor. I was doubtful of his success, but in promising him at least my neutrality, perhaps my active support, I was completely frank. Whatever may have been the storms in our relations, Servan-Schreiber seemed to me one of the rare men of the press who was capable of reviving a tired *Figaro*, and also capable of scandalizing our readers and losing at one blow several thousand of them for the pleasure of a provocation. Jean Prouvost, who had neither forgotten nor forgiven an abortive negotiation with Servan-Schreiber, flatly refused his offer. Robert Hersant also came to visit me; the conversation lasted about an hour and left me with mixed feelings. The man, in contrast to his public image as a press lord, has two weapons, one that no one should refuse to recognize and another that no one grants him, intelligence and charm. Robert Hersant knows how to use a charm that he owes principally to his voice (at least when he controls his will to power). His round face, his pink complexion like that of a healthy baby, his blond hair, and his blue eyes inspire first of all a kind of confidence: here is a good companion with whom I would like to work and even more to drink. But there should be no illusions: suddenly, with a word or a gesture, his sensuality and brutality break forth, the two most visible traits of his personality.

Obviously, on his activities during the war and his troubles with the courts and in the Assembly (he was disqualified once but triumphantly reelected by the voters of Oise), he was evasive. He gave me to understand that he had a good deal to say on those subjects and that he would say it to me one day (he didn't) but, at this first meeting the positive dominated the negative in my mind. For several years, *Le Figaro* had not been under any direction. Gabriel-Robinet, worn out by illness, had no control over the editorial staff, and I had the feeling that the administration was no better. Hersant had built a press empire: success is never due entirely to chance and luck. Perhaps he would stop the decline of this newspaper which still had one asset: its title.

Before making my decision, I asked for an audience with the President of the Republic and the minister of the interior. Valéry Giscard d'Estaing informed me, under a pledge of secrecy, of the origin of the funds Hersant had at his disposal (I don't believe his information was complete). The conversation once again confirmed my impression of the distance between politicians' public speech and their spontaneous reactions. The president made me feel that *Le Figaro* hardly deserved its current autonomy. Clearly sensitive to the criticism to which he was sometimes subjected in the paper, he seemed to me entirely indifferent to the function of the press as a countervailing power, a function on which he spoke with talent more than once. That the moral authority and the prestige of *Le Figaro* are more important than the conformism or impertinence of any particular article, even Giscard, in private, could not understand. He did not wish to know that Hersant's acquisition of *Le Figaro* would be a blow to the nonmaterial, symbolic capital of the paper. Michel Poniatowski allowed me to read a note that summarized the Interior Ministry's documentation on Hersant. The information on the war years told me little. Besides, Hersant was not yet twenty when war was declared; his youthful "mistakes" did not condemn him for ever. The wrongs committed, erased by the amnesty, did not dishonor the man who was guilty of them.

Finally, I approved Jean d'Ormesson's position, and I will quote part of his 3 June 1975 article: "In this complicated and briefly summarized situation, I would willingly defend the idea that, along with many difficulties, Robert Hersant presents at least two virtues. First, unlike the famous mare of the philosophers which had all qualities except for existence, I am perfectly willing to believe that Robert Hersant possesses many faults, but at least he exists. At the present time, he alone is capable of taking charge of the administration of *Le Figaro*. In the face of absence and the adventures of nothingness, presence is an advantage. Further, we must recognize that the celebrated statutes that are *Le Figaro's* bible grant many rights to the editors. In particular, they can oppose the designation of the editor-in-chief. But the very meaning of the statutes is to assure a break between ownership and the editorial staff. Would not granting the staff rights to determine ownership thereby provide a future owner rights over the editorial staff? . . . Robert

Hersant is what he is. I will say it clearly; I have not made an investigation of his activities. I am inundated, like many others, by pamphlets denouncing him. It is always difficult, in this kind of written or oral literature, to distinguish among truth, propaganda, and calumny. . . . Covered by the amnesty, Robert Hersant holds elective office. Should we be more demanding than the laws of the Republic and the popular will?"

One hundred eighteen votes out of two hundred ninety-five were in favor of a strike if Jean Prouvost did not give up his intention of selling the shares of *Le Figaro* to Robert Hersant—a minority, but a substantial one, which might have become a majority if Jean d'Ormesson and I had joined the potential strikers. From the Elysée and Matignon came discreet pressure in favor of the magnate who had built his fortune on *L'Autojournal*, then acquired a dozen small provincial papers, and created a few specialized magazines, and was now seeking, with *Le Figaro*, confirmation of his success and entry into the salons. *Paris-Normandie* which he had recently bought, was the last step before the conquest of Paris.

My own decision convinced Jean d'Ormesson (unless it was the other way around) and thus that of the staff as a whole. I cannot be certain of it, but I do not want to evade my responsibility: at bottom, I could not appease my troubled conscience whether I sided with those who favored or opposed a strike. My no would have shaken the yes of Jean d'Ormesson; in fact we made the same decision, and we made it together. As in other circumstances, the memory of my earlier decision weighed on me. In 1965, I had taken the lead among the friends of Pierre Brisson who imposed the continuation, in favor of Gabriel-Robinet, with minor modifications, of the 1949 agreement, in other words the preservation of the current organization until its original expiration date. During the crisis and the strike of 1969, I had expressed my solidarity with the editorial staff, but without enthusiasm and without playing an active role. I do not think I would have taken on editorship of the paper, even if Jean Prouvost had accepted a unanimous proposal from the editorial staff. In 1975, the problem, at least in appearance, had completely changed: Robert Hersant made a commitment to respect the legal structure of *Le Figaro*. The journalists arrogated to themselves supervisory power over the owner's decisions, while, on paper, they had no rights but those of blocking certain decisions of the executive committee of the management, particularly the nomination of the president of the directing group, in fact the paper's editor-in-chief. Jean d'Ormesson formally stated that they were in error, but neither he nor I was so naïve as to take Hersant's word that he would respect the letter and the spirit of the 1971 compromise. Would a "press entrepreneur," who was also an elected representative, for long refrain from influencing editorial policy as well as the administration of the newspaper?

Why did I think in 1975 that I should not repeat the battle of 1965? I was no longer sure that I had been right ten years earlier; only my loyalty to Brisson had inspired and justified the battle against Prouvost. The editorial staff had gradually disintegrated, morally and materially; the activist wing, led by Denis Perier-Daville, president of the Administrative Council of the Society of Editors, relied less on the legacy of Brisson than on their doctrine: a newspaper should not be put on sale like a commercial enterprise. A Robert Hersant ought not to buy *Le Figaro*, an intangible asset, as one might buy stocks in steel or electronics. It was an appealing doctrine, but one that was difficult to translate into reality. Unless journalists themselves have capital, there has to be an owner. If ownership falls to a union or a political party, freedom will be even further restricted. The least unacceptable solution is finally that of the Anglo-Saxon countries: the owner chooses an editor, to whom custom, public opinion, and a sense of appropriateness grant broad autonomy.

In 1975, other reasons led me to support the "candidacy" of Hersant. Despite last minute remorse, there was no other candidate. A strike supported by some of the journalists would not necessarily have prevented the sale of the newspaper. Above all, it would have revealed the real situation: the Brisson group was represented only by survivors who were more or less worthy of preserving the legacy; the unity of the editorial staff belonged to the past and to mythology. Struggles for position, rivalries based on vanity, ideological quarrels, all the causes of disunion on the paper reinforced one another. Collectively humiliated by the rise of *Le Monde* and the fall of *Le Figaro*, divided on the position to be adopted (center-right, solid right, center-left), some journalists opposed a man, others an act that symbolized a defeat that was moral as well as economic. With whom should I have allied myself? With Denis Perier-Daville and the militants of the Society of Editors? With the supporters of a center-left *Figaro*? With the survivors of the Brisson group, as concerned with certain perquisites as with the old principles of an organization that no longer existed? *Le Figaro* continued to hold a place, limited perhaps, but indispensable, in the national political sphere. All things considered, Jean and I were not wrong to take the risk of supporting Hersant.

The managing committee, of which I was now a part, met once a week. Thus, I often saw Robert Hersant, and I was struck, to be frank, by his natural intelligence; whatever the subject under discussion, I never heard him say anything foolish. The committee as a whole took on the thankless task of firing people (fewer than we had at first thought). Our deliberations often resembled unstructured conversations (if there had been anything but mineral water on the table, we could have been in a café). Hersant did not take these ritual meetings very seriously, even though important decisions about the newspaper were made there. Who should be sent to Washington, Rome, or Bonn?

During this period, Hersant scarcely intervened in editorial decisions, even though he had, early on, introduced to the meetings his "confidential assistant," or rather his "pen" (unless his function was to sign the papers he wrote himself): Charles Rebois. He added certain questions to the surveys that *Le Figaro* commissioned; he interpreted in his way, which was at least open to question, some of the survey answers. Was this an amateur's naïveté or deliberate manipulation? The first crisis broke out over an article written by Hersant himself on world politics. He developed the argument that the Soviet Union, threatened by the People's Republic of China, now sought to strengthen its security in the West, thus to increase its control over European countries, particularly France, by means of a socialist-communist government. The article, neither better nor worse than many others, smacked of uninformed after–dinner conversation. In 1974, the Soviet Union had shown some preference for Giscard d'Estaing over Mitterrand. But regardless of the quality of the article, a taboo had been violated: the owner was acting as a journalist.

Once again, I argued for tolerance. We had wagered on Hersant with the hope that, in essentials, he would play the game. Could we reject an article that we might have published if it had not been signed by the owner of the paper? Moreover, it seemed unlikely to me that he would often repeat his attempt at being a commentator (I might add that he received about fifty letters, most of which were favorable). After a few days of agitation, Jean-François Brisson left the paper. A model of honesty and rigor, he attempted to the end to defend and exemplify his father's legacy. He had fought against the intrusion of Prouvost. Among the directors of the paper, he was the only one who wished me to assume the leadership. Had he heard the same statements from his father as Wladimir d'Ormesson had? I don't think so; if he had heard them, he would have said so. I tried without success to keep him on: I was wrong, since, scarcely two years later, I followed his example.

In one of his books, Jean d'Ormesson has recounted the denouement, the last months of my time at *Le Figaro*, but curiously his narrative passes in silence over the beginning of the end, or the first scene of my revolt against Hersant. The three of us had had lunch at d'Ormesson's house in Neuilly, and we had had a reasonable discussion about the prospects for the 1978 legislative elections. Hersant set out his proposals for assuring the survival of his various publications in the event of a victory of the left. We then came to the months leading up to the elections, and I proposed to him—not at all in an aggressive or demanding tone—that I should, in practice, assume my role as political director. During the months between September and March, I told him, I would like to take my title seriously, spend every day at the paper, and in fact determine the line adopted by *Le Figaro*. Jean d'Ormesson could have taken offense at my request since it appeared to interfere with the authority of the chief editor. I do not think that he reacted in that way: he granted me the privilege of age and perhaps the advantage that I wrote about politics as a "professional." It was as a writer or novelist that he claimed to be a "professional." Of course, *Le Figaro* amused him, his leadership position satisfied his vanity; if I had participated in daily editorial conferences, he would willingly have cooperated with me, although he might have had to make hard choices if a disagreement surfaced.

This proposal provoked a response from Hersant that startled me: "I want to take over the political direction myself, and I will frequently write editorials." I answered rather sharply (I don't remember exactly what I said) and left a few minutes later; I had an appointment at the other end of Paris. An alarm had been set off in me: if he refuses to have confidence in me, and especially if he intends to write editorials for *Le Figaro*, then arguments of policy and efficiency are no longer valid. I have no choice but to resign.

In the course of the next few weeks, I asked for an audience with the President of the Republic; I met with Jacques Chirac and several other public figures. I said more or less the same thing to all of them: Robert Hersant has told me that henceforth he intends to write editorials. If he persists, I will leave *Le Figaro*, along with Jean d'Ormesson, who has always assured me that he would not stay without me. Now, *Le Figaro*, despite its decline, remains an irreplaceable forum in the realm of political conflict. It already lost part of its credibility the day it entered the Hersant empire; if it becomes his organ, it will drift into oblivion; my departure, and that of Jean d'Ormesson, and of others who will follow our example, will leave very little on the paper.

I repeat that this episode—the lunch at which Hersant declared his intention to write editorials himself—does not appear in Jean d'Ormesson's narrative of events. Even today, I wonder why he forgot or omitted it. On the other hand, he invents a three-person Parisian drama, none of whose participants appears totally sane: "Raymond Aron and Robert Hersant had only one point in common; they both believed that things would certainly be better if they were listened to more. Each of them had—it must be said, with an appearance of reasonableness—tendencies toward megalomania and paranoia. I was rather schizophrenic and, in any event, manic-depressive. Nothing will keep me from believing that Hersant had only one aim, to become President of the Republic. Raymond Aron, who was less mad, was nevertheless surprised that he had not become the French Kissinger. Let me say immediately that, had I been de Gaulle, Pompidou, or Giscard, I would have chosen Aron as an adviser. I am not quite sure that I would have elected Hersant as head of state if I had been the French people."

The passage is amusing, but it has only tenuous connections with reality. "Megalomania and paranoia": no one knows himself, but Jean d'Ormesson was neither schizophrenic nor manic-depressive. If one is to believe him, his only ambition was to have Hersant and Aron work together. But the question arose only after the lunch at Neuilly, which has mysteriously evaporated from his memory. I asked to exercise political influence over *Le Figaro* for a few months, without the slightest intention of imposing myself permanently. I never laid claim, as he has written, to the position of head of the editorial committee. Why would I ask for it at the age of seventy-two? I would in fact have been megalomaniacal if I had wished for or believed that I would accede to that position. What I wanted was at least a promise from Hersant that he would not compose political editorials in alternation with Jean and me.

Did this entirely personal reaction come to the fore too late or too soon? As Jean suggested to me, and as his brother, his guardian angel, told him directly: we should have opposed the nomination of Hersant as head of the editorial board. Since we had granted him the position held by Brisson and Gabriel-Robinet, what right did we have to dispute his entitlement to the privileges of that position? The argument was legally correct. But, by leaving to Jean and me, respectively, the titles of general director and political director, he seemed to have given up the exercise of some of the privileges held by his predecessors. Hersant, despite his position in the legislature (he almost never attended the National Assembly), appeared first of all as a press magnate, a capitalist; he was not known as a writer of editorials. Jean Prouvost never wrote editorials. Hersant's intentions, or his plan, were thus, for the paper and for me, a coup, legally less important than his official position, but psychologically much more serious.

The political personalities to whom I expressed my anxieties showed little interest in the constant crises of *Le Figaro* (except for Jacques Chirac). Valéry Giscard d'Estaing was aware of Hersant's political plans. If my memory serves me correctly, the President of the Republic advised me not to leave *Le Figaro*, but he seemed to me insensitive to the essential, that is, the loss of intellectual and moral authority for the paper that would be brought about by the departure of a few symbolic names. Only Jacques Chirac recognized the force of the argument, and he threatened Hersant with withdrawal of the support of the RPR if he forced the "intellectuals" of *Le Figaro* to resign. In fact, Hersant was officially endorsed by the RPR. Marie-France Garaud criticized me sharply when I told her that I supported Hersant's rival in the election, who refused to obey party directives and easily defeated Hersant.

As for the consequences of my departure for the future of *Le Figaro*, despite my megalomania, I never had any illusions. The example of François Mauriac would have instructed me if that had been necessary: no contributor to a newspaper, however prestigious he may be, carries a substantial number of readers with him. My departure depleted the political capital of *Le Figaro;* from 1977 on, that capital has continued, slowly and steadily, to decline. A dozen journalists left at the same time I did, relying on their right to break a contract on grounds of principle; they were vindicated in court. Jean d'Ormesson was with me for a few weeks. Summoned and accused by Chirac's advisers of the time, he returned as an editorial writer.

After my conversation with Hersant, and my conversations with political personalities, I had no choice but to resign. One Monday in April, in the morning, I met with Joseph Fontanet, former minister of education, who was launching a daily paper, *J'informe.* At the time, I did not rule out collaboration with this sincere, kind man of perfect integrity, a Catholic without a hint of clericalism or dogmatism. In the afternoon at exactly twenty minutes to three, I suffered a stroke: my right arm fell lifeless at my side, and I was no longer able to speak. A few weeks later, home from the hospital, I wrote my letter of resignation to Hersant.

2 1

POST-GAULLISM

In April 1969, I refrained from any commentary on the referendum organized by General de Gaulle both on decentralization and on reform of the Senate. After the nation's negative answer, I commented on the event, perhaps in an excessively banal style. "Eleven months after the 30 May speech and the Champs-Elysées demonstration, General de Gaulle, disavowed by the nation, has left the Elysée palace and returned to Colombey-les-deux-Eglises, 'powerful and alone.'" There followed an analysis of the origins of the event; the referendum he had abandoned on the insistence of Georges Pompidou; the extraordinary value he attributed to this kind of question of confidence posed to the nation; the memory of ideas that had long been considered by the General as president of the RPF: "He saw in decentralization a means of encouraging citizen participation in public affairs and simultaneously a first step toward reversing the age-old tendency toward administrative centralization." The General probably attached even more importance to the question of confidence than to the content of the reforms. Who had won the June elections, the president or the prime minister? "The referendum–question of confidence was designed to resolve all doubts and restore to the General the unquestionable authority without which he certainly prefers the solitude of his village to the trappings of power. . . . Like Antaeus, he needed to restore his strength by contact with the soil of the nation, with the will of the people." I explained General de Gaulle's failure, at least in part, by the inevitable evolution of the president, who had become, despite himself, the head of a moderate (or right-wing, if one prefers) majority. "It is nevertheless true, through an irony of history, that General de Gaulle, on this occasion, has been a victim of his philosophy of the referendum-plebiscite. Elected for seven years, with a solid majority in the Assembly, which may have been reticent but was resigned, he had nothing to fear but the gods or the mediocrity of social conflicts. Anyone else would have been content; he had to overcome the affront by a personal victory, or by a defeat, apparently unjust and absurd, and thereby the supreme ordeal for the hero. A return to Colombey in May 1968 would have been unworthy of France; in April 1969, it took on a certain melancholy grandeur, perhaps mysteriously granted to the Gaullist vision of the world."

In a second article, entitled "Elusive France," I analyzed in detail the link between the events of May 1968 and the definitive retirement of the General: "The 'events' had precipitated, if not determined, the separation between the two men. From this angle, General de Gaulle's retirement appears to be a consequence, distant if you like, of the conflagration ignited at Nanterre by a few hundred students. Since 11 May 1968, France has become elusive for General de Gaulle. The decisions that he has made, all intelligible from the perspective of his philosophy and his personality, have oddly turned against him. He himself will not be surprised by this ingratitude of fate and of men. Like all men of action, shaped by classical culture, he has meditated on fortune, whose inconstancy the hero can only dominate by accepting it with serenity."

I resisted the temptation of a summing up, or, more modestly, some remarks on the historical role of General de Gaulle. I had followed him only in his enterprise that had failed, the RPF. Even when I agreed with him on essentials, I did not willingly endorse his style. As a member of the RPF, I had continued to write studies according to my own philosophy, not his. During the last years of his reign, I had the reputation of being one of the non-Gaullists least tolerated by the Prince.

The compliments with which he showered me in response to my books mean nothing, or almost nothing. There is no lack of writers, major or minor, who have drawers full of letters of praise.

The first, handwritten, letter I received from him had to do with *The Century of Total War*, and was more revealing of his vision of the world than of his feelings about the book and its author (at the time a member of The National Council of the RPF): "Your book, *The Century of Total War*, that you have kindly inscribed for me, is full of ideas, facts, arguments. I admired it a great deal. It is both satisfying and alarming to consider the perspectives you present with so much talent, but perhaps the only victory that mind can carry out over matter in fusion consists in directly confronting the agitated situation and its consequences and not to agree to an abdication, which would, in any event, serve no purpose. But perhaps, on the contrary, struggle, effort and will shall finally be the masters. But clarity of vision is necessary. You have powerfully contributed to that."

Matter in fusion, the effort to master chaos, these expressions suggest the General's Bergsonism as well as his Nietzscheanism. The man of action measures himself against a disorder that he will attempt to shape into order.

Espoir et peur du siècle, published in 1957, and *La Société industrielle et la guerre*, published after his return to power, produced the same kind of praise, perhaps even more exaggerated. In the first book, I presented my ideas on decolonization and the independence of Algeria. He certainly made no issue of this.

The following book, *France Steadfast and Changing*, which analyzed the transition between the Fourth and Fifth Republics, touched him more directly. His courtesy this time was accompanied by a touch of irony: "In your book, I rediscover and I savor your agile and multifaceted thinking, your great talent for historical and psychological analysis, your truly excellent style. I admire and envy your ability to make immediate judgments about the events we are living through and the torrent that is bearing us along. As for me, I have not yet formulated my own philosophical understanding. That will not surprise you." It goes without saying that the words "I admire and envy" provided a lesson delivered without malice. The expression "the torrent that is bearing us along" expresses, I believe, a constant idea of the General's or, more precisely, the Bergsonian side of his vision of the world. Perhaps, in addition, on 19 May 1959, he did not yet know toward what solution his own policies were leading. When I sent him *Peace and War*, he alluded to my political positions in his finest style: "It happens that I am sometimes not convinced by what you write, and I know that from the outset you have rarely approved what I do. However, please believe that I admire the way in which your mind attempts to encompass the great flood that is carrying all of us toward an apparently measureless and, in any event, unprecedented fate." The polite formula repeated the one he had used in the preceding letter. This one referred to London ("from the outset") and repeated the same image, with "flood" replacing "torrent."

His response to *Dimensions de la conscience historique* contains no hint of any possible irritation. On the contrary: "Your philosophy of history, in particular when you apply it to the contemporary world, brings light into an abyss, and it is true, is it not, that the life of the nations is an abyss." The letter is dated 4 April 1961, and it does not appear to have been affected by my articles in *Preuves,* some of which, already published, criticized, at the least prematurely, the General's Algerian policy.

The next to last letter I received from him, still cautiously written, was in reaction to *The Great Debate,* and gave evidence of an irony that came close to disdain: "I have read *Le Grand Débat,* as I often read what you write in various publications on the same subject. It seems to me that you constantly come back to it with so much vivacity perhaps because the position you have taken does not fully satisfy you yourself. At bottom, everything: 'Europe,' the 'Atlantic Community,' 'NATO,' 'armaments,' and so on, comes down to a single question, should France be France? This was already the question at the time of the Resistance. You know how I have chosen, and I know that there is no rest for theologians." (In a final letter, in response to the *Essai sur les libertés,* he called me "cher maître.")

The letter of December 1963 on *Le Grand Débat* seems to me, among all those he wrote to me, the most Gaullist. Not because, for once, it omitted the ritual compliments, but because it directly confronted the subject, the strategic deterrent force. As I have pointed out, with documentary support, in a previous chapter, I never took a position against the French program of nuclear armament. But my unpardonable sin in the General's eyes was my attempt *not* to separate national defense through nuclear weapons from European and Atlantic defense. I concluded by acknowledging that I was looking for an impossible solution. The General, for whom the state was identified with the defense of the nation, applied his philosophy all the more to nuclear weapons, which are less susceptible than all others to be placed under the authority of a coalition. Alfred Fabre-Luce, in an article in *Le Monde* on September 1, 1966, criticized me for surrendering to *faits accomplis.* The conclusion of his article was: "In the meantime, the *force de frappe,* which has never been expressly approved by the Parliament, nor by a popular vote, is and must remain a subject for national controversy; we should not close off discussion at the close of an incomplete debate."

Although I was able to maintain intellectual relations with the General despite everything, I never did the same with Georges Pompidou. To be sure, in 1955, I sent him *The Opium of the Intellectuals,* and he thanked me with a warm letter that I have not been able to find. To other books, he replied with letters of thanks promising attentive reading. I wrote him a personal letter about an article on the Azores meeting and the agreement between the French and American presidents. I had committed a factual error, for which I apologized to him. He answered cordially.

With respect to my relations with the government, the replacement of General de Gaulle by Georges Pompidou brought about some changes. Political and media circles were aware of my "anti-Gaullism," and they attributed to the General a particular hostility toward me—with some exaggeration. Television producers hesitated to interview me, even on the subjects of my books. This fear was expressed only during the last two or three years of the regime. In the early 1960s, Pierre Desgraupes interviewed me several times; under the Fourth Republic, in *Espoir et peur du siècle,* I had had the occasion to develop my ideas on decolonization. There was another episode: I had been asked to deliver the opening address at a conference on the social responsibilities of the doctor. I accepted, but I let it be known that General de Gaulle might not consent to share a platform with me. A few weeks later, the organizer of the congress asked to see me. Recognizing his embarrassment, I did not give him time to discuss the situation and said to him immediately: "The General will not come if I deliver the speech. Do not apologize: I'm not surprised; it goes without saying that his presence is more important than mine." Jean Guitton spoke in my place. By an irony of history, as a war prisoner, he had rallied to the Marshal. When he entered the Sorbonne, the students prevented him from speaking for several weeks. I was among those who fought unconditionally for him, and even more for freedom and tolerance.

I appeared to be so "untouchable" that a government minister, who had been in the same tank company as I in July 1940, declined an invitation to lunch that a mutual friend wanted to organize. Ten years later, under the regime of Giscard d'Estaing, his memories returned and he carried on friendly conversations with me. Nor have I forgotten another scene, which was painful, to say the least. I had been invited to deliver a lecture at the opening session of a conference of weapons engineers in 1968. Pierre Messmer, minister of defense, was there, along with Jean Blancard, his weapons specialist. No one risked introducing me. After a few, interminable, moments of hesitation between two approaches—create a scandal by leaving, or go up to the platform and deliver my speech as though nothing were happening—I reasonably chose the second. A few days later, I received a letter of apology from Blancard, who had been alerted by Jean-Claude Casanova.

On the occasion of the 1969 presidential election, for the first time, I took a position on an electoral contest. Under the Fourth Republic, I kept my distance from party rivalry and government crises. From 1957 on, the Communist Party had ceased to belong to the political or parliamentary community. (In 1954, Pierre Mendès France declared in advance that he would not take Communist votes into account in calculating his absolute majority.) From 1958 on, General de Gaulle exercised sovereign authority, supported by an unquestionable majority of the nation. For the first time after the General's resignation, the French confronted a significant choice; on one side Alain Poher, president of the Senate, a sympathetic, moderate, cordial man, but lacking in the stature needed for a president; on the other, Georges Pompidou, who had been prime minister from 1963 to 1968. I did not hesitate to support the latter; I did not consider it in the national interest to devalue the function of the president so soon after the death of the General.

When Georges Pompidou died, Jean d'Ormesson had just assumed the editorship of *Le Figaro,* and he was subjected to pressure from all the Gaullist factions. He agreed with me on a stance of relative neutrality, up to the first round of the election, between Chaban-Delmas and Giscard d'Estaing; he presented the contest between the two representatives of the majority as the equivalent of primary elections in the United States. He was at first inclined to dissuade Giscard from dividing the majority, since Chaban had declared his candidacy first, with a haste that had rather shocked political circles, not to mention public opinion. During the first weeks of the campaign, every day, *Le Figaro* published an article in favor of the majority and another in favor of Mitterrand. A portion of the editorial staff leaned toward Mitterrand and favored a shift of the paper toward the center-left. Among articles written by Socialists, only one, I believe, was not published, an article by Pierre Joxe, which was insulting to me in the judgment of Jean d'Ormesson (I have never read it). I succeeded in convincing Jean that, during the last week, *Le Figaro* would stop presenting itself as an open forum and that we would take an unreserved position in favor of Valéry Giscard d'Estaing.

I had often met Valéry Giscard d'Estaing before the 1974 election, but I did not have a close connection with him. Many journalists, I am sure, knew him better than I, or at least had spoken more often with him, as journalists normally do with politicians.

I remember a few of our meetings: for example, a debate on the radio about one of my books, *Le Grand Schisme,* I think, which thus took place in 1948 or 1949. He had the book in his hands, hastily and incompletely cut.[1] He came once or twice to the debates on the economy organized by *Le Figaro* in the late 1940s or early 1950s; the matter under discussion was a stabilization plan to counter inflation. At the time, he spoke in favor of *ad hoc* measures rather than a general program (control of credit or reduction of the budgetary deficit).

A few years later, in 1955, I passed through his office on my way to see Edgar Faure, who was prime minister, in the midst of the Moroccan crisis. We spoke for a few minutes. To my surprise, he emphasized the inadequacy of French administrative structures in the protectorate rather than the nationalist movement. When he became an under-secretary, then minister of finance, I had the opportunity to meet and listen to him several times, since

I belonged at the time to the *Commission des Comptes*. A few days before a meeting of the Commission, I had criticized his policies, a series of immediate measures. He answered the article with so much vigor (an attack to which I replied as best I could) that Michel Rocard, who was secretary of the Commission, told me several years later that he had had a good deal of difficulty in resuming the discussion and smoothing over the rough points.

I have a final memory, a radio dialogue in 1968, about the events or about *The Elusive Revolution*. He was still in political limbo. Together we deplored the fragility of French institutions, shaken, dislocated, almost overthrown by a strong wind, which was not even a real storm. He insisted on the omnipotence of the General, or, more accurately, on the fact that the General came out of the crisis more than ever in control of the process.

In 1973, during the legislative elections, our relations took on a somewhat personal character. He telephoned me to compliment me on my article on the *Programme commun,* "Squaring The Circle"; he apologized for using many of my arguments in the evening's debate with François Mitterrand; I cannot do anything else, he told me, because you have developed all the arguments, or the best ones. I gave him a pleasant surprise that day by assuring him that I would support him at the next presidential election, scheduled for 1976. At the end of the seven-year term, in fact at the death of Georges Pompidou, he would be the best candidate for the majority. Seven years later, despite Mitterrand's victory in 1981, I have not changed my opinion.

In 1974, he invited me to attend, in the television studio, the final debate between the two candidates before the second round of the elections. His campaign director told me, with apparent sincerity, how much he had benefited from my articles in *Le Figaro*. That said, I became neither an adviser nor a familiar of the president. And I did nothing to become either.

A few weeks after his election, he organized a working lunch on the problems of nuclear strategy. Present at the lunch were the three people who had written books on the subject, General Gallois, General Beaufre, and I; two journalists who specialized in military questions, Jean Isnard of *Le Monde* and Jean-Pierre Mithois of *Le Figaro;* General Méry, at the time head of his military staff, who later became chairman of the joint chiefs; and two other generals whose names I have forgotten. From the beginning the president stated that he wanted to listen, not to talk, that he had until then hardly studied defense problems, and that he intended to do so. These remarks surprised me a little; as minister of economy and finance, he must have taken part in meetings of the Defense Council, in the course of which necessarily, certain aspects of defense doctrines had to have been mentioned and discussed, if not rigorously analyzed.

During the lunch, conversation was dominated by the generals (and writers) Pierre Gallois and André Beaufre. Gallois had arrived first; my arrival disturbed him because of our earlier polemics; his state of mind led him to exaggerate his arguments more than usually—those who know him can imagine how far he stretched his conception of the leveling power of the atom and the "sanctuarization" of national territory. I did nothing to moderate his argument, quite the contrary. I had the impression at the end of the conversation that the president would certainly not choose General Gallois as an adviser, that he reacted with spontaneous skepticism to the doctrinaire arguments for security through the threat, exclusive and permanent, of total catastrophe, massive reprisals. At one point, with clearly expressed irony, the president asked the three of us for our opinions on the significance of tactical nuclear weapons: nonexistent, answered General Gallois; you will say essential, said the president, turning with a smile to General Beaufre, I could only take an intermediate position. The president promised further conversations, which never took place. Toward the end of the lunch, he made a statement that has lodged in my memory: I cannot imagine, he said, under what conditions I should push the button.

On a completely different occasion, I had an hour's conversation with the president, in late 1974 or early 1975. Paris was rife with rumors about Valéry Giscard d'Estaing's private life; his early morning collision with a milk-wagon provided grist for the Parisian rumor mills. An article in Le Monde referred to this campaign of denigration, not to say defamation. One day, Yves Cuau of Le Figaro told me that at a lunch with journalists the president had accused the Israelis (or the Jews, I am not certain on this point) of conducting a campaign against him. I immediately took up my pen and wrote him a short letter: I criticized him for accusing the Israelis or the Jews of conspiring against him. Coming from you, I wrote, this accusation risks unleashing consequences that you would be the first to deplore.

The president telephoned me immediately and invited me to a conversation on the subject. I insisted on the seriousness of his accusations; he answered that his remarks were based on facts, not on hypotheses or speculations. The facts, as I can reconstruct them, boiled down to a telephone call from an Israeli journalist to Le Canard enchaîné. The Israeli ambassador assured me that his services wanted to have no connection with this suspect journalist of Israeli extraction. The president then asked me about the Jews of France, their numbers, and their feelings about Israel. He had just read the famous Balfour Declaration on the "Jewish homeland," one of the founding documents of the state of Israel. According to him, the situation could not fail to deteriorate at the expense of the Jewish state; the Israeli government was wrong in not accepting the solution offered to them, a Palestinian entity on the West Bank. One day, even their control over the territory within the 1967 borders would be challenged.

What struck me most in this friendly conversation was the total absence of pro- or anti-Jewish, pro- or anti-Israel feelings on Giscard's part. Apparently immune to the passions that had riven France at the time of the Dreyfus affair, and during and after the war, he had recently informed himself about the origins of the state of Israel. It was as though he lacked a faculty that would have permitted him to sympathize with the sensibility of French Jews even if he disapproved of Israel's actions. In the last part of his term as president, his chief of staff was a Jew whose father had disappeared in the Nazi camps. If he had asked this man for advice before his trip to the Near East, or after the terrorist attack on the rue Copernic, he would not have committed the errors that alienated a part of the Jewish community. At the end of the conversation, he alluded to nuclear strategy; I still have not completely mastered the arguments, he told me at the door of his office, we have to talk about this again. The discussion never took place. Several times, I was invited to official lunches or dinners, in honor of Chancellor Schmidt or President Senghor. I asked to see him only about *Le Figaro;* he never asked to see me, although he did call me on the phone.

The quarrel between the President of the Republic and his former prime minister over the mayoralty of Paris deeply disturbed those who anticipated the consequences of a break between the two parties and who wanted to prevent the "suicide of the majority" (the title of an article of mine published on 21 February 1977).

I had at first, at least in appearance, come out in favor of Jacques Chirac. The RPR, under its former title of UDR, held the majority in the municipal council of Paris and its chairmanship. In accordance with the reform imposed by the President of the Republic, the president of the municipal council became the mayor of Paris—a prestigious title that had fallen into disuse after 1871. The two parties of the then majority had been very close to agreeing on a single candidate for the mayoralty. For reasons that I have never understood, the agreed candidate, Pierre Taittinger, withdrew from the race. The President selected the mayor of Deauville, Michel d'Ornano, without securing the agreement of Jacques Chirac. Suddenly, Chirac threw his glove into the ring, directly challenging the President of the Republic by claiming the position of mayor of the city of light for himself.

Beforehand, on 2 January 1976, I had analyzed the implications of the now open rivalry between the head of state and his former prime minister. I knew hardly more than the man in the street about the causes of the break between the two men. I was not blind to Giscard's defects, but my irritation was calmed as soon as I compared him to the heads of government of Europe and America with whom he held discussions or negotiations. I knew Jacques Chirac very little, and from a distance, I never had the impression that he was a fascist type (despite what others may have said); he was Radical-Socialist in his manner of courting the peasants, a demagogue in large cities in his combative style and his almost infinite capacity to shake hands, always in search of an electoral slogan that he abandons a few days after having invented it, a force of nature and a political force from whom we can expect and fear a great deal. Of the two, in my eyes, only Giscard had the intelligence, the experience, and the authority of a head of state, but he made the fatal mistake of turning Chirac into an implacable enemy. Perhaps as early as 1977, the hostility between the two, a result of frustrated friendship on both sides, led the two adversary-allies toward a common defeat. I argued in vain against the "suicide of the majority," and I addressed the president because I was not in touch with the prime minister.

The president joined battle with passion, and he lost. Pressure from the presidency on television had never been so strong as it was during the Paris elections. The RPR municipal councillors occupied positions that were in some cases unassailable. Françoise Giroud was launched in an attack against one of these positions, that she was unable to win, despite support from *L'Express*. She lost everything because of an unfortunate episode involving a government decoration. My cousin Aron-Brunetière—she had served under him in the Resistance—spoke in her support. The president had asked her to head a slate in a particular district and promised to give her a cabinet post, whatever the voters might decide. The "scandal" of the usurped decoration freed her from her commitment.

The president took my advice very badly. Two of my articles favored Chirac simply because they recognized the legitimacy of his candidacy. I have no opinion about their eloquence. A few followers of Chirac in order to flatter me, asserted that without my article they would never have succeeded (hence fostering my "megalomania"). The anger of the president would also have flattered my vanity if I had hoped for this kind of influence. In Paris, among the well-to-do, *Le Figaro* is still in its rightful place. In my view, the articles had more effect on the political class than on the voters.

The president's staff wondered why I had struck a "low blow" against him. Some of his entourage attributed my attitude to the affair of Abu Daoud, one of the organizers of the terrorist attack against the Israeli Olympic athletes in Munich. I had vigorously, perhaps too vigorously,[2] criticized the speech with which the government, with the help of the justice system, had gotten rid of this inconvenient Palestinian. I was not surprised but struck by the refusal of professional politicians to imagine an approach that would not be determined by a more or less corrupt motive, resentment, or calculation. Moreover, *before* the offering, I had written that the President should not himself become personally involved in the fight over the Paris mayoralty, where he risked losing its prestige.

After these controversial articles, I met once or twice with Jacques Chirac, Marie-France Garaud, and Pierre Juillet. Chirac seemed to me to be charming; contact with him seemed easy, easier than with Giscard. In the end, I had no conversations with Giscard that were not strictly, totally political.

A few weeks after the municipal elections, I disappeared from circulation. Before my cardiac crisis, I had written a few articles on the "inevitable clash" of the spring of 1978, and I had referred to "a year to persuade"; the last article on domestic politics was published on 28 March. The four articles that marked the end of thirty years of contributions to *Le Figaro* were published between 23 and 27 April.

I wrote these four articles to say farewell to the readers of *Le Figaro*, to put myself to the test while my hand could barely outline the letters. These articles will be considered in the last part of this book, devoted to the years of reprieve that nature, with the help of the doctors granted me, and whose bittersweet flavor I occasionally taste.

NOTES

1. It may have been *The Century of Total War;* in that case, the dialogue took place in 1951 or 1952.
2. If I am to judge from readers' letters.

2 2

ON IDEOLOGICAL
CRITICISM

The Opium of the Intellectuals con-
cluded a phase of my existence, fifteen years during which I lived outside the
university as a journalist and a militant. Published in the spring of 1955, a
few months before my candidacy at the Sorbonne, the book was a provocation to the intellectual left, which was not a majority but was influential in
the university. Published a year before Khrushchev's secret speech to the
Twentieth Congress of the Soviet Communist Party, it was helped by circumstances, despite the anger it provoked: the Parisian intelligentsia was beginning to wonder about the Marxism-Leninism of the Soviet Union.

The criticism of ideologies, as I understand it, did not stop with *Opium*.
First of all, I carried on discussions with some of my opponents and tried to
define my positions precisely, to refute the accusation of skepticism or
nihilism for which so many readers reproached me. Moreover, the conclusion, "The End of the Age of Ideology?" provoked a more or less passionate controversy on both sides of the Atlantic. The publication in the early
1960s of the three short works on industrial society led me to establish
connections between the phases of economic and social development and
ideologies.

In retrospect, I sometimes wonder why I devoted so much time to ideological criticism, a category under which I include many articles, among them *The Industrial Society,* and two books—*D'une Sainte Famille à l'autre* (1969; English translation: *Marxism and the Existentialists* [London and New York: Harper & Row, 1969]), *History and the Dialectic of Violence* (Oxford: Blackwell, 1975).

I find some extenuating circumstances to justify what some have called polemical excess. Not that I had many illusions about the effectiveness of debate. Feelings survive for a long time after the ideologies through which they have been expressed and rationalized. Despite everything, intellectuals attempt to prove or to justify their faith; many of them never succeeded in adopting the Stalinist version of Marxism. Thus, I never had conversations with believers in "Dialectical Materialism."

The articles and books that I place in the category of ideological criticism are related to the goal I had set myself when I was young: to compare ideas to the realities that they express, deform, or transfigure; to follow both the course of events and the course of ideas. The first three chapters in *Opium* deal with the "sacred cows" *left, proletariat, revolution,* in order to analyze these equivocal notions and their various meanings as a function of particular historical contexts.

My critique was inspired by both Marx and Kant. The critique was Marxist, since Marx was always searching, beyond language and illusions, for authentic experience. How would he have judged a regime that claims to be proletarian, while granting the proletariat none of the freedoms granted by bourgeois democracy, if only the right to choose their own union representatives? My critique was Kantian, since it condemned the philosophy of history whose ambition goes beyond the limits of knowledge and of legitimate forecasts.

For thirty years, Parisian ideological fashions have always been accompanied by a reinterpretation of Marxism. The texts I include in the category of ideological criticism belong, at bottom if not apparently, to entirely different literary genres. *The Opium of the Intellectuals* still seems to me to be an essay for a cultivated public. *D'une Sainte Famille à l'autre* and especially *Histoire et dialectique de la violence* approach philosophy; I have never succeeded in eliminating jargon from the pages devoted to Sartre's *Critique de la raison dialectique.*

At about the same time as the "revolution of the carnations" in Portugal, Solzhenitsyn burst on the Parisian intellectual scene. I would not have participated in the disputes among left-wing intellectuals about the author of *The Gulag Archipelago* had my comment on a television program, *Apostrophes,* not provoked the wrath of Jean Daniel. The personality of the *zek* had touched me deeply: coming from another world, an extraordinary man, whose like would be difficult to find anywhere in the world, spoke to all of us, collectively and individually. Of the participants in the program, neither Pierre Daix nor Jean d'Ormesson had made much of an impression; they had not tried to. Jean Daniel had irritated me, but at the same time, I shared to some extent the humiliation he had inflicted on himself, attempting to compare his fights against French or American imperialism to the struggle Solzhenitsyn carried out against the Kremlin. I suffer, as a psychoanalyst has explained to me, from an inclination toward *entlehntes Schuldgefühl,* a borrowed feeling of guilt. Jewish comedy, sometimes that of the Marx Brothers, does not make me laugh; on the contrary, I feel myself as the butt of the jokes.

The editorial I wrote two days later (18 April 1975) attempted to express my ambiguous feelings; even today, I do not think it exceeds the bounds of legitimate controversy. If Jean Daniel considered my remarks excessive, what must he have thought of Sartre's article on me in May 1968? I present to the reader the elements of the dispute:

When Dostoyevsky returned from the "house of the dead," who would have suggested that he speak to a bureaucrat or a servant of the bureaucracy? In expressing regret that there was no member of the Communist Party on the television program the other day, Jean Daniel placed himself in a thankless position. Solzhenitsyn is not a political man, even if his statements, his work, and his life constitute political realities with all the force of his suffering and his genius. His convictions transcend politics because they inspire an extraordinary personality, because they are, in the last analysis, spiritual in essence: faith in freedom and unconditional devotion to the truth. By asking the author of *Cancer Ward* to express opinions about the events of the day, the editor of *Le Nouvel Observateur* lowered the dialogue to the ordinary level of Parisian debates. Who in the West is carrying on the same battle as Solzhenitsyn? The answer is simple because the question is indecent; no one. Neither the right nor the left. To carry on his fight, we would have to confront the same enemy, risk the long voyage through the system of concentration camps, derive from the same ordeals the invincible strength to resist the infernal machine. We have written articles and books in favor of Algerian independence, and we have no reason to regret that. Nor do we have the right to be proud of it when we meet the author of *A Day in the Life of Ivan Denisovich.* The judgments that Solzhenitsyn makes about Vietnam, Portugal, or Chile, of course, call for discussion, and the exile may be mistaken. The Salazar regime has left a population half of which is illiterate. The Chilean generals use and abuse repression and torture; captains and majors in Portugal will build more schools and open more factories than the previous authorities. The communists of North Vietnam will at least put an end to the war. If Solzhenitsyn is troubling, if he provokes indigestion, this is because he has touched a nerve, the lie of Western intellectuals; if you accept the great Gulag, he says to them, how can you be virtuously indignant about minor Gulags? Camps are camps, whether they are brown or red.

In his book of a few years later, *L'Ere des ruptures*, Jean Daniel still felt my remarks as a personal attack, unworthy of me and unjust to him. "I was not indifferent to the fact that Raymond Aron abandoned reasoned argument and waxed indignant, with uncharacteristic violence, because I had not bowed before an exceptional man."

I cannot detect in my text the slightest symptom of having abandoned reasoned argument. Nor did I ask him to bow before anyone. I observed that by regretting the absence of a communist from the dialogue, he assumed a "thankless role." I am no more ready than he is to accept all the judgments of Solzhenitsyn on the world situation. But, at the time, Jean Daniel had not yet completed his shift in position; he was still speaking of his "communist comrades." Even in his book, he attributes to the communists he knew personally virtues that make impossible any comparison between fascism and communism.

I did not criticize him for referring to the other authoritarian or more or less totalitarian regimes against which he had fought. But the French intellectual, concerned with preserving the "unity of the left," when confronting Solzhenitsyn, placed himself in a false position: there is a difference in nature between the Soviet Gulag and the Portugal of Salazar. I was not at all attacking Jean Daniel, because, as I said, the greatness of Solzhenitsyn would have crushed anyone at all. I criticized him for refusing to acknowledge the cardinal sin of the intellectual left. In Vietnam, Jean Daniel had been aware of only one enemy—American imperialism—an imperialism whose ultimate objective was to withdraw. Solzhenitsyn saw in Vietnam in addition a new communism and new Gulags, and he was right.

> I was in the Soviet Union at the time of the Paris agreements; all my friends were surprised, they did not understand how these agreements could be taken seriously. Look at today's situation. Suppose that South Vietnam had attacked the North. There would have been a general uproar. The counterrevolutionaries of the South would have been accused of violating the Paris agreements, even if these counterrevolutionaries had been resistance fighters who had combated the United States; North Vietnam invaded the South, and everyone was pleased. Or else, people prefer not to consider the problem, they propose that foreigners leave as soon as possible, leave Saigon and even Phnom Penh, since their safety can no longer be guaranteed. Do you know what the departure of the foreigners represents for me? It is the departure of the witnesses, of all those who might have seen, remembered, and repeated afterward what was going to happen after the victorious troops entered the cities. And consequently, the departure of the witnesses means a delay of several years in telling what I have seen elsewhere.

A few weeks later, in responding to an article in which Solzhenitsyn had criticized the Americans for not supporting the Vietnam War, I reiterated the fact that foreign policy was inevitably amoral to some degree. A democracy cannot and must not ignore the domestic systems of the states with which it deals; but it cannot and must not, on the other hand, conduct a crusade to spread its own institutions: "To fight always and everywhere a regime that is considered evil is to wish a crusade, if one is on the offensive, or battles lost in advance, if one remains on the defensive." And I set forth precise questions, addressed to Western governments, that do not admit of categorical or obvious answers: Should we support China against the Soviet Union? Against those who, in 1975 (and there were more and more of them), tended to place East-West rivalry in the background in order to emphasize North-South opposition, I reiterated an argument to which I still hold: "Whatever anyone may say, the historic rivalry between the Soviet Union and the liberal West remains the contest of the century, despite the opposing interests of the West and the Third World."

In an article published in 1977, I defined the term ideology in a precise and narrow sense, comparing it to a secular religion—a definition that presents more difficulties than advantages. Fanaticism and millenarianism come and go, with or without a total system for the interpretation of the world. The observer who grasps in a single view the alternative between faith and skepticism is struck by the fact that the same hopes, so often disappointed, can endlessly launch men to attack the same Bastilles, or the old Bastilles in new guise. In the early 1930s, Karl Mannheim feared that the desire for transcendence was giving way to a resigned acceptance of reality. Karl Popper, and many others, hoped that men would be able to discuss reasonably, according to scientific methods, the possible reforms of an always imperfect social order. The fears of Mannheim have been calmed, and the hopes of the social engineer disappointed.

Political discussions could be called ideological, even in the centuries when men at every level of the hierarchy invoked transcendental principles, truths of a religious order, if one includes within ideology theological arguments and the dogmas of the churches. In our time, in the regimes that no longer lay claim to a truth, to a higher will, politics has become specifically ideological, or, if you prefer another expression, ideological controversies have become the essence of politics.

The ancien régime was not based on the conclusions of debates among intellectuals. The legitimacy of the sovereign was barely distinguishable from the teachings of the Church, and the legitimacy of the nobility came from a long history. Once the Church and the tradition had been called into question or rejected, and the sovereignty of the people proclaimed, all parties and all social groups were drawn into a continuous debate about the regime that would be most in harmony with the dominant ideas (liberty and equality), the most conducive to collective wealth and individual well-being. The structure of these patterns of justification varies according to party and epoch. At one extreme, the ideal pattern of thought amounts to a more or less rigorous combination of facts and values; at another extreme, it is organized into systems that proclaim themselves to be total, judging the present and predicting the future. I had reserved the term *ideology* for the latter; I would hesitate to do the same today.

To be sure, I find it difficult to place in the same category the Stalinist catechism and the comparative analysis of various economic systems, in relation to various parameters (individual freedom, productive capacity, distribution of income, quality of life, and so on). On the one hand, the whole history of humanity, if not of the cosmos, is said to lead to classless socialism (or socialism with nonantagonistic classes); on the other, we consider the problems common to all modern economies, we study the various solutions, referring both to theory and experience, to explain the probable consequences of each of those solutions. Unity of fact and value, and the prophetic impulse on the one hand, dualism of what is and what ought to be, and a patient search for improvement on the other: the opposition had seemed to me so pronounced that I did not dare to describe the two attitudes with the same word.

What now leads me to change my vocabulary, I wrote in 1977, is first of all the multiplicity of cases that lie between the two ideal types, then the existence of orthodoxies, crude and imperious, derived from doctrines hostile to Marxism-Leninism, and finally the resemblance between the themes used by the social sciences and those used by propaganda, the ceaseless communication between the consciousness of themselves that modern societies derive from party rivalry and the consciousness they owe to so-called scientific disciplines. In so-called socialist regimes, this communication leads to identity: the ideocratic regime erects into a state truth a certain version of the world, derived from Marxism, or based on it. In the West, our societies have neither a synthesis of their knowledge of themselves nor a single vision of their future, nor an image of their ideal.

The Marxist-Leninist asserts, or better decrees a universal truth, refusing to distinguish between knowledge and desire; the liberal or critical thinker, aware of the traps set by his passions, aware of the ambiguity of reality itself, constantly calls his hypotheses and judgments into question. Skepticism? Not at all. The liberal constantly seeks the truth, and he will never budge from his ultimate convictions, that is, his maxims that are as moral as they are intellectual. I was not mistaken in contrasting my attitude to that of the true believers, the faithful of the secular religions. I was mistaken in calling one ideological and the other not. It is better to adapt a title used by Pascal: *Du bon usage des idéologies*.

2 3

HENRY KISSINGER
AND THE END OF
AMERICAN HEGEMONY

Between 1947 and 1958, my columns in *Le Figaro* dealt for the most part with economic concerns and developments in international diplomacy. The rivalry among the parties of the Fourth Republic held little interest for me, since the various governments, all coalitions, all carried out essentially similar policies. The Republican Front, victorious on paper after the dissolution of the Assembly in 1955, named Guy Mollet as prime minister; it was he who assumed the responsibility of sending draftees to Algeria. At the request of Pierre Brisson, I wrote a few articles on the theme "The Fourth Republic has to reform in order to survive." I foresaw the only reforms possible within the framework of the established regime—which severely restricted their scope. In reality, there had to be a shock, a national crisis, for the republic of the deputies to capitulate so that a constitution like that of the Fifth Republic became conceivable without a break in legal continuity.

Under the reign of General de Gaulle, I had the reputation of belonging to the "opposition." I felt no nostalgia for the "abolished regime." On particular points, I disapproved of the General's diplomacy, but in May 1968, I had no hesitation in deciding which side I belonged to. My criticisms, sometimes excessive or unfriendly, came in part from my conception of the duties of a political commentator, in part from my inclination to keep my distance from the Princes who govern us, and above all from my disagreement with the General's diplomacy.

During the dozen years of post-Gaullism, my courses at the Collège de France and my books mobilized my time and my interest much more than my participation in *Le Figaro*, and later *L'Express*. In the 1970s, all the systems established after the war, the Bretton Woods currency agreement, the system of state relations guaranteed by the power and will of the United States, by the rivalrous connivance of the two superpowers, by the nuclear superiority of the American Republic, were shaken by blows that appeared sudden but had in fact ripened throughout the 1960s.

During the years 1969 to 1975, one man was permanently in the forefront: Henry Kissinger. I knew him better than any other American secretary of state, better than any French foreign minister, with the possible exception of Maurice Schumann. I would even say, without hesitation, that he was a friend, on condition that it is recognized that the word changes meaning according to age and circumstances. I retain a nostalgia for my youthful friendships with Lagache, Sartre, Guille, Nizan, and Canguilhem, as I experienced them or as I remember them; we gave each other everything that we had, incapable of calculating, indifferent to apparent competition. Purity or an illusion of youth? I don't know. Even if politics had not broken them, these friendships would have grown old, deeper and more solid perhaps, but different, with all of us absorbed by our professions and family obligations, less available for interminable conversations.

The friendships established among adults are quite different. I met Manès Sperber in 1937 in André Malraux's little apartment on the rue du Bac. Our friendship was forged in the terrible prewar years. It continues today without interruption or faltering. We have carried on the same fight, against the same enemy, united in feeling even when our judgments were opposed.

Henry Kissinger had paid me a visit toward the end of the 1940s, when he was hardly out of Harvard. I met him from time to time in the course of the 1950s, in Paris or the United States. I followed his career from a distance, the success of his books, particularly the one that made his reputation, *Nuclear Weapons and Foreign Policy*. I respected the book, but it did not seem to me to deserve its reputation. He did, to some extent, stand out from other professors of international relations because of his acute awareness of the predominance of politics over technical considerations.

I spent time with him in Cambridge during my semester at Harvard. He asked me to lead one of his seminars. He has respect for me, no doubt, or, if you prefer, he does not apply to me the sense of his intellectual superiority which he is said to inflict on mere mortals. Because of the difference in our ages, he always adopted toward me the stance of a younger man, if not that of a student. He was never my student, but he learned from *Peace and War.* Like me, closer to history than to scientific models, he praised, sincerely I think, the qualities of the book.

I was not unaware that he had career ambitions—which meant in the United States in the early 1960s accession to an important position in Washington. He had not given up strictly intellectual success—he also wanted to be the best among specialists in international relations and strategy. But he would probably have said that political science, in its current form, was not sufficient in itself. Action, in this view, is worth more than theory. Einstein is greatly superior to a nuclear energy engineer, but a great secretary of state triumphs over the best professor of international relations. With some qualifications, I agree with this hierarchy of values.

Did I foresee the exceptional success of "Doctor Kissinger" in the jungle of Washington? Certainly not. Nor did I foresee failure. I merely had doubts. Would he succeed in imposing himself on the president, charming the journalists through flattery, forcing the respect of the Senate? I might have bet yes, but I would certainly not have bet my life.

Between 1969 and 1975, I met him several times in Paris and Washington. As I remember him, I saw him at the White House first in 1970, during the Cambodian crisis, and a second time in the spring of 1972 when the North Vietnamese offensive was threatening the South Vietnamese army. He remembered my previous visit, since he began the conversation by recalling it: "You bring trouble." When he came to Paris, we often had breakfast together. Once the AFP mentioned that Kissinger, during a stay in Paris, had met President Giscard d'Estaing and Raymond Aron. I have rarely mentioned my conversations with prominent figures, because they were infrequent and I derived little from them. Pandit Nehru received me for a half-hour in New Delhi in 1953. I have a vivid memory of the man; he told me nothing original or secret. President Park of South Korea granted me a whole hour, and I found him more interesting; in particular, he spoke sensibly about the division of Korea, pointing out that, for centuries, Korea had been divided into several kingdoms.

In our conversations between 1969 and 1978, Kissinger told me nothing that I could not have learned from the press, or from occasional leaks. Nevertheless, contact with the man who negotiated with the Soviets, the Vietnamese, the Israelis, and the Arabs helped me to interpret events. To some extent, I sympathized with Kissinger's way of thinking, in the strict sense of the term, placing myself in his position, experiencing the feelings he must have had. Moreover, in our conversations, he willingly explained the reasons behind his adoption of one attitude or another. Besides, everyone heard the plea for an honorable peace and his evocation of the cost of surrender. Even with me, he did not always say the same things about a particular subject, for example, on the importance (or lack of importance) of the balance of strategic nuclear forces. In 1969, he observed with hostility the beginnings of Willy Brandt's *Ostpolitik*. I cannot say whether he regularly read my articles. His collaborators probably sent them to him from time to time, the ones that criticized or explicitly praised him, I suppose; only once did he reply in writing to one of my articles, about Cyprus. I criticized him for not having immediately condemned the Greek *coup d'état*, for tolerating this initiative, which provoked the intervention of the Turkish army. An exchange of letters followed. In any event, our relations were the same during and after his reign; I agreed to join the informal study groups that he had created on his return to private life.

Was I more indulgent toward American diplomacy in 1969–75 because of my personal relations with one of its creators?

In leafing through the collection of articles I had written for *Le Figaro*, I noted with surprise and a feeling of guilt, that I had commented hardly at all on the first stages of American intervention in Vietnam (Kissinger, in his memoirs, confesses that he, too, had not paid much attention to the beginnings of an interminable war). My visit to Hanoi was the first occasion on which I heard of Ngo Dinh Diem, from the general secretary of the French administration. This high-level bureaucrat described Diem to me as the Americans' man, an Annamite mandarin who represented, according to this official, the final recourse, the last card. This conversation took place in October 1953, before Dien Bien Phu and the Geneva conference.

In the course of the years immediately following the Geneva agreements, commentary and debate focused on Franco-American friction; our allies were taking charge of Diem's ferociously anticommunist regime, and thereby eliminated the influence, and even the presence of the French. An American university replaced the Ecole Nationale d'Administration in the task of training the bureaucrats of the new state. French troops were the first to leave; counselors and teachers in turn left ample space for newcomers. At least this is the way the newspapers told the story of the withdrawal of the French, humiliated by the Viet Minh at Dien Bien Phu and forced out by the Americans.

The "free" elections provided for by the Geneva agreements did not take place. I was neither surprised nor scandalized: in North Korea and East Germany, the Communist regimes did not tolerate free elections. Would Ho Chi Minh have tolerated a public meeting in Hanoi organized by Diem? Would the Diem regime have resisted the shock of public meetings held by Ho Chi Minh and his lieutenants in Saigon or other cities? I did not pay enough attention to a fact that, during the Indochina War, I had often

referred to in the context of Parisian controversies: the Vietminh revolutionaries would never give up the objective they had set forth from the very
beginning of their enterprise: the unity of the three regions. For them,
Cochin-China, Annam, and Tonkin belonged to a single whole.

In 1954, the Vietminh had brought to the North a fraction of its supporters
in the South. Diem immediately attacked the communists in order to
eliminate them, or at least to make them harmless. Toward the end of the
1950s, the Communist Party of the North decided to resume the war against
the "puppets" or the "accomplices" of American imperialism. When
Eisenhower left the White House, there were fewer than a thousand American military personnel serving in South Vietnam; Kennedy acceded partially
to the pressure of the joint chiefs of staff, and the number of "advisers"
suddenly increased to more than 15,000. Why did he commit the United
States to the defense of a noncommunist state in South Vietnam? Did he
believe in the domino theory? Did he think, as de Gaulle reports in his
memoirs, that he was creating a pole of anticommunist resistance in Southeast Asia? Even now, I do not know what motives inspired Kennedy. Personally, I incline toward a rather primitive interpretation.

United States support of the Diem government is self-explanatory: it was a
simple application of the doctrine of containment. Since half of Vietnam had
been left outside communist domination, the West remained interested in
this still "free" half.

Europeans, supporters of the Atlantic Alliance, had approved American
action in Korea. Did the action in Vietnam belong to the same category? The
answer depended on many badly understood factors. We know, whoever has
visited South Korea knows, that south of the 38th parallel, there is a political
entity, a state, a people, ready to defend themselves against aggression from
the North. There is also a patriotism, which is inextricably both Korean and
anticommunist, which involves a condemnation of the 25 June 1950 invasion
and fully justifies Harry Truman and Dean Acheson. In 1954, or 1960, was
there a South Vietnamese patriotism? Is it legitimate or not to compare the
two Vietnams to the two Koreas or the two Germanies? No one doubts that
the East Germans, if they could express themselves freely, would choose the
condition of their brothers, "exploited by capitalism." And yet, if the West
Germans tried to reunite the two pieces of the old Reich, they would be
treated in the West as warmongers, by everyone, right or left. It therefore
did not seem to me just to call American participation in the survival of the
Republic of South Vietnam imperialist.

Another consideration necessarily influenced our attitudes. Did the gov-
ernment of the South deserve to be saved? Was it preferable to the one the
North Vietnamese brought with them? The Western press, particularly the
American press, unmercifully criticized the violations of democratic rules

under the government of the South. It reported the horrors of the camps—since there were camps in the South. Hence, the question arises: by fighting for South Vietnam, was the United States fighting for a strategic position, for the ideas of the West, or to preserve its prestige, or, according to Kissinger's expression, its credibility?

Personally, if memory does not deceive me, I inclined toward the following position: it would be desirable, for the South Vietnamese and the United States, for the Republic of South Vietnam to survive; but was the United States able to pursue this enterprise to the very end? The cost of the war would perhaps be greater than the value of what was at stake. In other words they risked not only committing a sin but a mistake. Divided by these divergent, if not contradictory, feelings and analyses, I sought refuge in one of my roles, that of spectator of human folly and misfortune.

The Vietnam war had an original aspect, when compared to previous so-called wars of liberation or to the Korean campaign. The North Vietnamese divisions did not cross a demarcation line as the North Korean troops had done. The "partisans" carrying on the "small war" in the South had access to logistical support, but also to constantly renewed reinforcements of soldiers recruited and trained in the North. In response to North Vietnamese aggression, the Johnson regime inaugurated a strategy inspired by the doctrine of escalation that was put into effect by the air force. The Americans did not seek out the troops and the industries of the North to fight against the former or to seize the latter; they bombarded the territory of a state with which they were not at war but one which was strengthening and supplying the fighters in the South.

What was the strategic significance of these bombings? Those directed against the Ho Chi Minh trail were aimed, if not at preventing Northern soldiers from reaching the South, at least at reducing their number. I remember a conversation with Robert McNamara at the Pentagon around 1966. As was his custom, he illustrated his ideas with diagrams. He drew three lines, one over the other: the first represented the number of people moving from North to South in the absence of bombing; the second the number in spite of bombing; the third, still lower, the number that would be necessary to change decisively the course of operations. The bombing, not on the Ho Chi Minh trail, but in North Vietnam, had the purpose of "punishing the enemy," devastating the opponent's territory—a return to the practice recorded throughout the centuries. In the last century, during the conquest of Algeria, the French did not refrain from similar methods, for example, poisoning wells and depriving caravans of their sources of water. The Washington leaders, Lyndon Johnson and his cabinet, informed Hanoi of their intentions to bomb the North if infiltration into the South and resupply of the Vietcong did not come to an end. They applied the doctrine, developed by professors in the context of nuclear strategy, of the progressive increase in the use of violence, in order to persuade the communists of Hanoi to abandon their enterprise.

I analyzed this original form of warfare, bombing gradually intensified against subversion, skeptical about the effectiveness of such a strategy. The bombings caused property damage and loss of life; they did not destroy the cities (when the Americans who had argued the cause of North Vietnam visited Hanoi after the Paris agreements, they noted with surprise that the city was essentially still standing, far from the pile of rubble that they had imagined).

The psychological effect of the bombing turned out to be as minimal as the bombing of Germany had been during the Second World War. The population "held." The threat of escalation did not shake the resolve of the North Vietnamese government. It did not take the warnings transmitted by the Canadians seriously. It did not doubt that the Americans would impose limits on themselves. "To make others believe in the demonetarization[1] of gold, the Americans had to believe in it themselves. To intimidate the North Vietnamese, the Americans should have taken seriously their own threat of escalation. In each case, the message confronted the incredulity of its recipient because of the very skepticism of its producers" (6 March 1968).

A few months ago, my friends Claudie and Jacques Broyelle asked me whether I had "approved" American use of napalm—something they had been told so as to cure them of their friendship for me. The question is no different in nature from the one asked by Dominique Wolton and Jean-Louis Missika: Did you condemn torture in Algeria? I answered, slightly irritated by the insistence of my questioners: I am not a "beautiful soul" (*eine schöne Seele*). In 1945, I hoped that France would consent to the unity of the three Kys. In 1965 or 1968, there was a South Vietnamese Republic which seemed to me preferable to the totalitarianism of the North; the American effort to preserve this republic, in a "dubious battle," did not arise from an imperialist impulse, but rather from an illusion of omnipotence. As for napalm, it had to be detested just as torture had been. Should soldiers have been able or obliged to refrain from using these means? From a distance, it is easy to answer: of course.

The battle was all the more dubious because the leaders in Washington themselves had no clear idea of why they were fighting. In the beginning, between 1954, and 1960, the support given to Saigon was an automatic expression of containment. In 1961 and 1962, Kennedy, humiliated by the disaster of the Bay of Pigs and by his Vienna meeting with Khrushchev, found a way to show that he was tough, to dissipate any illusions Khrushchev may have had as a result of the disastrous beginnings of the administration. When Lyndon Johnson visited Saigon as vice-president, he was prodigal in expressing variations on the theme of falling dominoes. As the United States became further involved in the impasse, the president and his advisers knew less and less why they were expending so many men and dollars, against whom or in view of what end they were sacrificing so many lives and so much wealth.

Walt W. Rostow, who was National Security Adviser between McGeorge Bundy and Henry Kissinger presented to me one of those *weltgeschichtlich* theories he is so fond of: Ho Chi Minh and Vietnamese expansion were the latest expression of revolutionary romanticism. American victory over this ideological conqueror would signify the end of an epoch. Other Washington advisers saw, behind Ho Chi Minh, Lin Piao and the surrounding of cities by countryside, or Chinese imperialism, others still the imperialism of the Kremlin. Events since then have confirmed the latter interpretation.

The Tet offensive was, in fact, a failure on the part of the Vietcong. Nowhere did the population join the "freedom fighters." Those fighters committed inexcusable activities. They forced victims to dig the ditches into which they hurled hundreds of officials and notables of the imperial city of Hue. My friend, Pham Duy Khiem, ambassador of South Vietnam to Paris in 1954, distributed through AFP on 13 April 1968 an indignant report on the conduct of the Vietcong in the regions they controlled for a few days. "These intellectuals failed to contemplate what remains of so many simple functionaries, innocent agents of the administration and their families, soldiers on leave, French priests, German teachers with their wives buried alive (around three hundred so far), or killed after mutilations and various tortures (around seven hundred), sometimes chained together with barbed wire." This report sank into indifference and oblivion. The cause transfigured the crimes of the North, it aggravated those of the South.

Beginning in 1969, the year that Nixon and Kissinger came to power, I confined myself even more to analysis. The Republicans had no responsibility for the role assumed by the United States in the Vietnam War. Nixon could have given in to the demands of the North and, in a few months, have achieved the peace demanded by public opinion, or at least by the most vocal spokesmen of public opinion. What were the demands of the North? They could be reduced to a formula: a "coalition government," from which, obviously, would be excluded the "gang of puppets," Thieu and his supporters, in other words those who were governing South Vietnam and symbolized the resistance. The members of the "provisional government of the South," created by the communists, the "third force," which some opponents of Thieu discussed in the cafés of the capital, were not an intermediary or a mediator between the men of Saigon and those of Hanoi; allies or accomplices consciously or not, they were indistinguishable from the Vietcong or, if you prefer, could not distinguish themselves from the Vietcong and the Communist Party of the North. The "coalition government" implied the elimination of the South Vietnamese government, and hence the capitulation of the United States. The American Republic "should have" forced Thieu and his allies to withdraw, in which case it would have betrayed them and their cause, confessed that they existed only by grace of the power of a foreign army.

Nixon and Kissinger knew that the voters expected them to end the Vietnam War, but neither the voters nor even the members of Congress had yet understood that North Vietnam was demanding the capitulation of the United States, scarcely veiled by the formula of the coalition government. Kissinger himself, in his memoirs, tells how he hoped to reach an agreement with Vietnam in less than a year. Nixon, who was more prescient, had strong doubts. Before being named National Security Adviser, Kissinger had presented the two sets of negotiations he anticipated in a *Foreign Affairs* article, one between the United States and North Vietnam, the other between the two Vietnamese governments. The North rejected the second set, since it did not "recognize" the Thieu regime, obliterated by the communist vision of the world, reduced to the pitiful role of imperialist "puppet." Thus in 1969, once the strategy of the Republican administration was known, I correctly foresaw a continuation of the war.

For example, on 2 July 1969, I emphasized primarily the impossibility of a political agreement between Hanoi and Washington: "If President Nixon *wants* both to withdraw from Vietnam and not to concede political victory to the enemy (a Vietcong government in Saigon), he will have difficulty in finding a replacement government for the South. And the North Vietnamese continue to reject, with the same firmness, dialogue with 'the puppets of Saigon.'" A little further on: "It is as though the North Vietnamese and the Vietcong were counting on the weariness of the American people in order finally to carry off their political victory. In the absence of a decision on the battlefield, the war has been transformed into a contest of wills. Whoever holds on for the last moments has won. If the war is not over in eighteen months, will Nixon be able to resist the opponents, who are more and more numerous and more and more violent?" And I concluded: "Do the Americans, today like yesterday, under Nixon as under Johnson, have any choice but that between political defeat and the continuation of hostilities? There might be a third way, on the day when the North Vietnamese considered their enemy as patient as themselves. But what miracle would enable them to make that judgment?" In other words, I correctly formulated the *alternative: defeat or prolonged war.*

In 1972, after the failure of the North Vietnamese offensive across the demilitarized zone, I hoped for a conversion of North Vietnamese diplomacy, the acceptance of an American-Vietnamese agreement without the liquidation of the Thieu regime, in other words a cease-fire without a political solution, a resolution that the North Vietnamese had resisted up to that point. It was in October 1972, in fact, that the North Vietnamese made the major concession, on the basis of which negotiations were to result in a resolution, which only the members of the Nobel Peace Prize jury confused with peace. The government of the South, whose existence was denied by Le Duc Tho, remained in place. "Leopard skin" was the expression used to describe South Vietnam after the Paris agreements.

We know what happened to these 1973 agreements: two years later, North Vietnamese divisions massively crossed the demilitarized zone. Thieu ordered a retreat in order to contract and strengthen the defense perimeter. The retreat changed into a rout and, within a few weeks, the Communist Party reached the goal that it had set itself when it launched the war against the French in December 1946, the unity of the three Kys under a Soviet-style regime.

Kissinger presented the Paris agreements as an almost unexpected success. Nixon and his advisers, to the end, refused surrender, that is, the overthrow of the Thieu government that the Americans had supported for years and for which they had fought. To assume the responsibility for dismissing him themselves would have been dishonorable. Dealing with North Vietnam, while leaving Thieu a chance of survival, was an honorable peace. "President Nixon and his advisers do not refuse to 'lose the war' at any price, if the arrival of the Vietcong to power defines defeat; they want to preserve a chance of not losing it and, above all, not to betray their commitments. Imposing a coalition government on Saigon would signify betrayal. And defeat would become a disaster if the United States betrayed or appeared to betray their allies. In any event, they would lose much more than a limited conflict, Vietnam, or face, they would lose the confidence of their friends and the respect of their enemies," I wrote in *Le Figaro* of 30 October 1969. I did not accept, but merely reproduced, the plea that I, like many others, had heard directly from Henry Kissinger. In the same article, I also quoted a few lines from a pamphlet by Robert Kennedy: he also considered an immediate and unconditional retreat of American forces to be impossible and disastrous. "Beyond Asia, a sudden and unilateral retreat would raise doubts about 'the credibility of the United States.'"

I may be asked why I did not recommend the "radical solution" to the United States, while I had favored Algerian independence, or at least the Algerians' right to independence as early as 1957, at a moment when the "rebellion" or the resistance was barely beginning to organize its troops.

In Algeria, the French wanted to maintain all or a part of a colonial situation; I thought that so-called liberal, compromise solutions would also lead to independence. In recommending recognition of the Algerians and their right to independence, I called on the very principles that France claimed to defend and illustrate: the right of peoples to self-determination. There was no comparison to the situation of the United States in Vietnam: the Americans did not want to stay, they wanted to leave. They were protecting a government that was independent, on paper at least. Was this government supported by the people? The answer was not self-evident. Did the people of the South wish to be "liberated" by their brothers from the North? They certainly did not participate in their own liberation; it was a military offensive that cast the Thieu regime onto the rubbish heap of history. Political judgment of this war, it is true, depended also on the capacity of the American Republic to withstand such an ordeal to the end; a mistake, an imprudent strategy, can become a sin for a statesman.

If I had joined my voice to the chorus that exalted the resistance of North Vietnam and angrily attacked American "imperialism," I would have found myself in strange company. The United States, in my view, was committing (or had committed) a mistake by committing their forces and their prestige in the rice paddies of Vietnam. But in 1969, should they morally, could they politically surrender, that is, themselves establish a government subject to Hanoi, a barely concealed communist government? After the fact, perhaps Kissinger would recognize that it would have been preferable for the United States to cut its losses in this fatal adventure in 1969 rather than in 1973. The four extra years aggravated disorder and dissension within the republic. The end result would finally have been less negative. I am not so sure. In any event, Kissinger would reply that, had it not been for the Watergate scandal, North Vietnam would not have launched a general offensive two years after the 1973 agreements. The Paris agreements did not definitively save the Republic of the South, but they implied its existence, which North Vietnam thus recognized for the first time.

Of course, no one celebrated on 26 January 1973. I entitled an article "Will the cease-fire be peace?" and I wrote: "The end of this war or the end of a war? No one can say. The future depends on the intentions and the wisdom of both sides. Thus President Thieu and the Provisional Revolutionary Government will find, if they wish, countless opportunities to accuse one another of violating an agreement that is probably inapplicable and certainly uncontrollable. Let us however forget, just for a moment, the rigors of analysis, without playing the role of interpreter of the conscience of the world, as some of our colleagues like to do, self-proclaimed moral arbiters. Since we all feel a kind of physical relief, let us not shut ourselves off from hope. Perhaps the Vietnamese, left to themselves, will discover together, intuitively, the secret path to peace, that reason alone is incapable of discerning."

Unfortunately, it was reason, again, that taught us the truth.

A few months later, management of the crisis provoked by the Yom Kippur War, further increased the prestige of Henry Kissinger, an *éminence grise* who drew all the light to himself and cast his principal into darkness. The Yom Kippur War divided the French, but it did not provoke passions comparable to those that had troubled them before and after the Six-Day War.

In 1967, I believed that Nasser was principally responsible for the fighting, even though Israel had struck first. In 1973, in my view, the roles had been reversed. Sadat had planned and prepared the operations and taken the Israelis by surprise, but Israeli diplomacy left him no alternative. Divided between hawks and doves, supporters and opponents of Greater Israel, the Israeli political class, incapable of proposing a solution to its enemies, took the path of least resistance; it decided that the Israeli army would remain in place, and it invited the Arab countries to negotiate directly with the Jewish state. Negotiations without preconditions, which would deal with everything at stake in the conflict. The Israelis, of course, were not aware that the Arabs would reject the invitation: after the disaster of 1967, a dialogue would have appeared to the Arabs as a surrender.

I remember a conversation in Jerusalem in 1971 with a semiofficial committee charged with the responsibility of studying the military and political prospects for the next ten years in the region. Sadat, I told them, could not indefinitely postpone the time of revenge; either Egypt would in some sense explode from within, or else it would explode by attacking on the outside, in order to accomplish a success in the absence of which Sadat could not follow the path of peace. Can we not at least grant him a "small victory?" In 1973, this small victory might have become significant.

In an earlier chapter, I have alluded to my diagnosis at the time; the Egyptians surprised the Israelis, crossed the Canal without resistance and resisted the premature counterattack of an Israeli armored brigade, which wanted to destroy the bridgehead. During the early days of the fighting, in a broadcast discussion, I expressed doubt as to whether the Israelis were capable of driving the Egyptians back across the Canal before the cease-fire.

In retrospect, I admire Sadat's strategy and Kissinger's conduct during the crisis. The Egyptian president was cornered: he could not deal with Israel without losing face, he did not believe that he had the necessary means to win a decisive victory over his enemy. He therefore prepared for a battle with a limited objective. By multiplying maneuvers, he, so to speak, lulled the vigilance of the Israelis, and succeeded, as the Israelis had in 1967, in creating a surprise effect. The Israeli army had not been mobilized; the order for mobilization was given only on the morning the Egyptian and Syrian troops attacked. On the Golan front, Israel was served by the heroism and the superior flexibility of a few dozen assault tanks confronting several hundred Syrian tanks. After crossing the Canal, the Egyptian troops would probably have taken the mountain passes if Sadat, against the advice of his military command, had not demonstrated excessive caution. Perhaps the military mistake was determined by political calculation. Sadat needed a military success in order to erase the humiliation of 1967, but he was not counting on revenge equivalent to the disaster of 1967. The great tank battle took place when the Israeli army, totally mobilized, had transferred most of its armored vehicles to the Sinai front. The bold advance of General Sharon, in the center of the front, gave the Israelis the opportunity to encircle the Second Egyptian Army. Kissinger managed to impose a cease-fire before the destruction of the encircled army. He was indifferent to the prospect of a resounding victory for Israel; he delayed the delivery of aid to Israel—he made the decision only on the day that, because of a food shortage, Israel was confronted by genuinely mortal danger.

Who had won? Israel had won in the sense that it had inflicted more losses than it had suffered; in a few more days, it would have put one of the Egyptian armies that had crossed the Canal *hors de combat*. Nevertheless, the Egyptians boasted of their initial successes; the uncertain outcome was enough to create the conditions for a peaceful Israeli-Egyptian settlement, for want of a general settlement with all the Arab states.

My article of 6 November 1973, entitled "Defeat of the Conqueror," provoked some more or less insulting letters from my coreligionists. I recapitulated the criticism I had made of Israeli policy in 1967: "By stationing its army on the Suez Canal, the Jerusalem government was issuing a challenge to the Soviet Union and, to an extent, to Western Europe itself. It was depriving Egypt of Sinai oil and revenues from the Canal. It strengthened the solidarity between Egypt and the rich countries of the Persian Gulf and invited the Soviet Union to increase its commitment; it made it impossible for any Egyptian government to accept the situation indefinitely." I repeated, on the military level, the objections that I had formulated in 1967, in my conversations with Israeli generals, against the establishment of the front on the Canal, a natural line of defense in appearance but not in reality. In 1973, for the first time, the Israelis needed material support from the United States during the hostilities themselves. They obtained it at the last moment, and their dependence on the United States became even more obvious.

Perhaps the fact that struck the Israelis the most, during these days of ordeal, was the refusal of all the Europeans to place their airports at the disposal of the Americans for the airlift—of all the Europeans except for Portugal on the eve of the revolution of the carnations, which allowed the American Air Force to use the Azores bases. For the Israelis, resupply was a question of days, if not hours. None of the major European countries took the risk of irritating the Arabs, oil producers, by however limited a participation in the rescue operation. Henry Kissinger did not conceal his "contempt," his "disgust" at the cowardice of the Europeans. The Europeans in turn felt humiliated; the dialogue between the Great Powers was taking place over their heads, whether that dialogue was leading to collusion or collision.

Henry Kissinger seemed to be an extraordinary manipulator. When the Soviets alluded to the threat of the intervention of airborne troops in the theater of combat, he convinced the president in the middle of the night to place all United States military installations throughout the world in a state of alert. Simultaneously, he took a plane to Moscow and made an agreement with Brezhnev on the cease-fire, which deprived Israel of part of its victory—which the secretary of state had always wished for without saying it. Then, with tireless shuttling between Jerusalem and Cairo, he laid the foundation for an Israeli-Egyptian settlement. At the time, the man who had negotiated with Zhou Enlai, Mao Zedong, Leonid Brezhnev, and Le Duc Tho, and who had always, after hours, days, months, or years, reached an agreement, appeared with the aid of the media, as a miracle man. The leaders of two African countries at war with one another thought of calling on the services of the itinerant diplomat. The Tarpeian Rock is never far from the Capitol.

The quadrupling of the price of oil and the temporary embargo imposed on the United States placed the energy crisis in the foreground. Vietnam, after the withdrawal of American troops, suddenly became a secondary episode in the historical expansion of the Marxist-Leninist movement. Kissinger's attempts to revive the Atlantic Alliance resulted only in bland communiqués. The creation of the Energy Agency was the occasion for a futile battle between Paris and Washington, Michel Jobert and Henry Kissinger. The press reported the excesses of language into which each of the two foreign ministers fell. France refused to be a part of the "Energy Agency": participation or nonparticipation seemed to me equally insignificant. Another academic quarrel developed over the diplomatic methods that should be adopted by Europe toward the United States. Should the United States be consulted before the Common Market nations adopted a common position? The United States did not want to confront a European bloc before its voice had been heard by its allies in the Atlantic Pact. It was in 1974, I think, that I was invited by State Department officials to speak in the Secretary of State Club. The secretary of the club asked me for the title of my talk. After a few moments' reflection, and consultation with the official, I proposed, "Why has the Secretary of State forgotten the ideas of Professor Kissinger?" In fact, Kissinger had no hesitation in writing, in the book published in France under the title *Malentendu transatlantique*, that the United States cannot count on the assent, the automatic acquiescence of a united Europe. The secretary of state had little patience for the inclinations toward independence that the professor had foreseen, and, in advance, considered inevitable and healthy. It is better to have a loyal and difficult ally than a satellite in a state of suppressed rebellion.

The club official had led me to expect an audience of a few dozen; I was awaited by almost two hundred department officers, sitting and standing. Perhaps some of them derived some pleasure from the freedom and irony I used in speaking of their boss. Perhaps as well, like all American audiences I had addressed, they showed their goodwill, their tendency, for the moment, to agree with the speaker—ready, on another occasion to extend the same sympathy to a speaker of a contrary opinion. I remember this occasion, both the speech and the questions, with pleasure.

Diplomatic storms, in themselves, hardly bothered me. The Europeans' refusal to offer their bases for the American airlift to Israel I thought of as a response to American diplomacy, focused on the dialogue with Moscow and Peking, without coordination with the Europeans. The secretary of state's contempt, justified or not, is not suitable for a disciple of Metternich and Bismarck. Moreover, he criticized them for a common declaration—a way of involving themselves in an affair concerning them, but at which they had remained, willy-nilly, mere spectators. Although I think I was excessively indulgent toward the Europeans, I cannot approve Kissinger's arrogance.

My admiration for the manager of the Yom Kippur crisis was qualified by concern over the scope of détente. Of course, the Nixon administration had not initiated the dialogue with Moscow, nor had it been the first to speak of détente. It is nevertheless true that, from 1968 to 1973, public opinion considered the administration responsible. The United States had re-established relations with Peking, improved relations with Moscow, signed the first agreement on the limitation of strategic weapons (SALT 1), and a text that, apparently, set out the spirit in which Moscow and Washington would conduct their external affairs. Two formulas summed up the essential points of this good conduct code: restraint, that is, moderation, and the agreement of the two Great Powers to refrain from seeking unilateral advantages. Taken literally, this text meant that the United States and the Soviet Union were putting an end to their global rivalry. No one, at least among professional commentators, thought in 1972, after Nixon's trip to Moscow, that the Soviet Union would stop supporting or manipulating movements of "national liberation."

The Yom Kippur War at least revealed, to those who had any illusions, the ambiguous character of détente. In November 1973, we did not know whether Brezhnev had urged the Egyptian president to push his troops beyond the Suez Canal. "What we do know is that Brezhnev was not stingy with material: assault tanks, cannons, Sam 3s, Sam 6s, individual antitank weapons. . . . Once battle had been joined, Brezhnev urged the Arabs to action (at least if the letter to President Boumedienne is authentic), and he established an airlift for the resupply of his allies a few days after the outbreak of hostilities, while the United States was still refraining from resupplying Israel. Did the Soviets thereby violate the spirit of détente, the principle of moderation, attempt to gain a unilateral advantage at the expense of their rival? Of course, but it took a good deal of naïveté to take this commitment literally." (*Le Figaro*, 5 November 1979). But in that case, what remained of the code of good conduct signed in Moscow the year before? The Europeans, Michel Jobert in particular, denounced both collusion and collision. According to the expression of the French foreign minister, the Great Powers shook hands above the airlifts.

At the same time, public opinion, perhaps as much in Europe as in the United States, was gradually becoming half-conscious of a change in the balance of forces in favor of the Soviet Union. In SALT 1, the United States had granted the Soviet Union a forty percent superiority in the number of launch vehicles, compensated by the American advantage in numbers of nuclear warheads (thanks to the MIRV technique, which the Soviets had not yet mastered). Three years later, when the Vladivostok negotiations set forth the broad outlines of an agreement, the Soviets had "MIRV" missiles that were superior in throw-weight, the explosive power of nuclear devices. When SALT 2, negotiated under President Carter, was submitted to the Senate, its opponents raised the question of balance. Nixon and Ford had both accepted the principle of equality in strategic weapons, but did American superiority at the highest level in the scale of violence not represent an essential element of American deterrence not for the security of American territory, but for Western Europe?

During the years when Kissinger appeared to be a superman, the Soviet Union became, for the first time, a superpower, a global power able to use its military might in any part of the world. When Ford lost the election, Kissinger returned to private life and wrote his memoirs, but he retained extraordinary prestige in the United States, particularly in Congress. But it is impossible not to wonder whether he had not disguised or transfigured through his talent, the retreat of American diplomacy, the decline of the imperial republic.

In early January 1977, I wrote for *Le Figaro* an analysis which attempted to provide an equitable assessment of his accomplishments and his legacy. I noted first his triumph through the media: "No secretary of state ever gave professional journalists or sensation-mongers so much material, no one ever devoted so much time to them. He was someone who cultivated his public persona. His knowledge of the facts was astonishing, his athletic performances impressive, and his calculated improvisations and outbursts of anger.

By turns accommodating and brutal, he conquered his adversaries through endurance. Israelis and Egyptians surrendered less to his charm than to his physical resistance, to his presence of mind after a sleepless night. . . . But this actor, in both senses of the word, had two strings to his bow, two irons in the fire. When events defeated his hopes, he accused them in the name of history. When Saigon fell and the efforts of four years went up in smoke, he returned to his youthful reading, meditating on the decadence of the West, and the loyal James Reston reported the morose reflections of this 'philosophical brute,' out of place in the circles of Richard Nixon and Gerald Ford, an improbable star who had conquered Washington."

Then, I noted Kissinger's unquestioned talent to manage crises. "Whatever judgment one may make about his global vision, he has been an incomparable manager of crises. In any event, his Machiavellian masterpiece (the adjective is meant to be ambivalent) will remain the Yom Kippur War, which had taken the Israelis by surprise and in which the Egyptians and the Syrians were to win a moral victory, even though their enemy did not really lose." The management of this crisis created the basis on which the Egyptian president launched his peace offensive and startled world opinion by his visit to Jerusalem.

I then came to the essential point: "In the last analysis, what is most important to him, and what will determine the judgment of history, is the global vision which is said to have inspired him and has been demonstrated simultaneously in détente and in his refusal to establish contact with the Italian Communists. In the interest of direct relations between Moscow and Washington, Henry Kissinger accepts Russian domination of Eastern Europe. To maintain the balance between the respective spheres of influence of the two superpowers, he was not above helping the enemies of President Allende in Chile or declaring the historic compromise in Italy unacceptable. A Pole made an ironic remark about this policy: supporting communists where they have made themselves hateful and fighting them where they have gained some popularity. To which he would answer: "How can they be removed from power where they are hateful?""

Kissinger's policies, apart from the rapprochement with China, are continuous with the policies of the United States since 1947, and especially since 1953. The combination of partial agreements with Moscow and resistance to local advances of the Soviet Union defines less Kissinger's method than the unwritten law of American diplomacy for the last thirty years. I nevertheless pointed out the novelty of "détente," or rather the change in the balance of military forces between the United States and the Soviet Union. In this context, it was hardly possible not to raise the question of the underlying inspiration of this balancing act.

When Ronald Reagan and, with him, the most anticommunist wing of the

Republican Party, returned to power, Kissinger was seen by the new administration as the man of détente and the SALT agreements, much more a dove
than a hawk in his actual conduct of foreign affairs.

Was this criticism (or praise) well founded? The answer is not self-evident.
Kissinger gave the impression of being fundamentally different from the
president's entourage, and from the American political class in general, by
his personal qualities, his ability to articulate his views, and his gift for
analysis, leavened by the humor that American journalists (and all American
audiences) find so attractive. Simplifying, one might say that his intellectual
superiority automatically imposed itself.

Does my judgment in 1982 differ essentially from that of 1977? For a half
century, I have limited my freedom of criticism by asking the question: In his
place, what would I do? Could Nixon accept the "coalition government" in
Saigon? If he could not, the prolongation of the war was inevitable. The fall of
Prince Sihanouk was almost a necessary result and hence the spread of
military operations to Cambodia. When I read Kissinger's memoirs, I am not
always convinced by his arguments, but I feel strengthened in my impressions as an observer. The President and his adviser, pressed by internal and
external enemies, attempted to bring about a negotiated peace. To pacify
internal opinion, they gradually brought back American forces; to save the
Republic of South Vietnam, they strengthened its army; to bring the North
Vietnamese leaders to compromise, they used their air force. The Paris
agreements preserved the appearances; in any event, the fall of Nixon cut
short the existence of those appearances.

The approaches to Peking and Moscow did not have to do exclusively with
the search for a way out of Vietnam. In any event, sooner or later, the United
States would have resumed diplomatic relations with Peking, relations all the
more normal and useful because the quarrel between the two capitals of
Marxism–Leninism, public since 1963, offered obvious opportunities to
American diplomacy. Moscow and Peking both aided North Vietnam, without reconciling their differences. The American dialogue with Peking could
influence Moscow's attitude toward the United States and toward Vietnam.

In retrospect, it does not appear that this diplomacy, which remains
completely intelligible, changed the course of events in Vietnam. In 1972,
the Communist regime in the North lacked neither artillery and missiles
against the bombers nor tanks and ammunition for the spring offensive. The
SALT 1 agreements ratified parity between the United States and the USSR;
the good faith requirements set out on paper did not prohibit Moscow from
offering "fraternal aid" to "national liberation" movements. Détente changed
to some extent the style but not the substance of the rivalry between the two
superpowers. If Nixon and Kissinger had not themselves been conducting
the diplomacy of the United States, they would have denounced the illusions

of détente. Thus, Nixon's 1981 book, *The Third World War,* develops a philosophy of international relations far removed from his enthusiasm for détente with Peking and Moscow.

Did Kissinger himself believe in détente, in the network of agreements through which he hoped to restrain and then tame the revolutionary monster? Perhaps, but he added that this policy required a strong, vigilant America, ready to respond to any attempt at aggression or subversion from Moscow. Once this policy appeared to be the expression of a divided America, weary of its imperial burden, it was condemned. Now, from 1973 to 1976, during and after the Watergate scandal, the Senate closely controlled all external affairs. It refused to appropriate the funds that Kissinger wanted to spend to avoid the victory in Angola of the party connected to Moscow and supported by Cuban troops.

Even after Nixon's resignation, while preaching firmness, he continued to advocate détente. He advised President Ford not to receive Solzhenitsyn. When I criticized him for his concern not to offend the sensibilities of the oligarchs in the Kremlin, he answered first: "What would we think if they received our dissidents?" I answered that we did not have the equivalent of their dissidents, and he did not insist on the point. At bottom, Kissinger in power oscillated between two attitudes that he considered, or hoped, to be compatible: on the one hand, the pursuit of the policy of containment in its most resolute form—to prevent Communists from coming to power in Chile, Italy, Angola—and on the other, strategic arms limitation treaties and commercial and technical agreements for Soviet-American cooperation. The Soviet Union as a revolutionary power, had to be contained; the Soviet Union, as one of the two great military powers, aimed to occupy a position in the world in conformity with its strength, and it was appropriate to grant it certain concessions, which the United States, incidentally, did not have the means to block. Resistance to an ideological–military imperialism on one hand, integration of the United States's alter ego into the concert of nations on the other—neither of these ideas calls for criticism. Unfortunately, the two ideas do not demand the same language—weakness can be fatal in a democratic society; and, because of circumstances—Vietnam, Watergate, domestic dissension—Kissinger achieved only imperfect success in both enterprises.

NOTES

1. They demonetarized gold in a certain sense, but the holders of the yellow metal had no reason to attack those who were responsible for this step.

2 4

ON HISTORICAL
CRITICISM

$\mathbf{T}$he two books, *The Imperial Republic: The United States in the World (1945–1972)* and *Thinking about War: Clausewitz,* have little in common, even though they are both derived from courses given at the Collège de France in the academic years 1970–71 and 1971–72. There were other differences between the two. I gave a course on foreign activities of the United States because I had signed a contract with an American publishing house. On the other hand, the course on Clausewitz finally led me to attempt the interpretation of a celebrated book, *On War,* of a strategist, and of his posterity.

My work on Clausewitz amounted to an investigation of the origins (or one of the origins) of modern strategy. The wars of the twentieth century and the atomic bomb have shattered classical ideas, at least in appearance, and have called into question both the art of diplomacy and the art of war.

A. *THE IMPERIAL REPUBLIC*

The Imperial Republic was my first attempt at a work of *history*, indeed the first *narrative* I had written. But how was it possible to present the foreign activities of the United States over the course of a quarter-century? The first difficulty was to establish clear temporal divisions. Could this period be separated from the two preceding centuries? I dealt with this first obstacle in a fifteen-page prologue entitled "The Island-Continent."

The notion of Island-Continent comes from a celebrated English geopolitical theorist, Halford J. MacKinder, who had provided an interpretation in his books, particularly in *Democratic Ideas and Reality*, of the struggle between land powers and maritime powers. A maritime power can maintain its superiority only if it has an economic base sufficient to provide it with adequate resources. Rome triumphed over Carthage because it gained control over the seas. England gained mastery of the seas after it became really an island; it ceased having a potentially hostile neighbor when Scotland was incorporated into the United Kingdom.

I considered 1898 as the end of the period during which the United States consolidated its position as an Island-Continent and the beginning of another, which ended in December 1941, with Pearl Harbor and American entry into the war. It was a curious, diverse, and contradictory period: the victory over Spain both expressed and fostered an inclination toward European style imperialism; the 1917 intervention, the Senate's refusal to ratify the Versailles Treaty, the neutrality laws, do not amount to a system, do not reveal any plan. The United States accomplished its "manifest destiny," it created in America a great English-language empire: In what direction would its ambitions turn? It began a European style colonization with Puerto Rico and the Philippines, but rejected it. In 1917–18, it placed its weight in the scale and determined the outcome of the Great War, Anglo-French victory, and then withdrew. In the 1930s, Congress passed laws intended to prevent the entry of the Republic into the war that they foresaw. The Americans too, on this occasion, entered the future with reluctance.

In chapter 1 of *The Imperial Republic*, entitled "In Search of the Guilty, or The Origins of the Cold War," I spoke as a historian about a period that I had lived through, if not as a participant, at least as a commentator. Twenty years later, do events appear to me in a different light? The "revisionists"—the name given to historians who place principal responsibility for the cold war on the United States—belong to an American tradition. In the United States, there was a revisionist school after the Mexican War, after the Spanish-American War. The first two wars had not had unanimous public support at the time, nor had the 1917 intervention. Ethical or political criticism recapitulated afterward the arguments that had been used at the time against the president of the party in power; it found other arguments as the background of events was revealed and official truths were called into question. The conversion of the Grand Alliance into the cold war had given rise only to a scattered and weak opposition. Resistance to Soviet expansionism had at first been accompanied by an anticommunist fervor that gave birth to McCarthyism, and the hateful "witch hunt," a persecution that was not comparable to the Soviet purges, but was unworthy of a democracy; less a matter of madness than of paranoia.

The second part of the book, "The United States in the World Market," presented different and generally more difficult problems of interpretation. The United States influences other economies in the world market by its existence as much as by its actions. It does not will all the consequences of its actions. To some extent, the analysis was developed on a well-trodden field. Through the Marshall Plan, the United States accelerated the recovery of European economies, just as it helped Japan to rebuild its cities. Later, the Japanese took control of their own affairs. Favored by the modesty of their military budget, they put on seven-league boots and beat all growth records. Fifteen years after the influx of dollars into Europe, the deficit of the American balance of payments replaced the theme of the "structural" penury of dollars. The external action of the United States immediately after the war, the Marshall Plan, the creation of international institutions, in retrospect no longer provoke polemics; it was both generous and far-seeing. "Enlightened egoism," if one prefers.

Philippics against "American imperialism" usually focus on Latin America, for two reasons: it is there that "Yankee imperialism," in the military sense, had been carried on for the longest time. The marines did not evacuate Nicaragua until 1934, when Franklin D. Roosevelt, proclaimed the "good neighbor" policy. It was to the Dominican Republic that Lyndon B. Johnson sent the marines to block a revolution that he feared would enter Castro's orbit. It was in Guatemala that John Foster Dulles launched an expedition to overthrow the left-leaning President Arbenz. Was this an application of containment to the Western Hemisphere? I see it rather as a continuation of the gunboat diplomacy that the American Republic conducted shamelessly in the nineteenth and even in the twentieth century, at the expense of some Spanish-speaking countries. The accusation of economic and political imperialism finds its best arguments in relation to this part of the world.

In both parts of the book, I did not formulate simple judgments, and I refrained as much as possible from making value judgments. With respect to diplomatic and strategic action, I presented it as it had happened, trying to make it intelligible on the basis of the intentions of the protagonists, the logic of the situation, and, inadequately, on the basis of the political system and the public opinion of the United States. In the second part, I attempted as well to analyze what had happened, the decisions that American leaders had taken in the world market and, even more, the external effects of the American economy, simply as a function of its reality. I sought less to judge than to understand; a relatively rare attitude in histories of the past, disappointing and even scandalous when the historian focuses on events that are so close that the feelings of participants and spectators are still alive.

B. *CLAUSEWITZ*

My course of thirteen lectures gave me the opportunity to reread *On War* and to familiarize myself with the literature on Clausewitz. Some officers, French and foreign, came to listen and asked for the text of the lectures, which did not exist. Once again I hesitated about the use of my notes and of the transcripts of my lectures. I decided not to repeat the precedent of the *Eighteen Lectures*, that is, to ask someone else to correct the transcript. My doubts had to do with the kind of book it should be: an essay, or a major work aiming at a general interpretation of Clausewitz. I chose the second. Since *Peace and War*, I had published only essays. The time had come once again to put myself to the test. It was a surprising decision: I was approaching the age of seventy, and a "Marx," or another study on the philosophy of history, would have corresponded more to the logic of my existence and my career.

To justify myself, however, I quoted a sentence from Croce in an article in *La Revue de métaphysique et de morale:* "Only the narrowness and the poverty of the general cultural level of philosophers, their unintelligent specialization, the provincialism, to speak clearly, of their habits of mind, can explain their indifference to, their distance from books like that of Clausewitz." The most celebrated and perhaps least studied treatise on strategy is a legitimate subject of investigation for a philosopher.

I set myself four principal goals: first of all, to present the biographical and historical data that would help to understand the man and the social and psychological context that shaped him; secondly, to illuminate Clausewitz's philosophical method; thirdly, to confront the most difficult and most important problem of interpretation: What did Clausewitz mean in his 1827 preface when he announced the revision of the text in the light of two themes: first, the distinction between two types of war, one whose aim is to defeat the enemy, the other only to carry off some victories on the border; second, the point of view according to which war is only the continuation of state politics by other means. Finally, analysis of the relationships between offense and defense led me toward the arming of the people and people's war. At the end of the course, I commented on the posterity, faithful or not, of the enemy and admirer of Napoleon, and I suggested some of the changes that nuclear weapons imposed, if not on the analytic theory, at least on the pragmatic implications of Clausewitz. The two courses of the following years—*Theory of Political Action* and *The Play and the Stakes of Politics*—continued the same research. The book also borrowed from these two courses.

In the first chapter, I briefly outlined the life of the strategist to whom fate refused the opportunity for a striking victory or a historic initiative. But he was involved in the great events of the Revolutionary and Imperial periods. He was struck, like most of his contemporaries, by the contrast between the limited conflicts and the campaigns of maneuvers characteristic of the eighteenth century on the one hand, and on the other the almost unlimited wars provoked by the fall of the monarch and the mass mobilization. The vagaries of history offered him the fact that was the point of departure, and remained at the center, of his reflection: the link between military and political phenomena. This link has a dual meaning: there is first of all a correlation, of a sociological order, between politics (the regime, the relations between the rulers and the ruled, the principle of legitimacy, and so on) and the way in which armies are organized and the way in which they fight; there is also an almost self-evident norm, the subordination of the conduct of military operations to political goals. War has a grammar of its own, not its own logic. The subordination of the military instrument to the political will took on, in Clausewitz's eyes, such importance that, when he planned a revision of the manuscript, he intended to emphasize the idea even more forcefully.

In order to make his method clear, in the course summary, I presented the first chapter of *On War* in the following terms: "At the outset, the simplest model leads to the theory of the movement toward extremes (*Steigerung bis zum Äussersten*) and of absolute war in conformity with this concept. In a second step, Clausewitz reintroduces the principal elements that the model has neglected: space (a state is not a wrestler, it possesses a territory and a population); time (the outcome of a war or a battle, the fate of a nation are not decided in a single moment); the asymmetry between attack and defense, which takes account of the suspension of operations; finally, politics, which fixes the goal of the war itself and, in consideration of the circumstances as a whole, the presumed intentions of the enemy, and the available resources, determines the plan of the war and the extent of the efforts made." The first chapter, a summary of the philosophy of the entire treatise, leads to a second definition, or rather to an articulation of the internal structure of the phenomenon of war "a strange triad of passion (the people), free activity of the soul (the military leader) and understanding (politics, the personified intelligence of the state)."

I worked on the book from 1972 to 1975 with alacrity, almost with enthusiasm. I spent time in the Bibliothèque Nationale, I read the French and German commentators on the treatise; I took pleasure in rediscovering old quarrels. I did not claim that I was putting an end to the controversies, but I was reconstructing Clausewitz's intellectual path through the various versions of his great work. I plunged into Clausewitz scholarship with the perhaps illusory conviction that I had demonstrated that the revision of Book VIII had preceded the composition of chapter 1, the most complete expression of the strategist's thought. Consciously, I had certainly not given myself a political mission; the idea had not occurred to me to enlist Clausewitz as one of the ideologists of the free world. The book became, in certain narrow circles of West Germany, a target of scientific–partisan debate.

Clausewitz's thought lends itself to two interpretations, which are not contradictory but divergent. Either one considers as the center of his thought the annihilating battle, his contemptuous statements about generals who are afraid of shedding blood, the notion of absolute war (or ideal, or in conformity with its concept), the inevitable movement toward extremes, the formulation according to which an army is never too large, and so on; or else, one focuses on the other side of his thought: war as the continuation of politics by other means, hence the primacy of the statesman over the military leader, the repeated affirmation that absolute or ideal war is the rarest form of warfare in history, that most wars, measured against absolute war, are only half-wars.

Most German military figures who were interested in Clausewitz inclined toward the first of the two possibilities. The victories of 1870 and 1871 illustrated the theory of the annihilating battle. Some interpreters, on both sides of the Rhine, challenged Clausewitz's assertion that defense is the strongest form of combat. A French officer who had his war of glory early in the century, Félix Gilbert, considered the asserted superiority of defense over offense to be in contradiction with the rest of the work.[1] It seemed easy to me to refute the asserted contradiction between the thesis of the virtues of defense and the praise of direct and brutal attack, the mass offense. The texts allow one to consider the course of his thought: a doctrinaire supporter during his youth, of offense, he discovered the resources of the defense in the course of the Napoleonic campaigns, in particular during the Russian campaign, and he more and more emphasized the historicity of war, the variety of wars dependent on the times, and hence the variety of strategies. The two kinds of war, one leading to sovereign dictation of the peace terms after the disarmament of the enemy, the other tending toward peace being granted as a consequence of military actions, present, so to speak, two ideal types, each of which is governed by its political aim and influences the conduct of operations.

If one follows this second side of the thought of Clausewitz one diverges from Liddell Hart, who called Clausewitz "the *mahdi* of the masses and of mutual slaughter," and evoked the "Prussian *Marseillaise*"; one also diverges from the dominant conception of the Prussian or German general staff, which claimed total freedom for the military leader during hostilities, from the declaration of war to the end of fighting (the text of the treatise was falsified to make it say, on this point, the opposite of what it said). But I do not have the impression that I neglected the admirer of Napoleon, the almost aesthetic enthusiasm that he felt for the image of an annihilating battle or the idea of a war in conformity with its concept. As a professional, he admired real war, and he seemed sometimes to feel contempt for quasi-wars, to prefer the heavy épée to the rapier. As a strategist, he never tired of emphasizing the advantages defense presented to the weaker side. As a teacher, he recommended neither total war nor quasi-war. He recommended to heads of state that they not be mistaken about the nature of war; he formulated this recommendation explicitly for the benefit of those who misconstrued the enemy's will to power. But he also wrote that total war is not an ideal to which the statesman or the strategist should aspire, or conform. In one sense, the nature and intensity of war are predetermined by the political context of the conflict; but if this determination left no place for the decisions of the head of state, Clausewitz would assert, implicitly, a total determinism in the context of the war hardly compatible with his exaltation of human will and the hero.

In the second volume, I sketched a history of the readings of Clausewitz, along with an interpretation of the wars of the twentieth century in the light of his concepts. The first chapter, entitled "From Annihilation to Exhaustion," shows how the First World War, which the military commanders on both sides hoped to end with an annihilating victory, was finally won by the coalition that was richer in resources, with the help of the exhaustion of the Central Powers. The second chapter analyzes the Second World War in a similar way. Lenin studied Clausewitz's treatise in Switzerland, and he drew some lessons from it. Thanks to him, Clausewitz became and remains a sacred author in the Soviet Union, quoted and discussed by all military writers. The third chapter begins with the army of the people, and I outline the various stages of the war conducted by ununiformed fighters.

In the second part of the second volume, I attempted to analyze the current situation by using some of Clausewitz's themes. "The debts of deterrence": Clausewitz taught that combat finally resolves credit transactions, like diplomacy and other maneuverings. With nuclear weapons, can deterrence remain effective without the resolution of combat, the exercise of the threats? "War is a chameleon": our century, in fact, presents simultaneously the most varied forms of combat, from the terrorist act to carpet bombing—war has never been so polymorphous, it has never been so omnipresent.

Compared to the twentieth century, the Revolutionary and Napoleonic periods seem to be only a pallid rehearsal for a full-blown spectacle of horror.

The transition between the two volumes, successful according to some readers, artificial or laborious according to others, is open to challenge. But I think it excessive to say, as some did, that hatred was foreign to Napoleonic war. Clausewitz himself points out that combat produces hatred in the spirits of the combatants. It is true that Gneisenau, who hated the French, could not imagine executing prisoners, women, and children, but he wanted Napoleon to be tried before a court. The French occupation of Europe cannot be compared to Hitler's occupation during the Second World War. Clausewitz favored the army of the people even though he foresaw their cruelty, on both sides. I repeated several times in the book the idea that the Napoleonic wars, compared to those of the twentieth century, still seem to us to have been civilized.

NOTE

1. Jean Jaurès used Clausewitz's thesis on defense as the strongest strategy against the French military authorities.

THE DECADENCE
OF THE WEST

I think of the 1970s—until the month of April 1977—as a period of intense activity and psychological peace: there were no polemics comparable to those provoked by the events of May 1968 or the Six-Day War. The Collège de France took most of my time and provided most of my work. The decline of Marxism-Leninism among the higher levels of the intelligentsia, begun with Khrushchev's secret speech to the Twentieth Congress of the Soviet Communist Party, became more pronounced. I was forgiven for my attitude in May 1968 as events faded into the past and the principal protagonists of those heroic weeks sank into the obscurity from which chance had taken them. A new generation of intellectuals arrived on the scene and immediately achieved notoriety; they were assisted by Parisian fashion, itself shaken by the Soviet dissidents, particularly Solzhenitsyn.

My election to the Sorbonne in 1955 had helped me to speak or to write my books about industrial society, international relations, and the major doctrines of historical sociology. My election to the Collège de France rejuvenated me, filled me with new enthusiasm; without the desire to deserve my place in that illustrious institution, perhaps I would not have had the courage to pursue my scholarly research on Clausewitz.

There are thirty years between *Le Grand schisme* and *In Defense of Decadent Europe*. The first corresponded to a need that I felt to analyze, in broad outline, the world situation as I saw it, in order to outline the framework within which my articles for *Le Figaro* would be placed. The *Defense* was born of weakness or inadvertence; I signed a contract with Robert Laffont for a book of vulgarization, designed to point out mainly obvious truths—the superiority of the free market over an economy planned by a centralized bureaucracy, and of the economies of Western Europe over those of the East. I had the illusion that I would write the book in collaboration with my friends. In fact, I wrote the book almost entirely by myself; Jean-Claude Casanova helped me significantly in the revision of the chapter on the Soviet economy and the preparation of statistics.

A half-century earlier, my conversion to sociology had begun with the study of Marxism. I had even considered a study of the intellectual and political posterity of Marx, carried out according to Marxist methods. I would have explained the Marxism of the Second International, essentially social democracy, by means of the socioeconomic context, and simultaneously have shown the influence over the conduct of social democracy exercised by the interpretation of Marx's thought by Engels and Kautsky. I had quickly abandoned the project because Marxist literature, particularly before 1914, was so discouraging. Leszek Kolakowski accomplished this project to a certain extent, but he adopted a non-Marxist method, that of the history of ideas.

In 1977, what struck me and dominated the first part of the *Defense*, was the dialogue between the Soviet dissidents and the more or less Marxist left of the West. Marxism remains the unavoidable philosophy of our time, said Sartre, even when he broke with the Communist Party. To the one whom he calls, ironically, the intellectual mentor of the West, Solzhenitsyn replies: "Marxism has fallen so low that it has simply become an object of contempt; there is not a single serious person in our country, not even among the students, who can speak of Marxism without smiling." Hence the question to which the first part of the book was intended to provide a response: Should we believe Russian exiles or French and Italian intellectuals? What explains the categorical certainty about conflicting interpretations from both sides? What is this doctrine or group of ideas invoked, sequentially or simultaneously, by the executioners and their victims, Bukharin before the tribunal that would send him to his death, as well as Stalin ensconced in his spider's web, Sartre the philosopher of freedom, and Suslov the guardian of Marxist-Leninist orthodoxy? Unlike Western intellectuals, the dissidents used an *ad hominem* argument: we know, because we have lived through applied Marxism. You in the West speculate on the thought of Marx, on his words and his dreams. Experience has taught us what you refuse to accept.

To which Westerners can object that Marxism plays opposite roles in East and West. There it serves to justify power, here to criticize it. The Eastern Europeans attack the doctrine in whose name they are oppressed, Westerners adopt some elements of the same doctrine, because it seems to them a basis for thoroughgoing critique of totalitarianism and a weapon against the most efficient economics, the most liberal societies. Does the Marxism of Marx not bear some responsibility for its posthumous fate?

Young philosophers at the time returned from Stalin to Lenin, from Lenin to Marx, from Marxism-Leninism to Marxism, either to exonerate or to accuse the "master thinker" of socialism. Although I did not present a detailed discussion of the idea of the distortion of Marx's legacy, I did present ways of thinking about the question. Marx's responsibility, I asserted, had to do with the combination of analysis and condemnation of capitalism on the one hand, with a prophecy of the socialist utopia on the other. His analytic tools—surplus value, exploitation—can be applied without distinction to any existing regime, whether property is private or collective, whether surplus value comes through businesses and individual incomes or through bureaucratic class.

The prophecy, contradicted both by the evolution of capitalism and by the experience of the so-called socialist regimes, remains as empty as it was at the beginning: How would the proletariat become the ruling class? Why would the proletariat become the ruling class? Why would collective ownership suddenly produce unprecedented efficiency? What magic wand would accommodate authoritarianism and centralized planning to personal freedom and democracy? What was to replace the market economy other than bureaucratic planning? The mystification began with Marx himself when he called his prophecy scientific.

We can translate these ideas into more abstract terms. The Marxist criticism of capitalism coincides with the criticism of political economy itself, as the subtitle of *Capital* suggests. It condemns interest because of the very fact that interest is not defined as legitimate remuneration for the use of money, but as an element of surplus value. Marx gives the name of commodity form to what we call the market and thus suggests the elimination of the market. In socialism, a stage preceding communism, in which everyone is rewarded according to his contribution, does the market measure each person's contribution to total production? If not the market, what will fulfill this function if not the community itself, with an arbitrariness that goes beyond that of the market?

Should we conclude that Soviet socialism derives logically from the thought of Marx? That it constitutes the authentic realization of the Marxist-socialist idea? Marx the man, who argued all his life in favor of freedom of the press, a rebel by temperament, can with difficulty be imagined as an apologist for a despotic state. But Lenin, who demanded all freedoms in opposition, destroyed them radically when he came to power. In his arguments in the Second International, Marx showed himself to be authoritarian and sectarian, a merciless polemicist against his rivals. The decisive question is of a different order. Does the socialist idea, pushed to the end, with the abolition of market relations, with equality as its objective, not end up necessarily, or at least logically, with a Soviet-style regime? Zinoviev makes this argument, and I would now support it.

The second part of the book compares the economies of the two parts of Europe, analyzes the means of growth of the Soviet system, and its inadequacy; I discuss the ideology of socialism, floating between the Soviet model and the various norms of social democracy; I analyze the theory, or the vocabulary, that presents the West as imperialist by nature because it is the center, the heart of the world economy, and purchases certain raw materials from the Third World, which it processes and without which it would suddenly be paralyzed. "Within the international political or economic system, the reciprocal dependence of nations involves an asymmetry in favor of the strong and the rich. But, if one denominates imperialism the very fact of the dependence of exporters of raw materials on the economic circumstances of the industrialized countries, one will end up by confusing under the same term that inevitable dependence and the use of Soviet tanks in Prague (or, if you prefer, the marines in the Dominican Republic). Propaganda systematically uses this confusion in order to make the Soviet empire stop appearing imperialist, while European countries—including Switzerland—continue to appear in that light, despite decolonization. In the midst of this tumult, one might forget that the fate of the Third World remains linked to the Atlantic nations and not to the Soviet bloc. Underdeveloped countries sell their raw materials to, and buy production equipment from, Europe, Japan, and North America; they receive almost all the aid they insistently demand from the industrialized, capitalist countries. What do they borrow from the Soviet Union, other than the ideology of imperialism, an indictment of all those from whom they have asked for everything and an apologia for those from whom they receive nothing?"

In the third part, one chapter analyzes, with an excess of optimism, the "new rules" of the world economy; a second reviews the specific crises of three Western European countries, Great Britain, Italy, and France; the third touches on the essential, the question that dominates and sheds light on the rest of the book: Is Western Europe, rich, brilliant, and creative, at the same time afflicted by an irresistible movement of decadence? Does it risk perishing as a result of internal disintegration or under the blows of the military empire that extends to the heart of the former territory of the Reich?

The title of the book, *In Defense of a Decadent Europe*, which surprised and did not satisfy Robert Laffont, sounds strange only in an age impregnated with Marxism or, more generally, with progressivism. Since the nineteenth century, the typical man of the left has not broken with his great predecessors; in a sense, he rejects instinctively the hypothesis of a contradiction between the course of history and the aspirations of men of good will.

From the beginning of the century, sociologists and economists had been considering the question of what kind of regime would be implied by public ownership of the means of production and by planning. Max Weber barely discussed the problems of a planned economy, but Joseph Schumpeter often dealt with them, trying to conceive of a rational planning based on the prices, in a free market, of consumer goods. None of the models of a planned economy involved, as a *necessary consequence*, equality of income or the freedom of citizens. In other words, the link between a noncapitalist economy and the values of socialist humanism has a purely ideological basis.

In an essay entitled "On decadence—French self-criticism a century ago and today,"[1] I compared the state of French awareness, before and after the defeat of 1870, with the national debate in 1957, during the last phase of decolonization. Prévost-Paradol's book *La France nouvelle* and Renan's studies on contemporary history reminded us of the partial blindness of writers who strove to be free of prejudice.

After Sadowa, Prévost-Paradol sensed the coming war and defeat. He noted the difference between the growth of the population in France, on the one hand, and in the rival countries, Germany, Russia, Great Britain, on the other. Among nations of the same intellectual level, it is, in the last analysis, size that decides the outcome. He did not believe in the superiority of the Germans in the long term: even exercising hegemony in Europe, the Germans would confront the coalition of the Russians and the Anglo-Americans—a coalition that would close off their access to world politics. Clairvoyant about the future tragedy of Germany, which had arrived too late at the first rank in Europe, he indulged in a dream, which was transformed a century later into a nightmare: a colonized Algeria would provide for France the space and the population in the absence of which it would sink into mediocrity and insignificance. The "natives," repelled but not exterminated, would give way to the colonists.

Ernest Renan argues in favor of colonization with a naïveté that now seems to us to be cynical:

Large-scale colonization is a political necessity of the first order. A nation that does not colonize is irrevocably condemned to socialism, the war between the rich and the poor. The conquest of a country of an inferior race by a superior race that undertakes to govern it is not at all shocking. England has carried out this kind of colonization in India, to the great advantage of India, of humanity in general, and of itself. . . . While conquest among equal races should be condemned, the regeneration of inferior or bastardized races by superior races conforms to the providential development of humanity. Among us, the man of the people is almost always a noble *déclassé;* his heavy hand is much more fit for handling a sword than a servile tool. Rather than working, he chooses to fight, that is, he returns to his original condition.

Regere imperio populos, that is our vocation. . . . Nature has made a race of workers, the Chinese, with marvelous manual dexterity and with almost no sense of honor; govern it with justice, while extracting from it an ample tribute for that government and in favor of the conquering race, and it will be satisfied; a race of workers on the land is the black race; be good and humane toward it and everything will be in order; the race of masters and soldiers is the European race. If you force that noble race to work in a dungeon like the blacks and the Chinese, it will rebel. . . .

Almost twenty years after *On War,* I devoted an entire course at the Collège de France in 1975–76 to the *Decadence of the West.* It was not worth publishing, even after revisions, but I used it here and there in the *Defense.* In the course, I attempted to explain the conditions necessary for an objective use of the term *decadence.* Jacques Chardonne saw in *Le Bonheur de Barbezieux* the masterpiece of the centuries, the excellence of human life. In his eyes, our age represented a perhaps definitive decline. Thousands and thousands of books, hastily produced by uncultured publishers, for readers incapable of appreciating superior and immaterial matters, are precipitating our societies toward coarseness, whatever may be their gross national product.

On the basis of other values, historians saw imperial Rome as decadent in comparison to republican Rome and its rustic virtues. Spengler presents "civilization" itself—the swelling of cities, mercantilism, utilitarian philosophy, the exhaustion of belief—as decadence, the final phase of a culture condemned to ripen and grow old like all living beings. I did not discuss Spengler's arguments; they are not open to discussion since they present themselves as irrefutable. I gave examples of illuminating intuitions, striking comparisons, that instruct or irritate. Whatever our judgment of Spengler, the fact remains that his principal work, essentially written before 1914, already predicted the great wars and vast empires, as well as the diffusion of critical thought, positivist and materialist, with as yet marginal, mystical reaction.

Arnold Toynbee,[2] who had neither the genius, nor the arrogance, nor the anger of Spengler, was in a way inspired by the resemblance between the Peloponnesian War and the 1914 war. From this matrix was derived the eleven volumes of the *Study of History,* which continues the enormous literature devoted to the fall of the Roman Empire, with the originality that the traditional reflection was broadened to a meditation on the fate of all civilizations. Toynbee, too, attempted to discern the pattern of development characteristic of civilizations, while granting each of them a margin of freedom. He created or diffused concepts that have now become banal; collapse or breakdown, times of troubles, battling states, internal or external proletariat, universal empire, universal religion, and so on. If one accepts the parallel—431 B.C., beginning of the Peloponnesian War; 1914, beginning of the degeneration of Europe—the time of troubles was to continue after the two great wars.

Without neglecting these broad perspectives, I restricted myself in the course, and especially in *In Defense of Decadent Europe*, to raising questions about the link between decline and decadence. Decline, defined by the reduction in relative power of a state or a nation, or of the contribution of a collectivity to the great works of humanity, is open to rigorous measurement, to quantitative limitations. The decline of France in the nineteenth century resulted from the relative weakness of the French birthrate in comparison to that of other countries. Similarly, the England of 1860, the imperial, financial, and industrial center of the world, could not maintain its unique position, which had to decline by itself, not through corruption of the imperial metropolis, but by diffusion of the secrets of its preeminence. In the same way again, the United States could not preserve the economic, financial, and military superiority it enjoyed in 1945, when its competitors in the world market had not yet recovered from their destruction, and its rival in international relations had not yet projected its power outside Europe. In each of these three cases, was it a question of decline or of decadence? And what does decadence mean? Machiavelli would have answered: the loss of *virtù*, or the loss of historical vitality; a notion that is certainly ill-defined but one that sociological analyses can clarify and enrich.

In the course, I attempted to criticize the literature dealing with French decadence, which was focused on the 1870 defeat. I noted brilliant formulations: "France is expiating its Revolution" (Renan). It is true that, since 1789, France has found neither a sovereign nor a regime that could be certain of its future and that was recognized as legitimate by the population as a whole; none of them felt sheltered from an accident, much less from military defeat. But the advance that the French had taken in matters of contraception over the other Europeans had nothing to do with the unpredictable occurrences of civil discord. In 1914, but not in 1870, France risked being overwhelmed by the superior numbers of the Germans. In 1870, the imperial army was destroyed in a few weeks; it was smaller[3] than the German army, had an inferior artillery, and a mediocre command. What explains the degradation of the French military? Contemporary historians provide at least the elements of an answer: the recruitment of officers, the contempt to which "intellectuals" were subject in the army; the memory of Napoleon's victories that fostered complacency; the break with the revolutionary and imperial practice of conscription to create a national army. Defeat on the battlefield in 1870 as well as in 1940, is explicable first of all in terms of military mistakes. To accuse the decline of warlike virtues in the French people, as Renan did, was a sacrifice to cheap metaphor. In other respects, he was more clear-sighted and hit the mark: war in our time has become a scientific matter. The generals who conquered Algeria and Marshal MacMahon had no such notions.

The military causes for a defeat are not in themselves a satisfying explanation; they lead the observer toward more general considerations. What explains the progress of military thought in the last third of the eighteenth century and its decline in the nineteenth century? Why were there no real universities throughout the nineteenth century?

The *grandes écoles,* the faculties of law and medicine provided education of quality, but one that was too exclusively directed toward the practical. To each of these questions, sociological analysis would bring at least elements of an answer; all of these elements together would suggest a semiliterary expression (or could be subsumed in such an expression): the society was incapable of meeting the challenges or of reforming institutions that were badly adapted to new phenomena. The decline in population did not necessarily bring about the defeat of 1870; nor does that decline appear to me to be the source of the military and scientific decline of the country.

After 1918, despite the victory, the anxiety of decadence continued to preoccupy the consciousness of the French, at least the most thoughtful among them. In the 1930s, the facade, which was still impressive after the war, crumbled, cracked, and gradually fell into ruin: the economy did not recover from the crisis; the French detested one another; many militants referred to foreign models—Moscow, Berlin, or Rome; by 1933 or 1934, the League of Nations in Geneva no longer meant anything. We lived through the decadence of the 1930s, and we saw its distinctive characteristic: the incapacity of the collectivity to respond to an external threat, because it lacked internal unity. The ruling class had neither understood nor mastered the world crisis. It had passively accepted the rise of Hitler toward conquest and war. The French lacked Machiavellian *virtù,* on which the greatness of empires is based and without which nations perish.

In the first of three television programs in October 1981, I referred to the "decadence" of the 1930s. I received a fine letter from André Fermigier; he, too, referred to the 1930s, of which he had a shining memory: "On another point, I listened to you with a certain surprise. This was when you spoke of the obsessive feeling of decadence that you experienced in the prewar years. Perhaps because of the lack of awareness of extreme youth, I have a rather more luminous memory of the time, and I often say that if you did not know

France before 1940, you do not know the joy of being alive. The kindness of people, the ease of life (I am not the son of an archbishop), the extraordinary beauty of everything, and the presence of civilization everywhere. Of course, conflict was present, about which little could be done, but there was also such an aspiration toward happiness, and such real, existing happiness: this is no doubt why the French did not want to fight (while the Germans had so little to lose). And I am not talking about the memory of a permanent cultural festival left by prewar Paris: Renoir, Jouvet, the *Nouvelle Revue Française*, the Opéra of Jacques Rouché, the French cinema *(heu! quantum mutatus ab illo!)*, Leiris, Gide, Montherlant (yes!), and even people who have since then driven me to distraction, what do we have that is comparable to offer today? Even in the harshly criticized exposition of 1937, there was more good architecture than in everything that has been constructed in France (and Europe) for the last thirty years. I thought of this while looking at the Martin du Gard exhibition at the Bibliothèque Nationale: toward the end, those are your years. Once again, I see the conflict, but where is the decadence?"

Fermigier correctly reminded me of the ambiguity of the notion of decadence. When he evokes "the reality of happiness," he forgets the harshness of workers' lives in 1933–36, and after the joyous exaltation of 1936, the fall into bitterness, the strikes, and the social tensions that left little room for happiness. Are things so very different as far as culture is concerned? The "renewed" France of the postwar period may perhaps be found wanting in comparison to the "decadent" France of the 1930s. Yes, we know that the novel, painting, the works of the mind and of art do not always flourish in the sunlight of military victories, no more than they always decline in the shadow of defeat. French painting in the nineteenth century continued through all regimes, perhaps influenced by glory or misfortune, but always creative and striking. Doctrinaire adherents to the theory of decadence generally tend to attribute the same fate to the polity and to its culture. The only people that can now be called imperialist, the Great Russian people, is certainly not experiencing a Periclean century. Perhaps the Paris of Jouvet shone with a brighter light than the Paris of Patrice Chéreau (and I'm not even sure of that). It may be that nonfigurative painting is approaching exhaustion, and no one will defend the cause of contemporary architecture. But the France of the 1930s, ignored the external world. How many books taught it its place in the world, the decrepitude of its economy, indeed of its universities and its science (with a few honorable exceptions)? The political and economic press of the 1930s was oddly feeble.

After 1945, despite the colonial wars, despite the loss of the empire, the French displayed a vitality entirely different from that of the prewar years. Misfortune was a better schoolmaster than the intoxication, short-lived, of a victory that had been too dearly bought. To be sure, our country participated in the "miracles" of European prosperity, although it was not in the front rank during the "trente glorieuses." The fact remains that a book by a Swiss historian, *A l'Heure de son clocher*, which was already something of a caricature when it was published thirty years ago, refers to a France that has disappeared. For better or worse, we have joined our century: industrialization, urban sprawl, the end of the peasants, computerization. Mathematics triumphs over the humanities. The French of the 1980s, the young, the bureaucratic elite who have spent time in American universities, the journalists, are no longer ignorant of the world. *Frankreichs Uhren gehen nicht anders.*[4]

In 1975–76, I outlined an analysis of the decline of Great Britain, and I attempted to take into account the relative influence of three evils, vague but obvious: the pride of success, the weariness of the inheritors, the handicap of being first. It goes without saying that these evils do not lend themselves to rigorous discrimination, but the effects of each of them are quite obvious. It is painful to liquidate an industrial sector that had experienced moments of glory (naval construction). Knighted entrepreneurs had developed a taste for the aristocratic life style and did not undertake the conquest of markets with the vigor of their fathers. A ruling class that has elevated its country to the pinnacle does not immediately recognize the first symptoms of decline.

In *In Defense of Decadent Europe*, I considered only the last phase of the decline of England. During the last quarter of the nineteenth century, it was Germany that took the lead in the rapidly expanding industrial sectors: chemistry and electricity. Between the wars, the management of the economy from 1919 to 1931, and the diplomatic reaction to the Hitlerian menace from 1933 to 1939, demonstrated blindness and weakness. After 1945, the decolonization carried out by the English seemed exemplary to us, on the other side of the Channel. But a rate of growth only half that of the principal countries of the continent brought about a decline of the United Kingdom in comparison to its traditional partners and rivals.

Decline *or (and)* decadence? Rates of growth do not measure the virtues of a community; the quality of life and of relations among people does not suffer from the relative slowness of economic expansion—on the contrary. That said, those who are nostalgic for Barbezieux or for villages nestled around the church tower may very well curse our century of steel and computers; economic performance, in our time, has become one of the clearest indicators of the *virtù* of a people, of its capacity for collective action. Tomorrow, if the per capita gross national product of the United Kingdom were to fall below that of Spain would British civilization, whose charm we feel as soon as we set foot on the island, resist class conflict and the emigration of the elite?

The paradox of the title—a brief in favor of decadence—can be explained by the contrast between the two Europes. If Western liberties were opposed to the effectiveness of the Soviet world, the situation would conform to the clichés of universal history: free Europe would represent Athens, and Marxist Europe Sparta (or, respectively, Greece and Rome). But the productivity of labor was found on the side of freedom; the other side, which laid claim to the ideology of abundance, reduced its population to rationing. Soviet Europe excels only in weapons; and even there it should be noted: excellence in the accumulation of weapons, in the high percentage of the gross national product devoted to the defense budget. Thus, the ambiguity of the title and of the book was identified with the ambiguity of the fate of Europe and of the West.

Although each of the nations of Western Europe continues to live through its own experience, it seems to me legitimate to consider them as a whole, as an object of analysis. The kinship of culture, by which Marcel Mauss defined a civilization, can clearly be observed among the countries of the European Community, in all its phases. Ethnic differences and differences in family structure persist, but social institutions (unions), economic institutions (business enterprises and the role of the state), and political institutions (parties and democratic representation) can be found in every country, essentially similar, though marked by a particular tradition in each country.

The European entity, now limited by the Soviet empire, was the nursery of Western culture, the agency of its expansion throughout the world. The maritime empires established in succession by the Spaniards, the Portuguese, the Dutch, and the English belong to the past. Retreat was even more rapid than expansion. In the East, the Romanov empire, now the Soviet Union, projects its shadow over yesterday's conquerors, deprived of their conquest; in the West, the Europeans have left in the Americas states comparable to the colonies the Greek city-states established throughout the Mediterranean. Of these colonies, the United States, favored by contiguous space, without hostile neighbors to the north or south, remains the chief representative. Between a military empire that has been superficially westernized and a colony that has become the heir of all Europe, the entity made up of nations that were once great, still more conscious of their particular vocations than of their common fate, is going through a difficult phase after the thirty years of postwar prosperity, incapable of defending itself, dependent on energy and raw materials transported over oceans that it no longer controls.

Europe has reestablished its place in the world market but not in the realm of international relations. Despite the Treaty of Rome, despite the progress of economic and even of diplomatic cooperation, the European countries do not attempt to act in common in the principal task of a state, defense. Perhaps the Europe of nations, which owed its prosperity to the plurality of states, and which certainly owes to the great wars the brutality of its collapse, is no longer capable of recovering the status of a subject acting on history. To be integrated into the imperial zone dominated by the United States, or to be dominated, if not absorbed, by the Soviet military empire— this seemed to me the historic choice confronting Europe when I reflected on decadence in my course of lectures or when I wrote *In Defense of Decadent Europe*.

The decline of the United States, from 1945 to 1975, flowed from irresistible forces. Economic supremacy and nuclear monopoly could not last. The leaders of Washington had wished for and fostered the recovery of European economies; the rise of Japan, as well, had its place in the vision of the world that inspired American diplomacy. How could that diplomacy have prevented the oligarchs of Moscow from accumulating weapons and manipulating their clienteles and their networks of terrorists? What I observed as early as 1975 was the threat of disintegration of the American imperial zone, which Toynbee perhaps assimilated to a universal empire.

For the United States, as well as for the European states, the question of decadence has to do with the *capacity for collective action*, hence with institutions and political and economic practices. Without formulating a categorical judgment, I noted symptoms of the disease now known as the English disease, but one which, to one extent or another, affects all the Western democracies: excessive power of lobbies, pressure groups, unions; weakening of the ideas or prejudices that hold a community together, and of the work ethic, which had appeared to be at the heart of American success; excess of legalism, that degenerates into abuse of the judicial process; preference of universities and scientists for basic research, relative lack of interest in the conversion of discoveries into commercial assets. In any event, the founding fathers of the American republic were not concerned to provide the Republic with the means for a worldwide diplomacy; as the degree of military superiority over its partner-competitors declines, the United States is no longer capable of assuring the security of the members of the imperial zone. The East Coast ruling class, which controlled policy after the war, split and committed suicide over the Vietnam War. The center of the United States has moved west, away from the old continent.

To conclude the course, I contrasted two panoramic views of human history, leading to two diagnoses of the current situation. According to one, two centuries ago in England, there occurred the most radical mutation in human society since the neolithic revolution; we are entering the third century of the industrial era; more or less rapidly, more or less painfully, the rest of humanity will join us; the United States remains the pioneer, but it risks losing its leading role, like Great Britain a century earlier. What men have done in the last two centuries, despite wars, they will continue to do. A century or two from now, they will stop following this path and will look for other reasons to live.

According to the other view, the European West, in the shadow of a military-ideocratic empire, is living a precarious existence, without will, without strategy. The American West is moving away from its European origins and losing the convictions that united an ethnically diverse population. The near future is not Atlantic civilization, but the reunification of Europe under an imperial authority that would pervert its culture and its inspiration.

In truth, these two views are not directly opposed; one includes continents and centuries in a perspective of the history of humanity, the other refers to only a fragment of humanity and a few decades. Optimism à la Herman Kahn does not exclude the disappearance of some peoples or the spread of totalitarianism. Pessimism about the survival of Western civilization does not exclude, in turn, the pursuit of the scientific and technical adventure. The notion of decline, as I used it, is entirely relative; the notion of decadence, applied to contemporary England, designates the inability of a nation to shake off its indolence or to reform its institutions or its habits. But the average Englishman lives better today than at the time of imperial splendor. The disintegration of the American imperial zone would resemble only distantly the fall of the Roman Empire. Separated from Europe, the American West would not enter an age of barbarism. Separated from the United States, Western Europe would fall under the Russo-Marxist-Leninist yoke. For how long? In what form? Is Sovietism an aberration or a necessary outcome of industrial or scientific societies in which transcendental religions and even the traditions of civility die?

A circumstantial book, attributable to the thoughtless signature of a contract, *In Defense of Decadent Europe* did not renew themes I had already treated. I thus accepted without protest, even within myself, the reactions that amounted to saying: "We already know all that," or "he already explained all that."[5]

NOTES

1. Published in *Espoir et peur du siècle* (1957).

2. Toynbee calls "civilization" what Spengler called "culture." Spengler gives the name "civilization" to the penultimate phase of development of all "cultures."

3. For institutional reasons, not because of differences in the populations of Prussia and France.

4. Herbert Lüthy's book, entitled *La France à l'heure de son clocher* in France, was called *Frankreichs Uhren gehen anders* in Germany: French watches work differently.

5. I should add that the reception was favorable in France and elsewhere. *Encounter* published a summary of the book that impressed Henry Kissinger.

The Reprieve

1977–1982

26

EMBOLISM

I left *Le Figaro* in the month of May 1977, but I would not have thought of this date as the beginning of the "reprieve" had it not been for an embolism in the month before that changed me for good. At the conclusion of my course at the Collège de France on "The Marxism of Marx," on the eve of leaving *Le Figaro*, eager for a new departure, unconcerned about my age, I felt myself suddenly a *Dasein Zum Tode*. Death, which had been an abstract notion, became a part of my daily existence.

I had a sudden attack and was promptly transported to the Cochin hospital. I had lost the ability to speak and write. Conscious—I would like to say fully conscious, but can I be sure?—unable to communicate, I indicated by gestures that I wanted paper and pencil; with great difficulty, left-handed, I wrote three words: *dying not afraid*. The intern on duty replied smilingly that there was no question of that. Was I playing a role? I don't think so; having suddenly become a spectator—a spectator of my body and my paralyzed speech—my self, my *pour-soi*, my "soul" resisted everything, apparently intact (an illusion, of course). The head of the service returned that very evening from the country and assured me that I would recover the faculty of speech, at least its essentials. The same evening I heard the three or four doctors discussing the situation: was my face twisted? They could not decide whether it was twisted toward the left or the right; their dialogue amused and reassured me. In the course of the evening, I spoke a few words. Doctor Monsallier told me later that, in a half-sleep, I had spoken in German. In the morning, for a few moments, I spoke again as though nothing had happened. This moment of grace did not last. The recovery of speech and writing demanded several weeks—an imperfect recovery.

According to the doctors, a blood clot had formed in an auricle of my heart because of a very slow pulse (50 to 55) and a cardiac arrhythmia. The attack was not the result of the rupture of vessels in the brain; the arteries were in the condition that might be expected at my age. If I could correct the cardiac arrhythmia, which I had already experienced and if I took precautions against coagulation of the blood, I could lead a normal existence. As for speech, it would return by itself, little by little, with benign after-effects.

I have a few memories of these first days in the hospital. The hospital neurologist came to see me. He showed me two objects: a *cap* that covered a bottle of mineral water and then the bottle's *neck*. I could find neither of the words, which I will never forget. He asked me to pronounce *extraterritoriality,* I suppose one of the most difficult words in the language. Despite these three failures, he said he was optimistic. I would be able to teach my course at the Collège de France in the following year.

Every time I remember this brief day of aphasia and the long days of deficient speech, I wonder why I suffered less than I would have imagined beforehand. When I told my friends of my experience, they all replied: "It must have been horrible." But, with complete sincerity, I said that it had not. From vanity? From insensitivity, pride, will? I don't accept any of these reasons. My self had suddenly taken up a position outside my body, and it was wondering, with more curiosity than serenity, what resources it would preserve. I should add that the next day a partial return of speech allowed minimum communication.

In a sense, I had more difficulty adapting myself to a partial and definitive deficiency than to the first shock itself. As early as fall 1977, I subjected myself to the test of improvisation on television. Before my accident, I had not agreed to participate on the program *L'Homme en question*. If I remember correctly, the program lasted for an hour: first a self-portrait of about twenty minutes, followed by a debate, usually with two attackers and two defenders. Roles were sometimes reversed. Anne Sinclair, thinking me capable of defending myself, confronted me with Maurice Duverger, Nikos Poulantzas, Philippe de Saint-Robert, and Alain de Benoist. The self-portrait, recorded in the professors' room at the Collège de France, was reduced to a monologue. The work was completed in the afternoon. Bernard

Bonilauri and Anne Sinclair seated next to me, asked or were supposed to ask questions. They did not have the opportunity. At the time, I was more concerned with form than with content. I stumbled over only two or three words in the course of this half-hour dialogue.

The discussion with my four interlocutors did not leave me with a pleasant memory. Poulantzas did not miss the opportunity for an attack against me, indispensable in the circumstances for a man of the left; if only to secure forgiveness from his comrades for having participated in the broadcast. A few years earlier, Philippe de Saint-Robert had written an article full of insults, in the style of Léon Daudet, without Daudet's truculence and talent. His physical presence repelled me even more than his writings. He reminded me of the Action française troops which disgust me, and he made me feel once again that these nationalists or reactionaries belong to a universe in which I could never breathe. Alain de Benoist played his part without an excess of aggressiveness. I barely remember the remarks from Maurice Duverger, critical but courteous.

In the course of the improvised discussion, I was stopped only twice by lapses in speech. The word "caricatural" refused to come out of my mouth; I did not insist and satisfied myself with "it's a caricature." My close friends and doctors who were interested in me were watching for typical symptoms: inversion of syllables, one word for another, a difficult word badly pro-nounced. The ordeal brought me some comfort: I was not barred from speaking in public. Of course, the time had long passed when, after the *agrégation*, the president of the jury had cautioned me against the rapidity of my speech, the risk that my students would not understand me. This rapidity had declined by itself. My facility of speech had in part resisted the passage of time. After all, the *Eighteen Lessons, Main Currents of So-ciological Thought,* even *The Elusive Revolution* had been spoken. What now remains of this luck that had allowed me, in the midst of my other obligations, to multiply lectures in French, English, or German, without a prepared text, with only a few notes or a brief outline in front of me?

In the 1977–78 academic year, I concluded, without ceremony, my teach-ing at the Collège de France. For the first time, instead of twenty-six lectures, I devoted half the required time to a seminar on "social justice," while the remaining thirteen hours of the course were titled "Liberty and Equality." I carried out the program to the end, noting that in the course of an hour I regularly stumbled over a few words, not always over difficult words that worried me beforehand—a fear that often proved self-fulfilling—some-times over an ordinary word that suddenly caught me short.

I had agreed to give a lecture at the London School of Economics, more precisely to students who published a journal of international relations, a lecture that took up the theme of the Auguste Comte Memorial Lecture delivered twenty years earlier, in the same basement lecture hall, on the theme of "War and Industrial Society." I did not risk improvising the lecture. Ralf Dahrendorf presided over an audience that was as large as, perhaps larger than, twenty years earlier. The speaker had changed; the lecture on the same subject, with the notation "a reappraisal," was not as good as the old one; instead of improvising and multiplying jokes that came to me spontaneously, especially when I was addressing an English or American audience, I read my text that had been written directly in English, incapable of freeing myself from my manuscript. To increase my misery, I was hoarse, and after a few minutes I gave the impression that I was fighting desperately not to lose my voice. Before the embolism, I had suffered from hoarseness at the Collège de France; cold affected my voice, a new problem for me. The same year, in the autumn of 1978, I gave the Alastair Buchan Lecture, named in memory of the founder of the Institute for Strategic Studies, who held the chair of international relations at Oxford. There too, I read, with a hoarse voice, a text that I had written in French. The ordeal was difficult, even more difficult for me, I think, than for the audience. Preparation for these two lectures had cost me a number of weeks, out of proportion to the result.

After five years, what remains of this temporary aphasia? For obvious reasons, I am a bad judge, according to the circumstances ready to dramatize my errors or forgetfulness, or on the contrary to convince myself that the ease of speech that had struck friends of the family when I was young survived the attacks of age and the wandering blood clot. I might set up the following assessment.

I need to be stirred by the public. I make more mistakes in private than in public; a monologue is easier for me than a dialogue. For several months after 1977, as the after effects of the attack persisted, I went to consult an orthophonist, a young, pretty, and charming woman; she had me read a difficult text, full of unusual words (by Bosco or Giono I think). To my own surprise, I read several pages without a lapse. The conversation lasted for a half-hour; there were two minimal "accidents" in all. The orthophonist dissuaded me from formal rehabilitation. Those who submit themselves to reeducation exercises do not even aspire to the level you have already reached, she told me. Perhaps she was taken in by my success; the examination itself had mobilized me.

I gradually recovered my former mastery—limited, of course—of English. I delivered a lecture at Oxford in 1981; I improvised it without looking at my notes. The preceding year, I had similarly improvised a lecture on Soviet diplomacy, at the Royal Irish Academy, where there were no mishaps to shake my composure. On the other hand, I remember with embarrassment confusions about the calculation of standings in tennis in the course of the television program with Anne Sinclair.

The hardest loss was that of German: I have few opportunities to speak German and, for lack of practice, even before 1977, I may not have been capable of improvising a lecture in that language. I still remember with some pleasure the lecture I read in Tübingen in 1965, on the occasion of the centenary of Max Weber's birth. The German Society of Sociology, to avoid possible arguments among its members, asked three foreigners to deliver the three major lectures: Talcott Parsons, Herbert Marcuse, and me. Parsons had been a student at Tübingen and knew German; he pronounced each separate word correctly, but the music of the sentence, the distribution of tonic accents escaped from him to such an extent that his reading of the lecture became strictly unintelligible, for foreigners as well as Germans. In a review, *Der Monat* contrasted the quality of my German with the failure of Parsons, who had wanted to honor his hosts by speaking their language; in recognition of this gesture, the audience had listened in silence, without stirring and without understanding, for nearly an hour and a half.

I can do without German; however, there were occasions on which I did feel the loss. In 1974, I had been elected to the Order of Merit for Science and Art, and I could improvise a response in German to the chancellor's welcoming speech. In 1977, I was supposed to deliver the speech presented by one of the members of the Order at the annual meeting. I had to excuse myself at the last minute; the invitation was renewed; in 1979, I accepted and read my text, with some difficulty but without making a fool of myself. I stumbled over difficult or long words. When I received the Goethe Prize in Frankfurt in 1979, my speech humiliated me; on reflection, my text seemed mediocre, and I read it even more badly than I had anticipated. Why have I not recovered German, which I had learned before English and which I knew much more thoroughly? Was it for lack of exercise, since reeducation consists of speaking? Is there a connection between the part of the brain affected and the storage of German? I don't know, I don't even know whether the second hypothesis can be taken seriously.

Am I excessively humiliated by these "speech problems," to use the vocabulary I had learned as a student? Am I wrong not to let go? How many of my "dear colleagues" whisper to each other: if the articles weren't signed by Raymond Aron, would readers appreciate them as they feel obliged to do? Yes, I was tempted by the example of Romain Gary but, for a journalist, such an attempt—borrowing someone's name to see if my writings would be appreciated if they were signed by an unknown author—would not, it seems to me, have any meaning. An editorialist or a columnist does not make an impression with one or two articles, the way a writer, who, with a single novel, can obtain the respect of the critics or the favor of the public. Even though, on *Combat*, I had the opportunity to write a successful series of articles on the political parties that immediately gained me the status of editorialist, it is only in the long run that the journalist earns his stripes, readers, and the attention of the governing classes. As for my collaboration on *L'Express*, I would say that a few articles—on the "new right," on *Le Monde*, on the terrorist attack on the rue Copernic—give me more confidence than the weekly editorials.

My writing, also, is from time to time disturbed by lapses, substitutions of one word for another, and even spelling mistakes. Luckily, errors in writing can be corrected without the reader suspecting. Errors in writing pique my curiosity. Are they accidental, or are they open to Freudian interpretation? In letters, the most frequent mistakes have to do with possessives, our for your, mine for yours. I rarely manage to discern a suppressed desire, an unavoided intention, bad faith. I imagine that, in this case, even a psychiatrist would concede the likelihood of a physiological explanation.

When I returned from the hospital, was I afflicted with anxiety about irremediable damage? Concern, to be sure, but not, I think, anxiety. Should I attribute to myself a certain strength of will, a tendency toward egocentrism, or naïve vanity? What explains my conduct in my eyes, a few weeks after the shock was the total continuity of my consciousness, of my "I"; my brain had been wounded, not me; the center of speech had been affected, not the center of thought; my right hand had become clumsy, but the infirmity of the tool did not affect the artisan. On one particular point, I had reason to be concerned. My writing is relatively abstract, more than is usually true even in the kinds of books I write. Abstract style tends toward a limited vocabulary. There was reason to fear that that limitation would increase.

I have not recovered, even today, the poetry that I used to know by heart. I have not maintained my spontaneous memory, of words or of lived experiences. On the other hand, the intellectual system, within which ideas and events are set—developed over the course of the last forty years, solid in 1977—essentially survived, I believe, the malignity of the blood clot. One day I attempted to remember a few lines of *La Jeune Parque:* "Tout-puissants étrangers, inévitables astres / qui daignez faire luire . . ." I had to refer to the text (in fact a copy in Simone Weil's handwriting that she had given to my wife). Fixed expressions still elude me.

All that said, I tried in some sense to live as I had before.

I remember the years 1976–77. At the Collège de France, the course on "The Marxism of Marx," despite its obvious imperfections, promised to produce a substantial essay on what, after so many years, I had come to consider as the kernel, the heart, of a thought that was as ambiguous as it was rich. The morning of that April day. I spoke with Joseph Fontanet as though, at seventy-two, I could still plant a tree, undertake a risky enterprise. I am convinced that, in any event, I would not have launched this unreasonable attempt, but the fact that I considered it seriously recalls my state of mind. At the time, I did not exclude the possibility of writing the two volumes that were supposed to follow *History and Dialectic of Violence*, and also a final volume on Marx himself. I believed that I still had enough time and the necessary strength. After April 1977, I questioned the time I had remaining and the strength that the cursed clot had left me.

A subtle change had taken place in me. Even though, in my inaugural lecture at the Collège de France, I had written that for me the game was up, I doubt that I thought so without reservation. I had not said it out of hypocrisy or coquettishness. At sixty-five, of course, the game is up, or *almost*. Reason did not dwell on the *almost*, but my emotional consciousness, so to speak, felt nothing but the *almost*. Of course, I was not going to renew my speculations on the theory of history, but these two volumes would complete the circle. From *Introduction to the Philosophy of History* to *The Historical Condition of Man*. Instead of summary presentations of Marxist thought, instead of polemics against the Parisian Marxisms, a synthetic analysis not of *the* Marxist thought, but of *various tendencies* of that thought, the origin of the historical movements that call themselves Marxist.

During the year 1978–79, my first year without university obligations, aside from various articles I had promised or to which I committed myself, I began to reflect again about a continuation of *History and Dialectic of Violence*. My plans were not yet set. During the summer of 1979, I wrote the first chapter of each of the three books I was thinking about: Marxism, philosophy of history, memoirs. The three essays demonstrated to me that unless I was going to make an extraordinary effort on myself, or rather against myself, I ought to choose the third. Not out of conscious choice but spontaneously, left to itself, my "I" wished to evoke my past.

Of all the projects, it was also the one that required the least intellectual effort. I did not ask myself whether my reluctance to talk about myself had authentically been transmitted into a need to confess. My close friends wondered if I would be able to write in a manner that was entirely new to me. I began, then, to recall the distant past without a firm determination to go on to the end. I asked Bernard de Fallois to read the first part, and he assured me that this combined evocation of events and opinions would interest a public, perhaps even the young, who know the last half-century only through biased history books or legends propagated by the victors. It is thanks to him that I reached the end.

2 7

L'EXPRESS

The rumor of my departure from *Le Figaro* was already circulating in Paris when I was temporarily incapacitated. The conversation I was supposed to have with Sir James Goldsmith on that April day took place three weeks later, after my stay in the hospital. I was once again speaking with enough ease to create the illusion of normality. I remember from one conversation the word "megalomania" or "megalomaniac," which stubbornly refused to come out of my mouth. Sir James, Jimmy as everyone on *L'Express* calls him, strikes one first of all by his intelligence. I do not subscribe to the idea that Alain liked to comment on: in the last analysis, everyone has lived the life he has chosen; but I can easily support an attenuated argument, an obvious one, even though it may be expressed in a paradoxical vocabulary: *success is always deserved*. Or else, success is explained uniquely by good fortune.[1] Sir James has become a great capitalist because he decided to earn a lot of money and because he had a tool of the highest quality, his intelligence. During the course of my first few months on *L'Express,* he held a meeting almost every week, in the course of which he discussed the preceding issue. He was mistaken as often as the others, if only because of his lack of experience with the press, but his criticisms and his often pertinent suggestions could rarely be ignored.

After my experience on *Le Figaro*, I was above all apprehensive about the proliferation of meetings, consultations, clans, fiefdoms, or quarrels. After *Le Figaro* and the physical shock of the month of April, I could have called an end to more than thirty years of journalism and devoted myself to my books. Since we had never changed our style of living—that of a mid-level civil servant—articles published in provincial newspapers through the agency of Opera Mundi were sufficient to supplement my income. Would this withdrawal from public life give me the time and the courage to write one or the other of the books I had planned? I was not sure. Much more, such a withdrawal would accentuate my lack of interest provoked by the proximity of death. I know that this lack of interest could also be characterized as serenity or wisdom. I thought, and I still think, that such an attitude on my part would have been a sign of abdication.

I have congratulated myself on my choice of *L'Express*. Would my existence have been more pleasant, richer, on *Le Point?* I don't know. I will simply say that once my role in the magazine had been clearly defined and strictly limited, everything worked out perfectly. Sir James himself let me know that I did not have to attend the editorial meetings dealing with the successive stages of putting the magazine together; it was gradually understood that the Monday meetings of the editorial committee would rarely have to do with the content or the direction of the last or the next issue. An editorialist, I assumed some responsibility as president of the editorial committee; but that responsibility, except for a few incidents, caused me no qualms of conscience.

On the eve of the 1978 elections, Sir James gave me a thankless task: to reread the texts of articles and to discuss them if they seemed incompatible with the officially defined line. He had forgotten to inform me that Olivier Todd had demanded and obtained in writing the right to compose editorials with a socialist slant. The result was a nightlong verbal squabble, interrupted by telephone conversations with Jimmy, who was in the Caribbean and threatened to cancel the next issue. *Le Canard Enchaîné*, in its usual style, commented on the incident; I did not appear in the best light.

The crisis came in May 1981. On the evening of 10 May, I came to the office with my grandchildren; I wanted to dictate the editorial I had written in advance on the victory of François Mitterrand. Jimmy was engaged in a discussion with Jean-François Revel, the editor, and other journalists. I did not feel the storm coming. The communiqué by Giscard d'Estaing on "premeditated betrayal," and the gathering of the former majority under the direction of Chirac, made it impossible for me to publish the article I had prepared. I was scheduled to go to the hospital on Tuesday the twelfth for a minor operation (removal of a diverticulitis from which I had been suffering for months, perhaps years, but which was causing me more and more discomfort). On the afternoon of the eleventh, I met Olivier Todd, agitated, beside himself; he blurted out that Jimmy had shown him the door. I had little knowledge of the underlying or superficial causes of the conflict between the owner and the staff that he had chosen. Once I was in the hospital, I called *L'Express* to make sure that my editorial would not be published— which had nothing to do with the crisis of the magazine. I convinced my friend Monsallier that my presence in the hospital on that Tuesday was not essential, since all the analyses would be done on the following day. I returned to *L'Express* and I had a two and a half hour conversation with Jean-François Revel and Jimmy. I did my best to calm passions.

Jimmy agreed without too much difficulty that *L'Express* could not and should not become the equivalent of a *Nouvel Observateur* of the right. For two reasons, each of which was equally decisive: one joined the left as one joins a religion; at the present time, there is no right comparable to the left, with the exception of the "new right," which has been excommunicated by the political establishment. On the other hand, many of the journalists come from the left and would not create a weekly designed to fight against the socialist government. In this conversation, Jimmy thought that Olivier Todd would remain on *L'Express*, but no longer as editor in chief, closest to the director, with whom he worked closely and on whom he certainly had some influence.

As for me, I had not been satisfied with the latest issues of the magazine, during the period of the electoral campaign. Jean-François Revel had written in his usual style against the communists, but he had written little against Mitterrand. I had been particularly irritated by the four articles on the eve of the first round of the elections, each with two columns, presented in the same way, two for Mitterrand, two for Giscard (in fact Revel's article was more against Marchais than for Giscard). I had a discussion that was close to a dispute, with Revel when he asked me to compress my three-column article, "Explanation of a vote," into two columns. I had already been surprised to hear from him in a meeting of the editorial committee that he regretted my support for Giscard and Max Gallo's for Mitterrand. There is no reason to intervene in the presidential battle, he said; what we have been writing for years should influence the choice of our readers more than last-minute appeals.

The issue in which the four articles appeared had troubled me much more than Revel realized at the time. A publication that wishes to be objective, but not neutral or disengaged, lowers itself, discredits itself, if it declares itself unable to take a position. I intended to give up the presidency of the editorial committee after the elections. There is no provision for arbitration between the direction and the president of the editorial committee. When Revel and I disagreed about a book by Bernard-Henri Lévy, we found a compromise: two articles on the same subject. Yves Cuau reminded me later that he had criticized, from a purely professional point of view, the juxtaposition of two editorials for Mitterrand with two for Giscard. I had given in over the telephone, and, in the presence of Max Gallo, I could not set forth my objections to the sudden elevation of a book reviewer to the status of political editorialist. We did not know—he hadn't told us—that he was aiming for a seat in Parliament (perhaps he didn't know it himself).

Despite my doubts over the orientation of *L'Express* over the course of the preceding months, I had confidence in Revel, although I intended to resign a presidency that had become fictitious. On 12 May, my only intention was to prevent a break between Jimmy on the one hand and Revel and Todd on the other.

The famous cover for the issue before the second round of the presidential election—Giscard looking old, Mitterrand above him, looking youthful— could at the least produce a misunderstanding. The best evidence of this was a note in *Le Canard enchaîné:* the owner of *L'Express* is already thinking of an alliance with the new masters. Perhaps this remark had something to do with the anger of Sir James. Those who produced this cover wrote to Jimmy, who showed me their letter, that they had followed directions.

I do not think that Jimmy held to a long-standing hostility toward Todd, even though his radical conservatism led him to detest, or rather to feel contempt for, the tepid social democracy of Todd. The deep cause seems to me anything but mysterious. Jimmy, like other businessmen, had thrown himself into journalism with conviction, a kind of naïve enthusiasm, not to earn money but to defend and illustrate his ideas.

L'Express had been a weekly of the left. It had fought against the Indochina War, against the Algerian War, against Gaullism, and against the UDR government. At the last minute, in 1974, Jean-Jacques Servan-Schreiber declared himself in favor of Giscard, and Françoise Giroud had to explain her vote for Mitterrand in *Le Provençal.* The editorial staff, which had resisted the shifts of line by the management, remained rather "on the left." Despite the time that had passed, there was a muffled tension between an owner who would have preferred a weekly that was resolutely "liberal" (in the European sense of the term), and the journalists who, with the exception of a few editorialists, oscillated between the two camps.

Mitterrand's victory did not really surprise Jimmy, but it drove him to distraction. Before the election, he was negotiating with the government about the future of the Hersant group, whose financial situation, according to him, required drastic measures. He was hoping to take control of *Le Figaro* and, thereby, to resolve certain personal and economic problems with *L'Express*.

After 10 May, the plan to shift some of the excess personnel of *L'Express* to *Le Figaro* collapsed. Moreover, Jimmy let himself be carried away by exaggerated pessimism, and he anticipated a 25 percent decline in advertising revenue. Logically, there was no connection between the role of Olivier Todd and the anticipated financial difficulties. But there was a connection, in Jimmy's mind, between the probable losses of the business and the political content of the magazine: if he was going to lose money to keep the magazine alive, at least it should defend his ideas, not those he despised. The cover compromised Jimmy, presented him as a turncoat, ready to collaborate with the socialists, while in reality he was thinking only of fighting them. All these feelings, some provoked by the shock of 10 May, others suppressed for years, exploded all at once, and Olivier Todd, with the cover, was the detonator and the victim. Finally, we should add that Jimmy had for a long time been thinking of promoting Yves Cuau and Yann de l'Ecotais (who had left *Le Figaro* at the same time as I did).

NOTES

1. I have written the same thing about Robert Hersant.

2 8

THE END
OF A GENERATION

By 1977, the debates of the 1950s (communism, the nature of Soviet society), the debates of the 1960s (the questioning of industrial society), belonged to the past; they had subsided for lack of combatants. Not that intellectuals devoted to Marxism-Leninism had disappeared; they were numerous in both secondary schools and universities. In Paris, in the "top intelligentsia," they hardly exist any more. In the course of the last few years, success has been won by young essayists who have rediscovered old-fashioned, or extremely old-fashioned, anticommunism. Accusations against technology, pollution, the city made of concrete, and modern power have not been abandoned or refuted. To all indications, such criticism will continue. Those who despise modern civilization have, in fact, attacked genuine evils or dangers. But the "major intellectuals," more or less close to these rebels, did not elevate "ecologism" to the level of philosophy. The *gauchisme* of the 1970s survives, but the *gauchistes* have taken divergent paths. Some have been absorbed by the communists, others by the socialists; still others have transferred their intransigence to the defense of human rights; a very small number are still perhaps tempted by direct action.

The Parisian intelligentsia did not, however, lack for controversies, limited to the narrow circle of weeklies and periodicals, that were nevertheless directly or indirectly, significant. I am thinking first of all of the "new right," whose leader, inspiration, and best representative is certainly Alain de Benoist (the author, under various pseudonyms, of countless articles). A prize awarded by the Académie française to one of his books, *Le Monde vu de droite*, drew attention to the two journals he had inspired, *La Nouvelle Ecole* and *Eléments*.

Alain de Benoist's group has not concealed its goal: to reconquer the ideological power that belongs to the left, even when so-called rightists govern the country. On this point, I agree with them. Except for the survivors of Action française and the nearly invisible fascists and Nazis, all parties generally lay claim to ideas of the "left," that is, liberal and democratic. Socialists criticize rightist governments for not reducing inequality (essentially income inequality), but the spokesmen of the right do not reply (or do so with embarrassment) that economic and political hierarchy is both inevitable and necessary for the common good. The "new right" totally condemns democratic-liberal conformism, of which I am proud to have been one of the advocates. Of course, I do not deny the importance of the authors that Alain de Benoist likes to analyze: Machiavelli and Pareto. I have not presented Western societies in the style adopted by true believers in democracy. I have "depoeticized," "disenchanted" both the rivalry of parties and the struggle between states. Alain de Benoist frequently refers to certain philosophers, like Karl Popper, to whom I feel very close in many respects. But on essential questions, on ideas that inspired policy, Benoist unfailingly recalls the fascists or the Nazis (I do not accuse him of having been one of them, I am simply saying that he frequently thinks in the same way as they do).

My position with respect to the new right recalls another matter of conscience: What is my situation, on the eve of my death, in relation not to my Jewishness, which I recognize without hesitation, but to Jewish organizations, to the younger generation, to the so-called movement of Jewish renewal? In an earlier chapter, dealing with the Six-Day War and General de Gaulle's press conference, I explained myself as sincerely as I could. But history did not come to a halt after 1967. Since the Algerian War, the Jewish community has swollen and been transformed by the Sephardic Jews of North Africa. The children or grandchildren of French Jews despise the discretion of their parents or their grandparents—discretion that they call prudence, if not cowardice.

Only one opportunity was offered to me to express myself on a particular case, the book by Bernard-Henri Lévy, *L'Idéologie française*. The "new philosophers" did not affect me personally. They do not represent an original way of philosophizing; they are comparable neither to the phenomenologists, nor to the existentialists, nor to the analytic philosophers. They write essays outside university guidelines. Their success has been fostered by the media and by the absence in present-day Paris of a judicious and recognized critical position. *Agrégés* in philosophy, they do not belong to the movement identified with Sartre and Merleau-Ponty; some of them were disciples of Althusser, whom they have abandoned without explicitly rejecting him. They created a sensation above all by their radical condemnation of Sovietism and indeed of Marxism.

Circumstances led me to criticize *L'Idéologie française*. The book touches on a sensitive area of French consciousness, and unlike Lévy's two earlier books, it deals with a current and lasting historical problem; the ancestors and the heirs of Vichy.

The Vichy regime was peculiar to France during the Second World War; alone among all the governments of occupied countries, it laid claim to its legality to the end, fought tooth and nail against the encroachments of the occupation authorities to the point of assuming the responsibility for doing itself dishonorable deeds (for example, the deportation of the Jews). Irrespective of the diplomatic decisions of 1940 and 1942, the leaders of Vichy proclaimed a particularly French doctrine, not dictated by the occupation forces. Where did Vichy ideology come from? Whose interests did it express? How can it be located in relation to Italian fascism, National Socialism, Francoism, Salazarism?

This is not the place to answer those questions. I devoted an article to *L'Idéologie française*, giving in to the urging of friends, mostly Jews who detested the book because of its very excesses and who were therefore apprehensive about misunderstandings. They did not wish that Bernard-Henri Lévy, denouncer of a French ideology that was shared by Maurice Thorez and Marshal Pétain, should appear to be the interpreter of the Jewish community.

Lévy's response to my article raised a serious question. Would the Jews be behaving as cowards if they were to obey what has been called, with reference to certain civil servants, the duty to be reserved? I have recalled how a friend, who was not at all an anti-Semite in 1937 or 1938, asked me to be "restrained" in French controversies about the proper way to approach Hitler's Germany. The existence of the state of Israel, as well, even though different from Hitlerian Germany, raised the question of dual loyalty.

Jews who have not lived through the years 1933–45 often look with disdain and condescension on their parents and grandparents, who continue to be concerned not to "provoke anti-Semitism"; the very concern appears to them to be futile and indeed contemptible. Anti-Semitism, as Julian Benta wrote, arises from the need to hate, from an aggressive desire, not from the conduct of the Jews themselves. To believe oneself obliged to maintain one's reserve, whatever the occasion, is to accept discrimination between oneself and the others. If one wished to be French, if one *is* French like all one's compatriots, why should one refrain from comment on any matter of interest?

The argument would carry conviction if Jews today wished for integration, if their Jewishness remained entirely spiritual. Once their consciousness connects them to Israel, a state among other states, even though it has particular characteristics, non-Jewish French citizens have the right to ask them to what political community they belong. As long as humanity remains divided among "states based on power," the Jews of the diaspora, free to determine their fate, must choose between Israel and their "refuge country," which has become their nation. As citizens of the French Republic, they legitimately maintain their spiritual or psychological links with the Israelis, but if these links with Israel become *political* and more significant than their French citizenship, they should logically choose Israeli citizenship.

Lévy denounces, with more vehemence than pertinence, all thinkers or writers who, in one way or another, have developed ideas close to those of Vichy, counterrevolutionaries, anti-Semites, doctrinaire promoters of communitarian and corporatist ideas, and so on. He attacks all those who have exalted a fleshly France, historical, defined by its land and its dead. He accepts only one France, that of 1789, the one symbolized by the *Fête de la Fédération*, the joint and free oath of all the provinces of the Republic, one and indivisible. All equal in rights and duties: this is the France that is born from the adhesion of its children, the only one that Lévy loves, as abstract as the love he feels for it. It is true that the notion of the rights of man and of the Revolution was challenged throughout the nineteenth century by many of the French, perhaps by a majority of them; anti-Semitism flourished in our country as much as it did in Germany. It was the Dreyfus Affair that woke Theodor Herzl from his dream of assimilation and inspired his Zionism. It is also true that the institutions, and even the moral bases, of the liberal democracies were mercilessly criticized, rejected, torn to pieces by the fashionable essayists of the 1930s. Robert Aron, Arnaud Dandieu, and Emmanuel Mounier detested plutocratic democracies in their fashion, to some degree related to that of the fascists. Vichy ideology of the first phase took its inspiration from Action française and also from the small groups, the "philosophical circles" whose influence on intellectual life was not negligible but which, before the war, remained marginal and did not lead to genuinely political action.

The French case is characterized not only by the number of ideas related to Italian fascism and National Socialism that prospered, but also by the fact that those ideas never produced an authentic fascism or National Socialism, not even a serious risk of right-wing authoritarianism, outside the exceptional circumstances of the Occupation. In the Académie française, anti-Semitism took the form of a discreetly respected quota; Action française and Maurras served as mentors for naval officers, provincial nobles, and good bourgeois society in Paris: neither the party of Colonel de la Rocque,[1] which came out of the Croix de Feu, nor the party of Jacques Doriot came close to critical mass. The Dreyfus Affair provides evidence of the resistance of French society to anti-Semitism and to "patriotic forgery" as well as to the virulence of the evil. As for the 1930s, they also provide evidence, in my eyes, of our nation's allergy to right-wing revolutions: our teachers, from those of Jules Ferry to those of the Second World War, held firm. Their patriotism at the beginning of the century was rooted in the Revolution, the doctrine of the rights of man, and nationalism. There was no lack of fascist or parafascist ideologies in France, but those ideologies had no crowds ready to adopt them and to fight for them.

In 1940, neither Emmanuel Mounier nor Hubert Beuve-Méry had the Gaullist reaction, that is, the simple conviction that the war would go on, that defeat in the battle of France had not determined the outcome of the struggle; one had to fight, and the moment to reform France had not arrived; reform, under the eyes of the occupation forces, would be discredited in advance. Like most of the French, these "new philosophers" of the 1930s did not immediately adopt the attitude that, in retrospect, seems best to us. An inquisitor, armed with his youth and eloquence, who arraigns all the suspects—those who did not reject the Marshal immediately or those who joined the underground only in 1943—should at least understand the revolt against the decadent Third Republic and the desire for another Republic, populated by fewer bearded and potbellied Radicals.

Lévy's book does not deserve all the polemics it has provoked, but the response it found in certain circles deserves some thought. Let us leave aside the erratic use of quotations. What strikes me are the feelings toward their "adopted country" expressed by the Jews who admire this pamphlet, an indictment of a great part of France and its culture. Have some Jews of the younger generation come to detest the country they have chosen?

Let us leave this book, which has taken too much space. I am thinking of the young Jews organized in commando groups who beat up the leader of a neo-Nazi sect and who threw acid at a peaceful citizen: a confusion in identity caused the loss of this man, who had nothing to do with anti-Semitism. This confusion brought to light the viciousness of the assault troops and their methods: the activists would have been no less inexcusable if they had disfigured the guilty man. I will be accused of blurring distinctions: on one side the rejection of a whole segment of French culture, on the other the use of violence against anti-Semites. There is no question of confusing these two actions, one intellectual, the other physical, but they derive perhaps from the same source: France had been for the Jews, despite the Dreyfus Affair, the first country that had freed them; in 1940, it became the only democratic country in Western Europe that established on its own, not under pressure from the occupation authorities, a status for the Jews modeled on the one the National Socialists had promulgated.

The Jews of the entire world, traumatized by genocide, have for the most part rediscovered a consciousness of Jewishness that the assimilated had lost. The Jews of France were also traumatized by Vichy, even though the French community was relatively spared, physically, in part because of the unoccupied zone.[2] Even more traumatizing than the Jewish law was the reaction, or rather the lack of reaction, of the juridical and moral institutions of the society. The Conseil d'Etat interpreted and applied the Jewish statute as though it were a law comparable to others, as though the violation of the principles of the republic could be accepted by jurists in response to any particular decision by the government.

I encounter Jews, old and young, who, so to speak, have not forgiven France, or the French, for the Jewish law and the roundup of the Vélodrome d'hiver by the French police (under the orders of Vichy or the occupation authorities). If they have not forgiven France, it is no longer their nation, but only the country where they live pleasantly. This is a normal attitude for the old, who cannot begin a new existence. But why do the young who have become indifferent to the fate of their "adopted country," their nation, not choose Israel? I can anticipate the reply: those who love will punish severely. Don't those who are harshest toward France have a much deeper attachment to France than the French who ask themselves no questions? This may be true, but these feelings, if they were repressed, would finally die out.

The "top intellectuals," or the intellocrats who controlled the media in the late 1970s, had given up semi-Sovietism; they sometimes continued to support the unity of the left, but they no longer practiced the cult of revolution, and they sometimes supported the Socialist Party, the only one capable of replacing the right-wing majority with a majority of the left. It was in this climate that I met Jean-Paul Sartre for the last time.

Claudie and Jacques Broyelle came up with the slogan: "A boat for Vietnam." I would like to say something about this ex-Maoist couple whom I respect deeply and who are my friends. Their book, *Le Deuxième Retour de Chine* had touched me because of the authenticity of its tone. I wrote to them to that effect. Their next book, *La Foi des pierres,* was even more striking: a personal contribution to elucidating the mystery of what is called belief. What does "believing" mean? What does a Stalinist or a Maoist believe in? What does he know of the facts that he will invoke tomorrow when he renounces his faith? In retrospect, the Broyelles shed light on the captive mind, the ruse of silence, the self-mutilation of the militant. The four of us met; Suzanne and Claudie hit it off. Olivier Todd and André Glucksmann immediately contributed their help and their authority to a humanitarian enterprise: saving some of the Vietnamese who were fleeing the regime the North had imposed on the South. I joined the movement with no hesitation. In the vast ocean of distress, what is represented by one boat and a few of those admirable *médecins sans frontières?* That kind of logic would lead all of us to do nothing. Did the "operation" also have a political meaning? Yes, of course. It was a so-called socialist regime that was pushing thousands of men, women, and children to risk their lives, in a sea infested with pirates, on rowboats or sloops, in search of freedom.

It was above all a humanitarian action, like something that could have been done by the Red Cross. I have been told that Glucksmann persuaded Jean-Paul Sartre. A press conference was organized, and I came. A few minutes later, Sartre arrived, supported by Glucksmann; I was seated, I turned toward him, Glucksmann told him my name, we shook hands, and I spoke the old greeting: "Bonjour, mon petit camarade." He said nothing, except perhaps hello. The photograph of our handshake was purchased in more than a hundred countries.

Claude Mauriac recounts this meeting in the following terms: "Glucksmann whispered a few words to Sartre while Raymond Aron held out his hand, which Sartre grasped, expressionless, with neither hostility nor warmth, while Aron looked tense, embarrassed, both anxious and happy. I heard Aron speak a few words of welcome, the only ones I could hear clearly being *camarade* or perhaps *vieux camarade*. And the expression, after such a long separation, seemed conventional, inadequate, maladroit, and touching." I read this account before it appeared in *Le Rire des pères dans les yeux des enfants*. I wrote him the following letter that he reproduced without comment in his book.

Dear Claude Mauriac,

I have read the passage of your diary that recounts my meeting with Jean-Paul Sartre on the occasion of the press conference for "Un bateau pour le Vietnam."

Allow me to make a few remarks. When I shook Sartre's hand, I said, *"bonjour, mon petit comrade,"* not *"vieux camarade."* It was a way of erasing thirty years and going back a half-century. For, in our group at the Ecole Normale, we called each other *"petit camarade."* If Sartre heard these words—which is not certain—he thought that I had said what I could and should say to him, neither inadequate nor touching.

As for my feelings, I think they were much simpler than they appeared to you. Seated side by side, neither one of us would have been embarrassed or annoyed; in fact, when I saw him, blind, almost paralyzed, I was overcome by an immense feeling of sympathy and pity. I had not seen him for years, and I had the feeling that he was dying. Cordially.

Was I right to think that he was "dying"? He died less than a year later, in April 1980, but a year earlier, did he still have the strength of intellect and will without which he would not have been himself? The question arises in connection with the conversations with Benny Lévy published in *Le Nouvel Observateur* on the eve of his death.

A few weeks after our meeting, a delegation of the group "Un bateau pour le Vietnam" was received by President Giscard. Two members of the delegation, André Glucksmann and Claudie Broyelle, spoke the most; they requested an increase in the number of Vietnamese admitted to France; they also asked for emergency measures. Jean-Paul Sartre said a few words in reply to a direct question from the president, introduced by the phrase "mon cher maître"; he confirmed his complete agreement with Glucksmann. I don't remember saying anything worth quoting. A statement by the president, reported by the members of the delegation, was a pretext for ironic commentaries. He had asked: Why are they leaving? or why do they want to leave? Didn't the very question reveal a total lack of understanding of the Soviet regime? I am not sure that the question revealed such naïveté: the refugees were not all impelled by the same motive. At the improvised press conference held at the Collège de France after the visit to the Elysée palace, Jean-Paul Sartre spoke for a few minutes: his voice had not changed, nor had his diction; a light, clear, and almost youthful voice; no pomposity, no transition from one statement to another; neither an orator nor a professor; I recognized him.

Quite obviously, the handshake did not put an end to thirty years of separation, neither in his eyes nor in mine. What significance should be attributed to this meeting that was both silent and ostentatiously public? After all, friends who have "quarreled" do not disappear from one another's view. Sartre wrote, without hypocrisy, eulogies for Camus and Merleau-Ponty, obituaries that clashed with the conventions of the genre. A few lines on Camus state the essential point: "In this century, and against history, he represented the latest heir of the long line of *moralistes* whose works constitute perhaps the most original contribution of French letters. His stubborn humanism, narrow and pure, austere and sensual, was engaged in dubious combat with the massive and formless events of the time. But conversely, because of the stubbornness of his rejections, in our time, against the Machiavellians, against the golden calf of realism, he reaffirmed the existence of moral reality."

With Camus, he said, the break was a way of living together. Something like that happened with Merleau-Ponty, I think. The quarrel followed publication of *Les Aventures de la dialectique.* The controversy, which was both political and philosophical, did not take on as personal a tone as in the case of Camus. Merleau-Ponty criticized Sartre for what he called ultra-Bolshevism, in other words substitution of the will of the party for that of the proletariat. Politically, the debate turned on the relation between class and party. Philosophically, according to Merleau-Ponty, there was a lack of mediation between class and party, between circumstances and decision. Absolute and unconditional freedom, the freedom of the Cartesian God, transferred to the *Pour-soi,* passed on to the party, which was thereby invested with the historical mission that Marx had assigned to the working class. Simone de Beauvoir replied that the criticism neglected the distinction between the ontological and the ontic: the ontological argument for absolute freedom did not exclude the entrapment of the *Pour-soi* or the party within historical circumstances, from which the will can escape not by a pure *fiat,* comparable to the decision of the Cartesian God, but through the long effort of the *Pour-soi* or the class to liberate itself from its alienations.

Camus, a "stubborn humanist, narrow and pure," Merleau-Ponty, an a-communist concerned with restoring mediations between circumstances and action, found an honorable place in the philosopher's gallery of the dead. He had spared neither the humanist nor the a-communist while they were alive, he praised them when they were dead, sincerely, or rather without going beyond the degree of bad faith that is tolerated in funeral orations. I do not think that he would have granted me a place, even posthumously, in his gallery of contemporaries. Olivier Todd relates that, in his last conversation with him, after the spectacular and fictitious reconciliation, Sartre repeated that I was a bourgeois, an enemy of the working class. Bourgeois in my origins and my way of living, without doubt. Enemy of the working class— the expression seems to me devoid of meaning. This rather stupid remark of Sartre's leaves little doubt as to his feelings toward me, at least as far as politics is concerned. In contrast, I should mention another anecdote. André Malraux had forced Gaston Gallimard to cease publishing *Les Temps modernes* after an article by Merleau-Ponty that had wounded him. "He calls me a coward, and he never fought anywhere but in his office," Malraux said to me. I told Sartre that I had nothing to do with this incident. He let me know that he had never suspected that I had.

Despite all this, does the handshake have a symbolic value for historians? I am not sure; Simone de Beauvoir, for one, responds without hesitation, no.[3] Sartre, who was essentially a moralist, came to consent to extreme forms of violence in the service of the good cause. He had long identified the revolution with the Communist Party and hence with the Soviet Union. From 1968 on, the young followed the other side of Sartre's thought, the crowd in fusion, the spontaneity of individual or collective praxis; he himself moved away from the revolution that had been crystallized in bureaucracy and the cult of personality. He rediscovered his true space, anarchy, not that of the parties that call themselves anarchist, but that of the individual who throws off all chains and rebels. At the same time, he no longer accepted the horrors committed in the name of a sublime goal. He no longer scorned the "tender souls" of the liberals, and he acknowledged sympathy with the victims of despotism, even Marxist-Leninist despotism. At this point, we could come together without either of us damaging ourselves, responding to the appeal of the Broyelles and of *Médecins sans frontières*.

I said and wrote as little as possible at Sartre's death. An article in *L'Express*, participation in the television program *Apostrophes*. I had so much to say that I would have preferred to remain silent.

When Jean-Paul Sartre received the Nobel Prize, Pierre Brisson asked me to write, for *Le Figaro littéraire*, a few pages on my early memories, our years and our conversations at the Ecole Normale Supérieure. I refused: Sartre detested academic eulogies, politics had separated us, and the event lent itself neither to a settling of accounts nor to a suspension of our differences. I offered Brisson a long article on the *Critique de la raison dialectique;* disappointed, almost desperate, he called it a university lecture. And yet, is not reading and discussing a philosopher's book an appropriate means of honoring a thinker whose power of thought one admires, without approving either his arguments or his positions?

Fifty years ago, jokingly, we made a commitment to one another. The one who survived would write the obituary for the other in the bulletin of former students of the Ecole Normale. The commitment no longer stands—too much time passed between student intimacy and the handshake of the press conference for the "Bateau pour Vietnam"—but some of it remains. I leave to others the thankless but necessary task of celebrating a work whose richness, diversity, and scope have astounded his contemporaries, of paying just tribute to a man whose generosity and disinterest no one has ever questioned, even though he was more than once involved in dubious combat.

I remember a conversation on the boulevard Saint-Germain, between the rue du Bac and the Ministry of War. At the time, Sartre had no sense of his own genius. I told him of my doubts, my uncertainty about the future. He said, roughly—I forget the exact words—that it did not seem so difficult to rise to the level of Hegel. In the same conversation, we broached the other question, revolution. I presented banal, prosaic objections. The oppressed, or rather those who represent them, easily adopt the role of those they have evicted from power. And, to cite the Marx of *The German Ideology,* the old mess will begin again. Probably, he answered, the same injustice, or a comparable injustice, will be established after the revolution, but if the revolution comes, I would like to serve it as a teacher in an elementary school.

This conversation took place after the end of our studies, when we were about twenty-five. I have recalled it more than once. Before Munich, Sartre was hardly interested in politics. Simone de Beauvoir recounts that neither of them expected anything from reforms, gradual improvements; only a revolution, brutal and total, could change the course of things, change life. For Sartre was, and remained throughout his life, deeply a moralist, even though he was led, by the logic of revolutionary absolutism, to compose texts on violence, like the preface to Fanon's book, which are worthy of inclusion in an anthology of fascist-leaning literature.

As a philosopher, he owes the essential aspects of his thought to himself. To be sure, he studied Husserl and Heidegger in Berlin in 1933–34; I had introduced him to phenomenology on a café terrace, and we know from Simone de Beauvoir's account how he had been overwhelmed by the revelation of a method that corresponded to his needs and his inspiration. However, neither phenomenology nor *Being and Time* gave him much more than a vocabulary, at most an approach. He had developed a *Weltanschauung*, structured by the *En-soi* and the *Pour-soi;* on the one hand, the thing in its inert materiality, its nonmeaning, on the other consciousness, always in search of itself, never coinciding with itself, and yet the principle and the creator of meaning. Without consciousness, nothing has meaning and it is itself, so to speak, only nothingness.

Sartre did not find the *Pour-soi,* transparent consciousness, free will in the image of God, in books, but in himself. Like Descartes, at least in his youth, he did not think that a psychoanalysis would teach him anything about himself. Sartre wished this proud *Pour-soi* to be simultaneously completely responsible for itself and for everyone else. Enclosed in its solitude, wearied by the vain search for being, the *Pour-soi* yearns to join the others, beyond the social comedy, in an authentic relationship, with neither party objectifying the other and thereby alienating the other's freedom.

L'Etre et le néant still seems to me by far the best of his philosophical books, the most faithful reflection of his vision of the world, charged with the contradictions of the human condition, rich in existential themes that fostered literary variations. The *Critique de la raison dialectique* denies *L'Etre et le néant* only in appearance, but he reestablished the *Pour-soi* in social reality, 'Marxizing' it by baptizing it *praxis;* he fills the empty freedom of the *Pour soi* with ways of being and acting derived from socialization, while attempting, with a dialectic more subtle than convincing, to preserve the transparent *Pour-soi,* condemned to freedom, of *L'Etre et le néant.*

Why did Sartre feel the need to decree that Marxism (which he probably did not study extensively) was an unavoidable truth, a historic moment in human thought? Let us leave aside the countless psychological and social interpretations that come to mind. Let the reader consider the Sartre who was ready, without illusions, to devote himself to the education of the people, if a revolution provided humanity with the opportunity for a new departure. Having achieved fame, with *La Nausée, Le Mur, Les Mouches,* and *Huis clos,* he found himself after the war in a France and a world torn apart not only by great power rivalry, but also, as Nietzsche had foretold, by philosophical conflicts. Sartre, who viscerally detested the bourgeoisie, could not choose the Western, American, capitalist camp. At times he favored the other camp, at times he dreamed of a third. This quest for the party or the countries devoted to revolution led him to Moscow and to Havana, toward strange pilgrimages, even though he never crossed the threshold. He behaved as a fellow traveler for some years, the worst years of Stalinism. Still in the *Critique de la raison dialectique,* that is, in the early 1960s, he hesitated between Marxism-Leninism and *gauchisme.*

The texts published recently by *Le Nouvel Observateur* do not belong to the work of Jean-Paul Sartre himself. But a few personal confessions correspond to my memories. He never resigned himself to social life as he observed it, as he judged it, unworthy of the idea he had of human destiny. Utopianism? Millenarianism? Rather the hope or the demand for a different form of human relations. We had both read Kant's *Religion within the Limits of Reason,* meditated on the choice that everyone makes of himself, once and for all, but also with the continuing freedom to transform himself. He never gave up the hope for a kind of universal conversion of humanity. But what was in between, the institutions mediating between the individual and humanity were never part of his thought, never integrated into his system. This was the drama of a moralist lost in the jungle of politics.

Why are you interested in politics, he asked me in the conversation I have recalled, if you don't believe in revolution, if you accept this society while ignoring its turpitudes? Perhaps the last term was more moderate, but the word is of little importance. I was probably marked by a phrase that Alain liked to quote: civilization is a thin film that can be torn apart by a single blow; and barbarism enters through the breach. Revolution, like war, risks tearing apart the film of civilization, formed slowly over the course of centuries.[4]

As for the television program *Apostrophes,* which made a stir, it did not seem to me to be a success. How could four people talk about Sartre in seventy minutes? I have a few memories of the program; I did not respond to the "bait" that Bertrand Poirot-Delpech periodically set before me, probably to distance himself from a man of the right. In the circumstances, his goal was useless. The left in general was grateful to me for having challenged Benny Lévy and declared categorically that the last texts, the conversations published in *Le Nouvel Observateur,* did not belong to the work of my little comrade. I argued with Glucksmann, who persisted in comparing Sartre with Solzhenitsyn. Friendship led him into an absurd argument. The *zek* detested the role played by the *maître à penser* of the Western world, his systematic indulgence toward parties or movements laying claim to the creation of a new man. I spoke without restraint, carried away by my feelings. Two of Sartre's intimates thanked me: Claude Lanzmann on the phone, Jean Pouillon with a note; Anne Philipe and Romain Gary did the same with personal dedications in their books.

Gary sent me *Les Cerfs-volants* with a flattering dedication. I thanked him a few days later, and as I was going through my files at the time, I offered to send him a letter from 1945, in which he had confessed to me his delighted surprise at the letters and articles of praise that he had received. The success I had predicted for him when I read the manuscript of *Une Education européenne* in London had already arrived. He answered that he would like to have this distant letter. Soon thereafter, having received the letter (I have not kept a copy), he sent me a note that I reproduce "despite everything"; "Thank you, dear Raymond Aron, for that letter which reminds me of the days when I still believed in 'all that': literary glory, fame, etc., etc. Everything has now become 'etc., etc.' I have followed with admiration your superb intellectual trajectory: your spirit illuminates so well these dark times that, reading you, one sometimes comes to believe in the possibility of escaping from them and in the existence of a path. It is rare that strength of thought goes along with strength of character. I say to you—I love this popular expression—'keep going.' Yours faithfully."

The note is dated 29 November 1980. He committed suicide on 2 December.

I have recently reread Sartre's conversations with Benny Lévy, which I had excluded from his work in that television discussion. Perhaps the antipathy I felt toward Benny Lévy inspired those harsh statements. After reconsideration and rereading those conversations, should these *ultima verba* be finally excluded from Sartre's work? The tone of these conversations does not echo that of my little comrade. He spoke in an entirely different manner five years earlier, in response to Michel Contat. On the other hand, Simone de Beauvoir and his intimate friends deny that his mind had weakened to such an extent that we can consider him not responsible. In 1975, in the conversation with Contat, he asserted that his intelligence had not been affected, that it remained as vigorous as in the past. There was only one symptom of aging: at times, he could not find the proper word.

According to the account by Simone de Beauvoir, the state of his health declined seriously between 1975 and 1980. Because of circulation problems, his legs gradually became paralyzed. It seems to me probable that his brain also suffered from the decline in his cardiovascular system. These afflictions, even without his blindness, would probably have prevented him from continuing his work, completing the *Critique de la raison dialectique* and his *Flaubert*. This obviously does not mean that his remarks in the interviews were forced on him by the interviewer and are a complete betrayal of his thought.

On certain points, the contradiction between the statements of 1975 and those of 1980 is so great that one would have to think some kind of conversion had taken place. He stated to Contat that thought is by nature solitary. In order to think, one has to be alone. There is no thought except that of a man alone. Referring to music, he has no hesitation in admitting that he does not like concerts and that he enjoys music only when he is alone. This is what he said five years later: "I was obliged to have dialogues because I could no longer write. And I suggested that you should be my secretary, but I realized right away that you couldn't do it, that I had to accept you within the meditation itself, in other words, that we would meditate together. And that completely changed my method of research, because until now I have always worked alone, seated at a table, with a pen and paper in front of me. While now, we are forming thoughts together. Sometimes we continue to disagree. But there is an exchange that I could probably not have thought of carrying on before my old age."

After reading these lines I am tempted to react immediately: this is not Sartre. For the first time, he accepts a "plural" thought, the expression of several people, in place of the thought of a man alone, speaking to everyone, universal at least in its aim. For the first time, he accepts meditation in common, into which he was forced by old age; he persuades himself, and tries to persuade his readers, that the constraint had become a blessing, since with the help of another he will criticize his past and outline the ethics that he never managed to write, neither after *L'Etre et le néant* nor after the *Critique de la raison dialectique*. To a similar effect are his remarks on progress, the approach of the ultimate end of mankind by means of partial failures. When they were young, Sartre and Beauvoir did not believe in total transformation; at seventy, he confessed to mistakes attributable to inadequate rather than excessive radicalism; at seventy-five: "I suppose that development through action would be a series of failures, out of which, unexpectedly, would come something positive, which was already contained within the failure but unknown to those who wanted to succeed. And it is these partial successes, local, hard to understand by the people who have done the work, which from failure to failure, would gradually bring about progress. This is how I have always understood history." He may have "understood" it in that way, but he certainly did not always "explain" it in the same way.

On the other hand, it does not seem to me illegitimate to associate some of his last statements with his personality and with certain tendencies of his thought. When he says that he was never "in despair," he is speaking the truth, according to the statements he made before the last years. A naturally happy man, he fulfilled most of his ambitions. In 1975, he felt satisfied with his existence, and he said so. And why should he not be? The philosopher replies to Sartre: "Man is a useless passion." The early Sartre was not personally in despair, but the metaphysician in him was without hope. He confessed to me, more than half a century ago, that he did not want to have a child because the human condition seemed to him to be hopeless.

The "second" Sartre, after the war, went beyond existential despair and scornful irony toward the masses, and he sought a way out of the impasse less in individual morality than in collective action. In the *Critique de la raison dialectique*, he combined despair with the hope necessary for revolutionaries. He maintained freedom as the ultimate aim, but the falling off of rebellion, the "beginning of humanity," seemed to be fated (would the second volume have shown that it was not fated?).

I think I can see Sartrean themes in these conversations, but they are more or less flattened out, made banal. Indeed, one looks in vain for firmness of tone, originality of thought or expression, even when he was repeating himself or when he was mistaken. Thirty years ago, cooling the harshness of his youth, he willingly admitted: "I have become 'soft-hearted,' 'benign.'" He became that in these final conversations; he had never been like that in the past.

When the old man rejects despair, denies a particular experience of anguish, he is perhaps revealing a part of himself. But this truth, if it is a truth, is expressed so poorly that it becomes vulgar, disorienting. "Note well that one notices very little despair in my work from then on. That was a moment. I see that in many philosophers with reference to despair and to any philosophical idea at all; they talk about it from hearsay in the first phase of their philosophy, they give it significant value, and then, gradually, they no longer talk about it, because they realize that the content does not exist for them, that they have taken it from others. I never felt despair. These are key notions of philosophy from 1930 to 1940. It also came from Heidegger, they were notions that were used all the time, but they didn't correspond to anything for me. . . ."

What makes the reading of these conversations painful and sometimes unbearable is the pressure, conscious or unconscious, exercised by Benny Lévy on an old man whose strength to resist had declined even more than his strength of intellect. Sartre prided himself on having no sense of guilt. His young disciple reminds him of the years 1952 to 1956, during which "the master thinker of the West," according to Solzhenitsyn's expression, behaved as a fellow traveler of Stalinism. Mercilessly, Lévy says to Sartre: "So, he gives up the ghost, your fellow traveler. I would like a death certificate. Who died? A sinister scoundrel, a fool, a time-server, or a fundamentally good person?" And Sartre answered: "I would say rather someone who wasn't so bad." And he excuses himself: "He wasn't a fellow traveler for long; it was secondary for him, the party made his situation impossible, when he resisted the party he wasn't so bad."

And then he presents his work as a failure and, like a vulgar humanist, declares that one must believe in progress, seeking the principle of the left and of morality in fraternity without terror. "What is needed for morality is to extend the idea of fraternity until it becomes the single and obvious relation among all mankind. . . ." He renounces his preface to Fanon's book and the cult of violence; he rewrites his essay on the Jews. "What was missing was the reality of the Jew. Note that this reality, which is in the end metaphysical, like that of the Christian incidentally, occupied little space in my philosophy. There was the consciousness of the self, from which I removed all particular characteristics that were supposed to come from within and which I had the self later receive from outside. Thus, deprived of metaphysical and subjective characteristics, the Jew as such could not exist in my philosophy. Now I see man differently."

It is true that in *La Question juive*, he ignored the Jews, whether their fate was metaphysical or not. What prevents me from recognizing an unknown Sartre in these dialogues is that he seems to me a victim of his younger interlocutor, more resolute than he, who makes him give in on the points at which he had demonstrated his genius, baroque as that may have been.

The conclusion of these conversations, about which historians will speculate, has a certain grandeur, even if it resembles none of the earlier Sartres. "The revolutionaries want to bring into being a society that would be human and satisfying for men, but they forget that a society of this kind is not a 'real' society, so to speak, but a legal one, that is, a society in which relations among men are moral. Well, this idea of ethics as the ultimate aim of revolution can only be thought of as a kind of messianism." Sartre was an anarchist with respect to institutions and a moralist with respect to individuals throughout his life despite the zigzags of his political career. On the eve of his death, tormented by Benny Lévy, he confessed, despite everything, one of his truths, the messianic hope in history.

In 1975, *Le Nouvel Observateur* had published conversations with Jean-Paul Sartre: "Self-Portrait at 70." A year later, Jean Daniel (or Bernard-Henri Lévy) requested an interview, which I readily granted. I talked for a few hours, with complete candor, with Bernard-Henri Lévy. We obviously spoke about the "two little comrades." In the text, published in the 15 March 1976 issue, the question is asked: "In the end, between Sartre and Aron, which one will have had the greater impact on the history of his time?" I answered: "The question does not arise. He has already had much more impact than I. First of all because he has behind him a work that is much richer than mine; his range includes novels, plays, philosophy, politics. Second, because part of what I have done is destined to disappear very quickly. As Maurois once said of one of my books: 'He would be our Montesquieu if he were able to step back from reality." Half of this statement is true: I have not stepped back far enough from reality."

Then I presented myself as an analyst and a critic. Now, writers of this kind can exercise a not insignificant influence on their contemporaries, but their work, tied to an ephemeral situation, disappears more quickly than that of the creators who, at the risk of error, construct cathedrals of concepts with the courage of imagination. At this point, Lévy interrupted me: "Even when they are wrong?" To which I responded: "What condemns me in the eyes of the intelligentsia is that I was right before the truth was obvious to others. I am also condemned because they have not forgiven me for not opening the way for the good society and not having attempted to teach the method for achieving it." Lévy: "And what do you think? Is it better, in that case, to be Sartre or Aron? Sartre the mistaken victor, or Aron defeated but correct?" At first, I refused to answer: "It's a question that has no real meaning." Lévy insisted: "Ask it in a different way. What good is Sartre if he is wrong? What good is Aron if he is right?" This time, reluctantly, I explained myself: "What I think is catastrophic, what he will one day be criticized for is for having used his dialectical virtuosity and generous feelings to justify the unjustifiable. For having, if you like, expended treasures of ingeniousness to attempt to demonstrate that one could not be against Stalin[5] and that, at least, one had to be close to him. On the other hand, one day it will be said, if people are still interested in him or in me, that I never justified the unjustifiable for dialectical reasons. I have never justified Pinochet. I have never justified Stalin and Hitler."

The left has often remembered from this dialogue only one peculiar proposition: it was better to be wrong with Sartre than right with Aron. I never thought or asserted that. At most, I explained why some do not reject this unreasonable preference. I see no virtue, even after the fact, in those who followed Sartre in his aberrations, even though admiration for the man to some extent excuses loyalty pushed to the extreme of blindness. I had nothing to do with these divagations of the philosopher of freedom. If someone rejected the role of fellow traveler, he was not therefore an Aronian, nor did he necessarily agree with me. It was enough that he encountered me, on occasion, when I was lucky enough to be right. The expression "better wrong with Sartre . . . ," improvised out of scorn, risks taking on a meaning that is even more hateful than it is absurd, as though it were dishonorable to be in the same camp as Aron. Do I need to add that my merits are minimal? Many others, before me, spoke the truth about the Soviet Union. Bertrand Russell grasped it in the early 1920s, after a journey to the USSR; Souvarine wrote the essential about Stalinism in the 1930s. The problem arises from the persistence in illusion or error of so many superior minds and generous souls. There is no reason to glorify those who were wrong with Sartre; if they did not want to meet me, they had a very wide choice in locating other companions.

The dialogue between the "two little comrades," that went on for thirty years, was the origin of three television programs in October 1981 and the publication of the script under the title *Le Spectateur engagé*. The producers of the programs wondered why I had followed a path different from that taken by the most celebrated of my cohorts. To clear up the matter, they decided to interrogate me.

Thus, in 1980, I became friendly with two young professors who belonged to the generation of 1968, one of whom had been a member of a Trotskyist party at the time, the other less engaged politically but equally attached to that festive rebellion. I met one of them, Dominique Wolton, in my office, on the occasion of an interview for *Le Monde*. He and Bruno Frappat questioned me, and asked me at the end if I would accept the imposition of three television programs devoted to my life and my thought. I accepted the offer without thinking. "Television amuses me, why not?"

Dominique came to see me with his friend Jean-Louis Missika, in principle so that we could agree on the plans for the three programs and the subjects to be discussed. They presented to me once or twice the general structure and the themes to be considered in each program. I listened distractedly and answered to everything: I agree, it's your business. I put my files at their disposal—essentially letters received on the publication of my books. We spoke about everything, very little about the programs. I was not concerned, because I do not like to prepare for an interview, particularly on radio or television. I authorized them to ask me any questions they wished me to answer, but I did not want to prepare my answers. I am not an actor: when I am obliged to repeat a sequence, the second version is usually worse than the first.

Why did Dominique and Jean-Louis charm Suzanne and me? The question is perhaps naïve and meaningless. Who can say why connections are made? Let us try nevertheless to understand, without considering those nonmaterial factors that can neither be touched nor illuminated. They came to see me out of intellectual curiosity, said Jean-Louis. For more than thirty years, since the end of the war, I had surrendered to none of the intellectual fashions of Paris. What was the logic of the positions I had taken? What political philosophy inspired my rejection of some things and my acceptance of others?

Was I affected by their curiosity? I was especially affected by their tone, their manner. At *L'Express*, even before the departure of Jean-François Revel, I felt isolated because of my age, because of the deference or respect that most journalists offered me, at least in appearance. Dominique and Jean-Louis talked with me as though they were talking with a comrade or a friend of their own age, while avoiding the familiarity that would have embarrassed all three of us. They differ but they are close, and they have conversations between themselves and with others. Dominique speaks more than Jean-Louis, but he does not cut his friend off; he gives the false impression that he is a man who is always in tune with people and situations;

Jean-Louis is not immune to Jewish anxiety, with which I have deep sympathy. We developed the habit of continuing our never-ending dialogue in hallways and building entrances. We became friends in a manner that had been forgotten in the course of the preceding half-century. Dominique and Jean-Louis, against all the odds, restored to me the affectionate comradeship fostered and renewed by conversations that alternated between discussion and confession.

They had asked me to keep two weeks for them, ten days of recording. I could not refuse Alain Peyrefitte's request, for the Friday of the first week, that I deliver a speech in Valognes on the occasion of the award of the Tocqueville prize to David Riesman. I returned by helicopter in order not to miss entirely a half-day of work. I need not have been so scrupulous. I caught a cold, and my voice was affected by it during the second week. Sometimes, my hoarseness made my statements hard to understand. This is why important passages about my Jewishness were not retained in the broadcast.

Dominique and Jean-Louis assumed responsibility for the editing; this task lasted for several weeks. In this case, too, I had complete confidence in them. The recording had lasted for more than twenty hours; at most, an hour and a half of my words was preserved for the broadcasts. When the script was typed, Dominique and Jean-Louis suggested that I make it into a book. At first I refused: why should I publish these conversations while I was writing my memoirs? Why should I perpetuate these improvised conversations that Jean-Louis and Dominique had prepared, but I had not? On he other hand, I had some hesitation in depriving them of a book that would be in part theirs and would clearly display their virtues. (They had read not only my major books but also many of my articles.) Bernard de Fallois played the role of arbiter and agreed with my friends. Albert Palle was in the philosophy class in the lycée of Le Havre in 1933–34 when I taught there; I had maintained my connection with him. He undertook the task of clarifying my statements while maintaining their spoken character. He accomplished his task admirably. The book, *The Committed Observer*, received a favorable response from the critics, my friends, and the public. It has been translated into German, Spanish, Italian, Portuguese, and English, even though the English and the Americans are skeptical about books of conversations.

For the first time, the press was unanimously favorable toward me (not without certain reservations, of course), except for that of the Communist Party. Consider the article in *Le Monde* by Michel Contat, a close associate of Sartre, who is preparing the *Pléiade* edition of his novels. This article— sympathetic as a whole, aggressive at the end—concluded, so to speak, thirty years of dialogue. "[T]he intelligentsia of the left, for whom he was so often the scapegoat, the despised adversary, now finds itself Aronian, or almost. . . . We must read this book, which restores dignity to a genre that is often distorted by servility: the interview of an exceptional personality. . . . [T]he dialogue [between Sartre and Aron] never stopped. Not that they wrote their books to respond to one another. . . . But these two antagonistic ways of thinking, despite their common culture (phenomenology, Marxism) are the two poles between which the intellectual debate of the century has been stretched to the breaking point . . . it is in our heads that . . . the two fraternally antagonistic voices confront one another, our two voices: one, stating what is desirable, proposes an unending project, and the other, reasonably countering with what is possible, stubborn reality, sets forth warnings. . . . [H]e still belongs to the family of the left, and, in a certain sense, this has always been true, even when he joined the opposition, because his arguments are always directed to the left, as though he wanted to remove their blinders. . . . He is a cool analyst who takes positions, a dispassionate partisan. . . ." Finally, there was the aggressiveness: "Can this geopolitical vision of the preferable and the hateful justify Aron's apparent blindness—despite his anticolonialist positions on Indochina and Algeria—about North-South relations, and to their creation of a holocaust through hunger . . . ?" The *médecins sans frontières* are worth more than I—more than Contat and Sartre himself. Would I have helped the hungry of Bangladesh or the Sahel if, like Contat's master, I had attributed fault to American opulence?

I refrain from comment on "the liberal pessimism" which, "in the tradition of his masters, Benjamin Constant and Tocqueville, is somehow discouraging, deadly." Finally comes the sentence that would be offensive if it were not stupid: "[O]ne can only agree with [the reality principle] as one agrees with Raymond Aron about everything except the essential: when the oppressed rebel, they do so on the basis of the only right that no one can deny them, unless he is himself an oppressor, the right to justice, whatever the risks for everyone else." Contat here changes his rhetoric and returns to the indictment that the "beautiful souls" constantly formulated against me. I was not right about everything (I have often been mistaken), but how has "the rebellion of the oppressed" been the essential thing that I have failed to see? Is there *one* rebellion of *all* the oppressed? The same in all latitudes, in all countries? And who will define the justice to which these oppressed have the right? "To recognize oneself as an oppressor," very well, like all of us, the privileged, Contat included. In June 1982, I met him, thanked him for his article, and I added: "Why did you feel the need to write the final, stupid, sentence, which charged me with a fictitious guilt?" "Cioran also criticized me for that sentence," he answered, and then he defended himself against my criticisms (I had mixed up two sentences, one on hunger, the other on rebellion) and pleasantly confessed: "One does not leave one's family easily." I could have answered: "I know something about that."

An article in *Le Quotidien* by a journalist who was a royalist by origin or training, Gérard Leclerc, criticized me not for my "liberal" or "deadly pessimism," but on the contrary for my *absolute confidence* in the pragmatism of an industrial society. "The climate is calming to the nerves, all the more because there are not many oases of this kind in the intelligentsia." My error was thus not in discouraging but in wrongly reassuring my readers. "The misfortune is that this perfect *honnête homme*, this just man, is also the unconditional defender of a civilization that bears its contradiction within itself."

The choice that I presented in the *Introduction* as initial, originating, the choice of the society or the regime that seems to me the best for all, resembles a scientific hypothesis in the sense given to that notion by Karl Popper—a hypothesis that justifies the attitude of the *social engineer*, reformism rather than revolution, at least in our historical context. On this point, did Sartre and I take opposite paths? When I returned from London, he gave me a copy of *L'Etre et le néant* with this inscription: "To my little comrade, this ontological introduction to the introduction to the philosophy of history." Commitment, on the ontological level, is deferred as a projection toward the future, a response to the challenge of the situation. It does not follow from a reasonable deliberation on the pro and the contra. It denies the present, but it is ignorant of the future that it is creating.

In a sense, on the ontological level if you like, commitment, as Sartre analyzes it, reflects the human condition, the servitude of action. Man is always ignorant of the effects of his acts. But, if one moves from analysis of the human condition to reflection on politics, it is not true that one commits oneself without deliberation; and the first stage of deliberation demands or presupposes a knowledge of our world and of other possible worlds. The historicity of modern man implies at least an awareness of the plurality of economic and political systems possible in our century, the knowledge of the universes within which people have found their homes and the meaning of their life.

Michel Contat attributed to me a certain blindness toward the "holocaust through hunger." Gérard Leclerc thinks that "in a nihilistic world, freedom on the basis of abandonment is no longer reasonable in any way." It is a pity, he writes, "that such an informed man has not recognized the limits of the liberal world." In his view, one ought to "invoke Nietzsche and Heidegger, beyond Tocqueville and Max Weber" and recognize that this society is more the child of desire than of reason—which I would be too reasonable to admit. The critics of *In Defense of Decadent Europe* also reproached me for speaking as *homo oeconomicus* when what was needed was metaphysics.

I confess that I get little help from philosophers or metaphysicians, in particular from those who are considered to be such in France. What light do they shed on the fate of our "liberal civilization," "limited" like all civilizations? The word nihilism appears from the pen of this young journalist, along with the name of Nietzsche. We are living in an age of nihilism, so it appears. God is dead; our conceptions of the world, our convictions, mask the will to power. Everyone chooses his faith according to his illusions or his ambitions. There is no more truth: How can it be discerned?

Western societies, particularly European societies do indeed suffer from what is called nihilism; thinkers find themselves unable to establish their beliefs and practices on a rigorous basis; many confess that they are incapable of making choices except from feeling, whim, or habit. This kind of speculation, which gave evidence of the discredit into which reason had fallen, dominated the intellectual scene during the last years of the Weimar Republic. A kind of skepticism has been gnawing at European consciousness since the decline of transcendental religions, and then of secular religions. Those who believe themselves to be and wish to be Catholic, for the most part, interpret the most fundamental dogmas of the Church in their own way. The vast majority of Europeans have been de-Christianized.

Economic and social progress has created a mass of petit bourgeois, concerned about their status, turned in on themselves or on a narrow circle, the family, a few friends. Nietzsche detested in advance what Tocqueville predicted: "tutelary despotism." Perhaps this will lead to the replacement of the word *despotism* by the welfare state, if only to distinguish between soft, social-democratic despotisms, and the violent and cruel despotisms of one-party states.

This rather banal analysis is afflicted with a Eurocentrism that is not conscious of itself. Nihilism does not trouble humanity as a whole. The peoples of the Third World, delivered from the European yoke, torn apart by the rebellions of poverty and faith, do not raise questions, even through their intellectuals, about nihilism. They often raise questions about their identity, about resistance to Western culture, or about the elements of that culture that they need to assimilate in order to survive. European nihilism emanates in part from the death of God, and as much, or even more, from historic awareness of the place of Europe in the contemporary world.

The limitation of liberal civilization is painfully obvious. At the United Nations, the democratic states in the European sense now represent only a small minority. However, India, after China the most populous country in the world, has preserved a part of the political legacy left by its former master. Liberalism has not conquered the earth, like machines or ideologies. Marx foresaw the "technicization" of the planet; in contemporary terms, he predicted that capitalism would circle the globe, crushing along the way age-old customs, sacred beliefs, the most precious refinements in human relations. Marx nevertheless accepted, indeed exalted this spread of capitalism, cruel and necessary. Capitalism, embodied by the British, would destroy the Asiatic mode of production, more or less self-sufficient villages exploited by the imperial administration. Heidegger emphasized the technicization in Marx's project. "Technicization" was a part of it, but if one rereads the Marxist corpus, it is clear that the vast majority of his writings deal with modes of production, and with economic mechanisms and contradictions. The Europeans have, to some degree, completed the mission that the philosopher of history can attribute to them. They have discovered the art of applying science to technology. Perhaps we should say that they have developed a metaphysics that contains within itself a science that was to transform nature through technology. Even today, the West, including the United States, is pursuing the expansion of knowledge and power. Precisely because their historic mission seems to be coming to an end, the Europeans have doubts about their fate and wonder which way to turn.

The more scientific truth is confirmed by the use made of it by engineers, the more epistemologists and scientists themselves wonder about the specific characteristics of the truths, entirely provisional, that triumph in and through the domination of nature. The more the means of communication, calculation, and intelligence at the disposal of humanity go beyond all fictions, the more the creators fear they have played the role of sorcerers' apprentices. Prophets assault us on all sides; the disciples of the Club of Rome, those who are obsessed by nuclear weapons, those terrified by pollution, or those who are kept awake by the population explosion, all prophesy the apocalypse. There is no lack of bearers of bad news. I need neither Nietzsche nor Heidegger to know that the development of humanity does not obey reason.

None of these anxieties is without foundation. The Europeans move from one fear to another; yesterday partisans of zero growth, today in revolt against the slowing of growth, they have lost the sense of a common project. The mass of Western Europeans, in a context of satisfaction and internal quarrels, live with the relative opulence that they demand from the welfare state. Is the Old Continent, aging because of its declining birth rate, leaving the dirty and underpaid jobs to the immigrants, already surrendering to the ideocratic empire, or does it offer the image of societies more or less reconciled to themselves?

Wise Europeans who hate war and say farewell to arms? Europeans who have been through all the adventures, the crusades, colonial conquests, the unending quest of science, attached to their freedoms out of habit, incapable of uniting to defend themselves or to create something? Will they go through the years of recession or stagnation that may await them between now and the end of the century without self-division or self-betrayal? From day to day, according to my mood, I lean in one direction or the other.

Nietzsche, the last metaphysician of the West, according to Heidegger, and Heidegger himself, who looks for the meaning of our age in reference to the history of philosophy, add another dimension to our historical diagnoses. Do they tell us anything more about our future? Does the fate of Western Europe depend more on the disappearance of the gods or on the decline of the birthrate? I still have enough taste for philosophical speculation not to give a categorical answer to these questions.

On the other hand, if we are talking about possible apocalypses, the threats hanging over humanity, I know where to look for faith and hope. Against the evils of industrial civilization, nuclear weapons, pollution, hunger, or overpopulation, I have no secret miraculous remedies. But I know that millenarian beliefs or theoretical ratiocinations will serve no purpose; I prefer experience, knowledge, and modesty.

If civilizations, all ambitious and all precarious, are to realize in a distant future the dreams of the prophets, what universal vocation could unite them other than human reason?

NOTES

1. Despite appearances, he was never a fascist. Colonel de la Rocque was unjustly accused of collaboration and imprisoned on his return from deportation to Germany. General de Gaulle wrote a letter to his family in which he paid tribute to the citizen and the patriot.

2. I do not want to enter into the polemic or the explanation of the fact that the percentage of victims of genocide was lower in France than in the other Western countries, Holland and Belgium. Because of the existence of an unoccupied zone? Thanks to Vichy or despite Vichy? It does not seem to me impossible to distinguish two elements of the problem; on the one hand, the unoccupied zone, as such, had certain advantages for the Jews; on the other hand, these advantages were not always the result of actions by the Vichy government.

3. In *La Cérémonie des adieux*.

4. *L'Express*, 25 April 1980.

5. I should have said against communism.

EPILOGUE

I was lucky enough in my youth to have three friends whose superiority I could not conceal from myself: Jean-Paul Sartre, Eric Weil, and Alexandre Kojève. I had doubts about the first for a few years; Malraux's reaction to *La Légende de la vérité*[1] made me fear that the fertility of his mind and his creative power, obvious by the early 1930s, instead of finding expression in works of genius, would be lost in the interstices between philosophy and literature. Our dialogue nevertheless was without difficulty. To be sure, Sartre was right to criticize me for being too afraid of making a fool of myself. Even in the so-called exact sciences, research cannot be accomplished without mistakes, and mistakes are often profitable. He, on the other hand, particularly in politics, made generous use of his right to be wrong.

Eric Weil, whose name is known to only a few thousand people, was exceptionally cultured, almost perfectly so. I argued with him several times about events rather than philosophy. But when our conversations turned to philosophy, I felt almost physically an intellectual force superior to mine, the capacity to go further, deeper, to set up a system. Even then, he knew the great philosophers better than I.

Alexandre Kojève always gave me the feeling that, if I risked expressing an idea, he had already thought of it. If he had not thought of it, he could have. He, too, impressed me by the breadth and depth of his philosophical culture, and his posthumous books confirm this impression. In 1938, he too, was mistaken about history in the making; a few months before the invasion of Poland, he did not believe war would come. I have already raised the question in another chapter: What did he mean in 1939, when he called himself a strict Stalinist? My familiarity with these three exceptional men, one of whom became a sacred monster while the two others lived in semi-obscurity, protected me from illusions. I never dreamed of measuring myself against the Greats of the past, I was on the contrary happy to quote them, interpret them, continue them. I envied Sartre who, at twenty-five, thought, without a hint of vanity, that Hegel's height was accessible to him; another in the same group, convinced that he would go beyond Max Weber if he devoted himself to economic and social research, left me skeptical; I envied, with a smile, Eric Weil, who seriously told me one day that he was going to bring philosophy to its conclusion. As for the texts of Kojève that would bring to an end, according to him, the cycle of thought and of history themselves, I read them today with the same feelings I had fifty years ago, although those feelings may now be even more ambiguous.

Of course, I was divided between admiration for these extraordinary minds and doubt. But admiration prevented me from aiming too high and, at the same time, from suffering from the distance between my ambitions and my work. A few weeks or a few months after each of my books, I distance myself from them. Perhaps my writer's satisfaction lasted longer with the *Introduction, The Opium of the Intellectuals, Peace and War*, and *Clausewitz*.

I am not fully satisfied with any of my books. The imperfection of all of them, even with reference to the level to which I aspire, does not weigh too heavily on me, now that the game is definitely up. The *Introduction* needed another year, and less tense, elliptical, constrained writing. Similarly, *Peace and War*, even though I planned the book for more than ten years, was written too quickly; its different parts were unevenly ripe. As for the judgments expressed in England and the United States on the publication of a collection of articles,[2] neither the most indulgent nor the harshest changed the idea I had of myself. I do not believe Bernard Crick when he presents me not as a disciple but as an equal of Tocqueville; nor do I feel overcome by a rather harsh judgment from a historian whom I respect, Felix Gilbert.

I would be lying if I said that the judgments others make about me and my work leave me indifferent; that cursed blood clot has not hardened my skin to the point that arrows bounce off it as though it were armor. But my sensitivity, which was excessive in my twenties, has fallen below the normal. I would suffer if I lost the friendship or the esteem of a few people, young or old, who now make up my universe. As for the others, they have the right to bury me. One of the few survivors of my generation, Georges Canguilhem, deserves the peace that he enjoys; his privateness, his modesty, the rare quality of his books reserved for the few, place him outside the battle for prestige or Parisian authority. By accident or out of perversity, I persist in not sinking into silence. I rightly receive blows, since I give them from time to time—as infrequently as possible because, for me, the time for polemics is over. But—who can say why?—I sometimes feel the need to unmask mystifications and to continue a battle that is much larger than I. I will eagerly pass the torch to others.

What makes Raymond Aron run? asked Viansson-Ponté in an article in *Le Monde* devoted to the *Main Currents of Sociological Thought*. What used to make me run was the mission that my father's misfortune had left me as a legacy. Not that that mission imposed on me the search for honors. It is true that my father would have liked to have the *Légion d'honneur;* it would in a sense have compensated him for all the rest, for the true object of his ambition, at which he had failed. I sought neither "honors" nor social success. Pierre Bourdan urged me to sign an application; I remained a chevalier of the *Légion d'honneur* for twenty-eight years, some kind of record; other honors came without my seeking. The witticism attributed to Winston Churchill suits me perfectly: never ask for them, never refuse them, never wear them. As for the dozen honorary doctorates, I had no reason to refuse them; refusal would have been evidence of misplaced pride. Sartre's revolutionary motive for refusing the Nobel Prize has no meaning for me. I was touched by the Goethe Prize of the city of Frankfurt, given to George Lukács three years earlier and to Ernst Jünger three years later.

Perhaps journalism, which did not help me with my university colleagues, brought me to the attention of foreign juries more than I deserved. Without my articles, professors would probably appreciate my books more, and foreign universities would think of me less often. It hardly matters. I gave my parents everything they expected of me; I await my last years with serenity, no longer thinking of their last years with pain.

Have I done the best with the means available to me? Having approached philosophers of the highest level, I knew that I would never be one of them. Of course, if I had returned to the university in 1945, if I had been elected to the Sorbonne in 1947, if I had given up journalism, I would have written other books. To mention the least doubtful example, instead of the three paperback volumes, I would have written a large book, which would have had fewer readers, but would have better answered to my aspirations toward rigor. I regret this volume, which would have been comparable to the *Introduction* or to *Penser la guerre*. My work as an analyst and a militant in the service of freedom compensates for these losses.

What are the books I regret not having written? Some readers will probably reply: a book on Marx. I would agree with this widespread assumption only with some hesitation. Marxism that has become Marxism-Leninism is of no interest to any serious person, to any scholar. To adopt an expression of my friend Jon Elster, under what conditions can one be simultaneously a Marxist-Leninist, intelligent, and honest? One can be a Marxist-Leninist and intelligent, but in that case one is not (intellectually) honest. There is no lack of sincere Marxist-Leninists, but they lack intelligence. Elster is writing a book that attempts to "make sense of Marx"; not an intellectual biography but an interpretation of Marxism, derived from the texts, which will, so to speak, sum up the Marxism that is valid, or at least usable today.

My project is, or was a few years ago, entirely different: to clarify the basic philosophical speculations of the young Marx, to grasp the broad outlines of economics as he presents them in the *Critique*, the *Grundrisse*, and *Capital*, and to derive from these two parts the various possible Marxes and the characteristics of the prophet-revolutionary. I doubt that I still have the time to write this essay, sketched in my 1976–77 lecture course at the Collège de France. It would fill an empty space in the body of my writings. But, all things considered, the loss does not seem to me to be serious, even for me.

As I write, a new Marxological dispute is developing. It has been provoked by the sudden interest that British analytic philosophers have taken in the Marxist philosophy of history. They are reconsidering the celebrated text of the *Preface* to *Contribution to a Critique of Political Economy*, the text that contained, according to Marx himself, the essentials of his conception of history, a text that the Marxists of the Second International had endlessly analyzed, and that Lukács, and following him, the existentialists, had despised. On the other hand, the economic works, written between the *Grundrisse* and *Capital*, have not yet been published. Understanding of the totality of Marx's economic thought would require many years of Marxology. Specialists are aware of an economist named Marx, richer, more subtle, and more interesting than the author only of *Capital*. But the useful Marx, so to speak, the one who may have changed the history of the world, is the one who propagated false ideas; the rate of surplus value that he suggests leads to the conclusion that nationalization of the means of production would allow recovery for the workers of enormous quantities of value seized by the possessors of the means of production; socialism, or at least communism, eliminates the category of "the economic" and the dismal science itself. As an economist, Marx remains perhaps the richest, the most exciting of his time. As an economist-prophet, as a putative ancestor of Marxism-Leninism, he is an accursed sophist who bears some responsibility for the horrors of the twentieth century.

I should also regret the development foreseen in the *Introduction* and in *History and the Dialectic of Violence*. Discussion of books by analysts no longer excites me very much. The two controversies that have produced the most verbiage, the so-called Hempel-Dray controversy, and the one concerned with the nature (or reality) of "social facts," seem to me somehow exhausted. I have referred several times to the former. It has to do with the dispute between *explanation* and *understanding*. On the one hand, historical explanation, patterned after the ideal type of scientific explanation, requires one or more general propositions from which one can deduce particular consequences. This scheme can often be found, not fully explicit, in the writings of sociological historians. But when there is a question of one decision, one man in a unique situation, the historian illuminates the decision through the logic of the situation along with the character of the agent. To understand Hitler's decision to attack the Soviet Union in June 1941 on the basis of his ambitions and his personality seems both easy and uncertain; to explain it as one would explain an embolism, a storm, or an earthquake seems to me logically and existentially mistaken.

The second controversy is of more interest to me. It has to do with societal facts, not to be confused with social facts. Can a postal system, a railway system, a church be assimilated to an entity, or simply to a subject capable of making decisions and of being characterized by adjectives, like a person? It is a subtle, complex, and perhaps inexhaustible controversy. A postal system or, in an archaic society, the system of reciprocal gifts, is not Peter or Paul, a human individual, a being of flesh and feeling. A "societal fact" includes individuals, stabilized, ritualized, or organized relations, behaviors that assure the permanence of the system. Does this system act and organize in the same way as an individual? I am tempted to answer, along with one of the most penetrating analysts, yes and no, or else yes or no, as you like. The various groupings that make up a society, narrow and archaic, or broad and modern, exist; the sociologist does not create them by observing them, but they do not exist in the same manner as a biologically delimited and particularized individual. In these "societal facts," a number of individuals are obviously interchangeable; a substitute mail carrier fulfills the same function as the regular one on vacation.

These analyses fascinate me, even though they seem to me to be rather frustrating. They are connected to the debate over methodological individualism[3] as well as to that over holism.[4] I would have liked to clarify my scattered remarks on social groups, the *Zusammenhänge* in Dilthey's expression, within which we are all integrated.

The debate, which is certainly not new, can already be found, with a different vocabulary, at the center of the dialogue between Durkheim and Tarde, between those whom Karl Popper calls *holists* and the proponents of methodological individualism (Hayek, for example). It takes another form when sociologists present society functioning by itself, with individuals as nothing but cogs, prisoners of an inflexible determinism. The courses I presented at the Collège de France tended to clarify both the nature of social groups and of the modalities of explanation, individualist or holist.

At the same time, I would have extended the *Introduction* and *History and the Dialectic of Violence*. When a sociologist studies the *functioning* of a society (or of a sector of a society), he immobilizes, so to speak, his object; he does not remove it from the process of development, but he grasps it at a particular moment. The more his attention is fixed on an immobilized phenomenon for methodological reasons, the less he is concerned with imperceptible changes affecting it or, on occasion, suddenly transforming it. I would have liked to connect system and history with one another. In *The Imperial Republic* (Englewood Cliffs, N.J.: Prentice-Hall, 1974), I pointed out the relative independence of international political relations from the world market rather than the connections between the two. Perhaps the scholarly and academic career of each individual is largely determined by social circumstances that constrain individuals. But whoever has lived in the century of Hitler and Stalin must be permanently blind to history if he denies the role of "heroes" and sees only the unfolding of a global, inflexible, and predictable determinism, where his contemporaries hear the sound, see the fury, and seek the meaning.

In our age of economy and of war, I should have—and perhaps I still will—sketched the equivalent of Spengler's *Jahre der Entscheidung*, or rather sketch out a skeptical philosophy of history for the end of the twentieth century. The two great wars of the century, the first preparing the way for the second, were leading to a third. This apparently logical sequence was interrupted by the technical innovation of nuclear weapons. Perhaps the great powers will never use these weapons against one another, because probable destruction so far exceeds the possible benefits of a victory.

Enough regrets. Assuming that someone takes the trouble to read me in the future, he will discover the analyses, aspirations, and doubts that filled the consciousness of a man who was impregnated by history: a French citizen, but a Jew whom a semifree French government had excluded from his country through a statute based on racial criteria; a citizen of a France that was a member of the European Community, one of the four centers of world science and the world economy, incapable of defending itself, hesitating between American protection and the Soviet peace that Moscow offered at the price of freedom; a Europe that was more liberal and libertarian than ever before, and tormented by a rebellion against the constraints of industrial society; a Europe that was perhaps decadent, because civilizations flourish in freedom and decay in unbelief; a Europe within a humanity that, despite the decline in economic growth between now and the end of the century, is condemned to the expansion of science and production.

More than these uncompleted tasks, I often regret that I did not deepen the question the *Introduction* formulated without providing an answer: What is the status of historicism? Are we prisoners of a system of beliefs that we internalize at a very early age and that governs our distinction between good and evil? Is the civilization that the West is spreading throughout the world worth more than the cultures it is stifling, flattening, and has more than once condemned to death? In a certain sense, I have remained a man of the Enlightenment. Of course, I do not eliminate with a word—superstition— the dogmas of the churches. I often sympathize with the Catholics, loyal to their faith, who demonstrate a total freedom of thought in all profound matters. The horror of secular religions makes me feel some sympathy for transcendent religions.

Do secular religions differ in nature from social beliefs in general? Our society constantly teaches us to judge men, actions, books; secular religions lay claim to a monopoly of ultimate values. In my view, they are a sign of regression in comparison to the differentiation of orders, ideas, systems. The West, at least in part, owes to the duality of powers, spiritual and temporal, its greatness and its fecundity; in the Soviet Union, pseudo-believers maintain a pseudo-religion, a so-called social truth that would bring together and assume leadership over secondary truths. For Western Europeans, the establishment of Marxism-Leninism as the truth of the state would mean more than a regression, it would be an abdication. The West lives and survives only through pluralism.

Marxism-Leninism can accurately be called a superstition in the full sense of the term. The dogmas of salvationist religions avoid refutation because they assert realities or truths that, by their very nature, are inaccessible to investigation conducted according to the rules of rational knowledge. On the other hand a dogmatism that lays claim to ultimate truth in an area susceptible to scientific analysis is subject to criticism.

I profess the systematic anticommunism that has been attributed to me with a clear conscience. Communism is no less hateful to me than Nazism was. The argument that I used more than once to distinguish class messianism from race messianism no longer impresses me very much. The apparent universality of the former has become, in the last analysis, an illusion. Once a class-based organization has come to power, it becomes involved with a national or imperial messianism. It sanctifies conflicts or wars rather than preserving, across frontiers, the fragile links of a common faith.

Intellectual or spiritual pluralism does not lay claim to a truth comparable to those of mathematics or physics; nor does it fall back to the level of ordinary opinion. It is rooted in the tradition of our culture; it is justified, and to some degree verified, by the falseness of beliefs that attempt to deny it. Iranian Shiites and Marxist-Leninists belong to the same family, since the Shiite clergy wants to rule over civil society as the Soviet Communist Party does. The Westerner is superior to the devotees of Khomeini or Lenin because he knows the difference between scientific truths, however provisional they may be, and religious beliefs, because he challenges himself, aware that our culture, in certain respects, is one among many. The refusal of doubt may strengthen the order of fighters, but it excludes pacification. The imam Khomeini, like the Marxist-Leninists, reminds us that "active faith" leads, even now, to a crusade. Contemporary Westerners, aware of the legitimate plurality of moral authorities, aware of the particularity of our culture, are the only ones who show the way toward a history that would have some meaning.

The secularization of politics leads logically to pluralism. Not that competition among parties can be placed on the same level as spiritual pluralism. What now seems to me implied by the exhaustion of inherited certainties is the questioning of the social order and the political system. It would be unreasonable to assert that it would be better to have a society subjected to permanent challenge than a society held together by uniformly shared convictions (better for whom?). I would say that political challenges are a necessary consequence of religious challenges. But political challenges are either repressed, suppressed, or stifled by varied levels of violence and manipulation; or else they are tolerated or organized with a view toward establishing a mode of government.

It is nevertheless true that the regimes I have called constitutional-pluralist can always be called the best or the only good ones, destined to be spread throughout the world. They correspond to the mental state of those whom Auguste Comte would have called the avant-garde of humanity. The right of everyone to participate in the political dialogue about the common fate flows from the abandonment of absolute truths, but certain societies cannot grant this right without dissolving.

Democracy, in classical philosophy, required citizens, virtuous citizens, that is, respectful of the Laws. Democracy in industrial societies establishes conflicts between producers and consumers, interest groups and political parties. The power that comes out of these inevitable rivalries, and which is limited by them, always risks decline, risks misunderstanding the demands of collective security.

It is convenient to argue that man preferred, and would still prefer, a sovereign separated from those who resemble him by the past that he embodies and the feeling that his subjects, in the course of centuries, have learned to offer to him. If one coldly compares the advantages and defects among various regimes, while considering all theoretically possible regimes, I do not know whether I would grant the first rank to the democracies of Europe or America. But what other system in the West could enjoy legitimacy? One-party states, in this view, would last only through scarcely veiled violence, and through the sullen resignation of the population. The countries of Eastern Europe provide us with a demonstration of that fact.

Even in politics, the debate over historicism retains an abstract, almost artificial character. If one raises the question of whether one should deplore the fact that humanity did not cease its development with neolithic societies or the Greek city-states, the answer seems to me impossible and the question devoid of meaning. The animal-man was programmed by his genetic inheritance for cultural evolution. At the various stages of this evolution, the organization of life in common took on various forms. This diversity in itself, does not pose a problem. What does create a problem, in the eyes of "historicists," is that evil in one place becomes good in another. Truth on this side of the Pyrenees, falsehood on the other.

Sociologists proclaim the diversity of languages and customs, the wealth of diverse human expressions. In the name of what value, according to what criteria can we choose among these "societies," giving each one a place at a particular level of the hierarchy, considering one of them as the best or as exemplary? In the same vein, Max Weber said: Which of the two cultures, French and German, is superior to the other? I reply: Why pose the question? To choose between them? Or to place one above the other?

It is true that diversity risks leading us into skepticism, if good and evil are reversed from one society to another. I do not at all think that this is true. Honesty, frankness, generosity, gentleness, and friendship do not change signs from one century to the next, from one continent to another, or by crossing borders. Of course, the same conduct can be considered aggressive in one group and healthily competitive in another. Neither behavior nor success is appreciated everywhere according to the same criteria. Within a particular society, there is no single image of the exemplary man. The knight, the priest, the intellectual do not aspire to the same kind of excellence. Everything that depends on culture, as ethnologists have defined it, is outside universalistic judgment. Anyone who would formulate such a judgment would necessarily belong to one of those cultures. There is no observer above the fray.

To some extent, the multiplicity of cultures resembles the multiplicity of arts: we should appreciate the diversity, not deplore the anarchy. We Westerners are, so to speak, in the soup. More than anyone else, we have become aware of this diversity, and we simultaneously aspire to universal truths or values. A contradiction that troubles, tears apart our historical consciousness, but which we are not unable to overcome, or at least to withstand.

Should we curse the Roman conquest of Gaul or celebrate it as the origin of France? Everyone will answer this question according to his feelings and his knowledge. A historical judgment of this kind should be left to the scholars, if they have the taste for it, to polemicists, or even to a philosopher like Fichte, possessed by the demon of propaganda. These historical judgments trouble us only when they become political judgments.

In our time, millions of people are living through and suffering from the acute contradiction between a culture that is dying and a culture that they simultaneously hate and desire because it offers the path to power and opulence. Nearly a half-century ago, I wrote that the West no longer knows whether or not it prefers what it contributes to what it destroys. Deprived of their empires, the Europeans no longer have the same responsibilities; they may still be committing ethnocide, but they do so less through their actions than through their very nature. The history of humanity is strewn with dead cultures, sometimes even cultures that have vanished in living memory.

History was tragic for the Indians, the Incas, the Aztecs? Who can doubt it? It tramples on the corpses of cultures as it tramples on the corpses of men. What is it leading to? Will what comes tomorrow even justify the suffering of those who fell along the way? Here too, no one can answer. Today, in this century, we have been freed from the provincialism characteristic of all past cultures, freed from naïve progressivism, and also from facile relativism. The truth of science, recognition of the dignity of all, nobles and commoners, form the basis of our convictions. The events of the century have dissipated our illusions: the progress of science is no guarantee of the progress of men or societies. The horrors of the regimes of Hitler and Stalin, contrary to current opinion, tear us away from a coarse form of progressivism. We know that everything, including the worst, is possible, but also that the worst is not morally indistinguishable from the acceptable.

By means of this approach, I would have arrived at a more thoroughly developed theory of "historical consciousness in thought and action."[5] How can one reconcile in thought the right of all cultures to exist and resolute adherence to one's own culture? How can I reconcile in practice my belonging to the nation of which I am a citizen and my loyalty to my Jewish ancestors? How can I accept the possibility of the use of nuclear arms against cities, in other words the annihilation of millions of innocent people? Could I fully accept the last sentence of the *Introduction:* "Human existence is dialectical, that is, dramatic, since it operates in an incoherent world, commits itself regardless of its duration, seeks a fleeting truth, with no assurance but that provided by a fragmentary science and formal thought"?

I would make a sharper distinction between social values and moral virtues, I would strengthen the foundations of scientific truth and human universalism. As for action, I would describe our historical condition more concretely, but not in fundamentally different terms. In quiet periods, within modern democratic societies, the citizen has few occasions to live through the terrors of adventurous decisions. When we hesitate between American and Soviet protection, we are involved in an incoherent world, we choose one social configuration against another, both of which are imperfect, and we resign ourselves to a possible horror that we should perhaps reject absolutely.

About fifty years ago, I wrote that our historical condition was dramatic. Should we say dramatic or tragic? In some respects, tragic is more appropriate than dramatic. Tragic is the necessity to establish security on the basis of the nuclear threat; tragic, the choice between the accumulation of conventional weapons and the nuclear threat; tragic, the destruction of old cultures by industrial civilization, but tragedy would be the final judgment only if a fortunate conclusion, beyond tragedy, was not even conceivable. I continue to think a happy end possible, far beyond the political horizon, an Idea of Reason.[6]

Have I felt regret for not having been the Kissinger of a Prince, as some have suggested, notably Jean d'Ormesson? I would answer them in a friendly way that they are wrong. Roger Martin du Gard, in his still unpublished memoirs, sketches an excessively flattering portrait of me, and explains why I "will not rule."[7]

As for me, I think that I simply never possessed the qualities necessary to exercise power, even at the level of an adviser. Prudent in my writings, I have difficulty in controlling my speech. I allow myself to express extreme ideas, to respond to circumstances or to express moods which do not represent my deepest thoughts and risk discrediting them. A political man has to hold his tongue as well as his pen. I am not incapable of adapting my words to my audience, but diplomatic language is painful to me. I like to speak without weighing my words, and even the most trivial lie costs me an effort: I lack imagination in refusing a dinner invitation or a request for a lecture.

There is more. I never claimed to have the competence of a professional economist. To be sure, most finance ministers themselves do not have the competence of those who teach or administer the economy. Why should a minister, if he were seeking an adviser outside the administration, choose a man like me, on the periphery of all disciplines, a free spirit inclined toward passions that are hardly compatible with the duties of adviser?

The case of Henry Kissinger obsesses commentators, because of my relations with him and his feelings toward me, which he expresses freely, even in my absence. My grandchildren will proudly preserve the copy of his

Memoirs with the inscription: "To my teacher" (unless historians remove Kissinger from his pedestal and I share with him in the fickleness of fate). Presiding over the National Security Council in Washington, informing the President of the United States every morning about the state of the world, negotiating for him in Peking or Moscow—such a role would have fascinated me if I had been an American citizen. All the more so because Bundy, Rostow, Kissinger, and Brzezinski, professors at Harvard or MIT, whose status was comparable to mine, acceded to the post without an electoral campaign, without laying siege to the Prince. Of course, as an American citizen, I would have sought the experience of power, but I would —I hope— have understood in time that I did not have the stuff of a Kissinger.

Intelligence, knowledge, and judgment are not enough. Performance is also required, of which I would most probably have been incapable: to impose oneself in the jungle of Washington disputes, personal and political, to seduce the press or at least avoid its hostility, to make or inspire often necessary decisions that send young men into battle and death. Not that I reject the use of force, in theory or in practice. But it is one thing to agree abstractly to the recourse to arms, and another to convince the president here and now to take that step. My scrupulous nature and my hatred of violence would have told against me in the post occupied by an exceptional intellectual like Kissinger.

Enough of these confessions about the unreal. Let us imagine a position in France comparable to that of adviser for diplomacy and defense. None of the presidents of the Fifth Republic has needed such an adviser, and none of them would have accepted him. And the position would not have been very exciting. A substantial part of General de Gaulle's diplomacy did not go beyond stage management. What remains from his journeys to Latin America, Rumania, or Poland, but the memory of acclaim? A few of his decisions remain: leaving the integrated command of NATO, attempting and failing at a Franco-German alliance designed to remove the two countries from "American hegemony," reestablishing relations with Moscow (neither understanding nor cooperation followed from this détente). Since then, French diplomacy has been composed of two aspects: permanent negotiations with our partners in the European Community and action in the rest of the world.

In Africa, France is attempting to preserve its sphere of influence, to maintain its links with Francophone countries. From time to time, crises arise, in Chad, the Central African Republic, Kinshasa. Decisions, correct or not, require neither clairvoyance nor uncommon courage. In the Near East, French diplomacy has hardly gone beyond declarations, for lack of the means necessary to have a direct effect on events. France is absent from no part of the world but, even though the presidents of the Fifth Republic, like American presidents, act as their own foreign ministers, they delude themselves. Since the death of the General, except for Britain's entry into the European Community, French diplomacy has remained in the same groove. This is not what gives France its place in the world; it is the French themselves, the quality of their work and of their culture.

I envisaged neither a ministry, nor an ambassadorship, even less a seat on the Conseil Constitutionnel, which was offered to me. What made me run and still occasionally awakens in me anxiety and hope is the question that I constantly asked myself: Did my teaching have some value for the young people who listened to me? Did the teaching contained in my articles serve my country, the instruction of my readers, the reputation of French journalism outside France? Did I serve some function for the thirty years during which, in all circumstances, I wrote at least an article each month?

During my dozen years at the Sorbonne, I felt little concern about the influence I might have. I brought to my students, Marxist or not, the theory of industrial society, the political philosophy of Spinoza, the sociological interpretation of Montesquieu, the study of international relations. This teaching may not have had the same value, in some respects, as the teaching of a specialist in questionnaires would have had for the few destined for careers as sociologists. But, given the student public in those years of transition between the Sorbonne of my youth and the Sorbonne that exploded in 1968, a more traditional professor, more prosaically and rigorously following the path from analysis to sociological explanation, would have done no better than I. Better for some, worse for most. Professionals emphasize technical training of sociologists all the more because they know its limits and, in the last analysis, its facile quality.

The question I asked myself more than once has to do with the moral or political content of my teaching, understood in the broadest sense. I have alluded to my contacts with the students of the Ecole Normale Supérieure of Saint-Cloud. A few months ago, in 1982, when this book was almost finished, I received from a former student at that school a few pages of a little book that he did not intend to publish, a book of memoirs in which I appear.

Here we are in the twilight of a curtained hall of the Sorbonne, for a meeting of the *Société française de philosophie* chaired by an Olympian Léon Brunschvicg, with an enormous forehead and a gaze that seems to penetrate beneath appearances. Raymond Aron—in an awkward body, with a face like a mask: elephant ears, prominent nose, a mouth both ironic and bitter—has just made a presentation, with cool detachment, on relativity in history, the fragility of democracy, the uncertainty of the future of humanity, views that provoke the massive Victor Basch. Basch, his whole body trembling, proclaims with a tribune's voice his unshakable conviction: freedom was born in Greece, it has constantly enlightened man in his progress, it is a light that will never go out; it will carry the day. His interlocutor replies with cold courtesy that nothing is determined in advance, that nothing is definitively established, that at most one might consider (but this concession is made grudgingly, almost wearily) that in the very long term, perhaps, reason and morality might win out through their coherence, more effective and more solid than passion and violence. . . . It is obviously Raymond Aron who is right.[8]

The session of the *Société française de philosophie* described here took place in June 1939. I have referred to it myself in an earlier chapter with mixed feelings. Of course I was right: the uncertainty of the future, the threat of war, the fragility of democracy. Victor Basch was living his faith, serene despite the gathering storm. And he was assassinated—because he was a Jew, because he believed in all the values that the Nazis and their French disciples wanted to destroy.

The "Cloutard" reports his memories of his philosophy professors:

We took the courses of the two professors jointly charged with teaching philosophy at the school, both Jews, but as dissimilar as possible. The conscientious Dreyfus-Lefoyer was always there; his course, which was thorough, even exhaustive, without challenge and without surprise, left us indifferent. The course of the relaxed Raymond Aron in which, completely outside the official program, he provided us with his reflections on the philosophers of history, from Machiavelli to Sorel and Pareto, with Hobbes along the way, was provocative and impressive. To idealist optimism, he contrasted the practice of political actors, whether or not concealed by speech—the *Realpolitik* of Bismarck that had inspired Hitler. He had just spent several years in Germany, when he had been able to observe the rise of Nazism that he obviously abhorred, while it fascinated him. He had been a socialist and had developed a deep understanding of Marx. He appreciated in Marx the rigorous economic critic, but he rejected the Manichaean prophetic stance, the source of unappealable condemnations. In the name of lucidity and realism, he cut through illusions. I did not want to give up my faith, but I recognized the power of his views. While we all wanted to continue to live in the nineteenth century, just as sunlight dissolves fog, his rigor did away with its myths, and we all found ourselves unarmed and naked on the edge of the abyss. We might almost have held it against him, as though he were the one who had led us there. And in fact, denouncing the Nazi danger that carried with it the threat of war, he was frightening at the same time that, emptying the revolutionary credo of all hope, he was demobilizing. . . .

It was not I who was frightening but the world as it appeared to me between 1935 and 1939, and as it was, as we know today. I was never cold, but I often gave that impression. Why? Because of my reticence? Because I maintained distinctions between teaching and friendship? Because I followed Spinoza's advice "not to ridicule human actions, not to deplore them or curse them, but to understand them"? Some or all of this was true, probably in addition to something else that was more mysterious. The statements I made when young, in the course of the 1930s, may have expressed a kind of intellectual delight, the awareness of having dissipated clouds and come close to the truth. If nostalgia for the beliefs I was attacking had been perceptible beneath my negations, my voice might not have been made cold by analysis but warmed by the rebellion, futile as it may have been, of consciousness against reality.

When I wrote *La tragédie algérienne*, François Mauriac came up with the same adjective as my student at Saint-Cloud. Why? A choice had to be made between war and peace, between the preservation of French sovereignty and the Algerians' right to independence; this dilemma had to be presented *mercilessly*. The analysis was neither warm nor cold, but it was either true or false. To be fair, on another occasion, François Mauriac thanked me with a warm letter for a lecture I delivered to several hundred Catholic students.

There remains the serious accusation that I was demobilizing. Was this true throughout my life? This should not be true, since I have not devoted myself exclusively to the austere task of science. I may have been demobilizing for my students at Saint-Cloud between 1935 and 1939.[9] But what opportunity did I have to do better? Fauconnet left me the choice between "desperate or Satanic"; the "Cloutard" and his friends considered me terrifying. I shook their certainties, I revealed to them the mortal danger that was upon us. I argued for a democracy which, even in its decrepitude, was better than the totalitarian regimes. "We are fighting for *Paris-soir* against the *Völkischer Beobachter*," Jean Cavaillès said one day, not in despair, but mockingly, and he was one of the purest heroes of the Resistance. I did not open for my listeners the path to revolutionary salvation. Was I wrong, when salvation bore the name of Stalin?

Have I been "demobilizing" since the war? It was indeed necessary to demobilize the believers, militants, fellow travelers of Stalin, Khrushchev, and Brezhnev. I devoted a good deal of time to this operation for mental health. Facts and fashions, not my arguments, have now tended to discredit the revolutionary hope that communism claims to embody. But, although the "Cloutard" in the 1930s could legitimately ask: "What can I hold on to?" Michel Contat does not have the right to pose the same question in 1982. Since the last war, the Western democracies have accomplished progress that those who hold them in contempt considered impossible: economic growth, personal freedom, the improvement of social relations. Who propagated "deadly" teaching, those who sought Mecca in turn in Moscow, Belgrade, Peking, and Havana, or those who, freed from soteriological beliefs, worked as hard as they could for prosperity and for the reform of liberal regimes, the least bad of our civilization, perhaps the least bad in history?

The critique of secular religions contained in itself certain affirmations, a broad position that some would attack as conformist. I accept the basic characteristics of established democratic and liberal regimes. In the *Essay on Freedom,* for which I have a certain affection, I attempted to set forth the necessary synthesis of two forms of freedom: the realm of autonomy left to individuals and the means that the state offers to the most deprived so that they might exercise their acknowledged rights. Modern democracies ignore neither freedom of choice nor freedom as capacity, the former assured by limitations on the state, the latter by social legislation. At their best moments, Western societies seem to me to have accomplished an exemplary compromise.

Nowadays, the dominant thinkers would not dream of calling me "Satanic or desperate." They would be more likely to denounce me as a conservative, indifferent to inequalities among individuals and nations, resigned to regimes of which no one, unless he is blind, can ignore the imperfections, if not the basic flaws. The rich and the poor still exist, along with the powerful and the humble. No "sociodicy" could justify our regimes any more than theodicies ever justified the Creator. Those who place equality above all, above freedom, criticize me for the small space I have devoted, in my books and articles, to the "scandals" of inequality.

I often discussed inequality in my Sorbonne lectures. One year, I devoted two hours a week to the theme. I never produced material for publication because my attempts left me so unsatisfied.

I am with all my heart egalitarian in the moral sense of the term: I loathe the too frequent social relations in which status hierarchy stifles the sense of fraternity. Is this a legacy of salvationist religions, of the equality of everyone before God? The arrogance or authoritarianism toward their students of a number of my colleagues, often on the left, shocks me. But, beyond these feelings, I confess that I do not know what is implied by social justice, nor what distribution of income, wealth, prestige, or power would meet the requirements of equity. Legal philosophers in the United States have been discussing the theme for several years. They are inclined to recommend the greatest equality compatible with the preservation of freedom. However brilliant these speculations may be, they neither suppress the obviousness of certain judgments on particular cases, nor the uncertainty about society as a whole.

Outside a society that is egalitarian in every respect, which is impossible in the absence of total despotism, the distribution of social goods follows no simple principle. Negative judgments are easier to make than positive ones. The advantages, monetary and otherwise, enjoyed by certain groups, professions, or individuals, are neither justified in themselves nor in comparison with those of other groups, professions, or individuals. It is easier to condemn an unjust situation than to define the notion of justice that should govern society as a whole. For every profession, in the abstract, one should take into account the cost of training, the painfulness of the work, the contribution to the common good, its effectiveness, without considering the moral value of each individual. On the basis of these considerations no one, not even the most sophisticated computational analyst, could give a categorical answer. The distribution of individuals in jobs is largely a matter of chance. The one who has not succeeded can blame fate and avoid his own responsibilities.

Everyone who wrote about politics out of a concern for truth was in some sense a demystifier. In an age dominated by the ideas of liberty and equality, sociologists belong more than ever to the school of suspicion. They do not take at face value the language that social actors use about themselves. The boldest or most pessimistic, no longer possessing an image or a hope of the good society, consider their own with merciless severity. The very society that proclaims equality of opportunity transmits, from generation to generation, its structure, its classes, its hierarchy; the members of these classes change over time, but familial continuity wins out. By means of their diplomas, the heirs add an extra component to their legitimacy.

Sociologists have formed diverse images of our liberal societies on the basis of the same facts. It is not surprising that the children of favored families have more chance of succeeding than the child of an industrial or agricultural worker. The more the educational system puts all students together in the same schools, hence in apparent conditions of equality, the more equality of opportunity appears out of reach. The illusions of the single school have vanished; but should we be indignant because opportunities are unequal, or congratulate ourselves because there are opportunities for many, if not for all?

Liberal society, like every society, "socializes" the young, inculcates in them certain values, a sense of good and evil. In this sense, those who have power, who lord it over others, also impose their symbols. Is it scandalous that the moral authority of the laws of the state strengthens, by legitimating it, the domination of the ruling class? Or else, should we marvel at the freedom of choice that the West, unbelieving and perhaps decadent, leaves to everyone? Scientific culture, universalist by nature, now holds the principal place in the education of the young. And the values propagated by the educational system tend to invite criticism of, rather than respect for, the established order.

Marxism no longer plays the role of crushing democratic-liberal regimes under the utopia of the classless society or the example of Soviet reality. It may help to foster a kind of nihilism. By insisting on the arbitrary nature of values and the inequality of interpersonal relations in communities that are, in relative terms, the least tyrannical, one ends up by not recognizing the most obvious facts: although modern society reproduces itself—it would not be a society if it did not reproduce itself—it is changing more rapidly than all past societies. And the liberal order remains different from the tyrannical order offered to us by the Soviet Union. Whoever sees only a difference in degree between the ideology of the state in Moscow and "symbolic violence" in Paris, blinded by "sociologism," finally obscures the fundamental questions of the century.

The philosophers of history who have adopted Toynbee's perspective assert that Europe will recover its strength only through faith, Christianity or even, specifically, Catholicism. I declare myself incompetent on the question. If I were a believer, Jewish or Christian, I would attempt to propagate my faith or my truth. Since I am not a believer of any church, I leave the space of transcendental faith empty, and I personally adhere to the faith of the philosopher, doubt rather than negation. The many attempts to establish harmony between Christian dogma and contemporary cosmologies may, without corresponding, coexist without contradicting one another. Science will never produce anything comparable to the Covenant of the Jewish people or the Revelation of Christ.

The sociology of religion methodologically abstracts from the supernatural dimension. Can it answer the question of whether the twenty-first century will be religious? Is a revival of the Catholic Church probable, and what form will it take? Will it move in the direction of the traditionalists or of the liberation theologians? I do not feel capable of deciding. I believe more in a Catholicism that preaches the salvation of each individual soul than in a Church as auxiliary of revolutionary movements (although in Latin America, the second possibility seems to me in some cases to be almost inevitable).

By leaving out of account traditional churches and concentrating my attention on secular religions did I miss the essential point? Was I wrong or unlucky in taking economics and war as subjects of reflection, as the principal phenomena of our time? I have just proposed a choice between error and bad luck. In fact, how could I have chosen otherwise? When I reached historical consciousness, the Great Depression was exacerbating German nationalism, driving Hitler to power, and Europe toward catastrophe. Marxism in power in Moscow, an antiproletarian revolution in Berlin, those are the events that dictated the direction of my research. I wanted to become the contemporary historian of those revolutions and those wars.

Bad luck. Did the inspiration I found in German historicism, in Kark Marx and Max Weber, turn me away from the right path, that of Durkheim and Tarde? Does my generation, "polluted" by German ideas, which Jean-Paul Sartre transfigured with incomparable brilliance, already belong to the past? This may be true, and I feel no bitterness about it. The best sociologists, however, use both Marx and Weber, both purified of their political passions, which conceal their complementary character from the scientific point of view.

Personally, I do not think that my passage through German culture, followed by my study of Anglo-American analytic philosophy, turned me away from France. Before 1939, Germany was our fate. Until the defeat of the Third Reich in 1945, ideas that had come from Germany had penetrated world history. Racism belonged no more to Germany than to other European countries, but Hegel, Marx, and their epigones, Nietzsche and his critique of ideologies, informed, illustrated, shed light on the great conflicts for world domination.

After the twilight of the Germanic gods, American-style democracy, pragmatic, without metaphysics, in search of semantic rigor, confronted nothing but a bastardized version of the Hegelian-Marxist tradition. The technicization of the planet was stimulated with a new impulse. Marxist myths finally dissipated almost by themselves, in the light of the facts. Even the change in the economic climate since 1973 (or perhaps a few years earlier) has not renewed perspectives on the future of humanity.

I see few reasons for optimism when I look at the present. The Europeans are in the process of committing suicide by means of their low birthrate. Peoples that do not reproduce themselves are condemned to growing old, and are therefore haunted by the state of mind of abdication, a *"fin de siècle"* sensibility. They can compensate for losses with foreigners, as they did during the thirty postwar years of prosperity, but they thereby risk increasing tension between immigrants and workers threatened with unemployment. The democratic-liberal synthesis and the mixed economy are threatened, probably by the end of the century, by the slowing of growth, inflation, monetary disorder, and the proportion of transfer payments in the national income. After an almost miraculous recovery, France is losing its place in the world, because it has not adapted to the rigors of competition, because it is half-paralyzed by internal quarrels and the persistence of anachronistic ideologies.

The United States has lost its military superiority. The Soviet Union has accumulated weapons, at first to intimidate, and also to intervene as soon as an opportunity arises. The political class of the American republic, the Eastern elite, that inspired and conducted diplomacy for a quarter-century, has committed suicide; responsible for the Vietnam War, it laid the blame on Richard Nixon, who had not brought it to an end quickly enough. Presidents Carter and Reagan have oscillated from one extreme to another. The consensus on foreign policy has disappeared. The country is no longer rich enough to finance both social legislation and rearmament. It still has scientific preeminence and an unequaled system of production, but it has become unpredictable for its enemies and for its allies.

In Europe, the Federal Republic of Germany, more than ever the keystone of the Atlantic Alliance, seems troubled. On the front lines, touching the Soviet empire, it attempts to maintain an American army on its territory without irritating the men in the Kremlin. The pacifism of millions of Germans has reduced the goverment's decision–making capacity: Does it express the legitimate fear of horrible weapons or the rejection of participation that the German people has more and more difficulty in accepting? The reconciliation of the French and the Germans remains solid and authentic. But has the day evoked in the controversies of the 1950s arrived? Socialist or conservative, the chancellor in Bonn looks both toward the threatening East and toward the protective West. In what direction will he turn in the end?

If I were to give in to my darker feelings, I would say that all the ideas, all the causes for which I have struggled seem to be in danger at the very moment when, retrospectively, it is granted that I was not wrong in most of my fights. But I do not want to surrender to discouragement. The regimes for which I have argued, in which some would see only a camouflage for power, by its essence arbitrary and violent, are fragile and turbulent; but as long as they remain free, they will possess unsuspected resources. We will continue to live for a long time, in the shadow of the nuclear apocalypse, divided between the fear inspired by monstrous weapons and the hope awakened by the miracles of science.

I would not like to end this too lengthy retrospective with reflections on history in the making. By definition, it goes on; the point at which it stops for me means nothing in itself or for others. My professional activity has not filled my life, neither articles, nor books, nor teaching. I owe to my wife, my children, my grandchildren, and my friends the fact that I have lived my "reprieve," since 1977, not in anguish but with serenity. Thanks to them, I have accepted death—that is easy—but also the consequences of the embolism and the infirmities of age—which is harder. I remember an expression I sometimes used when I was twenty, in conversations with friends and with myself: "to achieve one's secular salvation." With or without God, no one knows at the end of his life whether he is saved or lost. Thanks to those about whom I have said so little and who have given me so much, I remember this formula without fear and trembling.

NOTES

1. A manuscript rejected by Gallimard, which is soon to be published along with other unpublished works by Sartre.

2. *History and Politics* (New York: Free Press, 1978).

3. Methodological individualism consists in asserting that in the last analysis all social facts result from individual behaviors and that all explanations, in the social sciences, ought to go back to those individual behaviors.

4. This name has been given to the theory of totalities or of groups that cannot be reduced to the elements they contain.

5. A title I gave to two series of lectures in Aberdeen, the "Gifford Lectures."

6. In Kant's sense.

7. "Reading the works of Raymond Aron, one's first feeling of agreement is so strong that one would like to grant him absolute power and allow him to conduct affairs of state. He is the 'good dictator,' secretly desired since the death of Solon. But I imagine him in power. He is much too intelligent to govern! Not only would his intelligence disarm him in the face of his adversaries and oblige him to understand opposition too well to brush it aside or to combat it. . . ." The text is dated "summer 1957." Roger was probably thinking in particular of my positions on Algeria.

8. I showed the portrait I have quoted to another former student of Saint-Cloud. This other "Cloutard," who has since become a university professor, had attended neither my thesis defense nor the session of the *Société française de philosophie*, but he remembered me as a professor. He wrote: "At Saint-Cloud, before, during, and after classes, your features and your attitude were what they were but with something more that is missing from this portrait, your smile, your kindness, your good humor. It is true that you did not go to the *Société de philosophie* to be nice, but to defend your convictions. The fact remains that if I accept the 'ironic' mouth, I strongly challenge the bitter mouth. I have trouble finding an appropriate replacement for the word, but I never saw any bitterness on your ironic (but not always) mouth even when the Sorbonne chose Gurvitch over you, an evening when I happened to be visiting; I saw, to be truthful and you will forgive me, occasional sadness, but there was good reason for that." This second student became a friend in the prewar years; I was not the same for those who listened from a distance as for a friend who visited us in the little house where I was finishing my thesis and with whom I discussed *Esprit*.

9. Not for all of them, particularly not for the Catholics.

BIBLIOGRAPHY

This bibliography is neither complete nor scientific. It will allow the interested reader to refer to my works in the five periods into which I have divided these *Memoirs*.*

I. 1928–1940

La Sociologie allemande contemporaine. Paris: Alcan, 1935; reprinted in 1950, 1957, 1981. (*German Sociology*. Glencoe, Ill.: Free Press, 1957; reprinted 1982.)

Introduction à la Philosophie de l'Histoire. Essai sur les limites de l'objectivité historique. Paris: Gallimard, 1938. Reprinted in 1981 in the "Tel" series, with an appendix containing several articles on the same problems, notably "Comment l'historien écrit l'épistémologie" (*Annales,* Nov.–Dec. 1974) and "Récit, analyse, interprétation, explication: critique de quelques problèmes de la connaisance histori-que" (*Archives européennes de sociologie,* 1974) (translated in Raymond Aron, *Power, Modernity, and Sociology* [Aldershot: Edward Elgar, 1988], pp. 36–39); new edition 1986.

Essai sur une théorie de l'histoire dans l'Allemagne contemporaine; la philosophie critique de l'histoire. Paris: Vrin, 1938. Reprinted in 1950 and again 1970 in the

---

*Ed. note: Titles of English translations have been added to the bibliography; information on French editions has been updated to 1989.

"Points" series, Editions du Seuil, with the title *La Philosophie critique de l'Histoire;* new edition, Julliard, 1987.

Contributions to *Libres Propos* and *Europe,* between 1928 and 1933. Almost all articles dealt with Franco-German relations, the rise of National Socialism, and the Hitler revolution.

L'homme contre les tyrans. New York: Editions de la maison française, 1944.

De l'armistice à l'insurrection nationale. Paris: Gallimard, 1945.

L'Age des empires et L'avenir de la France. Paris: Tribune de la France, 1945.

II. 1945–1955

Le Grand Schisme. Paris: Gallimard, 1948.

Les Guerres en chaine. Paris 1951. (*The Century of Total War.* Garden City, N.Y.: Doubleday, 1954; Westport, Conn.: Greenwood, 1981.)

L'Opium des Intellectuels. Paris: Calmann-Levy, 1955. (*The Opium of the Intellectuals.* London: Secker & Warburg, 1957; New York: Doubleday, 1957; Westport, Conn.: Greenwood, 1977.)

Aside from my contributions to *Point de Vue* (1945), to *Combat* (1946–47), and to *Figaro* from spring 1947 on, I contributed to various journals:

Liberté de l'Esprit, in which I published: "Le pacte de l'Atlantique" (April 1949), "Imposture de la neutralité" (September 1950), "Réflexion sur la guerre possible" (December 1951, January 1952), "En quête d'une stratégie I. Le partage du monde, II. Les fausses alternatives" (March–April 1953). I also published in this journal some articles of ideological criticism which were reprinted in the collection *Polémiques* (Paris: Gallimard, 1955), namely "Messianisme et sagesse" (December 1950) and "Séduction du totalitarisme" (May–June 1952).

From 1952 on, I contributed frequently to *Preuves,* in which I published "Discours aux étudiants allemands" delivered at the University of Frankfurt on 30 June 1952 (nos. 18–19), "La Russie après Staline" (no. 32), articles on my return from Asia, and especially two articles that followed the controversy over *L'Opium des Intellectuels:* "Aventures et mésaventures de la dialectique" (no. 59) and "Le fanatisme, la prudence et la foi" (no. 63). (Translated in F. Drdus, ed., *History, Truth, Liberty: Selected Writings of Raymond Aron* [Chicago: The University of Chicago Press, 1985], pp. 119–34.)

III. 1955–1969

Dix-huit leçons sur la société industrielle. Paris: Gallimard, 1962; reprinted 1986. (*Eighteen Lectures on Industrial Society;* New York: Free Press, 1962; London: Weidenfeld and Nicolson, 1967.)

La Lutte de classes. Paris: Gallimard, 1964.

Démocratie et totalitarisme. Paris: Gallimard, 1966. (*Democracy and Totalitarianism.* New York: Praeger, 1969.)

These three books are corrected copies of courses presented at the Sorbonne in 1955–56, 1956–57, and 1957–58.

Espoir et Peur du siècle: Essais non partisans. Paris: Calmann-Levy, 1957. The book contains three essays, one on the Right, a second on decadence, and the third on war. (*On War: Atomic Weapons and Global Diplomacy.* New York: Norton, 1968.)

La Tragédie algérienne. Paris; Plon, 1957.

L'Algérie et la République. Paris; Plon, 1958.

La Société industrielle et la guerre, followed by *Tableau de la diplomatie mondiale en 1958.* Paris: Plon, 1958. (*War and Industrial Society.* Westport, Conn.: Greenwood, 1980.)

Immuable et changeante, de la IVᵉ a la Vᵉ République. Paris: Calmann-Levy, 1959. (*France Steadfast and Changing.* Cambridge, Mass.: Harvard University Press, 1960.)

Dimensions de la conscience historique. Paris: Plon, 1961; reprinted Julliard, 1985. The studies collected in this book, except for the first, "La Notion du sens de l'histoire," written in 1946 for *Chambers Encyclopedia* (translated in Raymond Aron, *Politics and History: Selected Essays,* ed. Miriam B. Conant [New Brunswick, N.J.: Transaction Books, 1984], pp. 5–19), date from this period; "Evidence et inférence" (French version of a lecture delivered in English at Harvard, translated in D. Lerner, ed., *Evidence and Inference* [Glencoe, Ill.: Free Press, 1959], pp. 19–47; "De l'objet de l'histoire," 1959, for the *Encyclopédie Française,* vol. XX; "Thucydide et le récit des événements," publiushed in *Theory and History* in 1961 (translated in Aron, *Politics and History,* pp. 26–40); "Nation et empire," *Encyclopédie Française,* vol. XI, 1957; "L'Aube de l'histoire universelle," 1960, French version of the third Lord Samuel Lecture (translated in Aron, *Politics and History,* pp. 212–33); "La Responsabilité sociale du philosophe," paper presented at the 1957 Warsaw Congress of the International Institute of Philosophy (translated in Aron, *Politics and History,* pp. 249–59).

Paix et Guerre entre les nations. Paris: Calmann-Levy, 1962. (*Peace and War: A Theory of International Relations.* Garden City, N.Y.: Doubleday, 1966.)

Le Grand Débat: initiation a la stratégie atomique. Paris: Calmann-Levy, 1963. (*The Great Debate: Theories of Nuclear Strategy.* Lanham, Md.: University Press of America, 1985.)

Essai sur les libertés. Paris: Calmann-Levy, 1965; reprinted by Pluriel, 1977. (*An Essay on Freedom.* New York: World Publishers, 1970.)

Les Etapes de la pensée sociologique. Paris: Gallimard, 1967. The book came out of courses given at the Sorbonne and mimeographed by the Centre de documentation sociale under the title: les *Grandes Doctrines de sociologie historique:* in 1960, volume 1, Montesquieu, Auguste Comte, Karl Marx, Alexis de Tocqueville; in 1962, volume II, E. Durkheim, V. Pareto, Max Weber. The book appeared first in English under the title *Main Currents of Sociological Thought* (New York: Basic Books, 1965; reprinted Doubleday, 1968–70).

Trois Essais sur l'àge industriel. Paris: Plon, 1966. (*The Industrial Society: Three Essays on Ideology and Development.* New York: Praeger, 1968.)

La Révolution introuvable. Paris: Fayard, 1968. (*The Elusive Revolution: Anatomy of a Student Revolt.* New York: Praeger, 1969.)

De Gaulle, Israël et les Juifs. Paris: Plon, 1968. (*De Gaulle, Israel and the Jews.* New York: Praeger, 1969.)

Les Désillusions de progrès. Paris: Calmann-Levy, 1969; reprinted Julliard, 1987. (*Progress and Disillusionment: The Dialectics of Modern Society.* New York: Praeger, 1968; Harmondsworth: Penguin, 1972.)

During this period, from 1958 to 1962, in *Preuves,* I published commentaries on the beginnings of the Fifth Republic and the Algerian policy of General de Gaulle. I published most of my sociological studies in the *Archives européennes de sociologie.* Most of these studies, at least those I found worth reprinting, are in *Etudes politiques* (Gallimard).

IV. 1969–1977

D'une Sainte Famille a l'autre. Essais sur les marxismes imaginaires. Paris: Gallimard, 1969. (*Marxism and the Existentialists.* New York: Simon and Schuster, 1970.)

De la condition historique du sociologue. Inaugural lecture at the Collège de France. Paris: Gallimard, 1970. ("On the Historical Condition of the Sociologist," in Aron, *Politics and History,* pp. 62–82.)

Etudes politiques. Paris: Gallimard, 1972. Collection containing in particular: "Machiavel et Marx" (translated in Aron, *Politics and History,* pp. 87–101); "Alain et la politique"; "Max Weber et Michael Polanyi" (translated in *The Logic of Personal Knowledge: Essays Presented to Michael Polanyi on his Seventieth Birthday* [London: Routledge and Kegan Paul, 1961], pp. 99–115; and analyses of international relations.

République impériale: les Etats-Unis dans le monde, 1945–1972. Paris: Calmann-Levy, 1972. (*The Imperial Republic: The United States and the World, 1945–1973.* Englewood Cliffs, N.J.: Prentice-Hall, 1974.)

Histoire et dialectique de la violence. Paris: Gallimard, 1972. (*History and the Dialectic of Violence.* Oxford: Blackwell, 1975; New York: Harper and Row, 1975.)

Penser la guerre: Clausewitz. Vol. I, *L'âge européen;* vol. II, *L'âge planétaire.* Paris: Gallimard, 1976. (*Clausewitz: Philosopher of War.* London: Routledge and Kegan Paul, 1983; New York: Simon and Schuster, 1986.)

Plaidoyer pour l'Europe décadente. Paris: Laffont, 1977. (*In Defense of Decadent Europe.* South Bend, Ind.: Regnery Gateway, 1979.)

V. The Reprieve

Les Elections de mars et la Ve République. Paris: Julliard, 1978.

Le Spectateur engagé. Conversations with Jean-Louis Missika and Dominique Wolton. Paris: Julliard, 1981. (*The Committed Observer.* Chicago: Regnery Gateway, 1983.)

From April 1977, I stopped writing for *Le Figaro.*

From September of the same year, I wrote a weekly editorial for *L'Express.*

It was in *Commentaire* that I published the following articles:

"Mr. X règle ses comptes avec son passé: l'isolationnisme de Georges Kennan." *Commentaire,* 1978 (I.2).

"Pour le progres : apres la chute des idoles." *Commentaire* 1978 (I.3) (translated in *The College* [January 1980], pp. 1–8.

"De l'impérialisme américain a l'hégémonisme soviétique." *Commentaire*, 1979 (II.5) (translated in *Encounter* [February 1979], pp. 10–21).

"Existe-t-il un mystère nazi?" *Commentaire*, 1979 (II.7) (translated in *Encounter* [June 1980], pp. 29–41).

"L'hégémonisme soviétique An I." *Commentaire*, 1980 (III.11) (translated in *The St. John's Review* 32, no. 3 [1981]: 14–23).

An English professor, Robert Francis Colquhoun, has written a biography which includes a bibliography: *Raymond Aron: Vol. 1, The Philosopher in History, 1905–1955; Vol. 2, The Sociologist in Society, 1955–1983* (London: Sage, 1986).

INDEX